Rachel Giora, Michael Haugh (Eds.)
Doing Pragmatics Interculturally

Trends in Linguistics
Studies and Monographs

Editor
Volker Gast

Editorial Board
Walter Bisang
Jan Terje Faarlund
Hans Henrich Hock
Natalia Levshina
Heiko Narrog
Matthias Schlesewsky
Amir Zeldes
Niina Ning Zhang

Editor responsible for this volume
Volker Gast

Volume 312

Doing Pragmatics Interculturally

Cognitive, Philosophical, and Sociopragmatic Perspectives

Edited by
Rachel Giora
Michael Haugh

DE GRUYTER
MOUTON

ISBN 978-3-11-065620-6
e-ISBN (PDF) 978-3-11-054609-5
e-ISBN (EPUB) 978-3-11-054393-3
ISSN 1861-4302

Library of Congress Cataloging-in-Publication Data
A CIP catalog record for this book has been applied for at the Library of Congress.

Bibliografische Information der Deutschen Nationalbibliothek
The Deutsche Nationalbibliothek lists this publication in the Deutschen Nationalbibliografie;
detailed bibliographic data are available on the internet http://dnb.dnb.de.

© 2019 Walter de Gruyter GmbH, Berlin/Boston
This volume is text- and page-identical with the hardback published in 2017.
Typesetting: Frank Benno Junghanns, Berlin
Printing and binding: CPI books GmbH, Leck
♾ Printed on acid-free paper
Printed in Germany

www.degruyter.com

Preface

We have edited this book, *Doing Pragmatics Interculturally: Cognitive, Philosophical, and Sociopragmatic Perspectives*, as a token of our appreciation of István Kecskés' scientific achievements. We have known Kecskés for many years now and think very highly of him. He is a phenomenal linguist whose impact on his various fields of expertise is unprecedented. For one, he is the forefather of **Intercultural Pragmatics**, a new field in linguistics which he started from scratch, and which has attracted numerous scholars in the years since its inception. Thanks to him, the field of Intercultural Pragmatics has now a journal of its own (*Intercultural Pragmatics*), its own international conference (*INPRA: International Conference on Intercultural Pragmatics and Communication*), and is also a key pillar of the bi-annual pragmatics conference in the Americas (*AMPRA: International American Pragmatics Association Conference*). Intercultural Pragmatics also has a seminal book of its own, authored by Kecskés (*Intercultural Pragmatics*, Oxford University Press, 2014), which provides a platform for the field, while also moving beyond traditional pragmatics. And what's more, now, thanks to Kecskés, Intercultural Pragmatics has also a book series of its own (*Mouton Series in Pragmatics*, with Kecskés as Editor-in-Chief). Add to this another three books he has co-edited on Intercultural Pragmatics (Kecskés & Assimakopoulos 2017; Kecskés & Horn 2007; Kecskés & Romero-Trillo 2013), and the extent of his impact on the field of Intercultural Pragmatics is self-explanatory.

István Kecskés has also contributed significantly to other research areas such as **Socio-Pragmatics and Cognitive Pragmatics,** in which his work on **bilingualism** features as a prominent strand. He is the founder and Editor-in-Chief of *Chinese as a Second Language Research*, as well as being President of *CASLAR* (Chinese as a Second Language Research Association), alongside being the co-director and founder of the biannual Barcelona Summer School on Bi- and Multilingualism. On top of all that, he has authored a number of books on bilingualism (Kecskés 2002, 2003; Kecskés & Papp 2000), in addition to (co-) editing a number of other volumes on the topic (Kecskés 2013; Kecskés & Albertazzi 2007). His most important contribution is his evidence-based finding that foreign language learning benefits from one's mother tongue. In his co-authored book *Foreign Language and Mother Tongue* (Kecskés & Papp 2000), Kecskés and Papp present empirical data garnered through a longitudinal study on the effects of foreign language learning on one's first language. While relying on psycholinguistic findings, Kecskés and Papp have further shown that the factor of salience (Giora 1997, 2003), found to affect children and adult L1 language comprehension and production, has observable bearings on how we interpret learners' difficulties with idioms, formulaic implicatures, and situation-bound utterances in L2 production and comprehension. In order for an adult L2 learner to perform adequately, s/he needs to be familiar with the conventional, frequent, and prototypical meanings of a situation-bound utterance in a given situation. This, however, is something L2 learners do not always have access to because of their insufficient common ground knowledge and conceptual fluency in the target language (Kecskés 2002).

Another area of expertise of István Kecskés is **Discourse Pragmatics** and **Cognitive Pragmatics**, in which he features dominantly. He has published extensively on the topic. He has authored and co-edited six books (Allan, Capone & Kecskés 2016; Kecskés 2014; Kecskés & Mey 2008; Kecskés & Horn 2007; Kecskés & Papp 1991, 1994) and written over fifty articles in refereed journals and books. A recent publication of his (Kecskés 2016) focuses on a highly original topic, arguing that deliberate creativity, which allows speakers to resort to nonformulaic language, is more pervasive among second language learners than native speakers. The latter, however, are creative in a different way.

His rich and varied expertise has allowed him to enrich linguistics both theoretically and empirically. Not least significant is his work developing the **Socio-Cognitive Approach to Communication**, through which he incorporates not only the cooperative, context-dependent aspects of interaction, but also its egocentric, untidy, trial-and-error features. He has already published several papers on this approach in the *Journal of Pragmatics, Pragmatics & Cognition*, and *Second Language Research*. Indeed, building on the "egocentrism" model (e.g., Keysar and Henly 2002; Barr and Keysar 2005, 2007), alongside the graded salience hypothesis (Giora 1997, 2003), Kecskés (2008) has been able to show that the tendency of language users to egocentrically anchor their judgments in available information, regardless of whether this information is actually useful for solving a given problem or not, may explain why, initially, hearers' and speakers' perspectives may not match. On such occasions, the actual context will come into play and serve as a basis for determining what the speaker means, regardless of degree of literalness.

In sum, István Kecskés' thorough acquaintance with different disciplines, his familiarity with a variety of research methods, his enthusiastic devotion to promoting new research topics, his immense impact on the international scientific community, and his long list of publications, including ten books in well-known publishing houses alongside many tens of articles in top international journals, make him a most conspicuous scholar in the field of cognitive and usage-based linguistics. He is committed to excellence, kindles intellectual interest in new fields of research, and is one of the most frequently invited lecturers and keynote speakers in pragmatics worldwide. The varied contributions of this book reflect on his diverse yet immensely rich expertise across multiple fields. And so, given the way in which Kecskés consistently advocates an approach in pragmatics that cuts across disciplinary divides, we present this volume as an attempt to do just that, thereby honouring both the spirit and intellectual content of the immense contribution he has made to the field of pragmatics.

Rachel Giora and Michael Haugh

Acknowledgement: We would like to thank Valeria Sinkeviciute for her editorial assistance in the later stages of this project.

References

Allan, Keith, Alessandro Capone & István Kecskés. (eds.) 2016. *Pragmemes and theories of language use*. Cham, Switzerland: Springer.
Giora, Rachel. 1997. Understanding figurative and literal language: The graded salience hypothesis. *Cognitive Linguistics* 8(3). 183–206.
Giora, Rachel. 2003. *On our mind: Salience, context, and figurative language*. New York: Oxford University Press.
Kecskés, István. 2002. One language is not enough. *American Journal of Psychology* 115. 1.
Kecskés, István. 2003. Situation-bound utterances in L1 and L2. Berlin & New York: Mouton de Gruyter.
Kecskés, István (ed.) 2013. *Research in Chinese as a second language: The acquisition of language and culture*. Boston & Berlin: De Gruyter Mouton.
Kecskés, István. 2014. *Intercultural pragmatics*. Oxford: Oxford University Press.
Kecskés, István. 2016. Deliberate creativity and formulaic language use. In Keith Allan, Alessandro Capone & István Kecskés (eds.), *Pragmemes and theories of language use*, 3–20. Cham, Switzerland: Springer.
Kecskés, István. 2017. Sequential structure of discourse segments shaped by the interplay of recipient design or salience. In Joanna Blochowiak, Cristina Grisot, Stephanie Durrleman-Tame & Christopher Laenzlinger (eds.), *Formal models in the study of language*, 243–260. Cham, Switzerland: Springer.
Kecskés, István & Liliana Albertazzi (eds.) 2007. *Cognitive aspects of bilingualism*. Heidelberg: London: Springer.
Kecskés, István & Assimakopoulos, Stavros. (eds.) 2017. *Current issues in intercultural pragmatics*. Amsterdam: John Benjamins.
Kecskés, István & Laurence Horn. (eds.) 2007. Explorations in pragmatics: Linguistic, cognitive and intercultural aspects. Berlin & New York: Mouton de Gruyter.
Kecskés, István & Jacob Mey. (eds.) 2008. *Intention, common ground and the egocentric speaker-hearer*. Berlin & New York: Mouton de Gruyter.
Kecskés, István & Tünde Papp. 1991. *Theoretical linguistics, applied linguistics, language teaching*. Budapest: TS Programiroda.

Kecskés, István & Tünde Papp. (eds.) 1994. *New technology supporting language teaching.* Durham, NC/Budapest: CALICO/Felsooktatási Koordinációs Iroda.

Kecskés, István & Tünde Papp. 2000. *Foreign language and mother tongue.* Mahwah, NJ: Lawrence Erlbaum.

Kecskés, István & Jesús Romero-Trillo. (eds.) 2013. *Research trends in intercultural pragmatics.* Boston & Berlin: De Gruyter Mouton.

Keysar, Boaz & Anne S. Henly. 2002. Speakers' overestimation of their effectiveness. *Psychological Science* 13(3). 207–212.

Contents

Preface —— v

List of contributors —— xii

Introduction

Rachel Giora and Michael Haugh
1   Introduction —— 3

Part I: Socio-cognitive and experimental pragmatics

Raymond W. Gibbs, Jr. and Herbert L. Colston
2   The emergence of common ground —— 13

Robert E. Sanders
3   Overcoming differences and achieving common ground:
Why speaker and hearer make the effort and how they go about it —— 31

Marta Dynel
4   "Is there a tumour in your humour?": On misunderstanding
and miscommunication in conversational humour —— 55

Victoria Escandell-Vidal
5   Notes for a restrictive theory of procedural meaning —— 79

Marit Sternau, Mira Ariel, Rachel Giora and Ofer Fein
6   Deniability and explicatures —— 97

Eline Zenner, Nane Mertens, Laura Rosseel and Dirk Geeraerts
7   The acquisition of loanword pragmatics: An exploration —— 121

Jonathan Culpeper, Michael Haugh and Daniel E. Johnson
8   (Im)politeness: Metalinguistic labels and concepts in English —— 135

Part II: Philosophical and discourse pragmatics

Laurence Horn
9 What lies beyond: Untangling the web —— 151

Kasia M. Jaszczolt
10 The true provenance of self-reference:
A case for salience-based contextualism —— 175

Wayne A. Davis
11 Transparent reports as free-form idioms —— 193

Jacques Moeschler
12 How speaker meaning, explicature and implicature work together —— 215

Chaofen Sun and Ming Chew Teo
13 Temporally closed situations for the Chinese perfective LE 了 —— 233

Jesús Romero-Trillo
14 Acategorical pragmatic markers:
From thematic analysis to adaptive management in discourse —— 255

Anita Fetzer
15 Contrastive discourse relations in context:
Evidence from monologic and dialogic editing tasks —— 269

Lluís Payrató
16 Pragmatics and multimodality.
A reflection on multimodal pragmastylistics —— 293

Part III: Interpersonal and societal pragmatics

Klaus P. Schneider
17 Pragmatic competence and pragmatic variation —— 315

Anne Barron
18 Offers in English —— 335

J. César Félix-Brasdefer
19 **The intercultural speaker abroad** —— 353

Jörg Meibauer
20 **Pragmatics and children's literature** —— 371

Jacob L. Mey
21 **Unloading the weapon: Act and tact** —— 389

Kepa Korta
22 **The meanings and contents of aesthetic statements** —— 399

Index —— 418

List of contributors

Mira Ariel is Professor of Linguistics at Tel Aviv University.

Anne Barron is Professor of English Linguistics at Leuphana University of Lüneburg.

Herbert L. Colston is Professor of Psychology at the University of Alberta.

Jonathan Culpeper is Professor of Linguistics and English Language at Lancaster University.

Wayne A. Davis is Professor of Philosophy at Georgetown University.

Marta Dynel is Professor of Linguistics at the University of Lodz.

Victoria Escandell-Vidal is Professor of Linguistics at UNED, Madrid.

Ofer Fein is a senior lecturer at the Academic College of Tel Aviv Yaffo.

J. César Félix-Brasdefer is Professor of Spanish Linguistics at Indiana University.

Anita Fetzer is Professor of Linguistics at the University of Augsburg.

Dirk Geeraerts is Professor of Linguistics at the University of Leuven.

Raymond W. Gibbs, Jr. is Professor of Psychology at the University of California, Santa Cruz.

Rachel Giora is Professor of Linguistics at Tel Aviv University.

Michael Haugh is Professor of Linguistics at the University of Queensland.

Laurence Horn is Professor Emeritus of Linguistics and Philosophy at Yale University.

Kasia M. Jaszczolt is Professor of Linguistics and Philosophy of Language at the University of Cambridge.

Daniel E. Johnson is an independent scholar.

Kepa Korta is Associate Professor of Philosophy at the University of the Basque Country.

Jörg Meibauer is Professor of German Studies at the University of Mainz.

Nane Mertens is a postgraduate student at the University of Leuven.

Jacob L. Mey is Emeritus Professor of Linguistics at the University of Southern Denmark.

Jacques Moeschler is Professor of Linguistics at the University of Geneva.

Lluís Payrató is Professor of Linguistics at the University of Barcelona.

Jesús Romero-Trillo is Professor of Linguistics at Universidad Autónoma de Madrid.

Laura Rosseel is a doctoral student at the University of Leuven.

Robert E. Sanders is Professor Emeritus of Communication at the University at Albany, SUNY.

Klaus P. Schneider is Professor of Linguistics at the University of Bonn.

Marit Sternau is a lecturer at Levinsky College of Education, Tel Aviv.

Chaofen Sun is Professor of East Asian Languages and Cultures at Stanford University.

Ming Chew Teo is Assistant Professor of Chinese Studies at the University of Houston.

Eline Zenner is Professor of Dutch Linguistics at the University of Leuven.

Introduction

Rachel Giora and Michael Haugh
1 Introduction

1 Doing pragmatics interculturally

Pragmatics is a large and diverse field encompassing a wide range of approaches, methods, and theories. What unites the field is a common focus on how language is *used* and the role of language in communication, whether this be mediated through various written modes, increasingly in digital forms, or in various modes of spoken interaction. Generally speaking, the field of pragmatics is conceptualized as either a *subfield* of linguistics, on a par with syntax, semantics, and the like, or as a particular *perspective* on language and communication that emphasizes the functions of language, whether these be cognitive, social, or cultural. While this is frequently couched in terms of a distinction between "Anglo-American" and "European Continental" pragmatics, in recent years, there have been increasing calls for increased dialogue and interaction amongst scholars to enable more empirically focused and more theoretically focused approaches to mutually inform each other and thereby further enrich the broader field (e.g. Culpeper and Haugh 2014; Ilie and Norrick forthcoming). The Intercultural Pragmatics movement represents one of the strongest voices in the field advocating just that sort of scholarly exchange.

Just as pragmatics can be conceptualized in two different, albeit not mutually exclusive ways, so too can intercultural pragmatics be understood in two different, complementary ways, either as a *subfield* of pragmatics or as a particular *perspective* on pragmatics. On the more traditional, disciplinary view, intercultural pragmatics involves the application of theories and methods from pragmatics to the analysis of the role of language in intercultural encounters. As intercultural pragmatics in the traditional sense lies at the intersection of the fields of pragmatics and intercultural communication, it brings together a wide range of different theoretical and methodological perspectives. As Kecskés (2014) points out, though, studying cognitive, social cultural aspects of language use in intercultural encounters has potentially much to offer broader attempts at theorization in pragmatics. This is partly because the "common knowledge" or "common ground" that underlies much pragmatic theorising cannot be straightforwardly presumed in such cases (if indeed it can be straightforwardly presumed in so-called intracultural encounters).

However, intercultural pragmatics has also been conceptualized as a particular *perspective* on pragmatics more generally that explicitly advocates scholarly debate between researchers representing different subfields of pragmatics

DOI 10.1515/9783110546095-001

(Kecskés 2004). As pragmatics has developed over the past fifty years, while it has continued to draw from its philosophical and linguistic roots, it has, at the same time, also been enriched through the addition of (socio-)cognitive, experimental, discursive, critical, interpersonal, social, and cultural perspectives on language use. While this has yielded a plethora of approaches, methods, and theories that highlight the inevitable complexity of our common object of interest, in becoming an increasingly diverse field, therein lies the danger that the field also becomes increasingly fractured. An intercultural pragmatics perspective actively resists the latter, drawing scholars together into a mutually informing and enriching dialogue across subfields and perceived boundaries. The aim of this volume is to showcase applications of intercultural pragmatics in this broader sense.

2 Overview of the book

While many of the chapters contained within this volume cut across boundaries, reflecting the call by Kecskés to do just that, we have nevertheless arranged the various contributions into three broad sections to enable the reader to navigate the admittedly rather complex landscape of modern pragmatics. These sections reflect the relative focus of these respective contributions on cognitive, linguistic, or socio-pragmatic aspects of language use.

The contributions in Part I, "Socio-Cognitive and Experimental Pragmatics", pick up on various themes addressed in Kecskés' sociocognitive approach to pragmatics. It begins with two chapters that offer different perspectives on long-standing debates about the role of "common ground" in communication. In Chapter Two, "The emergence of common ground", Raymond W. Gibbs Jr. and Herbert L. Colston review relevant studies in social psychology and cognitive science that support a dynamical systems approach to common ground. They argue that the abilities of people to coordinate their social interactions with one another emerge from self-organisational processes that operate with respect to goals interlinked across multiple different time-scales. On this view, there is no need for interactants to consistently try and explicitly align their own individual mental representations. The position taken on this matter by Robert E. Sanders in Chapter Three, "Overcoming differences and achieving common ground" is that it is always incumbent on speaker and hearer to overcome differences in common ground sufficiently to bring the matter at hand to a conclusion, but cautions that the amount of effort needed to achieve this is not consistently proportional to the extent of (presumed) background differences between speaker and hearer. In Chapter Four, "On misunderstanding and miscommunication in conversational humour", Marta Dynel proposes that we need to carefully distinguish between miscommunication and misunderstanding, and the different types of misunderstanding therein. She draws attention to differences between genuine misunderstanding, planned misunderstanding, and overtly pretended misunderstanding, using data from the television show, *House MD*, to illustrate her claims that the interface between misunderstanding/miscommunication and humour can both facilitate and hinder the emergence of humour

The focus then shifts to the discourse status of different types of pragmatic meaning. In Chapter Five, "Notes for a restrictive theory of procedural meaning", Victoria Escandell-Vidal outlines a set of arguments as to why retaining a linguistically-based distinction between conceptual and procedural meaning is important. She proposes that the notion of procedural meaning is best limited to the contribution of interpretable features that target computations in conceptual-intentional systems at different levels of representation, and that natural coded signs (e.g. smiles) are best treated as distinct from linguistic operations. This is followed, in Chapter Six, "Explicatures and deniability", in which Marit Sternau, Mira Ariel, Rachel Giora, and Ofer Fein introduce a new methodology for distinguishing between pragmatic inferences. Sternau and colleagues apply their Deniability test – an interactional corollary of Grice's cancelability – to various pragmatic inferences, and find support for both the maximalist and the minimalist positions: different types of explicated inferences vary in how easy it is for the speaker to deny having said them. Ultimately, the findings support Ariel's Privileged Interactional Interpretation level and Sternau's graded interpretation strength, whereby linguistic meanings are strongest, weak implicatures are weakest, and, in between, are what they call strong explicated inferences ('what is said' inferences), weak explicated inferences, and strong implicatures.

Experimental approaches are also employed in investigating evaluation of language use in the final two chapters in this section. In Chapter Seven, "The acquisition of loanword pragmatics", Eline Zenner, Nane Mertens, Laura Rossel, and Dirk Geeraerts investigate the way in which Dutch primary school children evaluate the use of English-loan words in a cartoon. A key finding is that while across different age groups the loan-words are consistently evaluated positively in that context, these attitudes become more systematically structured with respect to status, solidarity, and sociability as their age increases, and there is also increasing explicit awareness demonstrated on their part. Finally, in Chapter Eight, "*(Im)politeness*: Metalinguistic labels and concepts in English", Jonathan Culpeper, Michael Haugh, and Daniel E. Johnson report on the results of an experiment in which possible differences across *impoliteness*-related terms used in perception scales were examined. It was found that different metalinguistic labels had different relationships with each other, depending on the power relationships that were presumed to hold between the interactants. In other words, understandings of metalinguistic labels are dependent, in part, on the context in which they are situated and the specific purposes for which they are being used.

Part II focuses on current debates and topics in "Philosophical and Discourse Pragmatics". The first four chapters in this section take a broadly philosophical approach to pragmatics. In Chapter Nine, "What lies beyond: Untangling the web", Laurence Horn reviews the issues affecting the formulation of the distinction between lying and misleading and examines the arguments for linking that distinction to the one drawn in Gricean pragmatics between what is said and what is implicated. Focusing on the role of assertion as a criterion of lying, Horn marshals a range of evidence from the courtroom, the lab, and everyday conversational exchanges to challenge recent accounts according to which a speaker can lie (by implying a falsehood) while telling the truth. This is followed, in Chapter Ten, "The true provenance of self-reference: A case for salience-based contextualism", by Kasia M. Jaszczolt's discussion of self-reference as a test case for contextualist accounts of meaning (e.g., *Daddy will finish his dinner and will play with you in a moment*; *One tries to do one's best*). Specifically, Jaszczolt analyses natural language uses of self-reference and concludes that the pragmatic, contextualist approach better accounts for the variety of uses than the other alternative (e.g., syntax-based) approaches, which fail to provide for a comprehensive account. Next, in Chapter Eleven, "Transparent reports as free-form idioms", Wayne A. Davis contends that transparent, propositional attitude reports with that-clauses, termed "transparent reports", are "free-form idioms", conveying idiomatic interpretations. Although ambiguous, their ambiguity is semantic though not lexical or syntactic. Indeed, unlike prototypical idioms, transparent reports are not defined by a fixed form. Instead, they are highly, even if not entirely, compositional and productive. Finally, in Chapter Twelve, "How speaker meaning, explicature and implicature work together", Jacques Moeschler contends that scalar implicatures cannot capture the complexity of speaker meaning. Along the lines of Horn and Kecskés (2013), Kecskés (2017), and Moeschler (2017), he argues that "the recovery of speaker meaning requires much more than accessing defeasible meanings, as implicatures".

The focus then shifts to the pragmatics of particular linguistic phenomena in discourse. In Chapter Thirteen, "Temporally closed situations for the Chinese perfective LE 了", Chaofen Sun and Ming Chew Teo highlight the uniqueness of the Chinese perfective aspect marker *le* 了. They argue that, for this perfective aspect marker (termed here le_1) to be used correctly, it must occur in a temporally bounded (i.e., completed or terminated) context. Without such a telic context, this marker will not be capable of signaling the perfective aspect on its own. This is followed, in Chapter Fourteen, "Acategorical pragmatic markers: From thematic analysis to adaptive management in discourse", by Jesús Romero-Trillo's discussion of three types of acategorical pragmatic markers: those without an original grammatical ascription (e.g. [@:m], m, mhm); those whose original category is lexical (e.g. listen, well, good, fine); and those with at least one lexical item plus one or more grammatical items, termed phrases (e.g. I mean, you know, the thing is). His findings, based on studies of spoken discourse, show that acategorical pragmatic markers serve to cohere sequential segments; they link subsequent to prior discourse units, especially when they occupy the initial position of the tone unit, as they do in 87% of the cases tested.

The lens broadens to consider the pragmatics of linguistic phenomena at the discourse level in Chapter Fifteen, "Contrastive discourse relations in context: Evidence from monologic and dialogic editing tasks", in which Anita Fetzer argues that contrastive discourse relations signal a change in the flow of the discourse and play a particularly important role in argumentative discourses, the establishment of their common ground and their coherence. Finally, the importance of going beyond the traditional focus in pragmatics on analyzing language in isolation from its broader multimodal context is amply demonstrated by Lluís Payrató in Chapter Sixteen, "Pragmatics and multimodality: A reflection on multimodal pragmastylistics". A discussion of instances of additive, complementary multimodality is extended to a consideration of interactive, intersectional forms of multimodality through which new meanings, new communicative strategies and new identities for interactants are made possible. It is thus, in the spirit of the call by Kecskés for an interdisciplinary pragmatics that this section on philosophical and discourse pragmatics ends with a chapter exhorting us to analyse the ways in which meanings are created through multimodal text

The final section of the volume, "Interpersonal and Societal Pragmatics", shifts the lens to another ongoing theme in the work of Kecskés, namely, his interest in interpersonal aspects of language use and the pragmatics of interactions amongst second language and lingua franca speakers, which leads into a consideration of pragmatics at a broader societal level. The section begins, in Chapter Seventeen, "Pragmatic competence and pragmatic variation", with a call from Klaus P. Schneider to build in the inevitable variation in the ways in which pragmatic phenomena are accomplished across different social groups into our theorization of pragmatic competence. He points out, however, that to do so requires a vast empirical undertaking in order to map out the detailed "pragmaticography" of different languages. Schneider debates the contribution that experimental methods can make, and necessarily so, to this ambitious empirical program, thereby providing a tangible link back to the issues implicitly raised in some of the chapters in Section I. This theme is further elaborated in Anne Barron's chapter on "Offers in English" (Chapter Eighteen), where she analyses the ways in which offers are formulated by British speakers of English, using spoken data held in the British component of the International Corpus of English. A key finding is that particular types of offer types correlate with different strategy types: hospitable offers are commonly accomplished through preference strategies, that is, inquiring about what the hearer wants, while offers of assistance are more commonly accomplished through execution strategies, that is, stating what the speaker can do for the hearer. There are also striking differences in various types of modification that accompany these different offers. The chapter thus illustrates well the value of corpus-assisted analyses of speech acts for pragmatics.

The focus then shifts to research about the development of pragmatic competence in intercultural settings in Chapter Nineteen, "The intercultural speaker abroad". J. César Félix-Brasdefer introduces two key methods by which sociopragmatic awareness can be raised amongst second language learners: (1) critical analysis of impoliteness events recorded through diary or field notes, and (2) retrospective verbal reports following role-plays designed to highlight particular differences in sociocultural norms. He highlights the important pedagogical implications that such work has for second language classrooms. The development of pragmatic abilities amongst children is then considered in Chapter Twenty by Jörg Meibauer. In "Pragmatics and children's literature", Meibauer argues that studying the pragmatics of children's literature, which involves studying both the broader social situations and contexts in which children's literature is used, as well as specific pragmatic dimensions of the texts themselves, is important because it constitutes a key form of input into the development of pragmatic competence amongst children.

The move towards a broader societal lens is continued by Jacob L. Mey in Chapter Twenty One, "Unloading the weapon: Act and tact", in which he critically reflects on the ongoing importance of the metaphor of "language as a loaded weapon" for a pragmatics that embraces its historical and social underpinnings. Drawing from a wealth of experience, he reminds us of the hidden power of not only words themselves, but the tones and gestures that accompany them, in acting in ways that are, on the surface at least, ostensibly a matter of tact. The volume concludes, somewhat fittingly given the broad interests of Kecskés, with a chapter by Kepa Korta that explores the broader sociohistorical roots and implications of the language we use. In Chapter Twenty Two, "The meanings and contents of aesthetic statements", Korta outlines the complexity inherent to any claim that a particular piece of art is "beautiful". Rather than simply treating such a claim as a "subjective judgement", about which one can "faultlessly disagree", he suggests that a distinction needs to be drawn between aesthetically describing and aesthetically or artistically evaluating. This brings us full circle in that both the cognitive and linguistic underpinnings of an inherently social activity, namely, the appreciation of art, is brought into play by Korta.

In sum, the various chapters in this volume traverse a broad range of topics from a variety of different perspectives, which are mutually enriching and influential. This work thus collectively represents an example of what Kecskés has consistently advocated: not simply studying but *doing* intercultural pragmatics in very real and tangible ways.

References

Culpeper, Jonathan and Michael Haugh. 2014. *Pragmatics and the English Language*. Basingstoke: Palgrave Macmillan.
Horn, Laurence and István Kecskés. 2013. Pragmatics, discourse and cognition. In Stephen R. Anderson, Jacques Moeschler & Fabienne Reboul (eds.), *The language cognition-interface*, 355–375. Genève: Droz.
Ilie, Cornelia and Neal R. Norrick (eds.). Forthcoming. *Pragmatics and its Interfaces*. Amsterdam: John Benjamins.
Kecskés, István. 2004. Editorial: Lexical merging, conceptual blending, and cultural crossing. *Intercultural Pragmatics* 1(1). 1–26.
Kecskés, István. 2008. Dueling context: A dynamic model of meaning. *Journal of Pragmatics* 40(3). 385–406.
Kecskés, István. 2014. *Intercultural pragmatics*. Oxford: Oxford University Press.
Kecskés, István. 2016. Deliberate creativity and formulaic language use. In Keith Allan, Alessandro Capone & István Kecskés (eds.), *Pragmemes and theories of language use*, 3–20. Cham, Switzerland: Springer.
Kecskés, István. 2017. Sequential structure of discourse segments shaped by the interplay of recipient design or salience. In Joanna Blochowiak, Cristina Grisot, Stephanie Durrleman-Tame & Christopher Laenzlinger (eds.), *Formal models in the study of language*, 243–260. Cham, Switzerland: Springer.
Moeschler, Jacques. 2017. Back to negative particulars. A truth-conditional account. In Stavros Assimakopoulos (ed.), *Pragmatics at its interfaces*, 7–32. Boston & Berlin: De Gruyter Mouton.

Part I: **Socio-cognitive and experimental pragmatics**

Raymond W. Gibbs, Jr. and Herbert L. Colston
2 The emergence of common ground

1 The emergence of common ground

One of the most contentious debates in the study of linguistic pragmatics concerns whether or not people possess common ground knowledge and beliefs that are readily accessed during speaking and listening. Most people certainly share information (i.e., their "shared knowledge"), such as that the earth is round, people die, and the Pope is Catholic. However, sharing information is not the same as two or more people understanding, explicitly or implicitly, that both of them possess some information or belief implicitly or explicitly as part of their "common ground" (e.g., the belief that my sister and I share, and know that we share, about my father's birthday). Common ground generally refers then to information, beliefs, attitudes that some select group of individuals both share and mutually recognize that they possess in common.

The ways people produce and interpret language often requires that people possess common ground information. Consider the following simple exchange:

(1) Mary: "Are you going to Peter's party tonight?"
 Sally: "Didn't you hear that Chris will be there?"

Sally's response to Mary's question with a rhetorical question signals to Mary something about Sally's belief about Chris, enough so as to help Mary infer that Sally does not want to attend Peter's party (e.g., because Chris is Sally's old boyfriend who she does not want to see at a party). In this case, then, Mary and Sally both understand, and tacitly recognize that they both understand, what Sally feels about Chris. The mere mention of Chris by Sally activates this common ground information which then assists Mary in drawing the authorized conversational implicature from Sally's rhetorical question, namely that she will not go to Peter's party.

Linguistic pragmatic studies, including research in linguistics, philosophy and psychology, have long debated (a) whether it is even possible for two or more people to possess common ground information, (b) how people infer what is, or is not, part of their common ground with others, and (c) whether people automatically recruit common ground information as part of the context for pragmatic language use (Kecskés and Mey 2008). For example, scholars offer a range of opinions about the process by which people determine that some belief is truly established as common ground (e.g., the infinite regress problem), and whether common ground guides early language production and comprehension, as opposed to only being referred to at a later, non-obligatory moment in the course of speaking and listening.

This chapter explores these debates over common ground and acknowledges István Kecskés's unique contributions to understanding how common ground provides the background for, and emerges from, conversational interactions. Our agenda is to advance discussion on how dynamical-systems theory, and principles of self-organization, can explain the varieties of common ground experience in human cognition and communication. We first discuss Kecskés's scholarly ideas on common ground in a theory of linguistic pragmatics, review some of the extensive empirical and experimental research on how common ground may shape speaking and listening, and then finally offer our spin on a self-organizing approach to the emergence of common ground. Our conclusions are, to varying extents, consistent with Kecskés's writings on this complex problem.

2 István Kecskés's contributions to common ground theory

István Kecskés, often in collaboration with Fenghui Zhang, has offered a unique perspective on the debates over common ground in human communication. Kecskés and Zhang (2009, 2013) maintain that advocates for the necessity of common ground in linguistic behavior too often implicitly assume a model of communication-as-transfer-between-minds. Under this view, communicative intentions are seen as pre-existing psychological entities that are transferred from one mind (i.e., the speaker) to another (i.e., the listener) via the conduit of language. Listeners or readers must unpack the language encountered to infer what speakers' or writers' pre-existing intentions must have been given their personal understandings of the common ground existing at that very moment.

Kecskés (2008) has advanced an alternative framework for the theory of linguistic communication, called the "dynamic model of meaning" (DMM). This approach highlights the interplay of intention and attention given a socio-cultural background, which arises from prior and current experiences, all of which are essentially socio-cultural. In this manner, debates about when and how common ground operates in interpersonal interaction depend on the ways that intention and attention arise from socio-cultural factors. They go on to claim that common ground has two parts: core common ground (e.g., the relatively static, generalized common beliefs that exist within a certain speech community) and emergent common ground (e.g., the relatively dynamic, particularized knowledge that is co-constructed during the course of any conversation).

For example, consider two exchanges between Jill and John (Kecskés and Zhang 2013: 380):

(2) Jill: "I need some money."
    John: "There is an ATM over there."

John's use of "ATM" is based on his and Jill's "core" common ground given that ATMs are widely recognized as places to get cash in most countries, as well as John's understanding of Jill's declaration as a report of an immediate problem to be solved and not as a general statement about her financial status or as a request to John for a loan.

"Emergent" common ground depends on the actual situation, and is exhibited in the following conversation, from a British sitcom (Kecskés and Zhang 2013: 381):

(3) Jill: "I met someone today."
    Jane: "Good for you."
    Jill: "He is a police officer."
    Jane: "Are you in trouble?"
    Jill: "Oh no…"

Meeting a police officer may be typically regarded as a bad thing. Nonetheless, one possible interpretation of Jill and Jane's exchange is that Jill's meeting a man who is a police officer was not a problem, and even implies some possible romantic connection between Jill and the police officer. This example illustrates how some common ground emerges from the conversational interaction and is not just part of the prior knowledge speakers and listeners rely on when understanding one another.

Much of Kecskés and Zhang's efforts have been directed toward explicating the different sources and computations of common ground. One argument they make is that speakers can be both egocentric and cooperative at the same time. Thus, when Jill says, "He is a police officer", she is speaking egocentrically given her more complete understanding of the officer as someone who is not investigating her for being in any legal difficulty. Jane did not have access to this privileged information, which led to her question "Are you in trouble?" based on the culturally salient view of what often happens when encountering a police officer. Still, it would be a mistake to conclude that Jill was being entirely egocentric in her conversational style, as she clearly wanted Jane to construe her comments about the police officer in a positive manner, something that was soon made clear in Jill and Jane's conversational exchange.

A key part of Kecskés and Zhang's general approach is that communication is "more like a trial-and-error process that is co-constructed by participants" rather than "an ideal transfer of information" (Kecskés and Zhang 2009: 337). Meaning is constructed "on the spot" from conversational interaction rather than being buried inside speakers' minds and then fully expressed in the language they use. There may be occasions, then, when speakers do not necessarily seek to further modify and establish new common ground, and may be much more egocentric in what they say.

3 The interdisciplinary challenge

One reason for the lack of consensus over the role that common ground may play in communication is scholars' diverse disciplinary backgrounds. Contributions from cognitive science, cognitive psychology, social psychology and related fields, for instance, ground their arguments in phenomena from the mainstream literatures of those disciplines that may not be greatly familiar to scholars from other areas. Conversely, the linguistic, psychological and philosophical underpinnings of interpersonal communication may not always have impacted experimental psychologists as they attempt to define and measure common ground and its possible impact on linguistic interaction.

For example, establishing and relying upon common ground is actually modulated by a range of factors, as suggested by various studies in experimental psychology (Colston 2008, 2015). People tend to rely more on information that is first mentioned than on materials presented later on in both reading and listening. Most people will also tend to recall information in a more schematic manner than how it was originally presented. In some cases, people will even falsely remember some event as occurring, which they personally witnessed, when, in fact, this event was only imagined or verbally mentioned by another person in a different context. Speakers will also be biased toward remembering information that is most consistent with their current emotional or cognitive state, and fail to recall material that is inconsistent with what they now feel or think. Finally, people may falsely recall something as previously occurring when this possibility was only inferred, but not explicitly stated, from some earlier conversational interaction.

These, and many other, experimental findings on human memory suggest that there is no single way in which information is stored and accessed as part of people's common ground during interpersonal interaction. Even when people both assume to know that something is clearly mutually known, the process by which this knowledge is accessed will differ depending on the dynamics of the specific situation and the particular task that two or more people are engaged in. People may appear to be operating in a more or less egocentric or collaborative manner depending on some of the variations in human memory performance.

In addition to these various complexities about memory and common ground, we must also recognize a greater range of ways in which people typically converse with one another (Colston 2008). For instance, people are not always equally focused on the task when they are communicating. One individual's attention may drift during talk, and one participant may be reluctant to speak of certain matters or wish to completely avoid talking about some topics with some people. Speakers often allude to other people's ideas or talk, rather than state what is on their own minds directly. People sometimes engage in conversation for the pleasure of talking to a specific other rather than to solve some problem, as typically studied in psycholinguistics tasks, or use words and phrases precisely because these will be unknown to their conversational partner.

Linguistic and philosophical discussions of common ground and its possible role in linguistic pragmatics often fail to appreciate these nuances of real-world conversations, partly because they rely entirely on the words on the page in order to conduct their interpretive analyses. Psychologists have the advantage of being able to more finely explore how specific task demands (e.g., as seen in memory research) or people's orientations toward particular conversations (e.g., as seen in some psycholinguistics studies) affect the online course of speaking and listening. In general, there are multiple, interacting complexities that are not necessarily evident from the text alone which pushes people to speaking and understanding in more or less egocentric or cooperative ways.

4 Psycholinguistic perspectives on common ground

A central feature of many pragmatic theories is that people use language for coordinating both their individual and joint actions. The role that common ground has in this coordination process has become an important focus of research in experimental pragmatics. Most of these studies have participants perform some task together, usually with one person directing another to solve some problem, such as arranging cards or pictures in a certain order or constructing some toy building. The products of these conversations are analyzed to assess the extent to which the accrual of common ground enables speakers and listeners to more readily coordinate their intentional meanings in discourse. These different psycholinguistic results all show how people may possess not just core common ground, but very specific, idiosyncratic knowledge with others given both past and current experiences. In these ways, the empirical studies expand upon Kecskés and Zhang's idea on the divide between core and emergent common ground. Thus, even "core" common ground depends not just on generalized background knowledge but through knowledge emerging from, and then being relied upon, in very specific discourse settings.

Consider, for example, an experiment in which two persons talk to each other, but cannot see each other (Clark and Wilkes-Gibbs 1986). Both sit before schematic drawings of cartoon figures, called tangrams, which are new to both parties. One conversant describes a specific figure from her set of figures, and the other identifies the correct picture from his set using the heard description alone. Unsurprisingly, participants get better at this task over time. Speakers initially provide detailed descriptions of the figures to make initial identifications possible, but over time each pair of dialog partners eventually evolves a shared idiosyncratic lingo specific to the given task environment, allowing them to pick out figures more quickly. Thus, on a first trial, one speaker referred to a figure by saying, "All right, the next one looks like a person who is ice skating, except that they're sticking two arms out in front." But on the sixth trial in this study, the same speaker simply said, "The ice skater." These results suggest that understanding what a speaker intends to communicate, and the criteria by which listeners judge that they have understood that message, is a joint product requiring coordination and cooperation between listeners and speakers. As participants build up their common ground about the present task, their speech changes so that they no longer need to be as explicit in their references to different cards.

Another version of this card-sorting task examined the role of expertise (Issacs and Clark 1987). In these studies, pairs of people, some being from New York (experts) and some not (novices), attempted to arrange a set of postcards with pictures of different buildings and places in New York City. To the extent that the director and matcher could establish that each was from New York, more proper nouns (e.g., the Chrysler Building, Rockefeller Center) should be used to describe the postcard scenes. If both participants were novices (i.e., not from New York) far fewer uses of proper names would be expected. If an expert and a novice were paired, then the use of proper names should increase over time (or trials) as the experts taught the novices about the names for different postcards.

These predictions were all shown to be correct. There was also an increase in the efficiency of the conversations as shown by a decrease in the overall number of words used and the number of turns required to complete the task. Thus, in conversations between experts, proper names were used about 80% of the time while proper names were used less than 20% of the time between novices. When an expert was talking to a novice, the number of proper names initially decreased as it became clear to the expert that the novice did not know what some of the names referred to. When novices talked to experts, the number of proper names increased as some of the expertise "rubbed off" and the names of landmarks were learned from the expert partner. Experts and novices seemed to have discovered that they were talking to other experts or novices by the way the conversation proceeded, because in only 6 of the 32 pairs did participants actually ask or tell the other person whether they were New Yorkers. This study demonstrates, then, how people's assessment of what is in their common ground shapes what they say, but also how common ground changes their speech behaviors over time.

In certain contexts, participants in real-life conversations design their utterances so that specific listeners will not fully understand their pragmatic meanings, such as when a speaker wishes for one person to correctly interpret what is being communicated, but not some other co-present individual. One set of experiments explored this type of situation. In this particular case, participants in a card-arranging task had to communicate the ordering of photographs of Stanford University scenes, but there was a third person in the room, provided with the same set of pictures, and the two participants had to try to ensure that the third person did not succeed in the task (Clark and Shaefer 1987). Thus, the speaker had to ensure that the addressee understood, but had to conceal the identification of the real-world referent from the overhearer. All three participants were Stanford University students and thus "experts", but the two participants were friends and the overhearer was a stranger.

Because the three participants had the same community membership, it was expected that the conversant would use "private keys" or information that was part of their particular common ground, but which was unknown to the overhearer. Although there were certain instances when the speakers slipped up and uttered the name of a scene, the vast majority of references contained these private keys. For example, a speaker referred to a fountain on campus as "where someone wanted to put my teddy bear". Overall, the addresses were twice as successful in correctly arranging the photographs as were the overhearers, suggesting that speakers and listeners can often successfully hide what they are exactly talking about from some co-present individual. They accomplish this by speaking using only references that they know the addressees will recognize, but not the overhearers.

As Kecskés and Zhang, among others, have argued, conversations do not typically proceed in a ballistic manner in which people state what they mean and then hope for the best that the addressees will somehow understand them. Speakers actively, automatically monitor listeners' reactions to insure proper understanding of what was expressed, both linguistically and gesturally. For example, one study had pairs of participants assemble different Lego models with one person acting as the director and the other as the builder (Clark and Krych 2004). For one group of people, the director and builder could see each other and the builder's workspace. In a second group, the participants could hear but not see one another, and in a third group, the director gave only audio-taped instructions to the builder.

The participants performed the worst in constructing the specific Lego model when they communicated using an audiotaped message, and somewhat better when they could hear, but not see, each other. Not surprisingly, perhaps, people performed the assembly task best when they could both see and hear one another. Directors engaged in a host of actions when speaking with builders, including exhibiting, posing, and pointing, in addition to using eye gazes and head nods to communicate their in-the-moment messages. These different linguistic and nonlinguistic actions were also exquisitely timed given what the builders were doing at any moment. In many instances, directors altered their utterances midcourse when they sensed that the builders needed to reorient their specific actions to better complete the overall assembly task.

These findings drive home the important point that speakers produce language not only to express what they mean, but also to ordinarily ground what is said through a variety of linguistic and nonlinguistic devices. As Clark and Krych (2004) emphasize, speech planning is opportunistic in taking advantage of the online process of language production to alter what is said as problems arise. This conclusion is also directly in line with Kecskés's dynamic model of meaning in which conversational interactions unfold not along pre-existing communicative intentions. Instead, speakers and listeners work together in more of a trial and error fashion to construe meaning "on the spot" given the specific conversational situation or task, including socio-cultural factors.

Kecskés has also noted how difficult it is to always align a specific utterance with a distinct "thought in the head" intention. Consider a situation where a teacher attempts to get a student to do his homework by saying "We're going to have a big test next week. You better catch up doing all of your overdue homework" (Gibbs 1999). Although the teacher's primary goal may be to get the student to do his homework, she may also be concerned with other things as well, such as to motivate the student to take greater personal responsibility for his education. In this case, getting the student to catch up with his homework assignments would only be one of a broader set of possible communicative goals.

In some cases, it is even difficult to attribute specific intentions to speakers because many utterances in discourse are incomplete, with other speakers quickly chiming in with their own contributions, some of which take the talk in a new direction. Consider this brief excerpt from a discussion among people attending a "Friends of the Earth" club meeting (Gregoromichelaki et al. 2011: 208).

(4) A: "So what is that? Is that er ... booklet or something?"
     B: "It's a book."
     C: "Book."
     B: "Just ..talking about al you know alternative"
     D: "Om erm, renewable yeah"
     B: "energy really I think"
     A: "Yeah."

This exchange illustrates how people move in and out of the parsing and production roles so that it is not really possible to ascribe specific intentions to particular utterances. The meanings understood in conversation rest not just in the minds of individual speakers, but emerge from the collaborative process of interaction between conversational participants. Speakers sometimes offer their listeners a choice of construals, so when listeners make their choice, they help to determine what the speaker is taken to mean (Clark 1996). A speaker may present an utterance with one intention in mind, but when the listener misconstrues it, the speaker then changes his or her mind and accepts the new construal.

One instance of this is seen in a radio broadcast where a baseball announcer was being interviewed about the game to be played, and was asked by a journalist, "Who is behind the plate today?" referring to what player was taking the position of catcher (Gibbs 1999). But the announcer misconstrues this to be a question about whom the umpire was for the game (who stands behind the catcher), and began talking about the umpire, which the journalist accepted and then maintained this topic by asking other questions about the umpire. Later on, the journalist acknowledged that he wanted to know who was playing catcher on that day.

Speakers sometimes do not correct listeners' misunderstandings because they deem it too trivial, disruptive, embarrassing to correct, or because what listeners infer, and respond to, somehow works better in the situation (see Firth's 1996 "let it pass" principle). In this way, speakers' intentions can partly emerge from the process of negotiating meaning in conversational interactions, including even ignoring a salient interpretation of what was said, again as suggested by Kecskés and Zhang.

The interactive way in which common ground sometimes emerges from discourse does not necessarily imply that people are always directed toward the other's perspective during talk exchanges. There are various demonstrations showing how speakers may occasionally be egocentric in their talk. Under some circumstances, such as stress or high levels of cognitive burden, speakers can be more egocentric in their productions than the traditional common ground view would predict.

One set of studies specifically examined whether people took other's perspectives into account when interpreting sarcastic remarks (Keysar 1994). These experiments tested if readers could withstand their own privileged knowledge when judging whether a speaker meant something sarcastic or not. Participants read stories ending with comments (e.g., "Oh yeah, Professor Jones is a real nice guy") that only they knew were really intended as sarcastic by the speakers (i.e., participants knew that the speaker believed the professor was rude). The participants were, however, asked to make the sarcasm judgments from the perspective of a story character that did not have this privileged information most relevant to the speaker's sarcastic intention. Overall, people generally were far more likely to attribute a sarcastic interpretation on the addressees' parts than should have been the case had the participants recognized the presumed common ground existing between speakers and listeners in the story context. People apparently cannot suppress their own privileged knowledge about a speaker's sarcastic intent when trying to assess the likely interpretation of other listeners (see Shintel and Keysar 2009 for a more nuanced view of egocentrism).

This conclusion calls into question the idea that an evaluation of common ground information is an automatic part of language interpretation. Indeed, different studies illustrate that listeners do not consistently consider common ground in their comprehension (Barr and Keysar 2005). People frequently misjudge the effectiveness of their own communication precisely because they do not correctly assess what is, and is not, part of their common ground with others. Speakers who have learned the meaning of opaque phrases, for instance, sometimes overestimate the likelihood that other people know those meanings (Keyser and Bly 1995). Speakers also sometimes think their own utterances are less ambiguous and more effective than they actually are (Keysar and Henly 2002), which also implies a failure to adopt other people's perspective during interpersonal interaction.

Advocates of the interactive, collaborative view have taken issue with some of these experimental results. For example, some scholars argue that the methods and theoretical conclusions in Keysar (1994) were flawed, primarily because of a missing critical control group. Gerrig, Ohaeri, and Brennen (2000) showed that readers were just as likely to judge a speaker's remark as sarcastic given either negative privileged information or no privileged information at all. Thus, experimental participants can track story characters' knowledge and intentions as part of their ordinary recourse to common ground during linguistic processing. People may not, nonetheless, always correctly assess what is presumably in their common ground with others, which will lead to misunderstandings of speakers' communicative intentions. Thus, the failure to properly understand the other person's perspective does not imply that a speaker or listener never tried to take that individual's point of view into immediate account as conversation unfolds in real-time.

More recent experimental studies have expanded on the types of information that gives rise to common ground. For example, various experiments have explored the way that metarepresentations, and metalinguistic cues (e.g., my partner can see what I am doing, I have talked to my partner before) shape people's understanding of their partner's perspectives (Horton and Brennan 2016). People may, given particular tasks, only view what is part of the common ground in a gradient or probabilistic manner (e.g., "I am somewhat certain that my partner believes X) (Brown-Schmidt 2012). An increasing number of psycholinguists now maintain that common ground emerges from constraint-satisfaction processes, which explains how individual perspective-taking in conversation arises given multiple, interacting forces or constraints (Brown-Schmidt and Hanna 2011). We explore one version of this possibility later. Still, certain proposals are widely discussed which insist that common ground is only rarely relied upon (Barr 2004; Pickering and Garrod 2004), especially assuming that people can speak egocentrically because they share the same context with their partners.

5 The dynamical systems alternative

What is required, then, is a broad theoretical model that is sensitive to many of the regularities and variations in the ways common ground develops and is applied during linguistic communication. Our suggestion is that a dynamical systems approach to linguistic pragmatics offers the flexibility and power to explain diverse experimental findings, yet also points the way to seeing common ground as primarily an emergent phenomenon (Gibbs 2010). The genesis for this alternative comes from the large body of research demonstrating how human performance emerges as products of human self-organizing systems. Any system whose structure is not imposed from outside forces or from internal blueprints (e.g., internal mental representations) alone can be said to self-organize (Bak 1996; Juarrerro 2000). Self-organizing systems are capable of creating new structures because their dynamics are dominated by these interactions instead of by the activity of isolated components. Emergent mechanisms are temporary, or "soft-assembled," because they do not endure as passively stored representations within the system's dynamics. Soft-assembly processes operate in highly context-sensitive ways within particular environmental niches to create the very specific physical patterns and behaviors within each system (Gibbs and Van Orden 2010).

A dynamical systems approach has been applied to explain many types of within- and between-human performance. First, many experimental results demonstrate that people spontaneously coordinate their movements during different nonverbal tasks. For example, one study looked closely at this, using two people sitting next to one another in rocking chairs. Intrinsic rocking frequencies of the chairs were manipulated by positioning weights at the base of the chairs (Richardson et al. 2007). Participants observed each other's chairs or looked away from one another. Most interestingly, when participants looked at each other, they soon settled into a dynamic of rock synchronously, even when the natural frequencies of their chairs differed. Thus, people unknowingly rocked against natural frequencies in order to reach synchrony, an example of temporal self-organization, producing an emergent temporal structure, instead of some internal executive representation.

Second, self-organization patterns emerge when people are specifically communicating with one another, which is evident in different kinds of nonverbal behaviors, such as coordination in participants' eye gaze, acoustic patterns of speech, the movements of heads and hands, people's postures, and so on, all of which constrain the dynamics of their interpersonal interaction (Gibbs and Van Orden 2010). In these ways, people's implicit coordinated behaviors are clearly influenced by what they observe or hear from one another. Even when people are not trying to coordinate, their bodily systems naturally become "entrained" and function as a "coupled" system. Self-organization in behavior arises from the interplay of brain, body, and environment as a single "context-sensitive" system.

This same approach can be applied to explain how people's mere knowledge or beliefs about one another also contribute to the spontaneous emergence of shared cognitive states, such as their "common ground". Thus, people's attributions about each other, and not just their perceptual and motor interactions, give rise to coordinated, interpersonal activities, including conversation. Studies show, for example, that a whole array of nonlinguistic dimensions (e.g., posture, prosody) becomes self-organized the more two speakers agree with one another (Paxton and Dale 2012).

How does this self-organizational perspective explain the diverse ways that common ground influences interpersonal communication? Speakers' words, as well as their paralinguistic and bodily actions, are produced to simultaneously achieve a stack of goals, including, coordinating with others in the moment, making a specific comment in light of what else has just been said or occurred, relieving a sense of incompatibility between what you expected and what occurred, and perhaps re-establishing some equilibrium with others in context (e.g., the teacher talking to her student about doing his homework). These different goals act as constraints on what words are uttered and what bodily acts are undertaken, with each of these being sustained on different time scales. Some goals emerge from longer time scales (e.g., general coordination with others), some on shorter time scales (e.g., the immediate desire to understand that he needs to do his homework), with others operating along even faster time scales (e.g., saying specific words in particular ways to convey one's emotional state).

Characterizing the ways people use language in interpersonal communication must take into account all of these interacting forces, and not simply focus on only what are traditionally conceived as more immediate, or proximate factors, such as privately-held mental intentions. There is no overarching mechanism that decides the process of formulating or interpreting linguistic utterances. People's conversational behaviors are not simply driven by purely egocentric or collaborative processes. Instead, people's abilities to coordinate their interactions when communicating emerges from self-organizational processes operating along multiple, linked time-scales without the need to explicitly align internal mental representations between individuals. Coordination in linguistic communication is not accomplished from matching up discrete mental entities between speakers but arises, more simply, from self-organizational processes within and across individuals.

A dynamical systems approach to common ground in conversation is capable of flexibly explaining how coordination emerges between individuals under varying complex conditions. For example, it is not always clear whether a speaker is talking in an egocentric or other-centric manner at any one point. Consider one study that explored this issue in a spatial perspective-taking task (Duran, Dale, and Kreuz 2011). Participants were asked to respond to the instructions from a simulated partner, working from a different computer terminal in another room, who requested one of two folder iconic displays on a table top graphic. Their instructions were ambiguous because they could be presumed to be from the egocentric perspective of the simulated partner, or from the participant's own perspective. The ambiguous nature of the instructions were based on their specific orientation of the folders in the desktop, as well as the way the simulated partner and participant were positioned around the virtual table. For instance, the request "Give me the folder on the right" would be ambiguous if the participant and partner sat on opposite sides of the table. Participants could, therefore, interpret the instructions to get the folder on his right (i.e., an egocentric view) or the right side of the partner (i.e., the other-centric perspective). Across the entire experiment of 40 trials, one-half of the instructions were ambiguous, and one-half were given in situations in which both persons shared the same perspective.

Overall, most participants in most trials adopted the more difficult other-centric perspective, as shown by the long processing time to understand and fulfill the requests. In fact, even when the participant and partner shared the same point of view, people took longer to act because they made efforts to engage with their partner's perspective, despite the fact that they already shared the same point of view.

Finally, this study was also designed to explore why people probabilistically so frequently chose the other-centric interpretation. Some participants were told beforehand that their partners were real, and given a cover story to strengthen this belief (when, in fact, the partner's instructions were pre-recorded). The rest of the people, however, were told that their partners were not real, but simulated. Not surprisingly, and consistent with earlier findings, people adopted the other-centric perspective far more often given the simulated than the real person conditions. Thus, participants' assumptions that the simulated partner may not be capable of inferring the others' perspectives led the participants to generally take their "simulated" partner's point of view when interpreting and following the instructions.

This study illustrates a deeper reality of how common ground emerges and is used in conversation. People may actually adopt both the ego-centric and other-centric perspectives at different times, and in different ways, depending on a host of factors. Indeed, people may even simultaneously make use of both perspectives at any one moment of speaking and understanding, precisely as suggested by Kecskés and Zhang in their earlier writings.

A dynamical systems simulation of these results aimed to explore the different attributional factors shown to be critical in people's perspective-taking behaviors (Duran and Dale 2013). This simulation described how complex ego- and other-centric behaviors self-organize over time with participants' responses unfolding within a low-dimensional attractor landscape. More specifically, this model accounts for participants' responses on an individual trial basis over the entire experiment, and the time it took people to execute their bi-stable ego-centric and other-centric responses. Quite simply, the simulation accounted for the experimental results, particularly the response time patterns and participants' response choices. Thus, general principles of dynamical systems, such as the self-organization of behavior given context and other constraining variables, provided a quantitative explanation of human communication processes. People's "common ground" emerges as "coupled behavior" by rapidly integrating attributional constraints (i.e., people's beliefs about whether their partner was real or not) along with physical characteristics of the task environment. In this way, people do not adopt either an ego- or other-centric perspective because their coupled systems exhibit "multipotentiality" in which both perspectives are immediately integrated during their task performances.

6 Conclusion

Can we reach common ground regarding "common ground"? Despite proposals that people either always speak and understand egocentrically or collaboratively, there is a growing trend to view "common ground" as an emergent phenomenon given ongoing self-organizational processes in human behavior. This general model is consistent with other dynamical system accounts in psycholinguistics, such as those related to lexical access and sentence processing (Gibbs 2006; Spivey 2007), and is, more broadly related to the rise of constraint-satisfaction models in cognitive science. Dynamic models have the advantage of being capable of explaining how the interpretation of different perspectives during conversation can be expressed as a nonlinear function of response histories by participants over the course of a single experiment. Determining when and how people behave collaboratively or not depends on many perceptual, motor and attributional factors, as well as specific task demands associated with any communicative context.

One advantage of the dynamical perspective is that it abandons the traditional "meanings in the head" view that has long dominated the study of linguistic pragmatics. Linguistic utterances are not direct reflections of pre-existing intentions locked inside the minds of speakers and listeners. Instead, meaning is always dynamic and emergent and is shaped by the interaction of perceptual, motor, cognitive, linguistics and social-cultural factors. István Kecskés, and his colleagues, have offered their own analysis of common ground in interpersonal communication that is generally consistent with the probabilistic, dynamical systems view of human performance argued for in this chapter. Of course, as we noted earlier, there remain disciplinary preferences for what data and what kinds of analyses must be offered in order to count as good scholarship in, for example, linguistics, psychology, philosophy, cognitive science, etc. Our hope is that linguistic pragmatic scholars will begin to consider broader models of human behavior, such as the dynamical systems approach advanced here. There is no reason why complex linguistic phenomena cannot be given the same scientific explanations which have been successfully applied in many areas of the biological and physical sciences. Common ground, like many regularities and variations in human behavior, arises as the temporary emergent product of basic self-organizing processes.

References

Bak, Per. 1996. *How nature works: The science of self-organized criticality*. New York: Copernicus.
Barr, Dale J. 2004. Establishing conventional communication systems: Is common knowledge necessary? *Cognitive Science* 28. 937–962.
Brown-Schmidt, Sarah. 2012. Beyond common and privileged: Gradient representations of common ground in real-time language use. *Language and Cognitive Processes* 27. 62–89.
Brown-Schmidt, Sarah & Joy E. Hanna. 2011. Talking in another person's shoes: Incremental perspective-taking in language processing. *Dialogue Discourse* 2. 11–33.
Clark, Herbert H. 1996. *Using language*. New York: Cambridge University Press.
Clark, Herbert H. & Deanna Wilkes-Gibbs. 1986. Referring as a collaborative process. *Cognition* 22. 1–39.
Clark, Herbert H. & Edward F. Schaefer. 1987. Concealing one's meaning from overhearers. *Journal of Memory and Language* 26. 209–225.
Clark, Herbert H. & Meredith A. Krych. 2004. Speaking while monitoring addressees for understanding. *Journal of Memory and Language* 50. 62–81.
Colston, Herbert L. 2008. A new look at common ground: Memory, egocentrisim and joint meaning. In István Kecskés & Jacob Mey (eds.), *Intention, common ground, and the egocentric speaker-hearer*, 151–188. Berlin & New York: Mouton de Gruyter.
Colston, Herbert L. 2015. *Using figurative language*. New York: Cambridge University Press.
Duran, Nicholas D. & Rick Dale. 2013. Perspective-taking in dialogue as self-organization under social constraints. *New Ideas in Psychology* 32. 131–146.
Duran, Nicholas D., Rick Dale & Roger J. Kreuz. 2011. Listeners invest in an assumed other's perspective despite cognitive cost. *Cognition* 121. 22–40.
Firth, Alan. 1996. The discursive accomplishment of normality: On conversation analysis and 'lingua franca' English. *Journal of Pragmatics* 26. 237–259.
Gerrig, Richard J., Justina O. Ohaeri & Susan E. Brennan. 2000. Illusory transparency revisited. *Discourse Processes* 29. 137–159.
Gibbs, Raymond W. 1999. *Intentions in the experience of meaning*. New York: Cambridge University Press.
Gibbs, Raymond W. 2006. *Embodiment and cognitive science*. New York: Cambridge University Press.
Gibbs, Raymond W. 2010. Stability and variability in linguistic pragmatics. *Pragmatics and Society* 1. 32–49.
Gibbs, Raymond W. & Guy Van Orden. 2010. Adaptive cognition without massive modularity. *Language & Cognition* 2. 149–176.
Gregoromichelaki, Eleni, Ruth Kempson, Matthew Purver, Gregory Mills, Ronnie Cann, Wilfried Meyer-Viol & Patrick Healey. 2011. Incrementaility and intention-recognition in utterance processing. *Dialogue and Discourse* 2. 199–233.
Horton, William S. & Susan E. Brennan. 2016. The role of metarepresentation in the production and resolution of referring expressions. *Frontiers in Psychology* 7. DOI: 10.3389/fpsyg.2016.011
Isaacs, Ellen A & Herbert H. Clark. 1987. References in conversations between experts and novices. *Journal of Experimental Psychology: General* 116. 26–37.
Juarrero, Alice. 2000. *Dynamics in action: Intentional behavior as complex system*. Cambridge, MA: MIT Press.

Kecskés, István. 2008. Dueling context: A dynamic model of meaning. *Journal of Pragmatics* 40. 385–406.
Kecskés, István & Jacob Mey (eds.). 2008. *Intention, common ground, and the egocentric speaker-hearer*. Berlin & New York: Mouton de Gruyter.
Kecskés, István & Fenghui Zhang. 2009. Activating, seeking and creating common ground: A socio-cultural approach. *Pragmatics & Cognition* 17. 331–355.
Kecskés, István & Fenghui Zhang. 2013. On the dynamic relations between common ground and presupposition. In Alessandro Capone, Franco Lo Piparo & Marco Carpapezza (eds.), *Perspectives on linguistic pragmatics*, 375–395. Dordrecht: Springer.
Keysar, Boaz. 1994. The illusory transparency of intention: Linguistic perspective taking in text. *Cognitive Psychology* 26. 165–208.
Keysar, Boaz & Bridget Bly. 1995. Intuitions of the transparency of idioms: Can one keep a secret by spilling the beans? *Journal of Memory and Language* 34. 89–109.
Keysar, Boaz & Anne S. Henly. 2002. Speakers' overestimation of their effectiveness. *Psychological Science* 13. 207–212.
Paxton, Alexandra & Rick Dale. 2013. Argument disrupts interpersonal synchrony. *Quarterly Journal of Experimental Psychology* 66. 2092–2102.
Pickering Martin J. & Simon Garrod. 2004. Towards a mechanistic psychology of dialogue. *Behavioral and Brain Sciences* 27. 169–226.
Richardson, Michael J., Kerry Marsh, Robert W. Isenhower, Justin RL Goodman & Richard C. Schmidt. 2007. Rocking together: Dynamics of intentional and unintentional interpersonal coordination. *Human Movement Science* 26. 867–891.
Shintel, Hadas & Boaz Keysar. 2009. Less is more: A minimalist account of joint action in communication. *Topics in Cognitive Science* 1. 260–273.
Spivey, Michael J. 2007. *The continuity of mind*. New York: Oxford University Press.

Robert E. Sanders
3 Overcoming differences and achieving common ground: Why speaker and hearer make the effort and how they go about it

1 Introduction

Traditional pragmatic theory is founded on the tacit premise of sameness between speaker and hearer. On the premise of sameness, general, shared, principles and rules were theorized that tie the situated meaningfulness of utterances to their *im*personal context, making any idiosyncracies of speaker and hearer irrelevant. These are institutional, communal, interpersonal or discursive contexts that have become fixed and conventionalized across individuals, such as referred to in Searle's (1969) constitutive rules of illocutionary acts, and Hymes' (1974) "rules" of speech events. On this premise, we can expect uniformities in the composition of an utterance across speakers produced with the same intention about its situated meaning, and reciprocally, uniformities across hearers in their understandings of that utterance's situated meaning.[1]

The shortcomings of this premise of sameness have not been ignored over the years, but Kecskés' (2014) socio-cognitive model of intercultural pragmatics confronts them head on. He addresses critical shortcomings in this premise of sameness, and offers a remedy. My agenda here is to build on what Kecskés has proposed and go a step further.

This premise of sameness certainly includes language/utterance processing sameness, which is probably a universal and has not been a matter of serious contention. But the premise of sameness led to disregarding all the other ways in which people are inescapably different psychologically that affect understandings, for example in the associations they make between what is taking place

---

[1] There are a range of criteria for what constitutes "understanding", with early ones in pragmatics mirroring those in semantics of understanding as a correct interpretation of that utterance in that circumstance. But the criterion that most speakers and hearers evidently adopt, at least in practice, is an interactional one, and most theorists and analysts have adopted it as well. The criterion is that an utterance has been understood when it has been understood well enough for speaker and hearer to both be satisfied and move on from that one to the next. The term "understanding trouble" is employed here rather than "misunderstanding" to capture this, in that the term "misunderstanding" presupposes that an "incorrect" interpretation has been made. Instead, an understanding trouble arises when an utterance has not been understood well enough for hearer and/or speaker to move on to the next utterance, as indicated by either the hearer and/or the speaker not moving on and initiating repair instead.

"now" and their reservoir of experiences and memories, perceptual biases, processing habits, and so forth (e.g., Tversky and Kahneman 1974; Giora 2003; Keysar 2007).

The premise of sameness also includes linguistic sameness (typically the syntactic/semantic/lexical knowledge shared by native or fluent speakers of the same language). However, this premise is difficult to sustain in the context of globalization. We live in a world in which the language in which people interact may not be their native language, and which they may not know equally well, whether they be interactions between non-native and native speakers, or between all non-native speakers in a lingua franca (Firth 1996; Gardner and Wagner 2004; Mauranen 2012).

And less overtly in the literature but unmistakably, the premise of sameness includes what might best be referred to as cultural sameness – communally shared knowledge of the world, and of norms, rights and obligations, tasks and activities, customs and routines. This is knowledge in Hymes' (1974) sense, of speech events and how to participate in them; in Garfinkel's (1967), Goffman's (1959) and Gumperz' (1982) sense, of how the tasks and activities of everyday life are done; and in Schank and Abelson's (1977) sense, of conventionalized scripts and schemas. However, in a world in which people are less and less segregated into communities of sameness, this premise of cultural sameness between speaker and hearer is difficult to sustain.

Insofar as such "sameness" between speaker and hearer cannot be counted on, people face increased chances of understanding troubles and the need for efforts to overcome them. This has not been overlooked by work in pragmatics since its early days in the 1970s, but it has led our work to go in two directions. One is to more carefully and fully theorize the processing involved that depends on "sameness" to work, and to make sameness less a global condition and more contingent on the local realities of person and context, as most notably in relevance theory (Sperber and Wilson 1986) and politeness theory (Brown and Levinson 1987). The other path is to stress that understanding troubles and efforts to overcome them are to be expected, with a resulting focus on the achievement of understanding through interaction (e.g., Sanders 1987; Clark 1996; Arundale 2008; Haugh 2015; and of course, Kecskés 2014).

Kecskés has disputed the soundness of the theoretical premise of sameness and uniformities of production and interpretation by delineating sources of difference, and calling attention to the resulting efforts of speaker and hearer to work towards sameness as they discover difference. In his book, Kecskés (2014) calls attention to the various ways in which speaker and hearer may differ in their knowledge and experience of the world, of other people, of contexts and situations, habits and methods of processing information, and language. He reminds us that in addition to possible cultural differences (with which globalization increasingly faces us), people may also differ as psychological beings. He views us as being individuated by our alleged egocentrism (in Keysar's 2007 sense – but see Sanders, Wu, and Bonito 2013) and by what is salient at any moment against the backdrop of our personal histories, knowledge, interests, and focus of attention regarding the matters, discourse, and lexicon at hand (e.g., Giora 2003).

In line with Clark's (1996) approach, Kecskés' socio-cognitive model posits that it is a matter of discovery through interaction how much of such prior knowledge and experience, and habits and methods of processing information, speaker and hearer share. As Kecskés (2014) puts it, adopting the term from Clark (1996), it is a matter of discovering the extent of the "common ground" they have at the outset and then expanding that through interaction, presumably one or both aspects that Clark distinguishes – their "communal common ground" (what they know in common through a shared culture) and "personal common ground," or more accurately, interpersonal common ground (what they know in common through past experience with each other). The extent to which they do not have common ground is the extent to which they will encounter understanding and coordination troubles, with the remedy for those being to build greater common ground through interaction.

This brings me to my agenda here, to build on Kecskés' thesis by providing two codicils that address the questions of *why* and *how* speakers and hearers make the effort to cope with and remedy the understanding and coordination troubles their differences produce. The questions I address specifically are:

1. Remedying understanding and coordination troubles by building common ground is effortful and success is not assured, so *why* do people make the effort to do this instead of giving in to their differences and ending efforts to communicate?
2. In light of their differences, *how* do people go about building common ground when they do not have it sufficiently at the outset to avoid understanding and coordination troubles?

It seems from a close examination of naturally occurring interactions that there is more under the empirical surface of communication between persons than Kecskés delves into. In particular, Kecskés' model predicts that there will be a linear relationship between the degree of difference between speaker and hearer – linguistically, culturally, and/or psychologically – and how effortful communication between them is. But as some of the data examined here show, this relationship is not a constant and we have to be cautious about it. First, between persons who are "the same" by most measures, understanding troubles may still arise, just as much as for persons who are different. Second, between persons who are not "the same," even opposites, communication may occur without understanding troubles.

2 Codicil 1: *Why* people work at overcoming differences – the rhetorical covenant

In this section, I address the first question, why people make the effort to overcome differences instead of giving in to them and stopping the talk. In some cases, people persist even if their differences make communication effortful because there is a practical exigence that makes communicating obligatory. Failing to communicate at all, or doing so ineffectively, would have damaging, perhaps even dire, consequences; for example in collaborating on the operation of commercial aircraft, diagnosing a medical condition, or in a 911 call. But in many instances, communication is more optional – still a means to an end, but with consequences that are not dire if it does not have the practical or social benefit it was engaged in to bring about. And yet even if communication that is less consequential becomes effortful because of speaker-hearer differences, speaker and hearer generally persist in their efforts to overcome differences and make communication work.

I propose that the basis for such persistence, even when communicating is more optional, is that speaking, and being spoken to, make a special claim on us. This is because speaking to others is an inherently practical activity.[2] When people produce utterances, it is not ("normally") for the pleasure of hearing their own voice.[3] Aside from recourse to force and violence, speaking to others is our principal means of getting things done with each other, and bringing things about that depend on others' participation, support or acquiescence. Hence, we speak to others because, and when, there is something to be gained from it.[4] In

---

[2] Communication is practical in the sense of being a means to an end that benefits speaker, hearer, or both. In addition to such material practicalities as collaboration on material tasks and activities, giving or getting information, and making plans, decisions, and arrangements, I include such social practicalities as negotiating, supporting, affiliating or dissociating, gossiping, socializing, entertaining, and so forth.
[3] Of course, people are sometimes said to be doing just that, speaking for the pleasure of hearing their own voice, but this is an accusation of *wrongdoing*. It is a breach of their not having discernibly been speaking as people are expected to do, as arguably we have a social contract to do – speaking *to* others as a means of involving them in bringing something about, even just being respectfully or companionably co-present, and not be wasting their time.
[4] There is certainly cultural variability, and probably institutional, professional, relational and individual variability, in what is included under "something to be gained from it" that

general, this may involve a practical, social, intellectual, professional, or institutional matter, whether a matter of enduring consequence, of momentary gratification, or somewhere in between. The end result may be one that is mutually beneficial (a negotiated settlement; a celebration; a plan), or that benefits the hearer(s) (speaker provides instruction, assistance, entertainment), or that benefits the speaker (hearer complies with a request, redresses a grievance, gives advice).

A truism comes to bear here that applies to all creatures – that energy will be expended on something only if there is an exigence that requires it and will be resolved by it.[5] The presumption of "optimal relevance" in Relevance theory is an extrapolation from this truism, that an ostensive stimulus is presumed by the hearer to be worth the effort to process it to the extent of the effort a speaker puts into making it optimally relevant to the hearer. But that does not go far enough. It does not capture that *being spoken to* makes a special claim on us, nor that there is a social dimension in this, not just a cognitive one: We (people generally) take for granted that when someone speaks to us, even a stranger in passing, that (a) the speaker has reached out to us in particular, and (b) there is something to be gained from it that somehow involves us, so that (c) it would be irresponsible and/or anti-social of us to disattend it.

The evidence that speaking and being spoken to makes a special claim on us socially is plain,[6] much of it captured by Goffman's (1959, 1967) ideas about

---

warrants or necessitates speaking. For example, in some ethnic traditions, "something to be gained" includes ceremonial results in a context that for others involves mainly practical ones (e.g., Keenan 1973 on the betrothal ritual of the rural Malagasy). And what may be gained from speaking seems to be conceptualized relatively narrowly among American Indians, with a corresponding comfort with not speaking in the presence of an other (Basso 1986; Braithwaite 1990; Phillips 1982; Scollon and Scollon 1981); and conceptualized expansively among American "whites" with a corresponding *dis*comfort with not speaking in the presence of an other.

5 This truism was captured in a pair of signs under the first exhibit we came to years ago in the reptile house at the Brookfield Zoo in Chicago. The first sign asked "Why don't they move?" The second answered, "Why should they?"

6 The use of new technologies provides further evidence of the hold that being spoken to has over us, in that they give hearers ways to save themselves from being intruded on and/or having their time wasted when others speak to them. A ringing telephone and through that the caller's "summons" once made the same claim on the attention of the one called/addressed as being spoken to does, but telemarketers exploited that with calls that are a waste of the hearer's time. With the advent of caller ID on telephones, hearers can and often do shield themselves from being spoken to by anyone other than known contacts. And many users have shielded themselves further by having replaced phoning altogether with texting, arguably because a text, even from a known contact, does not make the same claim on us to stop what we are doing just then and attend to it that being called/summoned does.

facework, and the politeness theory Brown and Levinson (1987) developed from those. First, even though being spoken to is inherently intrusive, hearers do observably stop what they are otherwise doing, often reflexively, and attend when someone speaks to them. Second, for a hearer to ignore a speaker is often an affront, and may be met with anger. Third, speakers take for granted this receptiveness by hearers, in that they generally do not do anything more to gain the hearer's attention than to just start speaking, although sometimes content-free preliminaries are used such as "Excuse me" (to specific others) or "Can I have your attention" (to an assemblage) when the hearer/s is/are engaged with something else at the moment.

Fourth, speakers generally self-edit, rather than verbalize whatever and whenever thoughts or feelings occur to them, so that their utterances are directed to others as means to some situationally-relevant end (e.g., Goffman 1959, 1967) that is relationally, institutionally, professionally, and/or culturally "normal." Hymes (1964) made this point with reference to culture-specific "speaking rules" as to when speaking is obligatory, optional, or proscribed; to whom one may speak, about what, when and where, and so forth. Speakers who detectably fail to self-edit in those ways – who in the presence of others just speak, directed to no one in particular, about nothing of situational relevance – are likely to seem impaired or pathological.

This self-editing by speakers, combined with the general attentiveness of hearers when spoken to, and speakers' expectation of this attentiveness, all point to the same foundation – that *there is a tacit social contract among us that speaking will only be done when speakers deem that there is something to be gained from it, and that hearers when spoken to will therefore attend, process, and respond.*[7] On the basis of this social contract, speakers are accountable for there *being* something to be brought about by that speaking just then. And both speakers *and* hearers, hearers having become encumbered just by being spoken to, thereby become *jointly* accountable for bringing about whatever the speaking was done to bring about. This social contract goes beyond the premise of traditional pragmatics that speakers produce utterances with the intention that they will have a certain meaning and that hearers reciprocally presume the speaker has intended this. This contract presumes that speakers produce the utterances

---

[7] Put in these terms, it may seem to be entirely a matter of "politeness", or saving the face of self and other, that motivates speaker and hearer to make these efforts, so that there is no need to posit that there is a special social contract to explain them. But there would not be a face threat here if it were not for this social contract and the standing obligation it creates for speaker and hearer to uphold it by each making efforts for speaking once started to bring something about and not be a waste of time.

they do with the additional intention that they will *bring something about* by speaking and that hearers reciprocally presume the speaker has intended this in having said exactly that just then (see Sanders 2015 on the distinction between utterance-level intentions and activity-level intentions).

I refer to this social contract as the *Rhetorical Covenant,* a covenant that speaking will be crafted to be a means to some specific end that is consequential to hearers, an end often incumbent on hearers to assent to and even assist with bringing about. In ancient Greece and Rome, "rhetoric" was the study and practice of the art of persuasion to resolve civil disputes (as in the writings of Plato, Aristotle, Cicero, and Quintillian). It later became, more broadly, the art of adapting discourse to its end (George Campbell in eighteenth century Britain). I also include under this heading twentieth century ideas about rhetoric as the inherent influence of language/speaking on people and situations (Kenneth Burke 1945, 1950; and Richard Weaver [1953] 1985, in America); and that speaking is an action that reifies or constructs social realities (Ludwig Wittgenstein 1953 and J.L. Austin 1962 in Britain; and in America, Harvey Sacks' 1992 lectures in the 1960s; Erving Goffman 1959; Harold Garfinkel 1967; Dell Hymes 1974).

It is not a new idea that when someone speaks, speakers and hearers thereby become accountable for fulfilling certain obligations to each other, but most have focused either on the speaker's obligation (Sacks and Schegloff's 1979 concept of "recipient design"; Clark's 1996 concept of "optimal design") or the hearer's obligation (Grice's 1975 focus on the hearer's presumption of speaker cooperativeness; Wilson and Sperber's 2004 concept of "optimal relevance").

In contrast, what the Rhetorical Covenant makes obligatory is that *both* speaker and hearer collaboratively make something come of it when speaking is done at all and troubles arise, starting with producing an understandable utterance and making a relevant (and preferably for the speaker, a targeted) response. That mutual obligation applies as much when there are differences between speaker and hearer that make fulfilling the Rhetorical Covenant more difficult as when there are not, else (we presume) speaking would not have been done in the first place. For the speaker to not make a good faith effort to overcome differences that stand in the way of bringing about what he or she spoke to bring about – starting with the way each utterance is understood and responded to – is therefore an accountable matter. It could raise doubts among hearers and observers about the speaker's will or ability to uphold the Rhetorical Covenant and not be wasting the hearer's time. Conversely, for the hearer to not make a good faith effort is also an accountable matter, because not doing so would manifest the hearer's doubts about the speaker's will or ability to uphold the Rhetorical Covenant.

This predicts that no matter what the basis or extent is of differences between speaker and hearer, they will make notable efforts to overcome their differences once speaking occurs. This is not done for its own sake, but only if and when, and focused on remediating it, a trouble arises that stands in the way of bringing about whatever understanding and response the speaking was done to bring about, as we see in Example (1). Example (1) is from an interaction in English as a lingua franca between two non-native speakers, one Japanese (J) and the other Korean (K), that Kecskés (2014) used to make a point about topic change. But the interest in Example (1) here is the amount of effort speaker and hearer put into getting a question answered, even though the answer was not particularly consequential for either speaker or hearer, at least on the surface.

J and K were in an instructional environment that obligated them to interact, but not necessarily to persist in talk on a topic if it became effortful, and yet they did. We can assume that there are important differences in their common ground – cultural differences, and linguistic differences with reference to their knowledge of English – but these are not overt in this instance, nor the source of the understanding or coordination trouble that arose. The source of the trouble between J and K in this instance seems to have arisen from a psychological difference between them, that a linkage between referents was salient to K and not J.

(1) Kecskés (2014: 29), Albany lingua franca database
J: I play baseball with Japanese and Korean men.
K: Ah there must be a lot of competition no?
J: Hm?
K: You know like … You know like … You are going… things are bad in Korea because of history. So maybe competitions?
J: Competi-
K: Ok maybe you guys feel like ok we have to win. Japan has to win. No no?
J: No.
K: Ok that's good nice nice … Do you like American food?

The main source of the trouble here seems to have arisen from linkages between Japan and Korea that were made salient for K by J's reference to Japanese and Korean men playing baseball. The linkage, indicated by K's allusion in line 5 to history, is probably between Japan as a colonial power in Korea and Koreans as a subjugated people. With that linkage evidently in mind, K surmised that Japanese and Koreans engaged in playing baseball together would feel "a lot of competition" and is asking J whether this is so. This is a linkage that was evidently unapparent to J and so there was an understanding trouble; or alternatively, perhaps this linkage was quite clear to J but he found it a delicate matter, so that he resisted participating in this topical line, resulting in a coordination trouble.

J's response to the initial question about this displays (or feigns) an understanding trouble (line 3: "Hm?"). K attempts to clarify in lines 4–5 by alluding to the historical linkage between Japan and Korea that has evidently become salient to him and that, from this perspective, might provoke competition between persons of these two nationalities. J's response to this indicates he still does not understand well enough to answer the question, but now he identifies the source of the understanding trouble as the word "competition" (line 6: "Competi-"), either the meaning of the word "competition" or for K to refer to it at all. K's response indicates he regards the matter to be an understanding trouble, in that he defines the term "competition" as a concern with winning (line 7: "maybe you guys feel like ok we have to win"). But at the same time he attributes this desire to the Japanese in particular, bringing the delicate matter of Japan as a colonial power closer to the surface. J's response is a flat "No." If an understanding trouble was involved here, this response displays an understanding and ends the matter (though it is not certain that J did finally understand the question when he answered it, or just unobtrusively gave up and adopted the proffered candidate answer, "no"). Alternately, if a coordination trouble, not an understanding trouble, was involved here because this was a delicate matter to J, his response of a flat "no" both ends the matter and tacitly rejects the soundness of the linkage and a willingness to go any further with it.

It is the most obvious, but in this case not the only, manifestation of the Rhetorical Covenant that both K and J persisted in their respective efforts to get K's initial question understood and answered, or acknowledged and answered. In addition, a more subtle way in which the Rhetorical Covenant manifests itself is the way K responds in line 10 to J's answer. J's having answered with a simple "no" probably did not accomplish whatever K sought to accomplish by asking his question. It is minimal and uninformative about what K arguably wanted to find out (which seems to have been whether it was manifested in the dynamics among players that Japan had been a colonial power in Korea, specifically whether Japanese players felt they had to win in competition with Koreans). But K did not respond to J's simple "no" as being at all insufficient, possibly because doing so might have made it seem that he had been wasting their time, and thus not fulfilling his obligation under the Rhetorical Covenant. Instead, despite its shortcomings, K accepts J's answer in an over-built way[8] as being entirely satis-

---

8 To claim a response is over-built turns on a subjective judgment of whether it goes beyond what is called for to fulfill the Rhetorical Covenant. If one judges that J's response of "no" in Example (1) minimally fulfilled his obligations under the Rhetorical Covenant to help bring about whatever K asked his question to bring about, then a commensurate assessment would have been equally minimal (e.g., "OK"). On that basis, K's response seems over-built because

factory (line 10: "Ok that's good nice nice"), thereby heading off any inference that pursuing an answer and getting this answer to his question had been a waste of their time.

In addition, while K may have opted to close the matter there because it was so effortful to get the little he did from J thus far, he may (also/instead) have closed it there because to keep going on this topic risked a more blatant failure to fulfill his obligation under the Rhetorical Covenant to not be wasting their time. Pursuing the matter further risked getting no more from J than K already had, therefore a waste of their time, no matter whether J had answered with a simple "no" because he still did not understand, or because he had nothing more to say on the matter, or because the historical role of Japan in Korea was a delicate matter for him and he was uncomfortable with its even being alluded to, especially by a Korean. For that reason, the Rhetorical Covenant warrants K's having changed the topic just then, and moreover, changed it so completely (line 10: "Do you like American food?").[9]

3 Codicil 2: *How* people overcome differences – resources and processes

Given that the Rhetorical Covenant obligates speaker and hearer each, and jointly, to make a good faith effort to remedy understanding and coordination troubles to bring about whatever speaking was done to bring about, the main question here is how they go about doing so. The answer starts with the recognition that even if speaker and hearer lack the common ground needed to understand and respond to each other "effortlessly", that does not mean that they lack common ground entirely, as Kecskés makes clear. Kecskés refers to this as their "core" common ground, the samenesses two people have at the outset – presumably a composite of what Clark (1996) refers to as communal and [inter]personal common ground.

---

he made three assessments of that response, not one, moreover each more positive than the prior, adding up to enthusiasm – "OK" + "that's good" + "nice nice". Even if K actually did like knowing that Japanese did not feel a need to win when playing with Koreans, arguably only one positive assessment would do (e.g., "that's good").

9 K's topic change seems abrupt (at least to Kecskés and to me). But whether a topic change seems abrupt turns on a subjective judgment that it occurred before talk on the prior topic had brought about whatever it was produced to bring about, and thus before the Rhetorical Covenant had been (adequately) fulfilled. If one judges that J's answer of "no" to K's question does not actually bring about whatever the question may have been asked to bring about, despite K's acceptance of it, it makes changing the topic just then seem abrupt.

Kecskés argues that when understanding or coordination troubles arise, the remedy is for speaker and hearer to create an expanded common ground. Given that they already have common ground to build on, the question here is, how do they go about it each time they encounter an understanding or coordination trouble? To get at this, we first have to go below the surface of the concept of common ground to recognize that common ground is a multiplex, not unitary bodies of shared linguistic knowledge, communal knowledge, and [inter]personal knowledge. Within such bodies of knowledge and experience there are generally subareas or domains within which the extent of common ground between any pair of people may vary. I refer to each of these as a *common ground domain*. For example, the lexical common ground of any two speakers of a language is unlikely to be unitary, but to comprise multiple parts that are likely to vary in extent across various activity domains and epistemic domains (e.g., two neighbors may have much greater lexical common ground in the domain of home maintenance, and much less in their respective professional domains). When an understanding or coordination trouble arises from a lexical difference, it will be a difference in a particular domain. To remedy the trouble and replace difference with sameness, speaker and hearer can draw on their common ground *in that domain* once they identify the domain in which the trouble has arisen. We see this in Example (1), when J evidently had lexical trouble with the word "competition". To remedy it, K turned to expected lexical common ground in the domain of game-playing, and tied the trouble word ("competition") to words that were expectably in the activity domain of a lexical common ground, sports, specifically tying "competition" to a desire to "win".

The question we then come to is how speaker and/or hearer identify what the common ground domain is in which the trouble arose, so that they can remedy the trouble by reasoning forward from the common ground they *expectably* have in that domain to overcome the specific trouble that arose, replacing that difference with sameness. Identifying the domain is likely the more straightforward matter, insofar as there is a topic being talked about (e.g., in Example (1), playing baseball, therefore the domain of sports) or activity being engaged in (e.g., in Example (2) below, opening a phone call). The expectation or assumption of what common ground speaker and hearer have in a domain that they can draw on to remedy the trouble sometimes has a basis in their prior experience with each other ([inter]personal common ground in the domain), but they do not always have this. A more reliable basis for such expectations, often the entire basis, is culturally-grounded stereotypes of the language, knowledge, and experience in that domain of "persons like that" (stereotypes probably tied to such observables as age, gender, class, education, appearance and manner, native or foreign).

3.1 Common ground and understanding troubles of people who are minimally different

This process of analysis and remedy is likely to be the same regardless of the degree of difference between speaker and hearer (or the extent of their common ground). But it is of particular interest to examine what is done to remedy troubles between people who are minimally different, for all practical purposes "the same" from the perspective of traditional pragmatics. In addition to the light these examples shed on what contribution speaker and hearer may respectively make in resolving troubles, these examples are also instructive about the variety of ways that, as Kecskés anticipates, people may differ despite being the "same" in the common ways in which we compare people (language, culture, age and perhaps other demographics such as social class and economic status).

Examples (2)–(5) are a succession of troubles in a single telephone call between Angie and Harvey, who are minimally different, yet it seems, consequentially different. Each of those troubles arose in a specific domain of topic or activity, and the remedies arose from corresponding common ground domains. Across these four instances, there is some variation in the contribution Angie and Harvey each make to analyzing and remedying the trouble.

Angie and Harvey are older adults living in the Berkeley, California area in the mid-1980s. Harvey is the husband of Angie's close friend or relative, Rita. Angie is the caller, presumably to talk to Rita, but Harvey answered, and so they talked for a few minutes before Harvey called Rita to the phone. Based on evidence within the recording itself, Angie and Harvey speak the same language, and seem to be comparable in age, from the same class and culture, and well-known to each other. While Angie and Harvey could long since have developed all the common ground they need to achieve understanding and coordination, it seems they have not done so (contrary to Kecskés' expectation that as people with consequential differences interact over time, a "third" and new common ground/culture will emerge between them). In particular, it seems Angie has not, or cannot, learn how to adjust for and overcome differences between her and Harvey, despite almost certainly having often interacted with him beforehand. Perhaps this is because remedying a trouble in a specific instance may only address a specific source of trouble in a specific domain for current purposes without adding to their common ground in that domain, or may not be enough to overcome psychological differences that seem to be involved in Angie's and Harvey's interaction.

In their conversation, Angie seems to process talk-in-interaction faster than Harvey does, is more informed, with more sophisticated interests, experiences, and attitudes. As a result, in Examples 2–5, a recurrent source of trouble is the recipient design of Angie's utterances. She moves on before Harvey is ready to, refers to something as already known about that Harvey does not already know about, and so forth. And then when Harvey's response reveals an understanding trouble or coordination trouble, Angie has to "stop" and go back, and she and Harvey then work at identifying the source of trouble and remedying it well enough to go on.

Although Angie and Harvey do not need to spend much effort overcoming each one of these troubles, their conversation is cumulatively quite effortful because it is made up almost entirely of producing troubles and then overcoming them. Yet they persisted, both of them making the effort needed to fulfill their respective obligations under the Rhetorical Covenant to bring about what speaking was done to bring about.

The successive troubles in this conversation, and the sources of common ground Harvey and Angie draw on to overcome them, involve communally grounded knowledge of: how phone calls are opened, Example (2); that sending a card is a way to celebrate someone's birthday, Example (3); that colleges are venues where plays are performed, Example (4); and different genres of plays, Example (5).

3.1.1 Angie-Harvey common ground domain 1: How phone calls open

In Example (2), the trouble that arises involves Angie's having truncated the opening of their phone call to bypass identifiers and greetings in a way that is common among familiars (Hopper et al. 1990/91). It seems that Harvey cannot/will not go forward absent much of what Angie omitted, and he initiates the restoration of identifiers and greetings.[10] This trouble makes relevant their knowledge of the canonical opening of phone calls (Schegloff 1979, 1986), and both draw on this for a remedy.

---

[10] There could also be resistance to truncating the conventional opening sequence for the sake of preserving the ritual or etiquette of participating in it. *Anecdotal Evidence: S was driving through the French countryside, and was unsure which turn to make as he left a village, so he went back to ask for directions from two women he had seen socializing in front of a grocery. He opened with "Parl' Anglais?" The women looked at him in brief silence, and then the one to his left (L) smiled and extended her hand to shake his, saying "Bon jour." S inferred that L was giving him a lesson in manners by ignoring his question and initiating a different opening, an exchange of greetings, in her language, before getting to whatever business S might want them to attend to. S reciprocated her greeting; then L, in fluent English, asked how she could be of help.*

(2)   Hopper Archive, University of Texas: "Berkeley" ca. 1985

((telephone ringing))
Harvey: H'lo:.
Angie: Hi Harv,
              (0.7)
Angie: Yer [company the::re?
Harvey: [(Who is it) Angie?
Angie: ↑Yeah.
Harvey: How are ya?
Angie: Pretty ↑good. (0.2) Didjer company arrive?
Harvey: La-Yeah yeah, last night.

The canonical way in which telephone calls open is that identifiers and greetings are exchanged before anything substantive is said, although this opening may be truncated in some service encounters (Hopper et al. 1990/91). It may also be truncated if voice recognition (and/or Caller ID) make identifiers redundant.[11] Angie truncated the opening of this call by going directly to a greeting and substantive question without giving Harvey a chance to reciprocate and participate, evidently considering that identifiers in this case were redundant even then (mid 1980s), prior to Caller ID technology.

In greeting Harvey by name, Angie shows that she knows who it was that answered, perhaps from voice recognition alone, but possibly also from knowing he was the male resident in the home who would have answered the phone. And given that she conjoined her greeting with a substantive (and personalized) question, without identifying herself, Angie evidently expected her identity to be equally recognizable to Harvey. She may have expected this on the basis of voice recognition alone, but perhaps also from additional indicators she gave – that she is a female who knows Harvey well enough to recognize his voice, well enough to use a shortened form of his name that is probably reserved for friends

---

11 Openings may be more radically truncated than research has documented if identifications would be redundant and the caller and recipient know that caller has no other reason for call than to resume a prior line of talk or action, in which case the call may "start" by picking up where the parties left off, without any preliminaries at all, sometimes to be playful with openings. *Anecdotal Evidence: R asked S for the loan of some equipment, and S explained he kept it at a different site and would bring it home after he went to that site the following Tuesday. R said he would call on Wednesday to arrange to pick up the equipment. S had forgotten about R's request until he was reminded on Wednesday when he saw from Caller ID that it was R calling. S answered the phone by saying "I forgot," responding to the known caller and presumed reason for call. R was not confused by this. His first turn at speaking consisted of laughter at how truncated and to the point that opening had been.*

and relatives ("Harve" rather than "Harvey"), and well enough to have asked a substantive question that reveals an insider's up-to-date knowledge of and interest in Harvey's affairs (that he was expecting "company" to arrive).

But Angie was wrong. Harvey is not certain, or is unwilling to assume, who is calling despite the indicators she has given him. He makes this apparent in line 6 by speaking over her question about whether his company has arrived to ask who she is, adding the candidate answer "Angie?". As a result, the call opening does not go forward in the truncated way Angie had initiated. The remedy they both adopt is to fall back on knowledge they evidently expect to have in common of the canonical opening sequence. Harvey's solicitation of Angie's identity in line 6 reinstates the canonical opening sequence. Angie endorses and participates in this reinstatement by just affirming his candidate answer about her identity (line 7: "↑Yeah.") and nothing more, foregoing a reiteration just then of her question that Harvey stepped on. This clears the way for Harvey to continue the canonical opening by going on to a greeting (line 8: "How are ya?"), and Angie goes along by responding to this (line 9: "Pretty ↑good."). It is only then that she asks her question again, which now completes the canonical opening by doing the work of reciprocating his greeting, while also moving on to a substantive matter.

3.1.2 Angie-Harvey common ground domain 2: Celebrating a birthday

The second occurrence of trouble occurred within a few turns of the opening, after Harvey answers Angie's question to say that yes, his guests had arrived. Angie then introduces a reason for call, to thank Harvey (and his wife Rita) for the birthday card they had sent her son Jimmy. Angie evidently did not expect Harvey to be aware a card had been sent, but did expect that he and she have common ground knowledge that birthdays are celebratory occasions and that sending a birthday card is a way of celebrating them. On that premise, she appends to her thank you for the card the information that there had been a birthday to celebrate (Jimmy's). But despite that, it seems this was not enough for Harvey to know what Angie was referring to.

(3)   Hopper Archive, University of Texas: "Berkeley" ca. 1985

      Angie: ... ·hh Well I wanted to thank you for th- (.) Well, Jimmy oughta thank you for the ca:rd, and thank Rita.=Y'know it was his birthday Saturday.
      Harvey: (The) what?
      Angie: Jimmy had his birthday Saturday.
              (0.7)

Angie: Ya ↑sent him a ↑ca::rd.
         (0.7)
Angie: He had his [bir-
Harvey: [(Oh it was) (.) Ji<u>m</u>my's
Angie: Jimmy's birthday, yeah.
Harvey: Ji<u>m</u>my's birthday.

It seems that Harvey stopped listening after she said "thank you for the ca:rd" and indicates that either because of a hearing problem, semantic problem, or processing problem, he does not know that she was referring to a card at all, let alone a birthday card (line 17: "(The) what?").

Angie does not answer this question directly by repeating the word "card" although that would have been a remedy if there were a hearing problem. Instead she seems to have tacitly analyzed the trouble as being, as she anticipated, that if Harvey did not know that Jimmy had had a birthday, she could not tie her reference to a card to the common ground they expectably had in the domain of celebrating birthdays. Hence, her response to Harvey's question (line 17: "(The) what?") is to repeat in line 18 the information she gave in line 16 that it was Jimmy's birthday. When this is met with silence (line 19), Angie evidently shifts her analysis, now responding as if there might have been a hearing problem after all and reiterates "card" (line 20: "Ya ↑sent him a ↑ca::rd"). She does this with an exasperated intonation that implies she should not have to be telling him any of this. When this is again met by silence (line 21), indicating that Harvey still has not understood, Angie reverts to her analysis that the trouble was that Harvey (still) has not realized it was Jimmy's birthday, and she starts to repeat that for the third time. But finally Harvey evidently gets it. He cuts off this third informing. He starts this response with "Oh" that indexes his now knowing what she had been talking about – line 23: "(Oh it was) (.) Ji<u>m</u>my's".

Once Harvey indicates he has understood at least that Jimmy had had a birthday, Angie moves on. However, we cannot tell and presumably she could not tell whether she brought about what she spoke to bring about – for Harvey to now understand a card had been sent to Jimmy for which he was being thanked. It is possible that as J had done in Example (1), Angie settled for what she did bring about as good enough. It was good enough to fulfill the Rhetorical Covenant. Harvey now being informed Jimmy had had a birthday may or may not have brought about his being thanked for the card, but even if it did not do that, it brought something else about. It became a preface that opened the door for her to move on to a next, related topic, what "we" (her family or at least she and Jimmy) had done to celebrate Jimmy's birthday.

3.1.3 Angie-Harvey common ground domain 3: Venues where plays are staged

The third occurrence of trouble arose when Angie went on to tell Harvey about having celebrated Jimmy's birthday by going out "a couple of times", starting with having gone to see a play at "Chabot", a local college. It seems that the trouble is that Harvey does not recognize the name of the place Angie says she went, "Chabot" (line 35: "(Go t') Chab<u>o</u>t?"). But initially, Angie seems to attribute Harvey's trouble to a hearing problem, so that her remedy was to simply repeat and affirm the name (line 36: "Yeah, Chabo:t"). But it turns out this was not the trouble and not an adequate remedy.

(4)   Hopper Archive, University of Texas: "Berkeley" ca. 1985

      Angie: ... we went to Chab<u>o</u>::t ((pronounced /ʃəbow/, a community college in Hayward CA)) and they had a nice theater play.
                 (0.7)
      Harvey: (Go t') Chab<u>o</u>t?
      Angie: Yeah, Chabo:t, ah::m
      Harvey: Well that's a m<u>o</u>vie.
      Angie: No no Chabot c<u>o</u>llege.
      Harvey: Oh Chabot college.
      Angie: Right.

When Angie reiterates in line 36 that "Yeah", they went to "Chabot", Harvey responds in line 37 in a way that makes clear that he was not having a hearing trouble. His response is an objection, that whereas Angie has said "they had a nice theater play" there, it seems that Harvey does not recognize the place she is referring to as a place where plays are staged. It seems that "Chabot" sounds to him like the name of a movie theater or a movie title he knows (line 37: "Well that's a m<u>o</u>vie."), so that from his perspective there is an anomaly about the venue. This indicates that the trouble arose from a difference in the common ground domain of places where plays are staged, and in that way he steers Angie towards the remedy. Her remedy draws on common ground in that domain that she expects she and Harvey have, and apparently do have, that colleges are venues where plays are staged. Hence, in response to Harvey's declaration that "Chabot" is a movie, Angie does not simply dispute that with something like "no it's not"; rather she responds by just identifying the place she is referring to as a college, with vocal emphasis on "college" a quite different *type* of place than Harvey thought (line 38: "No no Chabot c<u>o</u>llege"). In saying just that, she is depending on their common ground domain about places where plays are staged to include knowledge that colleges are such places, thereby resolving the anomaly Harvey perceived. And this seems to have solved the problem, in that Harvey prefaces his reiteration of her identification of Chabot *as a college* with the change of state token "oh" (line 39: "Oh Chabot College").

3.1.4 Angie-Harvey common ground domain 4: Genres of plays

Immediately after Angie clarifies that the place they went to was a venue where plays are staged, a next trouble arises. Having now understood that Angie went to see a play that was staged at Chabot College, Harvey asks (line 39) "whadid they have there?". The question is ambiguous in that it could be about what specific play was staged there, or about what genre of play was staged. Angie understands it in the former way and replies by naming the play, "The Wayside Inn".[12] But again she got it wrong, this is not what Harvey wanted to know.

(5) Hopper Archive, University of Texas: "Berkeley" ca. 1985

```
Harvey:   Oh Chabot college. [Wh why=whadid they have there?
Angie:                       [Right.
Angie:    It was ca::lled, uh::, .hhh The Wayside Inn.
          (0.7)
Harvey:   The Wayside Inn?
Angie:    Yeah, and [it-
Harvey:             [A comedy?
Angie:    Ah- no:::, it was actually quite serious.
Harvey:   Yeah?
```

The title of the play Angie named was evidently not known to Harvey, and so was not informative about what it seems he wanted to know. His response seems to be a confirmation request (line 43: "The Wayside Inn?"), but from what followed, he probably intended it as a prompt to be told more. Nonetheless, Angie responded to the question as a confirmation request, and confirmed it (line 44: "Yeah"). This does not satisfy Harvey of course, and so he guides Angie towards a remedy by introducing the issue of genre (line 45: "A comedy?"). Harvey's having named a genre seems to have redirected Angie to the common ground domain of genres. Accordingly, she does not simply respond with "no" to the question of whether the play was a comedy, which would have been minimally

---

12 Angie has the title slightly wrong here. She must be referring to A.R. Gurney's play *The Wayside Motor Inn*, based on her subsequently telling Harvey they had seen another play by the same author, *The Dining Room*, and Gurney authored both.

informative about what Harvey wanted to know. She gives him the name of a contrasting genre (line 46: "Ah- no:::, it was actually quite serious"). This seems to be the information Harvey asked the question to get. He seems satisfied by that, in having replied simply with an acknowledgment token (line 47: "Yeah?"), after which he goes on to tell Angie of a related matter, that a theater he knew of had staged a comedy by Neil Simon.

In each of these successive four cases, then, an understanding or coordination trouble manifested itself that Angie and Harvey remedied by first tacitly analyzing what common ground domain was involved. And once that domain had been identified, drawing on the common ground they expectably had in that specific domain to remedy the trouble. In all four examples it was Angie's recipient design that created the trouble. But in the first two, (2) and (3), it was Angie's analysis of the trouble that led her to a remedy. In the second two, (4) and (5), Angie did not immediately recognize that there was a trouble, or what its source was, and Harvey had to lead her, wittingly or unwittingly, to the common ground domain involved from which she could then draw a remedy.

3.2 Common ground and understanding between people who are maximally different

If people who are minimally different can still have differences that produce understanding and coordination troubles, as in Angie's and Harvey's case, it seems reasonable to predict that the number and seriousness of such troubles will increase in proportion to how different people are, until they have no common ground, and interaction becomes impossible. But it turns out that the matter is more complicated than that. That prediction assumes that people who are maximally different (speakers of entirely different languages and natives of entirely different cultures) will have no common ground. But to the contrary, Sanders (1986, 1987) contends that even when speaker and hearer are maximally different, they are still able to improvise ways of communicating because they still have considerable common ground. If so, this cannot be common ground people have through the happenstances of shared linguistic, communal and [inter]personal knowledge. There must be something more, something more fundamental. And there is. There are universals that we all share that inhere in just being human and having lived in a human society (Sanders 1986, 1987). I refer to these as a guaranteed common-ground "floor".

The universals involved certainly include universals of vocal and bodily emotional display, as for example Ekman (1971) has found (besides such facial expressions as smiles and frowns, we might add happy voice and angry voice, relaxed and tense musculature, and so forth). These, coupled with such universals as situated pointing and miming, provide a means of communicating independent of a shared language, as Sperber and Wilson (1986) illustrate. In addition, there are surely universals of social organization that each involve universal common ground domains, although we have not compiled a reliable inventory of them. They likely include *physical settings* (e.g., a home, a business or restaurant, a clinic, a governmental office, a checkpoint, etc.), *activities* (e.g., regulatory, competitive or collaborative, providing/selling and receiving/buying commodities and services, information giving/getting, and so forth), *status and role-identities*, and *entitlements and obligations* (e.g., family/kinship, personal v. impersonal, expert and novice, resident and newcomer, possession and indebtedness, hierarchy/authority/power).[13]

Within each of those settings, activities, and roles, there are certain generic ways people are interdependent and depend on communication as a means to certain ends. Therefore, it may be equally apparent to people of entirely different cultures and languages what is exigent in a given situation, what the task or activity is, the role and interconnections of the parties, what speakers (generically) may undertake to bring about just then through speaking (or in some other modality, communicating), and what hearers (generically) may infer about what the speaker's speaking (communicating) was done to bring about.[14]

---

[13] Such universals of social organization surface in many diverse ways culturally and personally, but those diverse ways spring from a common, universal base. For example, there are numerous personal and cultural differences about what constitutes a "home" and what activities take place there, among what people, with what rights and obligations. But these diverse realizations of the construct of "home" do not alter the fact that they have a common, arguably, universal basis, across persons and cultures, from mansions to long houses to shanties – perhaps that "a home" is a private, physically bounded, place of residence within which the authorized occupant(s) have the right to shelter and sleep there at will, to control access, to make rules, to organize and delimit activities there, etc. and who is/are responsible for preserving this place and keeping it operational.

[14] There is an example of achieving communication without a common language that can be attributed to the obviousness of such generic exigencies in *Soundings*, a magazine for recreational boaters, in an article about cruising in a chartered sailboat in Cuban waters (Blakely 2016: 52): "The crew of *Valasquez* … caught a big red snapper while sailing off [the island of] Cayo Macho de Afuera. The cruising guide says locals on this small… island will cook up whatever you bring in, so the six crew members dropped anchor and jumped into the dinghy with the fish in a pail …. There was nothing that looked like a restaurant, but a local they met at the end of a long and rickety dock turned out to be the cook. …. 'They spoke no English, and we had no Spanish, but 30 minutes later we were all drinking our beer … and eating a lunch of fresh lobster tails and red snapper …'."

Hence, even people who are as maximally different as two human beings can be, who are not of the same community or speak the same language, and have little or no prior experience with each other, will still have a pre-existing common-ground "floor" to draw on – not just to remedy understanding or coordination troubles and work out a way to overcome their differences, but as in Example (6), to head them off and make themselves understood effortlessly. Sanders (1987) cites an example of the active reliance on that common-ground floor by an aphasic 6 year old Moroccan child, Saïd, who was being taught in a Belgian clinic to use nonverbal communication devices (NVCDs) in place of speech.

(6)   Lowenthal & Saerens 1986: 319

On June 27 [within weeks of starting to learn to use a particular NVCD] [Saïd] made a purposeful mistake and immediately looked at the experimenter's face. He obviously expected the usual "NO". The experimenter did not react and the child immediately put his hands in front of his face in a gesture apparently meaning "Oh! What have I done?", [sic] he then corrected his purposeful mistake, and looked, laughing, at the experimenter: the child adopted an attitude which apparently meant "This was a mistake, I know it and I did it voluntarily".

Certainly Saïd and the experimenter in Example (6) are maximally different, indeed opposites, relative to all the ways we have of comparing people: child v. adult, Moroccan v. Belgian, learner v. expert, speech impaired v. "normal," and whatever other individual differences there were between them. It is true that Saïd had likely gained some core common ground with the experimenter in the few weeks he had been working with that new NVCD. This would have mainly involved shared knowledge of the task. And he had probably long since learned that he was in the (universal) role of learner, whose use of the device was subject to being assessed by the experimenter in the (universal) role of teacher. Such knowledge alone gave Saïd the "vocabulary" and perhaps the motivation to communicate what he did, but is not what made it possible to communicate it, and to do so without producing an understanding trouble.

Following Lowenthal and Saerens' inference, it seems Saïd's claim was that he had a sufficient mastery of the task that he could be – and in this instance that he was – detached enough from the task to make a joke with it. His "method" was to make a mistake in using that device for communicating, and then showing his mastery of the task and that the mistake was deliberate by self-correcting it, and more than that, laughing. First, behaviorally, Saïd had to draw on universals regarding nonverbal displays. He covered his face as a display of embarrassment or shame, and in doing so just then, implicated his awareness that what he had done was shameful, i.e., incorrect; and he laughed at the end of the sequence after correcting his mistake, displaying happiness (with himself) or amusement (at his "trick") and/or especially, not-shame after all. Second, of particular importance to communicating what he did, Saïd made use of sequencing: first he made an overt mistake, then covered his face, then corrected the mistake, and then laughed, each of which has the meaning it does not just in itself, but because of what followed it and what preceded it. For example, it would have communicated something quite different if Saïd had started by laughing, then made his mistake, then covered his face, and then corrected the mistake. The importance of sequence to the situated meaningfulness of speech (and behavior) has been underscored by many writers, especially conversation analysts (e.g., Schegloff 2007), but the fact that Saïd organized a series of actions into the sequence he did makes a strong case that this is one of the universals included in a common-ground floor.

4 Conclusion

It is clear that a common element in all of the examples here is that, as Kecskés claims but does not go into deeply, speaker and hearer are not helpless in the face of understanding and coordination troubles created by linguistic, cultural and cognitive differences. They fulfill their obligation under the Rhetorical Covenant to bring about what speaking was done to bring about by making active efforts to tacitly analyze the source of the trouble when there is a trouble, and once found, remedy it, drawing from the resources of their core (experiential) common ground and their common-ground "floor". It seems likely that the burden for accomplishing this falls primarily to the speaker who produced the trouble, but not always, as we see among the examples examined here. The hearer may actively guide the speaker to the source of the trouble, as J did in Example (1), or even produce the remedy, as Harvey did in Examples (4) and (5).

The examples here also indicate that we need to be cautious about positing a linear relationship between the degree of difference between speaker and hearer – linguistically, culturally, and/or psychologically – and how effortful communication between them is. While it likely is a linear one generally, as Kecskés assumes and I have as well, the examples here indicate this is a contingent matter. At one end of the difference continuum, fully bearing out Kecskés' concern about the presumption of sameness between speaker and hearer, it can happen that troubles may arise and communication becomes effortful between speakers and hearers like Angie and Harvey, who are minimally different (arguably the "same" as traditional pragmatic theory conceived it). At the other end of the spectrum, there can be exceptions where a speaker who is maximally different from a hearer, like Saïd in Example (6), still has communicative means and a common ground "floor" to make him- or herself understood effortlessly.

References

Arundale, Robert. B. 2008. Against (Gricean) intentions at the heart of human interaction. *Intercultural Pragmatics* 5(2). 229–258.
Austin, John L. 1962. *How to do things with words*. New York: Oxford University Press.
Basso, Keith. 1986. *The Cibecue Apache*. Long Grove, IL: Waveland Press.
Blakely, Stephen. 2016. Cuba, now. *Soundings* August 2016. 52–56.
Braithwaite, Charles. 1990. Communicative silence: A cross-cultural study of Basso's hypothesis. In Donal Carbaugh (ed.), *Cultural communication and intercultural contact*, 321–327. Hillsdale, NJ: Erlbaum.
Brown, Penelope & Stephen C. Levinson. 1987. *Politeness: Some universals in language usage*. Cambridge: Cambridge University Press.
Burke, Kenneth. 1945. *A grammar of motives*. (reprinted ed.). Berkeley, CA: University of California Press.
Burke, Kenneth. 1950. *A rhetoric of motives*. Englewood Cliffs, NJ: Prentice-Hall.
Clark, Herbert. H. 1996. *Using language*. Cambridge: Cambridge University Press.
Ekman, Paul. 1971. Universals and cultural differences in facial expressions. In James. K. Cole (ed.), *Nebraska Symposium on Motivation 19*, 207–282. Lincoln NE: University of Nebraska Press.
Firth, Alan. 1996. The discursive accomplishment of normality: On 'lingua franca' English and conversation analysis. *Journal of Pragmatics* 26(2). 237–259.
Gardner, Rod and Johannes Wagner (eds.). 2004. *Second language conversations*. London: Continuum.
Garfinkel, Harold. 1967. *Studies in ethnomethodology*. Englewood Cliffs, NJ: Prentice-Hall.
Giora, Rachel. 2003. *On our mind: Salience, context, and figurative language*. New York: Oxford University Press.
Goffman, Erving. 1959. *The presentation of self in everyday life*. Garden City, NY: Doubleday.
Goffman, Erving. 1967. *Interaction ritual: Essays on face-to-face behavior*. New York: Anchor Books.
Grice, Herbert P. 1975. Logic and conversation. In Peter Cole & Jerry L. Morgan (eds.), *Syntax and semantics 3: Speech acts*, 41–58. New York: Academic Press.
Gumperz, John J. 1982. *Discourse strategies*. Cambridge: Cambridge University Press.
Haugh, Michael. 2015. *Im/politeness implicatures*. Boston & Berlin: De Gruyter Mouton.
Hopper, Robert, Nada Doany, Michael Johnson & Kent Drummond. 1990/91. Universals and particulars in telephone openings. *Research on Language and Social Interaction* 24. 369–387.
Hymes, Dell. 1964. Formal discussion. In Ursula Bellugi & Roger Brown (eds.), *The acquisition of language*, 110–112. Chicago: University of Chicago Press.
Hymes, Dell. 1974. *Foundations of sociolinguistics: An ethnographic approach*. Philadelphia: University of Pennsylvania Press.

Kecskés, István 2014. *Intercultural pragmatics*. New York: Oxford.
Keenan, Elinor. 1973. A sliding sense of obligatoriness: The poly-structure of Malagasy oratory. *Language in Society* 2. 225–243.
Keysar, Boaz. 2007. Communication and miscommunication: The role of egocentric processes. *Intercultural Pragmatics* 4(1). 71–84.
Lowenthal, Francis & Jos Saerens. 1986. Evolution of an aphasic child after the introduction of NVCDs. In Francis Lowenthal and Fernand J. Vandamme (eds.), *Pragmatics and education*, 301–330. New York: Plenum Press.
Mauranen, Anna (ed.). 2012. *Exploring ELF: English shaped by non-native speakers*. New York: Cambridge University Press.
Philips, Susan 1982. *The invisible culture: Communication in classroom and community in the Warm Springs Indian reservation*. New York: Longman.
Sacks, Harvey. 1992. *Lectures on conversation (Gail Jefferson, ed.)*. Oxford: Basil Blackwell.
Sacks, Harvey and Emanuel A. Schegloff. 1979. Two preferences in the organization of reference to persons in conversation and their interaction. In George Psathas (ed.), *Everyday language: Studies in ethnomethodology*, 15–21. New York: Irvington.
Sanders, Robert E. 1986. Communicating across the borders of speech communities. In William Gudykunst (ed.), *Intergroup communication*, 137–151. London: Wm. Arnold.
Sanders, Robert E. 1987. *Cognitive foundations of calculated speech: Controlling understandings in conversation and persuasion*. Albany, NY: SUNY Press.
Sanders, Robert E., Yaxin Wu & Joseph A. Bonito. 2013. The calculability of communicative intentions through pragmatic reasoning. *Pragmatics and Cognition* 21(1). 1–34.
Sanders, Robert E. 2015. A tale of two intentions: Intending what an utterance means and intending what an utterance achieves. *Pragmatics and Society* 6(4). 475–501
Schank, Roger C. & Abelson, Robert P. 1977. *Scripts, plans, goals, and understanding: An inquiry into human knowledge structures*. Hillsdale, NJ: Erlbaum.
Schegloff, Emanuel A. 1979. Identification and reception in telephone conversation openings. In George Psathas (ed.), *Everyday Language*, 23–78. New York: Irvington.
Schegloff, Emanuel A. 1986. The routine as achievement. *Human Studies* 9. 111–152.
Schegloff, Emanuel A. 2007. *Sequence organization in Interaction: A primer for conversation analysis I*. Cambridge: Cambridge University Press.
Scollon, Ron and Suzanne Scollon. 1981. *Narrative, literacy, and face in interethnic communication*. Norwood, NJ: Ablex
Searle, John R. 1969. *Speech acts: An essay in the philosophy of language*. London: Cambridge University Press.
Sperber, Dan and Deirdre Wilson. 1986. *Relevance: Communication and cognition*. Oxford: Basil Blackwell.
Tversky, Amos and Daniel Kahneman. 1974. Judgment under uncertainty: Heuristics and biases. *Science* 185. 1124–1131.
Weaver, Richard M. 1985 [1953]. *The ethics of rhetoric*. Davis CA: Hermagoras Press.
Wilson, Deirdre and Dan Sperber. 2004. Relevance theory. In Laurence R. Horn and Gregory Ward (eds.), *Handbook of Pragmatics*, 607–632. Oxford: Blackwell.
Wittgenstein, Ludwig. 1953. *Philosophical investigations*. Oxford: Blackwell.

Marta Dynel
4 "Is there a tumour in your humour?": On misunderstanding and miscommunication in conversational humour

1 Introduction

This essay addresses the topic of conversational humour with regard to misunderstanding and miscommunication. The aim of this chapter is to tease out a number of problems concerning the workings of humour, specifically related to humour that fails due to misunderstanding/miscommunication, and humour that capitalises on misunderstanding. In order to meet this objective, the author revisits the existing literature on misunderstanding and miscommunication, providing some rationale for why each comes into being and arguing in favour of making a distinction between these two concepts. The notion of failed humour is duly addressed, and a few manifestations of conversational humour based on misunderstanding are examined.

The discussion of misunderstanding/miscommunication and humour production and reception is illustrated with scripted examples sourced from the medical drama series "House MD", whose plot revolves around the life and work of the eponymous diagnostician and his co-workers. The series, credited to the producers Paul Attanasio and David Shore, originally ran on the Fox network for eight seasons (November 2004 – May 2012). For over a decade now, the series has also been aired internationally on other channels, streamed via the Internet, and syndicated on DVDs around the world.

Scripted data are frequently taken to be representative of everyday interactions and are used in tandem with real-life data (e.g. Kecskés 2013; Bell 2015 ; Haugh 2015). This methodological step is premised on the (typically, only tacit) assumption of the *verisimilitude* of contemporary fictional discourse (i.e. its qualitative similarity to real-life discourse), as well as the interpretative availability of scripted mass-mediated interactions (for discussion and references, see Dynel 2011a, 2017a).

Essentially, fictional interactions on the screen are the fruit of the labour of scriptwriters, that is language users who conceive characters' interactions based on the workings of real-life communication and its psychological underpinnings. For their part, by default making use of the same linguistic norms and assumptions as scriptwriters do, viewers (and academics) can make sense of the characters' interactions, underlying goals and intentions thanks to all the evidence purposefully made available to them. Production crews operate on the assumption that characters' interactions should be tacitly accepted by viewers as natural relative to the socio-cultural context and should not strike them as being artificial, even if statistically infrequent. Fictional discourse does show peculiar communicative/linguistic features, which is the result of contextual constraints. A case in point is Dr House's predilection for disruptive, antisocial behaviour, which can hardly be thought of as a commonplace in real interactions but is by no means impossible. The same applies to his use of humour (witty, albeit mostly aggressive) as a defence mechanism or a vehicle for self-amusement and an exhibition of superiority, rather than for the sake of standard entertainment of the interlocutors. Therefore, the lack of amusement on the hearer's part need not always be used a yardstick for whether humour is successful or it has failed. A disclaimer must also be made that the analysis does not take account of the humorous effects exerted on the viewers of the series, for whom the humour is, indubitably, constructed by the production crew (see e.g. Dynel 2016a).

2 Collaboration vs. egocentrism in interactions

An ideal view of human interaction is premised on an assumption of a collaborative process between the *speaker* and the *hearer*.[1] As Levinson (2000: 29) puts it, "communication involves the inferential recovery of speakers' intentions: it is the recognition by the addressee [main type of hearer] of the speaker's intention to get the addressee to think such-and-such that essentially constitutes communication." Human communication is intrinsically centred on the attribution of intentions and *accountability* (Haugh 2012, 2013 and references therein). As Haugh (2012: 173) aptly summarises, when producing communicative acts "we are presumed to be exercising our agency in producing them. This is why we are held accountable for producing them." By default, the hearer aims to decipher the speaker's intended meaning, and not just *any* meaning or inadvertent meaning. Consequently, the hearer tacitly assumes that the speaker intends to communicate the meaning he/she has gleaned even if this meaning should involve misunderstanding (see section 3). This fact may either emerge in the ensuing interaction or remain undetected. Needless to say, permanent conscious intention recognition would be cognitively unfeasible, with the inferential processes taking place below the threshold of awareness, unless communicative problems

---

[1] Unless indicated otherwise, the "speaker" and the "hearer" are here taken as generic terms referring to the two ends of the communicative process for each turn in an interaction. Each end may involve more than one individual, which is the case with multi-party interactions.

should arise, prompting the hearer to consciously ponder on the speaker's intention (see Dynel 2016a and references therein).

There is also no denying that speakers typically intend, not always consciously (cf. the conscious vs. unconscious intentions distinction e.g. Gibbs 2009; Haugh 2008), to construct their utterances so as to be understood by the hearers. The notions of "recipient design" (Sacks et al. 1974) and "audience design" (Clark and Carlson 1982; Clark and Murphy 1982; Clark and Schaefer 1992) embrace the various means speakers deploy to make their utterances comprehensible to the hearers. Among other things, interactants tend to take for granted a vast amount of *common ground*, which encompasses: mutual knowledge, mutual beliefs, and mutual assumptions (Clark and Brennan 1991; see also Lewis 1969; Clark and Marshall 1981; Clark and Carlson 1982).

These (and many other) pragma-cognitive accounts of the production and reception processes need to be merged for "only a holistic interpretation of utterances, from both the perspective of the speaker and hearer, can give us an adequate account of language communication" (Kecskés 2010: 51). This holds also for *humorous communication*, namely that which is orientated towards inducing amusement in oneself and/or others.[2] The speaker's (non-)humorous utterance forms a basis for the hearer's inference, for which the hearer holds the speaker accountable and which should prototypically be compatible with the speaker's intention. Unequivocal as this may be in theory, natural language data adduce evidence that communication problems are rife in human interactions, irrespective of the level of familiarity between interlocutors and their best intentions to reach mutual understanding.

A lot of evidence has accrued over the past decade testifying that speakers and hearers rely more on their individual knowledge than on their mutual experience (Kecskés 2013). In a nutshell, researchers argue that people are *egocentric* in their production and understanding of utterances, contrary to the presumption of mutual knowledge (see Keysar 1994, 2000, 2007, 2008; Keysar and Henley 2002; Keysar, Barr, and Horton 1998; Barr and Keysar 2005, 2006). The many studies bear out that speakers overestimate their ability to communicate meanings and their utterances' effectiveness and, simultaneously, underestimate their utterances' ambiguity, labouring under a misconception of shared salience and accessibility. Moreover, hearers have little consideration for the mental state of the speaker unless a communicative error arises. As Kecskés puts it, "*[e]gocentrism means that interlocutors activate and bring up the most salient information*

---

[2] This definition could be developed as follows: or that which induces amusement despite no such intent on the speaker's part, viz. unintentional humour (Dynel 2016a) which may be consequent upon a communicative problem.

to the needed attentional level in the construction (by the speaker) and comprehension (by the hearer) of communication" (2011: 86, emphasis in original).

Egocentrism appears to be the result of each individual's prior experience which determines automatic behaviour and salience[3] inherent in the first stages of language production and reception (e.g. Keysar and Bly 1995; Keysar 2007). This is in accord with the *Graded Salience Hypothesis* (e.g. Giora 1997, 1999, 2003), which predicts that salient meanings affect production and comprehension processes regardless of the strength of contextual bias towards a less salient (or non-salient) interpretation. This is also in line with Kecskés' dynamic model of meaning (2003, 2008), according to which prior conversational experience determines the production and reception of lexical items. As Kecskés and Mey (2008: 4) neatly summarise: "Smooth communication depends primarily on the match between the two [production and reception]. Cooperation, relevance, and reliance on possible mutual knowledge come into play only after the speaker's ego is satisfied and the listener's egocentric, most salient interpretation is processed." As can be envisaged, egocentrism may lead to misunderstanding, and hence miscommunication. Keysar aptly concludes that misunderstanding "is not what occasionally happens when random elements interfere with communication; it is not only a product of noise in the system. It can be explained systematically as a product of how our mind works" (2007: 72). Before the notions of misunderstanding and miscommunication are explained (see section 3), here is an example from "House" that illustrates the discussion so far.

(1) [Dr House has had a rough patch and wants to confide in his friend, Dr Wilson. House barges into the latter's office. Wilson is leaning against the cabinets by the wall. His arms are folded and his head is tilted down. Outside it is raining heavily.]

    1. House: Adams defied me. There's one more zealot in the world. [sits on the couch] And Dominika moved out. She was fun. She was hot. She fixed my blender. That is not a metaphor. You know any good fake divorce lawyers? I am surprisingly depressed by this. [During House's monologue Wilson pinches his lips together a few times but doesn't interrupt.]

---

[3] Despite these individual differences in evaluations, there must be some recurrent universal patterns in some words' salience production and recognition. This is evidenced, among other things, by the workings of canned jokes, i.e. free-floating humorous units comprised of set-ups and punchlines, that are told orally or in a written format (e.g. on social media websites) in slightly altered forms. Their success resides in language users' making the same interpretations, for example based on ambiguities displaying salient and non-salient meanings.

2. Wilson: I have cancer.
3. House: You were a little short with me the other day. You do need an excuse. Cancer may be overplaying it.
4. Wilson: Stage II thymoma. I didn't want to tell you until I had it confirmed. I got the tests back this morning. I have cancer, House.
5. House: [Stares blankly as the news sinks in.]

Episode 18, Season 8

House wishes to share a list of grievances with his friend (1). These concern one of his team members (Dr Adams) and House's wife (Dominika), whom he married so that she should be granted a Green Card but for whom he seems to have developed feelings since the wedding. Following the premise of recipient design, House makes a meta-linguistic comment purportedly to pre-empt Wilson's potential misunderstanding based on a metaphorical interpretation of the word "blender". It is as if Wilson might deem it the correct interpretation given the uncanny literal meaning[4] (with women being relatively rarely apt at fixing household equipment) and House's propensity to talk about sex-related matters. In actual fact, House only seems to want Wilson to discount a metaphorical reading, but in doing so, he deliberately encourages this reading. House recognises the potential for humour upon uttering the phrase "she fixed my blender" and seeks to capitalise on it. By denying its metaphoricity, House deliberately invites Wilson to ponder on what it would mean for this expression to actually be a metaphor, and to consider all the bawdy possibilities this would entail. Needless to say, given the grave circumstances, House's attempt at humour (produced mainly for self-entertainment anyway) falls on deaf ears.

A seeming misunderstanding on House's part and momentary miscommunication arises as a result of Wilson's contribution (2), which House takes as being humorous and overtly untruthful (see section 4). Specifically, he interprets Wilson's turn as making up an excuse for his previous unavailability (3). This is the consequence of House's egocentrism. On the one hand, he views his friendly interactions as allowing for humour, including black humour, i.e. a type of humour which revolves around the topics of suffering and sadness. On the other hand, he has a tendency to use humour as a defence mechanism; by laughing everything off, he tries to avoid facing his true feelings for those around him. Whether or not sensing that Wilson's turn (2) may actually be a truthful admission, House chooses not to take it as such, attempting to wittily

---

4 Technically, the literal meaning must be the salient one and will be activated first even in this non-conventional metaphor (see e.g. Giora 2008 and references therein).

turn the tables on the interlocutor (3). Wilson duly moves ahead with his own conversational agenda and provides the details of his illness (4), thereby ignoring House's humour or, at least, not engaging with it. It is only then that House fully acknowledges Wilson's plight, as indicated by his non-verbal response (5).

3 Misunderstanding and miscommunication

In folk knowledge, "misunderstanding" is considered to mean a communicative failure (as evidenced by explanations, such as "Sorry, but this must be a misunderstanding"), with the blame being diluted between the speaker and the hearer. This non-academic (emic) use may have affected academic parlance. Generally, the notion "misunderstanding" (e.g. Zaefferer 1977; Grimshaw 1980; Thomas 1983; Schegloff 1987; Dascal and Berenstein 1987; Vendler 1994; Bazzanella and Damiano 1999; Weigand 1999; Yus 1999a, 1999b; House, Kasper, and Ross 2003; Bosco, Bucciarelli, and Bara 2006; Schlesinger and Hurvitz 2008; Verdonik 2010) seems to be used more frequently than "miscommunication" (e.g. Dua 1990; Tzanne 2000; Coupland, Giles, and Wiemann 2001; Mustajoki 2012; Bell 2015). A survey of the relevant literature yields a conclusion that the notion "misunderstanding" tends to be used interchangeably with "miscommunication", both capturing all manner of problems at the production and reception ends. Also, the authors working in the field frequently draw on the scholarship devoted to both constructs, which are treated equivocally (e.g. Dua 1990; Tzanne 2000; House, Kasper, and Ross 2003). On the other hand, the choice of either label is sometimes dictated by the field of analysis, with "miscommunication" prevailing in intercultural studies and gender studies, and "misunderstanding" being more frequently used in cognitive linguistics and theoretical pragmatics, for example. Nonetheless, the two notions should be distinguished, and differentiated from other phenomena, such as "misspeaking" or "mishearing" (see Grimshaw 1980; Tzanne 2000; Dascal 2003; Kaur 2011; Padilla Cruz forthcoming).

Following a commonsense interpretation, miscommunication should be seen as being due to the speaker's (faulty) production or the joint product of the speaker and the hearer, whilst misunderstanding is a cognitive effect on the hearer's part.

According to Weigand (1999: 771), "the term *miscommunication* refers to an interactive phenomenon of both the speaker and the hearer." Needless to say, miscommunication may be either the speaker's or the hearer's responsibility (e.g. Grimshaw 1980; Dua 1990; Bell 2015), or the responsibility of them both. In practice, the source may sometimes be difficult to determine categorically. Weigand (1999) chooses to reserve the label "miscommunication" to the cases which are not subject to "repair" (cf. Schegloff 1987). However, it is here claimed that miscommunication may concern both clarified and unclarified communicative problems, i.e. those that remain after an interaction has been terminated (cf. Hinnenkamp 2003 on misunderstanding). In other words, if discovered, miscommunication may be solved (or not) after it has arisen, or it may remain covert. Here is an example to illustrate that a communicative problem may be addressed and resolved the very moment it arises. This does not deny its existence, though.

(2) [Drs House, Foreman and Chase and Cuddy, Dean of Medicine, are talking in a very crowded hallway, as an epidemic has broken out. House claims he has found a patient (a 12-year-old) to diagnose and cannot help with the many patients.]

1. Cuddy: You just don't want to deal with the epidemic.
2. House: That's right. I'm subjecting a twelve-year-old to a battery of dangerous and invasive tests to avoid being bored.
3. All: [stare at him, stunned.]
4. House: Okay, maybe I would do that, but I'm not. If it turns out she does have meningitis, you're right, you win, but if we go back downstairs and she dies... your face will be so red.

Episode 19, Season 1

House's reply (2) to Cuddy's accusation (1) is couched in irony, classified as surrealistic irony (Kapogianni 2011, Dynel 2013), which involves absurdity. Thereby, he means to implicitly dismiss the critical allegation as being unfounded. Essentially, House's utterance is based on a premise that no doctor of sane mind would put a child's life at risk, let alone do it for the sake of self-entertainment. However, even if the three hearers should share this interpretation of the utterance, they reject it in favour of the salient literal interpretation in the light of their background knowledge of the speaker (namely, his predilection for solving medical riddles for pleasure regardless of the risk for the patients), as indicated by their nonverbal response (3). Therefore, although they must recognise the speaker's communicative intention, their reaction suggests that this meaning has not been successfully communicated (albeit not misunderstood), which House duly explains (4).

In contrast to miscommunication, which is an interactional phenomenon, misunderstanding is a failure to understand correctly (Dascal 1999), and is thus inextricably connected to the hearer's cognitive abilities (Weigand 1999), even if it should also be interactionally based. Misunderstandings arise as "errors in the inferential tasks in comprehension (Yus Ramos 1999a, 1999b)" that "may result in interpretations whose seeming plausibility predisposes hearers to accept them as the speaker's meaning" (Padilla Cruz forthcoming: xx)." This is not to suggest, however, that it is the hearer that is (solely) responsible for misunderstanding, with egocentrism affecting both production and reception ends. This is neatly captured by a well-balanced definition of misunderstanding for which Tzanne (2000: 39) credits Humphreys-Jones (1986: 1): "a misunderstanding occurs when a communication attempt is unsuccessful because what the speaker intends to express differs from what the hearer believes to have been expressed."

Importantly, misunderstanding may show different degrees (cf. Vendler 1994; Bazzanella and Damiano 1999; Verdonik 2010). This seems to be related to various levels of implicated meaning that the speaker intends to communicate. Weigand (1999) also differentiates between misunderstanding and *non-understanding* (see also Bazzanella and Damiano 1999). The latter term captures the idea of difficulties in understanding of which the hearer is aware and which he/she chooses to either hide or reveal with a view to being enlightened. In contrast, the hearer is typically not cognisant of his/her misunderstanding, which may, nonetheless, emerge in the ensuing interaction (resulting in clarifications) or which may remain undetected (Gass and Varonis 1991; Weigand 1999; Yus Ramos 1999a, 1999b; Hinnenkamp 2003).

Overall, miscommunication is sometimes seen as a broader notion which encompasses misunderstanding (Gass and Varonis 1991; Padilla Cruz forthcoming), as well as a range of subordinate phenomena that may give rise to miscommunication (e.g. Grimshaw 1990). Therefore, miscommunication does not need to involve misunderstanding even if it frequently does, which explains why the two labels are commonly used with regard to the same scope of communicative phenomena.

Generally, the sources of misunderstanding and miscommunication have been classified and/or analysed from various linguistic vantage points with regard to different criteria (e.g. Zaefferer 1977; Thomas 1983; Schegloff 1987; Dascal and Berenstein 1987; Weigand 1999; Yus Ramos 1999a, 1999b; Bosco, Bucciarelli, and Bara 2006; Padilla Cruz forth). What is most important here is that Schegloff (1987) lists as one source of misunderstanding the hearer's taking a serious turn as nonserious and vice versa (see Example 1). In other words, misunderstanding may originate in the hearer's failure to recognise the speaker's humorous intention showing as *autotelic overt untruthfulness* (i.e. saying things that one does not believe to be true within a humorous frame, and, typically, intending the hearer to recognise this fact, see Dynel 2016b, 2017d). Alternatively, the hearer may read such an intention into an utterance which has not been devised as humorously untruthful (see Bell and Attardo 2010; Bell 2015). The fact that humour and non-humorous meanings frequently intertwine can lead to interpretative problems. On occasion, a distinction between utterances carrying an "only joking" meta-message and a serious truthful message cannot unequivocally be made (e.g. Dynel 2011b, 2017d; Bell 2015; Haugh 2016; and references therein). Overall, humorous communication is burdened with many other problems at the production and reception ends.

4 (Mis)communicating humour

Whenever humour is performed in interaction, it is amenable to the receiver's evaluation. Carrell (1997) proposes the distinction between "joke competence" and "humour competence". These labels may not be self-explanatory, as "joke" and "humour" do not really correspond to the problem at hand ("joke" is a text genre, a category of verbal humour, whilst "humour" is a blanket term for all manner of phenomena that (are meant to) induce amusement in the hearer), but they capture the important distinction between the ability to recognise the presence of humour, and the ability to find a given stimulus (e.g. a text or an utterance) amusing/funny. On this basis, an important distinction needs to be made between *humorousness* and *funniness*. Humorousness vs. non-humorousness is considered an objectively verifiable dichotomy: a stimulus either is or is not humorousin the light of its features. One of such is the presence of humorous incongruity, which may be roughly defined as a form of mismatch of some kind (e.g. form vs. meaning, set-up vs. the punchline, or juxtaposition of utterances). By contrast, funniness and non-funniness are two opposite poles of a continuum, which rely on an individual's sense of humour and idiosyncratic perceptions at a given time and in a given situation. Much depends on the hearer's cognitive safety and playful frame of mind (Apter 1982; Martin 2007), which facilitate the appreciation of humour.

Relevant in this context are Hay's (2001) scalar stages[5] of the hearer's humour reception (or "support", in her parlance): recognition of a humorous frame, understanding of humour, appreciation of humour (finding humour funny) and agreement (support of the messages associated with humour). Prototypical reactions to humour consist in the hearer's achieving all the four stages, albeit usually without his/her awareness of doing so. On the other hand, the hearer may not recognise the presence of humour at all and/or fail to understand it for various reasons. This will naturally lead to lack of humour appreciation or

---

[5] Hay (2001) conceives of these as "implicatures", which may be considered specious, given the technical understanding of this notion in accordance with Gricean thought (based on maxim floutings and the Cooperative Principle). What Hay must have meant is a set of tacit or implicit assumptions underlying the reception of humour.

agreement with the speaker regarding some touchy matters, each of which may also arise independently even when the previous stages have been completed successfully. A statement may be ventured that the completion of the final stage cannot be deemed a sine qua non for amusement. The hearer may be amused, signalling his reception of the humour per se, even if he/she should not display full agreement with the meanings the humorous stimulus purports to carry (notice the familiar practice of laughing at a joke and simultaneously saying "That's so gross", for instance). This has to do with the fact that at least some humour is processed in a *paratelic* mode (Apter 1982), a frame of mind associated with a detachment from serious and goal-oriented behaviour and conducive to unrestrained amusement. Moreover, the hearers may dissociate themselves from the meanings that humour operates with, having markedly different attitudes in reality (e.g. appreciating a sexist joke does not mean that one is a misogynist).

Needless to say, the stages of humour reception will be attained subconsciously and can be brought to the level of consciousness if the conversational context should require this, especially when the ideal model of smooth communication is violated. Therefore, conscious acknowledging or querying the speaker's intentions to produce humour may be indicative of its failure (Dynel 2016a). This sometimes shows on the level of metalinguistic expressions that probe the speaker's intentions or explicate them, as in conventional formulae such as "Are you kidding?" or "I was only joking" (see e.g. Haugh 2016). Here is a more complex example involving a metalinguistic comment on the success/failure of humour (see Sinkeviciute 2017, and references therein).

(3) [House and his subordinates, Drs Cameron, Chase and Foreman are brainstorming. Foreman has been planning to quit his job.]

    1. House: Well if I'm wrong, then so is her body, because it obviously thinks she's got an infection or it wouldn't have gotten better from the antibiotics. What is pandiculation symptomatic of?
    2. Foreman: Yawning is a symptom of fatigue or cholinergic excitation.
    3. Cameron: Does this have anything to do with Addie?
    4. House: Let's say yes.
    5. Chase: Cerebral tumour, epilepsy... Could also be a medication reaction to antidepressants or some meds for end stage liver failure.
    6. House: Let's say no.
    7. Foreman: [laughs]
    8. House: [looks weirdly at Foreman]

9. Chase: [looks weirdly at Foreman] You don't want to leave this job. Three years you've been here and you've never once laughed at anything he's said.
10. Foreman: Because I wasn't kissing his ass.
11. Chase: But now you are? No, now you're nervous, uncomfortable about your decision. It wasn't even that good a joke.
12. House: Oh crap.
13. Chase: Most of your jokes are excellent. [Cameron rolls her eyes.] I just meant in comparison.
14. House: Shut up. I think she may not have an infection. You better deal with her before she crashes.

Episode 22, Season 3

In this multi-party interaction, House produces conversational humour across his two turns (4 and 6) by making similarly formed utterances that signal his tentative agreement and, contradictorily, disagreement with the preceding closed questions (3 and 5). When one of the interlocutors, Foreman, bursts out laughing (7), whereby he expresses his amusement, a short discussion ensues between him and Chase. The latter tries to find the underlying rationale for this amusement, which he considers undue and not genuine (9), as does the author of the humour (8). Chase produces two metalinguistic comments evaluating House's humour (11 and 13), signalling the failure of the humour in the preceding turns.

Lack of success at any of the four stages proposed by Hay (2001), especially the first two, occasions *failed humour* (see Bell 2009a, 2009b, 2015; Priego-Valverde 2009; Bell and Attardo 2010). Failed humour comes into being when an utterance (or a non-verbal stimulus) produced for the sake of amusing a chosen individual does not elicit the expected reaction.[6] Failed humour involves misunderstanding and/or miscommunication of some kind. It must be stressed, however, that a listener may fully understand the speaker's meaning and communicative intent per se, yet not appreciating the humorous potential of that meaning for various contextual and/or idiosyncratic reasons. Improving on the previous typology (imperfect, as the author herself admits, due to methodological limitations) advanced by Bell and Attardo (2010), Bell (2015) proposes a full-fledged framework of the sources of miscommunication that cause humour

---

6 Therefore, failed humour does not encompass cases of disaffiliative humour in multi-party interactions (see Dynel 2013 and references therein) observed from the target's perspective, who is typically not meant to reap humorous rewards. Essentially, the speaker says something humorous for the sake of self-amusement and amusement of only chosen hearers, all disaffiliating themselves from the target.

(which she frequently presents under the label "joke", technically, only one category of humour) to fail through the speaker's and/or the hearer's fault. She depicts these miscommunication triggers as falling into two major categories: those which are specific to humour (i.e. incongruity, appreciation, (meta)messages, and humour support) and those which apply to non-humorous communication as well, as indicated in the literature (e.g. linguistic rules at the level of phonology or semantics, ambiguity, or pragmatic force, for instance, together with framing/keying).

Admittedly, the framing/keying category (see Dynel 2011b, 2017d and references therein) is also peculiar to humour, insofar as it concerns the recognition of its presence. The incongruity criterion pertains to sense-making crucial for the success of humour, the sense-making that goes beyond the basic semantic interpretation of an utterance, which as such may be successful (to an extent) even when the humour is lost on the hearer. These two notions correspond to Hay's (2001) model just as appreciation and humour support do. Nonetheless, Hay's (2001) view of "understanding" appears to be broader, covering the communicative components that Bell (2015) captures under different triggers not restricted to humour and spanning the many levels of linguistic analysis, from phonology to pragmatics. The "(meta)message"[7] factor concerns any kind of "serious" meaning, at social or discoursal levels, that may be communicated by dint of humour. Whilst Bell (2015) lists unsuccessful production/reception of a (meta)message as a source of failed humour, one may venture to claim that this kind of miscommunication does not affect the humorous potential of an utterance per se.

Bell (2015) rightly presents each of the triggers of failed humour as being the speaker's or the hearer's responsibility. If the notion of egocentrism is taken into account, the responsibility will frequently be on the part of both interlocutors, who are involved in a conversational tug-of-war. On a critical note, the triggers that Bell lists are not discerned along one criterion, which is why the categories are not independent and cannot be regarded as a well-formed taxonomy. For example, ambiguity can be considered a problem manifest on different levels of linguistic analysis (semantics or pragmatics), and it may be inextricably connected with incongruity. Needless to say, in practice, the various triggers may co-occur, being interdependent.

Here are two examples that help illustrate the few points made here, with the focus on the mechanics of miscommunication and misunderstanding.

---

[7] Bell's (2015) term should not be mistaken for the famous Batesonian "this is play" meta-message specific to some humour (see e.g. Dynel 2011, 2017d) or the use of meta-language with regard to humour (see Sinkeviciute 2017).

(4) [House has a mutilated thigh muscle and uses a cane. House and his team (Chase, Foreman and Cameron) are discussing a case as they are walking along the corridor. They enter the diagnostic office. It's Christmas time, and there are some candy canes on the table. As it turns out, it is Cameron that has put them there.]

1. House: [freezes] What the hell are those?
2. Cameron: Candy canes.
3. House: [with emphasis] Candy canes? Are you mocking me?
4. Cameron: [apologetically] No! It's Christmas and, and I, I, I thought –
5. House: [giving a smile] Relax. It's a joke.
6. Cameron [blinks, gobsmacked]
7. Foreman: Isn't the prognosis for Churg-Strauss a bit grim?

Episode 5, Season 1

House, who is generally against celebrations, produces a rhetorical question (1) most likely as a means of implying his criticism of the otiose token of Christmas in their office. Receiving a naïve reply (2) from Cameron (whether this involves genuine misunderstanding or pretend misunderstanding of the question, see section 5, is open to discussion), House decides to tease everybody, feigning offence (3). He may thus mean to attempt to deceive the others into believing that he does not take kindly to the sweet in the shape of a cane due to his disability. Logically, this polysemy-based rationale sounds preposterous, and House's attempt at deception should be discovered by the interlocutors, also given their rudimentary knowledge of his character streak. His team members know that he likes to produce humour and is impervious even to purposeful impoliteness targeted at him. This should suffice for the interlocutors to reach a conclusion that he is "only joking" and is not truthfully expressing his outrage. However, Cameron's egocentrism (kindness and empathy prioritised), in tandem with House's deadpan delivery, must suffice for her to take this comment as being indicative of genuine indignation. Whether it has been House's intention to produce humour grounded in deception that is instantly revealed, the so-called *put-on humour* (see Dynel 2017b), or humour centred on overt untruthfulness, no humorous reaction ensues. Cameron is more frustrated than amused (6) even after House has explicated his rationale via a metalinguistic comment (5). On the other hand, Cameron may be aghast at the realisation that she has failed to predict House's jocular reaction to candy canes. The other hearers do not show any signs of amusement (even though they may have recognised the presence of humour) either, and return to the non-humorous discussion of the patient's condition (7). This seems to indicate that humour may fail also because of the circumstances, for example a medical problem at hand to be solved, that have a bearing on each hearer's frame of mind (see also Example 8), or the interlocutors' decision not to be drawn into House's mind-games, which they can recognise.

(5) [House is doing his clinic duty. The current patient is a nerdy middle-aged man.]

    1. Patient: It's usually worse in the morning. Especially if I've slept on my arm. [He's massaging his shoulder as he talks to House.] If I sleep on my back or you know, with my arms out, I'm usually ok.
    2. House: So your arm only hurts after you lie on top of it all night.
    3. Patient: Yeah.
    4. House: Hmm. [seemingly pensive] Well, have you thought about, I don't know, not doing that?
    5. Patient: Yeah, but it's how I sleep. It's how I've always slept.
    6. House: Well there's always surgery.
    7. Patient: To do what? Like clean out some cartilage or something?
    8. House: You're not sleeping on some cartilage; you're sleeping on your arm.
    9. Patient: [shocked] You wanna remove my arm?
    10. House: [in a light-hearted manner] Well, it is your left, a guy's gotta sleep.
    11. Patient: Are you insane?!
    12. House: [returns a confused look]
    13. [The patient storms out of the exam room.]

Episode 6, Season 3

Having recognised the patient's ailment as being self-induced (1–2), and possibly perceiving the neurotic patient as a nuisance, House decides to tease him, primarily for the sake of self-amusement, albeit possibly inviting the interlocutor to join the humorous experience.[8] In his first suggestion, House overtly feigns hesitation. It simply cannot be genuine, given the obviousness of the idea that the patient should have arrived at himself (4). Thereby, House implicitly criticises the patient for not having solved his problem on his own. As the latter is adamant that he will not change his sleeping position (5), House decides to tease him further in order to point out to him the extremeness of his tenaciousness, which

---

8 The exchange reworks an old "Doctor, doctor" joke:
    Patient: Doctor, doctor, it really hurts when I do this
    Doctor: Then don't *do* that!

verges on stupidity ("I will not change my sleeping position even though my arm hurts as a result"). House ridicules the patient's stubbornness by making an implicit, albeit overtly untruthful, absurd suggestion across his turns (6 and 8) in the hope that the patient sees his own recalcitrance as equally absurd and extreme. The patient seems to be outraged by this advice (9), failing to recognise House's humorous intent based on what seems to be overt untruthfulness indicative of humorous framing. The patient's taking the doctor's suggestion at face value can be explained by the fact that the former is seeking medical opinion and is clearly not in the frame of mind facilitating humour reception (cf. his egocentrism), not to mention the fact that his reaction borders on sheer stupidity. House makes use of this fact, brazenly developing on the absurd suggestion he has made by rationalising about it (10), as well as non-verbally confirming the allegation of his insanity (12). At this stage, House must be convinced that the gullible patient will let himself be deceived into believing whatever he hears. Ultimately, House allows the patient to leave the clinic room with a false belief that the insane doctor has recommended that he amputate his left arm. Even if House may not have had any intention of deceiving the patient at the beginning, the latter's failure to recognise the humorous frame (or more specifically, the humorous overt untruthfulness) prompted him to produce more messages that he expected to be misunderstood by the hearer fixated on the seriousness of his problem. This example anticipates the concept of planned misunderstanding, which is introduced in the section that follows.

5 Misunderstanding as a source of humour

Whilst misunderstanding typically causes humour to fail, there are categories of humour that thrive on it. Misunderstanding is what promotes a few forms of conversational humour. Needless to say, such humour may fail for the same reasons as the other forms of humour.

Firstly, misunderstanding on the part of a naïve individual may be considered a source of superiority-based humour for other interlocutors or, in the case of televised discourse, television audiences (see Brône 2008). This can be conceptualised as a type of *unintentional* humour, specifically *involuntary* humour contrived by scriptwriters (see Dynel 2016a). Essentially, silly utterances signalling misunderstanding (of something obvious to most people) are subject to ridicule (see Examples 5 and 6). This humour technique shows in the prevalence of sitcom characters who fail to grasp what is communicated and cannot even acknowledge their misunderstandings with the benefit of hindsight, as people tend to do in real-life interactions.

Secondly, speakers may purposefully cause misunderstandings in their hearers (see also Banks, Ge, and Baker 1991; Hinnenkamp 2003; Zamborlin 2007). This is what Weigand calls "planned misunderstanding", i.e. a nonstandard type of misunderstanding by means of which the speaker is "deceiving his interlocutor by planning misunderstanding and wanting to profit from it" (1999: 764), which "must not be detected by the interlocutor" (1999: 765). Regrettably, Weigand (1999) does not dwell much on this notion, but it deserves more attention. Planned misunderstanding is tantamount to a special type of deception, whereby the hearer is led to nurture a false belief of some kind. At a glance, planned misunderstanding may be considered a misnomer since the hearer does arrive at an understanding devised by the speaker, and is thereby deceived in an act of a successful communication. In other words, the hearer has an understanding intended by the speaker but nurtures a false belief, which is the purpose of all forms of deception (see e.g. Mahon 2015; Meibauer 2014; Dynel 2016c; Horn this volume). Misunderstanding, therefore, if purposefully induced by the speaker, needs to be distinguished from faulty/wrong understanding. Overall, most misunderstanding consists in developing false beliefs, whether purposefully induced by the speaker in an act of deception, or acquired via an inadvertent act of misleading.

Technically, planned misunderstanding comes into being when the speaker is cognisant of alternative interpretations that his/her utterance invites, with the salient, i.e. more easily accessible one, being what the speaker believes to be false, which is ultimately conducive to a type of deception. Planned misunderstanding may capitalise on various forms of deceptive ambiguity. One strategy involves the speaker's showing his/her wit and superiority (giving humorous pleasure to himself or herself) over a hearer (whom the speaker knows to be) incapable of recognising the presence of a stylistic figure (e.g. metaphor or irony) and liable to take the speaker's utterance at face value (see Dynel 2016c).

(6) [House is diagnosing a clinic patient by the name of Jill.]

    1. Jill: My joints have been feeling all loose, and lately I've been feeling sick a lot. Maybe I'm overtraining; I'm doing the marathon, like, ten miles a day, but I can't seem to lose any weight.
    2. House: Lift up your arms. [She does so.] You have a parasite.
    3. Jill: Like a tapeworm or something?
    4. House: Lie back and lift up your sweater. [She lies back, and still has her hands up.] You can put your arms down.
    5. Jill: Can you do anything about it?

6. House: Only for about a month or so. After that it becomes illegal to remove, except in a couple of states. [He starts to ultrasound her abdomen.]
7. Jill: Illegal?
8. House: Don't worry. Many women learn to embrace this parasite. They name it, dress it up in tiny clothes, arrange playdates with other parasites.
9. Jill: Playdates?
10. House: [He shows her the ultrasound.] It has your eyes.
11. Jill: [The news sinks in.]

Episode 4, Season 1

House's diagnosis "You have a parasite" (2) displays a case of planned misunderstanding, which rests on a covert use of a metaphor. Essentially, House compares a foetus/child to a parasite, based on their common feature: living inside the organism and getting nutrients from it, which is detrimental to the host organism. He must be cognisant of the fact that the patient will not be able to make the relevant inference, likely deriving humorous pleasure from this. The salient interpretation of this utterance coincides with the literal reading, and it is this reading that the context seems to support (e.g. doctors typically use proper medical terms rather than resorting to unconventional metaphors, potentially offensive at that). It is then hardly surprising that the patient should understand House's utterance literally, as evidenced by her response (3). As the interaction unfolds, House elaborates on the features of the metaphorically described concept without explicitly mentioning it, though. Coupled with the non-verbal actions he is performing, House thus gives cues towards the metaphorical interpretation of his initial diagnosis. First, he implicitly refers to abortion (6), which the woman fails to recognise (7). In his consecutive turns (8 and 10), he lists some features of children, which are transparently not applicable to "parasites" (i.e. being named and dressed, having playdates arranged for them, showing resemblance to the "host"). Incidentally, the woman is very slow in grasping the implicit meaning, even when House has made it quite overt to her, likely because she nurtures a backgrounded assumption that she cannot possibly be pregnant.

Another peculiar case of planned misunderstanding may prove a useful notion in describing the workings of humour based on the *garden-path mechanism* (see Dynel 2009 and references therein). The speaker deliberately leads the hearer to make an interpretation contingent on the most salient meaning of a covertly ambiguous textual chunk. As the utterance unfolds, this salient meaning is duly revealed to be "wrong", as if it were based on the hearer's genuine misunderstanding, inasmuch as an alternative interpretation turns out to be the intended one, being congruent with the utterance's ending. In other words, garden-path humour relies on the hearer's making a salience-based/default interpretation, only to realise with the benefit of hindsight that a hitherto unobserved meaning, less salient/default as it is, is the "correct" one.

(7) [Wilson, House's best friend, suspects that House is attracted to Cuddy, Dean of Medicine. The two friends are now talking.]
  1. Wilson: If you want her... ask her out.
  2. House: My God, man! She's not some floozy in a bar. She's the floozy I work for. There's gotta be no radical steps here. Gotta be subtle. We happen to attend the same party... The chat happens to turn personal.
  Episode 7, Season 6

The opening part of House's reply (2) to Wilson's (1) piece of friendly advice seems to have one salient interpretation ("Cuddy is not one of those promiscuous women that I meet in bars"). However, as the turn unfolds, it transpires that there is another less salient interpretation, based on a different scope of negation that appears to be House's intended meaning ("Cuddy is a promiscuous woman I work for, not one I could meet in a pub") that is autotelically overtly untruthful. In other words, this meaning arises within the humorous frame, for it is dubious that House (or Wilson) genuinely believes Cuddy to be a promiscuous woman. This is actually why this kind of interpretation of House's opening utterance could not immediately be made by Wilson. It can be concluded that it must have been House's intention that Wilson should "misunderstand" this utterance by making the default inference only to have to reject in favour of an alternative meaning, thereby arriving at the "correct" understanding, which fosters humour.

Yet another way of exploiting misunderstanding for the sake of humour manifests itself in what Schegloff (1987) dubs "joke first" practice. This involves a speaker replying to a previous turn by means of a "joke" before producing a serious answer. According to Schegloff, "such 'joke first's are produced as intentional misunderstandings of the prior talk which has set the terms for the joking speaker's talk" (1987: 212). However, there is no genuine misunderstanding per se, insofar as it is only feigned and is perfectly strategic, capitalising on (punning or otherwise) ambiguity of the preceding turn (see also Grimshaw 1980; Dascal 2003; Hinnenkamp 2003; Schlesinger and Hurvitz 2008). Technically, what the speaker does is *overtly pretend* (see Dynel 2017c) to have misunderstood the preceding turn. This phenomenon has also been dubbed *hyper-understanding* (Veale, Feyaerts, and Brône 2006; Brône 2008). Veale et al. regard hyper-understanding as being a conversational situation when "the hearer demonstrates a fuller understanding of a speaker's argument than the speaker himself" (2006: 319). This "fuller understanding" involves the humorous speaker's recognition of an alternative reading of the preceding conversational turn. This alternative interpretation diverts from the intended speaker meaning, which the humorous speaker must have recognised as well, but which he/she chooses to ignore in the humorous reply (whether or not later producing a response relevant to the hitherto neglected meaning originally intended by the previous speaker).

(8) [Drs Foreman, Chase and Cameron have noticed a large patch of blood on the patient's bed, coming from the underside area of her lower half. The three doctors enter House's office. He is asleep and snoring but wakes up, wincing at the light.]
  1. Cameron: We've got rectal bleeding.
  2. House: What, all of you?
  3. The team: [standing still, deadpan]
  4. House: [moves his feet off the table and sits in his chair properly] So the monster is peeking out from under the bed, which either means she has a clotting disorder, or she has a tumor in her colon.

Episode 18, Season 2

House's reaction (2) to Cameron's report (1) on the patient's state is indicative of his humorous intent, being based on autotelic overt untruthfulness. House cannot possibly be taken to believe that the three doctors have developed the same symptom. What House does is then overtly pretend to have misunderstood Cameron's statement by taking it at face value, as if this were the most salient interpretation of her utterance. House's attempt at humour does not invite any humorous response (3), which is hardly surprising given the grave circumstances which inhibit any amusement on the three hearers' part. House duly returns to the topical talk (4), addressing the current patient's condition, and thereby he reveals his appreciation of Cameron's intended meaning.

6 Conclusion

This chapter has attempted to give some insight into the problem of miscommunication and misunderstanding with regard to conversational humour. The discussion was illustrated with scripted examples from "House MD". First, a succinct summary of background notions was provided, encompassing the problems of intentionality, salience and egocentrism. Secondly, some light was shed on misunderstanding and miscommunication, as discussed in the scholarship, the underlying argument being that differentiation should be made between the two. The next section addressed the problem of failed humour, which was attributed to miscommunication on the production and/or reception ends. Finally, misunderstanding was shown to be a source of humour in a number of cases: genuine misunderstanding in televised discourse; planned misunderstanding involving deceptive ambiguity, as in covert use of irony and metaphor or in garden-path humour; as well as the "joke first" practice involving overtly pretended misunderstanding.

The discussion presented in the course of this chapter may be concluded by analysing its title. The readers familiar with the pop song "Supreme" (lyrics written and performed by Robbie Williams) will perceive the allusion, finding it salient. Whether or not this intertextuality is recognised, arriving at the implicit interpretation of the unconventional metaphor (along the lines of "Is there something curbing your sense of humour/blocking your humour production or reception?") necessitates going through the stage of literal meaning recognition, which must be more salient than the interpretation intended by the present author and, most likely, Robbie Williams as well. No negative, painful connotations are intended. As regards the answer to the metaphorically posed question, lack of humour response is a matter of failed humour, consequent upon miscommunication of some kind. This miscommunication may involve misunderstanding, and/or any of the many different factors, some motivated the speaker's and/or the hearer's egocentrism, which concerns also his/her individual sense of humour.

Acknowledgements: I would like to thank the two anonymous reviewers for many useful comments that helped me improve the quality of this paper. Also, I am grateful to Rachel Giora and Michael Haugh for their kind invitation and their editorial work.

References

Apter, Michael. 1982. *The experience of motivation: The theory of psychological reversals.* London: Academic Press.
Banks, Stephen, Gao Ge & Joyce Baker. 1991. Intercultural encounters and miscommunication. In Nikolas Coupland, Howard Giles & John Wiemann (eds.), *"Miscommunication" and problematic talk*, 103–120. London: Sage.
Barr, Dale & Boaz Keysar. 2005. Making sense of how we make sense: The paradox of egocentrism in language use. In Herbert, L. Colston & Albert N. Katz (eds.), *Figurative language comprehension*, 21–43. Mahwah, NJ: Lawrence Erlbaum.

Barr Dale, & Boaz Keysar. 2006. Perspective taking and the coordination of meaning in language use. In Matthew Traxler & Morton Gernsbacher (eds.), *Handbook of psycholinguistics*, 901–938. Amsterdam: Elsevier.
Bazzanella, Carla & Rossana Damiano. 1999. The interactional handling of misunderstanding in everyday conversations. *Journal of Pragmatics* 31. 817–836.
Bell, Nancy. 2009a. Responses to failed humor. *Journal of Pragmatics* 41. 1825–1836.
Bell, Nancy. 2009b. Impolite responses to failed humor. In Neal Norrick & Delia Chiaro (eds.), *Humor in interaction*, 143–163. Amsterdam & Philadelphia: John Benjamins.
Bell, Nancy. 2015. *We are not amused. Failed humor in interaction*. Berlin: De Gruyter Mouton.
Bell, Nancy & Salvatore Attardo. 2010. Failed humor: Issues in non-native speakers' appreciation and understanding of humor. *Intercultural Pragmatics* 7(3). 423–447.
Bosco, Francesca, Monica Bucciarelli & Bruno Bara. 2006. Recognition and repair of communicative failures: a developmental perspective. *Journal of Pragmatics* 38. 1398–1429.
Brône, Geert. 2008. Hyper- and misunderstanding in interactional humour. *Journal of Pragmatics* 40. 2027–2061.
Carrell, Amy. 1997. Joke competence and humor competence. *Humor* 10. 173–185.
Clark, Herbert & Susan Brennan. 1991. Grounding in communication. Perspectives on socially shared cognition. In Lauren B. Resnick, John M. Levine & Stephanie D. Teasley (eds.), 127–149. Washington: American Psychological Association.
Clark, Herbert & Thomas Carlson. 1982. Hearers and speech acts. *Language* 58. 332–372.
Clark, Herbert & Catherine Marshall. 1981. Definite reference and mutual knowledge. In Aravind K. Joshi, Bonnie Webber & Ivan Sag (eds.), *Elements of discourse understanding*, 10–63. Cambridge: Cambridge University Press.
Clark, Herbert & Murphy, Gregory. 1983. Audience design in meaning and reference. In Jean Francois LeNy & Walter Kintsch (eds.), *Language and comprehension*, 287–299. Amsterdam: North-Holland Publishing Co.
Clark, Herbert & Edward Schaefer. 1992. Dealing with overhearers. In Herbert Clark (ed.), *Arenas of Language Use*, 248–273. Chicago: University of Chicago Press.
Coupland Nikolas, Howard Giles & John Wiemann (eds.). 1991. *"Miscommunication" and problematic talk*. Newbury Park, CA: Sage.
Dascal, Marcelo. 1999. Introduction: Some questions about misunderstanding. *Journal of Pragmatics* 31. 753–762.
Dascal, Marcelo. 2003. *Interpretation and understanding*. Amsterdam: John Benjamins.
Dascal, Marcelo & Isidoro Berenstein. 1987. Two modes of understanding: comprehending and grasping. *Language and Communication* 7(2). 139–151.
Dua, Hans. 1990. The phenomenology of miscommunication. In S. H. Riggins (ed.), *Beyond Goffman*, 113–139. Berlin & New York: Mouton de Gruyter.
Dynel, Marta. 2009. *Humorous garden-paths: A pragmatic-cognitive study*. Newcastle: Cambridge Scholars Publishing.
Dynel, Marta. 2011a. Stranger than fiction. A few methodological notes on linguistic research in film discourse. *Brno Studies in English* 37(1). 41–61.
Dynel, Marta. 2013. When does irony tickle the hearer? Towards capturing the characteristics of humorous irony. In Marta Dynel (ed.), *Developments in linguistic humour theory*, 298–320. Amsterdam & Philadelphia: John Benjamins.
Dynel, Marta. 2016a. With or without intentions: Accountability and (un)intentional humour in film talk. *Journal of Pragmatics* 95. 67–98.
Dynel, Marta. 2016b. On untruthfulness, its adversaries and strange bedfellows. *Pragmatics & Cognition* 23(1). 1–15.

Dynel, Marta. 2016c. Comparing and combining covert and overt untruthfulness: On lying, deception, irony and metaphor. *Pragmatics & Cognition* 23(1). 174–208.
Dynel, Marta. 2017a. Impoliteness and telecinematic discourse. In Miriam A. Locher & Andreas H. Jucker (eds.), *Pragmatics of Fiction*. De Gruyter Mouton Handbooks of Pragmatics, Volume 12, 455–487. Boston & Berlin: De Gruyter Mouton.
Dynel, Marta. 2017b forth. Lying and humour. In Jörg Meibauer (ed.), *Oxford handbook of lying*. Oxford: Oxford University Press.
Dynel, Marta. 2017c forth. No child's play: A philosophical pragmatic view of overt pretence as a vehicle for conversational humour. In Villy Tsakona & Jan Chovanec (eds.), *The dynamics of interactional humor: Creating and negotiating humor in everyday encounters*. Amsterdam & Philadelphia: Benjamins.
Dynel, Marta. 2017d. But seriously: On conversational humour and (un)truthfulness. *Lingua*. https://doi.org/10.1016/j.lingua.2017.05.004
Gass, Susan M. & Evangeline M. Varonis. 1991. Miscommunication in nonnative speaker discourse. In Nikolas Coupland, Howard Giles & John M. Wiemann (eds.), *"Miscommunication" and problematic talk*, 121–145. London: Sage.
Gibbs, Raymond. 1999. *Intentions in the experience of meaning*. Cambridge University Press, Cambridge.
Giora, Rachel. 1997. Understanding figurative and literal language: The graded salience hypothesis. *Cognitive Linguistics* 7. 183–206.
Giora, Rachel. 1999. On the priority of salient meanings: studies of literal and figurative language. *Journal of Pragmatics* 31. 919–929
Giora, Rachel. 2003. *On our mind: Salience, context and figurative language*. Oxford: Oxford University Press.
Giora, Rachel. 2008. Is metaphor unique? In Raymond Gibbs (ed.), *The Cambridge handbook of metaphor and thought*, 143–160. New York: Cambridge University Press.
Goffman Erving. 1974. *Frame analysis: An essay on the organization of experience*. New York: Harper & Row.
Grimshaw, Allen D. 1980. Mishearings, misunderstandings, and other nonsuccesses in talk: A plea for redress of speaker-oriented bias. *Sociological Inquiry* 40. 31–74.
Haugh, Michael, 2008. The place of intention in the interactional achievement of implicature. In István Kecskés & Jacob Mey (eds.), *Intention, common ground and the egocentric speaker-hearer*, 45–86. Berlin & New York: Mouton de Gruyter.
Haugh, Michael. 2012. On understandings of intention: a response to Wedgwood. *Intercultural Pragmatics* 9. 161–194.
Haugh, Michael. 2013. Speaker meaning and accountability in interaction. [Special Issue: Focus on the speaker]. *Journal of Pragmatics* 48. 41–56.
Haugh, Michael. 2015. *Im/Politeness Implicatures*. Boston & Berlin: De Gruyter Mouton.
Haugh, Michael. 2016. "Just kidding": Teasing and claims to non-serious intent. *Journal of Pragmatics* 95. 120–136.
Hay, Jennifer. 2001. The pragmatics of humor support. *Humor* 14(1). 55–82.
Hinnenkamp, Volker. 2003. Misunderstandings: Interactional structure and strategic resources. In Juliane House, Gabriele Kasper & Steven Ross (eds.), *Misunderstanding in social life: Discourse approaches to problematic talk*, 57–81. London: Sage.
Horn, Larry. 2017. What lies beyond: Untangling the web. In Rachel Giora and Michael Haugh (eds.), *Doing Pragmatics Interculturally*, 151–174. Boston & Berlin: De Gruyter Mouton.

House, Juliane, Gabriele Kasper & Steven Ross. 2003. Misunderstanding talk. In Juliane House, Gabriele Kasper & Steven Ross (eds.), *Misunderstanding in social life: Discourse approaches to problematic talk*, 1–21. London: Sage.
Humphreys-Jones, Claire. 1986. *An Investigation of the types and structure of misunderstandings*. Newcastle-upon Tyne: University of Newcastle-upon-Tyne dissertation.
Kapogianni, Eleni. 2011. Irony via 'surrealism'. In Marta Dynel (ed.), *The pragmatics of humor across discourse domains*, 51–68. Amsterdam & Philadelphia: John Benjamins.
Kaur, Jagdish. 2011. Intercultural communication in English as lingua franca: Some sources of misunderstanding. *Intercultural Pragmatics* 1. 93–116.
Kecskés, István. 2003. *Situation-bound utterances in L1 and L2*. Berlin & New York: Mouton de Gruyter.
Kecskés, István. 2008. Dueling contexts: A dynamic model of meaning. *Journal of Pragmatics* 40. 385–406.
Kecskés, István. 2010. The paradox of communication. Socio-cognitive approach to pragmatics. *Pragmatics and Society* 1(1). 50–73.
Kecskés, István. 2011. Salience in language production. In Kasia Jaszczolt & Keith Allan (eds.), *Salience and defaults in utterance processing*, 81–105. Berlin & New York: Mouton de Gruyter.
Kecskés, István. 2013. *Intercultural pragmatics*. Oxford: Oxford University Press.
Kecskés, István & Jacob Mey. 2008. Inroduction. In Kecskés, István & Jacob Mey (eds.). *Intention, common ground and the egocentric speaker-hearer*, 1–7. Berlin & New York: Mouton de Gruyter.
Keysar, Boaz. 1994. The illusory transparency of intention: linguistic perspective taking in text. *Cognitive Psychology* 26. 165–208.
Keysar, Boaz. 2000. The illusory transparency of intention: does June understand what Mark means because he means it? *Discourse Processes* 29. 161–172.
Keysar, Boaz. 2007. Communication and miscommunication: The role of egocentric processes. *Intercultural Pragmatics* 4. 71–84.
Keysar, Boaz. 2008. Egocentric processes in communication and miscommunication. In Kecskés, István & Jacob Mey (eds.), *Intention, common ground and the egocentric speaker-hearer*, 277–296. Berlin & New York: Mouton de Gruyter.
Keysar, Boaz & Anne Henly. 2002. Speakers' overestimation of their effectiveness. *Psychological Science* 13. 207–212.
Keysar, Boaz & Bridget Bly. 1995. Intuitions of the transparency of idioms: Can one keep a secret by spilling the beans?. *Journal of Memory and Language* 34. 89–109.
Keysar, Boaz, Dale Barr & William Horton. 1998. The egocentric basis of language use: insights from a processing approach. *Current Directions in Psychological Science* 7. 46–50.
Levinson, Stephen. 2000. *Presumptive meanings: The theory of generalized conversational implicature*. Cambridge, MA: MIT Press.
Lewis, David. 1969. *Convention. A philosophical study*. Cambrige MA: Harvard University Press.
Mahon, James Edwin. 2015. The definition of lying and deception, *The Stanford Encyclopedia of Philosophy* (Fall 2015 Edition), E. N. Zalta (ed.). http://plato.stanford.edu/archives/fall2015/entries/lying-definition/
Martin, Rod. 2007. *The psychology of humour. An integrative approach*. Burlington, MA: Elsevier.
Meibauer, Jörg. 2014. *Lying and the semantics-pragmatics interface*. Boston & Berlin: Mouton de Gruyter.

Mustajoki, Arto. 2012. A speaker-oriented multidimensional approach to risks and causes of miscommunication. *Language and Dialogue* 2(2). 216–246.

Padilla Cruz, Manuel. forthcoming. Interlocutors-related and hearer-specific causes of misunderstanding: Processing strategy, confirmation bias and weak vigilance. *Research in Language*.

Priego-Valverde, Beatrice. 2009. Failed humor in conversation: A double voicing analysis. In Neal R. Norrick & Delia Chiaro (eds.), *Humor in interaction*, 165–184. Amsterdam & Philadelphia: John Benjamins.

Sacks, Harvey, Emanuel Schegloff, Gail Jefferson. 1974. A simplest systematics for the organisation of turn-taking for conversation. *Language* 50. 696–735.

Schegloff, Emanuel A. 1987. Some sources of misunderstanding in talk-in-interaction. *Linguistics* 25. 201–218.

Schlesinger, Izchak & Sharon Hurvitz. 2008. The structure of misunderstanding. *Pragmatics and Cognition* 16(3). 568–586.

Sinkeviciute, Valeria. 2017 forth. Funniness and 'the preferred reaction' to jocularity in Australian and British English: An analysis of interviewees' metapragmatic comments. *Language & Communication*.

Thomas, Jenny, 1983. Cross-cultural pragmatic failure. *Applied Linguistics* 4(2). 91–112.

Tzanne, Angeliki. 2000. *Talking at cross-purposes: The dynamics of miscommunication*. Amsterdam & Philadelphia: John Benjamins.

Veale, Tony, Kurt Feyaerts & Geert Brône. 2006. The cognitive mechanisms of adversarial humor. *Humor* 19. 305–340.

Vendler, Zeno, 1994. Understanding misunderstanding. In D. Jamieson, ed., *Language, mind and art*, 9–21. Dordrecht: Kluwer.

Verdonik, Darnika. 2010. Beween undersanding and misuderstanding. *Journal of Pragmatics* 42(5). 1364–1379.

Weigand, Edda. 1999. Misunderstanding: the standard case. *Journal of Pragmatics* 31. 763–785.

Yus Ramos, Francisco. 1999a. Towards a pragmatic taxonomy of misunderstandings. *Revista Canaria de Estudios Ingleses* 38. 217–239.

Yus Ramos, Francisco. 1999b. Misunderstandings and explicit/implicit communication. *Pragmatics* 9(4). 487–517.

Zaefferer, Dietmar, 1977. Understanding misunderstanding: a proposal for an explanation of reading choices. *Journal of Pragmatics* 1. 329–346.

Zamborlin, Chiara. 2007. Going beyond pragmatic failures: Dissonance in intercultural communication. *Intercultural Pragmatics* 4(1). 21–50.

Victoria Escandell-Vidal
5 Notes for a restrictive theory of procedural meaning

1 Introduction

One requirement of a fully developed linguistic theory is that it should articulate the relations of its components in such a way that the resulting model is both descriptively adequate and explanatorily efficient. Among the notions that have recurrently attracted the attention of linguists and philosophers, the basic distinction in cognitive science between "representational structures in the mind and computational procedures that operate on those structures" (Thagard 2005: 10) has played a central role in understanding how languages work.

In relevance theory (Sperber and Wilson [1986] 1995) the distinction was presented as *conceptual/procedural*: an utterance is expected to encode both "information about the representations to be manipulated, and information about how to manipulate them" (Wilson and Sperber 1993: 1). This was an elaboration of the proposal in Blakemore (1987) that the theory of linguistic meaning should be split into two components:

> On the one hand, there is the essentially conceptual theory that deals with the way in which elements of linguistic structure map onto concepts – that is, onto constituents of propositional representations that undergo computations. On the other, there is the essentially procedural theory that deals with the way in which elements of linguistic structure map directly onto computations themselves – that is onto mental processes. (Blakemore 1987: 144)

In this view, procedural items encode sets of instructions about the specific inferential processes to be carried out during the course of utterance interpretation. The term *procedural* was initially applied to discourse markers, but soon broadened to cover categories such as mood and modality, pronouns, verbal tenses and intonation (for a historical view and references, see Escandell-Vidal, Leonetti and Ahern 2011; Wilson 2011, 2016; Carston 2016).

Several challenges have also been raised against this view. Some recent developments have suggested ways of approaching the distinction which could be understood as blurring it, on the assumption that all linguistic items can be envisaged as encoding processing instructions operating at various levels of representation (Espinal 1996; Nicolle 1997; Wilson 2011; Moeschler 2016). For other scholars, procedural elements operate at the level of inferential processes and hence must belong to pragmatics, not to semantics (Bezuidenhout 2004; see

Curcó 2011, Wilson 2016 for discussion). Finally, it has also been claimed that we can find procedural indicators guiding the process of utterance interpretation that are natural, non-linguistic in nature (Wharton 2003, 2009). The picture that emerges is, thus, one in which the original insight behind the notion of *procedural meaning* seems to have dissolved to some extent (cf. Carston 2016) and arguably lost some of its original appeal and explanatory power.

The aim of this paper is to sketch the main elements of a restrictive theory of *procedural meaning* as an essential component of a linguistic theory. More specifically, I will argue that the label *procedural meaning* should be applied only to a specific set of linguistically encoded features of functional categories that target the inferential systems. Only in this way will we be able to offer a principled account of how grammar constrains inferential processes, and thus benefit from the predictions of a sound theoretical explanation.

Three main points will organize the discussion:

- Functional categories encode computational instructions.
- The coexistence of conceptual and procedural features within a linguistic category always entails an asymmetrical relation.
- Natural signals activate procedures, but do not encode *procedural meaning*.

Finally, the consequences and implications will be brought together in the last section.

2 Functional categories and procedural meaning

The theory of meaning envisaged in Blakemore (1987) inspired the idea that there was a correlation between the conceptual/procedural distinction and the classical divide between *lexical* and *grammatical*, or *functional* categories (Escandell-Vidal and Leonetti 2000; Leonetti and Escandell-Vidal 2004). In this view, lexical categories encode concepts that map onto conceptual representations, whereas functional categories encode computational instructions. I think that, if adequately refined, the correlation is worth keeping.

2.1 Lexical and functional categories

Following the lines in Hauser, Chomsky, and Fitch (2002), I assume that a language can be seen as a system pairing complex phonological representations and complex semantic representations as the result of the operation of a recursive combinatorial engine. The recursive mechanism (narrow syntax) takes a finite set of simple elements and produces an infinite set of complex expressions, which are then mapped into two representational interface systems, namely the phonological system and the semantic system. Then the information feeds into other language-external systems related to language use, including processing mechanisms such as the sensorimotor systems and the conceptual-intentional systems.

Linguistic expressions can be expected to consist of attributes that can be read by the different sub-systems of the language faculty:

- *Phonological*, which map onto abstract phonological representations.
- *Computational*, which include information relevant to combinatorial processes.
- *Conceptual*, which map onto abstract conceptual representations.

Each of these three sets of features is readable, I suggest, by its own proprietary system. This view is compatible with both the generative programme (cf. Chomsky 1995: 230–241) and the relevance-theoretic perspective (Sperber and Wilson [1986] 1995: 86–92; Curcó 2011; see also Moeschler 2016 for a different proposal).

Languages seem to organize these bundles of attributes into two different patterns. The first pattern corresponds to what we call *lexical* categories; the second is the one we identify with *functional* categories.

Lexical categories consist of attributes of the three classes. The phonological information associated to a lexical item yields its abstract phonological representation; this representation is delivered to the sensorimotor system, responsible for the articulation and the perceptual identification of sounds. The semantic attributes map onto abstract semantic and conceptual representations, which in turn give access to encyclopaedic information about the kinds of entities that constitute the denotation of the concepts involved, including general world knowledge and experiential properties. The computational attributes include information relevant to combinatorial processes; in the case of lexical categories, this information takes the form of *labels* that specify inherent features, such as syntactic category, gender and inflectional properties.

A functional category, in contrast, encodes information of two classes only. It contains phonological information, which defines its phonological properties, and computational attributes, which consist of instructions issued to processing devices. Functional categories, thus, have phonological and computational attributes, but crucially lack conceptual features. As a consequence, unlike lexical items, functional categories do not map onto conceptual representations, nor do they give access to any sort of encyclopaedic information.

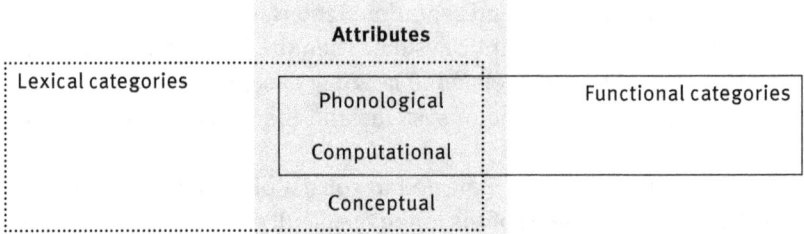

Figure 1. The structure of linguistic categories

This is not, however, the only difference between lexical and functional categories. The most significant one has to do with the nature of the computational attributes they encode. In the case of lexical categories these are tags or labels that specify the properties relevant to constituent order and phrase structure in syntactic combinatorial processes (such as grammatical category and inherent gender). Labels can specify the input conditions for an operation to apply, but they do not encode directions for computations. Crucially, the computational labels of lexical categories are relevant to syntactic processing only, and are not read by other components.

The computational attributes of functional categories, in contrast, consist of directions, functions or rules specifying the way in which other constituents are to be processed and fit together in composition. Computational attributes of functional categories are, thus, operational, not descriptive, and can be modelled as algorithms specifying input conditions, a logical operation and an output (Russell and Norvig 1995).

2.2 The domains of processing instructions

If the computational layer of functional categories can be conceived of as containing features that trigger operations to be performed by the various processing systems the language faculty consists of, one should expect to find computational instructions for all kinds of processes. This is exactly what we have.

Some features only play a role in determining the application of syntactic operations; these can be called 'syntax-internal features' (Adger and Svenonius 2011). Syntax-internal features are the driving force that creates and defines the hierarchical relations that build syntactic structures: this is the case, for example, for agreement heads in the verbal and the nominal domain. These features trigger the search for matching features; once a feature has been matched, it is deleted, so it does not reach any of the interface systems. This is why they are usually called 'uninterpretable' features within the minimalist programme (Chomsky 1995: 277).

Not all computational features are uninterpretable. In fact, most of them have a role in syntactic computation but also activate further processes at the interface systems (the semantic and the phonological systems). These are called 'interpretable' features (Chomsky 1995). For instance, the *Complementizer* position is assumed to host features determining syntactic modality and also constraining illocutionary potential (Rizzi 1997); similarly, a (contrastive) *Focus* position assigns a prosodic feature to a constituent at the articulatory system, but also triggers the inferential search for a relevant set of alternatives. *Inflection* encompasses modal, temporal and aspectual features that trigger syntactic operations of agreement (such as *consecutio temporum* and mood selection, for instance), and also help in locating the event and identifying its point of view. Finally, *Determiner* both defines the syntactic argumenthood of a noun phrase and contributes to establishing its reference. Features that play a role in both syntactic processes and phonological or semantic interpretation are called 'interface features' (Svenonius 2007).

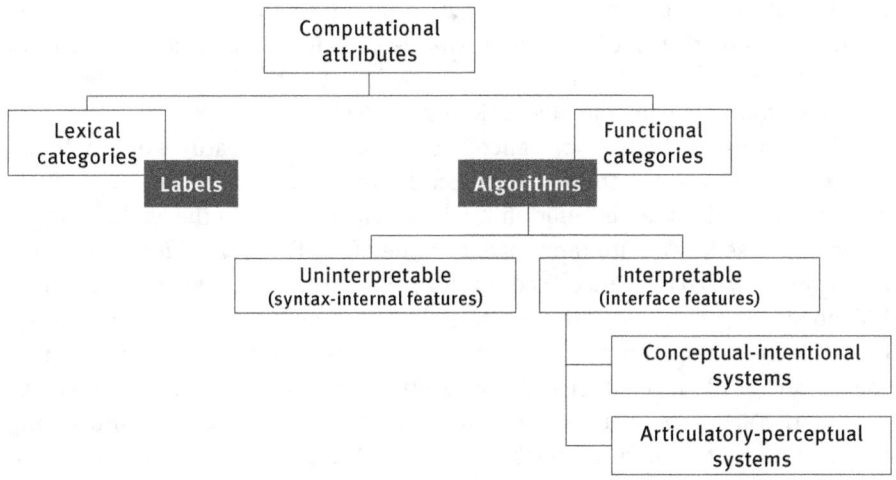

Figure 2. Linguistic categories and computational attributes

Interpretable features reaching the articulatory-perceptual system consist of indications for linearization, prosodic patterning and stress assignment; those delivered to the conceptual-intentional system drive inference by placing specific constraints on various pragmatic processes, including reference assignment, illocutionary force and implicature recovery, among others.

2.3 Procedural meaning

After the considerations in the previous sections, I suggest restricting the term *procedural meaning* (for lack of a better term) to the contribution of interpretable features that target the conceptual-intentional systems. In my proposal, procedural meaning is defined by three criteria that, taken together, select a well-defined class of linguistic elements: it is a formal attribute of (a subset of) functional categories; it can be modelled as a computational algorithm; and it reaches the conceptual-intentional systems. These three criteria are not shared by any other set of linguistic features. In this way, a definition in positive terms is provided, in contrast to the usual characterisations that focus on what procedural meaning is not (cf. Blakemore 2002).

This proposal has various consequences. Procedural meaning is a kind of encoded meaning. It thus belongs to the semantics of a language (Wilson 2011, 2016), because the systematic link between form and meaning is arbitrary and language-specific (Curcó 2011). The encoded procedure belongs to the linguistic system and is decoded and interpreted by the domain-specific module for linguistic decoding. The fact that the processing instruction encoded targets an external cognitive system does not modify its status as part of the semantic component of a language. As Wilson (2011) puts it, the nature of the encoding relation is to be distinguished from what is encoded. In addition, procedural meaning *stricto sensu* is restricted to a subclass of linguistic categories, so it cannot be found outside the linguistic system itself.

The processing instructions encoded in interpretable features of functional categories can operate on several logically different, though not necessarily sequential, levels of representation. One is the level at which the explicit proposition expressed by an utterance is determined (i.e., the *propositional*, or *lower-level explicature*, in relevance-theoretic terms; cf. Sperber and Wilson [1986] 1995; Wilson and Sperber 1993; Carston and Hall 2012). The inferential processes that contribute to establishing this propositional representation have a bearing on the truth-conditional content and have been called *primary* pragmatic processes (Recanati 2003). Determiners, pronouns and tense markers encode processing instructions that operate at this stage. The other is the level where the representations formed are related to other representations, either linguistically expressed or not. The inferential processes leading to establishing these connections have been called *secondary* pragmatic processes (Recanati 2003) and include all the inferences necessary to identify implicated premises and conclusions (*implicatures*), and also illocutionary intention and propositional attitude (*higher-level explicatures*, in relevance-theoretic terms; cf. Carston 2009). Discourse markers and illocutionary indicators encode instructions for this stage. Thus, languages have encoded procedures to guide the inferential systems.

This view provides solid support to the intuitive idea that there is a consistent correlation between linguistic categories and their semantic contribution. It is in this restricted sense of *procedural meaning* that the correlation can be maintained between lexical categories and conceptual meaning, on the one hand, and functional categories and procedural meaning, on the other. All the categories that have procedural meaning are functional, though not all functional categories necessarily have procedural meaning.

The existence of this correlation should not be surprising at all; on the contrary, it is exactly what one would expect to find in an efficient design of language: a neat division of labour between elements encoding representations and elements encoding directions for the various processing systems. If all this is right, then we have a reliable set of criteria for identifying linguistic categories specialized for encoding procedural meaning. A number of significant generalizations can be derived from this approach that would definitely be lost if the distinction is abandoned.

3 The coexistence of conceptual and procedural meaning

One of the main arguments against the distinction between conceptual and procedural meaning comes from the fact that many linguistic items seem to be hybrid, i.e., both kinds of meaning seem to be combined within the same item. If this is so, some scholars argue, the distinction is not worth maintaining. In this section I will discuss the various ways in which the coexistence obtains in order to show that they are not a problem for the generalization proposed.

3.1 Morphological composition

From a pre-theoretic point of view, it is usual to equate linguistic categories with words. In fact, the correlation is very high. However, it is important to recall that the form in which a given category is realized varies from language to language and is highly dependent on typological classes. In Romance and Germanic languages, for instance, lexical categories consistently occur as independent items, whereas grammatical categories can surface either as morphologically independent (conjunctions and pronouns), or as bound morphemes (case features; person and tense/mood markers). This fact, however, has no bearing at all on the status of the category. Thus, although an inflected verb form presents both lexical content and grammatical features assembled together in the same word, the categories involved are quite distinct. This is crucial for our current discussion, because this kind of coexistence of lexical and functional features in the same word by no means blurs the lexical/functional distinction (and hence the conceptual/procedural distinction), nor makes it a gradual one (Wilson 2011; Clark 2016). Similarly, even if tense, mood, person and number typically occur instantiated in a single portmanteau morpheme (as happens in inflectional languages), these categories are not to be mixed together. Therefore, when talking about linguistic categories, it is important to keep in mind that they are better conceived of as stable sets of features -not as words-, and in this way a unified treatment of all meaningful elements can be provided without the distortion imposed by an external device such as writing.

3.2 Procedural meaning with conceptual content

A more serious objection to the proposal of a clear-cut conceptual/procedural distinction comes from the fact that sometimes a functional category targeting the inferential system seems to include both processing instructions and conceptual representations. Consider the case of pronouns. A form like *she* activates the identification of a highly accessible referent with the property of being a female (or an entity conventionally assimilated to females in the given language, like ships, cars and cities). Thus, one could think that *she* specifies both the kind of computational operation to be performed and also some conceptual features, namely, 'accessible' and 'female'.

Saussure (2011) has convincingly argued that this concurrence of computational and conceptual features poses no problem at all for the hypothesis that functional categories encode processing directions. The algorithm expresses a logical function and this logical function can be further specified by adding specific conditions: the encoded procedure "takes the conceptual information as a parameter (...) and therefore the conceptual information is simply under the dependence of the procedure" (Saussure 2011: 65). Curcó (2011: 43) captures this fact by suggesting that procedural information is 'bracketed', so its conceptual content cannot be 'unpacked'.

The procedure encoded by the pronoun *she* contains a processing instruction and two specific restrictions. The processing instruction is a computational operation to the effect that the speaker S identifies (a representation of) an entity x and subsequently adds this representation to the explicature (i.e., the inferential development of the encoded propositional schema, in relevance-theoretic terms). The two parameters impose additional restrictions on the successful candidate for x, which should be both accessible and female. It is easy to see that these two requirements are not of a kind. The requirement to be female can be considered as a conceptual requirement, since 'female' – whatever its actual content is – can be an intrinsic attribute of a concept. The condition on accessibility, in contrast, is not an attribute of a concept, but a complex relation involving at least the addressee's mental representations and the discourse: the accessibility indication instructs the addressee "to retrieve a certain piece of given information from his memory by indicating to him how accessible this piece of information is to him at the current stage of the discourse" (Ariel 2001: 29). It is, therefore, a requirement restricting the search space of the encoded processing instruction (i.e., the operation has to take place within certain limits), rather than on the properties of the entity itself. Only the 'female' attribute, then, can be considered conceptual in some sense – though always keeping in mind that it is presented as an attribute of an entity, not as a concept *per se*.

The fact that some conceptual information can thus be part of the information encoded in a procedure does not mean that these two kinds of meaning are at the same level: the conceptual information is always hierarchically dependent. Conceptual attributes can specify input and output conditions for the algorithm to operate, but they always fall under the scope of the core operator, not the other way round. In addition, conceptual attributes occurring as parameters in an algorithm appear in the computational layer, not in the conceptual layer, so they will be read by the conceptual-intentional system as a parameter specifying a function, not by the semantic system directly, as in the case of lexical categories. This fact provides a natural explanation for the impossibility to 'unbracket' the procedure.

Thus, the allegedly 'hybrid' nature of some procedural expressions is not a real counterexample to the generalization suggested. The coexistence of rules and conceptual features under the same expression can be accounted for without abandoning the advantages of keeping a restrictive notion of procedural meaning.

3.3 Lexical categories and procedures

Another objection that can be raised against a clear-cut distinction between lexical and functional categories comes from the fact that some lexical categories seem to include procedures as well. Consider the case of verbs involving movement, such as *come* and *go*. *Come* means 'to move or travel towards a person who is speaking'. Now, identifying the specific direction of movement entails locating the speaker and orienting the movement towards him. In this respect, *come* seems to contain a deictic component – crucially, a procedure, not a semantic representation. After the considerations made in the previous section, it should be clear that the occurrence of a procedural bit among the semantic features of a lexical category is not a counterexample to the suggested generalization either. As in the previous case, the relation between the two features is asymmetrical. The core semantic attribute of *come* is the one that specifies movement, and this is indisputably a semantic feature; the deictic component occurs as embedded, dependent on that semantic feature, not on a par with it.

Some recent approaches have suggested that the semantic content of lexical categories is to be accounted for in terms of procedures: lexical items would encode not a concept, but directions to build one (see Wilson 2011, 2016; Carston 2016 for discussion). This idea comes from the observation that words used in discourse do not necessarily show the same denotational properties usually associated with their linguistic meaning; as a consequence, an inferential process has to be triggered to build an *ad hoc* concept.

I cannot consider the issue in detail here (but see the arguments in Carston 2016: 3.3); but suffice it to say that a model of ostensive-inferential communication, such as the one proposed within the framework of relevance theory, gets conceptual adjustment and *ad hoc* concept formation for free (as the result of inferential processes driven by considerations of relevance), so there is no need to postulate a specific mechanism to that very same effect. Encoded representations are but one kind of clue to direct the audience towards the intended set of representations, so there is no commitment to literalness that needs to be overridden by a specific, encoded procedure.

The discussion in this section has shown, then, that it is possible to maintain a systematic association between conceptual and procedural meaning, on the one hand, and lexical and functional categories, on the other: lexical categories have conceptual meaning, while procedural meaning will be found among functional categories only.

4 Procedures and encoding

The last question that I will address in this paper concerns the existence of procedural meaning outside the limits of grammar. It is well known that gestures, facial expressions and tone of voice suggest directions for the interpretation of an utterance, so it would be tempting to treat both linguistic and non-linguistic signals as different manifestations of the same notion.

Before proceeding, some considerations are at issue here. Paralinguistic signs are most of the time unconsciously produced. The audience can obtain valuable information from them by establishing causal relations between the observable behaviour and a potential cause. However, this does not count as communication in the technical sense, as has been convincingly argued in Wilson and Sperber (1993), since a crucial feature is missing, namely, intentionality. Only when deliberately exploited for communicative purposes, and when this deliberateness is intentionally shown, can a paralinguistic sign have communicative import and come with a presumption of relevance: in this case, intention and ostention together make a natural sign a communicative one, without ever changing its very status as a natural sign.

Wharton (2003, 2009) has suggested that, in addition to natural signs, there are also what he calls *natural coded signals*. In his view, these have evolved from natural signs with a specific communicative purpose. Smiles are a case in point of natural coded signals: a natural sign has been stylized, Wharton says, to conventionally point the audience in a certain direction. Thus, a smile activates a mental state in the audience that correlates with the mental state of the individual who produced the signal. The degree of this state in the addressee/audience is assumed to be analogue to the intensity of the signal produced. Crucially, Wharton claims that natural coded signals do not merely indicate, but encode information about the speaker's mental state – an information that is determinant in building higher-level explicatures.

I very much agree with Wharton on the idea that natural behaviours are a proper part of a theory of language use, and that a more articulated model is needed to account for the relations between linguistic and non-linguistic signals. I also agree that the contribution of natural signals is better captured in procedural, not in conceptual terms. This is not enough, however, to warrant considering them as having *procedural meaning* in the restricted sense I am presenting here. More specifically, I do not think that functional categories triggering specific inferential processes and paralinguistic signals can share enough relevant features so as to constitute a natural class from which significant predictions and generalization can be drawn. If we want to maintain that both linguistic expressions and natural signals are encoded, we have to be aware that the notion of code used is substantially different for each case.

A restricted notion of code seems to be essential to understand many significant properties of human languages. Hauser, Chomsky, and Fitch (2002) have argued that the core of the language faculty is a computational mechanism for recursion; this device is the only uniquely human component of the language faculty. Now, this recursion mechanism has the properties of discrete combinatorial systems (Pinker 1994: ch. 4): systems that generate an infinite number of combinations and permutations out of a finite number of discrete elements; the properties of the resulting combinations are quite distinct from the properties of their particular elements. As a precondition for recursion and productivity, the system has to work on a restricted set of minimal, discrete elements. Also arbitrariness of linguistic signs (i.e., the fact that there is no motivated link between form and meaning) seems to be a defining feature of human languages; in this sense, linguistic items are symbols and human languages are symbolic systems of representation. Discrete combinatorial systems are complex codes, with a lexicon and a set of combination rules.

Nothing of the sort can be said of natural signals. In a natural signal there may well be a conventionalized one-to-one mapping between a standardized natural behaviour and a standardized interpretation, but this falls short of being an element of a recursive complex code such as the one we use for human languages. Natural signals are mostly gradual (working on an analogical basis) and iconic (keeping a motivated connection between the form of the sign and its interpretation). Stylization and standardization of natural signs can be a precondition for conventionalization, but is not still enough for considering that the interpretation to which a natural signal is attached could be called *meaning* in the same technical sense we use for linguistic expressions. What is unique about the linguistic code is a set of properties that, taken together, are privative of human languages and are not found in any other information transmission system in the natural world, including natural signals.

The difference between the linguistic system and natural signals is even greater if the cognitive perspective is adopted. In one of his arguments, Wharton says that if natural signals are coded, then we would expect that they should be interpreted by specialized neural machinery. This prediction is borne out, he claims, as the existence of dedicated neural mechanisms for face recognition and facial expression understanding suggests.

However, the fact that there are dedicated, domain-specific systems for these tasks is by no means evidence for the claim that their input signals should be a code. Rather, what domain-specificity suggests is that there must be a well-defined set of data that constitute the proprietary domain of a specialized mechanism. But if this is so, then the evidence goes exactly in the opposite direction. There are no grounds for establishing that the devices for interpreting facial expressions when they are natural signals should be different from those that process natural signs; on the contrary, the prediction is that the very same mechanisms are responsible for attributing and understanding attitudes and emotions. Hence, the existence of dedicated neural systems cannot be a criterion for assigning the status of a code to natural signals.

Finally, recent research on emotion from a neuro-physiological point of view emphasizes the role of simulation in the experiential understanding of others' actions (see Gallese and Caruana 2016 for further details and references). In Gallese, Keysers, and Rizzolatti (2004), among others, compelling empirical evidence is presented for the idea that emotion recognition and understanding take places as through the activation of visceromotor centres as an instance of embodied simulation. This is exactly what all kinds of paralinguistic features do: they activate sensorimotor systems for emotion simulation. This process cannot be equated with decoding in any relevant sense.

Natural signs and natural standardized signals can serve the communicative function of guiding the addressee towards identifying various aspects of utterance interpretation, including propositional attitude and emotion. They can be crucial for identifying speaker's intention and, hence, speaker's meaning. This does not entail, however, that they are to be put on a par with specialized linguistic processing instructions. Procedural meaning is a component of a subset of linguistic categories that are discrete and symbolic; natural signals, even if partially conventionalized, are gradual and symptomatic. Natural signals may be "read", they may be interpreted, but surely they are not decoded in the same sense as linguistic expressions are.

5 Conclusions and implications

In this paper I have sketched a restrictive theory of procedural meaning. My proposal is built on the idea that the conceptual/procedural distinction is worth maintaining because it is the linguistic correlate of the cognitive, more general distinction between representation and computation, which is, ultimately, at the basis of all complex combinatory systems, including human natural languages.

The information contained in the entry of a lexical category has specific attributes that are readable by the various components of the language faculty: computational features are read by the recursion engine and determine syntactic computation, whereas phonological and conceptual features feed into the interfaces. Lexical categories contribute to utterance interpretation by providing conceptual representations that are read by the semantic system and feed into the inferential systems. Their meaning properties are found at the conceptual level.

The entry of a functional category, in contrast, contains information for the phonological and the computational systems only. Functional categories contribute to utterance interpretation by issuing processing instructions, either for syntax and/or the inferential system. Uninterpretable features trigger syntactic processes and ensure compositionality; interpretable features activate inferential processes.

The crucial difference between lexical and functional categories lies in the layer at which what we call *meaning* is located: the layer of conceptual features, in lexical categories; the layer of formal features, in functional categories. The distinction, then, concerns *encoded* meaning and hence is a linguistic distinction.

Functional categories constitute the core architecture of a language. In fact, they are language-specific and have been identified as the locus of parametric variation (Ouhalla 1991). They also are more difficult to master when learning an L2 than conceptual items (see also Wilson 2011, 2016; Carston 2016). In fact, encoded procedures are not isolated items; rather, they are part of a larger, language-specific computational system. We can expect to find cross-linguistic variation in the properties of the encoded procedures. Consider again the case of the pronoun *she*. Although we tend to consider that the Spanish pronoun *ella* is the straightforward translation of the English *she*, the two items do not encode exactly the same procedure. The core computational operation to be performed is the same for both, namely, to identify (the representation of) an entity. However, the additional conditions imposed on this operation by the grammar of each language are different. The accessibility requirement for Spanish is more complex and has to take other variables into consideration. In the cases where a null, silent pronoun is allowed, it is the null pronoun that would search the most accessible representation of a referent, so the overt form *ella* would exclude them and would only search among medium accessibility referents. Where no competition with the null pronoun is possible (for instance, when occurring as the complement of a preposition), the overt pronoun takes over the most accessible situations again (cf. Ariel 2001). The paradigmatic class to which a category with procedural meaning belongs creates a language-specific system of dependencies that mutually constrain the domains of each procedure. As for the 'female' requirement, it does not appear as such as a parameter in the procedure encoded by *ella*. What we find in Spanish is rather the more abstract grammatical feature 'feminine' (as opposed to 'masculine'), a value of an arbitrary label of nouns as a grammatical category, not a property of entities. Only when in competition with the null pronoun, the form *ella* selects female entities; otherwise, it can refer to any feminine noun. These facts then show that the information encoded in the formal layer of functional categories belongs to a structured system of discrete distinctions: categories with procedural meaning form structured networks of paradigmatic relations.

A linguistic procedure can be modelled as an algorithm to be read by processing systems. It cannot be adjusted, relaxed or modified in any sense to fit in with the requirements of either the context or other forms of representational content. Whereas conceptual content is flexible and can enter interpretive processes of adjustment, enrichment, elaboration and coercion (Wilson and Carston 2007), procedural meaning is rigid, as argued in Escandell-Vidal and Leonetti (2011) (see also Carston 2016). As a consequence, a procedural instruction must be satisfied at any cost. Procedural meaning always prevails.

A welcome consequence of this view is that a whole family of apparently unrelated interpretive phenomena can be explained as the result of the interaction between the various types of linguistic meaning and conceptual representations. The prediction is that "any possible mismatches between meaningful elements will always be solved obeying the constraints imposed by procedural ones" (Escandell-Vidal and Leonetti 2011: 87). Consider, for example, the case of definite determiners (see Leonetti 1996; Žegarac 2004; Scott 2011; Escandell-Vidal and Leonetti 2011 for details). A definite article encodes an instruction to build a mental representation of a referent that is univocally identifiable and that has the relevant conceptual properties encoded in the noun phrase. This instruction contains a guarantee of cognitive accessibility guiding the addressee towards the location of the intended referent. The accessibility requirement is easily satisfied when the referent has been previously introduced in the discourse. The procedural instruction, however, does not require an old referent, but an easily identifiable one. In an utterance like *Beware of the dog!* the guarantee encoded by the definite article triggers a process of *accommodation* by which the addressee has to introduce into the discourse an ad-hoc representation that contains a univocally identifiable dog. What is interesting here is that the accommodation triggered by these examples of first-mention definites is fully systematic and predictable, and derives directly from the need to satisfy the procedural instruction encoded by the definite article.

This effect of predictability and systematicity is found in various other types of grammatical phenomena, such as aspectual clashes, coercion phenomena with copulas, non-temporal uses of verbal tenses, and evidential interpretations of tensed sentences. Crucially, all these phenomena involve some sort of feature mismatch in which one of the non-matching items is procedural. The pattern is always the same: since the procedural instruction has to be satisfied at any cost, this forces specific interpretive solutions that affect conceptual representations, whilst the instruction encoded is always satisfied (see Escandell-Vidal and Leonetti 2011 for details).

All this constitutes, I think, a strong piece of evidence for the specifically linguistic, discrete and conventional status of procedural meaning, and is also a main element for an adequate understanding of the grammar/pragmatics interface.

Acknowledgements: This research was partially supported by grant FFI2015-63497-P from the Spanish Ministerio de Economía y Competitividad to the project SPIRIM (The Semantics/Pragmatics Interface and the Resolution of Interpretive Mismatches). I thank my colleagues Aoife Ahern, José Amenós, Manuel Leonetti, the volume editors and two anonymous reviewers for comments and criticism that greatly improved the manuscript.

References

Adger, David & Peter Svenonius. 2011. Features in minimalist syntax. In Cedric Boeckx (ed.), *The handbook of linguistic minimalism*, 27–51. Oxford: Blackwell.
Ariel, Mira. 2001. Accessibility theory: An overview. In Ted Sanders, Joost Schilperoord & Wilbert Spooren (eds.), *Text representation: Linguistic and psycholinguistic aspects*, 29–87. Amsterdam & Philadelphia: John Benjamins.
Blakemore, Diane. 1987. *Semantic constraints on relevance*. Oxford, Blackwell.
Blakemore, Diane. 2002. *Relevance and linguistic meaning. The Semantics and pragmatics of discourse markers*. Cambridge: Cambridge University Press
Carston, Robyn. 2009. The explicit/implicit distinction in pragmatics and the limits of explicit communication. *International Review of Pragmatics* 1(1). 35–62.
Carston, Robyn. 2016. The heterogeneity of procedural meaning. *Lingua* 175–176. 154–166.
Carston, Robyn & Alison Hall. 2012. Implicature and explicature. In Hans-Jörg Schmid (ed.), *Cognitive Pragmatics*, 47–84. Boston & Berlin: De Gruyter Mouton.
Chomsky, Noam. 1995. *The minimalist program*. Cambridge, MA: MIT Press.
Clark, Billy. 2016. Relevance theory and language change. *Lingua* 175–176. 139–153.
Curcó, Carmen. 2011. On the status of procedural meaning in natural language. In Victoria Escandell-Vidal, Manuel Leonetti & Aoife Ahern (eds.), *Procedural meaning. Problems and perspectives*, 33–54. Bingley: Emerald.
Escandell-Vidal, Victoria & Manuel Leonetti. 2000. Categorías funcionales y semántica procedimental. In Marcos Martínez Hernández, Dolores García Padrón, Dolores Corbella, Cristóbal Corrales, Francisco Cortés, José Gómez Soliño, Laura Izquierdo, José Oliver, Berta Pico, Luis Miguel Pino, Francisca Plaza & Germán Santana (eds.), *Cien años de investigación semántica: de Michel Bréal a la actualidad*, 363–378. Madrid: Ediciones Clásicas.
Escandell-Vidal, Victoria & Manuel Leonetti. 2011. On the rigidity of procedural meaning. In Victoria Escandell-Vidal, Manuel Leonetti & Aoife Ahern (eds.), *Procedural meaning. Problems and perspectives*, 81–102. Bingley: Emerald.
Escandell-Vidal, Victoria, Manuel Leonetti & Aoife Ahern. 2011. Introduction: Procedural meaning. In V. Escandell-Vidal et al. (eds.) *Procedural Meaning. Problems and Perspectives*, xvii-xlv. Bingley: Emerald.
Escandell-Vidal, Victoria, Manuel Leonetti & Aoife Ahern (eds.). 2011. *Procedural meaning: Problems and perspectives*. Bingley: Emerald.
Espinal, M. Teresa. 1996. On the semantic content of lexical items within linguistic theory. *Linguistics* 34. 109–131.
Gallese, Vittorio & Fausto Caruana. 2016. Embodied Simulation. Beyond the expression/experience dualism of emotions. *Trends in Cognitive Science* 16(2). 98–99.
Gallese, Vittorio, Christian Keysers & Giacomo Rizzolatti. 2004. A unifying view of the basis of social cognition. *Trends in Cognitive Sciences* 8(9). 396–403.
Hauser, Mark, Noam Chomsky & W. Tecumseh Fitch. 2002. The language faculty: What is it, who has it, and how did it evolve? *Science* 298. 1569–1579.
Leonetti, Manuel. 1996. El artículo definido y la construcción del contexto. *Signo y Seña* 5. 101–138.
Leonetti, Manuel & Victoria Escandell-Vidal. 2004. Semántica conceptual / Semántica procedimental. In M. Villayandre Llamazares (ed.), *Actas del V Congreso de Lingüística General*, 1727–1738. Madrid: Arco.

Nicolle, Steve. 1997. Conceptual and procedural encoding: Criteria for the identification of linguistically encoded procedural information. In Marjolein Groefsema (ed.), *Proceedings of the University of Hertfordshire relevance theory workshop*, 45–56. Chelmsford: Peter Thomas and Associates.
Moeschler, Jacques. 2016. Where is procedural meaning located? Evidence from discourse connectives and tenses. *Lingua* 175–176. 122–138.
Ouhalla, Jamal. 1991. *Functional categories and parametric variation*. London: Routledge.
Pinker, Steven. 1994. *The language instinct*. New York: Harper/Perennial.
Récanati, François. 2003. *Literal meaning*. Cambridge: Cambridge University Press.
Rizzi, Luigi. 1997. The fine structure of the left periphery. In Liliane Haegeman (ed.), *Elements of grammar: Handbook in generative syntax*, 281–337. Dordrecht: Kluwer.
Russell, Stuart & Peter Norvig. 1995. *Artificial intelligence: A modern approach*. Engelwood Cliffs: Prentice Hall.
de Saussure, Louis. 2011. On some methodological issues in the conceptual / procedural distinction. In Victoria Escandell-Vidal, Manuel Leonetti & Aoife Ahern (eds.), *Procedural meaning. Problems and perspectives*, 55–79. Bingley: Emerald.
Scott, Kate. 2011. Beyond reference: concepts, procedures and referring expressions. In Victoria Escandell-Vidal, Manuel Leonetti & Aoife Ahern (eds.), *Procedural meaning. Problems and perspectives*, 183–203. Bingley: Emerald.
Sperber, Dan & Deidre Wilson. 1995 [1986]. *Relevance. Communication and cognition*. Oxford: Blackwell.
Svenonius, Peter. 2007. Interpreting uninterpretable features. *Linguistic Analysis* 33(3–4). 375–413.
Thagard, Paul. 2005. *Mind: Introduction to cognitive science*, 2nd ed. Cambridge: MIT Press.
Wharton, Tim. 2003. Natural pragmatics and natural codes. *Mind & Language* 18. 447–477.
Wharton, Tim. 2009. *Pragmatics and non-verbal communication*. Cambridge: Cambridge University Press.
Wilson, Deidre. 2004. Relevance and lexical pragmatics. *UCL Working Papers in Linguistics* 16. 343–360.
Wilson, Deidre. 2011. The conceptual-procedural distinction: Past, present and future. In Victoria Escandell-Vidal, Manuel Leonetti & Aoife Ahern (eds.), *Procedural meaning. Problems and perspectives*, 3–31. Bingley: Emerald.
Wilson, Deidre. 2016. Reassessing the conceptual--procedural distinction. *Lingua* 175–176. 5–19.
Wilson, Deidre & Robyn Carston. 2007. A unitary approach to lexical pragmatics: Relevance, inference and ad hoc concepts. In Noel Burton-Roberts (ed.), *Pragmatics*, 230–260. Houndmills: Palgrave.
Wilson, Deidre & Dan Sperber. 1993. Linguistic form and relevance. *Lingua* 90. 1–25.
Žegarac, Vlad. 2004. Relevance theory and *the* in second language acquisition. *Second Language Research* 20(3). 193–211.

Marit Sternau, Mira Ariel, Rachel Giora and Ofer Fein
6 Deniability and explicatures

1 Introduction

In this chapter we focus on inferences that count as part of the Relevance-theoretic concept of 'explicature'. We propose to test the degree of commitment the speaker has regarding various types of explicated pragmatic contributions using a new tool – the Deniability test.

The chapter is divided into four sections. The first two sections (two and three) present the theoretical background, focusing firstly on the notion of explicatures, including the dispute revolving around it, and secondly – on the Deniability test, its rationale, aim and structure. The following section (four) describes a psycholinguistic experiment we conducted testing the ability of the Deniability test to distinguish between various types of explicated inferences with regard to the speakers' commitment. We sum up our findings and conclusions in section 5, and discuss the relevant implications from them.

2 Explicatures

Grice (1969 and onwards) was the first to distinguish between 'what is said' (linguistically encoded meanings, hereafter 'bare linguistic meanings') and implicatures (pragmatic inferences). The combination of these two, Grice's conveyed meaning, will be here referred to as the interpretation. All the pragmatic components associated with the speaker's utterance were defined as implicatures. However, while adopting the basic division into semantic versus pragmatic meanings, Grice and researchers following him, neo-Griceans and post-Griceans alike, have felt a need for an additional, intermediate level, richer than the bare linguistic meaning, but at the same time, not as pragmatically enriched as the conveyed meaning, which incorporates all pragmatic interpretations. This intermediate level is geared towards specifying the semantic content of the speaker's utterance, typically associated with all and only its relevant truth conditions.[1]

While the consensus in the field is that such an intermediate level should combine linguistic and inferred meanings there is an ongoing debate about the nature of this representation. To be sure, all researchers agree that the bare lin-

---

[1] It should be noted that when presenting Grice's theory, we sometimes take the liberty of doing so using our own terminology.

guistic meaning falls short of fulfilling the semantic goal set for this intermediate level, while the conveyed meaning contains more than is necessary. The controversy concerns how much pragmatic inferencing should be allowed into the representation. Minimalists, such as Grice (1989) and Borg (2004, 2016) argue for a 'what is said'$_{min}$ (terminology after Recanati 2001), whereby only grammatically mandated interpretations should be added on. Grice's assumption was that the linguistic meaning, thus (minimally) enriched, not only accounts for speakers' semantic competence, but is at the same time also sufficient for determining all the truth conditions associated with the proposition.

As is commonly recognized now, however, the linguistic meaning augmented by grammatically mandated completions (saturations) cannot exhaust the relevant truth conditional content associated with the speaker's utterance. Some Minimalists, such as Bach (1994) and Borg (2004) recognize this, but nonetheless have adhered to the concept of 'what is said'$_{min}$. This required them to give up the requirement that 'what is said'$_{min}$ guarantee the proposition's fully truth-evaluated content. Maximalists, such as Sperber and Wilson ([1986] 1995), Carston (2002), and Recanati (2004, 2007) have chosen a different solution. They chose to adhere to the truth-conditionality criterion, and gave up on a 'what is said'$_{min}$ representation. Maximalists see no role for 'what is said'$_{min}$, and adopt a 'what is said'$_{max}$ representation as their intermediate meaning level. The Relevance-theoretic explicature is, by definition, a complete proposition. In fact, explicatures are said to be explicit (to different degrees) despite the fact that they contain inferred elements. Here is Sperber and Wilson's ([1986] 1995) definition of explicitness:

> An assumption communicated by an utterance U is explicit if and only if it is a development of the logical form encoded by U. (Sperber and Wilson 1986: 182)

Unlike Grice, for whom the gap between the linguistic meaning and the truth-evaluable proposition ('what is said$_{min}$') is minimal, the gap between the linguistic meaning and the explicature is quite substantial according to Maximalists. Pragmatics has a far more important role in determining the speaker's intended proposition (see especially Wilson and Sperber 2002). Explicated inferences (Ariel's [2008] term for the pragmatic inferences incorporated into the explicature) are not necessarily grammatically triggered. Conceptual incompleteness equally calls for pragmatic enrichments. Moreover, these inferences are not geared towards providing the most minimal truth-evaluable proposition possible. Rather, they must develop the linguistic meaning precisely into the speaker's *intended* proposition on the specific occasion. At the same time, Maximalists are very clear that not all pragmatic inferences are explicated inferences. Particularized Conversational Implicatures are certainly excluded. Generalized Conversational Implicatures are the main point of contention between Minimalists and Maximalists. For example, temporal and causal enrichments associated with *And*-conjunctions are for the most part explicated, rather than implicated, according to Maximalists.

As opposed to post-Griceans who concentrate on the role played by the addressee in the communication process, Kecskés (2010) presents a socio-cognitive approach (SCA) to pragmatics, which focuses on the speaker. Aiming to provide a new explanation for interpreting an utterance as subjected to both current and prior contexts, the SCA differentiates between an Explicature, which is taken as a full proposition of the hearer's reconstruction, and the speaker's utterance, which constitutes a full proposition, which is the product of the speaker's prior knowledge and intentions. In other words, the enrichment of an utterance is ascribed to the speaker's "private and subjective treatment of the utterance in an actual situational context" (p. 63). Thus, by opting for a wider scope of the speaker's utterance, by his own admission, Kecskés takes the representation of an uttered proposition a step further. Unlike Relevance Theory's Explicature, the enriched utterance is not merely committed to by the speaker, but rather owned by her.

In addition to Minimalists and Maximalists, there are Multiplists, researchers who have opted for multiple intermediate meaning representations. Here we focus on Ariel (2002, 2008), who proposed the Privileged Interactional Interpretation representation (PII), which stands for the speaker's message for the purpose of truth-conditional content, as well as for discourse relevance. According to Ariel, PIIs mostly amount to explicatures, but, she has argued, both richer (implicated) and poorer (unenriched linguistic meanings) levels of interpretations sometimes serve as PIIs.[2] If so, multiple meaning levels, both conveyed meanings and 'what is said'$_{min}$ (and even less than that) can function as PIIs.[3]

In previous publications, we have supported Ariel's proposals and further developed them. Sternau (2014; Sternau et al. 2015, 2016) has argued for a scalar notion of strength of interpretations. Strength of interpretations was, therefore, measured by the propensity of some representation to constitute the PII, based on a number of experimental tests, probing participants' judgments regarding what the speaker said. It should be noted that in these psycholinguistic experiments, we tested inferences as to their discourse status as 'said' material, a status

---

[2] See Jaszczolt (1999 and onwards) for a similar, "primary meaning" concept. But whereas Jaszczolt defines her Primary Meaning by reference to a model speaker and a model addressee, Ariel's PII includes any actual use, manipulative uses included, provided they are speaker or hearer intended.
[3] Interestingly, as noted above, Bach (1994) considers himself a Minimalist, but his notion of Impliciture may be taken as a 'what is said'$_{max}$, as it resembles Sperber and Wilson's (1995) Explicature.

normally reserved for explicitly stated assumptions. Our aim was to examine whether interlocutors understand the inferred content included in the various levels of interpretation *as if* it has been said. The resulting scale showed that explicatures were strongest in that they were most often confirmed as having been said by the speaker, whereas weak implicatures came out as least likely to be confirmed as having been said. Strong implicatures occupied an intermediate position on the strength scale.

Our previous experiments have actually examined 4 meaning levels: bare linguistic meanings, explicatures, strong implicatures, and weak implicatures. We tested these representations with regard to degrees of textual coherence, the likelihood to be construed as what the speaker said, and the likelihood to be denied by the speaker later on. The idea behind these tests for PIIhood is that stronger interpretations better cohere with their context, are more often confirmed as having been said, and hardly allow a speaker to deny them later on.

We found evidence for the following two strength scales which are orthogonal to each other reflecting the strength of some representation within some specific context (the scale in 2 simply reflects the prototypical application of the scale in 1):

(1) Strongly communicated message > Weakly communicated message

(2) Bare Linguistic meaning > Explicated$_{max}$ > Implicature$_{[strong]}$ > Implicature$_{[weak]}$

But perhaps one can push scalarity even further. Note that the fact that explicated inferences (the pragmatic contribution to explicatures) are stronger than implicatures does not rule out the possibility that not all explicated inferences are equal. Just like the indirectly communicated implicatures vary in strength, so can (perhaps) the directly communicated explicated inferences. Primary candidates for stronger explicated inferences are those pragmatic inferences included under 'what is said'$_{min}$, namely, grammatically mandated enrichments, such as Reference resolution and Disambiguation. Temporal, causal, etc. *and*-enrichments, originally considered implicatures, but later on classified as explicated inferences by Relevance theoreticians (see Ariel 2012; Carston 2002), may nonetheless not constitute as strong interpretations as 'what is said'$_{min}$ types of saturation. Indeed, Doran et al. (2009) and Doran et al. (2012) found differences between the truth-conditional role played by different Generalized Conversational Implicatures, at least for a literal-minded interpretation of the utterances associated with those inferences.

The goal of this paper is to examine putative explicated inferences and compare the predictions made about them by Minimalists, Maximalists, and

Multiplists. Surprisingly perhaps, we shall see that each approach offers insightful observations, so our strength-based classification of inferences will incorporate aspects from all these approaches. First, the results of the experiment described strongly support the Maximalist approach in that *all* inferences classified as explicated share a unique discourse status, different from that of implicatures. Moreover, they are basically undeniable by the speakers whose utterances reasonably triggered those inferences (see section 2 for the Deniability test). This result clearly goes against Minimalists, who should predict a division between 'what is said'$_{min}$ inferences as a single category, and all other inferences (whether explicated or implicated) as a complementary distinct category.

At the same time, we do find differences within the category of explicated inferences. Moreover, these differences fall along the 'what is said'$_{min}$ versus 'what is said'$_{max}$ distinction. This distinction then supports the Minimalist insight that there is an inherent difference between grammatically mandated ('what is said'$_{min}$) inferences and inferences triggered due to conceptual incompleteness ('what is said'$_{max}$). By the same token, Multiplists too are vindicated in that they see a significant difference not only between two meaning representations, but rather, between three levels, namely, 'what is said'$_{min}$, 'what is said'$_{max}$, and implicatures. Finally, our own graded strength analysis, which proposes that pragmatic inferences come with different strengths, is supported in that pragmatic inferences pattern along a *graded* strength scale.

In order to show that various explicated inferences need not necessarily be equally strong, we use here the Deniability test ('Can a speaker deny later on having said that…?'), which has already been shown to function as an efficient tool for differentiating levels of interpretation (Sternau et al. 2016). We explain the test in section 2.

3 Deniablity

The idea behind the Deniability test is that in natural discourse, speakers are often committed to much more than that which semantics dictates: what is defined as cancellable, i.e., all pragmatic inferences, is not always easily deniable. While what is deniable is, by definition, also cancellable, what is cancellable is not necessarily deniable, or at least, not easily so.[4] The Deniability test

---

4 It should be noted that some researchers have argued against taking into consideration what is understood by the addressee as a criterion to grade the speaker's commitment to what was said. For example, Bach (2001) claims that "it is a mystery to me why facts about what the hearer does in order to understand what the speaker says should be relevant to what the speaker says in the first place" (p. 156). However, this study assumes that the speaker's commitment

may be best described as the pragmatic counterpart of Grice's (1989) cancellability criterion. The cancellability criterion is semantic in nature, and equally applies to all and only non-semantic interpretations, i.e. pragmatic inferences. All pragmatic aspects are cancellable, and it does not make sense to grade the degree to which they are cancellable.

A different way of treating the issue of cancellability is found in Burton-Roberts (2006, 2010). According to him, cancellability is crucially related to the speaker's intention. He proposes a revised cancellability criterion, which should be thought of as clarification of the speaker's intended meaning. The basis for his new version of Grice's criterion is the rudimentary distinction between levels of interpretation which, by definition, convey the speaker's intended meanings, and meanings which are retrieved by default, and therefore do not necessarily constitute the individual speaker's intended meaning. Burton-Roberts argues that the former, i.e., Grice's PCIs and Sperber and Wilson's explicated inferences, are not cancellable, whereas the latter, i.e., Grice's GCIs, are. His solution is that we should treat cancellation as an operation that cannot contradict *what was intended*, but only *what is inferred independently of the specific context*. As GCIs are to some extent context-independent, they are not bound by the speaker's intentions, and hence, are 'Burton-Roberts cancellable' (see also Capone 2009).

This proposal disagrees with basically both neo-Gricean and post-Gricean views, which assume the ability to cancel not only implicated, but also explicated materials. Since these materials involve inferred interpretations, they are by definition cancellable (Ariel 2008; Carston 1988, 2002). However, since they often include grammatically mandated inferences as well, and are very crucial to determining the truth conditions of the proposition expressed, 'Burton-Roberts cancelling' them may not be easy.

We find Grice's semantic cancellability criterion absolutely important, but see no reason for it to be equally important in determining the *discourse* status of interpretations. Rather, we propose a parallel interaction-based test – the Deniability test. Whereas the cancellability criterion aims to distinguish between all semantic meanings and all pragmatic inferences, the Deniability criterion aims to distinguish between stronger and weaker interpretations within discourse. It remains to be seen whether its application follows Burton-Robert's predictions regarding what we call 'Burton-Roberts cancellability'.

Deniability, as proposed in this study, is a discursive pragmatic correlate which pertains to the speaker's perceived ability to actually deny a potential message or inference somehow associated with her utterance in interaction. We

---

to the conveyed content, as understood by the addressee, is what both parties of the discourse consider as a pragmatic PII, especially when the conversation proceeds smoothly.

have already found (see Sternau et al. 2015) that, unlike cancellability, Deniability correlates with the strength of the potential inference, and that strength depends on pragmatic factors only. Hence, besides the semantic-pragmatic distinction, there is an additional important difference between cancellability and Deniability. Whereas the former may bear one of two values – cancellable or not cancellable, Deniability is gradable. Thus, it serves as a tool to differentiate between various types of pragmatic inferences to a finer degree. When an interpretation is easy to deny, we take it to be a weaker interpretation. When Deniability is (hardly) available, a stronger interpretation is involved.[5]

To see that cancellability and Deniability do not invariably yield the same results, let us consider the following example:

(3) Boss (in a job interview):
    You have small children. How will you manage the long hours of the job?
    H.D.: **I have a mother**   (Originally Hebrew 6.14.1996, Ariel 2008: 300)

H.D.'s explicature (here, close to the linguistic meaning) is true, as she indeed has a mother. However, in fact, her mother never helps her with the children. Thus, the strong implicature, that H.D.'s mother will help her take care of the children if she needs to work late, is false, and indeed – cancellable. However, when reporting this conversation, H.D. herself introduced it as a case in which she lied. That is, she seems to have considered the strong implicature as part of her PII, and felt that she could not deny its content.

Indeed, imagine a situation where H.D.'s boss, after hiring her, says to her: "I have to ask you to stay after 19:00 today. I guess you will have to make the necessary arrangements with your mother." Would H.D. be able then to respond: "I never said that my mother helps me take care of my kids."? We believe that in interactional terms the context in which H.D.'s utterance "I have a mother" was uttered, forces a commitment to the implicature as manifested by her own words. Due to these factors, the likelihood that H.D. would be able to deny ever saying the content of the implicature is very low.[6] Being highly relevant to the discourse is what makes the implicature in (3) a Privileged Interactional Interpretation, which then participates in determining the truth conditions of the utterance. These Privileged Interactional Interpretations depend on the speaker's intentions (as in 1) and in principle do not necessarily follow any given formula of explicated or implicated meanings (as in 2).

In example (3) the Deniability test seems stricter than the cancellability criterion, as far as an appropriate interaction might proceed. Namely, some of the

---
5 cf with the option of deniability which is retained by those who use sarcasm (Camp 2012).
6 See above our clarification regarding the 'said' quality that is being examined.

speaker's utterance interpretations are cancellable, yet hardly deniable or practically non-deniable. Obviously, semantics alone cannot provide all the actual intuitive truth conditions for each utterance on any occasion. There is a clear role for pragmatics, and the Deniability test proposed here addresses exactly that. At the same time, it also provides an appropriate pragmatic tool for differentiating interpretation strengths, since deniability comes in degrees, which we can establish by comparing the deniability of various levels of interpretation.

This gradability has been independently proposed by Jaszczolt (2005, 2009, 2010). She argues that

> [c]ancellation is difficult when the pragmatic enrichment is well entrenched and expected across contexts. In other words, when such enrichments are of the form of salient presumptive meanings...or strong social, cultural, or cognitive defaults..., they are harder to cancel explicitly in that they require a rather non-standard scenario. (Jaszczolt 2009: 12)

Hence, Jaszczolt expects these strongly entrenched pragmatic meanings, which are implicit, and yet, constitute the intended meaning, to be hard to deny.[7]

A strong basis for the gradedness of Deniability can be found in Ariel (2008) as well. Ariel proposes several parameters to distinguish between explicated inferences (i.e., the inferred part of explicatures), strong implicatures, and weak implicatures, as shown in Table (1):

Table 1. Ariel's (2008: 292) Parameters for distinguishing between explicated and implicated inferences

	Explicated inferences	Strong implicatures	Non-strong implicatures
Explicit	–	–	–
Cancellable	+	+	+
Indeterminate	+	+	+
Direct	+	–	–
Interactionally necessary	+	+	–
Truth-Conditional	+	+/–	–

Note Ariel's last two features. Pointing at their being interactionally necessary and truth-conditional, Ariel's observations (Table 1) assign priority to explicated

---

7 It should be noted that the inferences addressed here by Jaszczolt are not the ones which are "Burton-Roberts cancellable". Whereas she refers to PCIs, he argues that only GCIs are cancellable.

inferences and some strong implicatures over nonstrong implicatures. These features are highly relevant to Deniability. Hence, the predicted results of the Deniability test should depend on the ability of the inference to affect truth judgments and be taken by interlocutors as interactionally necessary. If an interpretation is considered as affecting truth judgments and as discursively indispensable, it stands to reason that it would be undeniable. Ariel, however, does not discuss degrees of strength for each feature. As illustrated by Table (1), she presents all features of inferences as dichotomous: (–) or (+).

Last, the experiment here reported, is somewhat similar to Doran et al.'s (2009, 2012) experiment. Both experiments address different types of pragmatic inferences, aiming to find whether they are part of 'what is said'$_{min}$, the explicature$_{min}$, as we would put it. Doran et al. (2009, 2012) presented participants with dialogs such as in (4), asking them to decide whether the underlined sentence is True or False, in view of a new fact, which disclosed potentially cancelling information:

(4) Irene: I heard you all went shopping. What did Harry buy?
    Sam: Harry bought four books.
    FACT: Harry bought five books.

    Given this FACT, the underlined sentence is:
    T or F

Here are some of their examples for different GCI types:

(5) a. Co-activities
       Irene: Can the guys come to the reception?
       Sam: No. George and Steve play squash at the gym until 6:00 everyday.
       FACT: George plays squash at the YMCA until 6:00 daily, and Steve plays squash at SPAC until 6:00 everyday.
    b. Argument saturation
       Irene: I heard something big happened in the art studio yesterday.
       Sam: Yeah! In a fit of rage, Rachel picked up a hammer and broke a statue.
       FACT: After grabbing a hammer, Rachel angrily kicked a statue, causing it to fall over and break.
    c. Repeated verb conjuncts
       Irene: What happened at Doctor Witherspoon's office?
       Sam: Sasha waited and waited for her appointment.
       FACT: Sasha waited 5 minutes for her appointment at Doctor Witherspoon's office.

    d. Conjunction buttressing
       Irene: I understand that George has had a really rough year.
       Sam: <u>Yeah. Last month, he lost his job and started drinking</u>.
       FACT: George started drinking on the 15th of last month and lost his job on the 20th of last month.

    e. Bridging inferences
       Irene: What happened when Sue came over?
       Sam: She walked into the bathroom. <u>The window was open</u>.
       FACT: The open windows are in the kitchen, and there are no windows in the bathroom.

The condition described above was the base-line condition, and it constitutes the condition which best resembles ours. However, they conducted this experiment under two *additional* conditions: the literal condition and Literal Lucy condition. In the literal condition participants were instructed to evaluate the truth value of each underlined sentence after they were told that "the fact <u>literally</u> states that…" (Doran et al.: 137). In the third condition participants were introduced with a character named 'Literal Lucy', who understands everything literally. The participants were asked to decide whether 'Literal Lucy' understands the speaker's last sentence as True or False. The results they focus on are this third Literal Lucy condition. However, as they point out, the other two conditions yielded the same order of GCIs.

Doran et al. (2009, 2012) assumed that if the participants decide that Literal Lucy approves the underlined sentence (Sam's answer in [4] above, for instance), i.e., says it is true in view of the new fact, then the tested type of inference, e.g., 'Harry bought exactly four books', is relatively easy to cancel. It means that the information in the new fact was irrelevant to the truth-judgment regarding the proposition expressed by Sam. If so, the GCI here is not part of what we would call 'Explicated'. On the other hand, if the participants decide that Literal Lucy finds Sam's utterance false in view of the new fact, it means that the information in the new fact was relevant to the truth-conditions of Sam's utterance. Hence, the tested GCI is part of the 'Explicated'. In addition to different types of GCIs (such as scalar quantifiers and argument saturations), the materials used by Doran et al. also included contradictions and entailments to establish a baseline, and Necessary Contextual Elements (NCEs): deictics, ellipses, indexicals, and pronoun resolutions as fillers. Although NCEs ('what is said$_{min}$' inferences, in effect) were treated as fillers by Doran et al., the results concerning this set of items are highly relevant to our study.[8]

---

[8] They were tested in our Experiment.

Contradictions cannot be rescued by cancellation, and entailments must be true. Indeed, results showed that entailments received only 7% "false" answers. And contradiction received 99% "false" answers. These findings show that Doran et al.'s participants understood the task. Regarding NCEs, they received 86% "false" answers, which suggest that Reference resolution, Indexicals and the like constitute an integral part of the 'Explicated'.[9] The various types of GCIs, however, demonstrated dramatically different behavior.[10] On average they got only 36% "false" answers, which was significantly different from all other types of materials. Interestingly, different types within this set of items, showed significantly different patterns of behavior as well. Doran et al. (2012) found that Co-activities, for example (see 5a above), had a 18% "false" answers, i.e., an 82% chance of being cancelled, while Argument saturation (see 5b above) had a 37% "false" answers, i.e., 63% chance of being cancelled. These two are therefore not part of the 'Explicated', presumably. On the other hand, repeated verb conjuncts (see 5c above), for example, had 82% "false" answers, i.e., only 18% chance of being cancelled, which suggests that they are a part of the 'Explicated'. These findings portray a *continuum* along which different types of GCIs and NCEs are ordered. Certain types of GCIs may strongly affect truth judgments, hence are to be considered part of the 'Explicated', while others have a relatively marginal impact on truth judgments, and are thus closer to implicatures. It should also be noted that Doran et al. (2009, 2012) did not find any significant differences within the different GCI types advocated by Levinson (2000) (I-based, M-based, and Q-based) as to their ability to constitute part of the 'Explicated'.[11]

Doran et al.'s findings therefore suggest a scale along which various explicated contributions to the bare linguistic meanings are ordered. As noted above, we also propose a scale, however, our experiment, as well as the Interpretation Strength Scale it supports, does not limit itself to Levinson's GCIs. On the contrary, aiming to show a significant difference between the strength of different explicated inferences, specifically between 'Explicated$_{min}$' and 'Explicated$_{max}$', we used additional pragmatic contributions to the Explicature.[12] Another crucial difference between our experiment and the experiments reported on in Doran et al. (2009, 2012) is that we did not ask for truth judgments, but rather, for deniability judgments. Thirdly, we did not ask for literal-minded judgments, as they did in

---

9 Although focusing on GCIs, Doran et al. also note that the significant difference between contradictions and NCEs suggested that "some participants...are distinguishing even those contextually-supplied elements of WHAT-IS-SAID from those that are supplied strictly
10 Results here are based on Doran et al., which focus on the Literal Lucy condition.
11 This finding, however, is incompatible with Katsos (2003), who did find such differences between these GCIs types.
12 We will address Doran et al.'s findings again when presenting our own.

their "literal condition" and "Literal Lucy" condition. Our participants were asked to judge, based on their own intuitions regarding the nature of appropriate interactions. As we see below, results were quite different, and we submit that there is no reason to impose literal-minded judgments when interaction is involved.

However, addressing their "baseline condition", which resembles our condition, comparison between some of Doran et al.'s findings and ours is possible in some aspects, as will be elaborated below.[13]

4 The Experiment

Deniability, as introduced above, is the interactional counterpart of Grice's (1989) cancellability. Deniability tests the extent to which a speaker is licensed to say that s/he has never said a specific content in a certain situation. We here restrict ourselves to various pragmatic contributions included within explicatures – the explicated inferences. An explicated inference can be the outcome of any one of a number of processes, such as reference assignment, *and* enrichment, etc. Are there any differences between these various explicated inferences, in terms of their degree of strength? Will these differences reflect a possibly different status for an Explicated$_{min}$ versus an Explicated$_{max}$? Our goal is to find out whether different explicated inferences are not equally strong, and if so, what may determine possible differences between them.

4.1 Aim

The aim of this experiment was twofold:
1. Replicating the results of previous experiments, which supported the relatively high degree of strength of explicatures, as far as deniability is concerned (Sternau et al. 2015, 2016).
2. Testing the continuum hypothesis by examining the behavior of four categories of explicated inferences (elaborated below): reference assignment, default (or salient in terms of being prototypical members of a category or a scenario) enrichments, e.g., *eating breakfast today*, completion of fragmentary answers and various *and* enrichments.[14]

---

13 As noted above, the results provided by Doran et al. are those received under the third condition (Literal Lucy). But they report that the other two conditions demonstrated the same order within the GCIs category, and the order, i.e. the gradation itself, is what interests us here.
14 Regarding *and*-conjunction, Levinson (1995, 1998, 2000) also includes them in his distinct category of GCIs, yet, his enriched meaning of *and* does not account for a wide range of relations, as were examined here.

4.2 Predictions

The strength continuum suggests the following prediction: although there is a significant difference between all explicatures taken together as a single category and all other meaning levels, some explicated inferences might be easier to deny than others, and thus might be ranked closer to strong implicatures. Other explicated inferences may be harder to deny, which would rank them as closer to linguistic meanings. If so, we may offer a continuum within the explicature category. In other words, the proposal is that we should find a scale of interpretations, far richer than first envisioned, organized according to their ease of deniability instead of the simple scale in (6), which was tested in Sternau et al. (2015):

(6) Bare linguistic meaning > Explicated$_{max}$ > Implicature$_{[strong]}$ > Implicature$_{[weak]}$

Rather, we may have more members on the scale, breaking down the conventional Explicature category we operated with so far, into sub-categories.[15] Tipped off by Minimalists' ideas, one might predict that the explicatures which result from the processes involved in Grice's (1989) 'Explicated$_{min}$', i.e., Lexical ambiguity resolution and Reference resolution (core inferences), will be relatively harder to deny. Such a result will lend support to the psychological reality of the Gricean 'Explicated$_{min}$', since it will place these two inference types closer to the linguistic meaning than other explicated inferences on the continuum (Berg 2002; Borg 2005; Grice 1989; Horn 1984, 2006; Levinson 1983, 2000). In an intermediate position we may find Levinson's *additional* 'presumptive meanings'. These 'periphery' inferences are predicted to be easier to deny.[16]
Following is the Minimalists' predicted scale:

(7) Reference resolution >
    Default enrichments/Fragments completion/Conjunction enrichments

However, since Levinson did not include all possible enrichments of *and*-conjunction, Minimalists should in fact predict that Conjunction enrichments are the easiest to deny, as most materials here are not confined to the temporal-relation-enrichment. Hence,

---

[15] It should be noted that also Relevance-theoreticians suggested gradability of strength, but their gradability depends on the relative contribution of the explicated inferences versus that of linguistic meaning, rather than on the nature of different pragmatic contributions.
[16] Note that a hierarchy of Levinson's (2000) GCIs was tested by Doran et al. (2009, 2012). However, their results were not compatible with Levinson's classification system.

(8) Reference resolution > Default enrichments/Fragments completion > Conjunction enrichments

Maximalists, on the other hand, have not offered a strength-based distinction between different types of explicated pragmatic enrichments. Thus, they seem to have no predictions as to the hierarchy of these pragmatic enrichments.

4.3 Participants

Participants were 32 students from Tel-Aviv University (19 women, 13 men), aged 20–29, both undergraduates and graduates. All were native speakers of Hebrew. They were paid 30 NIS for their participation.

4.4 Materials

The study described here is an off-line experiment, which enabled participants to read the texts over and over again. The participants were presented with 30 short texts, associated with five types of pragmatic contributions of the explicature. Below are examples of each of the pragmatic contributions to the explicature.[17]

(9) a. **Reference resolution**
Michal and Anat are talking about Gadi, a guy Michal fancies. Michal met Gadi at a party and it seemed to her that he was flirting with her.
Anat: Well, did you check up on him?
Michal: He's married.
Conclusion: Gadi is married.

b. **Default (or Salient) Enrichment**
Yonni and his friends went on a hike. At 10 o'clock Yonni begins preparing a late breakfast for everyone. He wants to know whether Smadar would like an omelet, but cannot find her.
He asks her friend Rinat: Would Smadar like an omelet?
Rinat: Smadar has already had breakfast.
Conclusion: Smadar has already had breakfast that morning.

---

[17] We should mention that six items summoning Disambiguation were also included in this experiment. However, after examining them thoroughly, we concluded that some of them might have triggered a 'narrowed' meaning of the intended meaning, and therefore this category was excluded from our final analysis. The two items, which we did not suspect of misleading the participants, provided the following results: 2.37 and 2.78.

c. **Fragment completion**
   Ran and Ofer are visiting the museum. Ran wants to show Ofer a picture he really liked.
   Ofer: Well, when are we going to see the picture you talked about so much?
   Ran: On your left.
   Conclusion: The picture I liked is on your left.

d. ***And-* (Enriched) conjunctions**
   Iris and Yonni go on a night trip in the Judean desert. The next morning, when Iris comes back alone, their friend Dror asks her: Where's Yonni?
   Iris: Yonni felt bad and went to the hospital.
   Conclusion: Yonni felt bad and therefore went to the hospital.[18]

All short texts were inserted into one questionnaire alongside 10 filler items, which included strong implicatures we did not use in our previous experiments. Each question was always followed by an explanation (here, as in the original questionnaire – in bold). For example:

(10) An example of an item

   Ran and Ofer are visiting the museum. Ran wants to show Ofer a picture he really liked.
   Ofer: Well, when are we going to see the picture you talked about so much?
   Ran: On your left.
   Conclusion: The picture I liked is to your left.

Question: Can Ran deny the conclusion? (= to what extent will Ran be licensed to say to Ofer in the future: "In that situation, I didn't say that the picture I liked was on your left.")

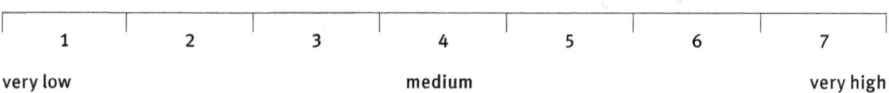

Figure 1. Deniability rating scale

---

[18] Noveck and Reboul (2008) and Pouscoulous and Noveck (2009) have already shown that a strongly biased context facilitates pragmatic inferencing, especially when scalar implicatures or the *and*-conjunction are involved.

Of the 24 short texts of the four categories of interest, six tested reference assignment (personal pronouns, demonstrative pronouns), six tested Default enrichments (some based on common examples from the literature (e.g. Bach 1994; Recanati 2004), six tested completion of fragmentary utterances, and six tested '*and*' enrichments (= 'and then', 'therefore' or 'nonetheless'). Again, some of these examples were also taken from the literature (Ariel, 2008; Carston, 2002). The questions were presented to the participants in a restricted random order. We made sure that consecutive items always concerned different types of explicated inferences.

4.5 Procedure

Participants were instructed to rate the degree of deniability of each target sentence taking into consideration *the circumstances under which it was uttered* (the phrase 'under these circumstances' was underlined in each question, *emphasis was added also by the experimenter while explaining the instructions out loud*). Given these specific instructions, we argue that what was rated was, in fact, perceived as the PII. The instructions were as follows:

> *Thank you for participating in this experiment.*
>
> *You are about to read a few short texts. At the end of each short text there is a conclusion derived on the basis of what a speaker in that text has just said. You are asked to rate, on a 7-point scale, the extent to which it is possible for that same speaker to deny having said (what is mentioned in) the conclusion, which could be implied from what s/he had said. You may change your mind and change your rating before submitting the questionnaire.*[19]

Following the instructions, two practice examples were presented followed by a comprehension question. Once the participant's understanding of the task was confirmed, s/he was left alone to finish rating the deniability of all the items.

---

19 As already noted above, it is the degree of 'saidhood', i.e. the discourse status, which is measured here. We are well aware of the fact that inferences are not uttered, and hence, are not 'said' in the conventional use of the verb.

4.6 Results

Table 2. Rating Mean and SD for Each Pragmatic Process

Pragmatic process	Mean	SD
Conjunction enrichment	2.89	1.21
Default enrichments	2.58	0.92
Reference resolution	1.92	0.74
Fragment completion	1.85	0.70

The results support the relatively strong status of explicated inferences. Note that the higher the mean is, the more deniable, and thus the weaker, the inference is. The deniability ratings of the explicated inferences tested here range between 1.85 and 2.89, clearly heavily skewed towards the non-deniable end of the scale. In fact, all of the explicated inferences scored significantly lower than 4 (all t's>5, all p's<.0001), which means that all were basically judged undeniable.

These results are illustrated in Figure 2:

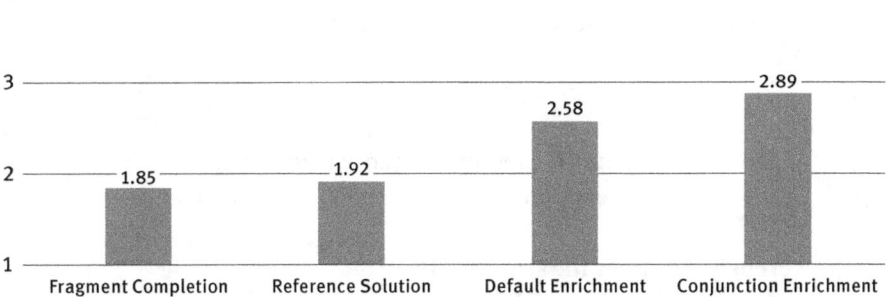

Figure 2. Rating mean for each pragmatic process

Subject and item ANOVAs show that there are differences between the four categories: $F_1(3,93)=16.52$, p<.001; $F_2(3,20)=3.41$, p<.05. Since, following Maximalists, we had no specific predictions as to the expected hierarchy of the Deniability of the various pragmatic contributions, we first employed a Helmert-contrast analysis (between each category and the mean of all subsequent categories), to establish the statistically significant gradation:

1. And-conjunction (mean of Default enrichments, reference assignment, completion of fragmentary answers): $F_1(1,31)=15.53$, p<.001; $F_2(1,20)=5.91$, p<.05.
2. Default enrichment (mean of reference assignment, completion of fragmentary answers): $F_1(1,31)=31.63$, p<.001; $F_2(1,20)=4.29$, p=.052.

3. Reference assignment-completion of fragmentary answers:
   $F_1(1,31)<1$, n.s.; $F_2(1,20)<1$, n.s.

Next, we examine the differences between each category of explicated inferences and the one(s) positioned next to it by employing a repeated contrast analysis:

1. Conjunction enrichment–default enrichment:
   $F_1(1,31)=2.37$, $p=.13$, n.s.; $F_2(1,20)<1$, n.s.
2. Default enrichment–Reference resolution:
   $F_1(1,31)=24.88$, $p<.001$; $F_2(1,20)=2.94$, $p=.10$, n.s.
3. Reference resolution-Fragment completion: $F_1(1,31)<1$, n.s.; $F_2(1,20)<1$, n.s.

It should be noted, however, that the analysis by subjects is much more meaningful here. This is because we had a relatively large number of participants but only six items per category.

Thus, in light of the results received from Subject ANOVA, the hierarchy of strength we got was:

(11) Fragmentary answers completion/Reference resolution
      > Default enrichment/Conjunction enrichment

Or:

(12) Group 1: Fragment completion/Reference resolution >
      Group 2: Default enrichment/*And*-Conjunction enrichment

Figure 3 crudely describes the scale in (11):

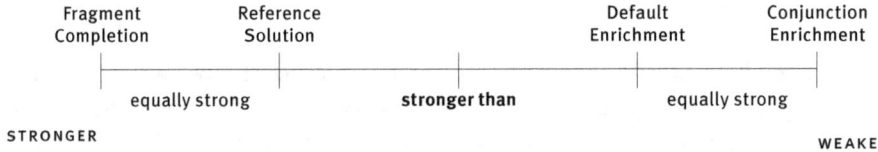

Figure 3. The deniability hierarchy within explicatures

As can be seen, results support a two-way division of degree of strength: Fragment completions are as strong as Reference resolutions, and both constitute a less deniable category; Default enrichments and *and*-conjunction enrichments are also equally strong, but they are easier to deny than Fragment completions and Reference resolutions.

5 Discussion and Conclusions

The results of our Deniability test can be seen as comprising two sets of findings, each supporting a seemingly different conclusion. But, as we see below, the conclusions are compatible with each other. Judging by the absolute means for deniable versus nondeniable, all the inferences here tested demonstrate a single pattern of behavior, and hence constitute a unified category. At the same time, a more fine-tuned analysis of the relative means reveals that the inferences can be divided into two sub-groups. It is the combination of these two findings that support our claim that while Maximalists are definitely vindicated, Multiplists and even Minimalists are also right. Let us see why.

All the inferences here tested were rated as *un*deniable. All four means (1.85–2.89) are significantly lower than 4, which is the cutoff point on our 7-point scale for deniable inferences. In other words, Reference resolution, Fragment completion, Default enrichment, and *And*-enrichments are all basically undeniable, which supports the Maximalists, both those who concentrate on the hearer (Sperber and Wilson [1986] 1995; Carston 2002 and onwards) and those who focus on the speaker (Ariel 2002 and onwards; Kecskés 2010). Indeed, any and all inferences involved in developing the linguistic meaning into the speaker-intended proposition *on the specific occasion* count as part of the explicature. All explicated inferences thus manifest a similar discourse status.

Nonetheless, the Minimalists' distinction between 'what is said'$_{min}$ inferences and other inferences, Recanati's (2004) distinction within his primary processes (roughly explicated inferences) between saturations and enrichments, and Burton-Roberts (2006, 2010) distinction between Burton-Roberts-cancellable and uncancellable inferences, all receive support as well. Reference resolutions and fragment completions are 'what is said$_{min}$' inferences for Minimalists, they are Saturations for Recanati, and they are inferences specifically intended by the addressee in the specific context, which makes them nonBurton-Roberts-cancellable. Indeed, these are the explicated inferences which are quite undeniable (means lower than 2 on a 7–point scale). The other inferences examined, Default enrichments and *and*-enrichments, are arguably at least less context-dependent. Inferences such as the 'eating' in *I've had breakfast* took place specifically 'this morning', and the temporal relation, for example, inferred for *And*-conjunctions depend much more on general knowledge about stereotypes and much less on the specific speech context. Indeed, the mean Deniability rate here is significantly higher (2.58, 2.89 respectively).

So, do the inferences here constitute a single homogenous explicated category, which follows the Maximalist analysis, or should we recognize two categories within our 'Explicated$_{max}$', namely, 'what is said$_{min}$' inferences, on the one hand, and "all other inferences", as advocated by Minimalists, on the other? Our claim is that the two positions are not as incompatible as they seem to be. While the Minimalist distinction between various inferences is supported by our data, we should emphasize that by no means do they argue against the Maximalist position, according to which all inferences required in order to develop the linguistic meaning into the speaker-intended proposition count as explicated. We claim that this requirement is quite compatible with further fine-tuned distinctions among the explicated inferences. In other words, all we need to do is introduce our strength gradedness into the category of explicatures. On our analysis, all the inferences here tested are quite strong (compatible with the Maximalist position), although some are stronger than others (compatible with the Minimalist position). Needless to say, once both Maximalists and Minimalists are vindicated, so are Multiplists, and especially our own graded strength position.

Before we move on to discuss the graded strength thesis, we should compare our findings to those of Doran et al.'s (2009, 2012). Once again, we will distinguish between relative and absolute results. The absolute criterion predicts that our undeniable inferences should correspond to their 'what is said' inferences, i.e., the utterances judged as false by their participants when the inferences were not true. Conversely, what our participants find deniable should not constitute part of 'what is said', in which case Doran et al.'s participants should judge the utterance as true despite the fact that the inference is not true. The relative criterion predicts that, to the extent that they are comparable, the ordering of the items on the scales, derived from the two experiments, should be the same. In other words, what is relatively less deniable on our scale should correspond to what prompts relatively more false judgments in their experiment, and vice versa: what is relatively more deniable on our scale should correspond to what prompts less false judgments in their experiment.

First, we should determine which inference types are reasonably comparable in the two experiments. We propose that their NCEs (Reference resolution Ellipsis, etc.), which they only included as a baseline, are similar enough to our Reference resolution and Fragment completion in that all are grammatically mandated on the one hand, and depend on the specific context, on the other hand. Next, their 'conjunction buttressing' cases are of course comparable to our *and*-enrichments. Finally, the inferences used to test the categories of 'argument saturation' (see again 5b) and 'bridging inferences' (see again 5e) at least resemble the inferences we used for our 'Default enrichments' category (see again 9b) in that all depend crucially on stereotypic scenarios.

Starting with the relative positions on our respective scales, the two experiments seem to be at least in partial agreement. Doran et al.'s NCEs are very clearly part of 'what is said', given that 86% of the participants' responses determined that the utterance was false when the inferred interpretation was false. Similarly, our participants graded as very low the possibility that speakers can later on deny Reference resolutions and Fragment completions (1.85, 1.92, respectively). Next, Bridging inferencing and Argument saturations are clearly less part of 'what is said' according to Doran et al.'s findings, as only a minority of their participants judged the utterances as false when the inference was false (39% and 30% respectively). This is clearly different from the NCE condition, where 86% of the participants judged the utterance as false on the basis of the false inference. Indeed, the results of our Deniability test show that Default enrichments are significantly more deniable than Reference resolutions and Fragment completions, scoring 2.58 on a 7-point scale. Doran et al. note that Conjunction buttressing differs from Argument saturation (21% of the cases judged false) but cannot determine whether the difference is significant. In our experiment *and*-enrichments are not significantly different from Default enrichments. All in all, then, to the extent that we can compare the *gradation* proposed by Doran et al. and by us, it seems that the two experiments are quite compatible with each other.

But this is not the case once we switch to the absolute status of 'what is said' and nondeniability. Recall that our findings are such that all the inferences tested for are quite undeniable, none of their means reaching the cutoff point of 4. While this nondeniability is echoed by Doran et al.'s findings for NCEs, it is not echoed by their target category, that of GCIs. Here, their results mostly point to an implicated status, since only a minority of the cases which the two experiments share received a false judgment. In other words, while the deniability test attributes a 'said' status to the inferences here examined, the True/False test attributes to them an implicated status.[20]

However, we must not forget the major differences between our study and that of Doran et al. First, Doran et al. asked for a True or False answer (i.e., cancellability), whereas we asked the participants to rate Deniability on a 7-point scale. Second, whereas Doran et al. focused on the literally-conveyed content, we directed the participants towards the Privileged Interactional Interpretation as perceived by the speaker, which is more discourse-dependent.[21] This explains why the *absolute* results we got are quite different. Most of the GCIs they tested for were classified as cancellable implicatures by their participants, whereas most of the inferences we tested for were classified as nondeniable by our par-

---

20 We use 'said' here, rather than the technical 'what is said' because Deniability is not recognized as a 'what is said' test.

21 One could argue that what we have here are strong implicatures, which would explain why they do not contribute to conditional aspects on the one hand, but are hard to deny on the other hand. But our research (Sternau 2014; Sternau et al. 2015, 2016) has shown that explicated inferences are less deniable than strong implicatures, let alone, than weak ones.

ticipants. One conclusion one could draw from these clear differences is that cancellability and deniability are simply different tests, the first – semantic, while the second – interactional. But the fact is that Doran et al.'s results are far from dichotomous, which may indicate that their participants, in effect, were also relying on a Deniability criterion, although they applied it more liberally, because of the instruction to make literal judgments.

Finally, we submit that the best account for our experimental results (as well as Doran et al.'s) is the reality of a strength hierarchy among various pragmatic contributions to explicature. This strength correlates with a variety of factors. One such factor is the source of the inference. The strongest source seems to be the grammatical one, which forces the interlocutor to complete an utterance up to a fully grammatical sentence expressing a proposition. The weaker source is the purely pragmatic one, which calls for completing sentences according to common or frequent scenarios. But once we take into account results we previously obtained for strong and weak implicatures (Sternau 2014; Sternau et al. 2015, 2016), the crucial role of the relevance of the inference becomes clear. The more relevant the inference to the speaker's intended message the stronger it is and the less deniable it is. This is why we found that while strong implicatures are relatively more deniable than explicated inferences, they are not actually deniable in absolute terms. Strong implicatures received a mean grade of 3.21, which is significantly lower than the cut-off point of 4 ($t(47)=5.45$, $p<.001$). The only category for which Deniability was confirmed in absolute terms is weak implicatures (mean grade of 4.39). Figure 4 reproduces a graph from Sternau et al. (2015), representing the relative strength of four types of interpretations: linguistic meanings, explicatures, strong implicatures, and weak implicatures:

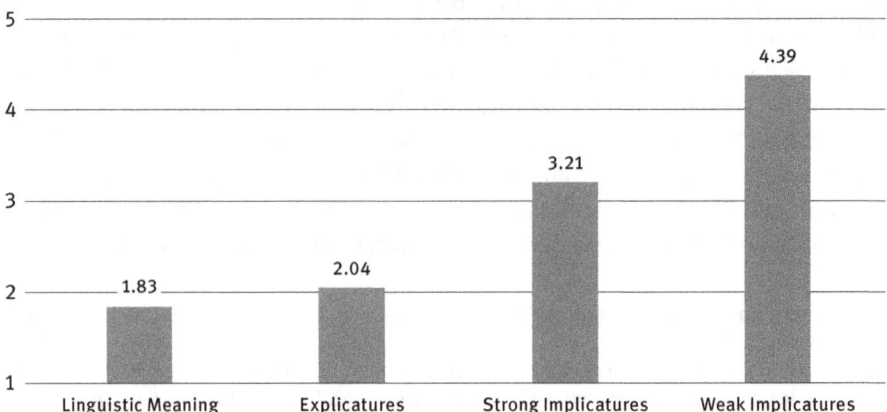

Figure 4. Rating mean for each level of interpretation (Deniability test)

This is why the Deniability test ultimately supports Ariel's Privileged Interactional Interpretation and Jaszczolt's Primary meaning. Above all, the findings presented here and elsewhere provide a solid basis for assuming a graded interpretation strength, whereby linguistic meanings are strongest, weak implicatures are weakest, and, in between, we have what we may call strong explicated inferences ('what is said'$_{min}$ inferences), weak explicated inferences (enrichments), and strong implicatures.

References

Ariel, Mira. 2002. Privileged interactional interpretations. *Journal of Pragmatics* 34(8). 1003–1044.
Ariel, Mira. 2008. *Pragmatics and Grammar*. Cambridge: Cambridge University Press.
Ariel, Mira. 2012. Relational and independent and-conjunctions. *Lingua* 122. 1682–1715.
Bach, Kent. 1994. Conversational impliciture. *Mind and Language* 9(2). 124–162.
Bach, Kent. 2001. Semantically speaking. In István Kenesei & Robert M. Harnish (eds.), *Perspectives on semantics*, pragmatics and discourse, 147–169. Amsterdam: John Benjamins.
Berg, Jonathan. 2002. Is semantics still possible? *Journal of Pragmatics* 34(4). 349–359.
Borg, Emma. 2004. *Minimal semantics*. Oxford: Oxford University Press.
Borg, Emma. 2005. Saying what you mean: Unarticulated constituents and communication. In Reinaldo Elugardo & Robert Stainton (eds.), *Ellipsis and nonsentential speech*, 237–262. Dordrecht: Kluwer.
Borg, Emma. 2016. Exploding explicatures. *Mind and Language* 31. 335–355.
Burton-Roberts, Noel. 2006. Cancellation and intention. *Newcastle Working Papers in Linguistics* 12–13. 1–12.
Burton-Roberts, Noel. 2010. Cancellation and intention. In Belen Soria & Esther Romero (eds.), *Explicit communication: Robyn Carston's pragmatics*, 138–155. London: Palgrave Macmillan.
Camp, Elisabeth. 2012. Sarcasm, pretense, and the semantics/pragmatics Distinction. *Noûs* 46(4). 587–634.
Capone, Alessandro. 2009. Are explicatures cancellable? Toward a theory of the speaker's intentionality. *Intercultural Pragmatics* 6(1). 55–83.
Carston, Robyn. 1988. Implicature, explicature and truth-theoretic semantics. In Ruth M. Kempson (ed.), *Mental representations: The interface between language and reality*, 155–181. Cambridge: Cambridge University Press. Reprinted in S. Davis (ed.) (1991), *Pragmatics: A Reader*, 33–51. Oxford: Oxford University Press.
Carston, Robyn. 2002. *Thoughts and utterances: The pragmatics of explicit communication*. Oxford: Blackwell.
Doran, Ryan, Rachel E. Baker, Yaron McNabb, Meredith Larson & Gregory Ward. 2009. On the non-unified nature of scalar implicature: An empirical investigation. *International Review of Pragmatics* 1. 211–248.
Doran, Ryan, Gregory Ward, Meredith Larson, Yaron McNabb & Rachel E. Baker. 2012. A novel experimental paradigm for distinguishing between what is said and what is implicated. *Language* 88. 124–154.
Grice, H. Paul, 1969. Utterer's meaning, sentence meaning and word meaning. *Foundations of Language* 4. 225–242.

Grice, H. Paul. 1989. *Studies in the way of words*. Cambridge, MA: Harvard University Press.
Horn, Laurence R. 1984. A new taxonomy for pragmatic inference: Q-based and R-based implicatures. In Deborah Schiffrin (ed.), *Meaning, form, and use in context: Linguistic applications* (Georgetown University Round Table on Languages and Linguistics), 11–42 Washington, DC: Georgetown University Press.
Horn, Laurence R. 2006. More issues in neo- and post-Gricean pragmatics: A response to Robyn Carston's response. *Intercultural Pragmatics* 3(1). 81–93.
Jaszczolt, Katarzyna M. 1999. Default semantics, pragmatics, and intentions. In Ken Turner (ed.), *The semantics/pragmatics interface from different points of view*, 199–232 Oxford: Elsevier Science.
Jaszczolt, Katarzyna M. 2005. Prolegomena to default semantics. In Sophia Marmaridou, Kiki Nikiforidou & Eleni Antonopoulou (eds.), *Reviewing linguistic thought: Converging trends for the 21st century*, 107–142 Berlin & New York: Mouton de Gruyter.
Jaszczolt, Katarzyna M. 2009. Cancellability and the primary/secondary meaning distinction. *Intercultural Pragmatics* 6. 259–289.
Jaszczolt, Katarzyna M. 2010. Default Semantics. In Bernd Heine & Heiko Narrog (eds.), The Oxford Handbook of linguistic analysis, 193–221. Oxford: Oxford University Press.
Katsos, Napoleon. 2003. An experimental study on pragmatic inferences: Processing implicatures and presuppositions. *Working Papers in English and Applied Linguistics* 9. 101–128.
Kecskés, István. 2010. The paradox of communication: socio-cognitive approach to pragmatics. *Pragmatics and Society* 1(1). 50–73.
Levinson, Stephen C. 1983. *Pragmatics*. Cambridge: Cambridge University Press.
Levinson, Stephen C. 1995. Three levels of meaning. In Frank Robert Palmer (ed.), *Grammar and meaning*, 90–115 Cambridge: Cambridge University Press.
Levinson, Stephen C. 1998. Minimization and conversational inference. In Asa Kasher (ed.), Pragmatics vol. 4: *Presupposition, implicature and indirect speech acts*, 545–612 London: Routledge.
Levinson, Stephen C. 2000. Presumptive Meanings: The Theory of Generalized Conversational Implicature. Cambridge, MA: MIT Press.
Noveck, Ira & Anne Reboul. 2008. Experimental pragmatics: A Gricean turn in the study of language. *Trends in Cognitive Sciences* 12(11). 425–431.
Pouscoulous Nausicaa & Ira Noveck. 2009. Going beyond semantics: The development of pragmatic enrichment. In Foster-Cohen S (ed.), *Language acquisition*, 196–215. Hampshire: Palgrave.
Recanati, François. 2001. What is said. *Synthese* 128. 75–91.
Recanati, François. 2004. *Literal Meaning*. Cambridge: Cambridge University Press.
Recanati, François. 2007. Truth conditional pragmatics. In Paolo Bouquet, Luciano Serafini & Rich Thomason (eds.), *Perspectives on contexts*, 169–186. Stanford: CSLI.
Sperber, Dan & Deirdre Wilson. 1995 [1986]. Relevance. Oxford: Blackwell.
Sternau, Marit. 2014. Levels of Interpretation: Linguistic Meaning and Inferences. Doctoral dissertation. Tel Aviv University.
Sternau, Marit, Mira Ariel, Rachel Giora & Ofer Fein. 2015. Levels of interpretation: New tools for characterizing intended meanings. *Journal of Pragmatics* 84. 86–101.
Sternau, Marit, Mira Ariel, Rachel Giora & Ofer Fein. 2016. A graded strength for Privileged Interactional Interpretations. In Keith Allan, Alessandro Capone & István Kecskés (eds.), *Pragmemes and Theories of Language Use*. In press.
Terkourafi, Marina. 2010. What-is-Said from different points of view. *Language and Linguistics Compass* 4(8). 705–718.
Wilson, Deirdre & Dan Sperber. 2002. Truthfulness and relevance. Mind 111(443). 583–632.

Eline Zenner, Nane Mertens, Laura Rosseel and Dirk Geeraerts
7 The acquisition of loanword pragmatics: An exploration

1 Introduction

The socio-cognitive approach to pragmatics ardently and eloquently advocated by István Kecskés (2010, 2014) ties in with a broader tendency in contemporary linguistics to combine sociolinguistic and psycholinguistic perspectives on language. Specifically also in the theoretical framework of cognitive linguistics, the last decade has witnessed the emergence of a tradition of cognitive sociolinguistics (Kristiansen and Dirven 2008, Geeraerts and Kristiansen 2015) that introduces notions and interests of cognitive linguistics into variationist linguistics and at the same time tries to sensitize cognitive linguistics to the importance of language variation.

A characteristic field of enquiry for this coalescence of sociovariationist and cognitive perspectives involves the cognitive representation of language variation: how is language variation and change perceived by language users, where 'perception' can be purely cognitive (the recognition of differences) or evaluative (the appreciation of differences, as in the broad field of 'language regard' as defined by Preston 2013)? And in addition, how does that perception change: how and when is knowledge of variation acquired, and how and when do evaluations develop in the individual?

Although the perspective of cognitive sociolinguistics has already been successfully applied to loanword research and contact linguistics (Zenner, Speelman, and Geeraerts 2012, 2014; Zenner and Kristiansen 2014), a specific focus on such acquisitional aspects has so far not been pursued. In this paper, then, we describe a small-scale exploratory study focusing on the perception of English loanwords in Dutch among primary school children. The starting-point is the widely accepted recognition (see Matras 2009) that prestige plays a role in borrowing processes. Borrowing is not only motivated by functional factors like the filling of lexical gaps, but may also be triggered by the prestige of the source language. The specific questions we will address then are the following:

- Are primary school children sensitive to the prestige of English loans in Dutch?
- If so, what are the attitudinal dimensions shaping that sensitivity, and how does it vary with age and other factors?

Methodologically speaking, tackling questions of this type requires a combination of a matched guise technique (Lambert, Hodgson, Gardner, and Fillenbaum 1960) with an onomasiological perspective on lexical variation (Grondelaers, Speelman, and Geeraerts 2007). The matched guise technique ensures that the stimuli presented to the test subjects differ only in the targeted linguistic variables, which in this case precisely take the form of onomasiological pairs of loanwords and their Dutch equivalents. The following sections of this paper are successively devoted to a more detailed description of the design of the experiment and to an overview of the main results. Conclusions are formulated in the final section.

2 Design

The investigation consisted of two components: a matched guise experiment with an attitudinal survey based on two guises of a cartoon hero, and a picture naming task. The first aimed to measure the general evaluation of a text containing English loanwords in comparison with the same text containing the Dutch synonyms of the borrowed words, and, more specifically, tried to identify the qualitative dimensions underlying the evaluations. The second component investigated the vocabulary knowledge of the children, checking whether the children know the correct meaning of the English words included in the mixed guise.

The tests were administered on March 17 and 18, 2016 in the Sancta Maria primary school in Aarschot, a historic town of 29,000 in the east of the central province of Flanders, the Dutch-speaking part of Belgium. Aarschot is a major regional center for primary and secondary education. In the set of test subjects, three age groups were distinguished: 28 subjects in the first grade (aged 6 or 7), 28 in the third grade (aged 8 or 9) and 34 in the fifth grade (aged 10 or 11). Of the total of 90 test subjects, 53 were girls and 37 were boys. A minority of tested pupils have a multilingual background, but it turned out to be difficult to include this factor in the analysis.[1]

In the matched guise experiment a cartoon hero (designed by means of the PowToon website, http://www.powtoon.com) introduced himself in two different guises, a Dutch guise and an English-Dutch mixed guise. Figure 1 gives an

---

[1] Information about the family background and home situation of the test subjects was gathered through a questionnaire administered to the parents, but the responses were not systematic enough to allow for inclusion.

impression of the cartoon character, at the same time showing the barcodes that were introduced to help the youngest age group (with only incipient reading skills) distinguish the two guises. All children were presented with the Dutch cartoon hero first, followed by the English cartoon hero. This could naturally influence the results and follow-up research will have to look into the effect of the order of presentation. However, given the relatively small test sample, we were not able to include sequentiality as a parameter in this stage of our research. As each test group is offered the cartoon's hero in the same order, it is however methodologically sound to gauge the differences between the three test groups (first, third and fifth grade).

Figure 1. Sterrenman / Starman, the cartoon hero

The text uttered in the two guises is rendered in Table 1, with italics indicating the linguistically contrasting items. In total, sixteen loanwords and loan phrases were offered to the children. These items were selected on the basis of various sources: (bilingual) popular television shows, specifically ones targeting a child audience such as *Dora the Explorer*, children's books, and information received from first grade teachers with regard to the English words that the pupils were likely to master. The synonymous Dutch expressions were checked against Koops et al. (2016), a normative list intended to counteract the 'unnecessary use of English'. The different lines in the table represent the successive frames of the cartoon.

Table 1. The text of the guises

Dutch-only guise	Mixed guise	Translation
Hallo kinderen! Ik ben Alistar maar jullie mogen mij *Sterrenman* noemen. Ik ben namelijk een *superheld*! *Tof*, hé?	*Hi kids*! Ik ben Alistar maar jullie mogen mij *Starman* noemen. Ik ben namelijk een *superhero*! *Cool*, hé?	Hi kids! I am Alistar, but you can call me Sterrenman / Starman. I happen to be a superhero! Cool, don't you think?

Table 1. (continued)

Dutch-only guise	Mixed guise	Translation
Dit is mijn *hulpje* en mijn *beste vriend*, Ziggy. Samen *genieten en ontspannen* we graag. Soms moeten we het in een spannend *gevecht* opnemen tegen *slechteriken*. Gelukkig heb ik een *rugzak* vol *leuke snufjes* en kunnen we de vijand makkelijk verslaan! En daarna geven Ziggy en ik telkens een groot *feestje*! *Dag*!	Dit is mijn *sidekick* en mijn *best friend*, Ziggy. Samen *chillen en relaxen* we graag. Soms moeten we het in een spannende *battle* opnemen tegen de *bad guys*. Gelukkig heb ik een *backpack* vol *coole gadgets* en kunnen we de vijand makkelijk verslaan! En daarna geven Ziggy en ik telkens een grote *party*! *Bye*!	This is my sidekick and best friend Ziggy. Together we like to chill and relax. Sometimes we have to wage an exciting battle against the bad guys. Fortunately I have a backpack full of cool gadgets, and we can easily beat the enemy. And then Ziggy and I always throw a big party! Bye!

After listening to the two guises, which took 40 seconds each, the children were asked to complete an attitudinal questionnaire featuring questions like the one illustrated by Figure 2: "Who could be your best friend – Sterrenman or Starman?".

Wie vind jij het liefst?

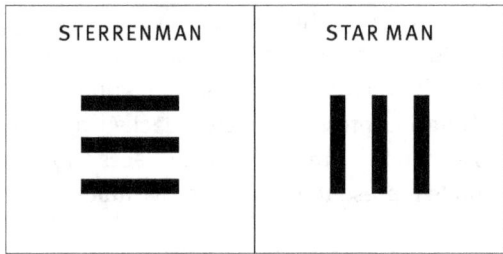

Figure 2. Sample attitudinal question

Apart from a question probing the overall preference of the pupils ("Who do you like most, Starman or Sterrenman?"), the questions asked in the attitudinal survey fall into three groups, according to the underlying dimension that we tried to cover. In line with existing attitude research, the following three dimensions of prestige were considered: solidarity, status and sociability. The questions included in the survey were read aloud in the classroom, and the next question was tackled when all students had answered the current one. The questions were categorized as follows:

- *Status-related questions*
  Who do you think is the smartest? Who do you think is the dullest? Who do you think is the dumbest?
- *Solidarity-related questions*
  Who could be your best friend? Who would you trust most? Who is the most friendly person? Who is the nicest person? Who is the most pleasant person?
- *Sociability-related questions*
  Who would have most friends in the playground? With whom would you share sweets and candy? Who is the funniest? Who would you invite to your birthday party?

Figure 3. Sample picture naming question

This classification has been based on the outcome of existing attitudinal studies that rely on factor analysis to cluster attitudes in dimensions (see e.g. Grondelaers and Van Hout 2010, Gondelaers, Van Hout, and Steegs 2010, Grondelaers and Speelman 2013). As our data set is too small for inferential techniques for such a bottom-up categorization, we will be careful not to overstate the importance of this three-tiered classification: the results for each question will be presented individually.

In addition to the structured attitudinal survey, the test subjects were invited to explain their preferences in an open question. A post hoc analysis classified the responses in five categories: responses indicating indecision ("I don't know"), responses referring to the name of the cartoon character ("I prefer Starman because he has a nice name"), responses referring to the personality of the cartoon character ("I prefer Sterrenman because he is funny"), responses containing a reference to one of the test pairs ("I prefer Sterrenman because he gives parties"), and responses referring to language ("I prefer Starman because he uses English and so you can learn English").

The Picture Action Naming Task (based on Johnson and Pearson's 1984 Listen and Locate Task) takes a form as in Figure 3: for each of the 28 items (*hi/ hello; kids/kinderen; star/ster; superhero/superheld; cool/tof; sidekick/hulpje; friend/vriend; chillen en relaxen/genieten en ontspannen; battle/gevecht; bad guy/ slechterik; backpack/rugzak; gadget/snufje; party/feestje; bye/dag*) the children are presented with a set of pictures from which they have to select the matching one. A number of fillers were inserted in the test. The items were presented in a scrambled order (i.e. not in pairs), but because our interest focuses on the children's knowledge of the English words, the English items of the pairs always appeared before the Dutch ones, to avoid interference of Dutch comprehension on the results for the English words. Again, the questions were read aloud in class, and the groups were taken through the questions on a step by step basis.

3 Results

Pending a more elaborate multivariate analysis, the following noteworthy results may be derived on the basis of binary analyses of the data.

[1] *Across all the age groups, the appreciation for the mixed guise is consistently, though not overwhelmingly, higher than the appreciation for the Dutch guise*, roughly stabilizing round a 60–40 distribution. The preferences are charted in Table 2. While the results in the first and third age group are nearly identical, the higher preference for the mixed guise in the middle age group is probably due to a technical problem during the experiment. The sound quality during the transmission of the fragments in the third grade class turned out to be slightly defective, and at least one pupil motivated his preference for the Starman guise by pointing to the fact that the Sterrenman fragment had been difficult to understand. It seems safe, therefore, to consider the higher results

for the mixed guise in the third grade as a spurious contextual effect. In what follows, the third grade results will be factored in when aggregating over the questions and respondents. When focusing in on more detailed analysis, results from the third grade will be discarded.

Table 2. Preferences for guises over age groups

	Starman	Sterrenman
First grade	57.14%	42.86%
Third grade	71.43%	28.57%
Fifth grade	58.82%	41.18%

These aggregative results, then, may be interpreted along two dimensions. First, if we attenuate the divergent pattern in the third grade, the results suggest that the preferences across the age groups are remarkably similar. Apparently, a specific appreciation of the linguistic guises is acquired early and remains stable throughout primary school. This result is in line with Kristiansen's (2010) findings relating to accent recognition, and Smith, Durham, and Richard's observations (2013) on the synchronicity of general language development and the acquisition of sociolinguistic competence.

Second, one should take care not to overinterpret the results. As they stand, they do not allow us to conclude that English in general enjoys a relatively high level of prestige, nor even that the English words in the fragments are slightly more appreciated as such than their Dutch counterparts. The data basically show that in the context of a cartoon of the kind used in the experiment, some English words have an evaluative edge over the Dutch synonyms. A conservative interpretation of this contextualized observation could take a stylistic perspective (Galinsky 1967): probably reflecting their familiarity with and exposure to cartoons as an international (i.e. predominantly English) format, the children seem to feel that for the cartoon genre, and more specifically for an animated character of the Superman type, the lavish use of English loans fits a little bit better than a Dutch-only speech style. To what extent genre expectations play a role should be studied in future research, assessing when children acquire which level of detail in language expectations when confronted with different genres. For instance, would the preference for the English guise be higher or lower when confronted with a documentary?

[2] *Structured attitudes appear with age, contrasting the sociability of the mixed guise character with the solidity of the Dutch guise character.* If we compare the attitudinal spectrum for the first and fifth grade, as in Figure 4 and 5 respectively, differentiation along attitudinal dimensions appears to emerge with age.

Whereas there are clear differences in the responses to the various questions in the older group, there is hardly any structure in the responses of the first age group.[2]

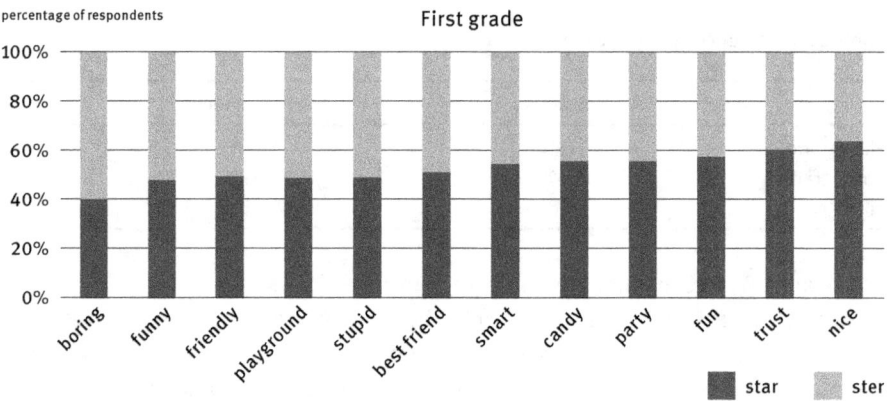

Figure 4. Attitudinal dimension in the first grade

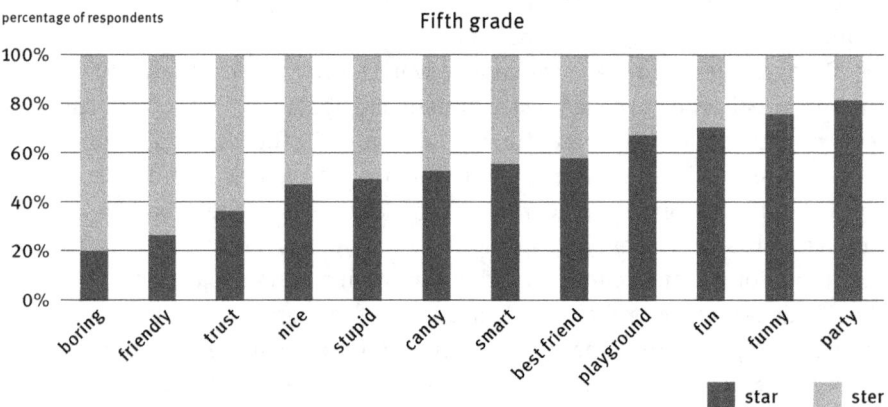

Figure 5. Attitudinal dimensions in the fifth grade

In qualitative terms, the distinction between the Starman guise and the Sterrenman guise that emerges in the older age groups, rests on an opposition between the dimension of solidarity and trust on the one hand and that of dynamism and divertingness on the other. Starman scores higher on features like being

---

[2] The third grade occupies a middle ground, but given the difficulties with the data collection, the results have to be treated with caution.

funny, being cool, having lots of friends, being invited to a party. Sterrenman by contrast scores high on features like being friendly and trustworthy (but also, in the status group, being boring). The dynamism attributed to Starman in the mixed guise fragment corresponds well with the contextualized perspective introduced above; the 'literary' quality of Starman (i.e. the way in which the character is framed in the stimulus fragment) is precisely one in which action and social interaction dominate.

But if these associations were triggered by the nature of the cartoon alone, they would appear indiscriminately in the two guises. In actual practice these features are attenuated in the evaluation of the Dutch guise fragment, which points to an independent association between language and evaluative dimensions. The specific association of the Dutch guise with solidity and solidarity rather than sociability reflects the familiarity and homeliness of the native language.

[3] *Boys score higher for a mixed guise preference than girls*, as shown in Table 3 (in which the results for the third grade should again be interpreted with extra care). This observation ties in with the stylistic interpretation of the results suggested above. If the preferences are primarily determined by expectations with regard to the genre or the character, it would not be surprising to find that a stronger affinity with the genre or character correlates with an increased preference for the typical speech style.

Table 3. Preferences for the Starman guise over genders and age groups

	Girls	Boys
First grade	28.57%	85.71%
Third grade	60.00%	100.00%
Fifth grade	47.37%	73.33%

The cartoon used in the experiment in fact has a decidedly masculine slant: the powerful Superman figure, the fight with bad people, the use of technology all evoke male stereotypes. If such features appeal more to boys than to girls, and if the use of English loans is experienced as the contextually appropriate style, it makes sense that girls consistently show a lower level of preference for the mixed guise.

[4] *The level of English vocabulary knowledge is high throughout and has no noticeable effect on the preferences*. The Picture Action Naming Task reveals that already in the first grade, the English words in the fragments are very well known. As shown in the boxplots in Figure 6, although the median score (cal-

culated straightforwardly as the number of correct answers out of 14 items) rises from the first to the third and from the third to the fifth grade, the scores are already quite high in the first grade: with a median of 11 out of 14 correct answers for the English words and a median of 12 out of 14 words correct for the Dutch words, the youngest group performs surprisingly well. Again, early acquisition and stability seem to be the regular situation.

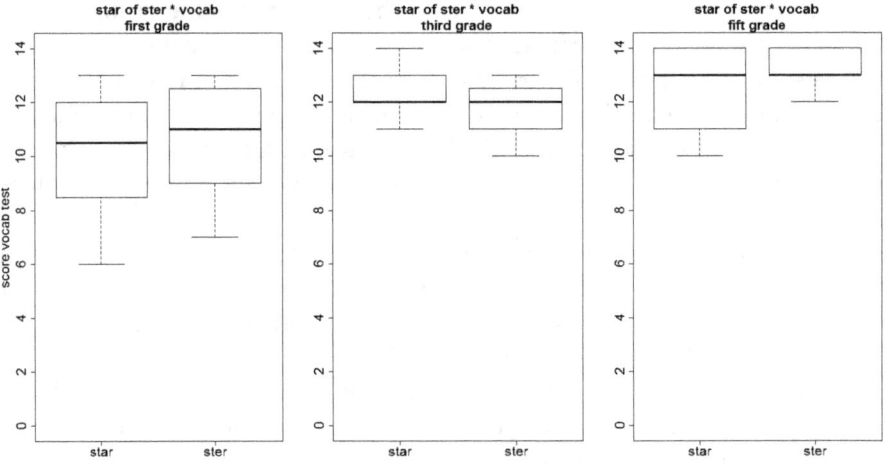

Figure 6. Preferences for guises by age group and vocabulary knowledge

At the same time, the level of vocabulary knowledge does not correlate with a preference for the Sterrenman or the Starman guise: it is not the case that informants with a mixed guise preference have a better command of the English items than those with a Dutch guise preference ($p > 0.05$ for t-test in each of the three cases).[3] If this were to occur, such a situation could be taken as indirect evidence for the importance of familiarity in the 'stylistic' interpretation of the results, to the extent that greater exposure could be assumed to be reflected in a stronger grasp of lexis. However, lexical proficiency turns out to be so high in both preference groups that possible differences due to exposure between the group preferring Starman and the group preferring Sterreman would be hidden by a ceiling effect.

It should be mentioned at this point that differences in exposure were probed by a number of questions in a questionnaire distributed among the parents of the participating pupils. The questions targeted the amount of time that the children

---

[3] The results remain the same when opting for Kruskal-Wallis, a non-parametric version of the unpaired t-test.

spent watching television, listening to music, gaming or using the computer. The response rate on the side of the parents was however too low to draw any valid conclusions concerning the effects of media exposure.

[5] *Explicit language regard increases with age.* Language awareness, in the form of explicit references to English as an argument for the informants' choices is absent in the first grade group, emerges in the third grade, and rises further in the fifth grade. This is shown in Tables 4 and 5, which summarize the results of the open question asking about the test subjects' reasons for the preferences they expressed. As the response rate for this part of the experiment was rather low, the figures should be interpreted carefully; representativeness for the group as a whole is not guaranteed. Even so, like the explicit differentiation of relevant dimensions, explicit sensitivity to the role of language seems to be a later acquisition than the basic evaluative stance. Interestingly, language-based arguments concentrate on English: even arguments in favour of the Dutch-only guise take the form of a rejection of English, rather than an endorsement of Dutch.

Table 4. Arguments for Sterrenman preferences over age groups

	First grade	Third grade	Fifth grade	∑
English	0 (0%)	3 (37.50%)	7 (53.85%)	10
Name	4 (33.33%)	1 (12.50%)	0 (0%)	5
Personality	5 (41.67%)	4 (50%)	5 (38.46%)	14
Test pair item	2 (16.67%)	0 (0%)	0 (0%)	2
Indecision	1 (8.33%)	0 (0%)	1 (7.69%)	2
∑	12/28	8/28	13/34	33/90

Table 5. Arguments for Starman preferences over age groups

	First grade	Third grade	Fifth grade	∑
English	0 (0%)	4 (20%)	8 (39.10%)	12
Name	5 (31.25%)	3 (15%)	0 (0%)	8
Personality	7 (43.75%)	11 (55%)	13 (61.90%)	31
Test pair item	0 (0%)	2 (10%)	0 (0%)	2
Indecision	4 (25%)	0 (0%)	0 (0%)	4
∑	16/28	20/28	21/34	57/90

One question that we cannot address at this point is whether children in the fifth grade show more advanced language awareness because they are increasingly understanding the *shared* attitudes towards language in their community.

Research on child-directed speech (see e.g. Van de Mieroop, Zenner, and Marzo 2016) reveals that parents style-switch more frequently between standard and vernacular when addressing their elementary school children than when addressing toddlers: they seem to be aiming at increasing their children's understanding of community norms, and to reveal which language is used best in which context. Whether or not such observations also play a role in the language of elementary school children with respect to code-switching between the mother tongue and Global English needs to be addressed in future research.

4 Conclusions

In the matched guise experiment reported on in this paper, we set out to explore the question whether primary school children are sensitive to the prestige of English loans in Dutch, and if so, what factors shape that sensitivity. In line with other work on early acquisition of responsiveness to linguistic variation, we found, first, that primary school children do indeed recognize the prestige of English in the context of the speech fragments presented to them, and that that recognition appears to be fairly stable across the three age groups included in the experiment. A knowledge of the pragmatic values of English, in other words, seems to be stably entrenched by the time children reach primary school. This does not mean, however, that age effects are entirely absent from the results: structured attitudes distinguishing dimensions like solidarity, status and sociability only appear in the older groups, as does an explicit awareness of the role of language in the preferences they express.

Secondly, both the qualitative analysis of the attitudes (with a dominance of the dynamic sociability dimension) and the external factors correlating with a preference for the mixed guise (viz. the higher score for English with boys) point to the highly contextualized nature of the prestige of English. It is not so much English as such that is experienced as prestigious, but for a cartoon featuring a superhero, the inclusion of English loanwords is appreciated as fitting the speech context better than a purely Dutch text – and all the more so when the test subjects are boys, who may have more affinity with the genre and the cartoon character than the girls. Loanword prestige, in short, is very much a stylistic, pragmatic phenomenon.

References

Galinsky, Hans. 1967. Stylistic aspects of linguistic borrowing. A stylistic view of American elements in modern German. In Boder Carstensen & Hans Galinsky (eds.), *Amerikanismen der deutschen Gegenwartsprache: Entlehnungsvorgänge und ihre stilistischen Aspekte*, 35–72. Heidelberg: Winter Verlag.

Geeraerts, Dirk & Gitte Kristiansen. 2015. Variationist linguistics. In Ewa Dąbrowska & Dagmar Divjak (eds.), *Handbook of cognitive linguistics*, 366–389. Boston & Berlin: De Gruyter Mouton.

Grondelaers, Stefan & Dirk Speelman. 2013. Can speaker evaluation return private attitudes towards stigmatised varieties? Evidence from emergent standardisation in Belgian Dutch. In Torre Kristiansen & Stefan Grondelaers (eds.), *Language (de)standardization in late modern Europe: Experimental studies*, 171–191. Oslo: Novus Press.

Grondelaers, Stefan, Dirk Speelman & Dirk Geeraerts. 2007. Lexical variation and change. In Dirk Geeraerts and Hubert Cuyckens (eds.), *The Oxford Handbook of cognitive linguistics*, 988–1011. New York: Oxford University Press.

Grondelaers, Stefan & Roeland Van Hout. 2010. Is Standard Dutch with a regional accent standard or not? Evidence from native speakers' attitudes. *Language Variation and Change* 22. 221–239.

Grondelaers, Stefan, Roeland Van Hout & Mieke Steegs. 2010. Evaluating Regional Accent Variation in Standard Dutch. *Journal of Language and Social Psychology* 29. 101–116.

Kecskés, István. 2010. The paradox of communication. Socio-cognitive approach to pragmatics. *Pragmatics and Society* 1. 50–73.

Kecskés, István. 2014. *Intercultural Pragmatics*. Oxford: Oxford University Press.

Koops, Bert-Jaap, Pim Slop, Paul Uljé, Kees Vermeij & Dick van Zijderveld. 2016. *2400x liever Nederlands: woordenlijst onnodig Engels*. http://www.ecoglobe.ch/language/nl/2400x.pdf

Kristiansen, Gitte & René Dirven (eds.). 2008. *Cognitive sociolinguistics: Language variation, cultural models, social systems*. Berlin & New York: Mouton de Gruyter.

Kristiansen, Gitte. 2010. Lectal acquisition and linguistic stereotype formation: an empirical study. In Dirk Geeraerts, Gitte Kristiansen & Yves Peirsman (eds.), *Advances in cognitive sociolinguistics*, 225–263. Berlin & New York: De Gruyter Mouton.

Lambert, Wallace E., Richard C. Hodgson, Robert C. Gardner & Stanley Fillenbaum. 1960. Evaluative reactions to spoken languages. *Journal of Abnormal and Social Psychology* 66. 44–51.

Johnson, Dale D. & P. David Pearson. 1984. *Teaching reading vocabulary*. New York: Holt, Rinehart & Winston.

Matras, Yaron. 2009. *Language contact*. Cambridge: Cambridge University Press.

Preston, Dennis. 2013. The influence of regard on language variation and change. *Journal of Pragmatics* 52. 93–104.

Smith, Jennifer, Mercedes Durham & Hazel Richards. 2013. The social and linguistic in the acquisition of sociolinguistic norms: Caregivers, children, and variation. *Linguistics* 51. 285–324.

Van de Mieroop, Dorien, Eline Zenner & Stefania Marzo. 2016. Standard and Colloquial Belgian Dutch pronouns of address: A variationist-interactional study of child-directed speech in dinner table interactions. *Folia Linguistica: Acta Societatis Linguisticae Europaeae* 50(1). 31–64.

Zenner, Eline, Dirk Speelman & Dirk Geeraerts. 2012. Cognitive Sociolinguistics meets loanword research: measuring variation in the success of Anglicisms in Dutch. *Cognitive Linguistics* 23. 749–792.

Zenner, Eline, Dirk Speelman & Dirk Geeraerts. 2014. Core vocabulary, borrowability, and entrenchment: A usage-based onomasiological approach. *Diachronica* 31. 74–105.

Zenner, Eline & Gitte Kristiansen (eds.). 2013. *New perspectives on lexical borrowing: Onomasiological, methodological and phraseological innovations*. Boston & Berlin: De Gruyter Mouton.

Jonathan Culpeper, Michael Haugh and Daniel E. Johnson
8 *(Im)politeness:* Metalinguistic labels and concepts in English

1 Introduction

This chapter deals with metalanguage in the context of pragmatics, more specifically, "impoliteness"-related metalanguage. Here, metalanguage seems particularly rich across numerous different languages. The English lexicon, for example, is stacked out with words such as *impolite, rude, discourteous,* and so on. Such items have been attracting increasing research attention. A key research question is: what can impoliteness-related metalanguage tell us about impoliteness concepts? Examining impoliteness-related metalanguage, both the specific expressions that are used and how they are used, is often assumed to give us a window into what users themselves are thinking. It is also a pertinent issue in experimental pragmatics work. Frequently researchers choose the words and expressions that shape test scenarios, rating scales, multiple choices, and so on (e.g. Ide et al. 1992; Suh 1999; van der Wijst 1995). But maybe those researchers are using terms that their informants would not actually use themselves, or maybe their choice of terms is creating a bias in the results.

The research reported in this chapter is a spin-off from a larger parent study investigating the degree to which informants considered particular utterances in certain situations impolite.[1] What that study did not do is investigate whether informants had treated its six different impoliteness rating scales in the same way. For example, there seems to be significant overlap between the meanings of the terms "impolite" and "rude", so maybe informants tend to treat scales labelled thus in the same way. Our null hypothesis is that there are no differences in the ratings given for scales labelled as *patronising, rude, aggressive,*

---

1 A report on this larger study is currently in preparation.

István Kecskés is one of the titans of the world of pragmatics. His intellectual contributions to pragmatics seem innumerable, spanning major work on formulaic language, second language acquisition, multilingualism, intercultural communication, and various theoretical aspects at the heart of pragmatics (some of which come together in his socio-cognitive approach to pragmatics). But his contribution has been more than intellectual: we have witnessed him galvanise research activity through the creation of journals, research associations, conferences, and more. This chapter connects with two of István's interests: his long-standing interest in the relationship between words and concepts (e.g. Kecskés 2002: chapter 1), and his more recent interest in impoliteness (Kecskés 2015).

DOI 10.1515/9783110546095-008

inappropriate, hurtful and *impolite* when informants perceive (im)politeness-related events (note that in this chapter the term *impoliteness* is used as a cover term for all related notions in English). We partly form this hypothesis on the basis of the way in which the literature sometimes uses these terms somewhat interchangeably. In this chapter, we therefore only describe the parent study in so far as it is necessary to contextualize our focus in this chapter, namely, the possible interactions amongst perception rating scales defined by impoliteness metalinguistic labels.

In the following section, we discuss notions of metalanguage, especially as they relate to concepts of politeness and impoliteness, and mention some of the work that has been done here. In section 3, we contextualize and introduce the method of our study. In section 4, we report our results, before going on to discuss them in section 5. We conclude by highlighting some implications of our work.

2 Metapragmatics and (im)politeness

The prefix meta- is used in various ways in English, but in the context of linguistics broadly conceived, it seems to denote that the item to which it is affixed is about the item to which it is affixed. Thus, "metalanguage" is language about language; "metadiscourse" is discourse about discourse; and "metapragmatics" is pragmatics about pragmatics. However, the linking word here, "about", does not fully capture the various ways in which terms like "metapragmatics" have been used. "About" seems to fall in with Jakobson's (1960: 356) use of "meta-" in his "metalinguistic" function: the use of language to "gloss" language (as one would find in a dictionary, for example). Pragmatics scholars need to engage in this too when they clarify or define terms. Interestingly, Hübler (2011: 107) cautions against using the term metapragmatics when the term pragmatics would suffice, the argument being that if pragmatics is about communicative behaviour, then any accounts of communicative behaviour informed by pragmatic theory will necessarily already be metapragmatic. Nevertheless, much discussion of meta- pragmatics clearly goes well beyond the limited "about" function.

The key focus of metapragmatics in the literature is reflexive awareness, that is, awareness on the part of users and observers of the pragmatic features of specific uses of language, and the potential meanings they have in context (see, for example, Culpeper and Haugh 2014: chapter 8). Hübler (2011) makes a useful division between studies that focus on explicit metapragmatics and those that focus on implicit metapragmatics. Explicit metapragmatics concerns expressions that are about some pragmatic aspect of the communication in hand, including speech acts (e.g. "Is that a threat?"), politeness (e.g. "that's so polite"), text structure (e.g. "to conclude ..."), and turn taking (e.g. "don't interrupt"). It involves the glossing focus discussed above, though not in the abstract: the focus is on the *usage* of such expressions. Implicit metapragmatics, in contrast, does not involve easily identifiable expressions or even a clear separation between communicative levels (i.e. one bit of communication being about another bit of communication). Instead, the focus is on indicators that interlocutors are metapragmatically aware that they are articulating beliefs and understandings about their use of language use through their use of language. A particular focus of that awareness is of the relationships between linguistic forms and situated contexts, especially the role of indexicals (Silverstein 2001). Our work on impoliteness-related expressions is centred in the realm of explicit metapragmatics.

The idea of focussing on explicit metapragmatics is in tune with work by some politeness scholars. Eelen (2001) and Watts (2003), for example, argue that "pseudo-scientific" classic politeness theories (e.g. Brown and Levinson 1987) seem remote from or pay little attention to the layperson's usage of politeness terms and what they might mean. Looking at politeness metapragmatic expressions and their contexts will, they suggest, provide a firmer ontological basis for politeness studies than has been the case. Despite this call to arms, only a limited number of studies have examined lay understandings of "politeness"-related terms.[2]

Early studies of lay understandings of "politeness"-metalanguage tended to use experimental techniques. Ide et al. (1992), for instance, conducted a multivariate analysis comparing terms associated with *polite* amongst American speakers of English with terms associated with *teineina* amongst Japanese speakers. A key finding was that while *friendly* is associated with being *polite* amongst American speakers of English, the equivalent (*shitashigena*) was not associated with being *teinei* amongst Japanese speakers.[3] Pizziconi (2007) found a somewhat different relationship holding between terms associated with *polite* amongst British speakers of English and *teineina* in Japanese emerged from multidimensional scaling, although once again it emerged that being *shitashigena* (cf. 'friendly') is not conceptualised as closely associated with being *teineina* by Japanese speakers.

More recent studies have tended to opt for corpus-based techniques. For example, Jucker, Taavitsainen and Schneider (2012), referring to their research method as "metacommunicative expression analysis", examined politeness-

---

[2] See Kádár and Haugh (2013: 188–194) for a useful summary of such studies.
[3] These glosses in English are only rough equivalents and there are important differences between these respective terms in English and Japanese (see Haugh [2016] for further discussion).

related terminology in the history of English, especially the terms *politeness* and *courtesy*, through corpus-based methods. Somewhat more work, however, has been done on impoliteness-related expressions. Culpeper (2009, 2011a: Chapter 3) uses corpus analyses to show that *impolite* is not completely synonymous with *rude* but more precisely matches a subset of its meanings (all with the exception of sex-related ones). Taylor (2015, 2016a, 2016b) has pioneered cross-linguistic/cultural work. Her studies show, for example, that English *sarcastic* and Italian *sarcastico* do not occupy the same semantic space, the English term being associated with behaviours that are more negatively evaluated.[4]

An interest in the study of (im)politeness metapragmatic expressions extends beyond, however, the potential they have to offer insight into people's thoughts about (im)politeness. The importance of such expressions is in both reflecting and constructing conceptions. This point has been forcefully made by sociolinguists with respect to attitudes and ideologies. Jaworski, Coupland, and Galasiński (2004: 3, original emphasis) put it in this way:

> How people represent language and communication processes is, at one level, important data for understanding how social groups value and orient to language and communication (varieties, processes, effects). This approach includes the study of folk beliefs about language, language attitudes and language awareness, and these overlapping perspectives have established histories within sociolinguistics. Metalinguistic representations may enter public consciousness and come to constitute structured understandings, perhaps even 'common sense' understandings – of how language works, what it is usually like, what certain ways of speaking connote and imply, what they *ought* to be like.

Of course, whilst the focus on metapragmatic expressions is new, the idea that meaning is dynamically constructed in the interaction between language and context is not. Kecskés (2002), for example, elaborates the point, commenting that the "dynamic behaviour of human speech and reciprocal process between language and context basically eliminates the need to ask the recurring question: which comes first [the situation or the language in the construction of meaning]?" (p. 31). Clearly, this dynamic interaction is the case for the majority of speech events.

Some events, however, abstract language away from interactive situations. Perhaps the paradigm case concerns literature. Reading a work of prose fiction involves the language creating the fictional world in the mind of the reader. Of course, there is, at a different level, interaction between the author's words and the reader's interpretation of them. Nevertheless, there is no explicitly shared

---

4 See Haugh (forthcoming b) for further discussion of corpus-based approaches to metapragmatics more generally.

situation or even common ground. Language has the upper hand. And so it is with many experimental pragmatics methods. Words are used to create fictional scenarios that informants read. Words are used to create the rating scales they use. And so on and so forth.

3 The studies and their methods

3.1 The parent study

In some respects, this study deploys a well-trodden method: the questionnaire. Informants were presented with a paper questionnaire, which contained scenarios and rating scales. However, there are two novel twists. One is that the test items were played aloud (from audio files embedded in a PowerPoint) rather than read by the informant. The other is that rating scales were not selected by the researchers but according to results of previous research that aimed to determine which impoliteness-related expressions people in this population, that is, British undergraduates, actually use. We will have more to say about the latter below.

The test stimuli were requests manipulated for directness and prosody. There were three forms of request: *you be quiet* [direct], *could you be quiet?* [conventionally indirect], and *you aren't being quiet* [non-conventionally indirect]. These categories of directness are, of course, rooted in Searle's (1975) notion of indirect speech acts, and have been popularized in cross-cultural research, most notably by Blum-Kulka, House, and Kasper (1989). Each request type was performed with one of three prosodies, which, broadly speaking involved a falling pitch (we labelled this "aggressive"), a fall-rise (we labelled this "neutral") and a rising pitch (we labelled this "tentative") (see Culpeper 2011b, for an overview of the literature on the "meanings" of these prosodies and also a discussion of global and local meanings). A pre-test was conducted to verify that each prosody was independently perceived in a way that justified the application of our labels. This resulted in nine test stimuli.

The stimuli were embedded within scenarios designed to allow for the manipulation of power extremes. Table 1 conveys the basic features of the three scenarios.

Table 1. The three scenarios

Setting	Low-power and high-power roles
Workplace	employee / employer
Army parade	private / sergeant
Courtroom	defendant / judge

As an illustration of what informants actually encountered, here is the army parade scenario. The context is read silently, and then the portion in square brackets and italics is where the pre-prepared sound file comprising a particular stimulus was played. The test was administered in a lecture theatre.

> At a parade ground gathering of army recruits, the sergeant-major is explaining the drill for the day. A recruit is chatting to fellow recruits about what they are going to do that night. The sergeant-major says to the recruit: "[*one of the three request forms with one of the three prosodies*]"

The above condition, with the sergeant-major speaking to the recruit, was called high-to-low power. A low-to-high power condition was created by reversing the participants in the final sentence of the scenario (e.g. in the case above, the recruit would speak to the sergeant-major). The three scenarios were not considered separately in the analyses, not least because testing showed that informants did not distinguish amongst them, but instead averaged their scores together to create an overall score for the power condition. Power was the only social variable under consideration because of the key role it plays in evaluations of impoliteness (see the references and discussion in Culpeper 2011a: 225–233), and to enable us to focus on the primary objective of this study, that is, to examine possible differences across *impoliteness*-related perception scales.

In total, 298 British undergraduate informants took the test. All were native-speakers of English who had been brought up in Britain, the vast majority in the north of England. However, the sheer number of test stimuli – 6 rating scales x 3 request types x 3 intonations x 2 power dynamics x 3 settings = 324 potential items – precluded running the whole test for each informant. Consequently, there were three data collection rounds, each according to the type of request:

Data collection 1 ('could you be quiet' – conventionally indirect): 134 questionnaires
Data collection 2 ('you aren't being quiet' – non-conventionally indirect): 100 questionnaires
Data collection 3 ('you be quiet' – direct): 64 questionnaires

3.2 The rating scales of the parent study and this study

The choice of labels on a rating scale in the pragmatics literature is usually a choice amongst metapragmatic expressions. But how do we know that the researcher's choice is the most relevant labels for the informants? To illustrate, should we label a scale *impolite* or *rude*? A corpus might give us a sense of what is generally familiar. In the 2 billion word Oxford English Corpus, *rude* occurs 18,387 times, whereas *impolite* only occurs 871 times. Of course, there is also the issue of meaning: we cannot assume that we can lump together scales with different labels, because they may be testing different notions. Corpus analysis can be used to reveal shades of meaning. It is, however, very difficult to find corpora that are large enough to reveal the words and meanings that are familiar to a very specific population (e.g. that consituted by our undergraduate informants). The solution adopted by the researchers conducting the parent study was to use five impoliteness-related terms, *patronising, rude, aggressive, inappropriate* and *hurtful,* precisely because they had been found, in a study reported in Culpeper's (2011a: 94), to be amongst the terms most frequently used by British undergraduates when they describe impoliteness events in which they were involved. To these five the parent study researchers also added the term *impolite*. These terms were not used to construct bipolar scales, but used as labels for agreement scales. Informants were asked to indicate their agreement with a statement in the format, "It was X", where 'It' referred to the scenario they had just read and the audio clip they had just heard, and 'X' was the metalinguistic term. The scales were 7-point Likert scales, varying from 'strongly disagree' to 'strongly agree'. Thus, for each informant, given the same conditions of power, prosody and directness, there is one judgment made for each of the six rating scales for each of the three scenarios (as noted above, the scores for the scenarios were averaged to create an overall mean score for the power variable).

We then used heat maps, including a hierarchical clustering dendrogram, to display the differences (distances) amongst the impoliteness rating scale scores. A heat map renders statistical values as colours in order to help visualize items with similar (or dissimilar) values. Hierarchical clustering dendrograms are an additional technique that helps visualize similar (or dissimilar) values by clustering them into a tree-like hierarchical structure. This can reveal which items are closely related, as they are in the same cluster, and which are not, as they are only linked higher up the tree. To achieve heat maps and clustering dendrograms, we cannot simply input the rating scale scores or calculate average differences. To illustrate, if half the informants scored *rude* 1 unit higher (e.g. 'agree') than *impolite*, and half the speakers scored it 1 unit lower (e.g. 'disagree'), the average difference would be zero. This, however, does not tell us the distance between the *rude* and *impolite* scores. We therefore focused on Manhattan distance, which involves absolute differences between scores, i.e. their distance from zero, without regard to whether they are positive or negative. In the hypothetical example given above, for instance, the mean Manhattan distance would be 1, as it is one unit from zero in both cases. For each participant, we calculated the absolute differences (Manhattan distance) between each rating scale score and the scores for the other rating scales, and then the average for each difference across all informants.

4 The study: Results

Figure 1 is a heat map of average absolute differences (Manhattan distances) between impoliteness-rating scores for low-to-high power scenarios, and this is followed by Figure 2, a heat map of average absolute differences among impoliteness-ratings for the high-to-low power scenarios. Both heat maps include a hierarchical clustering dendrogram of the columns, indicating the distances between values in the columns.

To illustrate how to read Figures, in Figure 1, the top rightmost cell contains 2.12. This is the average distance between *aggressive*, as indicated to the right of the row, and *patronising*, as indicated at the bottom of the column. To the left of this value, we see 2.05. This is the average distance between *aggressive*, and *rude*, as indicated at the bottom of the column. And so on. You may wonder why some cells have the value 0.00. This is, in a sense, a dummy value: for example, when *aggressive* is compared with *aggressive*, there is no distance between them, and so the value is necessarily zero. The heat map colourings give a sense of similar or dissimilar values. It is quite clear, for example, that *aggressive* and *hurtful* are generally similar. Regarding the column dendrogram, one must look at the tree structure in conjunction with the column labels at the bottom. Thus, the first cluster comprises *aggressive* and *hurtful*. The values that comprise this cluster are quite distant from the other values, as it is connected only by the topmost tree branch, and so on.

Regarding Figure 1, capturing average absolute differences between scale ratings in the low-to-high power scenarios, it is clear from the dendrogram clustering and the shading that the rating values for *aggressive* and *hurtful* are similar, and they both are relatively distinct from *rude*, *impolite* and *inappropriate*. *Patronising* roughly steers a middle course between these two groups (note that it has its own branch connecting only at a higher level with *inappropriate*, *impolite* and *rude*). *Impolite* and *rude* do indeed form a tight cluster, and they both have a close relationship with *inappropriate*. Regarding Figure 2, capturing

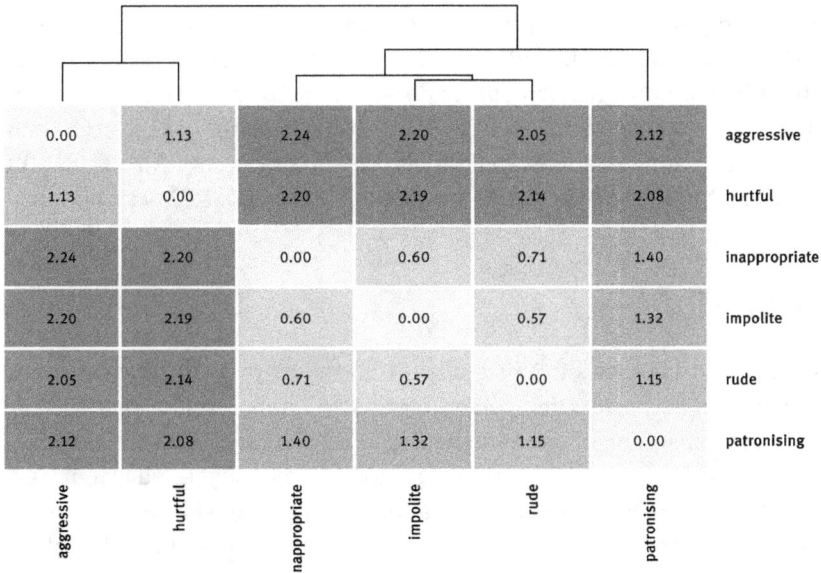

Figure 1. A heat map of average absolute differences among the impoliteness-ratings for the same low-to-high power scenarios

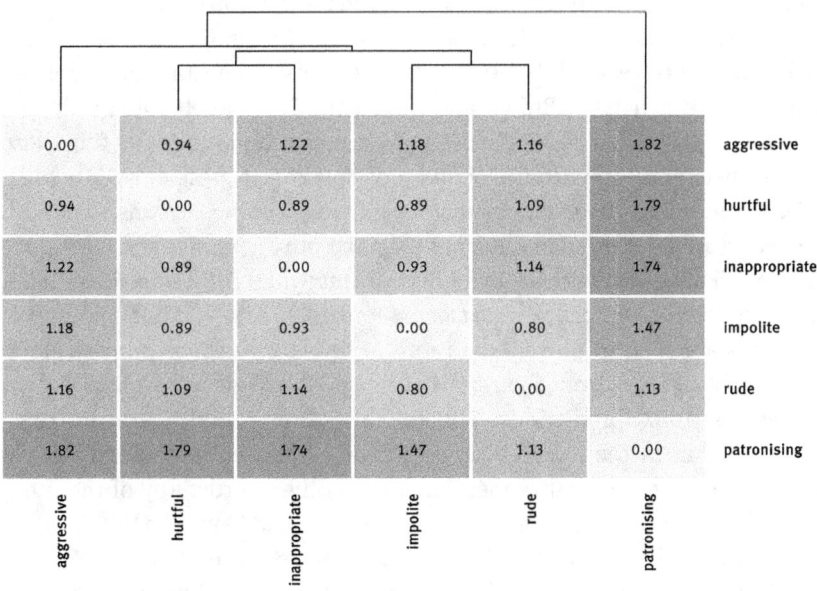

Figure 2. A heat map of average absolute differences among the impoliteness-ratings for the same high-to-low power scenarios

differences between scale ratings in the high-to-low power scenarios, now *patronising* is the most different (distant) from the rest, and *aggressive* and *hurtful* no longer pattern close together. *Impolite* and *rude* are still closely related, but they do not now have such a distinct relationship with *inappropriate*; in fact, they now have an equally strong relationship with *hurtful* and *aggressive*. Also, generally the differences between rating scales are smaller in the high-to-low condition.

5 Discussion

Clearly, the null hypothesis in this study – that there are no differences in the notions labelled as *patronising, rude, aggressive, inappropriate, hurtful* and *impolite* in the perception of (im)politeness-related events – must be rejected.

In the low-to-high condition, the two groups of scales suggested by our findings – *aggressive* and *hurtful* on the one hand, and *rude*, *impolite* and *inappropriate* on the other – are in fact in tune with some distinctions made in the literature. Both aggression and hurt are most frequently discussed in the context of work on anti-social interactions undertaken in social psychology or communication studies. Dailey, Lee, and Spitzberg (2007), for example, proposed the notion of "communicative aggression" as a term for capturing the interactional side of "psychological abuse". Vangelisti (2007) has pioneered research on the role of interpersonal messages in causing people emotional "hurt". In contrast, scholars using the labels *impolite* or *rude* tend to be based in linguistics or humanities-related disciplines (e.g. Leech 1983; Brown and Levinson 1987; Lakoff 1989; Culpeper 1996; Bousfield and Locher 2008). Also, amongst such scholars one can find those who have argued for the importance of inappropriateness (e.g. Meier 1995; Schneider 2012). Additionally, the emergence of these two groupings is consistent with the results of studies reported in Culpeper (2011a). Both *aggressive* and *hurtful* are associated with a higher degree of symbolic violence than *rude, impolite* or *inappropriate*, and, furthermore, are more closely connected to particular emotions.

Why does a switch in power condition to high-to-low cause *patronising* to emerge as most distinct from the rest? Let us consider this in terms of Brown and Levinson's (1987) predictions. Theoretically, Brown and Levinson (1987) would predict that in the low-to-high scenarios a speaker uses the "Don't do the FTA [face-threatening act]" superstrategy. In other words, any of the utterances should be deemed impolite. Conversely, Brown and Levinson (1987) would predict that in the high-to-low scenario a speaker uses the "Bald on Record" superstrategy. In other words, no additional politeness work should be required. Thus, the use of conventionally indirect or the non-conventionally indirect requestive forms, or indeed the tentative prosody could well have seemed superfluous in the high-to-low power condition, and this may have triggered a judgment that the politeness work is insincere, that it reflects a patronising attitude (preliminary analyses undertaken as part of the parent study suggest that this is indeed the case). However, whilst we think this is a plausible explanation, it awaits further research to substantiate it.

We noted how *impolite* and *rude* seem to attract the same kind of ratings regardless of the power condition. The similarity between these two concepts is not only reflected in the fact that some scholars use those terms interchangeably (e.g. Spencer-Oatey 2000), but also, as mentioned earlier in this chapter, in the results of Culpeper's (2011a: 82–88) corpus-based analyses of those two terms, which highlighted the many similarities between the terms. The few differences involve, notably, the sexual uses of *rude* (e.g. "rude picture postcard"), which can also be positive uses (e.g. "rude boy", meaning somebody who is sexually attractive). These other uses partly account for the more frequent occurrence of *rude*, as previously observed.

6 Implications

If this study has done nothing else we hope that it has raised awareness of the importance of metapragmatics, and in particular the use of metapragmatic terms in the field of pragmatics in general and in experimental work in particular. As far as the notion of impoliteness is concerned, its label, "impoliteness", can be used as a technical cover-term for various impoliteness-related phenomena, but it is important that its role as a cover-term is made explicit, as indeed we did at the beginning of this chapter. As our study demonstrates, impoliteness-related terms, of which impolite is one, form part of a semantic field in which related terms overlap, but also differ in often subtle but nevertheless important ways. This issue becomes even more acute when one starts to take into account potential differences in the sorts of metalinguistic labels and concepts across speakers of different varieties of English (Culpeper, O'Driscoll and Hardaker forthcoming; Haugh forthcoming a), as well as along other axes of metapragmatic variation.

This study also has implications for cross-linguistic studies of "(im)politeness". If terms in the same language are not interchangeable, what does that tell us about supposed equivalents across different languages? It is clear the "(im)politeness"-related metalanguage of different languages (and varieties therein) requires much more systematic attention from (im)politeness researchers than it has garnered to date. What this particular study tells us is that these sorts of metalinguistic understandings are inevitably dependent, in part, on how they are situated and for what purposes they are used.

References

Blum-Kulka, Shoshana, Juliane House & Gabriele Kasper (eds.). 1989. *Cross-cultural pragmatics: Requests and apologies*. Norwood NJ: Ablex.
Bousfield, Derek & Miriam Locher (eds). 2008. *Impoliteness in language: Studies on its interplay with power in theory and practice*. Berlin & New York: Mouton de Gruyter.
Brown, Penelope & Stephen C. Levinson. 1987. *Politeness. Some universals in language usage*. Cambridge University Press: Cambridge.
Culpeper, Jonathan & Michael Haugh. 2014. *Pragmatics and the English language*. Basingstoke: Palgrave Macmillan.
Culpeper, Jonathan. 1996. Towards an anatomy of impoliteness. *Journal of Pragmatics* 25(3). 349–367.
Culpeper, Jonathan. 2009. The metalanguage of impoliteness: Explorations in the Oxford English Corpus. In Paul Baker (ed.), *Contemporary corpus linguistics*, 66–68. London: Continuum.
Culpeper, Jonathan. 2011a. *Impoliteness: Using language to cause offence*. Cambridge: Cambridge University Press.
Culpeper, Jonathan. 2011b. "It's not what you said, it's how you said it!": Prosody and impoliteness. In Linguistic Politeness Research Group (eds.), *Discursive approaches to politeness*, 57–83. Boston & Berlin: De Gruyter Mouton.
Culpeper, Jonathan, Jim O'Driscoll & Claire Hardaker. forthcoming. Notions of politeness in Britain and America. In Eva Ogiermann & Pilar Garcés-Conejos Blitvich (eds.), *From speech acts to lay concepts of politeness. A multilingual and multicultural perspective*. Cambridge: Cambridge University Press.
Dailey, René, Carmen M. Lee & Brian H. Spitzberg. 2007. Communicative aggression: Toward a more interactional view of psychological abuse. In Brian H. Spitzburg & William R. Cupach (eds.), *The dark side of interpersonal communication* (2nd edn), 297–326. Mahwah, NJ: Lawrence Erlbaum.
Eelen, Gino. 2001. *A critique of politeness theories*. Manchester: St. Jerome Publishing.
Haugh, Michael. 2016. The role of English as a scientific metalanguage for research in pragmatics: Reflections on the metapragmatics of 'politeness' in Japanese. *East Asian Pragmatics* 1(1). 39–71.
Haugh, Michael. Forthcoming a. The metapragmatics of *consideration* in (Australian and New Zealand) English. In Eva Ogiermann & Pilar Garcés-Conejos Blitvich (eds.), *From speech acts to lay concepts of politeness. A multilingual and multicultural perspective*. Cambridge: Cambridge University Press.
Haugh, Michael. Forthcoming b. Corpus-based metapragmatics. In Andreas Jucker, Klaus P. Schneider and Wolfram Bublitz (eds.), *Methods in Pragmatics*. Boston & Berlin: De Gruyter Mouton.
Hübler, Alex. 2011. Metapragmatics. In Wolfram Bublitz & Neal Norrick (eds.), *Foundations of pragmatics*, 107–136. Boston & Berlin: De Gruyter Mouton.
Ide, Sachiko, Beverly Hill, Yukiko M. Carnes, Tsunao Ogino & Akiko Kawasaki. 1992. The concept of politeness: an empirical study of American English and Japanese". In Richard Watts, Sachiko Ide & Konrad Ehlich (eds.), *Politeness in language*, 281–297. Berlin & New York: Mouton de Gruyter.
Jakobson, Roman. 1960. Closing statement: Linguistics and poetics. In Thomas A. Sebeok (ed.), *Style in Language*, 350–377. New York: John Wiley & Sons.

Jaworski, Adam, Nikolas Coupland & Dariusz Galasiński. 2004. Metalanguage: Why now? In Adam Jaworski, Nikolas Coupland & Dariusz Galasiński (eds.), *Metalanguage: Social and ideological perspectives*, 3–8. Berlin & New York: Mouton de Gruyter.

Jucker, Andreas H., Irma Taavitsainen & Gerold Schneider. 2012. Semantic corpus trawling: Expressions of "courtesy" and "politeness" in the Helsinki Corpus. In Carla Suhr & Irma Taavitsainen (eds.), *Developing corpus methodology for historical pragmatics*. Helsinki: Research Unit for Variation, Contacts and Change in English.
http://www.helsinki.fi/varieng/series/volumes/11/jucker_taavitsainen_schneider/

Kádár, Dániel Z. & Michael Haugh. 2013. *Understanding politeness*. Cambridge: Cambridge University Press.

Kecskés, István. 2002. *Situation-bound utterances in L1 and L2*. Berlin & New York: Mouton de Gruyter.

Kecskés, István. 2015. Intercultural Impoliteness. *Journal of Pragmatics* 86. 43–47.

Lakoff, Robin Tolmach. 1989. The limits of politeness: Therapeutic and courtroom discourse. *Multilingua* 8(2/3). 101–129.

Leech, Geoffrey.1983. *Principles of pragmatics*. London: Longman

Meier, Ardith. 1995. Defining politeness: Universality in appropriateness. *Language Sciences* 17(4). 345–356.

Schneider, Klaus P. 2012. Appropriate behaviour across varieties of English. *Journal of Pragmatics* 44(9). 1022–1037.

Searle, John R. 1975. Indirect speech acts. In Paul Cole & Jerry L. Morgan (eds.), *Syntax and semantic. Volume 3*, 5–82. New York: Academic Press.

Silverstein, Michael. 2001. The limits of awareness. In Alessandro Duranti (ed.), *Linguistic anthropology: A Reader*, 382–401. Malden, MA: Blackwell.

Spencer-Oatey, Helen. 2000. Rapport management: A framework for analysis. In Helen Spencer-Oatey (ed.), *Culturally speaking: Managing rapport through talk across cultures*, 11–46. London: Continuum.

Suh, Jae-Suk. 1999. Pragmatic perception of politeness in requests by Korean learners of English as a second language. *IRAL* 37(30). 195–214.

Taylor, Charlotte. 2015. Beyond sarcasm: The metalanguage and structures of mock politeness. *Journal of Pragmatics* 87. 127–141.

Taylor, Charlotte. 2016a. *Mock politeness in English and Italian: A corpus-assisted metalanguage analysis*. Amsterdam & Philadelphia: John Benjamins.

Taylor, Charlotte. 2016b. Mock politeness and culture: Perceptions and practice in UK and Italian data. *Intercultural Pragmatics* 13(4). 463–498.

van der Wijst, Per. 1995. The perception of politeness in Dutch and French indirect requests. *Text & Talk* 15(4). 477–502.

Vangelisti, Anita L. 2007. Communicating hurt. In Brian H. Spitzberg & William R. Cupach (eds.), *The dark side of interpersonal communication* (2nd edn), 121–142. Mahwah, NJ: Lawrence Erlbaum.

Watts, Richard J. 2003. *Politeness*. Cambridge: Cambridge University Press.

Part II: **Philosophical and discourse pragmatics**

Laurence Horn
9 What lies beyond: Untangling the web

> Oh, what a tangled web we weave
> When first we practice to deceive!
>
> (Walter Scott, *Marmion*, Canto VI)

1 Introductory remarks

Recent years have seen an impressive flurry of publications exploring the domain Meibauer has deftly located in the title of his magnum opus on the topic: lying at the semantics-pragmatics interface. In particular, Meibauer has challenged the view of Saul (2012), to which I have also been sympathetic (Horn 2009, 2016, to appear), on which lying is to misleading as what is said (in the Gricean sense) is to what is implicated. On this view, the tradition going back to Augustine and Aquinas and formalized in Adler (1997) and Mahon (2008) is essentially correct: in order to lie that *p*, a speaker must *assert* and not merely imply or *implicate* that *p*. At the same time, recent research has also challenged the classical theory of lying on another point: is it only the putative liar's belief in the falsity of the

---

I am delighted to contribute to a tribute volume for István Kecskés, with whom I have collaborated on a number of fronts over the last decade. I am indebted to István for bringing me (as a representative of the "linguistic-philosophical" camp; cf. Horn and Kecskés 2013) into the fold of the intercultural pragmatics community. In this capacity, I participated in conferences devoted (de facto or de jure) to intercultural pragmatics in Shanghai (2005), Landau (2006), Charlotte (2013), Los Angeles (2015), and Split (2016), largely as a result of István's lobbying. I have also worked as a board member for *Intercultural Pragmatics*, the Mouton Series in Pragmatics, and the American Pragmatics Association, three of István's prodigal brainchildren. When I was asked to serve as Session Manager for Pragmatics, Discourse, and Cognition at the 19th International Congress of Linguists (Geneva, 2013), I accepted on condition that I could bring István on as co-organizer of that session, since as a pragmatic individual I know my own limitations. Pooling our complementary spheres of knowledge, we worked together smoothly and, I am confident in saying, productively to put together the session.

When I was considering topics for my plenary talk at 7th International Conference on Intercultural Pragmatics and Communication (INPRA 2016) in Split, it was István who persuaded me to speak on the topic of pragmatics and the lying/misleading distinction, a domain that has recently engaged the attention of several scholars in pragmatics, including fellow conference presenters Jörg Meibauer and Marta Dynel, whose work in the area has appeared recently under István's editorial aegis (cf. Meibauer 2011, 2014a, 2016; Dynel 2015). While István also urged me to submit my own response paper to Meibauer and Dynel for *Intercultural Pragmatics,* I trust that he won't object too strenuously to my including a version of that response, incorporating aspects of my plenary talk, between these covers instead.

DOI 10.1515/9783110546095-009

asserted proposition *p* that is required for the statement to count as a lie? On the revisionist view (Turri and Turri 2015), the actual falsity of *p* is also required.

In each case, the question has been put as to whether the appropriate definitions of the relevant notions allow, in the words of Meibauer (2014b: 97), for "lying while saying the truth".[1] In the former case, the issue is whether a speaker who says or asserts a proposition she correctly believes to be true can nevertheless be lying by virtue of implicating a false one. My position is that this is not possible. In the latter case, the issue is whether a speaker who says or asserts a proposition she believes to be false can nevertheless be innocent of lying by virtue of the fact that the proposition in question turns out to be true. Is such a speaker, in the words of the title of a recent study of the question (Wiegmann, Samland, and Waldman 2016), "lying despite telling the truth"? Despite the similar wording of the two questions, the circumstances to which they are intended to apply are quite different, and the answers I propose to give are different as well.

In section 2, I summarize the outlines of what I will call the standard theory of lying while also touching on some of the parameters of variation. In section 3, I focus on recent challenges to the tenet that (explicitly or implicitly) distinguishes lying from misleading by restricting the former category to situations in which the speaker actually asserts the proposition in question – the one that (she believes) is false – and thereby warrants its truth. In section 4, I turn to a different challenge to (some versions of) the classical theory that revolve around another criterion for what constitutes a lie, the one that takes lying to be essentially subjective, given its illocutionary status and thus its dependence on the intentions and knowledge of the liar, and not an objective fact, constrained by what is in fact true or false. In each section, I summarize the *positions prises* for the classical and revisionist views and try to demonstrate the superiority of the classical positions in accounting for natural language intuitions on what constitutes a lie and for the legal definition of perjury. I summarize my conclusions in section 5.

---

[1] The title of Meibauer 2014b is taken from a Blake couplet, *A truth that's told with bad intent/ Beats all the lies you can invent*. For Meibauer, this is an instance of "lying while saying the truth". But as I read the couplet, the point is that imparting ill-intentioned truths can do as much damage as telling lies. Gossip – e.g. A telling B out of sheer malice that B's spouse has been flirting with others – can be true or false, and true gossip is arguably more effective in harming B than false gossip, since it can't be as easily disproved.

2 Lying: the classic recipe(s)

Four criteria have standardly been invoked for what it takes for speaker S to lie to hearer H:

(1)   Criteria for lying
   (C1)   S says/asserts that p
   (C2)   S believes that p is false
   (C3)   p is false
   (C4)   S intends to deceive H

To *assert* something you *correctly believe to be false* with *the intent to deceive* (more precisely, as Wayne Davis (p.c.) points out, with the intent to deceive H into thinking that p is true) is surely to lie. But must all four criteria be satisfied? The Oxford English Dictionary (s.v. LIE, n., 2b), invokes **C3**, **C1**, and **C4**: a lie is "a false statement made with intent to deceive." Augustine endorses a different view in *The Enchiridon:* "Every liar says the opposite of what he thinks in his heart, with purpose to deceive"; thus we have **C1**, **C2**, and **C4**. Indeed, Augustine's requirement that the liar in stating p must believe not-p (**C2**) is more plausible than the OED's requirement that p be actually false (**C3**), a point to which we return in section 4. A more detailed argument is given by St. Thomas Aquinas (*Summa Theologica* II.II, q. 110):

> [I]f one says what is false, thinking it to be true, it is false materially, but not formally, because the falseness is beside the intention of the speaker so that it is not a perfect lie, since what is beside the speaker's intention is accidental...If, on the other hand, one utters falsehood formally, through having the will to deceive, even if what one says be true, yet inasmuch as this is a voluntary and moral act, it contains falseness essentially and truth accidentally, and attains the specific nature of a lie...We judge of a thing according to what is in it formally and essentially rather than according to what is in it materially and accidentally. Hence it is more in opposition to truth...to tell the truth with the intention of telling a falsehood than to tell a falsehood with the intention of telling the truth.

Some empirical support for the church fathers' subjective approach comes from a study by Coleman and Kay (1981), who provide their subjects with a multiplicity of scenarios variously manipulating the satisfaction of the three conditions I have labeled **(C2)–(C4)**. While the greatest unanimity of responses was by those reacting to "prototype" lies in which all three of these conditions were satisfied, in cases of partial satisfaction "falsity of belief is the most important element of the prototype of *lie*, intended deception is the next most important element, and factual falsity is the least important" (Coleman and Kay 1981: 43; cf. Meibauer

2014a: §2.3 for additional discussion). Note that **(C1)** is not manipulated in this study, but its satisfaction is presupposed.

For Chisholm and Feehan (1977), only two criteria are required:

(2) **L lies to D** $=_{df}$ There is a proposition *p* such that
 (i) *L* believes that *p* is false (or at least that *p* is not true); and
 (ii) *L* asserts *p* to *D*.

Crucial here are L's assertion of p (our **C1**) and L's belief in the falsity of p (our **C2**).[2] Not crucial are the falsity of p (our **C3**) or any attempt on L's part to get D to believe p (our **C4**).

Speech act theory distinguishes what is literally said or spoken in Austin's locutionary sense from what is asserted or otherwise put forth with illocutionary force (e.g. Searle 1969). The latter is the notion relevant for criterion **(C1)**. As Chisholm and Feehan (1977) point out, the illocutionary definition of *say* or *assert* relevant for characterizing lies must be narrowly defined enough to eliminate non-literal locutions in which no assertion is directly made: irony, sarcasm, banter, pretense, tall tales, (non-conventionalized) metaphor, and so on. At the same time, *say* cannot be too strictly defined:

> We must not take the word 'say' so narrowly that a man's speaking or writing is essential to lying. *L* can lie to *D* by nodding his assent,....or by using sign language, or by making smoke signals. (Chisholm and Feehan 1977: 149)

But it is the issue of narrowing down what counts and what does not count as saying that has proved the more elusive and controversial task.

As Chisholm and Feehan point out (1977: 155), a speaker can conveys a false proposition by implicature without lying, e.g. if I utter "My leg isn't bothering me *too* much today" when it's not bothering me at all I may succeed in misleading or deceiving you but – absent the assertion that my leg is bothering me – I do not lie. In the spirit of Chisholm and Feehan, we can characterize lying as the speaker's intentional representation of herself as committed to the truth of a proposition she believes to be false (see Adler 1997; Meibauer 2005, 2011, 2014a; Horn 2009; Saul 2012; and Stokke 2013a, b for defenses and critiques of this position).

---

[2] What if L neither believes that p is true nor believes that p is not true – or if L does not even care about the truth of p? What we have in that case is not a lie but an exemplar of, to use the technical term, *bullshit* (cf. Frankfurt 2005), although other terminology is sometimes employed:
> I play to people's fantasies. I call it truthful hyperbole. It's an innocent form of exaggeration – and a very effective form of promotion.
> Donald Trump (1987), *The Art of the Deal*

As such, lying constitutes non-natural meaning (meaning$_{NN}$) in Grice's sense and requires intentional illocutionary acts by human (or quasi-human) agents.[3] Misleading or deceiving can be accomplished either intentionally (agentively) or unintentionally (non-agentively) and is typically perlocutionary, defined by its effect on the addressee or victim. While lying may or may not be successful in its intended goal, *mislead* and *deceive* are "success" verbs (cf. Mahon 2007, Saul 2012: 71). Thus we have contrasts like those in (3):

(3) Sorry if I {misled you/deceived you/#lied to you}, I didn't mean to.
Don't let the blue sky {mislead you/deceive you/#lie to you} – it's bitterly cold out.
She {lied to me/#misled me/#deceived me}, but I didn't believe her for a minute.
I tried to {mislead/deceive/#lie to} her, but she was too clever to believe me.

Within the courtroom, the essential status of (**C1**) has long been recognized in defining perjury (we return below to the distinction between false statements and false implicatures) and the non-essential status of (**C4**), but questions about the other two conditions have been dealt with more subtly. Consider the 1911 U.K. Perjury statute in (4) and the 1975 revision in (5) concerning testimony not given under oath (emphasis added):

(4) http://www.legislation.gov.uk/ukpga/Geo5/1-2/6/section/1/enacted [1911, §1]
If any person lawfully sworn as a witness or as an interpreter in a judicial proceeding wilfully *makes a statement* material in that proceeding, *which he knows to be false or does not believe to be true*, he shall be guilty of perjury,...

(5) http://www.legislation.gov.uk/ukpga/Geo5/1-2/6/section/1A [1975, §1A]
If any person, in giving any testimony (either orally or in writing) otherwise than on oath, where required to do so by an order under section two of the Evidence (Proceedings in Other Jurisdictions) Act 1975, *makes a statement* –
    (a) *which he knows to be false* in a material particular, or
    (b) *which is false* in a material particular *and which he does not believe to be true*,
he shall be guilty of an offence...

---

3 As Marina Terkourafi reminds me, there is no illocutionary act of lying per se, since the speaker in general designs a lie not to be recognized as one; rather, a lie is essentially an intentionally defective performance of an illocutionary act – asserting or promising – with the sincerity condition unfulfilled.

In the forensic arena, actual falsity matters in the U.K., at least in the 1975 revision,[4] as seen in the conjunction of the highlighted passages in condition (b); Aquinas's "accidental truth" gets one off the hook here, however undeservedly. But under U.S. perjury law, as under the 1911 British statute, perjury can result from any testimony the defendant "does not believe to be true": cf. U.S. Code §1621, http://www.law.cornell.edu/uscode/text/18/1621 (thanks to Larry Solan for the pointer). Thus, "accidental truth" is not exculpatory. One wonders, however, if a witness is ever prosecuted in the U.S. for either (i) stating as true something she neither believes to be true nor believes not to be true (as in the case of dispensing bullshit) or (ii) making a statement she believes to be false that turns out to be "accidentally" true à la Aquinas.

We consider the roles of (**C1**) and (**C3**) in more detail in §3 and §4 respectively, but let us touch briefly on the status of (**C4**). Must a liar intend to deceive? This is a matter of debate, and debate it has sparked between deceptionists, who invoke (**C4**), and non-deceptionists, who do not. While the heritage of the deceptionist group harks back to Augustine's "purpose to deceive" and Aquinas's "will to deceive", it is not clear whether this is a necessary condition on all lies or just a marker of prototypic lies.

Knowingly false statements can be intended to deceive a third party without constituting lies to the primary or ratified addressee, so intention to deceive is not sufficient for lying if e.g. (**C1**) is not satisfied. At the same time, it is arguably not a necessary condition on lying either, since a knowingly false assertion can constitute a lie even if the liar assumes that the addressee will not be deceived. While Meibauer (2014a, b, 2016) is a member of the deceptionist camp, his allegiance may be attributable in part to his stance on assertion. Meibauer's characterizing of what it is to assert requires that "by uttering the declarative sentence σ S M-intended that an addressee H to whom S uttered p actively believes that p" (2014a: 99). But while this is faithful to Grice's original conception of assertion as part of speaker meaning, it does not take account of critiques by Searle (1969) and others who point out that S can assert even with the expectation or knowledge that H will not be persuaded that p is the case. All that is necessary is that S M-intends that H believe that S is committed to the truth of p, and if S does not hold that belief, she lies. I would maintain, contra Meibauer (2014a: 100) that assertions are not "essentially...a means to persuade the audience that p": I can assert (and lie) in order to go on record, whether or not I assert truthfully.

---

4 One puzzle in the interpretation of §1A is whether (a) can ever hold when (b) does not; it would seem that one cannot *know* p to be false without it being the case both that one *believes* p to be false and that p *is* in fact false.

Cassandra can lie as well as assert the truth even if she knows she will not be believed (cf. Pagin 2007 on asserting into the wind).

I will not review the status of "bald-faced lies" in detail here (cf. Sorensen 2007, Carson 2010, Meibauer 2014b: §2, Dynel 2015), but it might be worth noting an example of Meibauer's (2014b: 105) and a naturally occurring (though fictional) counterpart of it. In Meibauer's thought experiment, a husband who returns home at the crack of dawn with the excuse that he had to stay in the office that night "when it is mutually obvious to both him and his spouse that this is not true" does not commit a lie, "because the falsity of what is said is completely transparent to the interlocutors". Instead, this is "an act of verbal aggression", "a severe attack on the addressee's face". I would expect, however, that many lies qualify as face-threatening acts of verbal aggression.

Consider a slight variant of Meibauer's example, another transparently unbelievable alibi of an unfaithful spouse, and the author's characterization of the speech act involved:

> That he worked late she did not doubt, but she knew he did not sleep at his club, and he knew that she knew this...The regularity of his evening calls, however much she disbelieved them, was a comfort to them both...Even being lied to constantly, though hardly like love, was sustained attention; he must care about her to fabricate so elaborately. (Ian McEwan 2001, *Atonement*, p. 139)

Here, there is no true intent to deceive, no (perceived) severe attack on the spouse's face or blatant verbal aggressions, but to be sure there is indeed an instance of "being lied to".

3 Implicature and the (over?)extended definition of lying

3.1 Lying, misleading, and conversationally implicated falsehood

Consider the tale of the contentious first mate and captain, culminating in the captain's true log entry "Today, October 11th, the mate is drunk", followed three days later by the mate's log entry "Today, October 14th, the captain is not drunk", which serves in the context to induce a false implicature (via the maxim of Relation). Meibauer writes (2014a: 123; cf. Meibauer 2005: 1380), "The point is that the logbook entry of the mate is true. It is indeed the case that the captain is not drunk. However, a reader will understand that this is an exception because the captain is usually drunk…In this story we have a classical case of 'lying while saying the truth.'"

Similarly, if I tell you "X is meeting a woman this evening", thereby Quantity-implicating "that the person to be met was someone other than X's wife, mother, sister, or perhaps even close platonic friend" (Grice 1989: 37), I was lying – and not merely seeking to mislead you – if I know that the woman in question was in fact Mrs. X (Meibauer 2014b: 98).

"In order to capture the case of lying while saying the truth", Meibauer proposes an extended definition of lying (2014b: 98; cf. 2014a: 126):

(6) Lying (extended version)
 A speaker S lies iff
 (a) s/he asserts that p while not believing that p, or
 (b) s/he conversationally implicates on the basis of his/her assertion that q while not believing that q

Thus the first mate and I have both lied in these scenarios, based on clause (b). But is this prediction correct? Implicated truths and falsehoods have figured in a variety of ways within both ordinary and legal discourse. A good starting point is provided by implicatures associated with the observance or exploitation of the first Quantity submaxim: "Make your contribution as informative as is required (for the current purposes of the talk-exchange)" (Grice 1989: 26).

When it comes to acknowledging the overt or covert role of Quantity implicature, legal tradition has responded in different ways depending on the local goal and the overall context. In the first place, the tendency to recover unwanted implicatures can be *recognized* and *taken into account*, for example by cancellation. This can be seen in James Madison's 1789 letter to the House of Representatives on the need for the Ninth Amendment to the Constitution – "The enumeration in the Constitution of certain rights shall not be construed so as to deny or disparage others retained by the people" – to guard against an unwanted quantity-based implicature, which Madison derives as follows:

> It has been objected also against a bill of rights, that, by enumerating particular exceptions to the grant of power, it would disparage those rights which were not placed in that enumeration; and it might follow by implication, that those rights which were not singled out, were intended to be assigned into the hands of the General Government, and were consequently insecure.
> (http://constitution.findlaw.com/amendment9/amendment.html)

Judges often explicitly reason based on inferences from what was not said:

> In an amendment to the Public Health Service act, Congress in 1981 said that clinics receiving Federal funds for contraceptive services should, "to the extent practical," encourage family participation in their activities. If Congress had wanted to require parental notification, Judge Edwards said, it could have used more explicit language.
> (N.Y. Times 5/10/83, http://tinyurl.com/pvgqrev)

At the same time, implicature can either be explicitly incorporated into what is said for a specific legal context, such as the redefinition of *try* or *attempt* as entailing failure in performing the (criminal) act in question (see Horn to appear a for discussion and other examples) or it can be exploited and distinguished from what is said, in both forensic contexts and everyday life. We have encountered one case of such exploitation, Chisholm and Feehan's "My leg isn't bothering me *too* much today" uttered by someone whose leg bothers him not at all. Similarly in (7), from a web-posted story (whence the "Google gamma"), flouting a scalar implicature by understatement fails to yield a prototype lie (see Horn to appear b for the relation between lexical clones like *lie lie* and prototypes):

(7) γAnother not-really-a-lie-lie. I made it seem like this was just a slight headache when it was really more of a mild to really bad one.
(http://tinyurl.com/h5nshur)

For a more elaborate real world example, we turn to the fate of Picasso's "Guernica", the celebrated and moving canvas of the horrors of the Spanish Civil War, exiled to New York Museum of Modern Art during Franco's dictatorship but a target for repatriation once a democratic regime had been installed in Spain. Here is the New York Times account of a diplomat's "elaborate bluff" in accomplishing that repatriation:

> To demonstrate that the Spanish Government had in fact paid Picasso to paint the mural in 1937 for the Paris International Exhibition, Mr. Fernández Quintanilla had to secure documents in the archives of the late Luis Araquistain, Spain's Ambassador to France at the time. But Araquistain's son, poor and opportunistic, demanded $2 million for the archives, which Mr. Fernández Quintanilla rejected as outrageous. He managed, however, to obtain from the son photocopies of the pertinent documents, which in 1979 he presented to Roland Dumas, the Paris lawyer named by Picasso to determine when "public liberties" had been re-established in Spain, permitting delivery of the "Guernica" to the Prado.
> "This changes everything," a startled Mr. Dumas told the Spanish envoy when he showed him the photocopies of the Araquistain documents. "You of course have the originals?" the lawyer asked casually. "Not all of them," replied Mr. Fernández Quintanilla, *not lying but not telling the truth, either.* (Markham 1981, emphasis added)

What makes the diplomat's move an "elaborate bluff" rather than a lie is his exploitation of Quantity implicature to convey a falsehood that he did not utter. On Markham's diagnosis, this move constitutes not "lying while telling the truth" but neither of the two.

Fernández Quintanilla's ploy is part of a distinguished, or at least ancient, tradition dating back to Genesis. In his critique of (overt) lying, St. Augustine ("Against Lying", §23) cites the account (Gen. 20:12) of Abraham's deception of King Abimelech, where by asserting a connection of sisterhood he implicates a non-connection of marriage:

> [T]hey who assert that it is sometimes permitted to lie, conveniently do not mention that Abraham did this concerning Sarah, whom he said to be his sister. For he did not say, She is not my wife, but he said, She is my sister; because she was in truth so near akin, that she might without a lie be called a sister...Somewhat therefore of truth he left untold, not told anything of falsehood, when he left wife untold, and told of sister...It is not then a lie, when by silence a true thing is kept back, but when by speech a false thing is put forward.

They did not call him half-honest Abe for nothing.[5]

Within the legal domain, a landmark precedent in this domain is Bronston v. United States, 409 U.S. 352 (1973) (https://supreme.justia.com/cases/federal/us/409/352/case.html). Here is the crucial exchange:

> Bronston v. United States, 409 U.S. 352 (1973)
> https://supreme.justia.com/cases/federal/us/409/352/case.html
> BANKRUPTCY HEARING, JUNE 10, 1966
>
> > "Q. Do you have any bank accounts in Swiss banks, Mr. Bronston?"
> > "A. No, sir."
> > "Q. Have you ever?"
> > "A. The company had an account there for about six months, in Zurich."

As Chief Justice Burger notes for the majority in overturning an earlier perjury finding against Bronston for his responses here, the movie magnate's answers, while intentionally misleading given the personal account he had previously maintained at the International Credit Bank in Geneva, were nonetheless "literally truthful" at the time he was interrogated under oath:

---

[5] For more on the uses of silent deception and ways of hiding the truth ("cacher la vérité") without lying, see Pascal 1656; Roussel de la Tour 1763; Fauconnier 1979; Horn to appear a.

It is undisputed that, for a period of nearly five years, between October, 1959, and June, 1964, petitioner had a personal bank account at the International Credit Bank in Geneva, Switzerland, into which he made deposits and upon which he drew checks totaling more than $180,000. It is likewise undisputed that petitioner's answers were literally truthful.

(a) Petitioner did not at the time of questioning have a Swiss bank account.
(b) Bronston Productions, Inc., did have the account in Zurich described by petitioner.

Beyond question, petitioner's answer to the crucial question was not responsive if we assume, as we do, that the first question was directed at personal bank accounts. There is, indeed, an implication in the answer to the second question that there was never a personal bank account; in casual conversation, this interpretation might reasonably be drawn. But we are not dealing with casual conversation, and the statute does not make it a criminal act for a witness to willfully state any material matter that implies any material matter that he does not believe to be true.

Majority opinion written by Chief Justice Warren Burger (Page 409 U. S. 357–358)

Around the same time that Bronston and his lawyers prevailed on appeal, a similar verdict was returned in a case spinning off the Watergate scandal. As related in various news reports (see e.g. http://tinyurl.com/mf8tvyx), Texas attorney Jake Jacobsen was interrogated on May 3, 1974 concerning a $10,000 bribe he had allegedly offered to then Treasury Secretary John Connally on behalf of the lawyer's milk producer clients. A grand jury had determined that Jacobsen had lied, but U. S. District Judge George Hart Jr. dismissed the indictment because the "lie" denying the bribe was literally true. Prosecutor Sidney Glazer had prefaced his question "And is it your testimony that...", and Jacobsen had responded "That is correct." This led to the following exchange:

Judge Hart: "Jacobsen in this case gave a literally true answer to your question... You only asked 'is it your testimony?' You didn't ask him if it is true or false."
Glazer: "You don't have to ask him if his testimony is true or false when he's before a grand jury."
Judge Hart: "Not unless you're later going to indict him for perjury."

But it was the precedent established in Bronston v. U.S. in 1973 that was cited extensively by all sides during President Clinton's interrogation and subsequent impeachment hearings two decades later. Extensive discussion is provided by Tiersma (2003, 2005) and Solan and Tiersma (2006: 212–235), who stress that Bronston's violation concerned what is implicated (via the Quantity and Relation maxims) rather than what is literally said and posit the "Literal Truth Defense" against perjury charges, in contexts where lawyers fail to fulfill their responsibility of ascertaining the whole truth.

Bill Clinton's finesse at parsing the truth by misleading his accusers (on the meaning of *sexual relations* or of *is*) without actually lying was evidently passed on to an adept pupil. When Monica Lewinsky was asked under oath by Rep. Ed Bradley (R-TN) in a 1999 Congressional hearing whether portions of her affidavit in the Paula Jones case had been false, she responded "Incomplete and misleading", thereby (falsely) implicating that no portions of it were false. In reporting this exchange (http://tinyurl.com/n9xcp8t), Frances X. Clines commends Lewinsky's "Clintonian way with the meaning of words". But the tradition of exploiting the difference between what is implicated and what is said when in durance is much older, antedating even the notorious practices of the 17th century Jesuits (see Horn to appear a) on how to "hide the truth" without actually lying. Macintyre (1994: 336–337) cites Kant's dictum "that my duty is assert only what is true and that the mistaken inferences that others may draw from what I say or what I do are, in some cases at least, not my responsibility, but theirs". Macintyre recounts how Emperor Julian's agents accost St. Athanasius on the Nile demanding to know "Is Athanasius close at hand?" "Yes," replies Athanasius, "he is not far from here", and off they go in vain pursuit. Once again, whether perpetrated by sinners or saints, to mislead is not to lie.

3.2 Lying and cardinal sinn

Following Stuart Green, Meibauer points to an example in which the known falsity of a proposition that has standardly (since Horn 1972) been taken to instantiate quantity implicature intuitively yields a lie, and not merely an instance of intentional misleading:

> Imagine that A needs to borrow a car for the evening and asks B how many he owns. B, who in truth owns four cars, replies, "I have one car, and I'm using it this evening." Has B lied in saying that he owns "one car"? Has B made an assertion that is literally false, or has he merely led A to draw an improper inference from a misleading statement? It seems wrong to say that B has merely misled A...In terms of everyday morality, one who responds to a specific quantitative inquiry by baldly stating a numerical fact should be regarded as uttering a lie. (Green 2006: 146, quoted in Meibauer 2014b: 115; 2016: 117)

The claim in the last sentence is too absolute. Imagine that A and B have settled their differences about the use of B's car and decide to walk to the local watering hole; as they approach the entrance to the bar B asks how old A is and A assures him, "Don't worry, I'm 21." In this case, the falseness of the baldly stated fact (given that what's relevant in the context is whether A is *at least* 21 and so allowed to enter the bar) does not render her statement a lie (or even misleading).

But Green's (and Meibauer's) general point is well-taken, and it is the same point that Chief Justice Burger makes in distinguishing the hypothetical illustration invoked by the district court from bona fide cases of conversational implicatures like that in the actual Bronston case. This passage comes from the Supreme Court's decision overturning the District Court's conviction of Bronston:

> The District Court gave the following example "as an illustration only":
>
> > "If it is material to ascertain how many times a person has entered a store on a given day and that person responds to such a question by saying five times when in fact he knows that he entered the store 50 times that day, that person may be guilty of perjury even though it is technically true that he entered the store five times."
>
> The illustration given by the District Court is hardly comparable to petitioner's answer; the answer "five times" is responsive to the hypothetical question and contains nothing to alert the questioner that he may be sidetracked…Moreover, it is very doubtful that an answer which, in response to a specific quantitative inquiry, baldly understates a numerical fact can be described as even "technically true".

But this is precisely what is to be expected given the current consensus that cardinals – in particular when occurring as fragment or focused answers to question – express 'exactly n' and do not merely implicate the upper bound (cf. Kadmon 1984; Koenig 1991; Fretheim 1992; Horn 1992; Geurts 1998; and especially Bultinck 2005). Cardinals differ from other scalars in discourse:

> If you asked me whether 10 students passed and I knew that 15 did, I must first determine whether you were asking me if at least 10 passed or exactly 10 passed before knowing whether to answer positively or negatively; no such dilemma arises if you asked me whether some or most of the students passed. (Horn 2009: 8)

In addition, psycholinguists have demonstrated that the acquisition and processing of cardinals differs across various parameters from that of inexact scalar values like *some* (cf. Papafragou and Musolino 2003; Hurewitz et al. 2006).

A recent study by Weissman and Terkourafi (2016) poses the question – "Are false implicatures lies? – and answers primarily in the negative, providing evidence for the classical as opposed to the revisionist approach to the status of false implicatures within a theory of lying while also reinforcing the non-implicature-based analysis of cardinals. Weissman and Terkourafi devise an experimental study addressing the relation between the lying/misleading distinction (cf. Meibauer 2014a and work cited therein) and the distinction between what is said from what is implicated (drawing largely on Doran et al. 2012).[6] What they find is that, contra the predictions of Meibauer "extended definition" of lying, subjects tend to report that true statements with false (conversational) implicatures are largely (in 8 of 11 subtypes) not considered to be lies.

---

6 These same two strands of work are interwoven in Saul 2012, which is more of a philosophical inquiry than an empirical study.

There were, interestingly, three categories of (putative) implicatures whose falsity did produce a statistically significant judgment of lying on the part of subjects, illustrated by their examples reproduced in (8). (The background statement is given in brackets; the full scenarios are suppressed here.)

(8) a. [Where are the cupcakes?] "I ate 3; sorry." (when she actually ate 5)
b. [How'd the attic look?] "It was dusty and there were boxes and boxes of books." (when there was just one dusty box of books)
c. [Were you and Kelsey drunk?] "I drove, so I wasn't, but Kelsey drank and drank." (when Kelsey only had two drinks all night)

As noted in this section, the appropriate analysis of cardinals is not strictly implicature-based, so the sequence in (8a) confirms the point made by Green (2006) and Chief Justice Burger (in discussing the District Court's hypothetical) and does not affect the general alignment of the lying/misleading and what is said/what is implicated distinctions (Adler 1997; Horn 2009; Saul 2012). The cases involving Weissman and Terkourafi's "N and N" and "V and V" contexts in (8b,c) are certainly worth pursuing in more detail; perhaps speakers have conventionalized these constructions in such a way that 'multiplicity' is part of at-issue meaning rather than merely implicated.

In any event, the results of Weissman and Terkourafi's study are suggestive, and largely supportive of the classical position on lying. Subsequent work will need to address both the identity and heterogeneity of the class of conversational implicatures (see van Tiel et al. 2016 for an important step in this direction).

3.3 Lying, misleading, and conventionally implicating

On the topic of lies and implicatures, it should be noted that Meibauer cannot in fact defend the *iff* in his extended definition of lying (see (6) above) as a biconditional, since there are other circumstances satisfying neither of the clauses in (a) or (b) that he regards as instances of lying. In particular, consider the case of conventional implicatures. If the extended definition is intended to encompass conversational implicatures, which are usually (and I would argue correctly) taken to lie outside of linguistically encoded content on Grice's account, it surely extends *a fortiori* to knowingly false conventional implicatures. Indeed, Meibauer argues (2014: §4.6) that although such implicatures are not, for Grice, part of what is said, their falsity can result in lies even when the content of what is said is true.

But intuitions here line up with Grice (and with Augustine and Aquinas): since saying (in the relevant sense) is necessary for lying, one can *mislead but not lie via false implicatures*, whether conversational or conventional. Consider the examples in (9); for more on why these examples of adversative particles, second person pronoun forms, epithets, and German modal particles involve (Gricean) conventional implicatures (or the precursor notion defined and illustrated by Frege), see Horn 2013 and references therein.

(9) She's poor **but** she's happy: not a lie if she's both poor and happy
Even Hercules can lift the rock: not a lie if H. can lift it and he's the most likely to
Tu es beau/**Du** bist schön: not a lie if you're an attractive stranger
That **bastard** just got tenure: not a lie if I actually think he's a great guy
*Er is **ja/halt/doch** ein Linguist:* not a lie if he's a linguist, regardless of discourse factors

Meibauer quite correctly points out that the known falsity of certain putative conventional implicatures (as on the Potts 2005 characterization) may result in lies. If a candidate knows that Obama is a Christian born in Hawaii and nevertheless asserts (9) to a gullible audience, he has lied, regardless of the truth or falsity of the main clause claim.

(10) Barack Hussein Obama, who is a Muslim born in Kenya, cannot be trusted to defend America's interests.

But in fact, appositive or non-restrictive relative clauses are in fact secondary assertions (à la Frege 1892) and not true (Gricean) conventional implicatures; cf. Horn 2007 for elaboration.[7]

Relatedly, one can also intentionally misrepresent one's attitudes without lying by employing various non-linguistic or paralinguistic devices, from smiling and grimacing to intonation contours, which conventionally but non-truth-conditionally commit the speaker to aspects of encoded content. A passage from an internet story illustrates how paralinguistic markers like intonation can deceive but not lie:

(11) ꜛMy voice was dismissive, to deter Pietro from worrying. *Technically*, voice tone doesn't count as lying. (http://tinyurl.com/h5nshur)

---

[7] Material in appositive clauses can also constitute a non-assertive speech act, providing further evidence that such clauses are not presupposed or conventionally implicated. Thus, a Republican politician uttering (i) performs the two separate speech acts of endorsing and condemning:

  (i) Donald J. Trump, whom I hereby endorse for President, is an unprincipled racist demagogue.

The use of *technically* in (12) (italics in original) emphasizes the distinction between what counts or does not count as a technical lie (even outside the courtroom!) and what is only a "lie" in scare quotes or in loose or metaphorical speech, as when we say that someone pretending to be what he is not is "living a lie" or when Clancy Martin explains why "Good lovers lie":

> Relationships last only if we don't always say exactly what we're thinking. We have to disguise our feelings, to feint, to smile sometimes when we want to shout. In short we have to lie. (Martin 2015)

We could attempt to broaden the definition of lying beyond (6) to encompass all such extended uses from pretense to dissembling to flirtation to coy silence, but it is hard to know where to stop and even harder to know how we are to explain why ordinary speakers judge such non-asserted "lies" not to constitute actual lies or why jurists consistently restrict the application of perjury to cases in which (C1) is satisfied.

4 Where the truth lies?

A quarter-century after Coleman and Kay's seminal study, Turri and Turri (2015) revisit the experimental domain by devising a Mechanical Turk study that challenges one premise of what they deem the "folk theory" of lying (Augustine, Aquinas, Chisholm and Feehan, et al.). Their aim is to show that actual falsity, corresponding to (C3) – the criterion Coleman and Kay found to be least operative in their subjects' responses – is in fact crucial for determining the presence of a lie.

While Coleman and Kay's subjects were given only the response options "x is a lie" v. "x is not a lie", Turri and Turri found that when they multiplied the options to include "more flexible response options" encompassing "successful" and "unsuccessful" lying and truth-telling, or when they allowed subjects to choose between "he tried to lie and actually did lie" and "he tried to lie but only thinks he lied" (Turri and Turri 2015: 165), it becomes clear that lying requires actual (objective) falsity, not just believed (subjective) falsity.[8]

---

[8] An anonymous referee points me to an earlier consideration of the "true lie" due to Jean-Paul Sartre and Bill Lycan (working in indirect tandem). Lycan (2006: 165) explains:

> Sartre bemoans the fact that we have no simple expression for the following situation: *A* believes that not-*p*, but for selfish reasons wants B to believe that p. In a persuasive manner, *A* tells *B* that *p*: '*p*, B; trust me, old friend, would I ever lie to you?' Now in fact, *A* is mistaken, and it is true that *p*. *A* has tried to lie to *B*, and *A*'s character is that of a liar. But what *A* said was true, so it cannot be called a lie.

However, it is not at all clear that increasing flexibility of responses commensurately increases reliability of results, if the question is really whether or not a given utterance in a given context is a lie. If a subject chooses a subcategory providing more specific information, we cannot conclude that the superordinate category does not also apply: If I ask "Did he die or was he murdered?" and you reply "He was murdered", you do not thereby commit yourself to the proposition that he did not die. Similarly, coordinations like *lions and lionesses* or *cats or kittens* are entirely felicitous without yielding the result that lionesses are not lions or that kittens are not cats (see Rohdenburg 1985 for similar examples and Wiegmann, Samland, and Waldmann 2016 for further critiques of Turri and Turri 2015).

In presenting a forced choice between what counts as lying and what counts as "trying but failing to lie", Turri and Turri invoke a category that speakers do not otherwise volunteer. While Google searches do indeed pull up many hits for "failed lie", "x tried to lie", or "x unsuccessfully lied", such hits do not (as for Turri and Turri, or for Sartre's hypothetical Mr. A) involve agents who believe that they are lying but accidentally tell the truth. Rather, the agents in question are those whose attempts to deceive the addressee are unfruitful; i.e. they do lie but their lies are not believed. A terrible liar is not someone whose attempted lies end up being true but someone whose lies fail to convince. While we have seen that *lie* is not a success verb, liars do indeed aim to persuade, whether this holds definitionally (as it does for deceptionists) or prototypically (as it does for non-deceptionists).

Another problematic case for (C3) as a requirement on lying is one in which the agent has imperfect knowledge. If I make a statement that x will happen tomorrow, while you know I believe that x will not happen, you can correctly accuse me of lying today without needing to wait until tomorrow to see if x does in fact come to pass. In short, Aquinas's refusal to acquit the liar on the grounds of accidental truth is thus eminently plausible, although – as supported by the findings of Coleman and Kay (1981) – prototype lies do in fact satisfy the actual falsity built into (C3).

On many occasions I have mentioned this in my undergraduate classes, and every time, about 40% of the students balk at Sartre's judgment, and say they have no difficulty in calling *A* a liar. When I protest that a lie cannot be true, they say, 'Sure it can'; all that matters to them is the intent to deceive. On the basis of induction, I predict that 40% of my readers will likewise have rejected Sartre's complaint.

While Lycan sides with Sartre, the reader will recognize that the judgments of his 40-percenters echo those of Augustine and Aquinas. What we're dealing with here, Lycan concludes, is "simply a dialect difference", albeit one presumably not linked to regional or social factors.

A prototype approach to meaning is especially suited to a category like that of lying, in which different criteria are relevant for different contexts of evaluation. The "extended definition" of lying (Meibauer 2014a), about which I have been skeptical, might be seen as a definitional conduit taking us from literal, prototype lies to non-prototypical or non-literal ones. One argument for this is the distribution of the lexical clone, *LIE lie*. Cloning a noun tends to signal either a literal (as opposed to metaphorical) sense or a prototype category member (cf. Horn 1993, to appear b). We saw in (§3.1) that a speaker who understates the truth may mislead but does not LIE lie (cf. [7]). Other examples show that a prototypic lie is "malicious" (Aquinas) or "self-serving" (Meibauer), as opposed to a "white lie", one seen as justified on the basis of the perceived needs of the recipient (e.g. a child or medical patient; see discussion in Bok 1978, Horn to appear a). While satisfying all four criteria (**C1**)–(**C4**), such a justifiable untruth is not a LIE lie:

(12) Exchange on "Bones" (FOX TV), Episode 3x10; Seeley Booth is Parker's father and Temperance ("Bones") Brennan's fellow investigator (and romantic interest)

> BRENNAN: He's living a lie. You'd never do that.
> BOOTH: Well, not NEVER. I mean, I – I lie to Parker – especially this time of year.
> BRENNAN: What about?
> BOOTH: I tell him that Santa's coming.
> BRENNAN: Really?
> BOOTH: It's Santa Claus!... It's not a LIE lie, Bones. It's more like everybody agreeing that up to a certain age, kids deserve to live a different kind of truth.

Nor, if bloggers can be trusted, does a partial truth qualify as a LIE lie:

(13) γCould Cupid be real? Yes, but I don't know for sure sure. I didn't actually see the little god, so for me to tell you Cupid on Valentine's Day travels around shooting people with golden love arrows, well, that would be a lie. I mean, maybe not a lie lie, but not total truth.
(http://ilovefarmers.org/blog/2012/cupid-strikes-again)

γShe asked me at that time if I had been pursuant of something more than platonic friendship with her. Being a reasonable person, I of course straight up lied about it. I *didn't lie lie*...Just...kind of omitted the truth a little bit.
(https://adarkspot.wordpress.com/category/beauty/)

ʏShe looks down at her food, like any kid who's been caught in a white lie. You know, you didn't LIE LIE, but you kind of fibbed, like the dog ate my homework? It's *that* look.
(http://traciemcmillan.com/blog/what-i-learned-in-the-garlic-fields/)

On a more serious note, consider the case of National Intelligence Director James Clapper. Asked by Sen. Ron Wyden (D-Ore.) on March 12, 2013 whether the National Security Agency "collect[s] any type of data at all on millions or hundreds of millions of Americans", National Intelligence Director James Clapper replied, "No, sir…not wittingly." After later revelations, Sen. Wyden and others voiced reservations about the truthfulness of this answer, and Clapper conceded, in a June 10, 2013 interview with NBC's Andrea Mitchell, "I responded in what I thought was the most truthful, or least most untruthful manner, by saying no." He indicated that his response to Wyden turned on a definition of "collect": "There are honest differences on the semantics of what -- when someone says 'collection' to me, that has a specific meaning, which may have a different meaning to him" (http://tinyurl.com/lfct83z). While Clapper's doubletalk led directly to Edward Snowden's initiating the Wikileaks revelations revealing the NSA's efforts to gather data on ordinary Americans, Clapper continued to maintain that he had not lied to Congress, although his reasons for why his "least most untruthful" statement was not a lie shifted. Perhaps the subtlest of these is that what the NSA had been doing was not *collecting* data but *aggregating* it, given the technical definition of "collect" in use in the security services ("Data acquired by electronic means is 'collected' only when it has been processed into intelligible form").[9]

It is thus particularly interesting that according to one of his defenders (at https://fas.org/blogs/secrecy/2014/01/clapper-ssci/), Clapper could not have been lying because there was no intent to deceive (or at least he didn't lie to Wyden's committee because they knew the truth, although he may have lied

---

9 Clapper implicitly invokes the Jesuit doctrine of equivocation here: "It is permitted to use ambiguous terms, leading people to understand them in another sense from that in which we understand them ourselves" (Pascal 1656: 101–102). Lewis (1969: 193) might depict Clapper as practicing "minimal truthfulness": "A trickster is being truthful in this minimal way if, knowing that Owen is going to the shore of the river, he says 'Owen is going to the bank' during a conversation about Owen's lack of cash." A particularly elegant equivocation is due to the 13th century Dominican St. Raymond de Peñafort (patron saint of lawyers), who proposes deflecting a murderer at the door by swearing of his intended victim *"Non est hic"*, which the miscreant will interpret as the "virtual falsehood" 'He is not here' but which is "verbally true" in the alternate sense 'He does not eat here' (Cavaillé 2004; cf. also Cardenas 1702 in Roussel de la Tour 1763: 464).

to the general public). A respondent objects that the relevant statute is the one defining perjury, which as we have seen in §2, does not require the intent to deceive. The consensus of bloggers and commenters is that Clapper did lie, and that, in the words of one, "seeing someone in the position of James Clapper – the Director of National Intelligence – baldly lying to the public without repercussion is the evidence of a subverted democracy".

The last word might be ceded to commenter Jazusamo (http://tinyurl.com/zu2try8): "They'll tell us it wasn't a 'lie' lie... just a less than truthful version of the truth." Perhaps a follow-up study by Turri and Turri might add to their "more flexible response options" the possibility of judging a speaker's utterance as a lie but not a LIE lie.

5 Concluding remarks

If we are correct in viewing misleading not as a species of lying but as a distinct category, the question remains as to whether it is always better (or less egregious) to (intentionally) mislead than it is to lie. One consideration that may point in the opposite direction rests with the question of responsibility. In lying, the blame is attributable to the speaker for the illocutionary act of asserting the lie; in misleading (especially through the manipulation of conversational rather than conventional implicature), the deception is jointly constructed, with responsibility and blame shared between speaker and hearer. At the same time, as Carson (2006, 2010) has stressed, "every lie breaks a promise", the generally implicit promise to tell the truth (Carson 2006: 292, following W. D. Ross 1930) – while as we have seen one can intentionally mislead without breach of promise or trust.[10] In any case, whether or not the misleader may not be intrinsically on higher ethical ground than the liar, the distinction is crucial in forensic contexts, where a premium is placed on what counts as having been said rather than merely implicated (see Adler 1997; Saul 2012; and Solan 2012 for relevant discussion).

We might envisage an Optimality Theory of intended deception, with the context of assessment may determine the relative strength of the two constraints *LIE and *MISLEAD. In a legal context, *LIE is clearly the higher-ranked constraint, and is thus incorporated into the perjury statutes. But getting hearers to collude in their own deception is a real consideration as well.

---

10 As a referee puts the point, "[A]ttempting to deceive others doesn't necessarily involve trying to get them to trust one...[L]ying, unlike mere deception, involves breaking a promise and attempting to betray the trust of others and these are arguably morally relevant differences."

Current approaches to pragmatic enrichment allow for a domain of communicated content for which the input may be a variety of pragmatically derived aspects of meaning beyond implicature, and I cannot explore here the extent to which the explicatures of relevance theory or the implicitures invoked by Kent Bach (2001) may affect judgments of lying vs. misleading. (See Carston 2013 for a valuable discussion on the relation of legal interpretation to neo- and post-Gricean pragmatic theory and Dynel 2015 for useful remarks on these issues.)

I have maintained that a speaker who asserts truthfully and implicates falsely does not in fact lie while telling the truth, *pace* Meibauer. On the other hand, a speaker who believes she is asserting a false statement only to have it turn out to be, in Aquinas's sense, accidentally true does indeed lie while telling the truth, *pace* Turri and Turri.

Matczak (2016) has recently urged jettisoning "the Gricean paradigm in legal interpretation" in favor of "an externalist approach to language, one in which interpretation is based on conventions, not intentions" in the spirit of Lepore and Stone (2015).[11] But at least in terms of perjury law and fraud, as well as civil interaction, the central roles of intention, of belief, and of the classical Gricean distinction between what is said and what is implicated make it difficult to see how a shift away from intentionality is possible or why it would be desirable.

On the account defended here (and in more detail in Horn to appear a), work on the pragmatics of assertion and implicature informs our understanding of how lies (and non-lies) are assessed in both conversational and forensic domains, at least for English (and for Latin and French, to judge from the classical literature) (see Meibauer [2014a: 22–25] for interesting remarks on cross-linguistic diversity in this area). The (relatively) bright line between lying and misleading helps to illuminate the sometimes murky border territory dividing semantics from pragmatics. To determine what it is to lie helps us determine what it is to assert – and vice versa.

Acknowledgments. Thanks to those who attended and commented on earlier presentations of subsets of this material at conferences in Vancouver and Mainz, in Larry Solan's Yale Law School seminar, and in Ernie Lepore's semantics seminar at Rutgers. Thanks also to Barbara Abbott, Mira Ariel, Kent Bach, Elitzur Bar-Asher, Betty Birner, Emma Borg, David Braun, Tom Carson, Marta Dynel, Ben Farkas, Gilles Fauconnier, Bill Ladusaw, Ernie Lepore, Jörg Meibauer, Jennifer Saul, Larry Solan, Roy Sorensen, Dieter Stein, Marina Terkourafi, and Gregory Ward. I am particularly indebted to Wayne Davis and an anonymous referee for

---

11 See Horn 2016 and Szabó 2016 for critiques of Lepore and Stone 2015.

their comments on an earlier version of this paper; neither they nor anyone else named or unnamed here is necessarily on board with my arguments or conclusions. (Skeins of intellectual credit and debt can form their own tangled webs, though I trust benign ones.) This paper was given at the Intercultural Pragmatics Conference (INPRA 2016) in Split and I am especially grateful to István Kecskés and Jagoda Granić both for hosting an excellent conference and for inviting me. Finally, thanks to the volume editors Rachel Giora and Michael Haugh for their diligence and patience and to István Kecskés for his inspiration.

References

Adler, Jonathan. 1997. Lying, deceiving, or falsely implicating. *Journal of Philosophy* 94. 435–452.
Aquinas, St. Thomas. c. 1270. *Summa Theologica, Part II-II.* http://tinyurl.com/plgglrc.
Augustine, Saint. 420. Against lying. http://www.newadvent.org/fathers/1313.htm.
Bok, Sissela. 1978. *Lying: Moral Choice in Public and Private Life.* New York: Pantheon.
Bultinck, Bert. 2005. *Numerous Meanings: The Meaning of English Cardinals and the Legacy of Paul Grice.* Oxford: Elsevier.
Carson, Thomas. 2006. The definition of lying. *Noûs* 40. 284–306.
Carson, Thomas. 2010. *Lying and Deception: Theory and Practice.* Oxford: Oxford University Press.
Cavaillé, Jean-Pierre. 2004. *Non est hic:* Le cas exemplaire de la protection du fugitif. http://dossiersgrihl.revues.org/300?lang=en
Chisholm, Roderick & Thomas Feehan. 1977. The intent to deceive. *Journal of Philosophy* 74. 143–159.
Coleman, Linda & Paul Kay. 1981. Prototype semantics: the English word *lie. Language* 57. 26–44.
Doran, Ryan, Gregory Ward, Meredith Larson, Yaron McNabb & Rachel Baker. 2012. A novel experimental paradigm for distinguishing between what is said and what is implicated. *Language* 88. 124–154.
Dynel, Marta. 2015. Intention to deceive, bald-faced lies, and deceptive implicature. *Intercultural Pragmatics* 12. 309–332.
Fauconnier, Gilles. 1979. Comment contrôler la vérité. *Actes de la Recherche en Sciences Sociales* 25. 3–22.
Frankfurt, Harry. 2005. *On Bullshit.* Princeton: Princeton University Press.
Frege, Gottlob. 1892. On *Sinn* and *Bedeutung.* In Michael Beaney (ed.), *The Frege Reader*, 151–171. Oxford: Blackwell.
Fretheim, Thorstein. 1992. The effect of intonation on a type of scalar implicature. *Journal of Pragmatics* 18. 1–30.
Green, Stuart. 2006. *Lying, Cheating and Stealing: A Moral Theory of White-Collar Crime.* Oxford: Oxford University Press.

Grice, H. P. 1989. *Studies in the Way of Words*. Cambridge: Harvard University Press.
Horn, Laurence R. 1972. *On the Semantic Properties of Logical Operators in English*. UCLA dissertation. Distributed by Indiana University Linguistics Club, 1976.
Horn, Laurence. 1992. The said and the unsaid. *SALT II*, 163–192. Columbus: Ohio State U.
Horn, Laurence. 1993. Economy and redundancy in a dualistic model of natural language. In Susan Shore & Maria Vilkuna (eds.), *SKY 1993: 1993 Yearbook of the Linguistic Association of Finland*, 33–72.
Horn, Laurence. 2007. Toward a Fregean pragmatics: *Voraussetzung, Nebengedanke, Andeutung*. In István Kecskés & Laurence Horn (eds.), *Explorations in Pragmatics: Linguistic, Cognitive, and Intercultural Aspects*, 39–69. Berlin & New York: Mouton de Gruyter.
Horn, Laurence. 2009. Implicature, truth, and meaning. *International Review of Pragmatics* 1. 3–34.
Horn, Laurence. 2013. *I Love Me Some Datives:* Expressive meaning, free datives, and F-implicature. In Daniel Gutzmann and Hans-Martin Gärtner (eds.), *Beyond Expressives: Explorations in Use-Conditional Meaning*, 153–201. Leiden: Brill.
Horn, Laurence. 2016. Conventional wisdom reconsidered. *Inquiry* 59. 145–162.
Horn, Laurence. To appear a. Telling it slant: Toward a taxonomy of deception. In Dieter Stein & Janet Giltrow (eds.), The Pragmatic Turn in Law. Mouton Series in Pragmatics. Boston & Berlin: De Gruyter Mouton.
Horn, Laurence. To appear b. The lexical clone: Pragmatics, prototypes, productivity. In Rita Finkbeiner & Ulrike Freywald (eds.), *Exact Repetition in Grammar and Discourse*. Boston & Berlin: De Gruyter Mouton.
Horn, Laurence & István Kecskés. 2013. Pragmatics, discourse, and cognition. In Stephen R. Anderson, Jacques Moeschler & Anne Reboul (eds.), *L'interface langage-cognition: Actes du 19ème Congrès International des Linguistes*, 353–373. Geneva-Paris: Droz.
Hurewitz, Felicia, Anna Papafragou, Lila Gleitman & Rochel Gelman. 2006. Asymmetries in the acquisition of numbers and quantifiers. *Language Learning and Development* 2. 77–96.
Kadmon, Nirit. 1984. Indefinite noun phrases with cardinality indication. Unpublished ms., U. of Massachusetts.
Kant, Immanuel. 1799. On a supposed right to lie from altruistic motives. http://tinyurl.com/l528vof
Koenig, Jean-Pierre. 1991. Scalar predicates and negation: Punctual semantics and interval interpretations. *CLS 27*. 140–155.
Lepore, Ernie & Matthew Stone. 2015. *Imagination and Convention*. Oxford: Oxford University Press.
Lewis, David. 1969. *Convention: A Philosophical Study*. Cambridge, MA: Harvard University Press.
Lycan, William. 2006. The Gettier problem problem. In Stephen Cade Heatherington (ed.), *Epistemology Futures*, 148–168. Oxford: Oxford U. Press
Macintyre, Alasdair. 1994. Truthfulness, lies, and moral philosophers: What can we learn from Mill and Kant? *The Tanner Lectures*. http://tinyurl.com/k224o5p
Mahon, James. 2008. The definition of lying and deception. In Edward N. Zalta (ed.), *Stanford Encyclopedia of Philosophy*. http://plato.stanford.edu/entries/lying-definition

Markham, James. 1981. For Spain, 'Guernica' stirs memory and awe. *New York Times*, Nov. 2, 1981. http://tinyurl.com/omlwl8a

Martin, Clancy. 2015. Good lovers lie. New York Times column, February 14, 2015. http://www.nytimes.com/2015/02/08/opinion/sunday/good-lovers-lie.html

Matczak, Martin. 2016. Does legal interpretation need Paul Grice? Reflections on Lepore and Stone's Imagination and Convention. Unpublished ms., Warsaw University. http://papers.ssrn.com/sol3/papers.cfm?abstract_id=2716629

Meibauer, Jörg. 2005. Lying and falsely implicating. *Journal of Pragmatics* 37. 1373–1399.

Meibauer, Jörg. 2011. On lying: intentionality, implicature, and imprecision. *Intercultural Pragmatics* 8. 277–292.

Meibauer, Jörg. 2014a. *Lying at the Semantics-Pragmatics Interface*. Boston & Berlin: De Gruyter Mouton.

Meibauer, Jörg. 2014b. A truth that's told with bad intent: Lying and implicit content. *Belgian Journal of Linguistics* 28. 97–118.

Meibauer, Jörg. 2016. Topics in the linguistics of lying: a reply to Marta Dynel. *Intercultural Pragmatics* 13. 107–123.

Papafragou, Anna & Julien Musolino. 2003. Scalar implicatures: Experiments at the semantics-pragmatics interface. *Cognition* 86. 253–282.

Pascal, Blaise. 1656. *Les lettres provinciales*. Manchester: The University Press, 1920. English translation by Thomas M'Crie in *Pensées* [and] *The Provincial Letters*, New York: Modern Library, 1941.

Potts, Christopher. 2005. *The Logic of Conventional Implicatures*. Oxford: Oxford University Press.

Ross, William David. 1930. *The Right and the Good*. Oxford: Oxford University Press.

Roussel de la Tour. 1762. *Extraits des assertions dangereuses et pernicieuses en tout genre, que les soi-disans jesuites ont, dans tous les tems & perseveramment, soutenues, enseignées & publiées dans leurs livres*. Paris: Pierre-Guillaume Simon.

Saul, Jennifer. 2012. *Lying, Misleading, and What is Said*. Oxford: Oxford U. Press.

Solan, Lawrence. 2012. Lawyers as insincere (but truthful) actors. *Journal of the Legal Profession* 36. 487–527.

Solan, Lawrence & Peter Tiersma. 2005. *Speaking of Crime: The Language of Criminal Justice*.

Sorensen, Roy. 2007. Bald-faced lies! Lying without the intent to deceive. *Pacific Quarterly* 88. 251–264.

Szabó, Zoltán. 2016. In defense of indirect communication. *Inquiry* 59. 163–174.

Tiersma, Peter. 2003. Did Clinton lie? Defining "sexual relations". 79 Chi.-Kent L. Rev. 927 (2004). Available at http://papers.ssrn.com/sol3/papers.cfm?abstract_id=470645.

Tiersma, Peter. 2005. The language of perjury (focusing on the Clinton impeachment). http://www.languageandlaw.org/PERJURY.HTM

Turri, John & Angelo Turri. 2015. The truth about lying. *Cognition* 138. 161–168.

Van Tiel, Bob, Emiel van Miltenburg, Natalia Zevakhina & Bart Geurts. 2016. Scalar diversity. *Journal of Semantics* 33. 137–176.

Weissman, Benjamin & Marina Terkourafi. 2016. Are false implicatures lies? An experimental investigation. Ms., University of Illinois.

Wiegmann, Alex, Jana Samland & Michael Waldmann. 2016. Lying despite telling the truth. *Cognition* 150. 37–42.

Kasia M. Jaszczolt
10 The true provenance of self-reference: A case for salience-based contextualism

1 Overview

Referring to people, objects, or situations is an omnipresent feature of conversational interaction. While formal semanticists have been focusing on it in the ongoing attempt to improve the classifications of expressions used to refer so as to give them justice in truth-conditional analyses, the intuitive truth is that underneath the debates over direct reference, rigidity, descriptions vis-à-vis names, definite vis-à-vis indefinite descriptions, presupposing vs non-presupposing reading, quantifier vs name analysis of referentially used descriptions, and a plethora of other seminal pertinent discussions in the literature, lies a simple truth that natural language is so flexible that all such debates are always going to be limited at most to semantic properties of some standard uses. While these have been discussed in the literature, semanticists are still reluctant to take the big step of understanding semantics as a theory of the kind of meaning that does not reside *in* natural language but comes *with* natural language use, fully situated in the context or a purpose to which natural language happens to be put. In what follows I provide some arguments in favour of such concept-driven, rich semantics that at the same time does not depart from the prerequisite of compositionality and from truth conditions as a tool for analysing meaning. But neither does it underestimate the role of intentions and inferences, or the role of socio-cultural salient meanings and meanings that are salient due to the properties of mental states that underlie the production and comprehension of utterances. The importance of socio-cultural factors has been a leading thread of István Kecskés' research who proposed it for the so-called situation-bound utterances – a type of formulaic expressions (Kecskés 2000), showing how they utilise cognitive mechanisms such as conventional knowledge, metaphor or metonymy. It was subsequently offered as a model for analysing meaning in conversation at large (with special focus on intercultural communication), where, according to the socio-cognitive approach, pragmatics has to take into account societal factors such as cooperation but also individual factors such as egocentrism – and at the same time incorporate both the speaker's and the addressee's perspective (Kecskés 2008, 2010, 2014; Kecskés and Zhang 2009). The emphasis on both individualism and collectivism then requires a dynamic dimension which pays due attention to the fact that meaning is co-constructed by the interactants (see also Arundale 1999, 2010; Haugh 2008, 2010, 2012). But, according to the ideology pursued here, it also requires the philosophical analysis of intentions and their proposed reflection in produced and conveyed utterance content (see e.g. Haugh and Jaszczolt 2012).

In what follows I address the following question. Taking it as empirically given that analysing meaning in conversation requires all those aspects and dimensions, how does speaker reference fare with the standard philosophical debates concerning the semantic properties of expressions that speakers use to refer? In particular, I take on board one of the core topics currently in vogue among philosophers of language and formal semanticists, namely indexical expressions. To narrow the field further, I focus on first-person reference and how it is achieved in discourse. The answer that emerges is hardly a surprising one, but the one whose consequences have not yet been fully embraced in all (apart from truly radically contextualist) truth-conditional approaches to meaning. This answer is that referring is not a linguistic act and ought not to be analysed as such. Instead of focusing on direct reference vs contextual reference, names vs descriptions, or debates over natural language 'indexicals', we ought to focus on the functions various expressions that are used for referring can play when combined with other linguistic (structure, or co-text at large) and non-linguistic (salient meanings, situation-bound meanings, etc.) means of conveying reference. Not only does the semantic content in the case of self-referring not intuitively reduce to the referent of such acts as formal approaches assume, but, in addition, there appear to be different kinds of self-reference, conveying different aspects of the self and with different degrees of commitment or generalization, all of which is pertinent to the representation of meaning.

In this spirit, I shall ask the questions:

(i) Where does the meaning of self-reference come from?
(ii) What implications does the answer to (i) have for the indexical/nonindexical distinction?

and

(iii) What implications do the answers to (i) and (ii) have for the semantics/pragmatics boundary debates?

I address (i) and (ii) in section 2, and (iii) in section 3. I conclude with promoting the so-called Salience-Based Contextualism: a radical contextualist approach to meaning that does not shun acknowledging the diversity of means by which we express reference to the self, while retaining the assumption of compositionality of meaning that is accessible to the addressee without difficulty, despite its diversified and often complicated provenance. The socio-cognitive approach referred to above is at the core of this inquiry into referring.

2 Vehicles of referring to the self

Behind a fairly uniform façade where all languages have some standard and uncontroversial means of talking about oneself and expressing thoughts about oneself (called in the philosophical literature *de se* thoughts), there is substantial intra-language and inter-language variation. Although properties of pronouns and other self-referring expressions have been widely studied for particular languages and cross-linguistically[1], this variation is still in need of a fully explanatory classification. Relevant dimensions include the scales from the inner self to the public self, from self-denigrating to conveying a superior social rank, from speaking about individual experiences to generalizing to a wide group of individuals. Other dimensions, internal to the language system, can include (i) contextual shift of the self-referring subject, for example in direct quotation in English or in adopting a perspective of the object of conversation, like in Amharic, or (ii) self-reference using lexical, grammatical (including morphological) or entirely pragmatic means. In what follows I will not attempt to provide a full taxonomy of such dimensions, neither will I select a dimension for an empirical analysis of one or more languages with respect to it. These would all be very much needed enterprises but they are large-scale enterprises, requiring big data and specialist methods. What I attempt here is an argument that is more modest in scope but at the same time indispensable as a prerequisite to them. I will address the following question: Considering the significant diversity of forms languages use for self-reference on the one hand, and the swift, subconscious choices speakers make in selecting them on the other, what conclusions can we draw concerning the provenance of self-reference? Is there systematicity in the use of these forms that would suggest that self-reference is attained by employing the resources languages have to offer without any help from outside the language system, or, rather, does speakers' use of these forms suggest that there are multiple sources of information about self-reference at work, some linguistic and some extralinguistic, whose output is not reducible to a lexical or syntactic analysis?

The use of expressions that are not specialized for self-reference will be an important element in this discussion. English commonly uses so-called 'imposters' such as 'daddy', 'yours truly', or even 'mug' ('muggins'), testifying to the fact that expressions other than indexicals can perform the role of identifying a referent, as in (1)–(3).

---

1 See e.g. Jaszczolt 2013a for references.

(1) Daddy will finish his dinner and will play with you in a moment.
(2) Guess what. From next year yours truly will be the President of the Cambridge University Boat Club.
(3) They left the room in a mess and, as usual, muggins had to tidy up.

On the other hand, pronouns that, *qua* indexical expressions, are specified for picking out a referent, and *a fortiori* first-person pronouns that, *qua* indexicals, are specified for picking out the speaker or the writer, can perform other functions. The first example comes from the so-called 'fake indexicals' such as 'my' in (4) that can have a referential as well as a bound-variable reading.

(4) I'm the only one around here who can take care of *my* children.
    Kratzer (2009: 188, after Barbara Partee)

Looked from a (static) perspective of the functions the pronoun as an element of a language system can adopt, this is either a case of sematic ambiguity arising out of syntactic underspecification, where the latter has been subjected to different analyses, one of which allows for Kratzer's constructivist account on which bound-variable uses have functional heads as binders – or a case of semantic underspecification that, again, allows for various approaches to its precisification, some structure-driven and some free, top-down. Looked from a cross-linguistic pragmatic perspective, this is an example of a choice languages make for expressing quantifier-binding introduced by 'only': some, like English, utilise first-person pronouns, others, like Polish, use reflexives.

The second example comes from the so-called 'monster contexts'. According to Kaplan (1989), it is a necessary characteristic of an indexical that its semantic value be fixed in the context of the current speech act, except for its use in direct quotation. Putative contexts that would violate this rule are called by him 'monster contexts'. But in many languages this requirement is not fulfilled.[2] For example in the Amharic example (5), 'me' and 'I' refer to different individuals in spite of the lack of a directly quotative form.

(5) wändəmme käne gar albälamm   alä
    my-brother "with-me I-will-not-eat", he said
    My brother refused to eat with me.   (from Leslau 1995: 778)

---

[2] See Schlenker 2003; Roberts 2014; and on monster contexts e.g. Predelli 2014; Cappelen and Dever 2013, 2016; Jaszczolt and Huang, in press.

In (5), *albälamm* ('I will not eat') has the speaker's brother as its subject. It conveys the thought from the brother's (first-person) perspective. But preceding it, there is *käne gar* ('with me'), conveying the perspective of the speaker. It has recently become apparent to the researchers investigating this phenomenon that this is not a case of a curious context 'shift', or a case of a peculiar language that mixes the perspectives of different agents, but instead a perfectly natural phenomenon of focusing on the semantically prominent perspective – what de Schepper (2015: 147) calls 'speech-act roles', Roberts (2014) 'doxastic centers', and Mount (2015: 20) 'mutually-accepted perspectives of interlocutors'.

Next, in languages exhibiting honorification, such as Thai, Japanese or Korean, it is difficult to state what would count as a natural-language equivalent of the philosophical concept of an indexical expression. In this sense honorifics straddle the boundary between the two categories discussed above: like common nouns in the function of first-person reference, they convey some (arguably semantic) content in addition to performing the referring role – for example self-denigration in forms coming from 'slave', 'servant', or 'mouse'; like pronouns, their primary and default function, normally arrived at through the conventionalization process, is to identify the speaker or the writer. Since it appears that it would be difficult to identify one, unmarked equivalent of the English *I* in such languages based on any obviously applicable criteria,[3] the conclusion ought to be that both the referential and the social/expressive aspects of meaning constitute the semantic content. However, analogous to other types of expressions that have an expressive overlay, the scope of their truth-conditional content remains a topic for debate.

All in all, first-person indexicals can have non-referring uses or pick out some non-grammar-driven referents, while non-indexicals, such as common nouns, can slot into the role of first-person reference indicators. While this is a well-known fact, it demonstrates that the rigid linguistic criteria we try to impose on the ways of expressing *de se* thoughts cannot be sufficient. As I argued extensively elsewhere,[4] it also demonstrates that the concept of an indexical is an abstract without a reliable backing in natural-language lexicons: natural-language 'indexicals' either have other non-indexical uses in addition, or combine indexicality with other aspects of conveyed meaning like in the case of honorifics, or otherwise would have to be fundamentally rethought and revamped as a functional category where *the context, the intentions, the common ground, the goal, and other conversational factors decide whether an item is, or is not, an indexical expression on this occasion of use.*

---

3 See e.g. Heine and Song 2011.
4 See e.g. Jaszczolt 2013a, b, 2016, in press.

Now, starting with the evidence that there is no one-to-one correspondence between linguistic categories and types of semantic function in the domain of self-reference, or, in other words, that both pronouns and common nouns in languages in which these two categories can be distinguished each exhibit diversified behaviour with respect to referring function, and adding to it the fact that in some languages pronouns and nouns do not seem to form separate classes, we are left with the question as to whether analysing the conversational behaviour of elements of a language system suffices for analysing referring. On the one hand, the likely hypothesis seems to be that it *does* suffice. English personal pronouns refer by default; *I* is overwhelmingly used referentially, with an exception of fake indexicals. Arguably, bound-variable uses do not constitute strong evidence against their referentiality in that they do not occur frequently and they are prone to creating ambiguities anyway, as evidenced by (6), perhaps analogous to garden-path sentences in which the ambiguity sneaks in unnoticed by the speaker. Moreover, the phenomenon is strictly language-specific.

In (6), 'what I was wearing' can be read as referring to the speaker's ball outfit (referential use) or, in a reflexive manner, to anyone else's outfit (bound-variable use: no one else commented on what *they themselves* were wearing).

(6) We were talking about the May Ball. But only I commented on what I was wearing.

Next, imposters, in spite of being an open-class phenomenon, rely on conventionalisation when they are fairly semantically bleached ('yours truly', or 'mummy' in Child-Directed Speech), or add only expressive meaning to self-reference ('muggins', 'the idiot'), or, at the other end of the spectrum, strongly convey semantic content in addition to self-reference as in 'the person you elected as your spokesman' in (7), used for self-referring.

(7) We didn't reach an agreement. It has to be said that the person you elected as your spokesman failed to negotiate a deal for you.

But the affirmative answer to our question is now conditional on the explanation for this non-conventional end of the scale. Collins and Postal (2012) argue that first-person imposters, as DPs (or, in a more standard terminology, NPs), contain another hidden DP (NP) in their structure. This invisible DP is the first-person singular pronominal. Imposters are pronominal and have so-called 'sources' as antecedents: for first-person imposters this source is a concept AUTHOR. If we adopt this syntactic view, then the answer to the question as to whether the properties of the language system suffice for explaining self-reference remains 'yes' – at least on the basis of this one phenomenon and at the expense of complicating syntax with disputable external justification for this move. However, if we adopt the standard view according to which imposters are third-person nominal phrases, then the answer will depend on whether their self-referring properties can be accounted for by semantics or by pragmatics. Semantic solution that does not mirror, or stem from, the postulated structure is a non-starter (in addition producing a 'no' answer) in that we would have to postulate multiple ambiguities in the case of any description or name used for this purpose and as a result lose systematicity. We are then left with a pragmatic solution, founded on contextual information processed through the recovery of speaker intentions, and this sways our answer to 'no': properties of the language system alone do not give us sufficient insight into self-referring.

Looked at more closely, the negative answer gathers support on many more fronts. For example, the perspective-dependent first-person reference in Amharic is, by definition, resolved only when we establish the perspective (or Roberts' 'doxastic center'). The ambiguity of (6) can easily be used to support the opposite stance than the one we used it for above, that is, to show that only the recovery of the speaker's intention will allow the addressee to recover the meaning – if the addressee decides to attempt a recovery of the meaning at all, since, as Gricean pragmatics fails to emphasise but computational linguists frequently demonstrate, interactants sometimes leave meanings undetermined in order to get on with the main purpose at hand and move the conversation in the direction paved by the goals. Next, generic *one* or *you*, and arbitrary PRO (null pronouns) heavily rely on context and conventions of politeness in conveying self- or other-reference, as demonstrated by the pairs (8)–(9), (10)–(11) and (12)–(13) respectively.

(8) One tries to do one's best.

(9) One doesn't want to risk being a nuisance, does one?

(10) You sort of know that it would be a wrong thing to say.

(11) To get to Oxford, you have to change in London.

(12) [Speaker about one's emotional state:]
 It is infuriating to listen to these political squabbles.

(13) [Speaker to a tourist lost in an old town:]
 It is easy to get lost in these narrow streets.

While the context can bias their reference in different directions, (8) is standardly used as conventionalised (or at least standardised) expression of self-denigration when praised, while (9) would be easy to recognize as an attempt to criticize the interlocutor's behaviour, mainly in virtue of its structure ending with the question tag. In other words, it is not the degree of generalization beyond the self that motivates the uses of 'one' but rather sociopragmatic considerations such as the commonality of certain ways of expressing certain speech acts such as a response to praise (8) or criticism (9). While in both cases 'one' superficially conforms to what Moltmann (2006, 2010) calls *generalizing detached self-reference*, the purpose, at least in a not-strongly-biasing context, would be for the speaker to self-refer in (8) but to express, say, something to the effect of (9') in (9).

(9') If you stay any longer you will annoy the host.

Analogously, it is easy to imagine a non-biasing context in which 'you' is used for generalizing self-referring in (10) and for standard, second-person, albeit also generalizing, reference in (11). (12) and (13) exemplify the same phenomenon using uncontrolled PRO constructions. Differences are not qualitative, both expressions in each pair easily allow for the substitution of a generic *one*, but what matters to us here is that the intended primary reference can vary from context to context, allowing however for some standardised presumptions concerning first-, second-person or truly generic reference. In sum, our supporting argument comes from the considerable freedom with which *I*, *you*, *one*, uncontrolled PRO, or imposters are used. The same can be said of the use of substitutable forms in other languages that have been studied for this purpose, such as French, Polish, or Thai.[5]

To continue on the detached use of first-person markers, the next argument against the language-system-dependence of self-reference can potentially come from the phenomenon of immunity to error through misidentification, known in the literature as IEM (Shoemaker 1968; see also essays in Prosser and Recanati 2012). IEM is a characteristic feature of a subset of self-ascriptions of properties in the case of which it is not possible that these properties are in fact, unbeknownst to the speaker and contrary to the speaker's intention, predicated of a third party. For example, when the speaker's self-ascription is based on proprioception, it is referentially infallible – in the sense of being immune to IEM. But in situations where the speaker takes, so to speak, an external stance on herself, or represents herself as a subject (Recanati 2007, 2012), there is no such immunity; the speaker can mistakenly think that she is looking at her reflection in a mirror while, in fact, looking through a glass pane at, say, her twin sister or a lookalike. On such a scenario, (14) can be false – and when it is true, it is only contingently so.

---

5 See Huang, Srioutai and Gréaux, in press, and Jaszczolt and Witek, in press.

(14) I am wearing red lipstick.

As de Vignemont (2012: 224) aptly puts it, "[t]o be immune, my thought must be grounded in introspection", or in "a way of gaining information about one's mental states *from the inside*" – a definition she then defends against evidence from sufferers of somatoparaphrenia.⁶

Now, if IEM is a property triggered by or associated with particular linguistic items or constructions, then our argument from IEM fails. If, however, it is attached to situations or eventualities rather than linguistic units, we can use it as supporting evidence for the claim that the strength of self-referring, namely the potentiality of a referential error, is triggered outside of what the analysis of the language system can explain. Comparing (14) with (15) would suggest that our argument from IEM may be invalid: an observation about one's appearance will come, by default, with some degree of potential detachment, while an observation concerning one's pain will not.

(15) I have a sharp pain in my ankle.

Now, while (15) can be accepted as a case of IEM fairly incontrovertibly, the question arises as to whether IEM allows for mixed cases between immunity and its lack. Compare (14) with (14').

(14') I am wearing strawberry-flavoured lip gloss.

Imagine I am looking through a window pane, seeing my twin sister wearing a lip gloss, at the same time experiencing a sugary strawberry taste on my lips (which could equally be strawberry jam or ice cream). Here only a part of my self-ascription is immune to error – something that (14') does not reveal. We would have to break it up as in (14") to have the transparent linguistic, structure-driven representation of what is going on with IEM in this example. Only the part in italics exhibits immunity.

(14") *I am* wearing lip gloss and *experiencing strawberry taste on my lips* as a result.

Next, imagine that you see a lookalike through a window pane eating strawberries. At the same time you are putting red berries in your mouth without checking what fruit it is. If you are under the impression that you are looking at your-

---

6 Somatoparaphrenia is a type of delusion characterised by the patient's denial of ownership of his/her limb or side of his/her body.

self in the mirror, then, depending on the distinctness of taste, or level of focus or attention, your sense of taste could be confused as a result.

It appears that immunity is neither mirrored by structures nor invariably triggered by lexical items. Since it can be obscured by linguistic expressions, the answer to our question concerning the explanatory sufficiency of the language system has to be negative again.

Let us move from the IEM phenomenon to the knowledge attribution problem and the examples of the so-called low stakes/high stakes scenarios. Imagine that you invited guests for tea. You bought some cookies. One guest particularly likes cookies with nuts. He picks one cookie. You have made this type of cookies before, there are no nuts in the recipe you know, so you utter (16).

(16) This cookie has no nuts in it – I know, I made such cookies before.

On another scenario, one of your guests is allergic to nuts and you know he will suffer having eaten a cookie with nuts. He is searching for a cookie without nuts and picks one. *Ceteris paribus*, you utter (16). On the first scenario, the stakes were low: no danger would have occurred. On the second scenario, the stakes are high. But summing up, you would not want to say that in your self-attribution of knowledge you have been guilty of a contradiction, namely that you do and do not know (depending on the scenario) that there are no nuts in the cookies. Your self-ascription is situation-based. In the literature[7] the high and low stakes scenarios are used to discuss the question of truth-value attribution but here we are using them merely to show that the self-attribution of propositional attitudes also goes outside the language system and as such is heavily context-dependent. Discussions on the types of *ego* and types of self-consciousness so abundant in the philosophical and psychological literature further emphasise the importance of this context-relative or goal-relative perspective on the self.[8]

All in all, while thoughts about oneself are generically dubbed *de se*, there is variation on several dimensions in the functioning of various expressions in them that perform the role of first-person reference. And, what interests us here, pragmatics is indispensable for capturing this diversity. In representing the outcome of first-person reference in a cognitively plausible semantic theory, one must remember that this outcome is not easily reducible to the referent it picks out – but neither is it reducible to just one *de se* perspective. The provenance of self-reference is not uniform and neither is the meaning of self-reference itself.

---

[7] See DeRose 1992 and e.g. Stanley 2005; Blome-Tillmann 2013; Lutz 2014.
[8] For a recent account, see Peacocke 2014.

3 Implications for the semantics/pragmatics boundary

At this point it seems justified to assume that for the purpose of representing discourse meaning, reference belongs to thought and to cognitive mechanisms, not to language or a language system. The functional ambiguity of definite descriptions between referential and attributive, the ambiguity of indefinite descriptions between specific and nonspecific, the descriptive use of proper names, the descriptive or non-descriptive use of complex demonstratives, to name only a few core phenomena, provide more compelling arguments in favour of a functionalist or conceptual *qua* semantic analysis. There are no strictly referential terms in English and possibly there are none in natural language at large. To quote Hawthorne and Manley (2012: 245), "...reference turns out to be less prevalent than we thought – perhaps there are only a few expressions, like 'I', that are truly referential". As linguists, who are better informed than philosophers on this topic, have shown, and as we discussed in section 2, even this weak claim concerning *I* cannot be defended. Their proposal is worth quoting in full here:

> One pessimistic option is complete eliminativism about reference: just as no substance fits the role of "phlogiston" sufficiently well to count as its meaning, there is no semantic natural kind that will serve as the meaning of "reference".
>
> A more tolerant conclusion eschews any fundamental role for reference in compositional semantics, but brings it closer to the use of "refers" in ordinary language. On this approach, one thinks of reference as something that a speaker does on an occasion with a noun phrase, emphasizing that this can occur even if one's favored typology for formal semantics does not associate an object with that expression for the purpose of computing truth conditions compositionally.   Hawthorne and Manley (2012: 245–246)

While they propose to dissociate reference from compositional semantics, I would propose a different kind of dissociation. There is no doubt that truth conditions, or in general the idea of employing truth in the service of the explanation of meaning, provide the most powerful tool proposed to date for this purpose. This tool can be used for the purpose of analysing linguistic meaning associated with the devices of a natural language that produce sentences, that is the lexicon and the grammar, founded on a well acknowledged, theoretically well-defined, but in practice problematic principle of compositionality. But it can also be used for analysing a broader notion of discourse meaning that relies on aspects of meaning of very diversified provenance, where this notion of meaning is founded on a *not* well acknowledged, theoretically *not* well defined, but in practice absolutely necessary principle of compositionality. The first kind of semantics is of interest to those who research the properties and power of natural language and natural language systems. The other kind of semantics is of interest to those who research the principles underlying meaning in discourse and how it is composed in discourse interaction. By necessity, this kind of semantics will have to be radically contextualist in the sense of allowing for a substantial departure from standard meanings of words and standard meanings associated with linguistic structures. Radical contextualism that relaxes this dependence on logical forms offers here a way forward. It also offers a way of bringing together what is conceptually common to various cognitivist, functionalist, and contextualist approaches to meaning. The ways of expressing the self in discourse provide just one pertinent example in aid of the justification of such a discourse-oriented semantics.

One way of construing such a discourse semantics is to start with the Gricean picture of communication, acknowledge the central role of intentions, but question the centrality of the logical form. This is the approach initiated by post-Griceans in the 1970s in the Atlas-Kempson thesis (Atlas 1977, 1989; Kempson 1975, 1986) and taken up by Sperber and Wilson (1995 [1986]) and Carston (1988, 2002). But this centrality of logical form has to be weakened to a much greater extent than those postulating its enrichment or development suggest. Instead, discourse- and intention-based semantics that aims at representing the main intended message of the speaker's (and, if all goes well, also recovered by the addressee) ought to reject what Parikh (2010: 5) aptly calls an 'imbricated picture of meaning' (where different components of meaning 'overlap', so to speak, like roof tiles) and leap instead into speech acts that are primary reasons for uttering a sentence, no matter how remote their conceptual representation might be from the logical form of the uttered sentence. While Parikh's own Equilibrium Semantics executes this move by rejecting Gricean assumptions in the tradition of game theory (Lewis 1979), Default Semantics (Jaszczolt 2005, 2010, 2016) executes this move closer to home, in the spirit of Gricean principles of rational conversational cooperation, assuming that compositionality ought to be predicated about, and as a result sought on, the level of conceptual structures representing speech acts rather than on the level of natural language sentences or their enriched/modulated derivatives. What these views have in common is making full use of the fact that extra-linguistic sources of information contribute substantial chunks and aspects of information at every stage of the derivation of meaning. In identifying the sources of these meanings, interlocutors are driven by salience: "Human beings are usually quite adept at homing in on the right part of a shared scene or on what situation has been or is being described" (Parikh 2010: 278).

In Default Semantics, it is acknowledged that words and utterances often come with salient, automatically retrieved interpretations. The explanation is founded on the fact that language is a socio-cultural phenomenon, as well as a cognitive phenomenon. The use of language (i) leads to standards and conventions for a language community that produce one kind of salience (such as a shortcut in the processing of expressions that pertain to well-entrenched cultural and social common ground), and (ii) relies on properties of the mental states underlying the processed utterances that lead to a different kind of salience (such as a shortcut in processing potentially ambiguous expressions, assigning to them by default the reading with greater informativeness and stronger intentionality).[9] Adopting a contextualist approach to meaning will thus have to acknowledge, in addition to inference, these two routes based on salience – a view that I call Salience-Based Contextualism.[10]

All in all, when one carefully attends to the facts that (i) logical form is more peripheral to the intended meaning than Grice allowed; (ii) automatic, default recognition of meaning in context is as important as intention recovery; and in addition when one acknowledges that (iii) not all communication relies on truthfulness, informativeness, clarity, and so forth (Asher and Lascarides 2013) and that (iv) not all communication is equally other-oriented in making choices of some expressions over others (Kecskés and Zhang 2009), reconstructing speaker meaning is still best seen as an intention-driven enterprise – a Gricean view through and through.

Returning to the question of the provenance of self-reference, on this picture, supported with types of evidence discussed in section 2, reference is indeed conveyed in a process of establishing what was intended, à la Grice, but it would be wrong to represent it through what Parikh calls a 'linear pipeline view of meaning' (2010: 232), à la most post-Griceans; addressees do not shift from the meaning of a common noun to a presumed meaning of an intended 'functional' indexical, and neither do they shift from the current-content-based self-reference in Amharic when it becomes evident that this would lead to nonsense or a contradiction. Instead, they take one or the other perspective on reference. They do so either automatically or as a result of inference and both of these routes correspond to processes identified in Default Semantics. This perspective is informed by a lot more than the choice of a (potentially) referring expression, and in turn arguably contributes a lot more to the semantic representation than standard truth-conditional semantics that respects the indexical/nonindexical distinction and the associated direct reference view would allow.

---

9 The first are called in Default Semantics socio-cultural and world-knowledge defaults (SCWD) and the latter cognitive defaults (CD). See Jaszczolt 2005 for examples.
10 See Jaszczolt (2016: 50). See also Giora 2003, 2012 on Graded Salience Hypothesis and Giora, Givoni, and Fein 2015 on salience and defaultness.

To repeat, Parikh's semantic equilibrium, with its emphasis on derivation, is an alternative, non-Gricean route to the primary speech act. Yet another non-Gricean way would be to turn to phenomenology and, for example, propose that "[w]hat a speaker *means* is a folk-semantic notion" (Azzouni 2013: 352) – understood by interactants not in a Gricean way but directly as 's/he means that *p*'. These accounts depart from Grice not only on the dimension of the construction of the unit of analysis but also with respect to the hypotheses concerning the derivation process. The latter, however, is beyond our concerns here and, arguably, beyond the concerns of semantic theory *tout court*.

4 Conclusion

I have begun this paper by pointing out a well-known fact that self-reference in discourse can be attained by using a variety of tools, but have emphasised that the referential effect of using these tools does not undergo an adequate explanation when we limit the analysis to the lexical and grammatical properties of these devices alone. Imposters do not successfully yield to a syntactic view when our aim is explanatory adequacy, neither do generic *one*, *you*, or uncontrolled PRO allow for a fixed scale of generalization or detachment. Further, self-reference that is shifted from the current context for example in Amharic, and in a wide range of languages that behave in a similar manner, calls for entirely extralinguistic insights into focus and perspective. The first-person pronoun *I* in English allows for non-referential uses, and its referential uses can point to different strengths and aspects of *de se* thought, as IEM and high/low stakes scenarios demonstrate. All these, and other, factors point in the direction of a pragmatics-rich, contextualist account of reference and in the direction of conceptual or functionalist approach to semantic representations. While, as I pointed out, the Gricean perspective is not the only one that one could pursue with this evidence in mind, I argued here that when suitably divorced from the prejudice against abandoning the logical form as the backbone of the analysed material, and when it suitably attends to the role of salience and automatic interpretations, a Gricean account can be made to work. In the domain of self-reference, it points in the direction of rethinking the indexical/nonindexical distinction as a function-based rather than category-based dichotomy. It also allows for emphasising the importance of information other than providing the referent for the utterance meaning. Giving due priority to these facts allows us to opt for a functionalist, conceptual perspective on semantic representation.

Acknowledgement: Research leading to this paper was supported by The Leverhulme Trust grant *Expressing the Self: Cultural Diversity and Cognitive Universals* (Grant ID/Ref: RPG-2014-017) http://www.mml.cam.ac.uk/expressing-the-self.

References

Arundale, Robert. 1999. An alternative model and ideology of communication for an alternative to politeness theory. *Pragmatics* 9. 119–153.
Arundale, Robert. 2010. Constituting face in conversation: Face, facework, and interactional achievement. *Journal of Pragmatics* 42. 2078–2105.
Asher, Nicholas and Alex Lascarides. 2013. Strategic conversation. *Semantics and Pragmatics* 6. 1–62.
Atlas, Jay David. 1977. Negation, ambiguity, and presupposition. *Linguistics and Philosophy* 1. 321–336.
Atlas, Jay David. 1989. *Philosophy without ambiguity: A logico-linguistic essay*. Oxford: Clarendon Press.
Azzouni, Jody. 2013. *Semantic perception: How the illusion of a common language arises and persists*. Oxford: Oxford University Press.
Blome-Tillmann, Michael. 2013. Knowledge and implicatures. *Synthese* 190. 4293–4319.
Cappelen, Herman & Josh Dever. 2013. *The inessential indexical: On the philosophical insignificance of perspective and the first person*. Oxford: Oxford University Press.
Cappelen, Herman & Josh Dever. 2016. *Context and communication*. Oxford: Oxford University Press.
Carston, Robyn. 1988. Implicature, explicature, and truth-theoretic semantics. In Ruth M. Kempson (ed.), *Mental representations: The interface between language and reality*, 155–181. Cambridge: Cambridge University Press.
Carston, Robyn. 2002. *Thoughts and utterances: The pragmatics of explicit communication*. Oxford: Blackwell.
Collins, Chris & Paul Martin Postal. 2012. *Imposters: A study of pronominal agreement*. Cambridge, MA: MIT Press.
DeRose, Keith. 1992. Contextualism and knowledge attributions. *Philosophy and Phenomenological Research* 52. 913–929.
Giora, Rachel. 2003. *On Our Mind: Salience, Context, and Figurative Language*. Oxford: Oxford University Press.
Giora, Rachel. 2012. The psychology of utterance processing: Context vs salience. In Keith Allan & Kasia M. Jaszczolt (eds.), *The Cambridge handbook of pragmatics*, 151–167. Cambridge: Cambridge University Press.
Giora, Rachel, Shir Givoni & Ofer Fein. 2015. Defaultness reigns: The case of sarcasm. *Metaphor and Symbol* 30. 290–313.
Haugh, Michael. 2008. The place of intention in the interactional achievement of implicature. In István Kecskés & Jacob Mey (eds.), *Intention, common ground and the egocentric speaker-hearer*, 45–85. Berlin & New York: Mouton de Gruyter.
Haugh, Michael. 2010. Co-constructing what is said in interaction. In Eniko Németh & Károly Bibok (eds.), *The role of data at the semantics/pragmatics interface*, 349–380. Berlin & New York: De Gruyter Mouton.

Haugh, Michael. 2012. Conversational interaction. In Keith Allan & Kasia M. Jaszczolt (eds.), *The Cambridge handbook of pragmatics*, 251–273. Cambridge: Cambridge University Press.

Haugh, Michael and Kasia M. Jaszczolt. 2012. Speaker intentions and intentionality. In Keith Allan & K. M. Jaszczolt (eds.), *The Cambridge handbook of pragmatics*, 87–112. Cambridge: Cambridge University Press.

Hawthorne, John & David Manley. 2012. *The reference book*. Oxford: Oxford University Press.

Heine, Bernd & Kyung-An Song. 2011. On the grammaticalisation of personal pronouns. *Journal of Linguistics* 47. 587–630.

Huang, Minyao, Jiranthara Srioutai & Mélanie Gréaux. In press. Charting the speaker-relatedness of impersonal pronouns: Contrastive evidence from English, French and Thai. In Minyao Huang & Kasia M. Jaszczolt (eds.), *Expressing the self: Cultural diversity and cognitive universals*. Oxford: Oxford University Press.

Jaszczolt, Kasia M. 2005a. *Default semantics: Foundations of a compositional theory of acts of communication*. Oxford: Oxford University Press.

Jaszczolt, Kasia M. 2010. Default Semantics. In Bernd Heine & Heiko Narrog (eds.), *The Oxford handbook of linguistic analysis*, 215–246. Oxford: Oxford University Press.

Jaszczolt, Kasia M. 2013a. First-person reference in discourse: Aims and strategies'. *Journal of Pragmatics* 48. 57–70.

Jaszczolt, Kasia M. 2013b. Contextualism and minimalism on *de se* belief ascription. In Neil Feit & Alessandro Capone (eds.), *Attitudes de se: Linguistics, epistemology, metaphysics*, 69–103. Stanford: CSLI Publications.

Jaszczolt, Kasia M. 2016. *Meaning in linguistic interaction: Semantics, metasemantics, philosophy of language*. Oxford: Oxford University Press.

Jaszczolt, Kasia. M. In press. Pragmatic indexicals. In Minyao Huang & Kasia M. Jaszczolt (eds.), *Expressing the self: Cultural diversity and cognitive universals*. Oxford: Oxford University Press.

Jaszczolt, Kasia M. & Minyao Huang. In press. Monsters and *I*: The case of mixed quotation. In Paul Saka and Michael Johnson (eds.), *Semantic and pragmatic aspects of quotation*. Dordrecht: Springer.

Jaszczolt, Kasia M. & Maciej Witek. In press. Expressing the self: From types of *de se* to speech-act types. In Minyao Huang & Kasia M. Jaszczolt (eds.), *Expressing the self: Cultural diversity and cognitive universals*. Oxford: Oxford University Press.

Kaplan, David. 1989. Demonstratives: An essay on the semantics, logic, metaphysics, and epistemology of demonstratives and other indexicals. In Joseph Almog, John Perry & Howard Wettstein (eds.), *Themes from Kaplan*, 481–563. New York: Oxford University Press.

Kecskés, István. 2000. A cognitive-pragmatic approach to situation-bound utterances. *Journal of Pragmatics* 32. 605–625.

Kecskés, István. 2008. Dueling context: A dynamic model of meaning. *Journal of Pragmatics* 40. 385–406.

Kecskés, István 2010. The paradox of communication: Socio-cognitive approach to pragmatics. *Pragmatics and Society* 1. 50–73.

Kecskés, István. 2014. *Intercultural pragmatics*. Oxford: Oxford University Press.

Kecskés, István and Fenghui Zhang. 2009. Activating, seeking, and creating common ground. *Pragmatics and Cognition* 17. 331–355.

Kempson, Ruth. 1975. *Presupposition and the delimitation of semantics*. Cambridge: Cambridge University Press.
Kempson, Ruth. 1986. Ambiguity and the semantics-pragmatics distinction. In Charles Travis (ed.), *Meaning and interpretation*, 77–103. Oxford: B. Blackwell.
Kratzer, Angelika. 2009. Making a pronoun: Fake indexicals as windows into the properties of pronouns. *Linguistic Inquiry* 40. 187–237.
Leslau, Wolf. 1995. *Reference grammar of Amharic*. Wiesbaden: Harrassowitz.
Lewis, David. 1979. Scorekeeping in a language game. *Journal of Philosophical Logic* 8. 339–359.
Lutz, Matt. 2014. The pragmatics of pragmatic encroachment. *Synthese* 191. 1717–1740.
Moltmann, Friederike. 2006. Generic one, arbitrary PRO, and the first person. *Natural Language Semantics* 14. 257–281.
Moltmann, Friederike. 2010. Generalizing detached self-reference and the semantics of generic *one*. *Mind and Language* 25. 440–473.
Mount, Allyson. 2015. Character, impropriety, and success: A unified account of indexicals. *Mind and Language* 30. 1–21.
Parikh, Prashant. 2010. *Language and equilibrium*. Cambridge, MA: MIT Press.
Peacocke, Christopher. 2014. *The mirror of the world: Subjects, consciousness, and self-consciousness*. Oxford: Oxford University Press.
Predelli, Stefano. 2014. Kaplan's three monsters. *Analysis* 74. 389–393.
Prosser, Simon & François Recanati (eds.). 2012. *Immunity to error through misidentification: New essays*. Cambridge: Cambridge University Press.
Recanati, François. 2007. *Perspectival thought: A plea for (moderate) relativism*. Oxford: Oxford University Press.
Recanati, François. 2012. Immunity to error through misidentification: What it is and where it comes from. In Simon Prosser & François Recanati (eds.), *Immunity to error through misidentification: New essays*, 180–201. Cambridge: Cambridge University Press.
Roberts, Craige. 2014. Indexicality: *De se* semantics and pragmatics. Ms, Ohio State University.
de Schepper, Kees. 2015. Separating interlocutor phenomena from grammatical person. *Journal of Pragmatics* 88. 137–147.
Schlenker, P. 2003. A plea for monsters. *Linguistics and Philosophy* 26. 29–120.
Shoemaker, Sydney. 1968. Self-reference and self-awareness. *Journal of Philosophy* 65. 555–567.
Sperber, Dan & Deidre Wilson. 1986. *Relevance: Communication and Cognition*. Oxford: Blackwell. Reprinted in 1995. Second edition.
Stanley, Jason. 2005. *Knowledge and practical interests*. Oxford: Oxford University Press.
de Vignemont, Frédérique. 2012. Bodily immunity to error. In Simon Prosser & François Recanati (eds.), *Immunity to error through misidentification: New essays*, 224–246. Cambridge: Cambridge University Press.

Wayne A. Davis
11 Transparent reports as free-form idioms

1 Introduction

Propositional attitude reports with that-clauses have transparent as well as opaque interpretations. Such reports are semantically ambiguous, I argue, but the ambiguity is neither lexical nor syntactic. The different interpretations are not due to different syntactic structures or any ambiguity in verbs like *believe*. This is possible, I argue, because transparent reports differ from opaque reports in being *idioms*: noncompositional compounds. Unlike *kick the bucket* and other prototypical idioms, however, transparent reports are not defined by a fixed form. Idioms display a wide range of compositionality and therefore productivity. Some are completely noncompositional, like *by and large*. Others have one or two compositional elements, like *cook Sam's goose* and *What is this fly doing in my soup?* I have argued that irregular or "metalinguistic" negations are even more compositional idioms, with few lexical or syntactic constraints beyond the negative particle. They are "free-form" idioms: highly, but not completely, compositional and productive. Like irregular negations, transparent reports have many "exceptional" properties; for example, *S believes that p* and *S does not believe that p* may both be true. Because *S does not believe that p* on its transparent interpretation is noncompositional, it is an irregular negation. It differs from the other irregular negations in that its root is also idiomatic, but the idiomaticity of the negation is not simply that of its root.

In sections 2–5, I summarize my prior work on irregular negatives, word and sentence meaning, compositionality, and idioms, showing what free-form idioms are, and illustrating their wide range. In section 6, I distinguish between the transparent and opaque interpretation of propositional attitude and speech act reports, making the case that, like irregular negatives, such reports have a semantic ambiguity that is not due to any lexical or syntactic ambiguity, and that they are free-form idioms.[1]

---

[1] This paper began as a plenary lecture at INPRA 6 in Split, Croatia, June 10, 2016, and is drawn from Davis 1998, 2003, 2005, 2016a, 2016b. I thank Larry Horn and Mitch Green for saving me from a number of errors and unclarities.

2 Regular vs irregular negatives

The term 'negation' can denote either interpreted sentences, or the propositions they express. I will use it to denote a sentence containing the word *not* or an equivalent that is used to express the negation of a proposition. The same sequence of words may be a negation on one interpretation and something else on another. An example is *John did not pass the exam because he studied all night*. On one interpretation (*The reason John failed to pass was that he studied all night*), it is an explanation of a negation. On another interpretation (*It is not the case that the reason John passed was that he studied all night*), it is the negation of an explanation.

The sentence that results from removing the negative morpheme will be called the *root* of the negation. I describe a negation as *logically regular* if it expresses the negation of the proposition expressed by its root. A negation is *logically irregular* if it expresses the negation of some other proposition. On its most natural interpretation, *The sky is not blue* is a regular negation. It expresses the negation of the proposition expressed by *The sky is blue*. Consequently, *The sky is not blue* conforms to the standard logical rules for sentences expressing the negation of a proposition, including truth-value reversal: *The sky is not blue* is true iff its root is false, and false iff its root is true. The two sentences, and the propositions they express, are *contradictory*. I use 'Not-p' as a place-holder for any negative sentence, and '–p' as in logic for a regular negation.

Table 1 presents six examples representing large and distinct classes of sentences that have both a regular and an irregular interpretation. (1) is an example:

(1) The sun is not larger than some planets.
Regular: –(The sun is larger than some planets).[2]
Irregular: –(The sun is larger than just some planets).

On the regular interpretation, (1) is true only if the sun is not larger than *any* planets. On the irregular interpretation, it may be true if the sun is larger than some but not all planets. The irregular interpretation would be the most natural interpretation of Bob's response in (2):

(2) Alan: The sun is larger than some planets.
Bob: The sun is not larger than *some* planets, it is larger than *all* planets.

---

[2] I am taking the 'some' in (1) to have a narrow scope. (1) has a wide-scope interpretation on which it means "Some planets are such that –(The sun is larger than them)". On this interpretation, (1) is syntactically regular but not a negation. It expresses an existential proposition rather than the negation of a proposition.

On its regular interpretation, Bob's response is contradictory. On the more charitable irregular interpretation, both *The sun is not larger than some planets* and its root *The sun is larger than some planets* are true. The logically irregular interpretation is also *syntactically* irregular: it is not the interpretation predictable from the syntactic structure of (1) and its syntax alone. It is not *compositional*.

Table 1. Logically and Syntactically Irregular Negations

Denial Type	Sentence	Interpretation
Limiting-Implicature	The sun is not larger than *some* planets	The sun is not larger than just some planets
Ignorance-Implicature	The water is not *at most* warm	The water is known (not) to be less than warm
Strengthening-Implicature	Mary did not meet *a man* at the bar	Mary did not meet an unrelated man at the bar
Metalinguistic-Implicature	That's not a *tomäto*	That's not properly called a *tomäto*
Evaluative-Implicature	Midori's solo wasn't somewhat flawed.	It isn't bad that Midori's solo was somewhat flawed.
Presupposition-Canceling	Vulcan is *not* hot	*Vulcan is hot* is not true.

Horn (1989: 362–364, 370–375) discussed most of the types displayed in Table 1, and called them "metalinguistic negations". This term is appropriate for the *tomäto/tomāto* example. If Alan says "That is a tomäto," and Bob responds "That's not a *tomäto*, it's a *tomäto*," Bob is saying that Alan mispronounced the word *tomato*. But none of the other examples are statements about language. (1) is about the sun and its relationships to the planets. In (2), Bob is responding to something Alan said, but this is neither essential to nor distinctive of the irregular interpretation of the negation.

I have argued that what all the irregular negations in Table 1 have in common is that *they deny an implicature of their root*. (1) is analyzed in (3):

(3) The sun is not larger than some planets.
    Root: The sun is larger than some planets.
    Implicature of Root: The sun is larger than just some planets.
    Root-Implicature Denial: The sun is not larger than just some planets.

The implicature denied in this case is commonly called a *scalar* or *quantity* implicature. To avoid various theoretical associations, I call it a *limiting* implicature. So on the irregular interpretation given, (1) is a limiting-implicature denial. It is because limiting-implicature denials deny an implicature of their root rather than the proposition expressed by their root that they are logically and syntactically irregular.

The six different types of irregular negation presented in Table 1 deny different root implicatures. *That is not a tomäto* denies a metalinguistic implicature of its root, namely, that *tomato* is properly pronounced *tomäto*. We commonly pronounce one word (or other syntactic unit) in a sentence in a particular way to implicate that it is a proper way to pronounce it. We express the belief, but do not say, that the pronunciation is proper. We imply that it is proper by the way we say what we do. So this is similar to a Gricean (1989: 27) Manner implicature.

Even though the six interpretations given are logically and syntactically irregular, they are conventional. It is conventional to use a sentence containing *not* to deny a limiting, ignorance, strengthening, metalinguistic, evaluative, or semantic implicature of its root. By *convention* here I mean "customary practice" – the sense in which the meanings of words are conventional. Conventions in this sense are common actions with two key features: (i) they perpetuate themselves for a number of reasons, including precedent-following, social acceptance, normative force, individual habit and association, traditional transmission from one generation to another, and success in achieving common goals; (ii) they are arbitrary to some extent, meaning that there are other actions that could achieve the same goals and perpetuate themselves in the same ways. In the case of linguistic conventions, the most important goal is communication.

One fact illustrating the arbitrariness of implicature-denial conventions is that not all root implicatures can be denied using a negation.[3] Contrast: (4) and (5):

(4) Ned did not *make* the car stop. (✓ He stopped it in the usual way.)
Root: Ned did make the car stop.
Root Implicature (strengthening): Ned made the car stop in an unusual way.
Root-Implicature Denial: Ned did not make the car stop in an unusual way.

(5) Ned did not *stop* the car. (✗ He stopped it in an unusual way.)
Root: Ned did stop the car.
Root Implicature (strengthening): Ned stopped the car in the usual way.
Root-Implicature Denial: Ned did not stop the car in the usual way.

(4) can be used to deny the implicature that Ned stopped the car in an unusual way, but (5) cannot be used to deny that Ned stopped the car in the usual way.

---

[3] This was observed by Horn (1989: sections 3.3.1 and 6.3.2), although it conflicts with his thesis that metalinguistic negation could be used to reject a previous utterance on any grounds whatsoever (Horn 1989: 363). See also Geurts (1998: 281–283); Huang (2014: 61–62).

Hence (4) could consistently be followed by the sequent in parentheses, but not (5).

There are in English at least three other irregular negatives, illustrated in Table 2, but these are significantly different.[4]

Table 2. Other Syntactically Irregular Negatives

Type	Negative	Irregular Interpretation
NR Contrary	John does not believe there is a god.	John disbelieves there is a god
Litotes Contrary	It is not good the ice caps are melting.	It is bad that the ice caps are melting.
NL Contradictory	Every cat is not black.	Not every cat is black.

The interpretations in Table 2 are all syntactically irregular. For example, on its compositional interpretation, *John does not believe there is a god* expresses the negation of the proposition that John does believe there is a god, and so is true iff John fails to believe there is a god. But the sentence has another conventional interpretation on which it means the stronger proposition that John *disbelieves* there is a god, which entails that he believes there is not a god. On this interpretation, the sentence expresses a *contrary* of the proposition expressed by its root, not the negation. Moreover, it does not express the negation of *any* proposition. It is an irregular *negative*, but not an irregular *negation*. I call it the "NR contrary" interpretation, after "neg-raising", but without implying that the generative grammar account is correct. Litotes is a conventional figure of speech, and similarly involves expressing a contrary of its root rather than its negation.

Every cat is not black illustrates a different type of irregularity. On its compositional interpretation, the sentence expresses a proposition that is true iff every cat is non-black. So it expresses the Aristotelian **E** contrary of its **A** root. It is not the negation of any proposition.[5] But the sentence has another conventional interpretation on which it means *Not every cat is black*, and thus expresses the negation and contradictory of its root. So on its *syntactically irregular* interpretation, it is a *logically regular negation*. I call this the "NL contradictory" interpretation, after "neg-lowering".

---

4 See Horn 1989: 228, 303–304, 308–330, 355–360, 494; 2015.
5 "Every cat is non-black" is *equivalent* to the negation of "Some cat is black," but not *identical*. It is a universal generalization, not a negation.

These three negatives are as conventional as those in Table 1. The irregular contraries are also used to deny implicatures of their roots, but not the irregular contradictories, which deny the roots themselves.

I said above that the syntactically irregular interpretations are not compositional, meaning that they are not completely compositional. A completely compositional compound means what it does solely because of its syntactic structure and the meanings of its components. The compound gets its meaning from the meanings of its components and its syntax alone. Consequently, replacing a constituent with another term (with no change in syntax) will change the meaning if and only if the new term has a different meaning, and any change in the meaning of the compound will reflect the difference in meaning of the terms. The irregular interpretations of the nine sentences in Tables 1 and 2 do not have this property. Consider for example (6)(a).

(6) a. Mary did not meet a man at the bar
 b. Mary did not meet an adult male human at the bar.
 c. Mary did not meet a human at the bar.
 d. A man was not met by Mary at the bar.

(6)(a) has an interpretation on which it denies a strengthening implicature of its root and means that Mary did not meet an *unrelated* man at the bar. (6)(b) results from (6)(a) by replacing the word *man* with the synonymous phrase *adult male human*. Even though the meanings of their components and their syntax are the same, (6)(b) does not have the irregular interpretation of (6)(a). Similarly, replacing *man* by a term with a more general meaning as in (6)(c) changes the regular meaning predictably, but completely eliminates the irregular meaning. Furthermore, syntactic transformations that do not affect the regular meaning may eliminate the irregular meaning, as (6)(d) illustrates. With regard to the presupposition-canceling negation in Table 1, the syntactic and lexical differences between *Vulcan is not hot* and *Vulcan is non-hot* cancel out, resulting in their regular interpretations being equivalent. *Vulcan is non-hot* does not have the presupposition-canceling interpretation, however. And it is especially clear that replacing *tomāto* with the synonym *tomāto* changes the metalinguistic-implicature denial interpretation completely.

3 Semantic vs pragmatic ambiguity

One of the principal issues concerning irregular negatives is whether they are semantically or pragmatically ambiguous. On my account of linguistic meaning (section 5), that depends on whether the irregular interpretation is meant directly or indirectly. As we have noted, sentences like *The sun is larger than some planets* are conventionally used with a limiting implicature, that the sun is not larger than *just* some planets. This is something speakers mean by uttering the sentence, but not something the sentence means. Why not? Because it is meant indirectly, by meaning something else. Speakers who utter *The sun is larger than some planets* mean that the sun is not larger than just some planets *by saying* that the sun is larger than some planets. They express the former thought by expressing the latter.

In two of the nine cases illustrated in Tables 1 and 2, the irregular interpretations have the indirection characteristic of implicature. The first is *litotes*. In this familiar figure of speech, what we say is weaker than what we mean. We are engaging in a form of understatement. Suppose S used litotes in (7); then (a)–(c) are true.

(7) S: It is not good that the ice caps are melting.
    a. S expressed the thought and said that it fails to be good that the ice caps are melting.
    b. S thereby meant that it is bad that the ice caps are melting.
    c. S did not say that it is bad that the ice caps are melting.

Note that if S really believed that it was neither good nor bad, then S was misleading his audience but not lying. Because of the indirection, what S meant by uttering the sentence is something S implicated, but not something S said or something the sentence means.

The second irregular negation with the indirection characteristic of implicature is evaluative-implicature denial. While not a familiar figure of speech, it is also a case in which what we mean is not what we say. The meaning is modeled on that of the idiom, *The glass is not half empty, it is half full*. If S's negation in (8) is an evaluative-implicature denial, as indicated by the sequent, then (a)–(c) are true.

(8) S: Midori's solo was not somewhat flawed. It was nearly perfect.
    a. S expressed the thought and said that Midori's solo failed to be somewhat flawed.
    b. S thereby meant that it wasn't bad that her solo was somewhat flawed.
    c. S did not say that it wasn't bad that her solo was somewhat flawed.

In (8), if S did think it bad that Midori's solo was a bit flawed, he was misleading his audience but not lying.[6] Because of the indirection, what S meant by uttering the

---

[6] (8) differs from (7) in that S did not mean what he said. As a result, S did not *assert* that Midori's solo was not somewhat flawed.

sentence is something implicated, not meant. Since the irregular interpretations of negative sentences used as litotes or evaluative-implicature denials are meant indirectly, the sentences are pragmatically rather than semantically ambiguous.

In the other cases, there is no indirection. Consider NR contraries, represented by (9), in which S utters 'John does not believe there is a god' and (a) and (b) are true:

(9) S: John does not believe there is a god.
    a. S meant that John disbelieves that there is a god.
    b. S did not meant that by meaning that Jack lacks the belief that there is a god.

NR contraries differ markedly from litotes in not being cases of understatement. In (9), S would be lying if he thought John had no opinion on the matter. Consider also limiting-implicature denials, represented by (10):

(10) S: The sun is not larger than some planets.
    a. S meant that the sun is not larger than just some planets.
    b. S did not mean that by meaning that the sun is not larger than any planets.

It would have been very natural for S to have followed his utterance in (10) by "It is larger than all planets". But this sequent would not have been natural, indeed it would have resulted in contradiction, if S had said or expressed the thought that the sun was not larger than any planets. Moreover, S would have been lying if he said and meant that the sun was not larger than any planets. Since the NR contrary and strengthening-implicature denial interpretations are both conventional and direct, they are meanings of the negative sentences. So these sentences are semantically rather than pragmatically ambiguous.

A puzzle now arises. *Why* are the sentences S uttered in (9) and (10) ambiguous? There is no relevant *lexical* ambiguity. The word *not* has no ambiguity that would account for the ambiguity of these sentences, or any of the others in Tables 1 and 2. Moreover, there is no relevant *syntactic* ambiguity. In this respect, the sentences are different from *John did not pass the exam because he studied all night*, in which *not* could have within its scope either *pass the exam* or *pass the exam because he studied all night*. How can the sentences be semantically ambiguous if there is no relevant lexical or syntactic ambiguity?

Another puzzle. If the sentences S uttered are semantically ambiguous, so that S meant by uttering them something the sentences mean, then (9)(c) and (10)(c) should also be true. But (9)(d) and (10)(d) are clearly not true.

(9) c. S said that John disbelieves that there is a god.
    d. S did not say literally that John disbelieves there is a god.

(10) c. S said that the sun is not larger than just some planets.
    d. S did not say literally that the sun is not larger than just some planets.

If S did not literally say these things, does that not mean that (9)(c) and (10)(c) are not literally true?

4 Idioms

Are there any known semantic ambiguities that do not arise from lexical or syntactic ambiguity? Indeed there are many: *idioms*. Consider a prototypical case:

(11) kick the bucket.

(11) has two meanings in English. On its regular, compositional meaning, it means to do something to a particular bucket, namely, kick it. But it also has the idiomatic meaning "die". The ambiguity is not due to any ambiguity in *kick*, *the*, or *bucket* or their syntactic relations. Because of this, the idiomatic meaning is *noncompositional*. It cannot be predicted from the meanings of the component words and the syntactic structure of the phrase alone.

Idioms also show that *say literally* is stronger than *say*. For when S utters (12) with its idiomatic meaning, (b) is true but (c) is false.

(12) S: Ted kicked the bucket.
    a. S meant that Ted died.
    b. S said that Ted died.
    c. S said literally that Ted died.

(12)(b) is true when *said* has its literal meaning. So (b) is literally true even though (c) is false. To say something literally is not just to literally say it. To say p literally is to say p in a particular way: by using a sentence for which "p" is its literal or compositional meaning.[7] The way S said that Ted died was by using an idiom.

An idiom is a syntactically structured expression whose meaning is not predictable from the meanings of its components and its syntax alone, that is, whose meaning is non-compositional. So the evidence presented about (9), (10),

---

[7] Things are more complex when 'p' contains indexicals. See Davis 2016b: section 9.

and the other direct irregular negatives supports the conclusion that they are idioms. They are non-compositional to some extent, they have an ambiguity that is not due to lexical or syntactic ambiguity, and they are used to say things in a non-literal way. The literal meanings of all the negatives in Tables 1 and 2 are their regular meanings.

While irregular negatives are *partially non*-compositional, they are nonetheless *highly* compositional. The results of replacing words with synonyms sometimes eliminates the irregular meaning, as illustrated by (6)(a) and (b). But replacement of any other word in (6)(a) with a synonym leaves the irregular meaning intact, as illustrated by (13)(a) and (b):

(13)   Mary did not meet a man at the bar.
      a. Mary Kennedy did not meet a man at the bar.
      b. Mary was not in the company of a man at the bar.
      c. Jane did not meet a man at the diner.
      d. It is not the case that at the bar Mary met a man.

And while replacing some words with non-synonyms eliminates the irregular meaning entirely, as (6)(c) illustrates, replacing other words with non-synonyms changes the irregular meaning predicably, as (13)(c) illustrates. Finally, while syntactic alteration sometimes eliminates the irregular interpretation as (6)(d) illustrates, other syntactic alterations have no effect on the irregular interpretation, as (13)(d) illustrates.

The facts illustrated by (13) raise another question: How can irregular negations be idioms if they are so highly compositional? The answer lies in recognizing that while *kick the bucket* may be the prototypical idiom, it differs markedly from many other idioms. Being an idiom requires *not being completely compositional* rather than *being completely noncompositional*. Relatively few idioms are completely noncompositional.[8] I call them *fixed-form* idioms of *Type I*, illustrated by (14):

(14)   **Fixed-Form Idioms, Type I**.
      a. *by dint of*
      b. *by and large*
      c. *over the hill*

Type I idioms are completely fixed. Any substitution eliminates the idiomatic meaning, as does any syntactic transformation. *Large and by* has no meaning,

---

8 See Fraser 1970: 23; Wood 1986; Nunberg, Sag, and Wasow 1994: section 3.1; Kay and Fillmore 1999; Espinal and Mateu 2010; Kay and Michaelis 2012: 2273, 2275–2278.

for example, even though conjunctions are regularly commutative. *Through dint of* similarly has no meaning even though *through* is synonymous with *by*. Type II idioms are those like *under the radar*, whose form is fixed except for having the variant *below the radar*.

Type III idioms allow verb inflection as well as some variants, as illustrated in (15):

(15) **Fixed-Form Idioms, Type III.**
    a. *kick**s** the bucket*
    b. *cut**s** and run**s***
    c. *hit**s** the hay/sack*

I bolded the 's' in (15) to indicate that the inflection can vary. Thus *kicked the bucket* and *kick the bucket* stand in the regular semantic relation to *kicks the bucket*. The '/' indicates that *hits the sack* is a variant with the same idiomatic meaning as *hits the hay*.

Type IV idioms not only allow inflectional variation and some variants, they also have a "compositional variable": replacing one term with another in that position changes the idiomatic meaning predictably. Thus in (16)(a), *cut his teeth on* is related semantically to *cut one's teeth on* as *his* is related semantically to *one's*. *One's* can be replaced by any possessive pronoun, but not by other possessive nouns. Even when the subject is *John*, *cut John's teeth on* does not have the idiomatic meaning.

(16) **Fixed-Form Idioms, Type IV.**
    a. *cut one's teeth on*
    b. *cook someone's goose*
    c. *kick someone's butt/ass*

(16)(b) differs from (a) in that *someone's* can be replaced by any possessive noun; *cook John's goose* does have the idiomatic meaning. (16)(b) differs further in the syntactic transformations it allows. *It was John's goose that was cooked* is predictably related to *cook John's goose*, but *It was John's teeth that were cut on Mt Baldy* lacks the idiomatic meaning of *John's teeth were cut on Mt. Baldy*. Note how arbitrary it is what variation is possible.

Type V idioms have *two* compositional variables.

(17) **Fixed-Form Idioms, Type V.**
    a. *play one's heart out*
    b. *shove/ram something down someone's throat*

    c. *Watch someone win.*[9]
    d. *What is someone doing there?*

Someone in (17)(c) can be replaced by *him*, *Trump*, or *the president*, or *win* can be replaced by *lose*, *strike out*, or *die*, and the meaning of the idiom will change predictably. Like irregular negatives, (17)(c) and (d) are full sentences.

    Finally, *free-form* idioms have only a few fixed features.[10] They have a recognizable but irregular form.

(18) **Free-Form Idioms.**
    a. *The more Bill drinks, the less he remembers.*
    b. *Bush is more dumb than mendacious.*
    c. *The sun is not larger than some planets.*
    d. *That's not a tomäto.*
    e. *John does not believe there is a god.*
    f. *Every cat is not black.*

The common form of (18)(c), representing limiting-implicature denials, is fairly simple to identify: the sentence must contain *not* with its English meaning along with a term that can be modified by *just*, and its root must have a limiting implicature. Otherwise the sentence can be varied, and the result will have the predictable meaning; consider *Some mountains in North America are not smaller than Mt. Everest* (all are) and *Einstein was not smart* (he was a genius).

5 Foundations of semantics and pragmatics

In section 3, I relied on my account of what it is for expressions in a natural language to have a meaning or an implicature to classify the irregular interpretations of litotes contraries and evaluative-implicature denials as implicatures, and those of the other seven irregular negatives in Tables 1 and 2 as meanings. On my view (Davis 2003, 2005), meaning is the expression of ideas, for both speakers and expressions. Ideas are defined as thoughts or parts of thoughts. Propositions are thoughts with a declarative structure. To express an idea, roughly, is to perform an observable action as an indication that the idea is occurring to one.

---

[9] The idiomatic meaning of "Watch Trump win" is "Trump might surprise us and win."
[10] See Fillmore et al. (1988) and Kay and Michaelis (2012) for discussion of (18)(a) and (b). I disagree with their account of such idioms, however (see Davis 2016a: sections 6.6, 7.5, and 7.6).

Expression can be direct or indirect, as we observed in section 3. Both expressions and ideas can be simple or complex. Complex expressions and ideas have structures or forms of different types.

The fundamental principle of the theory is that expressions have meaning in virtue of conventions among speakers to use words, phrases, and sentences to directly express ideas. The definition that assigns meanings to expressions (in a particular living language at a given time) is recursive. The *base clause* of the definition says that some expressions have a particular meaning because it is conventional (in the customary-practice sense described in section 2) for speakers to use them to directly express particular ideas. Thus *tigress* means "female tiger" because it is conventional for speakers of English to use *tigress* to mean or express the idea "female tiger". *Bilingual* means "having two native languages" because it is conventionally used to express that idea. The *recursion clause* of the definition says that an expression has a meaning if (i) its components have meanings, and so directly express particular ideas; and (ii) there is a convention to use expressions of its form to directly express ideas with a particular structure; as a result, the expression expresses the complex idea with those components and that ideational structure. Thus even if the phrase *bilingual tigress* has never been used before, and so cannot be assigned a meaning by the base clause, it means "female tiger having two native languages" because of what *bilingual* and *tigress* mean and because of the convention to use phrases with the 'Adj N' structure to express ideas with the structure common to the ideas "biennial election", "poisonous apple", "wooden table", and so on. The base clause assigns meanings to a finite set of unstructured expressions or morphemes in the language; the recursion clause assigns meanings to an infinite set of expressions with forms of unlimited complexity.

The base clause also assigns idiomatic meanings to fixed-form idioms of Type I. *Over the hill* means "past one's prime" not because of what its components mean or the idea structure associated with its syntactic structure, but because it is conventionally used with those component meanings and that syntax to express the idea "past one's prime". The idiomatic meanings of all the other idioms are given by the recursion clause, by virtue of conventions to use expressions with a particular form to express ideas with a given structure. These conventions, however, give expressions meanings that are non-compositional to some extent. Limiting-implicature denials have their idiomatic meaning because it is conventional to use a sentence containing *not* with its English meaning along with a term that can be modified by *just*, and whose root has a limiting implicature, to express the negation of that implicature. The recursion clause assigns regular meanings to idioms in virtue of the conventional pairings of expression structures defined by syntax alone with idea structures.

Sentences have implicatures in virtue of conventions to (a) use sentences with a particular form to express beliefs with a certain structure by (b) expressing another thought and saying something else. Thus *The sun is larger than some planets* implicates "The sun is not larger than just some planets" because it is conventional to use any sentence 'p' containing *some* and expressing a particular proposition P to indirectly express belief in a related proposition P′, where P′ is the proposition that results from replacing the concept "some" in P with "just some".[11] The implicatures of a sentence are not meanings because they are expressed indirectly.

6 Transparent vs. opaque reports

Belief and other propositional attitude reports have two interpretations.[12] For the sake of a familiar and effective example, let us assume that the Superman story is true. A key fact is that Lois Lane does not realize Clark Kent is Superman. Consequently, (19)(a) is true and (b) is false on their most natural interpretation.

(19) a. Lois believes that Superman can fly.
     b. Lois believes that Clark can fly.

This is the *opaque* interpretation on which substitution of coreferential terms may change the truth value of a sentence.

There is another interpretation of (19)(b), however, on which it is true because (a) is true in the opaque sense, given that Clark is Superman. It is easier to hear this interpretation of (19)(b) if we imagine it uttered by Clark's adoptive parents – who always think of him as Clark, and recognize him whether he is in street clothes or his Superman uniform – when enumerating what Lois knows or suspects about his unusual powers. On this *transparent* interpretation, substitution of coreferential terms does not change the truth value of the sentence.

I believe the transparent interpretation can be defined in terms of the opaque. The definition is not quite so simple, but (20) will suffice as a first approximation for belief.[13]

(20) 'S believes that p' means S believes something equivalent by substitution of coreferential concepts to the proposition that p.

---

[11] See Davis 2016a: section 2.5 for more details.
[12] For a good sample of the vast literature, see Berg 1988; 2012: 8–9; Richard 1997; McKay and Nelson 2010.
[13] See Davis 2016a: section 7.4 for refinements.

In this definition, 'proposition that p' is intended to be opaque. The proposition that Superman can fly differs from the proposition that Clark can fly because their subject concepts are different. In the case of (19)(b), we can express the transparent meaning less formally as follows:

(21) 'Lois believes that Clark can fly' means "Lois believes that someone (who is Clark) can fly."

Approximation (20) is generalized in (22) to cover a large set of propositional-attitude and speech-act verbs 'V', including *believe, know, think, desire, hope, regret, say, deny, remind,* and *warn.*

(22) *'S ±V p' means S ±V something equivalent by substitution of coreferential concepts to the proposition that p.*

The reason for '±' will be apparent shortly.

For readers of the Superman story, the transparent interpretation of (19)(a) may be hard to hear. So let us work with another example. Superman's biological father Jor-El and mother Lara knew him as Kal-El, as did others from Krypton. Lois does not know Superman came from Krypton, and has no idea who Kal-El is. Consider now (23):

(23) Lois believes that Kal-El is a reporter.

It is easy to hear (23) as something that is false because Lois has no idea who Kal-El is. It is also easy to hear it as true because she believes Clark is a reporter – to hear it as something Jor-El would say if he saw Kal-El interacting with Lois in his street clothes.

Now compare (23) to (24):

(24) a. Lois believes that Kal-El as Kal-El is a reporter.
    b. Lois believes "Kal-El is a reporter."
    c. Lois believes that Kal-El as Clark is a reporter.
    d. Lois believes "Clark is a reporter."
    e. Lois believes that Clark is a reporter.

Unlike (23), (24)(a) and (b) are unambiguously false, while (24)(c) and (d) are unambiguously true. (24)(a) and (b) only have an opaque interpretation, and are equivalent. (24)(b) is just a syntactic variant of (23) on its opaque interpretation. (24)(c) and (d) are also opaque and equivalent. (23) is true on its transparent interpretation because (24)(a) and (b) are true, given that Clark Kent is Kal-El. (24)(e) on its opaque interpretation is equivalent to (24)(d), and is true on its transparent interpretation because (24)(d) is.

Pronouns force the transparent interpretation of reports with that-clauses.

(25) a. Lois believes "I am a woman."
    b. Lois believes that I am a woman.

(25)(a) is true: Lois identifies herself as a woman. It is also opaque: it may be true even if Lois suffers a bout of amnesia and no longer has any idea who Lois Lane is and so does not believe "Lois Lane is a woman". (25)(b) is false because Lois knows nothing about me. She believes no proposition equivalent to "Wayne Davis is a woman". (25)(b) has no opaque interpretation – no interpretation on which it is equivalent to (25)(a). (25)(a) has no transparent interpretation.

Both interpretations of a sentence like (23) are conventional and direct. So propositional attitude and speech act reports with that-clauses are semantically ambiguous. What is the source of this ambiguity? It is not lexical. That is, there is no ambiguity in the word *believe*. If there were, (24)(b) should be as ambiguous as (23). And there is no relevant ambiguity in any other words in (23). The ambiguity also is not syntactic. The syntactic structure of (23) is not ambiguous. In (23) as in (24)(b), *Clark is a reporter* is a clause subordinate to the main verb *believes*. In these respects, the ambiguity of belief reports with *that* clauses is like the ambiguity of irregular negatives.

On the transparent interpretation, (23) is true. It is something Jor-El might say to his wife if he recognizes that Clark Kent is Kal-El. The surprising and puzzling fact is that on its transparent interpretation, (26) is also true.

(26) Lois does not believe that Kal-El is a reporter.[14]

(26) would be something the evil General Zod from Krypton would say if he recognized that Superman is Kal-El and knew nothing of Clark Kent. The joint truth of (23) and (26) on their transparent interpretation follows from the joint truth of (27)(a) and (b):

(27) a. Lois believes "Clark Kent is a reporter"; Clark Kent is Kal-El.
    b. Lois does not believe "Superman is a reporter"; Superman is Kal-El.

---

14 This sentence is also subject to the ambiguity illustrated by *John does not believe there is a god* in section 2. Both *Lois fails to believe that Kal-El is a reporter* and *Lois disbelieves that Kal-El is a reporter* have transparent interpretations. I am taking (26) to mean the former but it could also mean the latter.

The joint truth of (23) and (26) when transparent also follows from the joint truth of (28)(a) and (b):

(28) a. Lois believes *he* is a reporter (pointing at a photo of Kal-El in his Clark Kent outfit).
b. Lois does not believe *he* is a reporter (pointing at a photo of Kal-El in his Superman outfit).

Given that (26) is a negation whose root is (23), how can they both be true? They appear to be just as contradictory as (29)(a) and (b).

(29) a. Lois believes "Kal-El is a reporter."
b. Lois does not believe "Kal-El is a reporter."

(29)(a) and (b) say that Lois does and does not believe a particular proposition, which is impossible. How could transparent reports differ so radically?

Sentences (23) and (26) appear to be contradictory because (26) is a negative sentence whose root is (23). They appear to be related semantically the same way (29)(a) and (b) are. As we learned earlier, however, we can infer that (23) and (26) are contradictory from their syntactic relationship *only if they are completely compositional*. The conclusion to draw is that on their transparent interpretation, one or both is *not* completely compositional. Indeed, if the analysis of transparent reports given above in (22) is correct, both are non-compositional. The '±V' in (22) stands for positive verbs like *believes* as well as their logical complements like *does not believe*. What (23) and (26) mean, on their transparent interpretation, is not completely predictable from their syntax and the meanings of their components:

(30) a. There is something Lois believes that is equivalent by coreferential substitution to the proposition that Kal-El is a reporter.
b. There is something Lois does not believe that is equivalent by coreferential substitution to the proposition that Kal-El is a reporter.

Unlike (29)(a) and (b), (30)(a) and (b) are not contradictory because different propositions can make them true. (30)(a) can be true because Lois believes the proposition that Clark is a reporter, while (30)(b) is true because Lois does not believe the proposition that Superman is a reporter. Note that (30)(a) and (b) are not contradictory or contrary: they are *subcontraries*. They can both be true as we have seen, but cannot both be false. If (30)(a) is false, (30)(b) has to be true. For (29)(b) is true in that case. And if (30)(b) is false, (30)(a) has to be true. For (29)(a) is true in that case.

The conclusion I draw is that the transparent interpretation is idiomatic. Transparent reports are free-form idioms. (26) is another irregular negative, one that is the subcontrary of its root. Table 3 thus adds one more row to Table 2.

Table 3. Other Syntactically Irregular Negatives

Type	Negative	Irregular Interpretation
NR Contrary	John does not believe there is a god.	John disbelieves there is a god
Litotes Contrary	It is not good the ice caps are melting.	It is bad that the ice caps are melting.
NL Contradictory	Every cat is not black.	Not every cat is black.
Transparent Subcontrary	Lois does not believe that Kal-El is a reporter	Lois does not believe that someone (who is Kal-El) is a reporter

We noted earlier that one of the ways irregular negations are "extraordinary" is that ordinary logical relationships fail. For example, (31)(a) and (b) hold when the negative sentences are regular, but not when they are irregular.

(31) a. *'p' and 'Not p' are incompatible.*
b. *'A is not B' and 'A is non-B' are equivalent.*

We similarly find that ordinary rules for belief sentences such as (32)(a)–(e) hold only on their opaque interpretation.

(32) a. *'S believes that A is B' is equivalent to 'S believes "A is B."'*
b. *'S believes that A is B' and 'S does not believe that A is B' are contradictory.*
c. *'S believes that A is B' and 'S believes that A is not B' cannot both be true, unless S is irrational or psychotic.*
d. *'S believes that A is B' entails that S has the concepts "A" and "B."*
e. *'S believes that A is B' normally implies that S is introspectively aware of believing that A is B.*

We observed that (32)(a) and (b) fail on the transparent interpretation. To see that (c) fails, note that *Lois believes that Kal-El is a reporter* is true because she believes "Clark is a reporter," and *Lois believes that Kal-El is not a reporter* is true because Lois believes "Superman is not a reporter". Their joint truth implies that Lois is ignorant of something, but not that she is irrational in any way. Both sentences are true on their transparent interpretation even though Lois does not have the concept "Kal-El". And both are true even though she is not aware of it.

The predictive and explanatory power of propositional attitude reports is also severely restricted on their transparent interpretation. Consider (33):

(33) Lois Lane wants to kiss Superman.
Lois Lane believes the man she is with is Superman.
∴ Lois Lane is motivated to kiss the man she is with.

On the most natural interpretation of the premises in (33), they would provide strong support for the conclusion. If the premises were true, we would be very surprised if the conclusion were not true. But when transparent, the joint truth of the premises provides little if any reason to believe the conclusion. The belief premise might be true even though Lois does not realize the man she is with is Superman. If she is in love with Superman, and believes "The man I am with is boring old Clark", we would in fact predict that the conclusion of (33) is false.

The failure of (32) and (33) on the transparent interpretation of belief reports seems extraordinary, but is so only if the reports are interpreted literally. When we recognize that the transparent interpretation is idiomatic, it is no harder to understand why transparent reports have these properties than it is to understand why irregular negations are extraordinary.

Since only a few features of transparent reports are fixed, such as the presence of propositional-attitude or speech-act verbs 'V' and the absence of quotation marks around the subordinate clause, they are free-form idioms. The subject to which 'V' is applied and the clause subordinated to it are compositional variables. The sentences can be transformed syntactically the same way opaque reports can be. For example, *That Kal-El is a reporter is believed by Lois* has the same transparent interpretation as (23). Unlike other irregular negatives, however, their positive roots also have an idiomatic interpretation. So we can add two more free-form idioms to (18), (34)(g) and (h).

(34) **Free-Form Idioms.**
 g. *Lois believes that Kal-El is a reporter.*
 h. *Lois does not believe that Kal-El is a reporter.*

Reports of the form 'S ±V that p' get both their opaque and their transparent interpretations from the recursion clause of the definition of meaning. There are two conventions pairing sentences with this structure to thought structures. One pairs 'S ±V that p' with the thought structure that 'S ±V "p"' is paired with. The other pairs it with the thought structure given by (22): "S ±V something equivalent by substitution of coreferential concepts to the proposition that p."

7 Conclusion

The puzzling ambiguity of propositional attitude reports, and the extraordinary properties of transparent reports, can best be explained by the hypothesis that the transparent reports are free-form idioms. When opaque, 'S ±V that p' means that S ±V the proposition expressed by 'p,' making it fully compositional if 'p' is. When transparent, 'S ±V that p' means (approximately) that S ±V some proposition equivalent by co-referential substitution to the proposition expressed by 'p,' making it partially compositional. Since the meaning of 'S ±V that p' varies predictably with the meaning of 'S,' 'V,' and 'p' in all cases, the transparent interpretation is still highly compositional, making it a free-form idiom. In this respect, transparent reports are markedly unlike fixed-form idioms such as *by and large*, but just like limiting-implicature denials and NR contraries. The ambiguity of propositional attitude reports is puzzling because it is neither syntactic nor lexical. But that is true of idioms generally. Transparent reports have extraordinary properties because they are indefinite. Unlike opaque reports, they do not identify the specific proposition to which the subject bears the propositional attitude expressed by the verb. As a result, their predictive and explanatory powers are limited, and pairs of the form 'S Vs that p' and 'S does not V that p' are non-contradictory despite their syntactic relationship.

References

Berg, Jonathan. 1988. The pragmatics of substitutivity. *Linguistics and Philosophy* 11. 355–370.
Berg, Jonathan. 2012. *Direct belief: An essay on the semantics, pragmatics, and metaphysics of belief*. Boston & Berlin: De Gruyter Mouton.
Davis, Wayne A. 1998. *Implicature: Intention, convention, and principle in the failure of Gricean theory*. Cambridge: Cambridge University Press.
Davis, Wayne A. 2003. *Meaning, expression, and thought*. New York: Cambridge University Press.
Davis, Wayne A. 2005. *Nondescriptive meaning and reference*. Oxford: Oxford University Press.
Davis, Wayne A. 2016a. *Irregular negatives, implicatures, and idioms*. Cham: Springer.
Davis, Wayne A. 2016b. A theory of saying reports. In Alessandro Capone, Ferenc Kiefer & Franco Lo Piparo (eds.), *Indirect Reports and Pragmatics: Interdisciplinary Studies*, 291–332. Cham: Springer.
Espinal, M. Teresa & Jaume Mateu. 2010. On classes of idioms and their interpretation. *Journal of Pragmatics* 42. 1397–1411.
Fillmore, Charles J., Paul Kay & Mary Catherine O'Connor. 1988. Regularity and idiomaticity in grammatical constructions: The case of *let alone*. *Language* 64. 501–538.

Fraser, Bruce. 1970. Idioms within a transformational grammar. *Foundations of Language* 6. 22–42.
Geurts, Bart. 1998. The mechanisms of denial. *Language* 74. 274–307.
Grice, H. Paul. 1989. *Studies in the way of words*. Cambridge, MA: Harvard University Press.
Horn, Laurence. 1989. *A natural history of negation*. Chicago: University of Chicago Press.
Horn, Laurence. 2015. Lie-Toe-Tease: Double negatives and unexcluded middles. *Philosophical Studies* 174(1). 79–103.
Huang, Yan. 2014. *Pragmatics*. Oxford: Oxford University Press.
Kay, Paul & Charles J. Fillmore. 1999. Grammatical constructions and linguistic generalizations: The *What's X doing Y?* construction. *Language* 75. 1–33.
Kay, Paul & Laura A. Michaelis. 2012. Constructional meaning and compositionality. In Claudia Maienborn, Klaus von Heusinger & Paul Portner (eds.), *Semantics: An international handbook of natural language meaning*, 2271–2296. Boston & Berlin: De Gruyter Mouton.
McKay, Thomas & Michael Nelson. 2010. Propositional attitude reports. In Edward N. Zalta, *Stanford encyclopedia of philosophy*. Stanford, CA: Stanford University Press.
Nunberg, Geoffrey, Ivan A. Sag & Thomas Wasow. 1994. Idioms. *Language* 70. 491–538.
Richard, Mark. 1997. Propositional attitudes. In Crispin Wright & Bob Hale (eds.), *A companion to the philosophy of language*, 197–226. Oxford: Blackwell Publishing.
Wood, Mary McGee. 1986. *A definition of idiom*. Bloomington, IN: Indiana University Linguistics Club.

Jacques Moeschler
12 How speaker meaning, explicature and implicature work together

1 Introduction

In this paper I would like to address a specific issue, which is the relation between speaker meaning, implicature and explicature. The main claim defended here is that the logical properties of pragmatic meaning do not provide a complete picture of speaker meaning. I will show that speaker meaning, in one well-known case, i.e. the meaning of the implicature triggered by *or*, corresponds to what Grice has called "what is conveyed", that is, the addition of "what is said" and "what is implicated". However, another classical case – scalar implicatures triggered by particular quantifiers – does not allow the same type of reasoning, because defining speaker meaning as the addition of what is said and what is implicated makes it impossible to explain why a speaker will choose a positive instead of a negative utterance, that is, *some* vs. *some not*.[1] This difficulty will lead to an alternative solution, argued for in a recent paper (Moeschler 2017), where scalar implicatures of particular quantifiers are reinterpreted as explicatures of the logical form of the clause, that is, fully developed and disambiguated propositions.

---

1 The issue of the lexicalisation of quantifier is not at issue here. See Horn (2004) and Moeschler (2017) for a detailed analysis.

I am particularly indebted to István Kecskés, who is at the origin of my international 'career'. He kindly invited me to contribute to the first issue of *Intercultural Pragmatics* (Moeschler 2004). From this moment on, István has been a strong reference for my work in pragmatics, mainly when I understood that theoretical issues, such as implicatures, explicatures, procedural meaning, etc. should be thought of in a wider context. His challenging ideas about speaker-oriented pragmatics, for instance, made me consider pragmatic meaning in a wider sense, including semantic meaning, such as entailment and presupposition, and reflect upon the role of implicature and explicature in social contexts. Last but not least, his funny examples, about equivocal situations, gave rise to strong ideas about how linguistic meaning, context and cognition are intertwined. As he told me after my talk at the second AMPRA meeting at UCLA that I was a contextualist (à la Recanati), I would like to use Rachel and Michael's invitation to show István that I am a moderate contextualist, and as Dan Sperber mentioned after one of my talks twenty years ago: "isn't it like an augmented-code model à la Grice?". Therefore, I would like to tell István how much I owe him for all the opportunities he offered me to work with him and to thank him for being so supportive and helpful.

This paper is organized as follows. Section 2 is devoted to the classical definition of what speaker meaning is from a Gricean and a post-Gricean perspectives. Section 3 addresses the issue of logical connectives, and more precisely the <*and, or*> Hornian scale, allowing a description of *or*-pragmatic meaning as *not-and*. Section 4 raises the question of how far particulars can be analysed along these lines forming Hornian scales as <*all, some*> and <*none, some not*> and the limits of the debate. Finally, section 5 discusses the implications of such discussions for the theory of meaning. The conclusion summarizes the findings and addresses new research questions for theoretical and empirical pragmatics.

2 Speaker meaning

Since Grice, pragmatics is mainly about *speaker meaning*. Grice defines speaker meaning *via* the notion of non-natural meaning: "'A meant$_{NN}$ something by *x*' is (roughly) equivalent to '*A* intended the utterance of *x* to produce some effect in an audience by means of the recognition of this intention'" (Grice 1989: 220). In other words, in order to produce the intended effect, the audience must not only recognize the speaker's intention to produce an effect, but also her intention to obtain this result *via* the recognition of this intention. So, for Grice having an intention is actually having two intentions, and this relates to the distinction between *informative intention* and *communicative intention* in Relevance Theory. The informative intention is "the intention to inform the audience of something", whereas the communicative intention is the intention "to inform the audience of one's informative intention" (Sperber & Wilson 1986: 29).

In Relevance Theory, informative and communicative intentions have a precise function, i.e. they make ostensive-inferential communication possible, they constitute a system of communication which completes the code model, mainly used to account for linguistic communication. As Sperber & Wilson (1986: 63) put it, "The communicator produces a stimulus which makes it mutually manifest to communicator and audience that the communicator intends, by means of this stimulus, to make manifest or more manifest to the audience a set of assumptions {*I*}". The set of assumptions {*I*} describes the communicator's informative intention, and the stimulus's being mutually manifest corresponds to her communicative intention.

A question arises concerning the relation between speaker meaning and implicature. It seems that what Grice had in mind regarding his famous example about B's answer to A's question on how C is getting his job in a bank (*Oh quite well, I think; he likes his colleagues, and he hasn't been in prison yet*) was that speaker meaning can be grasped due to the notion of implicature:

> The answer might be any one of such things as that C is the sort of person likely to yield to the temptation provided by his occupation, that C's colleagues are really very unpleasant and treacherous people, and so forth. It might of course, be quite unnecessary for A to make such an inquiry of B, the answer to it being, in the context, clear in advance. I think it is clear that whatever B implied, suggested, meant, etc., in this example, is distinct from what B said, which was simply that C has not been in prison yet. I wish to introduce, as terms of art, the verb *implicate* and the related nouns *implicature* (cf. *implying*) and *implicatum* (cf. *what is implied*). (Grice 1975: 43–44)

While what is said can be grasped as what Austin (1962: 94) called *sense* and *reference*[2] (cf. Moeschler 2012: 410), what is implicated gave rise to lots of debates, leading to a convergent conclusion that implicatures are the result of an inferential process, general pragmatic principles, and context. In the classical Gricean framework, generalized conversational implicatures are triggered by the use or the exploitation of a conversational maxim, whereas particular implicatures (what typically corresponds to the above example) are triggered by both conversational maxims and context.

In Grice's article, the notion of *conveyed meaning* is introduced when discussing his famous *Peccavi* example, where a British general implicates, in a very subtle way, that he has taken the town of Sind (*Peccavi* = *I have sinned*, which is homophonous to *I have Sind*):

> Whether or not the straightforward interpretant ('I have sinned') is being *conveyed*, it seems that the nonstraightforward must be ['I have Sind']. There might be stylistic reasons for *conveying* by a sentence merely its nonstraightforward interpretant, but it would be pointless, and perhaps also stylistically objectionable, to go to the trouble of finding an expression that nonstraightforwardly conveys that *p*, thus imposing on an audience the effort involved in finding this interpretant, if this interpretant were otiose so far as *communication* was concerned. (Grice 1975: 55; author's emphasis)

Thus, for Grice, what is conveyed is the combination of what is meant in a straightforward and nonstraightforward way, that is, as it has been interpreted in the pragmatic literature: what is said + what is implicated.

So the crucial question is *what is the nature of what is implicated*? Does it correspond to speaker meaning? In what follows, I would like to show that this is not the case. There are indeed good reasons, that is, logical and pragmatic ones, to make a clear distinction between speaker meaning and implicated meaning. The argument will be developed using logical connectives (section 3) and positive and negative particulars (section 4).

---

[2] "…'meaning' in the favourite philosophical sense of that word, i.e. with a certain sense and with a certain reference" (Austin 1962: 94).

3 The case of logical connectives

Logical connectives represent a good testing ground for quantitative or scalar implicatures, and more precisely for the meaning of *and* and *or*. In the classical view of scalar implicatures, conjunction and disjunction belong to a semantic scale (a Hornian scale, Horn 1976). They have the following properties: (i) they can be analysed in the logical square; (ii) they are examples of clausal implicatures (Gazdar 1979).

(i) In the Hornian scale, the upper-bound expression unilaterally entails the lower-bound, whereas the lower-bound expression quantitatively implicates (Q-implicates) the negation of the upper-bound. For instance, in a semantic scale <S, W>, where S is a strong predicate and W a weak one, (a) S(x) entails (→) W(x) and (b) W(x) Q-implicates (+>) ¬ S(x), as illustrated in (1) for the <*and, or*> scale:

(1) a. cheese and dessert → cheese or dessert
    b. cheese or dessert +> it is not the case that cheese and dessert

These relations can be made explicit in (2) and in Figure 1, which represents the logical (Aristotelian) square:

(2) a. *P and Q* unilaterally entails *P or Q*
    b. *P or Q* conversationally Q-implicates *not(P and Q)*
    c. *P or Q* and *not(P and Q)* are subcontraries: (i) they cannot be false together, but can be true together; (ii) if they are true together, this excludes states of affaires (SoAs) where *P and Q* is true and *P or Q* is false (cf. Table 3 below).

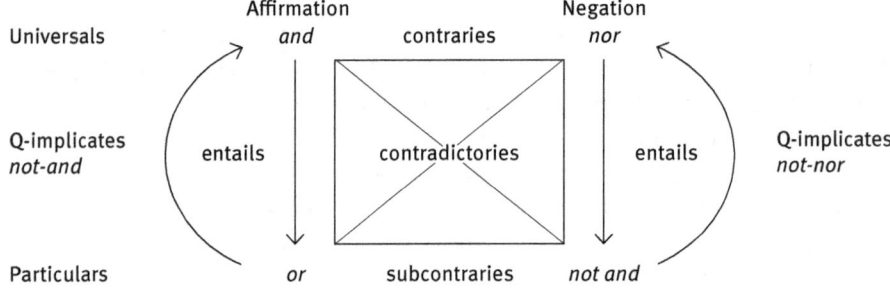

Figure 1. The logical square for logical connectives

What this figure states is that any complex proposition of the form *P or Q* Q-implicates *not(P and Q)* – as in *cheese or dessert* – as well as a logical form of the type *not(P and Q)* Q-implicates *not(P nor Q)*, which is equivalent to *P or Q*.

There is a second version of the relation between the logical connectives *and* and *or*, based on another fundamental pragmatic relation between these two connectives.

(ii) In Gazdar's theory of clausal implicatures, *or* and *if* are weak forms of *and* and *since*. In other words, the logical connectives *if* and *or* clausally implicate the set of propositions $\{\Diamond P, \Diamond \neg P, \Diamond Q, \Diamond \neg Q\}$.

It means that whereas *or*-scalar implicature states that the speaker knows that *P and Q* is not the case, *or*-clausal implicature simply indicates a mental state of ignorance by the speaker: she does not know whether *P* is possible or not, and whether *Q* is possible or not.

Table 1 makes this analysis explicit:

Table 1. Scalar and clausal implicature of *or*

Strong forms	Weak forms	Scalar implicature	Clausal implicature
P and Q	P or Q	K¬(P∧Q)	$\{\Diamond P, \Diamond \neg P, \Diamond Q, \Diamond \neg Q\}$

In this analysis, the clausal implicature meaning is a weaker meaning than the scalar one, and it resembles the free choice meaning. For instance, in (3), the addressee has the choice between tea and coffee, and the speaker does not know whether the addressee will choose tea or coffee, letting open the possibility that he will choose tea or coffee or both:

(3) For breakfast, do you want tea or coffee?
    Free choice implicature: you can choose tea, coffee, or both.

The ignorance reading of *P or Q* – a classical example by Grice (1978) – is of the same kind, and triggers a clausal implicature:

(4) *Daughter*:   Where is mom?
    Father: In the bathroom or in the kitchen.
    Clausal implicature: The father does not know where his wife is.

The question is whether here we are talking about speaker meaning. In the case of clausal implicature, *P or Q* conveys the reason why a speaker cannot choose between *P* and *Q*: she does not know or is not allowed to supply the information she is aware of concerning which proposition is true. On the contrary, the description of *or*-scalar implicature states that the speaker cannot assert a stronger proposition for whatever reason, which is *P and Q*. She can only assert her ignorance about the truth of one or the other disjunct either. If a waiter has *cheese or dessert* on the menu, it is because, for the price required, he cannot offer *cheese and dessert* (generally a menu with *cheese or dessert* is cheaper than a menu with *cheese and dessert*).

This difference is easily understandable because the contexts of a conjunction and a disjunction are not the same: the context of a conjunction requires that both conjuncts be true, because *P and Q* entails *P*, on the one hand, and *Q*, on the other, whereas the context of a disjunction pragmatically requires that only one of the disjuncts be true. This state of affairs has practical consequences, and gives rise to a very nice paradox. If a waiter offers a menu with *cheese or dessert*, then he must have both. So, from the waiter's point of view, stating on his menu *cheese or dessert* implicates that both are available, exactly as the upper-bound conjunction does for reasons of semantic entailment (*cheese and dessert* entails *cheese* and entails *dessert*).

Now comes the big issue with the *or*-scalar meaning, that is, the *not-and* interpretation. From a logical point of view, the *not-and* interpretation is compatible with a situation where the disjunction is false, implying that both disjuncts are false. In our example, it means that the *or*-implicature would be true even if the restaurant has neither cheese, nor dessert. This immediately falsifies the practical consequence of *P or Q*, because no one would expect that if a restaurateur offers a menu for 20€ *cheese or dessert*, he would be cooperative in a situation where he has neither cheese, nor dessert.

Let us first examine how it could be possible for the *or*-scalar implicature to lead to an implausible situation, and how we can explain and correct this misleading reading.

First, what is excluded in the *not-and* interpretation is the inclusive interpretation of *or*, that is, the interpretation where both disjuncts are true. This makes sense because in the case of *cheese or dessert*, the waiter cannot offer both: he is offering two menus, one with *cheese and dessert* and a cheaper menu, with only one of the items. However, the meaning of a scalar implicature makes possible a situation where both disjuncts are false. How is this possible? How can the *or*-scalar implicature mean that there will be neither cheese, nor dessert? The answer is straightforward if we use a truth table: Table 2 shows the truth conditions of the *or*-scalar implicature.

Table 2. *Or*-scalar implicature truth conditions

P	Q	P∧Q	K¬(P∧Q)
1	1	1	0
1	0	0	1
0	1	0	1
0	0	0	1

So the scalar implicature reading of *or* makes a correct prediction: when both disjuncts are true, the disjunction is false, and when only one of the disjuncts is true, the disjunction is true. But it also makes a false prediction: when both disjuncts are false, the disjunction is true, even if it should not be. Clearly, this case shows that scalar implicature meaning is something different than speaker meaning: unless we have good reasons to think that the waiter is a crook, we expect that all possible states of affairs (SoAs), where both disjuncts are false, will lead to falsehood.

How can we explain this? Fortunately, there is a classical answer, saving what we expect to be the scalar meaning of *or* (Horn 1976). If the truth table of the scalar implicature gives a bad result, conjoining the scalar implicature meaning and the inclusive disjunction meaning yields the right result, that is, the exclusive disjunction meaning. So the resulting logical computation (the exclusive meaning) is what Gricean pragmatics predicts (5), as Table 3 shows:

(5) What is said (inclusive meaning) + what is implicated = what is conveyed

Table 3. *Or*-exclusive meaning

P	Q	P∧Q	¬(P∧Q)	P∨Q	(P∨Q) ∧ ¬(P∧Q)	P▽Q
1	1	1	0	1	0	0
1	0	0	1	1	1	1
0	1	0	1	1	1	1
0	0	0	1	0	0	0

In other words, what we expect after the computation of *or*-pragmatic results in its exclusive meaning, that is, describing a possible state of affairs in which only one disjunct is true. Note that this is true for the ignorance reading, but not for the free choice one, which corresponds to the inclusive reading. Therefore, the positive point is that the paradox is solved: the *or*-scalar implicature is not speaker meaning, because speaker meaning is obtained via the conjunction of what is said and what is implicated. Figure 2 makes this general picture explicit:

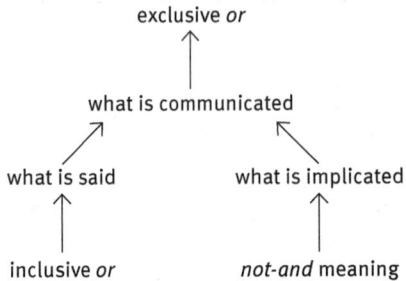

Figure 2. How to compute speaker meaning

4 *Some* and *some...not*: an alternative analysis of particular quantifiers

So far we have had a positive result, but this result is unfortunately not strong enough to state a generalization with respect to speaker meaning. The reason is that the argumentation holding up to now (speaker meaning = what is conveyed = what is said + what is implicated) cannot be used in the case of the scalar implicatures triggered by quantifiers, and more precisely by positive (*some*) and negative (*some not*) particulars.

Let us start with Horn's model of scalar implicature, where *some* implicates *not all* and *some not* implicates *some*. In Horn's model (Horn 1989, 2004), *some* and *some not* are subcontraries and their upper-bound counterparts are *all* and *none*. If we use the logical square, we obtain the following analysis:

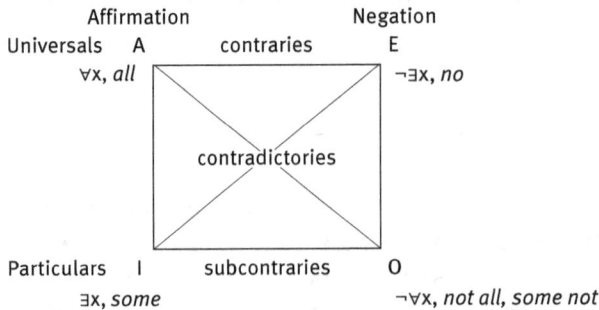

Figure 3. The logical square for quantifiers (from Horn 2004)

The main assumption of this analysis is that *some* and *some not* (*not all*) are subcontraries. Is this prediction correct? My answer is that Horn's (1989, 2004) analysis of particulars as subcontraries is logically consistent, but pragmatically problematic. Why? The main reasons are that the description of particulars as subcontraries gives rise to a possible one-sided "at least" reading (*some if not all, some not if not none*) and to a counterintuitive reading of speaker meaning as what is said + what is implicated. The cause of these undesirable consequences is the assumption that *some* and *some not* are subcontraries.

If two propositions are subcontraries, what is excluded is that they are false together, whereas (i) they can be true together or (ii) only one is true, the other false. When both subcontraries are true, they receive their two-sided readings (*some but not all, some not but not none*), and their one-sided readings (*some if not all, some not if not none*) is ruled out. The one-sided reading is due to the possible cancellation of conversational implicatures, and justifies the description of particulars as subcontraries. The implicature cancellation is illustrated by (6) and (7):

(6) Some students passed, and in fact all of them passed.

(7) Some students did not pass, and in fact none of them passed.

Where is the problem? The problem lies in lines 2 and 3 of the truth table of subcontraries (Table 4), which is the truth table of a disjunction. In line 2, *some* means *all*, and in line 3, *some not* means *none*, as the following truth table shows:

Table 4. Truth table for subcontraries

Line number	some X are Y	some X are not Y	Subcontraries relation
1	1	1	1
2	1	0	1
3	0	1	1
4	0	0	0

Is it a real issue? From the logical point of view, *some* is compatible with *all*, and *some not* with *none*, and this satisfies the definition of subcontraries. However, from the pragmatic point of view, this should not be an issue, because the implicature of *some* ('not all') as well as the implicature of *some not* ('some') are cancellable, satisfying the definition of subcontrariety (lines 2 and 3). So what is problematic here? The issue is that if a particular quantifier receives its two-sided reading, then lines 2 and 3 should not yield a positive truth value (1), but a negative one (0).

However, it could be argued that this is exactly what we expect, because implicatures are cancellable. Nevertheless, in this case, it would be weird to define a pragmatic property with logical properties (being a subcontrary). As we will see later, what Table 4 states is only the logical or semantic properties of particulars, and says nothing about their pragmatic meaning. From the pragmatic point of view, if we assume that the pragmatic meaning of *some* is restricted to *not-all*, and the pragmatic meaning of *some not* to *some*, then *some* and *some not* are not, pragmatically speaking, subcontraries, and their relation is that of a conjunction, as Table 5 shows:

Table 5. Truth table of the pragmatics of particulars

Line number	*some X are Y*	*some X are not Y*	Subcontraries relation
1	1	1	1
2	1	0	0
3	0	1	0
4	0	0	0

As it appears, positive and negative particulars are in a conjunction relation, meaning that the truth of one of them implies the truth of the other. So the proposed alternative analysis claims that particulars are not subcontraries. On the contrary, they are defined as implying each other, and not as implicating each other. This means that in order to obtain a particular reading, *both particulars* (*some* and *some not*) *must be true together*. As a consequence, each particular implies the other one – when one is true, the other one must be true as well – warranting for the partition of the semantic domain to be obtained at the *explicature* level, not at the implicature one.

However, there is a non-trivial consequence for the computation of the meaning of quantifiers, which can be an explanation of this explicature-based analysis: it is dependent on relations of incompatibility at the semantic and the pragmatic levels. At the semantic level, the incompatibility is given by the contradiction relations between one particular and its contradictory universal. In other words, the logical reading of the quantifier is warranted by its contradiction relation to its counterpart. This means that *some not* is semantically incompatible with *all*, and *some* with *none* (cf. Figure 3).

At the pragmatic level, the incompatibility lies between the two-sided and the one-sided readings. So *some* is pragmatically incompatible with *all*, and *some not* with *none*, both receiving, in their two-sided readings, a restricted meaning, made explicit by the operator *only*, as Figure 4 shows:

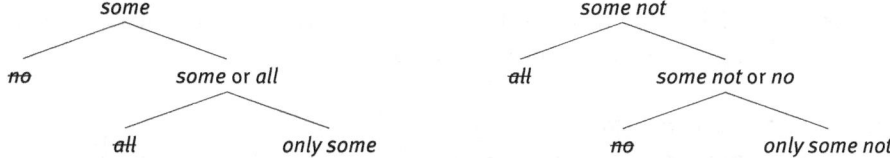

Figure 4. Semantic and pragmatic incompatibility for *some* and *some not*

Figure 5 makes the difference between semantic and pragmatic incompatibility explicit:

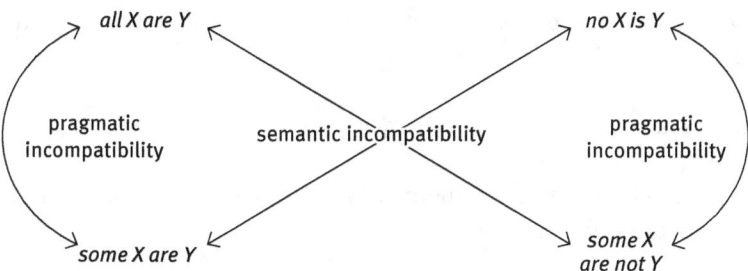

Figure 5. Semantic and pragmatic incompatibility between universals and particulars

As a consequence, the two-sided readings are not implicatures anymore, they are *explicatures*, which are restrictions of the logical meaning of particulars.

The second argument against the said + implicated analysis is given by a Boolean semantic analysis of the denotation of quantified sentences. In the classical analysis, *some* and *some not* make a partition of a set of individuals, the two subsets being represented by what is said and what is implicated. This is represented in (8) and (9):

(8) Some linguists know logic
   a. What is said: $\lambda x.\text{linguist}(x) \wedge \text{know\_logic}(x)$
   b. What is implicated: $\lambda x.\text{linguist}(x) \wedge \neg \text{know\_logic}(x)$

(9) Some linguists do not know logic
   a. What is said: $\lambda x.\text{linguist}(x) \wedge \neg \text{know\_logic}(x)$
   b. What is implicated: $\lambda x.\text{linguist}(x) \wedge \text{know\_logic}(x)$

In other words, what is said in (8) is what is implicated in (9) and vice versa. Moreover, the said + implicated analysis predicts that what is communicated is the addition of what is said and what is implicated. This way the denotation of the whole set of linguists (Horn 2004: 11) is described. From a pragmatic point of view, this gives rise to an uninformative result:

(10) *What is communicated*
[λx.linguist(x) ∧ know_logic(x)] ∧ [λx.linguist(x) ∧ ¬know_logic(x)]
= λx.linguist(x)

Fortunately, there is a possible alternative analysis which makes sense of choosing the positive vs. negative particular to convey speaker meaning. At the pragmatic level, that is, the explicature of the utterance, the alternative analysis defines the partition of the set of individuals that the speaker is talking about, here the set of linguists. Therefore, each subset defines the domain making the propositions true.

(11) Explicature of *some linguists know logic*:
λx.linguist(x) ⊄ λy.know_logic(y)
The set of individuals who are linguists is not properly included into the set of individuals who know logic.

(12) Explicature of *some linguists do not know logic*:
[λx.linguist(x) ∩ λy.know_logic(y)] ≠ ∅
The intersection between the set of individuals who are linguists and the set of individuals who know logic is not the empty set.

Table 6 makes the difference between the semantics and the pragmatics of *some* and *some not* explicit:

Table 6. Semantics and pragmatic of *some* and *some…not*

	Semantics	Pragmatics
some X are Y	X ∩ Y ≠ ∅	X ⊄ Y
some X are not Y	C(X ∩ Y) ≠ ∅	X ∩ Y ≠ ∅

The alternative analysis (Moeschler 2017) allows for a different description of the pragmatics of positive and negative utterances, as shown in Table 6. It means that the choice of a positive vs. a negative utterance is truth-conditionally motivated, and that their semantics is defined by their logical meaning, allowing the possibility of a one-sided meaning. For instance, (X ∩ Y) ≠ ∅ (*some*) is compatible with the universal reading (*all*), where *X* is properly included in *Y* (X ⊆ Y), as well as the semantics of *some not* – C (X ∩ Y) ≠ ∅, i.e. the complement of the intersection *X* and *Y* is not empty – it is compatible with the negative universal reading of *none* – the intersection between *X* and *Y* is the empty set (X ∩ Y ≠ ∅). In other words, the proposed alternative analysis explains the one-sided, as well as the two-sided readings of particulars.

However, the main advantage of the alternative analysis is that what is expressed at the explicature level clearly shows that the positive and negative particulars do not have *the same truth value* as pragmatic meaning. This point is crucial because it explains why a speaker will choose between the positive and the negative particular. Examples (13) and (14) show in which contexts a speaker will prefer *some* to *some...not*:

(13)　Anne:　　How was your exam in Pragmatics?
　　　Jacques:　Some of my students passed.
　　　　　　　　Explicature:　Only some of my students passed.
　　　　　　　　Implicature:　The result is good, because I expected none of my students to pass.

(14)　Anne:　　How was your exam in Pragmatics?
　　　Jacques:　Some of my students did not pass.
　　　　　　　　Explicature:　Only some of my students did not pass.
　　　　　　　　Implicature:　I expected all of my students to pass, and I am disappointed.

5 Implications for a theory of meaning

Is this analysis a possible contribution to the theory of meaning? I would like to come back to the initial issue, that is, the relation between speaker meaning and implicature. What logical connectives and quantifiers show is that implicature is only one part of speaker meaning, but cannot be equated with it.

Is this surprising? I would like to give two possible answers, one follows from what has been argued in this chapter, the other coming from a prediction I have made on intercultural pragmatics (Moeschler 2004, 2007).

The first answer is that implicatures are non-truth-conditional meaning, and as such, do not warrant any type of speaker commitment (cf. Moeschler

2013). The speaker commits herself to entailments and presuppositions, and certainly to the explicatures of her utterance, either basic (propositional form) or higher-ordered ones (illocutionary force and propositional attitude, cf. Sperber and Wilson 1986; Wilson and Sperber 2004, 2012). For instance, the speaker cannot deny having implied or presupposed propositions that are entailed or presupposed. Otherwise this would lead to contradictions – cf. (15) and (16):

(15) # I bought a Chow, but not a dog.
(16) # My daughter is in Japan, but I have no daughter.

However, the speaker can deny having implicated a proposition, as in (17), as well as one of the possible but not intended explicatures of her utterance because she wants to avoid misunderstanding (18):

(17) Today, I will offer you both cheese and dessert in the menu *cheese or dessert*.
(18) It's raining today, I mean, not here at home, but at Geneva.

The second answer has a more practical grounding. As argued in Moeschler (2004, 2007), intercultural communication is mainly based on explicatures and certainly not on implicatures: hints, *sous-entendus*, innuendos, and even puns are in most cases not grasped in intercultural communication. It means that in order to obtain speaker meaning, the addressee must access the utterance explicature; if this condition is not met, communication fails and gives rise to misunderstanding.

Now, these arguments could be thought as too narrow or too broad. Too narrow because the truth-conditional meaning vs. non-truth-conditional meaning issue has been discussed on very specific problems (particular quantifiers) and too broad, because the function of explicature has been claimed to be central in utterance understanding, as in intercultural communication. I would like to make this point clearer, because any type of scientific discussion must be explicit on its scope and domain of prediction. What I have tried to target in this paper is the general contour for pragmatics, combining formal, cognitive, but also social constraints. It is unfortunately generally believed that any type of formal approach to language and language use is disconnected from cognitive and/or social issues. I would like to claim that this view of language and language use is not correct. A formal approach, based on a precise and robust formalisation, aims to model cognitive processes and social practices. Concerning cognition, we are now in a good position, because experimental pragmatics has gained in expertise and confidence, and is now able to assess predictions of theories. For instance, as far as scalar implicature is concerned, it is clear that the debate about default inferences (Neo-Gricean) and contextualist approaches (Post-Gricean) has received a straightforward answer from an experimental perspective: we know now that the contextalist approach makes better predictions, because implicatures are costly and context dependent (Noveck and Reboul 2008 for a review, and also Zufferey 2015 as regards the acquisition of pragmatics). As the social issue is concerned, the debate is not as straightforward as for the first issue, mainly because several variables are at stake. For instance, it is difficult to predict which general cognitive constraints impact social behaviours. However, we can hypothesize that the increasing development of cognitive abilities in *homo sapiens* is certainly at the origin of our language faculty, and that using language as a communicative means has contributed to the development of our cognitive abilities (see Reboul 2017).

6 Conclusion

In this chapter, I showed why speaker meaning cannot be reduced to implicature, and why things are more complex. The arguments based on the semantic and pragmatic properties of logical words could be seen as rather narrow in scope, but in fact they show that an important part of the meaning conveyed is based on computations which are for some of them independent of the use of language, and for others triggered, the latter being monitored by the need to recover the speaker's informative intention.

It is also clear that some aspects of meaning go far beyond this type of interplay between conventional and pragmatic meanings. If I had to project the type of meaning complexity onto some properties of meaning tackled by István Kecskés in his work (see for instance Horn & Kecskés 2013 for a general survey of the relation between formal and socio-cognitive approaches to pragmatics, and Kecskés 2016 for a development of the socio-cognitive approach), it becomes clear that the recovery of speaker meaning requires much more than accessing defeasible meanings, as implicatures. In one of his favourite examples, Kecskés (2014) has shown that the speaker is not necessarily aware of some of the consequences of conventional or literal meaning. One example is *I would like to see you without your clothes*, uttered to a policewoman by a man sitting in the police car and meaning "with ordinary clothes". The first and conventional accessible meaning would be "naked". In this by now classical example, it is obvious that the man meant something very specific, which is completely accessible in the context of work, as the policewoman is wearing her uniform. But what makes the utterance critical, and this seems to be out of the speaker's control in Kecskés' perspective, is that *without your clothes* has a first and accessible meaning which triggers a completely different interpretation. In my opinion, what has to be explained is not the ambiguity or vagueness of this utterance, but why this non-preferred reading becomes the most accessible one.

If we come back to Grice's comment on *Peccavi*, which deals with the same issue, but has different encoding and inference strategies, the British general wants to hide his intention. In doing so, his intention must have a degree of accessibility to make it possible to be grasped because he is looking for successful, though inferential, communication. In the case of Kecskés' example, the man's first intention is not to implicate that he wants to see the policewoman naked, but that he wants to be with her in a different setting in which she wears non-professional clothes. The short-circuited interpretation is certainly based on social stereotypes, and also triggered by a stereotypical type of situation (a sitcom context), mainly based on the potential and general ambiguity of some utterances, especially those having sexual connotations. Does it mean that the man is aware of what is really meant? Who knows, and this is the secret of the show: the man is not only clumsy towards his addressee, but also funny for the sitcom audience as what he has communicated has gone far beyond what he actually meant.

This is not restricted to fictional settings: very often, as speakers, we realize *too late* that what we communicated went far beyond what we had meant. Is it because we are pragmatically or linguistically incompetent? Slips of tongues are not the way in which our 'unconscious' (*das Unbewusste*) speaks for us; on the contrary, they happen because our words are primed by some relevant accessible information, which is unfortunately and contextually unhappy.

If I am right, it means that what Grice called *straightforward interpretation* is not always what the speaker means: there are biases, and biases exist because natural languages are codes, rich but imperfect codes (Sperber and Origgi 2010, Scott-Philipps 2015). I do not think that we are systematically and generally pragmatically incompetent. For instance, the imperfection of linguistic codes mainly realized in polysemy and structural ambiguity is what makes it possible to play with language: puzzles, humour, teasing, etc. are just a couple of ways for speakers to exploit the imperfection of language to varying degrees of pleasure on the part of the audience.

Acknowledgements: This paper belongs to a series of publications written during the Swiss National Science Foundation project LogPrag, project n° 100012_146093, 2014–2017. Many thanks to Joanna Blochowiak, Karoliina Lohiniva and Cristina Grisot for their comments and corrections. Many thanks to Gabi Soare for her rephrasing and careful reading.

References

Austin, John L. 1962. *How to do things with words*. Cambridge, MA: Harvard University Press.
Gazdar, Gerald. 1979. *Pragmatics. Implicature, presupposition, and logical form*. New York: Academic Press.
Grice, H. Paul. 1975. Logic and conversation. In Peter Cole & Jerry L. Morgan (eds.), *Syntax and semantics 3: Speech acts*, 41–58. New York: Academic Press.
Grice, H. Paul. 1977. Further notes on Logic and conversation. In Peter Cole (ed.), *Syntax and semantics 9: Pragmatics*, 113–127. New York: Academic Press.
Grice, H. Paul. 1989. *Studies in the way of words*. Cambridge, MA: Harvard University Press.
Horn, Laurence R. 1976. *On the semantic properties of logical operators in English*. Bloomington: Indiana University Linguistic Club.
Horn, Laurence R. 1989. *A natural history of negation*. Chicago: University of Chicago Press.
Horn, Laurence R. 2004. Implicature. In Laurence R. Horn & Gregory Ward (eds.), *The Handbook of Pragmatics*, 3–28. Oxford, Blackwell.
Horn, Laurence & István Kecskés. 2013. Pragmatics, discourse and cognition. In Stephen R. Anderson, Jacques Moeschler & Fabienne Reboul (eds.), *The language cognition-interface*, 355–375. Genève: Droz.
Kecskés, István. 2014. *Intercultural Pragmatics*. Oxford: Oxford University Press.
Kecskés, István. 2016. Sequential structure of discourse segments shaped by the interplay of recipient design or salience. In Joanna Blochowiak, Cristina Grisot, Stephanie Durrleman-Tame & Christopher Laenzlinger (eds.), *Formal models in the study of language*, 243–260. Cham: Springer.
Moeschler, Jacques. 2004. Intercultural pragmatics. A cognitive approach. *Intercultural Pragmatics* 1(1). 49–70.
Moeschler, Jacques. 2007. The role of explicature in communication and in intercultural communication. In István Kecskés & Laurence R. Horn (eds.), *Explorations in pragmatics. Linguistic, cognitive and intercultural aspects*, 73–94. Berlin & New York: Mouton de Gruyter.
Moeschler, Jacques. 2012. Conversational and conventional implicatures. In Hans-Jörg Schmid (ed.), *Cognitive Pragmatics*, 405–433. Boston & Berlin: De Gruyter Mouton.
Moeschler, Jacques. 2013. Is a speaker-based pragmatics possible? Or how can a hearer infer a speaker's commitment? *Journal of Pragmatics* 43(1). 84–97.
Moeschler, Jacques. 2017. Back to negative particulars. A truth-conditional account. In Stavros Assimakopoulos (ed.), *Pragmatics at its interfaces*, 7–32. Boston & Berlin: Mouton de Gruyter.
Noveck, Ira A., & Reboul Anne (2008). Experimental pragmatics: a Gricean turn in the study of language. *Trends in Cognitive Sciences* 12(11). 425–431.
Reboul, Anne. 2017. *Cognition and communication in the evolution of language*. Oxford: Oxford University Press.
Sperber, Dan & Gloria Origgi. 2010. A pragmatic perspective on the evolution of language. In Richard K. Larson, Viviane Déprez & Hiroko Yamakido (eds.), *The evolution of human language: Biolinguistic Perspectives*, 124–131. Cambridge: Cambridge University Press.
Sperber, Dan & Deirdre Wilson. 1986. *Relevance: Communication and cognition*. Oxford: Basil Blackwell.
Scott-Philipps, Thomas C. 2015. *Speaking our minds. Why human communication is different, and how language evolved to make it special*. Basingstoke: Palgrave Macmillan.

Wilson, Deirdre & Dan Sperber. 2004. Relevance Theory. In Laurence R. Horn & Gregory Ward (eds.), *The Handbook of Pragmatics*, 607–632. Oxford: Basil Blackwell.
Wilson, Deirdre & Dan Sperber. 2012. *Meaning and relevance*. Cambridge: Cambridge University Press.
Zufferey, Sandrine. 2015. *Acquiring pragmatics. Social and cognitive perspectives*. Abingdon & New York, Routledge.

Chaofen Sun and Ming Chew Teo
13 Temporally closed situations for the Chinese perfective LE 了

1 Introduction

The character, *le* 了, is among the top five most frequently used Chinese characters in modern Chinese texts (Institute of Linguistics, Beijing Language and Culture University, 1985). A good understanding of it is, therefore, most important in any grammatical theory, be it for theoretical linguistics or CSL, as it is a grammatical form that any beginning Chinese class unavoidably must deal with. In order to reach a wider audience, this paper will keep the use of metalanguage out of the discussion so that both linguists and non-linguists can understand how this Chinese verbal suffix works in actual use.

This paper claims that the correct use of the perfective marker *le* 了 (Li and Thompson 1981) in Chinese (in this paper *Chinese* stands for present-day standard spoken Chinese known as *Putonghua* "common speech" in China) must match a temporally bounded context, i.e., either completed or terminated. That is, the perfective marker *le* 了, without an appropriate matching context, is never sufficient to signal the perfective aspect. In other words, as an aspectual marker, it is rather weak and does not have the ability to impose an end point to a clause where it occurs. This matching nature of the Chinese perfective has been neglected in previous literature but is necessary because inappropriate uses like the example in (1b), where the verb *chi* "eat" marked by the perfective le_1 is followed by a bare noun without le_2, cannot be properly explained (Lin 2006, Soh 2014). In this paper, this Chinese perfective is transcribed as le_1 and glossed as PFV so that it is distinguished from the sentence-final clitic le_2 in (1c), which, according to Li and Thompson (1981) and Comrie (1976), is a perfect marker indicating a currently relevant state (glossed as CRS).[1]

---

[1] An anonymous reviewer suggests a preference for data taken from authentic sources. While such a preference is perfectly understandable, examples in the paper, unless otherwise stated, are based on the authors' knowledge of Chinese because it is impossible to find minimally contrastive examples in corpora data. Nevertheless, parallel examples in the following are found in the Modern Chinese corpus of the Center for Chinese Linguistic at the Peking University.

(1) 我买菜, 烧饭, 干杂事 (Examples with bare objective nouns)
    wo mai cai,   shaofan, gan za shi
    1st   buy food cook   do   chore
    'I buy food, cook, and do chores.'

(1) a. 我吃饭
 wo chi fan
 1st eat rice
 "I eat."
 b. *我吃了饭
 wo chi-le_1 fan
 1st eat-PFV rice
 c. 我吃了饭了
 wo chi- le_1 fan le_2
 1st eat-PFV rice CRS
 "I have eaten."

As most studies have neglected the significance of the unacceptable -le_1-marked verb phrases with a bare objective noun like *fan* 饭 in (1b), it is rather unclear how the Chinese form-and-meaning pairs involving perfectivity can be explained either theoretically or for language education purposes. This paper examines the contexts in which -le_1 is appropriately used and demonstrates that -le_1 is a much weaker marker than the Russian perfective marker, and the failure in using -le_1 in the verb phrases with a bare objective noun is probably due to its inherently atelic temporal structure. The Chinese case may constitute a special perfective that requires matching with a temporally telic situation (a situation with an endpoint, either completed or terminated) but does not impose an end point on a temporally open situation on its own like the Russian perfective aspect marker. It is proposed in this study that accomplishment, achievement, and multi-point closed scale types of verb phrases are all telic. A clause can also be temporally bounded, or telic, by the sentence-final perfect marker –le_2 or a following clause.

Section 2 reviews some available literature with respect to perfective aspect. Section 3 discusses the proposed solution to the Chinese perfective. Section 4

(2) 我吃了饭就来 (The first clause is bounded by a second clause)
 wo chi- le_1 fan jiu lai
 1st eat-PFV rice then come
 'He will come after eating.'

(3) 他吃了豹子胆了! (Example with le_1 and le_2)
 ta chi- le_1 baozi dan le_2
 3rd eat-PFV leopard gall CRS
 'He has eaten a leopard gall! (Meaning: He has plucked up some courage)'

(4) 他养了一只很大的斗鸡 (Example in which the object is quantified)
 ta yang-le_1 yi-zhi hen da de dou ji
 3rd grow-PFV a-CL very large DE fighting cock
 'He kept a very large fighting cock.'

demonstrates the explanatory power of the proposed theory with respect to some controversial cases that may be a multi-point closed scalar type, a non-traditionally recognized situation type. Section 5 is the conclusion of the paper.

2 Perfective aspect cross-linguistically and Chinese perfective

In modern linguistics, the term *perfective aspect* came to eminence mostly from the study of Slavic languages. It has been noted by many (Comrie 1976; Binnick 1991; Smith 1997, etc.) that there are two sets of opposing forms, called imperfective and perfective cross-linguistically. Binnick (1991) observed the oppositions of the two aspects and pointed out that none of the features in (2) alone can completely capture the essence of the opposition.

(2)   *Perfective*   *Imperfective*
        non-progressive   progressive
        semelfactive   iterative
        punctuative   habitual
        dynamic   static
        transitory   permanent   (Binnick 1991: 154)

For instance, in (3a) the Russian imperfective form *čitala* can be roughly translated as progressive "she was reading" in English, and the perfective form *pročitala* as "she had read".

(3)   a.   *čitala*   read   imperfective   a non-complete action
           'she was reading'
     b.   *pročitala* read   perfective   a completed action
           'she had read'   (Binnick 1991: 136)

Furthermore, multiple readings would commonly follow once these two aspect markers are interactive with past, and non-past, tenses, as were observed by Binnick (1991) with the examples given in (4). Thus, depending on a context, the past perfective may mean simple past or pluperfect, whereas the past imperfective may mean simple past, past progressive, present perfect, or present perfect progressive. On the other hand, the non-past perfective unambiguously refers to future, whereas the non-past imperfective is still ambiguous with two possible readings, simple present tense or present progressive. In other words, the meanings of an aspect marker can vary significantly depending on the tense of an utterance, supposedly used in accord to the reference time of a given situation in which it occurs.

(4) Perfective Imperfective
Past *podumali* *dumali*
'(we, you, they) thought, had thought' '(we, you, they) thought, were thinking, have thought, have been thinking'
Non-past *podumayut* *dumayut*
(they) will think '(they) think, are thinking'

(Binnick 1991: 138)

The important takeaway from the Russian examples is that the actual interpretation, or various uses, of the perfective, or an imperfective, aspect marker may be the same in different contexts, although the basic meanings of perfective and imperfective are opposite given in (2). A proper interpretation cannot be divorced from a specific context.

With the Russian examples in mind, let us look at the Chinese perfective aspect marker -le_1. The Chinese verbal system does not have a comparable grammatical tense system. For example, in (5b) morphologically speaking the Chinese translations for the English verb *eat, ate,* and *will eat* are an invariant *chi* 吃.

(5) a. eat   ate   will eat
       present   past   future
    b. *chi* 吃 *chi* 吃 *cchi* 吃

A past, or non-past, situation in Chinese is primarily signaled by means of non-verbal elements, like *zuotian* 'yesterday' in (6a), or by the pragmatics of the aspectual markers, as well as a number of linguistic factors to be discussed later. For instance, the adverbial of time 'yesterday' marks it as a past situation. Furthermore, the clause is semantically ambiguous, though not in the Russian ways. The first reading *I ate a bowl of rice yesterday* simply implies a past event that was completed yesterday. But in a different context, when a speaker means "I wanted a bowl of rice yesterday" but "today I want two", it does not necessarily imply a completed event, but rather a past-future reference. It may very well be the case that the speaker did not get to eat any rice yesterday in spite of the fact that he wanted one bowl of rice (leading the speaker to have developed a much bigger appetite for it today). So (6a) can be interpreted as a past event, or simply an unfulfilled desire, even though boundedness is literally asserted by *yi-wan fan*. With the presence of the perfective -le_1 the sentence in (6b) is unambiguously a temporally bounded event (more on boundedness later) in a past event.

(6) a. 我昨天吃一碗饭
       wo zuotian   chi yi-wan fan
       1st yesterday eat a-CL   rice
       'I ate a bowl of rice yesterday.'
       'I (would like to) eat a bowl of rice yesterday,' (but I only want half a bowl today)
   b. 我昨天吃了一碗饭
       wo chi- le_1 yi-wan fan
       1st   eat PFV a-CL   rice
       'I ate a bowl of rice.'

What makes Chinese more challenging is that the aspectual meaning of a clause, without any aspect marker, can be interpreted in ways that may, or may not, be a present situation. Although the sentence in (7a) seems to have only one perfective reading, i.e., a completed situation, with $-le_1$, the one with neither $-le_1$ nor *zuotian* is at least two ways ambiguous, indicating either an intention (7b) or a habitual situation, but not a realized event.

(7) a. 我吃了一碗饭
       wo chi- le_1 yi-wan fan
       1st   eat PFV a-CL   rice
       'I ate a bowl of rice.'
   b. 我吃一碗饭
       wo chi yi-wan fan
       1st   eat a-CL   rice
       'I will eat a bowl of rice'   (intention)
       'I (always) eat a bowl of rice.'   (present and habitual)
       * 'I ate a bowl of rice.'   (completed)

Lin (2006) said that the default aspect for (8) is perfective and has a past interpretation. As a matter of fact, the past interpretation is only one of at least two possible readings for the verb *dai* 'take'. There is also a possible reading of intention that does not exist in English (Liu, Wenyue, and Ye 2004), as in the context for (8b) in which the speaker does not want to go to Taipei, even if the person, signaled by the subject, has the intention to take the speaker along to *Taipei*, 他带我去台北, 我不去.

(8) a. 他带我去台北
         ta   dai   wo   qu   taibei
         3rd take 1st go   Name
         'He took me to Taipei.'
     b. 'He (wants to) take me to Taipei.' (Lin 2006: 3)

Lin (2006) proposed an interesting context-based formal analysis as he considers -le_1 to be open to perfective and imperfective interpretations depending on the semantics of different Chinese propositions in various contexts. However, if the semantics of -le_1 is truly vacuous with respect to perfectivity, it should be expected to occur freely in either bounded or unbounded situations. We will demonstrate that in many cases this is not the case.

The examples in (9) are among the examples Lin (2006: 13) uses for -le_1's two-aspect hypothesis. If I understand his formal semantic analysis correctly, the claim is that a certain static result stage of Lisi's breaking his leg in the past still holds at speech time, and, with this piece of evidence, -le_1 should be a case of imperfective. On the other hand, (9b) is perfective as there is no result stage holds at the time of utterance.

(9) a. 李四跌断了左腿
         Li Si   die-duan-le_1 zuo tui
         Name   fall-break-PFV   left leg
         'Li Si has broken his left leg.'
         (Lin 2006: 13)
     b. 李四喝了酒, 也唱了歌
         Li Si   he-le_1 jiu,   ye   chang-le_1 ge
         Name   drink-PFV   wine,   also   sing-PFV   song
         'Li Si drank and sang.'   (Lin 2006: 12)

However, it seems unclear what exactly the result stage holding at speech/narrative time is for (9a). It seems that more natural data are needed to substantiate the analysis that was described primarily in metalanguage. Suppose that Lin's perfective analysis about *he- le_1 jiu* in (9b) is correct, then it cannot distinguish the perfective from imperfective -le_1 in both (10a & c), as the following clauses *cannot walk now* and *cannot drive* show that there seems to exist a resultant stage for both. What exactly are they? I will say the result stages are only implications but not explicitly expressed: *Lisi is under the influence* in (10a), and *Lisi is incapable of walking* in (10c). But neither is openly asserted by the initial clauses in (10). In what way is the result stage empty and not holding in (10a) but must be interpreted as holding in (10c)? As far as the issue of a result stage relevant to the speech/narrative time is concerned, the same can be said about the past tense *drank* in (10b), as the implication is that a result stage, possibly *being under the influence*, of the past event of drinking is holding at speech time, and, therefore, the subject should not drive. But is the current relevancy explicitly asserted by the verb *drank*? No. It is only implied and can be inferred from the context.

(10) a. 李四喝了酒，现在不能开车
    Li Si he-le_1 jiu, xianzai bu neng kai che
    Name drink-PFV wine, now not can drive car
    'Li Si drank, (he) cannot drive now'
  b. He drank and cannot drive now.
  c. 李四跌断了左腿，现在不能走路
    Li Si die-duan-le_1 zuo tui, xianzai bu neng zoulu
    Name fall-break-PFV left leg, now not can walk road
    'Li Si has broken his left leg, (he) cannot walk.'

(11) further demonstrates that nothing asserted in (10a) seem to indicate a result stage holding at the time of utterance of the second clause. What is asserted is simply the stage *die-duan-le zuo tui*, and nothing more.

(11) a. 李四跌断了左腿，*还在跌
    Li Si die-duan-le_1 zuo tui, hai zai die
    Name fall-break-PFV left leg, still Prog. fall
    'Li Si has broken his left leg, (he) is still falling.'
  b. 李四跌断了左腿，*还在断
    Li Si die-duan-le_1 zuo tui, hai zai duan
    Name fall-break-PFV left leg, still Prog. break
    'Li Si has broken his left leg, (he) is still breaking.'
  c. 李四跌断了左腿，*还在跌断
    Li Si die-duan-le_1 zuo tui, hai zai die-duan
    Name fall-break-PFV left leg, still Prog. Fall-break
    'Li Si has broken his left leg, (he) is still breaking.'

Examples in (11) thus cast a doubt on the imperfective hypothesis, as most clearly such a static resultant stage is not asserted as holding at the time of utterance, neither *die* 'to fall' nor *duan* 'to break', or *die-duan* together as a compounded verb. In order for Lin's imperfective hypothesis to hold, he needs to demonstrate it more convincingly with more relevant Chinese data. Other achievement situations in (12) show that the result state that holds is a consequence in (12b & d) similar to the English *drank* in (10b), which can be inferred but is not explicitly asserted as part of the resultative verb compound *zhao-dao* "to find" or a monosyllabic *si* "to die" in (12a & c).

(12) a. 他找到了李四了，*还在找到
    ta zhao-dao-le_1 Li Si le_2, hai zai zhao-dao
    3rd seek-arrive-PFV Name CRS, still Prog. seek-arrive
    'He found Li Si, *(he) is still looking for (him).'
  b. 他找到了李四很久了，早就不找了
    ta zhao-dao-le_1 Li Si hen jiu le_2, zao jiu bu zhao le
    3rd seek-arrive-PFV Name very long CRS, early then not seek CRS
    'He has found Li Si for a while, (he) stopped looking for (him) long ago.'
  c. 他死了很久了，*还在死
    ta si-le_1 hen jiu le_2, hai zai si
    3rd die-PFV very long CRS, still Prog. si
    'He died long ago, *still dying.'
  d. 他死了很久了，没有人还记得他了
    ta si-le_1 hen jiu le_2, meiyou ren hai jide ta le_2
    3rd die-PFV very long CRS, no people still remember 3rd CRS
    'He has died long ago, nobody still remembers him.'

Therefore, the -le_1 in *die-duan le_1 zuo tui*, in spite of its inference, should be construed not as a static imperfective but a perfective aspect marker for this completed dynamic achievement type event (Vendler 1954; Smith 1997).

Pertaining to the meaning of the Chinese perfective, it is necessary to understand the reason for the co-occurrence constraint between -le_1 and a bare objective noun. Lin (2006: 13) notes the oddity of example (13a) in contrast to the acceptability of example (13b). Unfortunately, he decides not to pursue an explanation, saying "[i]t is not clear to me why this is the case. Yet to the extent that such patterns are interpretable, they have a past interpretation." In other words, it is unclear why -le_1 in (10a), or (13b), is acceptable as a perfective but not in (13a).

(13) a. *李四喝了酒
    lisi he-le_1 jiu
    Name drink-PFV wine
    'Lisi drank.'
  b. 李四喝了酒就唱歌
    lisi he-le_1 jiu, jiu chang-le_1 ge
    Name drink-PFV wine, then sing-PFV song
    'Lisi sang after he had drunk.'

喝酒 he-jiu "to drink wine" and 唱歌 chang-ge "to sing" in (13), as well as 吃饭 chi-fan "to eat" in (1a), can be related to the so-call 离合词 liheci "separable words" (Lu, Z 1957; Lu, S 1979), in which a verb and a bare objective noun are used together so much so that they in (14) are treated by many Chinese linguists as a Chinese word. Very often, the object in this kind of construction is best not translated into English as it is typically not referential. Following my previous studies (Sun 2014, 2015), I will call them phrase-like compounds for the sake of convenience.[2] However, with the presence of -le_1 without additional language, none of them in (14) is acceptable as complete statement like the -le-less phrase-like words.

(14) a. 毕业 'to graduate'   *毕了业
        bi-ye   complete-affair
    b. 睡觉 'to sleep'   *睡了觉
        shui-jiao sleep-sleep
    c. 抽烟 'to smoke'   *抽了烟
        chou-yan   suck-smoke
    d. 开刀 'to operate'   *开了刀
        kai-dao   open-knife

As phrase-like words, the internal morphemes of this type of compounds can be separated and expanded into acceptable verb phrases in (15), where the verb phrases can be said to be bounded with a temporal end point in two ways. In (15a and b) the expanded VP bi-le ye 'to graduate' or shui-le jiao 'to sleep' are bounded by a following event jiu hui jia 'then go home' or jiu you jingshen 'then re-energized' respectively. That is, for (15a), graduation must occur before going home. As to (15c & d), the expanded VP chou-le yi-zhi yan "to smoke a cigarette" or kai-le yi-ci dao "to have a surgery" contains a numeral classifier construction that makes the objective noun quantified and referential.

(15) a. 我毕了业就回家
        wo   bi-le_1 ye   jiu   hui jia
        1st complete-PFV affair then go   home
        'I graduated and then went home.'

---

[2] It is proposed in Sun (2014, 2015) that there exist two categories such as word-like words and phrase-like words in Chinese between a phrase and a free morpheme, which is traditionally considered to be a word.

b. 睡了觉就有精神
 shui-le_1 jiao jiu you jingshen
 sleep-PFV sleep then have spirit
 '(He) slept a nap and then felt re-energized.'

c. 他抽了一支烟
 ta chou-le_1 yi-zhi yan
 3rd suck-PFV one-CL cigarette
 'He smoked a cigarette.'

d. 我开了一次刀
 wo kai-le_1 yi-ci dao
 1st open-PFV one-CL knife
 'I had a surgery.'

The examples in (16) show that a Chinese bare nominal in the object position can be interpreted as specific or non-specific depending on a context. In (16a) the noun *shu* is most likely used as a noun without referring to any specific book as the sentence implies that either I am simply someone who habitually buy books or I have the intention to buy a random book or book(s). In both readings, the book is non-specific, i.e., the speaker does not have any specific book in mind. However, in (16b) the same bare noun *shu* can refer to any book (non-specific as an intention), a specific book, specific books, definite book, or simply non-referentially books. The key is that a bare objective noun in Chinese can be referential, or non-referential, completely depending on a given context. Its interpretation is context-dependent (Chen 2003; Sun 1988). However, when the sentence is marked by a perfective marker, the noun *shu* must have a referential reading (16c), be it specific-indefinite or definite, because *wo mai-le_1 shu gei ta* can no longer be taken as an intention of buying him a book.

(16) a. 我买书
 wo mai shu
 1st buy book
 'I buy books.' (habitually)
 "I (would like to) buy any book/books." (intention)

b. 我买书给他
 wo mai shu gei ta le_2
 1st buy book give 3rd CRS
 'I (would like to) him a book/the book/books.' (intention)
 'I am buying him a book/the book/books.' (progressive)

c. 我买了书给他
   wo mai-le_1 shu   gei   ta
   1ˢᵗ   buy-PFV   book   give   3ʳᵈ
   'I bought him a book/the book/the books.'
d. 我在买书
   wo zai   mai shu
   1ˢᵗ   Prog.   buy book
   'I am buying a book/the/the books.'

Thus, there is a correlation between a dynamic perfective event and a referential reading of the bare objective noun in Chinese. In this light, it follows to say that the unbounded phrase-like words are generally atelic (or an activity that is inherently without an end point), when they are not quantified. These dynamic activities without an end point can easily co-occur with an imperfective/progressive aspect *zai* 在, *zai mai shu* (16d).

The examples from (14) to (16) show that only in bounded situation, the verbal suffix $-le_1$ can co-occur with a bare object NP. Otherwise, it must co-occur with a quantified noun with a numeral classifier that makes the noun referential. In section 3, this will be taken as strong evidence to treat $-le_1$ as an agreement-like perfective marker, as it does not have the power to impose an end point to the predicate.

3 Telicity matching

The Chinese co-occurrence constraint between the perfective $-le_1$ and a quantified objective noun may not be universal. It appears that it is quite all right for Russian to have the same object noun in either perfective or imperfective aspect in (17), as the objective noun *knigu* 'book' can occur in both aspectual contexts.

(17) a. čitala knigu   (imperfective)
         She read the book
     b. pročitala knigu
         She had read the book   (perfective)
         (from Binnick 1991: 136)

Although I am not in a position to explain what exactly is at work in Russian, the difference between Chinese and Russian makes it necessary to define the Chinese perfective aspect in a slightly different way.[3]

Linguists generally agree (Smith 1997; Smith and Erbaugh 2005; Lin 2006; Soh 2014, etc.) that the meaning of a perfective aspect is temporally bounded, i.e., an event that contains an end-point. Informally, it makes visible a completed event. A thorough definition of boundedness, though important, is beyond the scope of the current paper. I will simply discuss Smith's (1997: 266) definition:

a. $I\ F/E$
  ////////(RVC)
b. *Le* (S) makes visible a situation S at interval I. For times $t_{i,j}$, t_n, included in I: there is a time t_i that coincides with *I* and a time t_j that coincides with *F*, or a time t_j that coincides with *E*. There is not time ti_{-1} in I that precedes *I/E*.

In Smith's schematic statement above, *I* and *F* denote endpoints of the situation and *E* denotes a single-stage event (or an instantaneous event such as *to find (something)*, *die-duan tui* (10 & 12). In other words, the perfective applies to non-stative situation and spans their initial and final end.

Why, then, in this light is *shu* 书 after the verb *kan* 看 in (18c) unacceptable whereas similar Russian sentences are perfectly good in a non-stative situation? Sybesma (1997) notes that no Chinese verb is inherently bounded. So the following focuses on the object of the verbs in this kind of verb phrases. The multiple readings that a Chinese bare noun can have in different contexts may tell us something interesting. In (18a) *shu* book is non-referential and forms a phrase-like word for an activity "to read" with the verb *kan* 'to look'. The situation of the clause is temporally open, i.e., without an end point. With a perfect clitic, or currently relevant state, le_2, the same bare noun *shu* must be interpreted as definite in (18b). Temporally speaking, the situation marked by -le_2 is viewed as bounded, perhaps by speech/narrative time. In (18d), the same bare noun *shu* has a definite interpretation when it is bounded by another verb phrase. Then, the unacceptability of (18c) obviously has something to do with the indeterminacy of the referential status of *shu*. Even though a bare noun can be referential

---

[3] A reviewer who is a native speaker of Russian questioned whether the systems of the two languages are actually directly comparable. We appreciate this comment and do agree that Chinese and Russian perfectives are not the same. However, a systematic analysis of Russian aspectual system will take us far beyond the scope of the current paper. The Russian examples are cited to show a simple fact that a bare nominal in the objective position can, for whatever reason, occur in Russian perfective aspect. Thus, the purpose is to show the Chinese perfective suffix –*le* is different from the Russian perfective in this respect, although they are both commonly treated as perfective markers by many scholars (Binnick 1991; Comrie 1976; Smith 1997).

or non-referential, in *ta kan shu*, a habitual and unbounded activity in (18a), it is temporally open and, thus, incompatible with a perfective situation. The addition of the perfective -le_1 in (18c) is ungrammatical as the verbal suffix does not seem to make visible the referential property of the bare objective noun *shu* or changes it into a telic situation on the ground that, without the verbal suffix -le_1, (18c) is identical with (18a). The *ta kan shu le_2* and *ta kan-le_1 shu* in (18b and d) are temporally bounded by the meanings associated with the currently relevant state clitic le_2 and the clause *jiu hui mingbai*, and the referential readings of the bare noun *shu* are then made visible in these situations.

(18) a. 他看书
    ta   kan shu
    3rd look book
    'He reads.'   (habitual)

  b. 他看书了
    ta   kan shu le_2
    3rd look book CRS
    'He has read the book/is reading the book now.'

  c. *他看了书
    ta   kan-le_1 shu
    3rd look-PFV book

  d. 他看了书就会明白
    ta   kan-le_1 shu   jiu   hui   mingbai
    3rd look-PFV book then will understand
    '(If) he has read the book, (he) then will understand.'

  e. 他看了书了
    ta   kan-le_1 shu le_2
    3rd look   book CRS
    'He has read the book.'

Then, it becomes evident that the perfective marker le_1 by itself does not impose an end-point to a situation. Rather it must match an asserted telic situation, such as the match between le_1 and le_2 in (18e) or between le_1 and the following clause *jiu hui mingbai* in (18d). That is, the Chinese perfective marker must occur in a situation that is telic on its own. (18c) is not acceptable, because -le_1 itself does not bound. In a way, this phenomenon can be compared to the use or not of English plural marker –s that must agree with a third-person singular subject in present tense. That is, -s simply does not occur without an appropriate sentential subject in present tense. In Chinese, the perfective marker must occur with an appropriate telic situation. *kan-le_1 shu* (18c) is bad because le_1 fails to find a match. The temporally atelic Chinese phrase-like words that can only co-occur with a progressive imperfective marker *zai* in *ta zai kan shu* "He is reading" but not the perfective -*le*$_1$. From this, we can also tell that -*le*$_1$ is not an imperfective marker. Otherwise, as an imperfective marker, the context should have been right for it. But it is not.

In the light of the above discussion, the words *makes visible* of article b of Smith's definition given above should be revised to *matches* in (19):

(19) b. *Le*$_1$ (S) **matches** a situation S at interval I. For times $t_{i,j}$, t_n, included in I: there is a time t_i that coincides with *I* and a time t_j that coincides with *F*, or a time t_j that coincides with *E*. There is not time t_{i-1} in I that precedes I/E.

Wu notes (2005) that –*le* can denote completion, termination, and inception by proposing a SigP (Significant Point) that –*le* identifies. It is nevertheless totally unclear why a SigP is needed in Chinese perfective, but not so in Russian. The proposal in (19) explains Wu's observation as a matching process in terms of a cross-linguistic understanding of a perfective aspect. In so doing, the meaning of the Chinese perfective is not that much different from what a general perfective aspect is. *Le*$_1$ is perhaps simply a typologically weaker perfective marker in the sense that it does not make visible such a situation but rather needs to match a situation that is already temporally bounded on its own, thus obviating the need for an arbitrary SigP identification process.

4 What constitutes a matching situation for the perfective *Le1*

(20b) shows that a matching situation may be a temporally bounded clause (signaled by the numeral classifier construction) where it occurs, and (20a) shows that temporally indeterminate verb phrases with a bare nominal object can co-occur with -*le*$_1$ only if the clause is temporally bounded by a following clause. The following is some further discussion on what boundedness should be taken with respect to more Chinese data.

First of all, recall that *kan-shu* look-book is a phrase-like word with a non-referential noun. It makes up an activity meaning "to read". It is nevertheless unacceptable with the addition of -*le*$_1$ without clarification. It was also noted above that a Chinese phrase-like word is separable and expandable. This will allow the perfective marker to occur between the verb and the noun. But in so doing, the object noun cannot be bare unless it is followed by another clause like *jiu zou le* (20a).

Accordingly, an object noun modified by a numeral classifier also entails a bounded situation. The reason is simple and straightforward. *Reading a book* is an event that inherently contains a beginning point and an end point (20b). Thus, it is generally called an accomplishment situation (Vendler 1957; Dowty 1979; Smith 1997) that is always temporally bounded. Therefore, when the object of a verb is quantified, the clause can always co-occur with the perfective marker. So an accomplishment situation, or a quantified verb phrase, can match -le_1. There are, however, two possible readings for the two examples in (20), completed or terminated (Smith 1997; Peck, Lin, and Sun 2016). In these cases the final point has been reached in different senses. For the completion reading, Li Si finished reading the book from beginning to end. And for the termination reading, Lisi finished the event by just looking at it briefly without reading it from the first word to the last word.

(20) a. 李四看了书就走了
 Name kan(-le_1) shu
 Li Si look-PFV book
 'Li Si looked at the book and then left.'
 'He read the book and then left.'
 b. 他看（了）一本书
 ta kan(-le_1) yi-ban shu
 3rd look-PFV a-CL book
 'He read a book.'
 'He looked at a book.'

Secondly, an instantaneous achievement event in which the initial point and end point co-occur is also inherently telic, or bounded, and a suitable match for le_1.

(21) 李四跌断了左腿，现在不能走路
 Lisi die-duan-le_1 zuo tui, xianzai bu neng zo ulu
 Name fall-break-PFV left leg, now not can walk road
 'Lisi has broken his left leg, (he) cannot walk.'

Stative events can be changed (or coerced into achievement as Lin [2006] notes) into an achievement type. As a psych-verb that does not imply a change of state, *zhidao* without -le_1 is static and simply entails a certain state without asserting a change, i.e., "the entire school knows this". However, once it co-occurs with a perfective marker, it indicates an instantaneous situation (22) in which the beginning point and end point co-occur.

(22) 全校都知道(了)这件事
 quan xiao dou zhidao-le_1 zhe-jian shi
 entire school all know-PFV Dem-CL matter
 'The entire school knows this.' (without the perfective)
 'The entire school came to know this.' (with the perfective)

This is actually a very robust operation to form a type of Chinese achievement situation commonly known as inceptive, or inchoative, (Lin 2006; Smith 1997), i.e., an instantaneous change to start a new state. Chinese adjectives that function as the predicate of a clause without the need of a copula like English can also do this. *Hao* "good", which is a static adjective used as a predicate implying a permanent static situation in (23a), actually represents a large set of common adjectives with a similar predicative function, *gao* "tall", *hong* "red", *kuai* "quick", *gaoxing* "happy", etc. However, once it is combined with a perfective, it signifies an instantaneous change of state. That is, the perfective -le_1 matches this bounded situation somewhat like the more typical achievement type in (21). (23c) shows that current relevance can only be inferred but probably not asserted.

(23) a. 他很好
 ta hen hao
 3rd very good
 'He is very good.'
 b. 他好了很多
 ta hao-le_1 hen duo
 3rd good-PFV very much
 'He has got much better.'
 c. 他好了很多 (了),*还在好
 ta hao-le_1 hen duo le_2, hai zai hao
 3rd good-PFV very much CRS, still Prog. good
 'He has got much better, *(and) is still getting better.'

The examples in (24), representing a tricky set of data, nevertheless pertains to how situation types, thus boundedness of situations, should be looked at in Chinese more generally. This type involves data like *yang yi-tiao yu* in (26a), which, without an obvious change-of-state (or affectedness) of the object, is not a typically dynamic event, even when its object *yu* fish is quantified.[4]

---

[4] Other similar Chinese examples are VPs like *zu yidong fangzi* "to rent a house", *tui yiliang che* "to push a cart", etc.

Before we look at the examples in (26), let us consider *yang yu* 'to keep fish' in (24a) that is perhaps an activity like the phrase-like words above as it can co-occur with a progressive marker *zai* in (24b). It refers to all the activities that one may have to do in order to keep a fish. The ungrammatical (24c) demonstrates that *keeping a fish* is not a stative predicate like *hao* in (23) or an achievement predicate *die-duan zuotui* in (21) that do not co-occur with either a progressive or an imperfective marker *-zhe*.[5]

(24) a. 我养鱼 (activity)
 wo yang yu
 1st grow fish
 'I keep fish.'
 b. 我在养鱼
 wo zai yan yu
 1st Prog. grow fish
 'I am keeping fish.'
 c. *我在好
 wo zai hao
 1st Prog. good
 d. 我在养一条鱼
 wo zai yang yi-tiao yu
 1st Prog. grow a-CL fish
 'I am keeping a fish.'
 e. 我在看一本书
 wo zai kain yi-ben shu
 1st Prog. look a-CL book
 'I am reading a book.'

---

5 Achievement situations generally do not co-occur with *zai* 在 or *zhe* 着 (Chen 1991).

*他在跌断左腿
ta zai tie-duan zuotui
3rd Prog. fall-break left leg

*他跌断着左腿
ta tie-duan-zhe zuotui
3rd fall-break-IMP left leg

*他在好 or *他好着
ta zai hao ta hao-zhe
3rd Prog. good 3rd hao-IMP

With achievement and stative possibilities out, we need to find if *yang yi-tiao yu* is an activity or an accomplishment. An easy way to distinguish the two is to use a time adverbial. Normally, an accomplishment situation is correlated to an in-adverbial, and an activity to a for-adverbial (25).

(25) a. accomplishment: I read a book *for/in an hour.
     b. activity: I read in for/*an hour.

First, as a grammatical statement in Chinese, (26a) does not mean "I keep a fish," as it is a questionable statement in English.[6] It is good in Chinese and must be interpreted as an intention that I (want) to keep a fish in response to "How many fish do you want to keep?". The addition of a time adverbial *yinian* 'a year' in (26b) appears to have an in-adverbial interpretation only when it means that the speaker (wants to) keep a fish every year, as it certainly does not have the for-adverbial meaning, "I will keep a fish for a year". Rather, (26b) means something habitual, as if fish-keeping would continue with a different fish each year. It is, therefore, an in-adverbial reading. Interestingly, with the addition of a perfective -le_1, (26c) means that "I kept (or started to keep) a fish within a year". But this is not what we should expect from either an activity or an accomplishment situation, as neither would have the "start" sense that associated with inchoative. Note that an inchoative (23c) does not allow a *still*-phrase, but it is perfectly good in (26d), implying something that may hold at the time of utterance. So we are here back to the issue of imperfective. Is -le_1 an imperfective, even though we have been trying to argue away it?

(26) a. 我养一条鱼
        wo yang yi-tiao yu
        1st grow a-CL   fish
        'I (want to) keep a fish.'   (intention)
     b. 我一年养一条鱼
        wo yinian   yang yi-tiao yu
        1st one year grow a-CL   fish
        'I keep a fish (within) each year.' (intention, habitual)

---

6 Lin (2003) argues that –le_1 here is a realization marker compatible with both perfective and imperfective aspects (Lin 2006).

他养了一条金鱼
ta yang le   yi tiao jinyu
3rd grow-PFV one-CL   goldfish
'He is keeping a fish'   (Lin 2003: 266)

c. 我一年内养了一条鱼
 wo yinian nei yang-le_1 yi-tial yu
 1st one year in only grow-PFV a-CL fish
 'I kept a fish within a year.'   (in-adverbial, and bounded)
d. 我去年养了一条鱼，现在还在养
 wo qunian yang-le yi-tiao yu, xianzai hai zai yang
 1st last-year grow-PFV a-CL fish, now still Prog. grow
 'I kept a fish last year and (I) am still keeping it.'
 'I kept a fish last year and (I) am still keeping fish.'

However, it is probably a terminated situation. Following a recent multi-point closed-scale analysis on English verbs with incremental-theme (Rappaport Hovav 2008; Kennedy 2012; Lin 2011; Peck, Lin, and Sun 2013, 2016), we propose a multi-point closed-scale analysis to the Chinese termination reading of verbs of creation, consumption, and affectedness[7] that have been found difficult to be reconciled as an accomplishment. That is, (27) in Chinese is ambiguous between completion and termination. If it is used meaning *ate a cake*, it is an accomplishment situation (completion) just like what the English *ate a cake* means. But a completed event is not supposed to be compatible with a reading that can be cancelled by *but I have not finished it*. However, in Chinese it was found by Tai (1984) that it is quite possible to have a termination reading, i.e., *ate a certain cake*. In this case, (27) can be followed by 可是没吃完 *keshi mei chi-wan* "but (I) have not finished (it)."

(27) 我吃了一个蛋糕
 wo chi-le_1 yi-ge dangao
 I eat-PFV a-CL cake
 'I ate a cake, (*but I did not finish it).'
 'I ate a certain cake, (but I did not finish it).'   (Soh and Kuo 2005: 204)

As a multi-point closed scale event, it implies "some" but not "maximal" change even though these verb phrases lexicalize inherent endpoints. In other words, *yang-le yi-tiao yu* may very well be like (26) to contain a maximal end point, the entire life-span of a fish. However, when a speaker reports to someone his new hobby in keeping a fish, the speaker usually is not concerned about the moment when a fish would end its life. So typically, it implies "some" change, including the initial point and a certain point on a multi-point closed scale, and it can still be negated as only a certain point (before the maximal end point) has been

---

7 Peck, Lin, and Sun (2016) actually use the term "affection" instead of "affectedness."

reached. That is, in order for *yang-le yi-tiao yu* to make sense, a certain change has to have happened realizing the state "I am keeping a fish" from "I did not have a fish". It is then a termination point of a multi-point closed scalar event that does not entail a maximal change. Even though its entire scope is closed and inherently bounded, a termination occurs some point after the initial point, but before the inherent end-point on a multi-point scale is reached. This then explains why there seems to be a result stage unattained at the time of utterance because the terminated point is not the maximal, inherent end point. The attraction of the termination understanding is that we can say that *yang yi-tiao yu* is a bounded situation and can match the perfective le_1 without any problem. This is a closed situation on a scale with multiple points.

In sum, (28a & c) are both activity type situation, but (28b & d) are multi-point closed scale situations involving verbs of affectedness in *kan yi-ben shu* "read a book" (Peck, Lin, and Sun 2016) and *yang yi-tiao yu* "keep a fish" that allows a termination reading without including the inherent end-point. Lexically speaking, there is a propensity for *yang-le yi-tiao yu* (28d) to have a termination reading than *kan-le yi-ben shu* (28b). Therefore, they are in a position to match the telic restriction of the Chinese perfective $-le_1$.

(28) a. 我看书 (activity)
       wo kan   shu
       1st look book
       'I read'   (habitual or intention)
    b. 我下午看了一本书 ...   (multi-point closed scale)
       wo xiawu   kan-le_1 yi-ben shu
       1st afternoon look-PFV   a-CL   book
       'I read a book in the afternoon, *(I did not finish the entire book but will continue to read tomorrow)*
    c. 我养鱼   (activity)
       wo yang yu
       1st grow fish
       'I keep fish.'   (habitual or intention)
    d. 我去年养了一条鱼   (multi-point closed scale)
       wo qunian   yang-le_1 yi-tiao yu
       1st go-year grow-PFV   a-CL   fish
       'I kept a fish last year, *(the fish is still alive and I will continue to take good care of it in the future.*'

5 Conclusion

In conclusion, this paper has demonstrated that the Chinese verbal suffix -le_1 is a perfective aspect marker without any imperfective meaning. Its uses can be explained in terms of a cross-linguistic understanding of a perfective aspect. It is, however, different from its counterpart in Russian, as it requires a matching operation between the perfective and a temporally bounded context in Chinese, as it does not impose an end point. The stative analysis of certain Chinese data in the past was probably due to our general failure to recognize the scalar property of the Chinese verbs with incremental themes. In the light of the new insight on multi-point closed scalar verb phrases, the uses of the Chinese perfective -le_1 can then be explained in a manner that is much simpler and closer to fact. Pedagogically speaking in CSL, this analysis will enable us to teach the Chinese verbal suffix -le_1 without having to make students learn how to figure out how to choose between perfective and imperfective aspects. In the final analysis, it is simply a perfective aspect marker that must occur in an already bounded (telic) situation.

References

Binnick, Robert. 1991. *The Time and the Verb: A Guide to Tense and Aspect*. Oxford: Oxford University press.
Chen Ping 陈平.1988. 论现代汉语时间系统的三元结构 (On tripartite organization of the temporal system in Modern Chinese). *Zhonguo yuwen* 中国语文 6. 401–422.
Chen, Ping. 2003. Indefinite determiner introducing definite referent: A special use of "yi 'one' + classifier" in Chinese. *Lingua* 113(12). 1169–1184.
Comrie, Bernard. 1976. *Aspect*. Cambridge, England: Cambridge University Press
Dowty, David. 1979. *Word meaning and montague grammar*. Dordrecht: D. Reidel.
Kennedy, Christopher. 2012. The composition of incremental change. In Demonte, Violeta & Louise McNally (eds.), *Telicity, change, state: A cross-categorial view of event structure*, 103–121. Oxford, England: Oxford University Press.
Li, Charles and Sandra Thompson. 1981. *Mandarin Chinese: Functional reference grammar*. Berkeley: University of California Press
Lin, Jingxia. 2011. *The encoding of motion events in Chinese: Multi-morpheme motion constructions*. PhD dissertation, Stanford University.
Lin, Jo-Wang. 2003. Temporal reference in Mandarin Chinese. *Journal of East Asian Linguistics* 12. 259–311.
Lin, Jo-Wang. 2006. Time in a language without tense: The case of Chinese. *Journal of Semantics* 23. 1–53.
Liu, Yuehua, Pan Wenyue & Gu Ye. 2004. 《实用现代汉语语法》(A practical grammar of modern Chinese), Beijing: Commercial Press.
Lu, Shuxiang. 1979.《汉语语法分析问题》*Issues in the analyses of Chinese grammar*. Beijing: Commercial Press.

Lu, Zhiwei. 1957. 《汉语的构词法》 *Chinese morphology*. Beijing: Kexue Chubanshe.
Peck, Jeeyoung, Jingxia Lin and Chaofen Sun. 2016. A scalar analysis of Chinese incremental them VP. In Eom and & (eds.), *Language Evolution and Changes in Chinese, Journal of Chinese Linguistics* monograph series 26. 216–246.
Peck, Jeeyoung, Jingxia Lin & Chaofen Sun. 2013. Aspectual Classification of Mandarin Chinese Verbs: A Perspective of Scale Structure, *Language and Linguistics* 14(4). 663–700
Rappaport Hovav, Malka. 2008. Lexicalized meaning and the internal structure of events. In Susan Rothstein (ed.), *Theoretical and crosslinguistic approaches to the semantics of aspect*, 12–42. Amsterdam: John Benjamin.
Smith, Carlotta. 1997. *The parameter of aspect*. Dordrecht, The Netherlands: Kluwer Academic Publishers.
Smith, Carlotta & Mary Erbaugh. 2005. Temporal interpretation in Mandarin Chinese. *Linguistics* 43. 713–756.
Soh, Hooi Ling. 2014. Aspect. In C.-T James Huang, Y.-H. Audrey Li & Andrew Simpson (eds.), *The Handbook of Chinese Linguistics*, 126–155. West Sussex, UK: Wiley Blackwell.
Soh, Hooi Ling & Jenny Yi-Chun Kuo. 2005. Perfective aspect and accomplishment situations in Mandarin Chinese. In Angeliek van Hout, Henriette de Swart & Henk Verkuyl (eds.), *Perspectives on aspect*, 199–216. Dordrecht: Springer.
Sun, Chaofen. 1988. The discourse function of the numeral classifiers in Mandarin Chinese. *Journal of Chinese Linguistics*, 16(2). 298–322.
Sun, Chaofen. 2014. The pragmatics of the Chinese marker *de: wo de baba* "my dad" versus *wo baba* "my dad". *Chinese Language and Discourse* 5(1). 7–24.
Sun, Chaofen. 2015. The Uses of *De* 的 as a noun phrase marker. In William S-Y. Wang and Chaofen Sun (eds.), *Oxford Handbook in Chinese Linguistics*, 362–378. Oxford University Press
Sybesma, Rint. 1997. Why Chinese verb-le is a resultative predicate, *Journal of East Asian Linguistics* 6(3). 215–261
Tai, James H.-Y. 1984. Verbs and times in Chinese: Verdler's four categories. In Testen, David, Veena Mishra & Joseph Drogo (eds.), *Papers from the parasession on lexical semantics*, 289–297. Chicago: Chicago University Press.
Vendler, Zeno. 1957. Verbs and times. *The Philosophical Review* 66(2). 143–160.
Wu, J.-S. 2005. The semantics of the perfective LE and its context-dependency: An SDRT approach. *Journal of East Asian Linguistics* 14. 299–336.

Jesús Romero-Trillo
14 Acategorical pragmatic markers: From thematic analysis to adaptive management in discourse

1 Introduction: a history of pragmatic markers

In recent years the publications on the structure, function and cognitive value of pragmatic markers have increased and have provided new theoretical and applied perspectives. Although it is not the objective of this article to present the multifaceted literature on discourse/pragmatic markers and on their various theoretical approaches, as this has been discussed elsewhere (Romero-Trillo 2012), I think it is useful to mention what I consider the main epochs of their study. In the initial stages, many scholars tried to account for the somehow negative function of discourse/pragmatic markers in speech and described their 'vague' function that distorted the syntactic structure of the clause (Schenkein 1972; Jefferson 1978). A second stage, led by conversational analysts, tried to describe the use of the markers within the structure of conversation. Schlegoff (1984), for instance, called them 'continuers' because their main function was to show the listener that the surrounding words were part of a complete discursive unit in progress.

A third, and very influential discourse analysis perspective, was proposed in the seminal work by Schiffrin (1987: 31), when she said that "markers are sequentially dependent elements which bracket units of talk". Her approach to these elements can be summarised as follows: 'Discourse markers... not only differentiate subordinate and coordinate parts of a text from each other; they help speakers express interactional alignments towards each other and enact conversational moves' (1985: 281). Subsequent studies have also delved into the discursive role of the markers, as for example in Fraser (1999: 938): [they] "impose a relationship between some aspect of the discourse segment they are a part of, call it S2, and some aspect of a prior discourse segment, call it S1." Levinson, for instance, suggested that the key to their identification was that they should have "at least a component of meaning that resists truth-conditional treatment" (1983: 87–88).

Later, other studies analysed these elements from a cognitive stance as essential signals of language processing in speech (Romero-Trillo 1994), or as 'cue phrases' that constitute cognitive pegs for text readers (Knott and Dale 1994). In any case all descriptions delved into the identification of the functions that could be performed by these elements accompanied by a continuous and fruitful debate on the linguistic essence of which elements could be included

DOI 10.1515/9783110546095-014

in the category, and on what theoretical grounds. Current research focuses on the description of the markers as a substantial part of linguistic theories that can contribute to their development: variation studies (Aijmer 2013), relevance theory (Blakemore 2002), grammaticalisation (Brinton 1996), discourse studies (Norrick 2009), prosody (Romero-Trillo 2014, in press), etc.

2 Theoretical background: acategorical pragmatic markers and adaptive management

The purpose of this paper is to analyse 'acategorical pragmatic markers' as the epitome of the liaison between thematic structure, context and cognition (Romero-Trillo 2001, in press).

Acategorical pragmatic markers are one of three types, together with lexical and lexical composites, described by Romero-Trillo (2001, in press):

- Acategorical items: those markers that do not have an original grammatical ascription, e.g. *[@:m], m, mhm*, etc.
- Lexical items: those markers whose original category is that of lexical items, e.g. *listen, well, good, fine*, etc.
- Lexical composites: those markers that are phrases composed of, at least, one lexical item plus one or more grammatical items, e.g. *I mean, you know, the thing is*, etc.

The elements classified within the categories of lexical items and lexical composites undergo what has been described as 'discourse grammaticalisation' (Romero-Trillo 2001: 531), a phenomenon that has a direct positive correlation with their frequency of use in language. In other words, the more an element is used as a pragmatic marker the more its original meaning is effaced. Acategorical Pragmatic Markers, on the other hand, are free from any pre-existing grammatical or lexical meaning and function as prototypical elements in adaptive management by weaving the net of discourse between the addresser, the addressee, and the context of a message.

The theoretical premise behind the analysis is that pragmatic markers are inextricably linked to cognitive processes and, as a result, contribute to the structure of the utterances in which they appear through adaptive management. Adaptive management is a process inherent to spoken language that can be described as "the capacity of a speaker to adapt the grammatical, lexical and pragmatic parameters of discourse through a series of remedial elements and through a principled process, in order to comply with the demands of a new cognitive stage in a conversation via a cognitive standardised process" (Romero-Trillo 2007: 83). In other words, adaptive management is related to the speaker's capacity to engage in a negotiating linguistic process by which s/he is able to convey meaning, notwithstanding the cognitive difficulties, thanks to the implementation of remedial strategies to avoid misunderstanding.

In fact, to dodge misunderstanding is one of the goals of any interaction and is achieved through "contextual sifting", i.e. "the process of cognitive filtering that leaves out the incorrect assumptions in a given communicative situation, and sieves through the correct elements to guarantee successful communication" (Romero-Trillo and Maguire 2011: 234). Contextual sifting is, therefore, a demanding process for speakers and a crucial element of pragmatic competence in a language. As all other elements of pragmatic competence, its development is linked to intra- and extra-linguistic factors that are especially important in the development of a second or foreign language, as linguistic competence sometimes develops at a faster pace than pragmatic competence with the unwanted result of 'pragmatic fossilisation' (Romero-Trillo 2001). In other words, adaptive management functions at the interface between the message, the speaker-hearer interaction, and the context.

One of the linguistic models that has emphasised the relationship between these three elements of discourse is the Dynamic Model of Meaning (henceforth DMM) (Kecskés 2008). For DMM the resulting meaning of an utterance is the corollary of a cognitive process construed in context with a division into three elements: private, situational and linguistic context. In order to reflect the inherent dynamic nature of context in conversation in Kecskés' model, Romero-Trillo (2014: 124) introduced adaptive management as the element that guarantees the ongoing remedial processes by continuously sifting the incorrect assumptions, be they of a private, lexical or situational context nature. Figure 1 illustrates adaptive management in discourse:

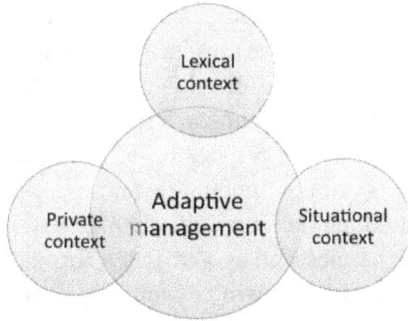

Figure 1. Adaptive Management in discourse

In this sense, the three features that I consider essential to understand the nature and function of pragmatic markers in adaptive management are the following (Romero-Trillo 2007, 2015, in press; Romero-Trillo and Maguire 2011; Maguire and Romero-Trillo 2017):

- The interpretation of propositional meaning;
- The communicative dimension between addresser and addressee;
- The role of context in the process of adaptive management in discourse.

The shift from conceptual to procedural meaning, to use the Relevance Theory terminology (Wilson and Sperber 1993), is one of the most salient features that can be perceived by any speaker in some of the pragmatic markers. The use of expressions such as 'look' or 'listen' to draw the attention of the addressee in a conversation rarely implies that the addresser has to obey and start looking or listening to some visual or aural input. Moreover, the realisation and distribution of these pragmatic markers in conversation in different languages also prove their non-conceptual meaning (Romero-Trillo 1997).

In addition, the present study intends to reorient the traditional theme-rheme description of Systemic Functional Grammar, based on the clause as the unit of analysis, and proves, with the help of corpus data, the role of acategorical pragmatic markers as fundamental elements in the tone unit and, therefore, in the cognitive processing of speech.

Traditionally, Systemic Functional Grammar (henceforth SFC) has advocated the division of the clause into 'theme' and 'rheme' (Halliday 1994) in the realization of the textual metafunction. According to this theoretical model, the 'theme', the first element of the clause, can be subdivided into 'multiple themes'. Being elements that appear at the beginning of a linguistic sequence, multiple themes may include certain expressions whose function can be equivalent to the functions realized by pragmatic markers. Nevertheless, in my opinion, one of the main caveats of SFG is that the description of the 'theme' is mainly conceived for the analysis of written texts and not for the analysis of spoken discourse (Romero-Trillo 1994). The reason for this inadequacy is the pervasive presence of pragmatic markers in speech with their fully-fledged prosodic value and elusive nature that render thematic analysis impossible to perform in SFG canonical terms.

Pragmatic markers do not restrict their role to the realization of continuative themes, as proposed by Halliday (1994: 53). In fact, pragmatic markers can expand their function and become a topical theme (Romero-Trillo 1994), i.e. the element that construes the topic, processes the message and carries it through the conversation. This function can be seen in the following example from the London-Lund Corpus, which shows it with the use of '[@:m]' at the beginning of the tone units. The pragmatic marker is used to link the information conveyed in the previous tone unit with the forthcoming information in which the rheme follows the marker that is used as the start of that specific tone unit. In this sense, acategorical pragmatic markers are cognitively used to connect forthcoming and previous discourse and mark mental processing in search of the exact words to follow:

1 1 4 630 1 1 A   11   ^y=es# -   /
1 1 4 640 1 1 A   11   **[@:m]** . ^one \other thing S/am# -   /
1 1 4 650 1 1 A   11   **[@:m]** - ^De!l\aney# -   /
1 1 4 660 1 1 A   11   a Ca^n/adian#

In the present article I will concentrate on the analysis of acategorical pragmatic markers as topical themes vis-à-vis their specific role in cognition and interaction (Boomer 1965; Goldman-Eisler 1958, 1961; Henderson 1974; Maclay and Oswood 1959; Natale, Entin, and Jaffe 1979). Acategorical pragmatic markers are, especially when they appear in thematic position, the prototypical elements that realise adaptive management as they are used by speakers to reformulate, think and plan in advance, observe the addressee's reaction to the message, etc. In fact, pragmatic markers play an essential role in the initial position of the tone unit and "their appearance always coincides with the element that initiates the development of the message in the tone unit, characterised in this case by the cognitive entropy for syntactic and semantic accuracy of the forthcoming discourse liaised with the preceding one" (Romero-Trillo 1994: 499).

3 Analysis of pragmatic markers as topical themes

The present section will present the prosodic analysis of the three types of pragmatic markers when they appear in thematic position in the London-Lund Corpus (Svartvik and Quirk 1980) (henceforth LLC). The corpus offers a detailed prosodic transcription of 50,000 words of naturally occurring casual conversation from British English. The prosodic symbols used in the transcription are the following:

#	end of tone unit
^	onset
/	rising nuclear tone
\	falling nuclear tone
/\	rise-fall nuclear tone

V   fall-rise nuclear tone
_   level nuclear tone
[ ] enclose partial words and phonetic symbols
.   normal stress
!   booster: higher pitch than preceding prominent syllable
=   booster: continuance
(( )) unclear
* * simultaneous speech
-   pause of one stress unit

The total number of acategorical pragmatic markers in the corpus is 6,921, of which 5,996 appear in initial position of the tone unit, thus realising the function of topical themes, and 925 appear in non-initial, i.e. medial or final, position of the tone unit.

3.1 Acategorical pragmatic markers as topical themes

The total number of acategorical pragmatic markers realising the topical thematic function is 5,996 and have the following distribution:

- [m]   = 109
- [@:m] = 2,921
- [@:]   = 2,966

The appearance of these elements can be inside a turn in which the speaker ends a tone unit and starts the following with one of these markers, as in the following examples:

(1) **[m]**
  B 11 3 ^\ah#   /
  A 13 3 and ^that`s [dhi] ^that`s [dhi] *((. ^wh\at do you/
  A 13 3 **[m]** 'call it#))*   /
  B 11 3 *^that`s the "g\auleiters#*

(2) **[@:m]**
  A 14 *[dhi] the ^other the ^other the ^other* the ^other/
  A 14 m/an# .   /
  A 12 **[@:m]** - ((who ^[rou?] 3 to 4 sylls)) I ^th\ought# /
  A 11 was ^going to get you :wV/ild# -   /
  A 11 was ^P\otter# - -

(3) **[@:]**
    a   20 1did you meet . ((Fuller))   /
    B 11 1^y/es#   /
    B 11 1it was ^he who in!v\ited _me# -   /
    B 11 1**[@:]** - - - and [@:] . it was a ^v\ery _pleasant /
    B 11 1_day# .

The elements can also appear across turns when the new speaker starts with a marker, as in the following examples:

(4) **[m]**
    B 11 1th\ey _said {^n\o#}# .   /
    a   20 1they said no   /
    B 11 1**[m]** . ^very !qu\ickly _I _mean#   /
    B 11 1[wi] with ^no ((waiting)) at !\all#

(5) **[@:m]**
    B 11 1 at ^this _very !m\oment#   /
    a   20 1 get [@:m] a bookseller such as Blackwell /
    B 11 1 ^Blackwells to h/andle it#   /
    a   20 1 **[@:]** or IUB *.* and [@m - @] it shouldn`t be too /
    a   20 1 bad an

(6) **[@:]**
    A 11 [@:m] - - De^laney`s the Ca:n\adian . st/udent /
    A 11 {re^m/ember#}#   /
    A 11 ^last y/ear#   /
    B 11 ^[mh/m]#   /
    A 11 **[@:]** he ^should have had his . dissertation \/in# /
    A 11 ((at the)) be^ginning of M\/ay#

From a prosodic perspective, I would like to highlight that all acategorical markers appear without tonicity (i.e. without prosodic focus), realising what Romero-Trillo (2001) described as Tone 0 to include the absence of tonicity as one important addition to Halliday's model of intonation (Halliday 1967, 1970). This fact indicates that these markers realise unmarked themes, i.e. without focus, and follow the most frequent theme-theme structure in which the focus typically falls on the last lexical item of the tone unit. Unmarked tonicity also indicates that the information conveyed by these markers is related to some previous information already shared with the interlocutors.

It is also important to highlight that most acategorical thematic markers in topical position tend to follow tone units that have a rising tone, both inside the turns and across turns, which points to the fact that they are cognitive mechanisms to process and think about a previous question or non-assertive statement.

3.2 Acategorical pragmatic markers in non-initial positions of the tone unit

In this section, I will describe the acategorical pragmatic markers under study when they appear in non-initial position of the tone unit.

The total number of elements in non-initial position (middle or final) found in the LLC is 925 for the three pragmatic markers, with the following distribution:

- [m] = 14
- [@:m] = 456
- [@:] = 455

and their prototypical realisations are the following:

3.2.1 Analysis of [m]

The pragmatic marker [m] appears 14 times in non-initial position of the tone unit in the LLC. Here follows an example of its use in middle position:

(7) B   11 1{re!v\ised} consti:t\ution#   /
    B   11 1^f\or#   /
    B   11 1[dhi] ^School of Y/iddish# .   /
    B   11 1in ^which . [@:m] the main !p\oint#   /
    B   13 1of ^my . of ^my **[m]** ^what triggered the whole thing/
    B   13 1!\off#   /
    B   21 1*((was when))*

And in final position:

(8) A   21 **^think** 'T`ll just 'have to   /
    B   11 **^[\m]#**   /
    A   11 ":say I((`ll)) just 'do the ":miracles :this t/ime#/
    A   11 and we`ll ^have an!other 'go at the ((**[m]**))   /
    A   11 mor/alities#   /
    A   11 ((^l\ater#))

3.2.2 Analysis of [@:m]

The pragmatic marker [@:m] appears 456 times in non-initial position of the tone unit in the LLC. An example of its appearance in middle position is the following:

(9) a 11 it is ^{g\oing to a'mount to} :{s\omething 'like} /
    a 11 :twenty-one and a 'half m\illions# .   /
    a 11 of ^which in !!th\is 'college#   /
    a 11 ^this . 'really . 'means . **[@:m]** :s\/omething /
    a 11 ar'ound# .

And an example of this marker in final position is the following:

(10) q7 11 ^m\any 'people 'in this H/ouse#   /
     q7 11 would ^h\ope#   /
     q7 11 that ^this 'statement would !n\/ot be **[@:m]#** . /
     q7 11 ^dribbled :\out#   /
     q7 11 in the ^last few d\ays#

3.2.3 Analysis of [@:]

The element [@:] has a frequency of 455 hits in non-initial position of the tone unit, which is almost equal to the element [@:m]. An example of the marker in middle position is the following:

(11) B 11 it`s ^not 'worth the tr\ouble# - - -   /
     B 11 ^not 'worth the tr\ouble# - - -   /
     B 11 ^this is **[@:]** ((the)) :little . :fellow (([ae] in))/
     B 11 the department of sty:listics at . :B\urgos#

And here follows an example of this pragmatic marker in final position:

(12) B 11 3 ^\isn`t it# .   /
     A 11 3 ^n\o# - -   /
     A 11 3 [@:m - - - w@ @:] . ^we`ve got to **[@:]** - - - /
     A 11 3 dec/ide# -   /
     A 11 3 ^what the :structure of :faculty b/oards#

4 Discussion

The analysis of the data indicates that acategorical pragmatic markers mainly concentrate in the initial position of the tone unit, 87% of the cases, as Figure 2 shows:

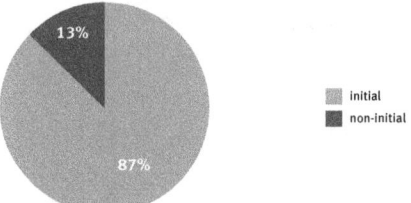

Figure 2. Distribution of acategorical pragmatic markers in topical position

The analysis of the results for the pragmatic markers [m], [@:m] and [@:] shows a similar proportion of use (between 86% and 89%), as can be seen in Figures 3 to 5.

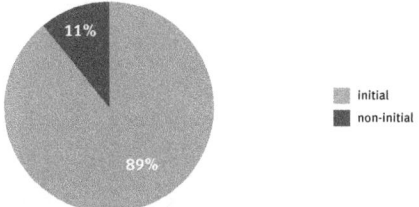

Figure 3. Distribution of the pragmatic marker [m]

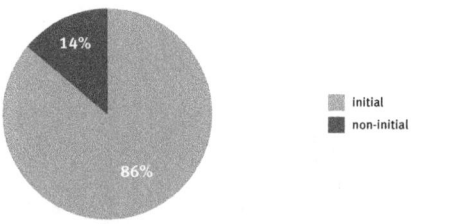

Figure 4. Distribution of the pragmatic marker [@:m]

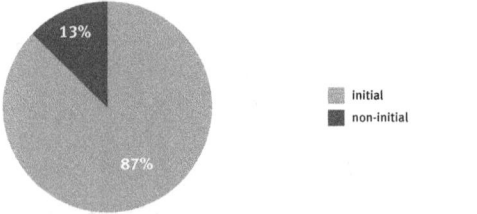

Figure 5. Distribution of the pragmatic marker [@:]

As far as position is concerned, the results show that there is an overall preference for the appearance of acategorical pragmatic markers in initial position, realising the function of topical themes. However, the chi-square test did not render statistically significant differences in the use of the markers as topical themes (chi-square= 0.49; p=0.7). This fact indicates that although there is an overwhelming use of these markers in initial position, they have a consistent presence in non-final position as elements that contribute to adaptive management.

In terms of prosody, the results show that all instances of acategorical pragmatic markers are realised with Tone 0. This shows the topical dependence on a previous given contextual element shared by the interlocutors. In the case of acategorical pragmatic markers in non-initial position, these elements also appear without tonicity in middle and final position. I would like to highlight that the number of markers with a long vowel sound in initial position, [@:m] and [@:], is very high: 5,887 instances, and that the number of elements with only a consonant sound, [m], is 109 instances. This preponderance of long vowels (98.12%) in thematic position of pragmatic markers may indicate their possible role in cognitive processing. Also, the proportion of long vowel markers is much higher (98.48%) than with the consonant sound, which reinforces the use of long vowel acategorical markers to signal word search also in non-initial position.

5 Conclusions

The present article has described the role of acategorical pragmatic markers as elements that realise adaptive management to construct meaning in discourse. The study has analysed their role as topical themes for adaptive management and their overwhelming appearance in first position in the tone unit, thus showing this preference in comparison with their appearance in non-initial position. The examples have shown how these elements can appear in initial-topical position and are used by the speaker to link the cognitive content of the previous tone unit to anchor the following discourse without the need to use lexical or grammatical cohesive devices. This fact proves their function for adaptive management as elements that guarantee communication vis-à-vis the lexical, situational and private information in interaction, while maintaining the prosodic and interactional context. Phonologically speaking, the study has shown the prevalence of the elements that are realised with a long vowel, and their possible role in language processing. Also, the results prove that acategorical pragmatic markers do not convey tonicity and are, therefore, realised with Tone 0. The study has also shown that the pragmatic markers follow the theme-theme classical structure in

Systemic Functional Grammar, in which unmarked themes are unstressed and the tonic usually falls on the last lexical item of the tone unit.

To conclude, I believe that acategorical pragmatic markers have a fundamental role in intercultural pragmatics and, as a result, must be considered essential elements in the teaching of English as their discursive and cognitive role in conversation may have different realisations in other languages.

Acknowledgement: This research was supported by the Ministerio de Economía y Competitividad (Spain) with the Grant: FFI2016-75160-R

References

Aijmer, Karin. 2013. *Understanding pragmatic markers: A variational pragmatic approach.* Edinburgh: Edinburgh University Press

Blakemore, Diane. 2002. *Relevance and linguistic meaning: The semantics and pragmatics of discourse markers.* Cambridge: Cambridge University Press

Boomer, Donald S. 1965. Hesitation and grammatical encoding. *Language and Speech* 8. 148–158.

Brinton, Laurel J. 1996. *Pragmatic markers in English: Grammaticalization and discourse functions.* Berlin & New York: Mouton de Gruyter.

Fraser, Bruce. 1999. What are discourse markers? *Journal of Pragmatics* 31. 931–952.

Goldman-Eisler, Frieda. 1958. Speech production and the predictability of words in context. *Quarterly Journal of Experimental Psychology* 10. 96–106.

Goldman-Eisler, Frieda. 1961. A comparative study of two hesitation phenomena. *Language and Speech* 4: 18–26.

Halliday, Michael Alexander Kirkwood. 1967. *Intonation and grammar in British English.* The Hague: Mouton.

Halliday, Michael Alexander Kirkwood. 1970. *A course in spoken English.* Oxford: Oxford University Press

Halliday, Michael Alexander Kirkwood. 1994. *An introduction to functional grammar* (2nd Edition). London: Edward Arnold

Henderson, Alan I. 1974. Time patterns in spontaneous speech, cognitive stride or random walk? A reply to Jaffe et al. (1972). *Language and Speech* 17. 119–125.

Jefferson, Gail. 1978. What's in aNYEM. *Sociology* 12. 135–139.

Knott, Alistair & Robert Dale. 1994. *Using linguistic phenomena to motivate a set of coherence relations. Discourse Processes* 18. 35–62.

Levinson, Stephen P. 1983. *Pragmatics.* Cambridge: Cambridge University Press.

Maclay, Howard & Charles E. Oswood. 1959. Hesitation phenomena in spontaneous English speech. *Word* 15(1). 19–44.

Maguire, Laura & Jesús Romero-Trillo. 2017. Adaptive Management and bilingual education: A longitudinal corpus-based analysis of pragmatic markers in teacher talk. In István Kecskés & Stavros Assimakopoulos (eds.), *Current issues in intercultural pragmatics,* 347–365. Amsterdam & Philadelphia: John Benjamins.

Natale, Michael, Elliot Entin & Joseph Jaffe. 1979. Vocal interruptions in dyadic communication as a function of speech and social anxiety. *Journal of Personality and Social Psychology* 37. 865–878.

Norrick, Neal R. 2009. Pragmatic markers: Introduction. *Journal of Pragmatics* 41. 863–865.

Romero Trillo, Jesús. 1994. Ahm, ehm, you call it theme? A thematic approach to spoken English. *Journal of Pragmatics* 22. 495–509.

Romero Trillo, Jesús. 1997. Pragmatic mechanisms to obtain the addressee's attention in English and Spanish conversations. *Journal of Pragmatics* 28. 205–221.

Romero-Trillo, Jesús 2001. A mathematical model for the analysis of variation in discourse. *Journal of Linguistics* 37. 527–550.

Romero-Trillo, Jesús. 2002. The pragmatic fossilization of discourse markers in non-native speakers of English. *Journal of Pragmatics* 34. 769–784.

Romero-Trillo, Jesús. 2007. Adaptive management in discourse: The case of involvement discourse markers in English and Spanish conversations. *Catalan Journal of Linguistics* 6. 81–94.

Romero-Trillo, Jesús. 2012. Pragmatic markers. In *Encyclopaedia of applied linguistics*. Oxford: Blackwell-Wiley: 4522–4528.

Romero-Trillo, Jesús. 2014. 'Pragmatic punting' and prosody: Evidence from corpora. In María de los Ángeles Gómez, Francisco José Ruiz de Mendoza Ibáñez, Francisco Gonzálvez García & Angela (eds.), *The functional perspective on language and discourse: Applications and implications*, 209–221. Amsterdam & Philadelphia: John Benjamins.

Romero-Trillo, Jesús. 2015. 'It is a truth universally acknowledged'…you know? The role of adaptive management and prosody to start a turn in conversation. *Pragmatics and Society* 6. 117–145.

Romero-Trillo, Jesús. In press. Prosodic modeling and position analysis of pragmatic markers in English conversation. *Corpus Linguistics and Linguistic Theory*. DOI: 10.1515/cllt-2014-0026.

Romero-Trillo, Jesús & Laura Maguire. 2011. Adaptive Context: the fourth element of meaning. *International Review of Pragmatics* 3. 228–241.

Schegloff, Emanuel A. 1984. On some questions and ambiguities in conversation. In Atkinson J. Maxwell & John Heritage (eds.), *Structures of social action*, 28–52. Cambridge University Press.

Schenkein, James N. 1972. Towards an analysis of natural conversation and the sense of 'heheh'. *Semiotica* 6. 344–377.

Schiffrin, Deborah. 1985. Multiple constraints on discourse options: a quantitative analysis of causal sentences. *Discourse Processes* 8. 281–303.

Schiffrin, Deborah. 1987. *Discourse markers*. Cambridge: Cambridge University Press.

Svartvik, Jan & Randolph Quirk. 1980. *A corpus of English conversation*. Lund: Lund University Press.

Wilson, Deidre & Dan Sperber. 1993. Linguistic form and relevance. *Lingua* 90. 1–25.

Anita Fetzer
15 Contrastive discourse relations in context: Evidence from monologic and dialogic editing tasks

1 Introduction

Discourse has been analysed from quantitative and qualitative perspectives, examining the linearization and concatenation of its constitutive parts on the one hand, and concentrating on the construal of discourse coherence on the other. Discourse relations are important for the analysis of the quantity and quality of discourse, providing relevant tools for relating the constitutive parts of discourse in discourse semantics and discourse pragmatics. Contrastive discourse relations are particularly important as they signal some kind of discontinuation in the flow of discourse, such as a rejection or modification of a prior argument or a renegotiation of already accepted presuppositions. In English discourse that kind of discontinuation is generally signalled by a negative discourse connective or by pragmatic word order and therefore assigned the status of a marked configuration (cf. Doherty 2003; Fetzer and Speyer 2012; Speyer and Fetzer 2014).

The goal of this chapter is to contribute to the analysis of contrastive discourse relations in a case study comprising two sets of data and one set of metadata from an experimental situation. Based on a 'bare' source text, which has been stripped of almost all of its adverbials of adjunct, conjunct and disjunct while still containing its original argumentative sequential organization and default configuration of events, the linguistic realization of the coordinating discourse relation of Contrast and of the subordinating discourse relation of Corrective Elaboration is analysed in nine dyadically edited texts and in nine monadically edited texts. All of the participants were asked to produce a well-formed argumentative text based on one source text. The co-edited data are supplemented by metadata, i.e. a kind of editing-aloud protocol, which documents the dyad's negotiation of what kind of linguistic material needs to be added to turn the bare text into a well-formed argumentative text. Particular attention is given to the linguistic realization of the two contrastive discourse relations in this study, to their signalling with discourse connectives – or to employ Systemic Functional Grammar terminology, textual and interpersonal themes realized in the theme zone – and to their local linguistic contexts. The study is methodologically compositional across functional approaches to discourse grammar (Givón

1993; Halliday 1994), discourse semantics (Asher and Lascarides 2003) and discourse pragmatics (Fetzer 2013a; Maier, Hofmockel and Fetzer 2016). Context is accommodated explicitly in the analysis: social context is accounted for through the discourse genre of commentary, linguistic context is accounted for through local and not-so-local adjacency, and cognitive context is accounted for through inference.

The chapter is structured as follows: The following part *Discourse: theory meets practice* addresses the question of quantity, i.e. granularity, and quality, i.e. discursive glue, and argues for a relational conception of a discourse unit as carrier of content, force and metacommunicative meaning. Part 3, *Contrastive discourse relations*, discusses the underlying definition of discourse relations, considering their linguistic realization, and relates them to other coherence strands. It also presents the results of the dyadic and monadic sets of data and contextualizes them with respect to the negotiation and joint construal of discourse coherence as documented in the metadata, and with respect to its impact on the construction of discourse common ground. The final part summarizes the results of the editing tasks and concludes.

2 Discourse: theory meets practice

Discourse – like context – has become more and more relevant to the analysis of meaning, and like context, the concept is used in diverging frameworks referring to different theoretical constructs. Discourse has been used synonymously with text, a linguistic surface phenomenon, denoting longer stretches of written and spoken language, including other semiotic codes, and it is frequently used to refer both to a theoretical construct and to its instantiation in context, i.e. type and token. While there has been some controversy about the question whether the analysis of discourse should be based on semantics or pragmatics (e.g., Fetzer 2013b), there is general agreement about a quantitative conception of discourse as "language patterns above the sentence" (Widdowson 2004: 4) – with the more or less explicit premise that patterned linearized sentences (or clauses) constitute discourse. The questions of the quality of the 'language patterns above the sentence' and their granularity as regards the basic unit of investigation – that is the micro discourse unit on the one hand, and the delimiting discourse unit on the other, i.e. paragraph, episode, sequence or discourse genre – remain controversial. Neither is there agreement about discourse units (DUs) being discrete or fuzzy entities.

An analysis of discourse needs to address two fundamental issues: (1) the question of granularity, that is, what is the minimal unit of investigation, is there a maximal unit of investigation and are there in-between units of investigation, and which necessary conditions need to be fulfilled for a linguistic unit to count as a DU?; and (2) what is discourse, or rather which necessary conditions need to obtain for a 'stretch of language (use)' to count as discourse? It has already surfaced that there is no general agreement about a definition of discourse in the heterogeneous discourse community – except for the quantity-anchored 'language patterns above the sentence'. This is also true for the question of granularity, in particular for the basic unit of investigation, which may differ from paradigm to paradigm – in spite of the fact that the DU and how it is conceived of, for instance as (a) carrier of content, (b) carrier of force, (c) carrier of metacommunicative meaning, (d) carrier of content and force, or (e) carrier of content, force and metacommunicative meaning, is indispensible to discourse analysis in general and to the analysis of the structuring of discourse in particular.

2.1 Discourse unit

Discourse is a multifaceted and multilayered construct, which has been approached from quantitative and qualitative perspectives. Approaches based on text linguistics assign the syntactic unit of sentence the status of a micro DU (e.g. De Beaugrande and Dressler 1981), and functional-grammar-anchored paradigms (e.g. Dik 1997; Givón 1993; Halliday 1994) consider the clause as their micro DU. Discourse semantics takes propositions as its unit of analysis, and more dynamic models also integrate illocutionary force (e.g., Asher and Lascarides 2003; Moeschler 2002) and use speech acts, propositions and utterances as their units of analysis.

The dynamics of discourse and its status as both process and product is based on the premise that DUs are relational by definition. Hence, DUs never form isolated parts, but are always constitutive parts of a larger whole, paving the way for the discourse to follow while at the same time providing context for the production of discourse. For this reason, DUs are not only relational, relating local DUs with less local DUs and with discourse-as-a-whole, but also doubly contextual. For the discursive concept of adjacency this means that adjacency does not only refer to structural adjacency, i.e. adjacency position, but also to semantic adjacency, i.e. adjacency relation, and to pragmatic adjacency, i.e. adjacency expectation, as is captured by the discursive constraint of dovetailedness put forward in *logic and conversation* (Grice 1975). Grice specifies the constraint for the unit of conversational contribution as "such as is required, at the stage at which it occurs, by the accepted purpose or direction of the talk exchange[1] in which you are engaged" (Grice 1975: 45), implying that conversational contributions are linked by one or more common goals manifest in prior and succeeding contributions. In discourse, conversational contributions have the status of a discursive contribution, which may be composed of smaller DUs, such as minimal DUs, that is discourse connectives, comment clauses or parentheticals, and micro DUs, or a combination of both. The discursive constraint of dovetailedness holds for minimal DUs, micro DUs, more complex DUs, such as sequences, and discourse-genre-as-a-whole.

Discourse coherence feeds on DUs and their connectedness as captured by the more general constraints of adjacency and dovetailedness, and it feeds on the delimiting frame of discourse genre, as pointed out by Thibault (2003: 44):

> Rather, genres are types. But they are types in a rather peculiar way. Genres do not specify the lexicogrammatical resources of word, phrase, clause, and so on. Instead, they specify the *typical* [original emphasis] ways in which these are combined and deployed so as to enact the typical semiotic action formations of a given community.

Discourse genre is thus some kind of blueprint in accordance with which interlocutors produce and interpret texts; they may deviate from the blueprint and act in dis-accordance with the discursive constraints locally (cf. Fetzer 2000 for the discourse genre of political interview), but they cannot act in complete dis-accordance with its discursive constraints. Connected intrinsically with '*typical* ways' of doing things with words in a discourse genre – or in an activity type in Levinson's parlance – are inferential schemata, as stated by Levinson (1979: 370):

> ... there is another important and related fact, in many ways the mirror image of the constraints on contributions, namely the fact that for each and every clearly demarcated activity there is a set of *inferential schemata* [original emphasis]. These schemata are tied to (derived from, if one likes) the structural properties of the activity in question.

The communicative value of DUs and of the discourse relations (DRs) holding between them can be implicit in these '*typical* ways' of doing things with words in discourse and in the corresponding '*inferential schemata*'. However, the communicative value of DRs holding between DUs can also be done in 'untypical ways', for instance by adding more cohesive ties to an already overtly realized DR, such as discourse connectives or pragmatic word order, or by the non-realization of a discourse connective which would be 'typical' for a DR holding between DUs, as would be the case with non-signalled contrastive DRs in English.

---

[1] Alternatively, the linearization of discourse, as this chapter proposes.

2.2 Discursive glue

Qualitatively oriented discourse studies share the assumption that discourse as a linearized whole of concatenated units comes in with the presumption of being coherent (cf. Bublitz, Lenk and Ventola 1999; Gernsbacher and Givón 1995), while quantitatively oriented studies tend to focus on the linearization of DUs. In qualitative studies it is not 'language patterns above the sentence' and their semantic well-formedness and pragmatic felicity which make them cohere but rather participants, who negotiate the meaning of DUs, who negotiate the nature of their local and not-so-local connectedness and who negotiate the meaning of discourse-as-a-whole, thereby construing discourse coherence. Hence, discourse coherence does not lie in the discourse itself but rather in participants' minds and therefore is a socio-cognitive construct. This view is also implicit in cohesion-based analyses of texture (e.g., Halliday and Hasan 1987), in which discourse coherence is connected intrinsically with cohesion and cohesive ties, that is linguistic items which signal, if not encode, the nature of the connectedness between the constitutive parts and the whole. Discourse coherence is also connected intrinsically with the sociocognitive constructs of DRs (Asher and Lascarides 2003) and coherence strands, that is referential continuity, temporal and aspectual continuity, spatial continuity and action continuity (Givón 1993), and it feeds on the more general discursive constraints of adjacency and dovetailedness (Grice 1975; Fetzer 2013b) and on the delimiting frame of discourse genre[2] discussed above in section 2.1.

Linguistics-based analyses of discourse have focused on the structure of discourse, for instance Segmented Discourse Representation Theory (Asher and Lascarides 2003) and Rhetorical Structure Theory (Mann and Thompson 1988), concentrating on the representation of discourse (or coherence) relations. Frequently, DRs have been discussed in the framework of idealized, prototypical scenarios and defined accordingly (but see contributions to Gruber and Redeker 2014). To apply such frameworks to real data is a challenging, but necessary step towards validating the theories underlying those frameworks and to develop them further towards applicable tools.

Contrastive discourse analyses have concentrated on the linguistic realization of DRs based on quantitative and qualitative investigations of parallel corpora, generally translations of literary texts (e.g. SPRIK[3]) or of institutional

---

[2] Discourse genre is used as an umbrella term comprising activity type (Levinson, 1979), communicative genre (Sarangi, 2000) and communicative project (Linell, 1998), to name but the most prominent kinds.
[3] Språk i kontrast (http://www.hf.uio.no/ilos/english/research/projects/sprik/)

discourse (e.g. EUROPARL Parallel Corpus; UN Parallel Corpus v1.0). They do not only allow for the examination of language-preferential realizations of DUs and DRs across languages, but also for differences between spoken and written modes, and between discourse genres, accounting for local constraints, such as adjacency. In spite of the differences in granularity and methodology, all approaches share – more or less explicitly – the premise that discourse is a parts-whole configuration in which the whole is more than the sum of its constitutive parts (cf. Fetzer 2013b).

Discursive glue is made manifest through discourse connectives[4], generally realized in the peripheries of micro DUs or as autonomous minimal DUs, through coherence strands realized within DUs (Givón 1993), and through DRs indexed within DUs and signalled by periphery-positioned linguistic material. In Segmented Discourse Representation Theory DRs are described as logical relations between two discourse segments, i.e. complex linguistic units with propositional content and illocutionary force of their own. Any discourse segment p2 usually stands in a logical relation to at least one other preceding segment p1 (or rather: the addressee construes a logical relation between them, in order to vouchsafe coherence). The propositions p1 and p2 are in the DR if the inferences the addressee makes and the logical connection s/he draws between p1 and p2 are in accordance with the ones defined for R. As discourse is not a purely linear phenomenon, but is hierarchically structured, two kinds of DRs are distinguished: coordinating relations that keep the discourse on the same level, and subordinating relations that introduce a deeper level in the discourse hierarchy. A DR can hold between two adjacently positioned DUs, but also between two DUs that are not adjacently positioned.

In line with functional grammar DRs are conceived of as socio-cognitive constructs, whose linguistic realization is constrained by the semantics of the DR, its sequential status as adjacently or non-adjacently positioned, and discourse genre (cf. Speyer and Fetzer 2014; Speyer and Fetzer accepted). From a DU-internal perspective, DRs are cued by references to coherence strands, which are made manifest through (a) topic continuity, (b) tense and aspectual coherence (including modality), (c) lexical coherence, and (d) default grammatical word order vs. pragmatic word order. Givón's units of investigation are clause – micro DU in our terms – and larger text-structures – meso and macro DUs in our terms:

> These strands are clearly the most concrete, salient, observable links between clauses in coherent discourse. But the phenomenon of discourse coherence is richer yet. First, coherence strands may connect – or **ground** [original emphasis] – the clause either to the

---

[4] Discourse connective is used as an umbrella term including pragmatic markers and discourse markers, to name but the most prominent ones (cf. Fetzer 2012).

current text, to the current speech situation, or to generic-lexical knowledge. Second, coherence strands may extend either locally, between adjacent clauses, or globally, across larger text-structures. Third, coherence strands may be either semantic or pragmatic in nature. Finally, the strands may ground the clause in either an anaphoric or a cataphoric direction. (Givón 1993, 287, vol. 2)

A systematic analysis of coherence strands may not only explain higher or lower degrees of glueyness (cf. Maier, Hofmockel, and Fetzer 2016) and thus of discourse coherence, but also predict syntactic formatting, which is relevant to the linguistic realization of DUs: "The more thematically connected a conjoined clause is with an adjacent clause – the more strands of thematic coherence it shares with that adjacent clause – the more likely it is to appear reduced, less finite, syntactically integrated with that other clause" (Givón 1993: 318, vol. 2), a claim which has been substantiated in grammaticalization and pragmaticalization research (e.g., Aijmer 1997; Traugott 1988).

The qualitative paradigm concentrates on discourse coherence, whereas the quantitative paradigm is more concerned with the structuring of discourse considering linearization and granularity. Both are relevant to defining DRs in general and contrastive DRs in particular.

2.3 Discourse relations

DRs have been defined as logical relations holding between two or more DUs with the inferences made by the addressee being in accordance with the ones defined for the DR. Coordinating DRs keep the discourse on the same level, while subordinating relations introduce a deeper level in the discourse hierarchy.

Logical relations have been operationalized within a pool of defining conditions and particularized features, which are indexically referred to in discourse, and are assigned the status of discursive glue (cf. Maier, Hofmockel and Fetzer 2016). The defining conditions and particularized features can be cued at the peripheries of a micro DU – and sometimes they may even form a minimal DU of their own – for instance with discourse connectives or parentheticals, also referred to as extra-clausal constituents (Dik 1997), and they can be cued in the core domains of a DU with Givón's coherence strands.

The defining conditions and particularized features of the most important DRs for the analysis of argumentative discourse are systematized in Table 1,[5] which is adapted from Maier, Hofmockel and Fetzer (2016: 66–67):

---
5 Abbreviations indicate the sources as A & L (Asher & Lascarides, 2003), G (Givón, 1993), and H (Halliday, 1994).

Table 1. Defining conditions and particularized features of DRs in English.

	Discourse Relation	Defining conditions	Particularized features
Coordinating	Continuation	Common topic (A & L)	• referential continuity (G; H) • topic continuity (A & L; G; H) • temporal coherence (G; H) • aspectual coherence (G; H) • lexical coherence (H)
	Narration	Common topic (A & L) Temporal sequentiality (A & L)	• referential continuity (G; H) • topic continuity (G; H) • aspectual coherence (G; H) • lexical coherence (H)
	CONTRAST *	Semantic dissimilarity between p2 and p1 (A & L)	• referential (dis)continuity (G; H) • topic (dis)continuity (A & L; G; H) • shift in temporal coherence (G; H) • shift in aspectual coherence (G; H) • lexical coherence: scalar antonyms (H)
	Background	p2 forms the background of p1 (A & L) Common topic (A & L)	• Spatio-temporal overlap (A & L) • Shift in aspectual class A & L) • Referential continuity: PRO-based co-reference (A & L; G; H) • topic continuity (A & L; G; H) • aspectual overlap (A & L; G; H) • lexical coherence (H)
Subordinating / Superordinating	Result	p1 gives reason for (parts of) events in p2 (A & L) Connecting two sub-events (A & L) Temporal precedence of cause (A & L)	• referential continuity (G; H) • topic continuity (A & L; G; H) • temporal coherence (G; H) • aspectual coherence (G; H) • lexical coherence (H)
	Comment	p2 selects p1 as topic; or: p1 selects p2 as topic (A & L)	• referential continuity (G; H) • temporal coherence (G; H) • aspectual coherence (G; H) • lexical coherence (H)
	ELABORATION **	Topic of p2 specifies topic of p1 mereologically (A & L)	• referential continuity (G; H) • temporal coherence (G; H) • aspectual coherence (G; H) • lexical coherence (H)
	Explanation	p2 gives reason for (parts of) events in p1 (A & L) Temporal consequence (A & L)	• referential continuity (G; H) • topic continuity (A & L; G; H) • temporal coherence (G; H) • aspectual coherence (G; H) • lexical coherence (H)

* Contrast is differentiated with regard to discourse-internal contrast, as defined above, and Contrast of Expectation, which requires the obligatory realization of a discourse connective (A & L).

** If Elaboration contains one or more contrastive elements, it counts as *Corrective Elaboration* (A & L); if there is functional synonymy between p2 and p1, it counts as *Equative Elaboration* (our term). If p2 refers to reported / quoted speech or thought of the agent of p1, signalled by an inflected speech-act / cognitive verb, it counts as *Projective Elaboration* (our term).

DRs may be fully specified[6] by indexical reference to all of their defining condition(s) and to all of their particularized features and then would have a higher degree of 'glueyness', and they may even be overspecified if a discourse connective is added to their fully specified linguistic realization, or if their theme zone is configurated non-congruently, or if a discourse connective is added and their theme zone is configurated non-congruently; their degree of glueyness would then be even higher. DRs may also be underspecified by indexical reference to their defining condition(s) and/or to some particularized features and then would have a lower degree of 'glueyness'. In the case of underspecification, DRs holding between DUs permit multiple interpretations. To preempt possible overlaps, underspecified DRs may be signalled with discourse connectives, and to ensure speaker-intended interpretation, fully specified DRs can be supplemented by discourse connectives and by non-congruently configurated theme zones. Depending on the number of features and conditions indexed, DRs can be fully specified or they can be underspecified to various degrees. In the latter case, multiple interpretations are possible, unless the DR is signalled with one or more connectives.

The DR with the lowest number of shared features is Contrast, differing from others not only in its defining condition but also in its particularized features. For this reason, this relation shows a high degree of specification. This is not the case for Continuation and Narration, which share the defining condition of common topic as well as all of their particularized features. Since there is only one condition that differentiates Continuation from Narration, dual assignment is possible. Comment and Continuation share all of their particularized features, but differ in their defining conditions, i.e. topic continuity and a whole proposition being the topic of Comment. For this reason, dual assignment is unlikely. Elaboration and Explanation share almost all of their particularized features, except for Explanation-specific topic continuity. While the defining condition of Explanation provides reasons for the events in the two DUs to be related and signals temporal consequence, the defining condition for Elaboration is mereological topic specification. Corrective Elaboration needs to contain at least one contrastive element and is – like coordinating Contrast – the subordinating DR with the lowest number of overlaps.

---

6 Specification is seen as a purely structural phenomenon and calculated by the number of conditions and features indexed in discourse.

2.4 Contrastive discourse relations

The coordinating DR of Contrast is defined as expressing semantic dissimilarity, which may be manifest in topic and/or referential discontinuity, a shift in temporal and/or aspectual coherence, scalar or complementary antonyms, contrastive discourse connectives or non-congruently configured theme zones. Subordinating Corrective Elaboration is defined as expressing semantic dissimilarity, which may be manifest in mereological topic specification of the second DU, referential discontinuity, a shift in temporal and/or aspectual coherence, scalar or complementary antonyms, contrastive discourse connectives or non-congruently configured theme zones.

The research reported in this chapter builds on the examination of the linguistic realization of DRs in a contrastive analysis of discourse, in which English written argumentative discourse, that is, commentaries from the British newspaper *The Guardian*, and German written argumentative discourse from the *Frankfurter Rundschau*, was compared. The two sets of data showed slight differences for the encoding and signalling of Contrast: in the English data, Contrast was not only fully specified throughout the data, but also signalled overtly with a contrastive discourse connective and sometimes also with a non-congruently configured theme zone, while in the German data Contrast was encoded and signalied overtly in 78.6% of the tokens (Fetzer and Speyer 2012). Similar results were obtained for the linguistic realization of Contrast in English and German written personal narratives. Again, Contrast was encoded and signalled throughout the English data, while the rate of encoded and signalled Contrast in German was 80% for adjacently positioned DUs realizing Contrast and 100% for non-adjacently positioned DUs realizing Contrast (Speyer and Fetzer accepted). To corroborate and refine the results obtained by also accounting for subordinating Corrective Elaboration, and to shed more light on the assumption that discourse genre is a kind of blueprint in accordance with which interlocutors produce and interpret texts, a case study has been undertaken to find out whether the results for the coding and signalling of DRs in an experimental setting based on an editing task were similar to the ones obtained for newspaper commentaries.

3 Method

To examine the encoding and signalling of DRs in the context of the argumentative discourse genre of commentary – and to compare it across two different production formats: monadically and dyadically edited texts – a pilot study was designed which allows the elicitation of data from speakers' realizations of connectivity in an empirically replicable fashion. This is achieved through the format of an editing-based task: participants are provided with the 'bare' text, together with information about medium and genre of the original text (cf. appendix). Their task is to use and edit – or co-edit – the 'bare' text and construct a coherent and well-formed text of identical genre, with the single constraint that the original sequence of DUs has to remain unchanged. The DUs of the 'bare' text have been stripped of almost all of its adjuncts, subjuncts, conjuncts and disjuncts, reduced in this way to their necessary minimum of propositional content, but still containing the sequential organization and default configuration of events. The participants can add or alter linguistic material to construct a text of a specified genre which they consider to be well-formed. The main interest of our study was not whether or even how a relation between two given units was realized, but rather the variation between different realizations of identical DR potential. Whenever an underspecified DR is encountered, participants – in both production formats – need to choose both the DR to employ and the degree of overtness in which to realize it (cf. Maier, Hofmockel, and Fetzer 2016). To provide more in-depth information about the elicited data, additional metadata was collected: dyads – that is pairs of participants – were recorded while carrying out the task together and their negotiations of what needed to be added were transcribed. The requirement to collaborate makes it necessary for the participants to externalize their expectations for well-formed discourse, and to re-negotiate and adapt them accordingly. With regard to the dyadically edited texts, the discourse about its execution qualifies as metadata, which allows insights into discourse processing.

We expected our participants to adhere to the constraints of the argumentative genre of commentary in their encoding and signalling of DRs. Intrinsic guiding criteria for the selection of additional material are (1) discourse genre as a blueprint, and (2) the sociocognitive construct of discourse common ground (Fetzer 2007) with intended readers of the resulting text. Evidence for the hypotheses of discourse genre as a kind of blueprint and sociocognitive discourse common ground as an administered record of a current communicative event related to other records as well as to presupposed Background (Searle 2010) is expected to be obtained from (1) the kind of linguistic material added to the bare units, which is seen as relevant to the construal of discourse common ground, and (2) the dyad's negotiation of what needs to be added to the bare units to transform them into a well-formed text. The added linguistic material allows for the reconstruction of imported context and explicated background assumption, while the dyad's negotiation of what needs to be added promises insights into the processing of discourse, the construal of discourse coherence and the construction of discourse common ground.

Discourse common ground is a context-dependent notion which administers the contextualization of discourse, in particular discourse processing, negotiation of meaning and construal of discourse coherence. Discourse common ground has a dual status: on the one hand, it is a particularized category anchored in one particular communicative event; it can be further categorized into individual discourse common ground, administering an individual's processing of discourse and construal of discourse coherence, and collective discourse common ground, administering the participants' ratification of the processing of discourse and the joint construal of discourse coherence; both types of discourse common ground overlap but may also diverge, to some degree. Discourse common ground is also a generalized category: it administers other kinds of discourse common ground, which the interlocutors have construed and administered in previous communicative events and interactions. All of these kinds of discourse common ground form some kind of network, which is related dialectically.

Discourse common ground is not only relational, but also dynamic. The dual status of discourse common ground as (1) generalized discourse common ground and thus as a base in which interlocutors anchor their discursive contributions, and as (2) emergent particularized discourse common ground is a bridging point with Kecskés's differentiation between core common ground and emergent common ground: "*Core common ground* [original emphasis] refers to the relatively static (diachronically changing), generalized, common knowledge and beliefs that usually belong to a certain speech community as a result of prior interactions and experience, whereas *emergent common ground* [original emphasis] refers to the dynamic, particularized knowledge created in the course of communication and triggered by the actual situational context" (Kecskés 2014: 160). The goal of communication – and of the monadic and dyadic editing task – is to activate the generalized discourse common ground, facilitating access to both generalized discourse common ground and to emerging particularized discourse common ground. Against this background, "[c]ommon ground is an assumption that we make in the course of actual communication. Both core common ground and emergent common ground are integrated parts of this assumed common ground" (Kecskés 2014: 164).

3.1 Data

The dataset comprises nine monadically edited argumentative texts, nine dyadically edited argumentative texts, and nine metadata texts, i.e. transcriptions of the dyads' negotiations of the linguistic material which needs to be added to the bare units to jointly construct a well-formed text. The monadically edited texts contain 281 DRs, the dyadically edited texts 160.

3.2 Procedure

Participants for the dyadically edited texts were adult native speakers of English, volunteering from the academic community of Augsburg University. They included two native speakers of American English, two native speakers of British English, and one native speaker each of Canadian English and Irish English. All of them were from an academic background and all of them can be considered to be familiar with how to produce and edit argumentative discourse. For the monadically edited texts, students from British universities and US universities volunteered to participate in the study – some gained extra credits for their courses, others just participated. They were provided with a 'bare' text, together with information about medium and genre of the original text (cf. appendix). Their task was to use and edit – or co-edit – the 'bare' text and construct a coherent and well-formed text of identical genre, with the single constraint that the original sequence of DUs had to remain unchanged.

An analysis was conducted of 18 texts produced by 9 monads and 9 dyads, focusing specifically on the linguistic material added to the bare units in the dyadic and monadic settings. In the edited texts, the linguistic material added was examined and classified as expanding the bare unit with discourse connectives or adverbials, or as forming additional discourse units, which stand in one or more DRs with a bare unit. All units were coded for DRs and analysed with respect to their realization of DRs in the framework of the defining conditions and particularized features systematized above in Table 1.[7] DRs encoded in coherence strands in accordance with their defining conditions and particularized features were classified as implicit, and DRs additionally signalled with discourse connectives or non-congruently configured theme zones (Halliday 1994; Fetzer 2008) were classified as overt. The metadata were transcribed by student assistants and checked against delivery. Their analysis focussed on those incident where the adding of discourse connectives and adverbials was negotiated, as well as on those where participants discussed the appropriate use of tense and its reference to time.

3.3 Results

The monadically edited texts contain 63.71% of the overall number of DRs, while the dyadic texts contain 36.29%. Their degree of overtness is also higher: while

---

[7] To ensure interrater reliability, the coding of DR was undertaken by the author and Carolin Hofmockel, a postgraduate research assistant (University of Augsburg).

50% of the DRs are realized overtly in the dyadically edited texts, it is 63.3% in the monadic texts, as is systematized in Table 2:

Table 2. Distribution and overt realization of DRs

DR	Commentaries (monadically edited)			Commentaries (dyadically edited)		
	N_{total}	N_{overt}	% overt	N_{total}	N_{overt}	% overt
Contrast	40	40	100%	15	15	100%
Continuation	32	13	40.6%	35	20	57.1%
Explanation	14	11	78.5%	11	8	72.7%
Elaboration	123	62	50.4%	54	17	31.4%
Corrective Elaboration	17	17	100%	11	11	100%
Comment	25	20	80%	13	1	7.6%
Sum	*251*	*163*	*64.9%*	*139*	*72*	*51.7%*
Background	25	13	52%	9	4	44.4%
Result	5	2	40%	12	4	33.3%
Sumtotal	**281**	**178**	**63.3%**	**160**	**80**	**50%**

Continuation is the only DRs in the data which is realized overtly less frequently – with 40.6 percentage points – in the monadically edited data, and 57.1 percentage points in the dyadic data. All the other DRs are more frequently realized overtly in the monadic data, which is reflected in an overall degree of overtness of 63.3% in the monadic data and 50% in the dyadic data. The difference in the degree of overtness is especially true for Comment, whose overt realization is 80 percentage points for the monadic data and only 7.6 for the dyadic data. Contrastive DRs, which are the focus of investigation of this paper, are realized overtly throughout the data.

In the two edited sets of data contrastive DRs are cued DU-internally and additionally furnished with contrastive discourse connectives, non-congruently configurated theme zones, or with both. The preferred contrastive discourse connective for Contrast is *but*, and the preferred initial constituent for non-congruently configured theme zones is a temporal adjunct. Frequently the contrastive discourse connective is embellished with a non-congruently configured theme zone, in particular temporal adjuncts, for instance 'but now'. The multiple cueing of Contrast contributes to varying degrees of overspecification. For Corrective Elaboration, the preferred discourse connective is *however*, followed by *though* (positioned DU-initially and DU-finally) and *despite*, and single occurrences of *instead of, yet* and *even better*. DU-internal cues are referential and/or topic (dis)continuity – or mereological topic specification for Corrective Elaboration –, a shift in temporal and aspectual coherence (e.g., 'nowadays' – 'in the past / in the post-war era'; 'London of former days was' – 'London of today is much more'; 'there was a time when NP was' – 'today this NP has changed'; 'last time NP came here' – 'now it's much more exciting!'), and scalar or complementary antonyms as regards lexical coherence. The DRs of Background and Explanation are also sometimes added to intensify the degree of glueyness for the contrastive DRs in the edited texts: Background was more frequent in the monadic data, and Result in the dyadically edited data. In the monadically edited texts Background and Explanation generally co-occur with contrastive DRs, supplementing not only causal contrast with temporal contrast but also providing further subjectified accounts for semantic dissimilarity or contrasting mereological topic specification.

3.3.1 Contrast

In the following, the cueing and specification of contrastive DRs is analysed; the dyadically edited examples are supplemented with extracts from their negotiation-of-production protocols. Examples[8] (1) and (2) are from the dyadically edited texts, and (3) and (4) from the monadically edited texts:

(1) #2/2 [*In the past*], London *was* a DOWDY place of tea-houses and STALE rock cakes,
    #2/3 [***but** now*] it*'s* MUCH MORE EXCITING.

(2) #1/7a [[**While** some Londoners *might find* these foreign tongues THREATENING,]]
    #1/7b I *delight* in hearing them mingled with snatches of French, German, Spanish, Italian, Japanese …

---

8 Within examples, *italic* typeface indicates *adverbial* status; simple underlining marks coreferential items; SMALL CAPS marks items connected via semantic relations; **boldface** indicates discourse connectives. Wherever relevant to the discussion, single square brackets ('[ ]') indicate added lexical material, double square brackets ('[[ ]]') added DUs, and curly brackets ('{ }') deleted material.

In the metadata, **boldface** indicates lexical material relevant to the immediate process of editing and to its negotiation, and *italics* refers to the 'edited'.

In (1) and (2), Contrast is cued by the defining condition of semantic dissimilarity between #2/2 and #2/3, and #1/7a and #1/7b with the particularized features of topic and referential continuity in (1) and topic discontinuity ('some Londoners' – 'I') and referential continuity ('foreign tongues' – 'them') in (2), temporal discontinuity (cued by tense and adjunct) in (1) and temporal and aspectual continuity, but modal discontinuity in (2), antonyms ('dowdy'; 'stale' – 'exciting'; 'past' – 'now'; 'some' – 'I'; 'threatening' – 'delight'), and contrastive discourse connectives ('but' and 'while').

Semantic dissimilarity and the cueing of Contrast-specific features is also an object of talk in the dyads negotiating the linguistic material which needs to be added to turn the 'bare' text into a well-formed whole:

B_1: {05:24} so here it says see also **this is present** | and **then** *London was a dowdy place* **but now and now** *it's much more exciting* so we have put this in the right context so we could start with the british **had seemed** or **in the past** (2s)

B_1: {06:31} erm (2s) erm (3s) i wrote i used now already see **but now** *it's much more exciting* | **but today** how about **today**'s *much more exciting* now how about if we do that but today

A_1: mhm *but today it's*

B_1: *much more exciting* now walking

Participant B_1 does not only mention the contrast to be cued with respect to tense and temporal adverbials, but also uses them ('this is present'; 'then'; 'had seemed'; 'in the past'; 'but now'; 'but today') when s/he talks about the linguistic material to be filled in. A very similar negotiation takes place between the second dyad, referring to tense ('a jump from the present to the past'). B_2 uses a contrastive discourse connective in their talk ('while'), contextualizing 'rock cake', which seems to have caused some partial understanding only:

B_2: {03:30} **yeah there's a jump from the present to the past** right so there are hm hm case it's true that *london was a dowdy place* **but now** *it's much more exciting* or

A_2: yeah

B_2: **while** it is tr-

A_2: in the past

B_2: *rock cake* is erm like a scone but larger and hard | (2s) buttery

A_2: uh huh {04:00} *and stale rock cakes* **but now** it's more exciting?

B_2: mhm *much more exciting* yeah

A_2: yeah *it's much more exciting*

In the monadically edited examples (3) and (4), Contrast is cued by the defining condition of semantic dissimilarity between #D/2 and #D/3, and #M/2 and #M/4 with the particularized features of topic and referential discontinuity in (3) and topic discontinuity ('London' – 'this negative perception') and referential discontinuity ('typical view' – 'recent survey') in (4), temporal continuity and aspectual change in (3) and temporal discontinuity and aspectual change ('was' – 'has changed') in (4), antonyms ('fairly similar – 'dramatically"; 'be' – 'change'), and the contrastive discourse connective 'but' in (3) and pragmatic word order with a fronted temporal adjunct in (4):

(3) #D/2 The landscape *may look* FAIRLY SIMILAR
    #D/3 [**but**] how we *live*, how we *move* around, how we *work* and who we *live* with *has changed* DRAMATICALLY.

(4) #M/2 [***There was a time***] when the typical view of the overseas visitor was that London *was* a DOWDY place of tea-houses and STALE rock cakes.
    #M/4 [***Today***], according to a recent survey of tourists conducted by the London Bureau of Tourism, this negative perception *has changed*.

The coordinating DR Contrast is – structurally speaking – overspecified in both the dyadically and monadically edited texts, in spite of the fact that Contrast is the DR with the lowest number of overlaps for defining conditions and particularized features, corroborating the results obtained for non-edited argumentative discourse.

3.3.2 Corrective Elaboration

The subordinating DR Corrective Elaboration is defined by the defining condition of topic of p2 specifying topic of p1 mereologically and by some contrast in its particularized features of referential continuity, temporal and aspectual coherence, and lexical coherence. In a contrast-loaded linguistic context, mereological topic specification may count as yet another contrastive device, signifying that just a specific part of the whole – that is the mereological specification – is relevant to the current discourse, but not the whole topic explicated in the prior DU. In the dyadically edited texts (examples [5] and [6]) and in the monadically edited texts (examples [7] and [8]), all Corrective Elaborations are signalled with the contrastive discourse connective *however*:

(5) #2/8   [Some would argue that] London *has become* the capital of linguistic diversity.
    #2/9   [**However,**] one important group *seems to be leaving itself out*:

(6) #3/8   [Surprisingly,] London *has become* the capital of linguistic diversity.
    #3/9   [**However,**] one important group [which] *seems to be [excluding] {leaving} itself {out}*

Mereological topic specification is reflected in the parts-whole configuration of 'London' and 'one important group' in (5) and (6), which implies some kind of contrast. It is made an object of talk in the dyad's negotiation of the well-formed realization of the text ('it is a contrast because this is' – 'it's a bit weird with like in fact and then however'). Contrast is also manifest in a shift in temporal and aspectual coherence ('has become' – 'seems to be leaving itself out'). The degree of contrast is embellished in (6) with the attitudinal disjunct 'surprisingly', which has also been an object of talk in the dyad's negotiation process:

A_2: yeah but otherwise how would you link it?
B_2: yeah
A_2: i could just well I mean I'm just thinking |
B_2:   well I well ok i can you know or (5s) ok yeah &&& [stuttering] **it is a contrast because this is ah|**
A_2: she can do this because she can do that|
B_2:   because she can yeah |
A_2: (3s) i'm changing the text &&& [mumbling] **however** *one*
B_2:   &&& (mumbling) namely students
A_2: (3s) **it's a bit weird with like in fact and then however**
B_2: yeah
A_2: it's like | a bit too much |
B_2:   mhm   mhm well just leave it out in fact
A_2: yeah (5s) it's like overdoing the transition | a bit |

B_1: {08:01}ok and how about *london has become the capital of linguistic diversity* &&& **surprisingly** we need something in there | we need an adverb in there **surprisingly** or i don't know
A_1:   yeah yeah let's put in surprisingly

The monadically edited data display very similar patterns of linguistic realization, but provide more contextual background, that is the source of the claim that London has become the capital of linguistic diversity, 'her husband', and an Explanation signalled with the discourse connective 'while' in (7). In (8) mereological topic specification is reflected in 'an inquiry' and its specification as 'an inquiry into the impact of Tory educational policies' signalled with an inverted configuration introduced by 'even better', which can also function as a contrastive discourse connective. Contrast is also inherent in shifts in tense and modality ('is under way' – 'would be better'):

(7) #M/8   [Her husband interjected], "<u>London *has become*</u> the capital of linguistic diversity".
    #M/9   [**However**] [#10 **while** linguistic diversity might be a salient feature of the nation's capital,] <u>one important group</u> *seems to be leaving itself out*:

(8) #S/13   <u>An inquiry</u> *is underway* – is not bureaucracy wonderful?
    #S/14   [**Even better**] *would be* <u>an inquiry into the impact of Tory educational policies</u> on closing more and more students out from a university education.

The subordinating DR Corrective Elaboration is – like coordinating Contrast – overspecified in both dyadically and monadically edited texts, corroborating the results obtained for non-edited argumentative discourse.

4 Discussion

The linguistic realization of contrastive DRs has been investigated in monadically and dyadically edited texts, and in both production formats they are not only encoded in DR-specific coherence strands, but also additionally signalled with contrastive discourse connectives and/or non-congruently configurated theme zones. Coordinating Contrast has been described as the DR with the lowest number of shared features, differing from other DRs not only in its defining condition but also in its particularized features. For this reason, this relation shows a high degree of specification. The high degree of specification also holds for subordinating Corrective Elaboration, whose particularized features are almost identical to coordinating Contrast but differ in its defining condition by the specification of semantic dissimilarity as mereological topic specification. In the negatively loaded linguistic context of contrastive DRs, mereological topic specification is very likely to obtain a contrast-based interpretation as a specification of a topic that has been conceptualized in too general terms. In addition to the negatively loaded context, contrastive DRs are intensified by contrastive discourse connectives and/or non-congruently configurated theme zones, expressing yet a higher degree of negativity. From an economy-based perspective on the encoding and signalling of DRs, the encoding and signalling of semantic dissimilarity in the linguistic realization of contrastive DRs displays some degree of redundancy and thus is classified as overspecified; this corresponds to observations for the genres of editorial and personal narrative (Fetzer and Speyer 2012; Speyer and Fetzer accepted).

The encoding and signalling of semantic dissimilarity anchored in the particularized features of the contrastive DRs is also made an object of talk in the dyads' negotiations as regards discursive well-formedness, referring to tense, aspect and lexical coherence. And as has been the case with the edited texts, the encoding and signalling of Contrast is also multiply cued in the negotiation-of-well-formedness sessions.

Structural overspecification seems to be the default for the encoding and signalling of contrastive DRs in argumentative discourse. But why would language users opt for overspecification for contrastive DRs which share only very few particularized features with other DRs? We assume that the degree of overspecification has several reasons. Firstly, structural overspecification is an attention-guiding device and thus related closely to sociocognitive salience. Secondly, speakers/writers intend to secure the speaker-intended interpretation of contrastive DRs, which signal a change in the direction of discursive flow and therefore require particular attention, and thirdly, contrastive DRs have a decisive impact on discourse processing as they signal a change in the administration of the current discourse common ground. In communication, the construal of discourse coherence and the assignment of DRs are constitutive parts of discourse processing – for both individual discourse common ground and negotiated and ratified collective discourse common ground. Both are negotiated and updated continuously, i.e. confirmed, modified or restructured, by storing new information and by updating already stored information, which may require some restructuring of the participants' individual and collective discourse common grounds. The discourse common grounds anchored to a current communicative event are related to other discourse common grounds and those less immediate discourse common ground may also need to undergo restructuring.

The overspecification of DRs provides as much discursive glue as possible and aims to ensure the activation of defining conditions and particularized features, and thus an interpretation of the DR as intended by the speaker. It can thus be understood as a strategic device to increase the salience of a particular DR by making it optimally relevant for the hearer. As for contrastive DRs, they may not only have a local impact on the administration of current discourse common ground, but they may require some restructuring of already stored discursive information in the current discourse common ground as well as in more remote discourse common grounds of other communicative events.

5 Conclusion

Discourse is a multilayered, complex construct, and so is its linearization. The sequential organization and linearization of discourse is not only a linguistic-surface phenomenon, but rather depends on the sociocognitive construct of discourse common ground, which is updated and administered continuously. Contrastive DRs have an important function in discourse in general, signalling some change in the flow of discourse, and they have an important function in argumentative discourse in particular, making manifest that one or more arguments may be controversial. The structural overspecification of contrastive DRs makes these changes manifest locally in the flow of discourse and guides the hearers/readers in their processing of discourse, construal of discourse coherence and the administration of discourse common ground. Structural overspecification is used strategically to contribute to the activation of defining conditions and particularized features, foregrounding them, making them salient through overt marking and assigning communicative relevance to them.

The focus of the analysis of the monadically and dyadically edited 'bare' texts and of the metadata documenting the dyads' negotiations of discourse-genre-specific expectations about discursive well-formedness has been on the linguistic realization of contrastive discourse relations. Throughout the data, semantic dissimilarity has not only been encoded in discourse-unit-internal coherence strands, but also signalled in periphery-anchored discourse connectives and non-congruently configurated theme zones. Frequently semantic dissimilarity has been multiply signalled. Overspecification thus seems to be the default for Contrast and Corrective Elaboration in the argumentative genre of commentary. An application of the editing-based-task approach to the examination of different discourse genres may provide further insights into discourse processing, construal of discourse coherence and discourse-genre-specific expectations for the linguistic realization of discourse relations.

References

Aijmer, Karin. 1997. I think – an English modal particle. In Toril Swan & Olaf Jansen (eds.), *Modality in Germanic languages. Historical and comparative perspectives*, 1–47. Berlin & New York: Mouton de Gruyter.

Asher, Nicholas & Lascarides, Alex. 2003. *Logics of conversation*. Cambridge: Cambridge University Press.

Bublitz, Wolfram, Uta Lenka & Eija Ventola (eds.). 1999. *Coherence in spoken and written discourse: How to create it and how to describe it. Selected papers from the international workshop on coherence, Augsburg, 24–27 April 1997*. Amsterdam: John Benjamins.

Dik, Simon. 1997. *The theory of functional grammar* (2 vols). Ed. K. Hengeveld. Amsterdam & Philadelphia: John Benjamins.
Doherty, Monika. 2003. Discourse relators and the beginnings of sentences in English and German. *Languages in Contrast* 3. 223–251.
Fetzer, Anita. 2000. Negotiating validity claims in political interviews. *Text* 20(4). 1–46.
Fetzer, Anita. 2007. Reformulation and common grounds. In Anita Fetzer & Kerstin Fischer (eds.), *Lexical markers of common grounds*, 157–179. London: Elsevier.
Fetzer, Anita. 2008. Theme zones in English media discourse. Forms and functions. Journal of Pragmatics 40(9). 1543–1568.
Fetzer, Anita. 2012. Contexts in interaction: Relating pragmatic wastebaskets. In Rita Finkbeiner, Jörg Meibauer & Petra Schumacher (eds.), *What is a context? Linguistic approaches and challenges*, 105–127. Amsterdam & Philadelphia: John Benjamins.
Fetzer, Anita. 2013a. The pragmatics of discourse. *Topics in Linguistics* 11. 5–12.
Fetzer, Anita. 2013b. Structuring of discourse. In Marina Sbisà & Ken Turner (eds.), *Handbooks of pragmatics. The pragmatics of speech actions. Vol. 2*, 685–711. Boston & Berlin: De Gruyter Mouton.
Fetzer, Anita & Augustin Speyer. 2012. Discourse relations in context: Local and not-so-local constraints. *Intercultural Pragmatics* 9(4). 413–452.
Gernsbacher, Moton-Ann & Givón, Talmy (eds.). 1995. *Coherence in spontaneous text*. Amsterdam & Philadelphia: John Benjamins.
Givón, Talmy. 1993. *English Grammar: a function-based introduction* (2 vols.). Amsterdam & Philadelphia: John Benjamins.
Grice, Herbert Paul. 1975. Logic and conversation. In Peter Cole & Jerry L. Morgan (eds.), *Syntax and semantics*, 41–58. New York: Academic Press.
Gruber, Helmut & Gisela Redeker (eds.). 2014. *The pragmatics of discourse coherence: Theories and applications*. Amsterdam & Philadelphia: John Benjamins.
Halliday, Michael A. K. 1994. *Introduction to functional grammar*. London: Arnold.
Halliday, Michael A. K. & Ruqaiya Hasan. 1987. *Cohesion in English*. London: Longman.
Kecskés, István. 2014. *Intercultural pragmatics*. Oxford: Oxford University Press.
Levinson, Stephen C. 1979. Activity types and language. *Linguistics* 17. 365–399.
Linell, Per. 1998. *Approaching dialogue*. Amsterdam & Philadelphia: John Benjamins.
Maier, Robert M., Carolin Hofmockel & Anita Fetzer. 2016. The negotiation of discourse relations in context: Co-constructing degrees of overtness. *Intercultural Pragmatics* 13(1). 71–105.
Mann, William C. & Sandra A. Thompson. 1988. Rhetorical structure theory: toward a functional theory of text organization. *Text* 8(3). 243–281.
Moeschler, Jacques. 2002. Speech act theory and the analysis of conversations. In Daniel Vanderveken & Susumu Kubo (eds.), *Essays in speech act theory*, 239–261. Amsterdam & Philadelphia: John Benjamins.
Sarangi, Srikant. 2000. Activity types, discourse types and interactional hybridity: The case of genetic counseling. In Srikant Sarangi & Malcolm Coulthard (eds.), *Discourse and social life*, 1–27. Harlow: Longman.
Searle, John R. 2010. *Making the social world: The structure of human civilization*. Oxford: Oxford University Press.
Speyer, Augustin & Anita Fetzer. 2014. The coding of discourse relations in English and German argumentative discourse. In Helmut Gruber and Gisela Redeker (eds.), *The pragmatics of discourse coherence: Theories and applications*, 87–119. Amsterdam & Philadelphia: John Benjamins.

Speyer, Augustin & Anita Fetzer. Accepted. "Well would you believe it, I have failed the exam again": Discourse relations in English and German personal narratives. *Pragmatics and Society*.

Thibault, Paul J. 2003. Contextualization and social meaning-making practices. In Susan L. Eerdmans, Carlo L. Prevignano & Paul L. Thibault (eds.), *Language and interaction. Discussions with John J. Gumperz*, 41–62. Amsterdam & Philadelphia: John Benjamins.

Traugott, Elizabeth Closs. 1988. *Approaches to grammaticalization*. Amsterdam & Philadelphia: John Benjamins.

Widdowson, Henry. 2004. *Text, context, and pretext. Critical issues in discourse analysis.* Oxford: Blackwell.

Appendix

Discourse editing task

Below, instructions and the skeleton text handed to the dyads in our experiment have been reproduced:

> The following 15 clauses form the backbone of a commentary from the Guardian. You may add or delete any linguistic material which you consider necessary to transform the current text into a well-formed coherent whole, but you may not change the order of the given clauses.
>
> The solitary monoglots
> 1   the British seem set on isolation from the world
> 2   London was a dowdy place of tea-houses and stale rock cakes
> 3   it's much more exciting
> 4   I can hear people speaking in all the languages of the world
> 5   was that Pashto or Hindi
> 6   I can just about differentiate Polish from Lithuanian
> 7   I delight in hearing them mingled with snatches of French, German, Spanish, Italian, Japanese…
> 8   London has become the capital of linguistic diversity.
> 9   one important group seems to be leaving itself out
> 10 students
> 11 foreign language learning at Britain's schools has been in decline for decades
> 12 the number of universities offering degrees in modern languages has plummeted
> 13 an inquiry is under way
> 14 the number of teenagers taking traditional modern foreign languages at A-level fell to its lowest level since the mid-90s.
> 15 it's a paradox

Lluís Payrató
16 Pragmatics and multimodality. A reflection on multimodal pragmastylistics

1 Introduction. Purposes and aims

John L. Austin closed the third of his famous lectures at Harvard University with the statement "we must at all costs avoid over-simplification, which one might be tempted to call the occupational disease of philosophers if it were not their occupation" (1962: 38). Austin had begun the first lecture saying that "[w]hat I shall have to say here is neither difficult nor contentious; the only merit I should like to claim for it is that of being true, at least in parts." In the pages that follow I would like to maintain the spirit of both these quotations in my discussion of verbal and non-verbal pragmatic resources and strategies for creating and understanding meaning. The point seems true and should not be over-simplified: a pragmatic theory of language must accept a multimodal component because language usage, in both the production and the reception phase, is founded in multimodality. Austin himself noted that we are perfectly capable of doing many things in many ways, not only through verbal language. He states clearly that even illocutionary power is not limited to the word, but can be extended to non-verbal acts. This assertion was acknowledged many years ago in one of the foundational texts of the discipline, and so it is rather difficult to understand why pragmatics has remained relatively untouched for the designs of semiotic companions.

Multimodality is a new term which in many respects has substituted the more classical one of non-verbal communication (Payrató 2009). My first aim in this paper is precisely to focus on the impact that non-verbal communication (the traditional term) and multimodality (a recent neologism) may have on pragmatic theory and practice. Secondly, I will discuss some of the questions that multimodal pragmastylistics must confront as its initial challenges.

2 Many terms, clear concepts? Where does multimodality begin?

Throughout "mainstream" linguistics, canonical and classical definitions distinguish – apparently in a clear way – between *verbal* and *non-verbal* items and *vocal* and *non-vocal* channels. Today, these can be reinterpreted as verbal and non-verbal *modes* and vocal and non-vocal *media*. Broadly speaking, we could say that modes are equivalent to production tools and media to dissemination tools. In spite of the apparent simplicity of the divisions, the concepts are less clear when the terms *language* (as a noun) and *linguistic* (as an adjective) come into play and combine with the previous terms, and still more with others such as *prosodic* or *paralinguistic* items. Is human language *entirely* verbal? Are we going to treat *linguistic* and *verbal* as exact synonyms? Are suprasegmental cues vocal, linguistic, prosodic and also *verbal* items? Of course, suprasegmental features are linguistic, but they are also non-verbal (except if we use *verbal* as a synonym not for *word* but for *linguistic* or "language mode").

Lyons (1972) proposed to establish different degrees of "linguisticness" to be able to manage the relations between these concepts. Today, the meaning of *prosodic* cues is no longer clear; the meaning of the term changes in the work of different researchers and traditions. Equally, *paralinguistics* may refer to (only) paralinguistic vocal items or, in a more general sense, to vocal and kinetic resources alongside prototypical verbal items. In fact, none of the terms *text*, *style*, and *multimodality* can be defined precisely and easily, and so combining them is no easy task. Nevertheless, the case for regarding gesture as a part of language has been taken up by many researchers (McNeill 2000; Kendon 2004; Müller et al. 2013), and despite their manual nature, sign languages have received consideration from linguists for many years.[1]

The first step in a simple (but not over-simplified) analysis is to try to describe or to shape the prototype of a single mode (or code), that is to say, the *unimodality* pole of the idealized continuum of unimodality-multimodality. In the non-verbal domain, we can imagine such examples as an extremely simple code based on colors or the expression of affect through facial expression. In the first case, we might think of a traffic light as a code with three meanings: red (meaning "stop"), amber (meaning "caution"), and green (meaning "go"). In the second case, we might think of several (universal or cultural) expressions associated with facial configurations, the most habitual in the research on this topic being "happiness", "sadness", "surprise", "anger", "disgust", and "fear". Apart from cultural specifications, no more considerations need to be added to this pole of unimodality, and actually many other languages or codes work in a similar, simple, way. However, if we examine the code not as an abstract, acontextual domain (as before) but in the way it is actually used, we will see that the way we understand the signals is neither isolated nor simplistic. For instance, traffic lights can be reinforced by other means beyond the simple type of color: the intensity of the light, or its intermittent nature; therefore, a temporal dimen-

---

[1] See in this case Vigliocco, Perniss, and Vinson (2014), and Perniss, Özyürek, and Morgan (2015).

sion is added to the static one. Similarly, displays of affect are not restricted to the face; they also depend on posture (even changes in skin color, such as blushing) and can be complemented by vocalizations or verbalizations. Thus, what we find in many cases are a series of complex signals produced at one and the same time by different codes and perceived by different sensory channels. In sum, what we have been describing is obviously the displacement from an abstract unimodal code to real multimodal processes.

The complexity is greater in the case of human language. First of all, if, in agreement with the most widespread theoretical option today, we consider that verbal language is a unique code or mode (or *core* mode/code), then we have three submodes and three media of *inscription* or materialization of the core, primary code: (a) the oral one (human language by default), with a vocal-auditory channel and a set of "design features" that have been highlighted and analyzed many times; (b) writing, a system that was born around 5000 years ago, which in turn has different formats and supports (including a tactile one); and (c) signing characteristic of sign languages, which also follows a visual channel. Starting with the last of these media, perhaps multimodality is at first glance less visible here, but we must remember that sign language production does not exclude other kinds of standard gestures and facial expressions; therefore we have more than a simple, unique coding. In writing, multimodality appears with many options in terms of the kind of alphabet (and sometimes even the option of choosing the alphabet), typography, layout, and so on. Finally, in the field of oral language multimodality combines three dimensions: verbal language, vocal paralinguistics and kinesics, which form what Poyatos (see inter alia 2004) called the triple structure of human language. Language, multimodality, and communication are necessarily embedded and embodied, and their development and evolution have been seen from a common perspective ever since their inception (Levinson and Holler 2014). No inscription of human verbal language can be materialized without engaging in a multimodal usage, in both the production and the reception of messages. No illocutionary values are manifested through exclusively verbal means, and so pragmatic theory must encompass the multimodal ways for creating meaning associated with the use of verbal language.

3 Then what is a multimodal text?

One of the results of the large-scale expansion of multimodality studies is that the concepts of text and discourse need to be reconsidered. Similar conceptual reassessments have been made in the classical ethnography of *speaking*, reborn and renamed as the ethnography of *communication*. As in the case of *speech* act

– seen as a *communicative* act, not as an exclusively verbal act – or a *speech* event – conceived no longer as a verbal event but as a *communicative* event – now we must see textual products as communicative products, and discourse analysis must be seen necessarily as a multimodal task. The text is no longer a simple verbal artefact but a semiotic construction, the result of the confluence of several codes and the connection of several channels in communicative interaction. Meaning is created not exclusively or "univocally" by verbal language, and language is not isolated, and so we should assess communicative samples from a different perspective from that of traditional linguistics. Günter Kress and Theo Van Leeuwen (2011: 4) defined this difference in a book that today is seen as one of the cornerstones of the intertextual chain of studies on multimodality:[2] "[t]he traditional linguistic account is one in which *meaning* is *made once*, so to speak", and in contrast, "we see the multimodal resources which are available in a culture used to make meanings in any and every sign, at every level, and in any mode."

Written discourse combines the meaning of verbal items with the meaning of layout, color, typography, and so on (see Machin 2007: 63–158). The crucial question is no longer whether the colors or the typography are indeed the *text* or the *paratext* or any other similar concept, nor the indefinite variety of (sub)types of texts (written communicative pieces), but how meaning is created through these multimodal resources and their combinations. Oral discourse associates segmental verbal items with suprasegmental linguistic items (pitch, quantity, accent), with paralinguistic items (vocal quality, intensity, vocal sounds), and with kinesic items (manual/facial/head gestures). This last dimension comprises gestures (mostly manual) or non-verbal acts of different types: coverbals (cospeech gestures, iconic or metaphorical), emblematic gestures or emblems (which can function without speech), interactive gestures, and rhythmic gestures.[3] While linguistic items are sequential, many of these other non-verbal items are simultaneous to each other and to other items such as affect displays (basically through facial expression) and items related to the management of time (chronemics), space (proxemics) and touch (haptics). Once more, the point is not the vast body of infinite kinds of texts (oral communicative pieces) that can be found in oral human interaction (see section 5), but how different modes are manifested and combined. This is also highly relevant for a multimodal pragmastylistics and for any pragmatic theory as a whole.

---

[2] For a general view see, inter alia, Jewitt (2009, 2014).
[3] The classification of gestures is far more complex than is suggested here; it cannot be summarized in a few lines. See inter alia Kendon (2004) and McNeill (2000).

4 Pragmatic theory and multimodality: Conventional acts

As a general tenet, if we accept that linguistic meaning is mediated by processes of social interaction in situational contexts, and also that human language is materialized or inscribed in several media during these processes in association with other communicative modes, then a pragmatic theory of language must be a multimodal pragmatic theory; that is, it must explain how language is used and how it functions together with other semiotic mechanisms.

As a concrete case or sample, if, like Austin (1962: 121–122), we accept that "for example, acts equivalent to the illocutionary act of warning or the perlocutionary act of convincing" can be "brought off non-verbally" (through a "*conventional* non-verbal-act"), a theory of pragmatic acts should also take into account at least those non-verbal acts that are usually materialized in association with linguistic ones or as a substitute for them.

Many similar cases can be adduced. In fact, many examples of the close relation between non-verbal (communicative) phenomena and the pragmatic (linguistic) domain are traceable throughout the history of the discipline (for a summary, see Payrató 2009). The notion of *pragmatic gesture* is not new, but it remains unclear (Payrató and Tessendorf 2014). What is beyond doubt is that researchers today consider gesture and speech as two synchronized models for producing meaning in human interaction (Kendon 2004; McNeill 2000). We already have examples to suggest that pragmatic gestures will be a key notion in multimodal pragmatics (Bolly 2015).

Because of the change of perspective, some recent pragmatics textbooks have included references or even entire chapters on the topic (see especially Archer, Aijmer, and Wichmann 2012 and Senft 2014). There have also been extensions of certain pragmatic theories that make it possible to focus on non-verbality (or at least on gestures in particular) from a specific pragmatic point of view, such as relevance. Wharton (2009) shows how the concept of relevance can be particularly useful for explaining different aspects of non-verbal behavior. The significance of the notion of relevance in studies of non-verbal communication was briefly but explicitly discussed in McNeill (1992) and Payrató (2003). McNeill stresses the need to discuss relevance, and Payrató emphasizes relevance theory and other cognitive models that could also be applied to the study of non-verbal communication (prototype theory and the concept of family resemblance). Taking into account the vast amount of information that interactants must manage in daily interactions, a notion of relevance (context-dependent relevance) is essential to distinguish what is communicatively substantial from what is trivial; for instance, meaningful gestural behavior from merely functional movements that are not deliberately (ostensively) communicative. It is no surprise that the analysis of the interactions between native speakers and second language learners, particularly when there is a considerable cultural distance between them, often reveals difficulties in tasks of this kind.

5 Pragmatic theory and multimodal pragmastylistics: Infinite features in the future?

The idea of style connects a product and the features that make it a specific entity with the individual who is responsible for it. The multiple meanings of the term become apparent from a review of the definitions in both standard and specialist dictionaries. To arrive at a precise definition of style is very difficult: as hinted in Count Buffon's famous adage, "Le style c'est l'homme même" ('the style is the man himself'). Thus, style matches the person with the character of the text. Style is a personal brand when behaving and a trace when creating a product; if this product is multimodal, the style must necessarily be treated also in terms of multimodality.

We live in a multimodal world. This is a commonsense assertion of a fact that has been obvious for many years. Our society is becoming increasingly multimodal, as life, communication, and culture grow in complexity. Maybe the complexity of multimodal communication was already visible in some traditional art forms such as opera and theater, but today its everyday presence is overwhelming, through the mass media and new technologies. We constantly receive vast amounts of information from many simultaneous sources, and we live surrounded by worlds born or founded on screens, from televisions to computers, smart phones, electronic devices, and videogames for adults or children.

A representative body of evidence that would create a reasonable basis for a stylistic typology of multimodality is too difficult to imagine, but at the other extreme, over-simplifications are not productive. The maps or the models of a multimodal pragmastylistics must also avoid the tendency to pay too much attention to petty details. Taking the analysis of oral language as the domain par excellence (and by default) in human communication, we can begin by reviewing the many variables that may have a prominent affect on the development of a multimodal stylistic typology:

1. Textual/discourse genre (and subgenres), where the sample is included: scope (private, public, institutional etc.), purpose (not literary, expressive/aesthetic etc.), structure (dialogic or multimanaged/monologic), number and type of modes or codes involved (along a spectrum of varying multimodality).

2. Type of text in question: orientation (narrative, descriptive, explanatory, argumentative, directive), materialization, i.e., the composition/nature (extension, nominal/verbal etc.), organization and informative structure (explicit/implicit, tied/untied, kinds of superstructure/macrostructure etc.), thematic development, degree of unity (cohesion) and types of cohesive mechanisms used, and keys for and degree of interpretability (coherence).

3. Dialectal variation manifested, determining permanent and constant features of interactants: historical (contemporary or not), geographical (local/regional/standard/not checked), sociocultural (class/ethnic group/educational level/generation/gender/acquisition-dependent).

4. Functional variation manifested, determining rather nonpermanent features of interactants but typical of communicative situations: subject or field (specialized/non-specialized or current), codes (and channels: oral/written; degree of planning), purposes or tenors (functional: interactive/informative; personal: subjective/objective, involved/distant), tone or degree of formality (informal/semiformal/formal).

5. Management of prosodic, vocal and paralinguistic aspects: non-verbal linguistic dimension, i. e., intonation (melodic contour, terminal sequences, focalizations), quantity (extensions), and stress; paralinguistic dimension, i.e., intensity, rhythm, emphasis (expressive resources), voice quality.

6. Management of gestures (kinesics): facial expression, gestures of the head, gaze, posture, coverbal gestures (iconic or metaphoric), emblematic gestures, interactive gestures, pragmatic gestures, deictic gestures.

7. Management of proxemic aspects (space management, personal and collective; environmental management), of chronemics (time management: interaction rates and latency on responses), and other modes or channels: physical personal traits, aspects of clothing and grooming, physical contact with partners (haptics), physical characteristics of objects or products (dimensions and texture, color, font, etc.).

8. Management and interaction of semantic and rhetorical devices: combination of types of meaning (natural/non-natural, propositional/non-propositional, iconic/non-iconic), salience, preference and type of expressive and cognitive strategies (comparisons, metaphors, metonyms), points of views or perspectives (direct style, indirect style, free indirect style), external objectification/representation of characters, type of modalization and involvement/detachment, strategies of implication/intensification/mitigation.

9. Management of relational and interpersonal aspects: facework (positive/negative) and (im)politeness strategies, construction /maintenance of social relations, construction/maintenance of identities (gender, generation, ethnic, social group/class, etc.), construction/maintenance of conversational/discursive/virtual identities.

10. Choice of modes and the interaction between them: number and type of modes of production (monomodality/multimodality), means of dissemination (monomediality/multimediality), cognitive mechanisms involved (monostrategical/multistrategical); degree and type of interaction between modes (dominance/complementary modalities, addition and intersection/fusion procedures).

No (single) pragmatic theory can assume all these stylistic variables at one and the same time, no linguistic theory can explain the complexity of language in its entirety, and no semiotic theory can tackle all the possible processes of creation of meaning. Nevertheless, we must contrast microanalyses based on variables such as the ones listed above with explanatory theories: perspectives focused on microevents with those which try to frame the entire (macro) panorama. What future research on a typology of multimodality should bring out is the evidence of empirical cases that allow (theoretical) generalizations, i.e., well-documented tokens for proposing well-established types or categories. For instance, if we look at the variables grouped in (10), we see how relevance is substantiated in every speech event, in every communicative act: how relevance depends on contextualization cues assumed by partners in situational, sociocultural contexts. Moreover, we can analyze the kinds of operations that can be found between modalities, whether verbal language prevails against imagistic language (or vice versa) and, in all cases, what kinds of (inter-/intra-) cultural patterns (maybe universal patterns) emerge. This dialectic is the testing ground defined by the coordinates of multimodality, pragmatics, and ethnography of communication.

Obviously, the construction of a theory of multimodal pragmastylistics should take into account the important early contributions to the field, but there is no room for a review of these studies here (we refer the interested reader to, inter alia, Hickey 1993 and Black 2006). Moreover, the concepts of communication, intention and meaning should be defined. Communication is conceived here as a set of multi-coding (multimodal) processes combined with inferential processes in which the recognition of intentions is essential. These intentions (mental states directed towards an action) confer (natural/propositional/iconic) meaning on communicative acts, which are recognized by principles of relevance (Sperber and Wilson 1986, 1995; Wharton 2009). Applied to the case of autonomous or emblematic gestures, an approach of this kind was outlined in Payrató (2003).

The examples in the following sections aim to describe some of the suggested connections, whether multimodality is based on the addition of codes (usually synchronized, parallel or converging codes, section 5.1), or on the intersection (the merging or blending) of modalities to create new meanings ("intermodes"). The latter is a particularly interesting case because it exploits exclusive opportunities born in the deliberate crossing of codes (section 5.2).[4]

5.1 Additive multimodality: Parallel and converging forms

The myth of the unimodality or monomodality of verbal language is based on a traditional linguistic mainstream focused on written language, standard registers, expository texts, and an undisguised interest for grammar and content analysis. Example (1),[5] an "open" formal letter left in a mailbox, is a rather monomodal text, a product at the left-hand pole of the monomodality-multimodality continuum; so are examples (2), flyers distributed by seers/healers, although they include a few more multimodal resources than (1).

The tendency to conceive texts like (1) (or even those in [2]) as completely monomodal is also based on the fact that they are not compared to others, and many multimodal features that they contain (calligraphy in this case, for example, or layout) go unnoticed. If, as in any functional variation analysis, we compare this text with other samples, these features acquire strong salience. This also happens if we compare (1) with (2) and especially (1)/(2) with leaflets from retail shops (3).

---

[4] Many variables are interrelated; the list is not exhaustive and other features could also be included. See for instance the proposal of Stöckl (2004) on mode distinctions and on the semiotic principles across modes, or the concept of modal density proposed by Norris (2004); see also applied examples in O'Halloran (2004) or Eckkrammer (2004). More recent developments include many other examples, inter alia Jewitt (2009, 2014), Müller et al. (2013, 2014), Norris and Maier (2014).
[5] I deal with these examples in more detail in Payrató (2013).

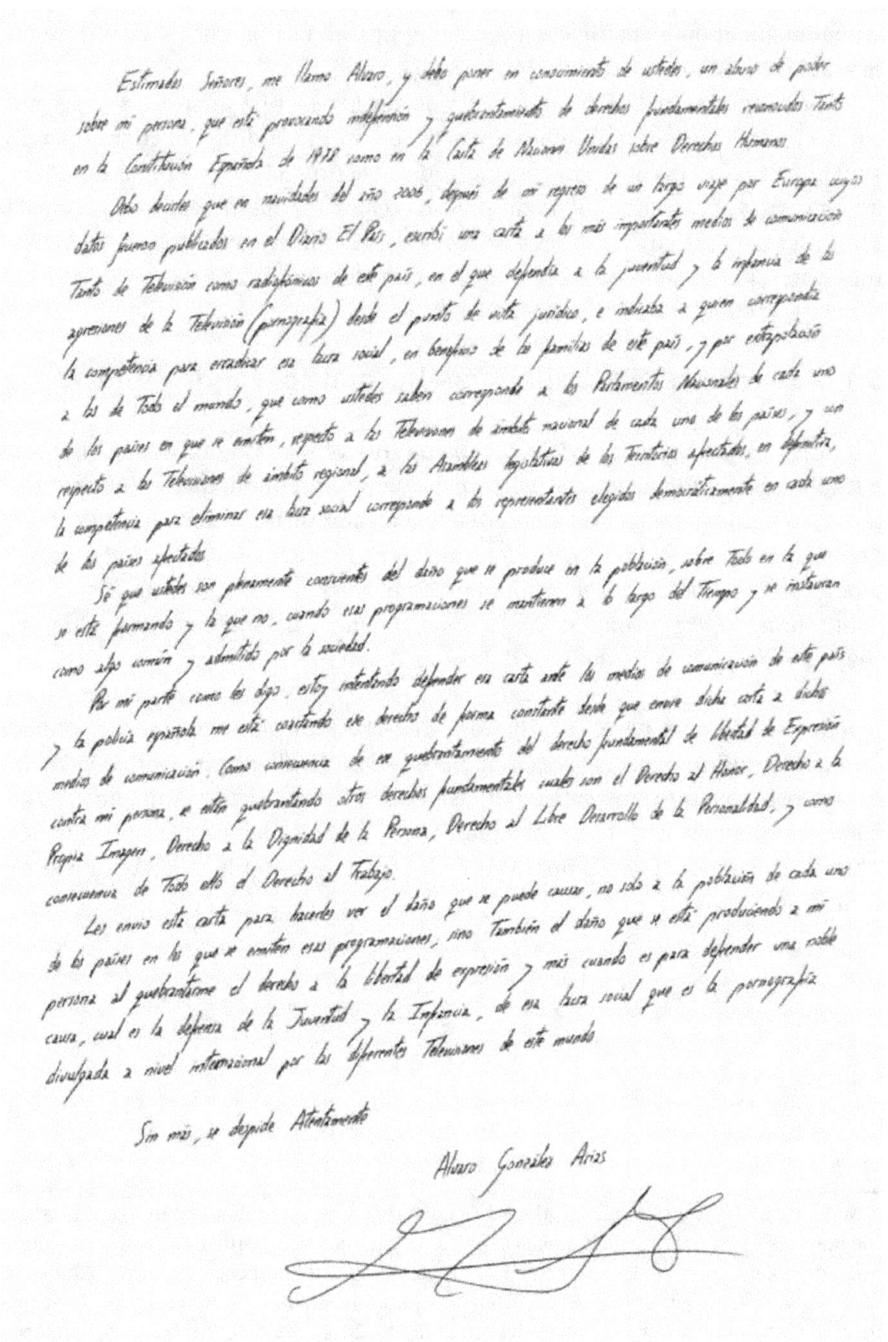

Estimados Señores, me llamo Alvaro, y debo poner en conocimiento de ustedes, un abuso de poder sobre mi persona, que está provocando indefensión y quebrantamiento de derechos fundamentales reconocidos Tanto en la Constitución Española de 1978 como en la Carta de Naciones Unidas sobre Derechos Humanos

Debo decirles que en navidades del año 2006, después de mi regreso de un largo viaje por Europa cuyos datos fueron publicados en el Diario El País, escribí una carta a los más importantes medios de comunicación Tanto de Televisión como radiofónicos de este país, en el que defendía a la juventud y la infancia de las agresiones de la Televisión (pornografía) desde el punto de vista jurídico, e indicaba a quien correspondía la competencia para erradicar esa lacra social, en beneficio de las familias de este país, y por extrapolación a las de Todo el mundo, que como ustedes saben corresponde a los Parlamentos Nacionales de cada uno de los países en que se emiten, respecto a las Televisiones de ámbito nacional de cada uno de los países, y con respecto a las Televisiones de ámbito regional, a las Asambleas legislativas de los Territorios afectados, en definitiva, la competencia para eliminar esa lacra social corresponde a los representantes elegidos democráticamente en cada uno de los países afectados

Sé que ustedes son plenamente conscientes del daño que se produce en la población, sobre Todo en la que se está formando y la que no, cuando esas programaciones se mantienen a lo largo del Tiempo y se instauran como algo común y admitido por la sociedad.

Por mi parte como les digo, estoy intentando defender esa carta ante los medios de comunicación de este país y la policía española me está coartando ese derecho de forma constante desde que envié dicha carta a dichos medios de comunicación. Como consecuencia de ese quebrantamiento del derecho fundamental de libertad de Expresión contra mi persona, se están quebrantando otros derechos fundamentales cuales son el Derecho al Honor, Derecho a la Propia Imagen, Derecho a la Dignidad de la Persona, Derecho al Libre Desarrollo de la Personalidad, y como consecuencia de Todo ello el Derecho al Trabajo.

Les envío esta carta para hacerles ver el daño que se puede causar, no solo a la población de cada uno de los países en los que se emiten esas programaciones, sino También el daño que se está produciendo a mi persona al quebrantarme el derecho a la libertad de expresión y más cuando es para defender una noble causa, cual es la defensa de la Juventud y la Infancia, de esa lacra social que es la pornografía divulgada a nivel internacional por las diferentes Televisiones de este mundo

Sin más, se despide Atentamente

Alvaro González Arias

Figure 1. "Open" letter left in a mailbox

Figure 2. Flyers of seers/healers, left in the mailbox or handed out in the street. Actual sizes (each card): 10.5 x 7.8 cm.

Figure 3. Advertising leaflet from a computer/electronics store: 1st page, 4th page, and central (double) page. Actual sizes: 41.5 x 29.5 cm (1st /4th) and 41.5 x 59 cm (central page).

While flyers (2) are quite simple and make very little use of multimodal resources, multimodality is immediately manifested in examples (3) with a burst of images and colors: the black and white of examples (1) and (2) now turns into a variety of colors; the tiny images of (2) into a string of photographs; minimal aesthetic resources into multiple visual resources, etc. The contrast is even more obvious if we compare the examples included in (1) and (2) with the advertisements in (4) and (5):

Figure 4. Flyer advertising a bus tour (left in the mailbox)

Figure 5. Flyer advertising a bus tour (left in the mailbox)

The verbal nature or dimension of examples (4) and (5) is lost, to the benefit of color and images. The name of the destination (Cardona) is hard to locate in (4) and it is impossible to find in (5), because there is no mention of it. The relevance of the event lies in the gifts (a vacuum, the impressive bottle of oil, a great cheese, and so on) not in the destination. Non-verbality tells us this immediately with the salience of the images.

In examples (1) and (2), the (very limited) multimodal meaning comes directly from the process of selection and inscription of verbal language in a (written) media. In examples (3), (4) and (5) the process of creation of meaning rests mainly on the juxtaposition of items of different (but parallel) modes, words and images, with color and other graphic resources acting as demarcative or expressive devices. We find other cases of juxtaposition in photographs/captions, paintings/titles, illustrated books and so on. There are only a few small mechanisms of convergence in (3) (in the double page, with lines and bubbles indicating adscriptions), but real convergences are to be found in other kinds of combinations between words and images such as comics, posters or other graphic designs, where the kind of meaning (natural, propositional, iconic) should also be analyzed.

In spoken language, multimodality rests mainly on the addition of mechanisms, usually with convergent forms in the sense that different modes (verbal, vocal paralinguistic, kinesics) are synchronized to elaborate coherent messages. Apart from exceptional cases of divergence (like non-verbal undisguised lies),[6] the combination of modes and channels results in a synchronization which has been highlighted by pioneers in the field of non-verbal studies.[7] The habitual metaphor for comparison has been dance: speech and gesture dancing in time from a pragmatically planned orchestration, with different, but above all consistent, individual and cultural styles. McNeill (1992) even suggests laws for describing the timing of verbal and gestural elements in detail, and Kendon (2004) has also highlighted this convergence on many occasions.

The combination of channels cannot be understood in a hierarchical sense in favor of either verbality or gesture. Rather it is the result of complementary ways of creating meaning. In (6), for example, a speaker verbally describes a frog moving away, while using an iconic manual gesture to depict the movement made by the animal (jumping):[8]

(6) i quan es desperta_
     l[a gra**nota ma**rxa_]
     COSPEECH GESTURE
     And when he wakes up the frog leaves

---

[6] See Arndt and Janney (1987) and what they call cases of contradiction and contrast: for example, between emotional reactions and prosodic or kinesic items; in the usual examples what is found is reinforcement, in which different codes corroborate the same meaning.

[7] See more references to the work of Condon, Birdwhistell, or Kendon himself in Payrató (2009) and Kendon (2004).

[8] The example is analyzed in Lloberes & Payrató (2011). The gesture is performed simultaneously with the fragment of verbal text in bold.

The gesture provides iconic meaning that is not in the verbal statement. It adds information, and multimodality is achieved by addition. This same complementary combination occurs with many emblematic gestures (for instance the one for "TO BE CRAZY"[9]), with the particularity that non-verbal and verbal items may appear juxtaposed, simultaneously (as in 7a), or in a sequence (as in 7b or 7c):[10]

(7) a. **En Joan està boig!**
 John is crazy!
 EN JOAN ÉS BOIG (EMBLEM)
 JOHN IS CRAZY (EMBLEM)
 b. En Joan està...
 John is...
 BOIG (EMBLEM)
 CRAZY (EMBLEM)
 c. En Joan...
 John...
 ÉS BOIG (EMBLEM)
 IS CRAZY (EMBLEM)

Emblems and coverbal gestures join together in the framework created by verbal utterances. This suggests the presence of a common procedure of elaboration and the existence of comprehensive grammars that treat the two channels together (vid. Fricke 2013 and Alturo, Clemente, and Payrató 2016). This case is very similar to what Slama-Cazacu (1975) named *mixed syntax*, one of the first contributions by a linguist to the analysis of the phenomena of verbal and non-verbal confluence.

5.2 Intersectional multimodality: Merged or blending forms

Taking a step further, we can approach cases in which multimodality becomes intersectional, i.e., it acts as a significant potential, as a strategy, and as an expressive resource of a semiotic nature to create new meanings. Sometimes these processes can be carried out with the simple change of a single element, such as a typographical sign; in other cases we find subtle and more complex arrange-

---

[9] In the Catalan emblem (also in Spanish, Italian, and French), the index finger gently taps the temple.
[10] See Payrató (1993). At least according to this proposal, an emblem can be defined as an autonomous gesture that has illocutionary value in its prototypical usage.

ments with multiple intersections and mergers, such as combinations of verbal items, vocal paralinguistics, facial expression, gaze, proxemics and haptics.

One of the clearest examples of these combinations occurs in gesture deictics, as already noted by Levinson (1983), as in (8), and in less studied cases like those of modal deixis, as in (9), in which the movement of the gesture represents the way expressed by deictic form or indexical. Other examples are found in vocal and gestural combinations, such as (10), in which the backwards movement of the head is accompanied by a click of the tongue, meaning a clear denial or refusal (a similar move to one found in cultures that do not use the lateral displacement of the head, for instance those of southern Italy, Greece or Bulgaria):

(8) I would like… *this one.*

(9) Ho va fer *així*
 He did it *this way*

(10) Què dius! NEGACIÓ + CLIC LINGUAL
 What are you saying! NEGATION + LINGUAL CLICK

While in the examples (6) or (7a) gesture and speech are coupled and complemented, now the combination goes a step further and in (8) and (9) we find merged forms. The consistency and interpretability of the speech act relies on the simultaneous use of verbal and gestural mechanisms: they cannot be separated. The intention of the speaker is not recognized unless verbal and non-verbal information is combined. The verbal statement (*I would like this one*) needs a gesture, and vice versa. In examples like (9), the hand and the arm represent the movement referred to by the indexical form, which is devoid of meaning out of context. In (10) the fusion is also evident, but it occurs not between a verbal item and a kinesic item, but between a vocal sound and a kinesic item.[11]

Deictic gestures are cultural, as many studies have shown (see references in Kita 2003), but the combination of a verbal item and a gesture creating a complex sign is surely a universal form, and possibly one of the first forms of multimodality by intersection found in children's acquisition of communicative competence. The combination by intersection and merger of verbal and kinesic patterns is common in many emblematic gestures, which can be seen as ethological displays (Payrató 1993; Senft 2014), as between verbal and vocal patterns in interjections.

---

[11] Enfield (2009) reports many cases of composite utterances involving fusion of this kind in deictic and illustrative components of moves. See another excellent example in the work of Özyürek (1998) on Turkish demonstratives.

In the case of written language, an example of basic, minimal, creative, and intersectional multimodality is found in (11). The example reproduces graffiti denoting a new interpretation of the content of the conventional reading of (12), located towards the pole of unimodality, or by the interpretation of (13). This last example is another clear case of multimodality, but the multimodality is achieved here through complementary functions or reinforcements (by addition) – not as in (11), where the creation of meaning through merging is very successful:

(11) El hombre de mi vida soy ♀o
      lit. *The man of my life am ♀/I*
      ♀ am the man of my life

(12) El hombre de mi vida soy yo
      I am the man of my life

(13)

The multimodal resource created in (11) should not be interpreted as a trivial game of substitution between elements of different codes (graphic codes in this case), such as, for instance, short texts like "I ♥ [love] New York", or emoticons or smilies embedded in electronic mails. Nor should it be interpreted as a resource borrowed from the technical language of mathematics found in example (13), where a woman is raised to the power of ten: Cat. d♀na^{10} (w♀man^{10}). What is pragmatically relevant in (11) is that a new kind of (merged) utterance from common (12) is interpreted in a new way. This is possible thanks to the fact that the intersection of a "foreigner" symbol (♀) and the original word (Sp. *yo*, "*I*") creates a new word, a new meaning ("I" female), and in fact a new identity and its corresponding interpretation by the receiver.

Finally, as the last step on our tour, we move from the typographic and symbolic exchange of (11) to a more complex graphic game like the one in (14), an advert that combines a verbal message (related to the selling of objects), the background of a photographic image and the foregrounding of a finger (which makes an obscene gesture) bearing a ring:[12]

---

[12] The example is reproduced from Payrató (2013). In (14b) a later, more politically correct version of the advert is shown – the word *amor* (*love*) substitutes the word *hombre* (*man*) – with some changes in the color and format.

(14)   a.      b.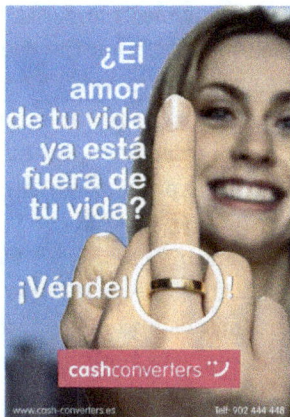

Multimodality is key to the prominence of the message, and multimodal blending contributes to the creation of identity and ideological meanings. In the image, fully locked into the verbal statement, the *o* of the clitic around the finger suggests the ring to be sold, while the finger insults the man (in 14a) or the person (in 14b) who presumably gave her the ring: "Is the man in your life (or the love of your life) now out of your life? Sell it/him!"

This type of intersectional multimodality contributes decisively to the prominence of the messages and the creation of new identities. In this case, a new female identity, happy and smiling (facial expression), dismisses the man (or the person, in [14b]) who is no longer the love "of her life" in a provocative, masculine way using an impudent gestural emblem. Multimodality, in short, goes far beyond the simple means of expression and appears as a pragmatic strategy with a huge potential significance, rooted in the ideology and the identities of a particular sociocultural group.

6 Conclusion

Alongside a purely inscriptive multimodality, which is unavoidable in the performance of oral/written language, more functional and significant cases can be found. Firstly, there is an additive, complementary multimodality, with descriptive or depictive functions. The juxtaposition or convergence of modes can be associated with different concepts of anchorage between texts and images, as we often see in the press, or in the matching of gestures and verbal items. Secondly, there is an interactive, intersectional multimodality, in which the fusion of modes allows the appearance of new meanings, new communicative strategies, and thus new identities for the interactants.

Today multimodality is the rule rather than the exception, and the fundamental fact is that the combination of different communicative modes contributes to the creation of new meanings in social interaction, either through (core) oral language or through written language (or both). The concept of globalization is perfectly applicable to many aspects of the world of communication. The need to expand pragmatic and discourse studies to the analysis of multimodality, their styles and the impact of these styles in the social world is one of the outstanding challenges we face in this field in this new century. More specifically, the way meaning is created through multimodal texts deserves analysis. Pragmatics and a multimodal pragmastylistics must play an important role in this analysis, both to deepen our understanding of communicative phenomena and to equip all speakers with strategies that enable them to critically encode and decode the multimodal messages of human interaction.

Acknowledgements: This study was undertaken with funding from the grants 2014 SGR 918 and FFI2014-56258P.

References

Alturo, Núria, Ignasi Clemente & Lluís Payrató 2016. Notes for a multilingual and multimodal functional discourse grammar. In Marta Fernández-Villanueva & Konstanze Jungbluth (eds.), *Beyond language boundaries: Multimodal use in multilingual contexts*, 3–33. Boston & Berlin: De Gruyter Mouton.

Archer, Dawn, Karin Aijmer & Anne Wichmann. 2012. *Pragmatics*. London: Routledge.

Arndt, Horst & Richard W Janney. 1987. *InterGrammar: Toward an integrative model of verbal, prosodic and kinesic choices in speech*. Berlin & New York: Mouton de Gruyter.

Austin, John L. 1975 [1962]. *How to do things with words*. Cambridge: Harvard University Press.

Black, Elizabeth. 2006. *Pragmatic stylistics*. Edinburgh: Edinburgh University Press.

Bolly, Catherine. 2015. Towards pragmatic gestures: From repetition to construction in multimodal pragmatics. Communication at the 13th International Cognitive Linguistics Conference (http://hdl.handle.net/2078.1/161982)

Eckkrammer, Eva M. 2004. Drawing on theories of inter-semiotic layering to analyse multimodality in medical self-counselling texts and hypertexts. In Eija Ventola, Charles Cassily & Martin Kaltenbacher (eds.), *Perspectives on multimodality*, 211–226. Amsterdam & Philadelphia: John Benjamins.

Enfield, Nicholas J. 2009. *The anatomy of meaning. Speech, gesture, and composite utterances*. Cambridge: Cambridge University Press.

Fricke, Ellen. 2013. Towards a unified grammar of gesture and speech: A multimodal approach. In Cornelia Müller, Alan Cienki, Ellen Fricke, Silva H. Ladewig, David McNeill & Sedinha Tessendorf (eds.): *Body – Language – Communication (Volume 1)*, 733–754. Boston & Berlin: De Gruyter Mouton.

Hickey, Leo. 1993. Stylistics, pragmatics and pragmastylistics. *Revue Belgue de Philologie et d'Histoire* 71(3). 573–586.

Jewitt, Carey (ed.). 2014 [2009]. *The Routledge handbook of multimodal analysis*. London: Routledge.

Kendon, Adam. 2004. *Gesture. Visible action as utterance*. Cambridge: Cambridge University Press.

Kita, Sotaro (ed.). 2003. *Pointing: Where language, culture, and cognition meet*. Mahwah: Lawrence Erlbaum.

Kress, Gunther & Theo Van Leeuwen. 2001. *Multimodal discourse*. London: Arnold.

Levinson, Stephen C. 1983. *Pragmatics*. Cambridge: Cambridge University Press.

Levinson, Stephen C. & Juduth Holler. 2014. The origin of human multi-modal communication. *Philosophical Transactions of the Royal Society B* 369 (1651).

Lloberes, Marina & Lluís Payrató. 2011. Pragmatic coherence as a multimodal feature: Illustrative cospeech gestures, events, and states. In Lluís Payrató & Josep Maria Cots (eds.), *The pragmatics of Catalan*, 215–246. Boston & Berlin: De Gruyter Mouton.

Lyons, John. 1972. Human Language. In Robert A. Hinde (ed.), *Non-verbal communication*, 49–85. Cambridge: Cambridge University Press.

Machin, David. 2007. *Introduction to multimodal analysis*. London: Bloomsbury.

McNeill, David. 1992. *Hand and mind*. Chicago: The University of Chicago Press.

McNeill, David (ed.). 2000. *Language and gesture*. Cambridge: Cambridge University Press.

Müller, Cornelia, Alan Cienki, Ellen Fricke, Silva H. Ladewig, David McNeill & Sedinha Tessendorf (eds.). 2013. *Body – Language – Communication (Volume 1)*. Boston & Berlin: De Gruyter Mouton.

Müller Cornelia, Alan Cienki, Ellen Fricke, Silva H. Ladewig, David McNeill & Jana Bressem (eds.). 2014. *Body – Language – Communication (Volume 2)*. Boston & Berlin: De Gruyter Mouton.

Norris, Sigrid. 2004. *Analyzing multimodal interaction*. London: Routledge.

Norris, Sigrid & Carmen Daniela Maier (eds.). 2014. *Interactions, images and texts. A reader in multimodality*. Boston & Berlin: De Gruyter Mouton.

O'Halloran, Kay L. 2004. On the effectiveness of mathematics. In Eija Ventola, Charles Cassily & Martin Kaltenbacher (eds.), *Perspectives on multimodality*, 91–117. Amsterdam & Philadelphia: John Benjamins.

Özyürek, Asli. 1998. An analysis of the basic meaning of Turkish demonstratives in face-to-face conversational interaction. In Serge Santi, Isabelle Guaïtella, Christian Cave & Gabrielle Konopczynski (eds.), *Oralite et Gestualite: Communication multimodale, interaction*, 609–614. Paris: L'Harmattan.

Payrató, Lluís. 1993. A pragmatic view on autonomous gestures. A first repertoire of Catalan emblems. *Journal of Pragmatics* 20. 193–216.

Payrató, Lluís. 2003. What does 'the same gesture' mean? Emblematic gestures from some cognitive-linguistic theories. In Monica Rector, Isabella Poggi & Nadine Trigo (eds.): *Gestures. Meaning and use*, 73–81. Porto: Universidade Fernando Pessoa.

Payrató, Lluís. 2009. Non-verbal communication. In Jef Verschueren & Jan-Ola Östman (eds.), *Key notions for pragmatics*, 163–194. Amsterdam & Philadelphia: John Benjamins.

Payrató, Lluís. 2013. Textos, estils i multimodalitat: cap a una pragmaestilística del text multimodal. In Lluís Payrató & Neus Nogué Serrano (eds.), *Estil i estils. Teoria i aplicacions de l'estilística*, 51–86. Barcelona: AEAU – Universitat de Barcelona.

Payrató, Lluís & Sedinha Tessendorf. 2014. Pragmatic gestures. In Cornelia Müller, Alan Cienki, Ellen Fricke, Silva H. Ladewig, David McNeill & Jana Bressem (eds.): *Body – Language – Communication (Volume 2)*, 1531–1539. Boston & Berlin: De Gruyter Mouton.

Perniss, Pamela, Asli Özyürek & Gary Morgan. 2015. The influence of the visual modality on language structure and language conventionalization: Insights from sign language and gesture. *Topics in Cognitive Science* 7(1). 2–11.

Vigliocco, Gabriella, Pamela Perniss & David Vinson. 2014. Language as a multimodal phenomenon: implications for language learning, processing and evolution. *Phil. Trans. R. Soc. B* 369 (1651).
Poyatos, Fernando. 2004. Nuevas perspectivas lingüísticas en comunicación no verbal. In Lluís Payrató & Núria Alturo (eds.), *Les fronteres del llenguatge. Lingüística i comunicació no verbal*, 57–91. Barcelona: Universitat de Barcelona – PPU.
Senft, Gunter. 2014: *Understanding pragmatics*. London: Routledge.
Slama-Cazacu, Tatiana. 1976. Non-verbal components in message sequence: 'Mixed syntax'. In Willam C. McCormack & Stephen A. Wurm (eds.): *Language and man: Anthropological issues*, 217–222. The Hague: Mouton.
Sperber, Dan & Deirdre Wilson. 1995 [1986]. *Relevance: Communication and cognition*. Oxford: Blackwell.
Stöckl, Hartmut. 2004. In between modes. In Eija Ventola, Charles Cassily & Martin Kaltenbacher (eds.), *Perspectives on multimodality*, 9–30. Amsterdam & Philadelphia: John Benjamins.
Wharton, Tim. 2009. *Pragmatics and non-verbal communication*. Cambridge: Cambridge University Press.

Part III: **Interpersonal and societal pragmatics**

Klaus P. Schneider
17 Pragmatic competence and pragmatic variation

1 Introduction

Pragmatic competence and pragmatic variation are key notions in current debates (e.g. the contributions in Beeching and Woodfield 2015). There is, however, considerable controversy as to how these two constructs should be defined (e.g. Félix-Brasdefer and Koike 2012, Sickinger and Schneider 2014) and how the relationship between them should be conceptualized (e.g. Schneider 2012b). These issues are addressed in the present paper.

Pragmatic competence, though much discussed, is a relatively vague concept of disputed status (cf. Kecskés 2014: 61–80 for some discussion). It is often reduced to the utterance level and contrasted with a range of further and related competences, including, among others, communicative competence, interactional competence, intercultural competence, sociolinguistic competence, and discourse competence (e.g. Kasper and Ross 2013; Timpe 2014). To advance the ongoing debates, two questions will be discussed: First, which aspects of language use should be included in pragmatic competence? And second, what exactly is (for lack of a better term) the 'substance', or what are the 'contents', of pragmatic competence, i.e. the particular regularities underlying pragmatic performance in a given language? Furthermore, there is the methodological issue of how pragmatic competence is best studied und which methods are best employed to examine its contents. The present paper is aimed at providing answers to these questions, especially as there is a lot of theorizing about the nature of pragmatic competence in general and not enough systematic empirical work on the regularities, i.e. norms and conventions, underlying pragmatic performance.

Language users do not use language in uniform ways but vary in their performance depending on the language and the variety they use, and also the situation they are in and who they are talking to (e.g. Schneider 2010; Barron 2014). Yet, while pragmatic variation undeniably exists, it is often abstracted away or at least not fully accounted for in conceptualizations of pragmatic competence. This is particularly true for pragmatic competence in a foreign language. Evidence of different practices that learners could orient to is not sufficiently available. The situation calls for more data analysis and descriptive work.

These issues are elaborated in the following sections. Section 2 provides a general discussion of pragmatic competence and its organization and contents, while section 3 examines different types of pragmatic variation. In section 4, the case of responses to thanks is used to exemplify crucial methodological and descriptive issues. Section 5 includes a brief discussion of the development of pragmatic competence in a foreign language and the aims of teaching L2 pragmatics and pragmatic variation. The paper concludes with a summary of the main points.

2 What is pragmatic competence?

Needless to say, any conceptualization of pragmatic competence crucially hinges on a definition of pragmatics. Pragmatics has been defined in many different ways, broad and narrow, as the study of language use, meaning in context, communicative functions of utterances, speaker intentions, hearer interpretations, participant practices, talk-in-interaction, relational work, displays of identity, and so on (cf. Bublitz and Norrick 2011). Each of these definitions reflects a particular tradition. Grabowski (2016: 165), writing from an applied perspective, aptly summarizes the situation as follows:

> While language theorists have produced exhaustive volumes on what constitutes pragmatics, and this body of research contains much of the history of the hypothesized elements under the domain of pragmatics, there still seems to be no ultimate consensus as to a hierarchical or organizational structure of these elements in language.

There is indeed no general agreement about the internal structuring within pragmatics and accordingly in pragmatic competence. Nor is there agreement about the relationship between pragmatic competence and further competences needed to successfully use language in communication. The overarching question is what it means to know a language – a question relevant not only to teaching and testing of (foreign) languages, but also to assessing and treating language disorders in a native language. 'Knowing', in the present context, does not mean explicit or declarative knowledge, but procedural knowledge, i.e. knowing how to do things with words in communication.

In this paper, I would not like to discuss alternative conceptualizations of pragmatics, e.g. Crystal's popular definition (Crystal 1997: 301), Verschueren's famous comprehensive view (Verschueren 1999: 7), or Huang's much quoted distinction between the narrow Anglo-American tradition and the broad Continental European tradition (Huang 2007: 4; cf. Schneider 2010: 240). Nor am I interested in discussing different notions of pragmatic competence or disentangling the jungle of competing terms and concepts, some of which are mentioned in the introduction. Instead, I would like to advocate an all-embracing notion of pragmatic competence which complements grammatical competence, as suggested by Thomas (1983: 92), who defines the latter as "'abstract' or decontextualized knowledge of intonation, phonology, syntax, semantics, etc.", and the former as "the ability to use language effectively in order to achieve a specific purpose and to understand language in context". These two components make up any language user's 'linguistic competence' (Thomas 1983: 92; also Leech 1983: 4), which in turn I consider the verbal component of communicative competence, complementing the component of non-verbal competence.

It is worth noting that Thomas's definition of pragmatic competence is much less detailed than her definition of grammatical competence, for which she specifies at least four subsystems. This imbalance is a disadvantage considering the primacy of pragmatic competence over grammatical competence. After all, grammar is not an end in itself (though teachers find it much easier to teach and test it), but a means to the end of effective communication. The underspecification of pragmatic competence can, however, be remedied by introducing a range of distinctions which expand the notion beyond the limitations of early constructs, notably the reduction to the utterance level and the narrow focus on spoken communication, both resulting from the origins of linguistic pragmatics in speech act theory. It has to be taken into account that utterances do not occur in isolation, as long established in discourse analysis and conversation analysis, and that written communication is, of course, also purposeful and intentional, and usually interactive in its own specific way. Against this background, I would like to minimally suggest the following components within pragmatic competence. A first distinction can be made analytically (if only for the purposes of research and teaching) between utterance-based micropragmatic competence (knowing how to perform a communicative act) and discourse-oriented macropragmatic competence (knowing how to behave in interaction or, more generally, in discourse) (cf. Schneider 2003: 63–68; Cap 2011; Barron and Schneider 2014: 1–3). In each case, further relevant distinctions include speech and writing competence (e.g. Johnstone 2008: 7), production and comprehension competence (e.g. Fraser 2010: 15), and pragmalinguistic and sociopragmatic competence. This last distinction, which has been referred to extensively in empirical and applied work, goes back to Thomas (1983: 99), who differentiates between language-specific pragmalinguistics, providing the linguistic resources relevant to a purpose, and culture-specific sociopragmatics, specifying the respective social norms.

Regarding this construct, I would like to argue that (1) any fully competent language users possess all of these competences, (2) not all native speakers of a language are equally competent, and (3) non-native users of a language are not necessarily pragmatically less competent than native speakers of this language. In this context, a question of central concern is what exactly competent users of a language know, what exactly they do, what exactly they acquire and learn in the course of their language development and socialization – in short, what the 'contents' of all of their pragmatic abilities are, for instance, how to apologize in a particular language for a specific offence in a given social situation in line with the relevant norms, or deliberately against these norms. We do not know nearly enough to answer these questions, let alone answer them exhaustively. What is needed is empirical work on essentially all communicative acts, discourse genres and situation types. This definitely presents an enormous challenge and may seem a ridiculously huge task, yet I am convinced that this is what ultimately needs to be done and clearly a project requiring the collection and analysis of big data.

In this context, it seems productive to introduce a further differentiation. The term 'pragmatics', like 'grammar', 'syntax' or 'semantics' etc., is systematically ambiguous. These terms refer either to a particular level of language (e.g. the semantics of a word, the syntax of the English language) or, on a metalevel, to the study of a particular level of language, or both. To disambiguate these terms, 'pragmatics' can be used to refer to the language level alone, or more adequately, to language use, as opposed to language system, in line with the broad understanding of pragmatics adopted in this paper. By contrast, the term 'pragmatology' can be used to exclusively refer to the theoretical study of pragmatics. Furthermore, by analogy to 'grammatology' versus 'grammaticography', the term 'pragmaticography' can be employed to refer to the systematic description of the pragmatics of a particular language, which has to go beyond merely illustrative examples and must be based on systematic and ideally coordinated empirical work.

In section 4, I will exemplify the type of research needed for pragmaticography, by focusing on responses to thanks, a speech act of limited complexity which also allows to demonstrate that pragmatic variation is an empirical fact, even among competent native speakers of the same language and in the same situation, and how it can be investigated as an aspect of pragmatic competence. Before presenting this example, a few general points about pragmatic variation will be discussed in section 3.

3 What is pragmatic variation?

Languages are not monolithic or homogenous wholes (cf. Weinreich, Labov, and Herzog 1968), although in applied contexts of language teaching and learning they sometimes might appear to be. Variation and change occur, however, in all aspects of language, including pragmatics. While in the early stages of pragmatics researchers concentrated on the foundations of human communication and pragmatic universals, the focus later shifted to the study of pragmatic differences, especially after the publication of Wierzbicka (1985), in which speech act theory, conversation analysis and early politeness theory were accused of ethnocentrism, "mistaking Anglo-Saxon conversational conventions for 'human behaviour' in general" (Wierzbicka 1985: 146). Competent language users, be they multilingual or monolingual, must know that pragmatic variation exists, e.g. that conversational conventions are not shared by all humans. This they do not know naturally and "automatically", this they have to be taught, language learners and native speakers alike. It has been found that native speakers of a language are fairly tolerant towards foreign language learners, expecting them to have an accent and make grammatical and lexical errors. At the same time, native speakers are much less tolerant towards pragmatic errors, tacitly assuming that all humans share the same ideas about e.g. directness, politeness and appropriateness. Hence, native speakers tend to interpret pragmatic errors as rude behaviour and attribute them to character flaws, rather than to pragmatic differences between languages and cultures (e.g. Crandall and Basturkmen 2004). Therefore, it is generally emphasized that learners and non-native users of a language must be made aware of the existence of pragmatic variation and acquire pragmatic competence in their L2. It is, however, also important that native speakers develop an awareness of pragmatic differences.

Different types of pragmatic variation can be distinguished, most of which are immediately relevant to the present discussion of pragmatic competence. What is not considered relevant here is historical pragmatic variation, more relevant to academic expertise, which ordinary language users do not, as a rule, possess (cf. Jucker and Taavitsainen 2010). Contemporary pragmatic variation occurs between languages (inter-lingual variation), but also across varieties of the same language, i.e. between native speakers of a given language (intra-lingual variation). Concerning intra-lingual variation, a further distinction can be made between micro-social and macro-social variation. Micro-social variation is also known as situational variation (Barron and Schneider 2009). Sociopragmatically competent language users behave in different ways in different situations, depending on how they perceive or wish to define a situation they are in and especially the relationship between the participants. Familiarity, also referred to as social distance, and the relative social status of language users vis-à-vis their interlocutors or readers, also known as power, are two micro-social factors which have received considerable attention in the literature, especially in projects based on Brown and Levinson's politeness theory (1987 [1978]) or the *Cross-Cultural Speech Act Realization Project* (Blum-Kulka, House, and Kasper 1989). Power and social distance are, however, not the only situational factors which have been found to systematically influence language use (Spencer-Oatey 2008: 33–40).

The examination of macro-social pragmatic variation, on the other hand, is more recent (Schneider and Barron 2008). Macro-social factors include, for instance, age, gender, ethnicity, region and social class, in other words factors whose influence on language use has long and extensively been studied in sociolinguistics and dialectology, yet not from a pragmatic perspective. While originally conceptualized as relatively stable properties of language users, they are now interpreted as aspects of identity which can be differently displayed, perceived and negotiated in discourse (Haugh and Schneider 2012: 1017). Macro-social pragmatic variation occurs across national and regional varieties of a language and across social groups and communities, and is therefore a type of intercultural variation. This type is studied in variational pragmatics (Barron 2014). While the main focus in this field is on the impact on the individual factors and their interaction, it is also about the interplay of macro-social and micro-social factors (Barron and Schneider 2009). The ultimate aim is to establish the patterns of language use that are relatively invariant across varieties and situations and thus may be seen to form the pragmatic core of a language, and those patterns that vary in systematic ways and can therefore be seen as pragmatic variables. For each of these variables, the variants have to be identified, which is an empirical task (Schneider 2014). Since some of these variants are variety-specific or even variety-exclusive, they are, as a rule, not known to all speakers of a language.

4 Pragmatic competence and variation: The case of responses to thanks

The example of responses to thanks serves to illustrate a number of issues addressed in the above discussions. These include what it means to know how to respond to thanks in English, how the contents of the relevant competences can be established empirically and in a methodologically sound way, to arrive at generalizable patterns arguably underlying pragmatic performance (Schneider 2012b), which can be used for teaching purposes or for corpus searches to generate big data about language use. In short, the case of responses to thanks is used to demonstrate which type of work is required for the purposes of pragmaticography (cf. section 2).

Responses to thanks may appear to be a peripheral speech act, as it can be realized by employing only a handful of formulaic expressions or, to use Kecskés's term, situation-bound utterances (SBUs) (Kecskés 2014). Responses to thanks have, however, received a lot of attention, not least recently, in a range of empirical studies carried out with different methodologies, in different theoretical frameworks, and covering different languages, different varieties and different contexts (e.g. Aijmer 1996; Schneider 2005; Talla Sando Ouafeu 2009; Mulo Farenkia 2012; Rüegg 2014; Bieswanger 2015).

In English, several options are available for realizing responses to thanks. In the literature, a range of different expressions are listed, including the following forms and variations thereof, as a rule without any comments about their use: *You're welcome, My pleasure, Don't mention it, Not at all, Anytime, That's okay* and *No problem*. This appears to be a relatively high number of very different realizations for such a seemingly unimportant speech act, and the question arises how these options differ, how they are used, and whether they can be used interchangeably. A valid answer can only be given empirically. I would therefore like to discuss two studies on responses to thanks in English, which report diverging evidence and can be used to exemplify important theoretical and methodological issues. These studies are Schneider (2005) and Bieswanger (2015).

4.1 Findings from a questionnaire-based study of responses to thanks

Schneider (2005) addresses the following questions: (1) Are all realizations included in the literature used by native speakers of English? Are these realizations used with different frequencies? Are further expressions used? (2) Does the use of realizations differ across national varieties of English? (3) Does situational variation occur? The first question pertains to pragmalinguistic competence essentially on the micro-pragmatic level, the third one to sociopragmatic competence, whereas answers to the second question may reveal differences concerning either or, in fact, both these competencies. The data for this study were collected by employing two discourse completion tasks which are part of a written mixed-task multi-focus questionnaire including a total of fifteen tasks altogether designed to elicit data on eight different pragmatic phenomena (for details, cf. Schneider 2005: 110–111). The two tasks included to elicit responses to thanks appear in positions 4 and 12 in the questionnaire, thus reducing the risk that informants would repeat the same expressions.

    4)   Please complete.
    A: *Thank you very much for the lift.*
    B: _____

12) Please complete
A: *Thanks for the coffee.*
B: _____

The instructions in these two tasks are minimal. Only the thanking acts are given, and no information provided about the social contexts. The two thanking acts are phrased in different ways to evoke different types of situations. In task 4, the full form *Thank you*, followed by the intensifier *very much* is to indicate a relatively formal situation. In task 12, by contrast, the unmodified short form *Thanks* is supposed to indicate a more informal situation. In both tasks, the thankable is explicitly named as a further hint at the situation in which the dialogue might occur. In interviews after the completion of the questionnaire, informants said that they perceived a difference in formality, imagining the dialogue in task 4 to occur between acquaintances, e.g. workmates, perhaps in an asymmetrical relationship, with the thanker in the inferior position. The dialogue in task 12, on the other hand, was perceived as occurring between friends, in a private context or a cafeteria. This shows that the way in which a speech act is realized triggers a situational scenario, without any further information, pointing to the interplay of pragmalinguistic and sociopragmatic competence.

The questionnaire was completed by a total of 180 native speakers of English, 60 each from England, Ireland and the United States of America. Region, age and sex were controlled. All informants were adolescents; the average age was 15. All speakers of a variety lived in the same place (Tadcaster in Yorkshire, Carlow in Co. Carlow, and Knoxville in Tennessee), to preclude subnational regional variation. All informants from England and Ireland were female; the American population, however, comprised 34 female and 26 male informants, since the Knoxville sample did not include 60 female adolescentss. Sex-based differences were, however, not considered.

The responses given by the informants provided realizations which could be grouped together into ten realization types, henceforth represented by short labels in all capitals. For instance, WELCOME stands for the full form *You are welcome*, contracted *You're welcome*, elliptical *Welcome*, and intensified *You're very welcome*, and so on. In addition to the types and tokens usually listed in the literature, four further types were found in the elicited data. These are THANKS (returned), SURE, YEAH and DON'T WORRY.

Moreover, the results reveal clear varietal preferences. Across the national varieties and situations under inspection, only four of the ten response types occurred frequently, at 17.2 % and more. The remaining six types occurred with frequencies of 3.2 % and less, and were thus rather insignificant. These six minor types included the four additional types, but also PLEASURE and

DON'T MENTION IT, commonly quoted in the literature. NOT AT ALL, another commonly listed type, did not occur in the data at all. The most frequent type was WELCOME, at 34.6 %, followed by OKAY, ANYTIME and NO PROBLEM, with similar frequencies between 19.9 and 17.2 %.

Furthermore, both regional and situational variation could be observed. Patterns emerged showing that the contents of the pragmatic competence of native speakers differ across national varieties of English, regarding both their choice of realizations (pragmalinguistic competence) and their distribution across situations (sociopragmatic competence). Table 1 summarizes the pragmalinguistic preferences, and Table 2 the sociopragmatic preferences (for further details, cf. Schneider 2005: 114–127).

Table 1. National preferences of the four major realization types

EngE		IrE		AmE	
OKAY	(51.2%)	WELCOME	(34.2%)	WELCOME	(53.5%)
WELCOME	(16.3%)	ANYTIME	(25.5%)	NO PROBLEM	(20.2%)
ANYTIME	(12.4%)	NO PROBLEM	(24.2%)	ANYTIME	(18.6%)
NO PROBLEM	(6.2%)	OKAY	(9.4%)	OKAY	(0.8%)

Table 2. Situational distribution of the four major realization types

	EngE		IrE		AmE	
	4) LIFT	12) COFFEE	4) LIFT	12) COFFEE	4) LIFT	12) COFFEE
WELCOME	57.1%	42.9%	64.7%	35.5%	50.7%	49.3%
OKAY	53.0%	47.0%	21.4%	78.6%	0%	100.0%
ANYTIME	68.8%	31.2%	60.5%	39.5%	66.6%	33.4%
NO PROB	75.0%	25.0%	63.9%	36.1%	65.4%	34.6%

In combination with, or occasionally in place of, a realization type, supportive moves were used, i.e. less formulaic phrases, literally suggesting a follow-up meeting or offering the opportunity for reciprocation, e.g. *Let's do it again sometime*, or *You can buy me one next time*. Overwhelmingly, supportive moves were used in the less formal COFFEE situation, once again bearing witness to the existence of situational variation and the speakers' sensitivity to situational differences.

In a follow-up study involving native speakers of English from Canada yet another picture emerges (Schneider and Sickinger 2014). In this study, the same questionnaire was completed by adolescents in the same age group, all from the same town in eastern Canada (Truro in Nova Scotia). In this case, the regional preference for the four major realization types was markedly different from the patterns established for the populations from England, Ireland and the USA. The Canadian preferences (relevant to the ensuing discussion) were: NO PROBLEM (44.2%), WELCOME (27.9%), ANYTIME (14.6%) and OKAY (0.9%).

4.2 Findings from a field note-based study of responses to thanks

Bieswanger (2015) is an empirical study based on Schneider (2005). Bieswanger is also interested in regional variation on the national level, specifically in differences between American English and Canadian English. His study is explicitly focused on methodological issues, discussing the validity of DCT data and the results in Schneider (2005). Bieswanger collected his data in New York City and in Vancouver by employing an ethnographic method. His study is, in fact, a quasi-replication of Labov's famous department store study (Labov 1966), adapted in an innovative way to elicit material for the examination of regional pragmatic variation. Instead of asking for goods sold on the fourth floor, Bieswanger asked directions to some well-known sight, thanking the interlocutors for the information and, as soon as they had left, wrote down their response to his thanks. While taking field notes in this fashion is not very reliable as far as the exact wording is concerned (cf. e.g. Jucker 2009), recording verbatim what was said in the case of responses to thanks should be possible, given the brevity of their realizations. In each of the two cities, Bieswanger elicited responses to thanks from 30 male and 30 female informants, attempting to create as homogeneous a population as this is possible based on outer appearance. All informants approached were "white", probably middle class (as they were wearing "business casual"), and approximately between 30 and 50 years old (Bieswanger 2015: 536). This procedure, incidentally, illustrates how people are often perceived and categorized and identities ascribed based on judgements of outer appearance alone (cf. also Haugh and Schneider 2012: 1017).

Bieswanger finds some striking differences between his Vancouver data and his New York City data (2015: 538–540), providing further evidence of regional pragmatic variation among native speakers of English. Bieswanger also finds differences between his and Schneider's American data (Schneider's Canadian data were not available to Bieswanger), readily attributed to the effect of the data collection method. For instance, Bieswanger observes a large number of non-verbal responses (a nod or a smile), which cannot easily be elicited by employing written DCTs. He furthermore identifies vocal grunts as an additional response type, which he labels "MH-HM". This type, which does not occur in the DCT data either, is, however, relatively infrequent at 3.2%. It is much more frequent in Bieswanger's Canadian data (11.4%), whereas non-verbal responses are comparatively rare in this variety (8.6%). Apart from that, essentially the same realization types occur in both sets of American data, and on closer inspection there are also some similarities between Bieswanger's and Schneider's results. First, SURE, DON'T WORRY and NOT AT ALL do not occur in either of the two data sets. Second, other types which do not occur in Bieswanger's data or only at a low frequency, also occur with a very low frequency (3.1% or less) in Schneider's data. This applies to OKAY, DON'T MENTION IT, PLEASURE and THANKS. There are three exceptions: YEAH, which is much more frequent in Bieswanger's data, and NO PROBLEM and ANYTIME, both more frequent in Schneider's data. Third, WELCOME is by far the most frequent American response type in either data set, albeit with a lower frequency in New York City. Interestingly, WELCOME has the same frequency in Bieswanger's and Schneider's Canadian data, at 27.1% and 27.9% respectively.

4.3 Issues of comparability

Concentrating on the differences between the findings in Schneider (2005) and his own study, Bieswanger concludes "that there are fundamental differences between the data types" and argues that his study "presents further confirmation that written production questionnaires do not allow us to study authentic spoken language" (Bieswanger 2015: 543). Yet the differences found may not result from the different types of data collection, but from a range of crucial differences in the design of the two studies compared, which are thus not immediately comparable. These differences include the following:

(a) The thankables are crucially different. In Schneider (2005), these are a service (lift) and a material good (coffee). In Bieswanger (2015), by contrast, the thankable is a verbal good (giving directions). It has been observed in the literature that acts of thanking for a verbal good do not receive a verbal response. For instance, Edmondson and House (1981: 167) write that responses to thanks "are not used when the Thanks was occasioned by a preceding *verbal* act" (original emphasis). Accordingly, thanks referring to e.g. compliments, congratulations or condolences are not responded to either. This is part of a native speaker's pragmatic competence. The fact that Bieswanger's thankable is a verbal good may account for the high frequency of smiles and nods. Bieswanger acknowledges that the situations differ, but only in terms of formality, and not categorially, claiming that giving directions "might be situated between the two questionnaire situations with respect to formality" (2015: 540).

(b) In Schneider's study, the interlocutors are friends or acquaintances; in Bieswanger's study, they are total strangers. In many studies, social distance has been found to be an influential micro-social factor accounting for different linguistic choices and variation in verbal behaviour, e.g. in the *Cross-Cultural Speech Act Realization Project* (Blum-Kulka, House, and Kasper 1989) or Brown and Levinson's politeness theory (1987 [1978]). According to Wolfson's Bulge Theory (1988), investment of politeness is particularly high among acquaintances and friends and very low with maximal social distance, i.e. between strangers, especially between strangers unlikely to ever meet again.

(c) In Bieswanger's case, the thanker is a non-native speaker of English, whereas in Schneider's case the default reading is that the interlocutors are native speakers. This may also have a bearing on the responding behaviour.

(d) There is a marked age difference. Bieswanger's informants are adults, between 30 and 50 years old. Bieswanger justifies approaching people only in this age range by explicitly saying that he deliberately wanted "to avoid what could be called 'youth language'" (2015: 536). Yet the population in Schneider's study consists exclusively of adolescents, i.e. speakers using youth language. This may explain the comparatively frequent occurrence of NO PROBLEM in Schneider's results, which seems to be especially popular among the youth (cf. also Dinkin 2016). In general, age has been identified as an important macro-social factor impacting verbal behaviour and responsible for pragmatic variation (cf. e.g. Schneider 2012a; Farr and Murphy 2009). Bieswanger (2015: 540) does acknowledge the age difference between his population and Schneider's population, but does not take it into consideration when comparing the results.

(e) Apart from regional pragmatic variation on the national level, there is also regional pragmatic variation on a sub-national level (cf. e.g. Placencia 2011; Schneider and Placencia in press). Bieswanger collected his American data in New York City, Schneider's data were collected in the south of the USA. The varieties of English spoken in NYC and in the South are, however, particularly salient regional varieties of American English and known to be radically different, not only according to dialectologists and sociolinguistics, but also as established in perceptual dialectology as a branch of folk linguistics (e.g. Niedzielski and Preston 2000: 41–126). Similarly, Bieswanger's and

Schneider's Canadian data were elicited in significantly different locations, namely respectively in the major city on Canada's west coast and approximately 7,000 kilometers away in a provincial town on Canada's east coast. What probably also plays a role here, apart from the different regions and the geographical distance, is the urban–rural divide, which has, however, not yet received sufficient attention in pragmatics (cf., however, Cramer 2016; Evans 2016).

The discussion of Schneider (2005) and Bieswanger (2015) underlines the central importance of comparability as a methodological principle in variation studies in general and the investigation of pragmatic variation in particular (cf. Schneider 2010: 252–253; Schneider 2014). As has been shown, careful control of all relevant factors is necessary. Therefore, experimental methods permitting such control, as e.g. DCTs, are, despite all well-known shortcomings (e.g. Kasper 2008), recommended, at least in the initial stages of a project. Experimental data can later on, once searchables have been generated, be triangulated with naturally occurring material from corpora. Moreover, the findings from the two studies seem to suggest that patterns of use have to be identified for each type of situation separately. Finally, it can be argued that experimental data such as DCT answers, in which informants say what they would or should do, reflect norms and conventions represented in pragmatic competence more immediately than the accidentialities and peculiarities of particular real-world situations (e.g. Schneider 2012b).

5 Consequences for the development of pragmatic competence

Knowing a language means knowing, among other things, how to "participate in conversations the way speakers of the language do" (Johnstone 2008: 7). Without being explicit about it, Johnstone obviously talks about L2 pragmatic competence and recommends native speaker behaviour as a model for non-native speakers. The question is, however, which native speaker model should be chosen in teaching pragmatics, e.g. which national variety. If language learners stay in a target language culture, then the answer to this question is obvious. It is generally assumed that a longer sojourn in a target language environment is beneficial to improving L2 proficiency. Yet it is not entirely clear how effective a stay abroad really is. There is a growing body of literature specifically focused on the impact of a stay abroad on the pragmatic competence in an L2 and its development (Barron 2003; Schauer 2009; Devlin 2014; Mitchell, Tracy-Ventura, and McManus Mitchell 2015; Ren 2015).

Schneider (2015) reports on a group of 132 German learners of English, aged 15–16, going to school in Canada for five or ten months. Before leaving Germany, then after five months and finally after ten months the pragmatic competence of these learners was assessed by using the questionnaire described in section 4, which was also completed by 114 Canadian peers who went to the same school in Truro, Nova Scotia. Table 3 shows the results for the responses to thanks produced by the Canadians and by the German learners before their stay abroad (GerE-pre) and after ten months (GerE-10).

Table 3. Preferences of the four major realization types of Canadian native speakers and German learners (before their stay in Canada and after ten months)

CanE	GerE-pre	GerE-10
NO PROBLEM (44.2%)	WELCOME (65.4%)	WELCOME (65.8%)
WELCOME (27.9%)	NO PROBLEM (32.6%)	NO PROBLEM (26.6%)
ANYTIME (14.6%)	OKAY (3.1%)	ANYTIME (15.8%)
OKAY (0.9%)	ANYTIME (0.8%)	OKAY (0.0%)

The most obvious result is the dramatic increase of ANYTIME in the learner responses, from 0.8% to 15.8%, its frequency resembling native speaker use (14.6%). Further, OKAY, infrequently used before and only rarely used by the Canadians, has vanished altogether. On the other hand, WELCOME is still clearly preferred by the learners as before, and the frequency of NO PROBLEM, the preferred realization of the Canadians, has even gone down. On closer inspection, however, the learners have acquired a number of features which make their responses to thanks more Canadian: Elliptical forms of WELCOME are not used anymore, nor combinations of WELCOME + NO PROBLEM or the erroneous transfer of *please*. Instead, intensifiers are employed (*very, at all*), which had not been employed before, and in combinations ANYTIME, which is clearly preferred in the more formal situation (lift), always occurs in second position. So the stay abroad has definitely modified the learners' L2 pragmatic competence and has made their performance more formulaic and thus more native-like. As Kecskés (2014: 71) emphasizes, "formulaic language use makes language use native-like", and also "[f]ormulaic language is the heart and soul of native-like language use".

Arguably, the effect could have been stronger, had the learners not only been exposed to native language use, but also explicitly taught pragmatics, since "metapragmatic awareness will help [learners] to adapt to whatever variety they might encounter" (Martínez Flor and Usó Juan 2010: 159). Therefore, raising the learners' awareness of culture-specific language use conventions is essential. It is essential more particularly for those learners who do not have the opportunity to stay in a target language culture for some time. It is crucial more generally because the aim of language teaching, and especially of teaching pragmatics, is not to imitate native speakers. While it is certainly true that "[m]astery of discourse conventions should be a high priority in second-language teaching ..." (Palmer and Sharifian 2007: 3), the idea is not that learners simply adopt these conventions. On the contrary, learners must be given "the knowledge to make an informed choice and allowing her/him the freedom to flout pragmatic conventions", which is a political, i.e. emancipatory issue; hence, the highest priority has to be that "the learner knows what s/he is doing" (Thomas 1983: 110), and what the consequences might be. This position has been repeated to this date (for a discussion, cf. Kecskés 2014: 63). While there seems to be general agreement about the aims of developing pragmatic competence, there is not enough research about the pragmatic conventions learners may wish to follow or intentionally violate. These conventions are not sufficiently known. While it is a good start to inform learners that pragmatic conventions exist which may differ across languages and cultures, regions and social groups, what is needed are descriptions of data as an input for teaching and awareness raising. A particularly sustainable way to develop pragmatic competence would be to empower learners to discover pragmatic conventions themselves.

6 Conclusions

This paper has argued for more systematic empirical work in pragmatics. While there is a lot of theorizing about the make-up of pragmatic competence and how it may be developed, what is needed are deeper insights into the contents of pragmatic competence. Specifically, more concrete descriptions of language use conventions and preferred patterns of pragmatic performance are required to develop pragmatic competence in a foreign language, and also in a native language.

Initially, a broad notion of pragmatics is advocated and, based on this, a comprehensive construct of pragmatic competence. It is argued that pragmatic variation must be accounted for in this construct, since language use differs across situations and cultures. Responses to thanks serve to exemplify some of these issues. In particular, it is shown how native speakers of English from England, Ireland, the USA and Canada vary their behaviour across situations, and how their preferences differ in the same situation, revealing culture-specific differences in their pragmatic competence.

Furthermore, methodological issues are addressed. By comparing two empirical studies of regional variation in English responses to thanks, it is demonstrated that comparability is a central concern in data-based work on pragmatic variation. It is emphasized that relevant situational factors have to be carefully controlled, which may be easier when experimental methods are employed, and that doing so also seems to provide more direct access to conventions and norms and, thus, to pragmatic competence.

Finally, the consequences of these discussions for the development of L2 pragmatic competence are briefly considered. Given the overall aim of language teaching to enable learners to use their L2 as they choose as individuals with their specific values and identities and not to copy native speakers, it is stressed again that more empirical research on pragmatic conventions is necessary, as learners have to know what the target culture expectations are, before they can decide whether or not they wish to observe them.

References

Aijmer, Karin. 1996. *Conversational routines in English: Convention and creativity*. London & New York: Longman.
Barron, Anne. 2003. *Acquisition in interlanguage pragmatics: Learning how to do things with words in a study abroad context*. Amsterdam & Philadelphia: John Benjamins.
Barron, Anne. 2014. Variational pragmatics. In Carol A. Chapelle (ed.), *The encyclopedia of applied linguistics: Electronic version*, 1–7. Oxford: Wiley-Blackwell.
Barron, Anne & Klaus P. Schneider. 2009. Variational pragmatics: Studying the impact of social factors on language use in interaction. *Intercultural Pragmatics* 6(4). 425–442.
Barron, Anne & Klaus P. Schneider. 2014. Discourse pragmatics: Signposting a vast field. In Anne Barron & Klaus P. Schneider (eds.), *Pragmatics of discourse*, 1–33. Boston & Berlin: De Gruyter Mouton.
Beeching, Kate & Helen Woodfield (eds.). 2015. *Researching sociopragmatic variability: Perspectives from variational, interlanguage and contrastive pragmatics*. Basingstoke: Palgrave Macmillan.
Bieswanger, Markus. 2015. Variational pragmatics and *responding to thanks* – revisited. *Multilingua* 34(4). 527–546.
Blum-Kulka, Shoshana, Juliane House & Gabriele Kasper. 1989. Investigating cross-cultural pragmatics: An introductory overview. In Shoshana Blum-Kulka, Juliane House & Gabriele Kasper (eds.), *Cross-cultural pragmatics: Requests and apologies*, 1–34. Norwood, NJ: Ablex.
Brown, Penelope & Stephen C. Levinson. 1978. Universals in language usage: politeness phenomena. In Esther Goody (ed.), *Questions and politeness*, 56–311. Cambridge: Cambridge University Press.
Brown, Penelope & Stephen C. Levinson. 1987. *Politeness: Some universals in language usage*. Cambridge: Cambridge University Press.

Bublitz, Wolfram & Neal R. Norrick (eds.). 2011. *Foundations of pragmatics*. Boston & Berlin: De Gruyter Mouton.
Cap, Piotr. 2011. Micropragmatics and macropragmatics. In Wolfram Bublitz & Neal R. Norrick (eds.), *Foundations of pragmatics*, 51–75. Boston & Berlin: De Gruyter Mouton.
Cramer, Jennifer. 2016. Rural vs. urban: Perception and production of identity in a border city. In Jennifer Cramer & Chris Montgomery (eds.), *Cityscapes and perceptual dialectology: Global perspectives on non-linguists' knowledge of the dialect landscape*, 27–54. Boston & Berlin: De Gruyter Mouton.
Crandall, Elizabeth & Helen Basturkmen. 2004. Evaluating pragmatics-focused materials. *ELT Journal* 58(1). 38–49.
Crystal, David. 1997. *English as a global language*. Cambridge: Cambridge University Press.
Devlin, Anne Marie. 2014. *The impact of study abroad on the acquisition of sociopragmatic variation patterns: The case of non-native speaker English teachers*. Oxford: Lang.
Dinkin, Aaron J. 2016. It's no problem to be polite: Change in apparent time in responses to thanks. Paper presented at the conference *New Way of Analyzing Variation 45*, Vancouver, Canada, 3–6 November 2016.
Edmondson, Willis J. & Juliane House. 1981. *Let's talk and talk about it: A pedagogic interactional grammar of English*. München: Urban & Schwarzenberg.
Evans, Betsy E. 2016. City talk and Country talk: Perceptions of urban and rural English in Washington State. In Jennifer Cramer & Chris Montgomery (eds.), *Cityscapes and perceptual dialectology: Global perspectives on non-linguists' knowledge of the dialect landscape*, 55–72. Boston & Berlin: De Gruyter Mouton.
Farr, Fiona & Bróna Murphy. 2009. Religious references in contemporary Irish English: 'For the love of God almighty. I'm a holy terror for turf.' *Intercultural Pragmatics* 6(4). 535–559.
Félix-Brasdefer, J. César & Dale A. Koike. 2012. Introduction: Pragmatic variation in first and second language contexts. In J. César Félix-Brasdefer & Dale Koike (eds.), *Pragmatic variation in first and second language contexts: Methodological issues*, 1–16. Amsterdam & Philadelphia: John Benjamins.
Fraser, Bruce. 2010. Pragmatic competence: The case of hedging. In Gunther Kaltenböck, Wiltrud Mihatsch & Stefan Schneider (eds.), *New approaches to hedging*, 15–34. Bingley: Emerald.
Grabowski, Kirby C. 2016. Assessing pragmatic competence. In Dina Tsagari & Jayanti Banerjee (eds.), *Handbook of second language assessment*, 165–180. Boston & Berlin: De Gruyter Mouton.
Haugh, Michael & Klaus P. Schneider. 2012. Editorial: Im/politeness across Englishes. *Journal of Pragmatics* 44(9). 1017–1021.
Huang, Yan. 2007. *Pragmatics*. Oxford: Oxford University Press.
Johnstone, Barbara. 2008. *Discourse analysis*, 2nd edn. Malden, MA: Blackwell.
Jucker, Andreas H. 2009. Speech act research between armchair, field and laboratory: The case of compliments. *Journal of Pragmatics* 41(8). 1611–1635.
Jucker, Andreas H. & Irma Taavitsainen (eds.). 2010. *Historical pragmatics*. Berlin & New York: De Gruyter Mouton.
Kasper, Gabriele. 2008. Data collection in pragmatics research. In Helen Spencer-Oatey (ed.), *Culturally speaking: Culture, communication and politeness theory*, 2nd edn., 279–303. London: Continuum.
Kasper, Gabriele & Steven J. Ross. 2013. Assessing second language pragmatics: An overview and introductions. In Steven J. Ross & Gabriele Kasper (eds.), *Assessing second language pragmatics*, 1–40. Basingstoke: Palgrave Macmillan.

Kecskés, István. 2014. *Intercultural pragmatics*. Oxford: Oxford University Press.
Labov William. 1966. *The social stratification of English in New York City*. Washington, DC: Center for Applied Linguistics.
Leech, Geoffrey N. 1983. *Principles of pragmatics*. London: Longman.
Martínez Flor, Alicia & Esther Usó Juan. 2010. *Speech act performance: Theoretical, empirical and methodological issues*. Amsterdam & Philadelphia: John Benjamins.
Mitchell, Rosamond, Nicole Tracy-Ventura & Kevin McManus (eds.). 2015. *Social interaction, identity and language learning during residence abroad*. European Second Language Association. http://www.eurosla.org/monographs/EM04/EM04tot.pdf (accessed: 25 July 2016).
Mulo Farenkia, Bernard. 2012. Face-saving strategies in responding to gratitude expressions: Evidence from Canadian English. *International Journal of English Linguistics* 2(4). 1–11.
Niedzielski, Nancy A. & Dennis R. Preston. 2000. *Folk linguistics*. Berlin & New York: Mouton de Gruyter.
Palmer, Gary B. & Farzad Sharifian. 2007. Applied cultural linguistics: An emerging paradigm. In Farzad Sharifian & Gary B. Palmer (eds.), *Applied cultural linguistics: Implications for second language learning and intercultural communication*, 1–14. Amsterdam & Philadelphia: John Benjamins.
Placencia, María Elena. 2011. Regional pragmatic variation. In Gisle Andersen & Karin Aijmer (eds.), *Pragmatics of society*, 79–113. Boston & Berlin: De Gruyter Mouton.
Ren, Wei. 2015. *L2 pragmatic development in study abroad contexts*. Bern: Lang.
Rüegg, Larssyn. 2014. Thanks responses in three socio-economic settings: A variational pragmatics approach. *Journal of Pragmatics* 71. 17–30.
Schauer, Gila A. 2009. *Interlanguage pragmatic development: The study abroad context*. London: Continuum.
Schneider, Klaus P. 2003. *Diminutives in English*. Tübingen: Niemeyer.
Schneider, Klaus P. 2005. 'No problem, you're welcome, anytime': Responding to thanks in Ireland, England, and the U.S.A. In Anne Barron & Klaus P. Schneider (eds.), *The pragmatics of Irish English*, 101–139. Berlin & New York: Mouton de Gruyter.
Schneider, Klaus P. 2010. Variational pragmatics. In Mirjam Fried, Jan-Ola Östman & Jef Verschueren (eds.), *Variation and change: Pragmatic perspectives*, 239–267. Amsterdam & Philadelphia: John Benjamins.
Schneider, Klaus P. 2012a. Appropriate behaviour across varieties of English. *Journal of Pragmatics* 44(9). 1022–1037.
Schneider, Klaus P. 2012b. Pragmatic variation and cultural models. *Review of Cognitive Linguistics* 10(2). 346–372.
Schneider, Klaus P. 2014. Comparability and sameness in variational pragmatics. In Silvia Mergenthal & Reingard M. Nischik (eds.), *Anglistentag 2013 Konstanz: Proceedings*, 361–372. Trier: Wissenschaftlicher Verlag Trier.
Schneider, Klaus P. 2015. What do learners need to know? A focus on pragmatic competence. Plenary lecture at the *XXVI Annual International Academic Conference "Language and Culture"*, Tomsk State University, Russia, 28–30 October 2015.
Schneider, Klaus P. & Anne Barron. 2008. Where pragmatics and dialectology meet: Introducing variational pragmatics. In Klaus P. Schneider & Anne Barron (eds.), *Variational pragmatics: A focus on regional varieties in pluricentric languages*, 1–32. Amsterdam & Philadelphia: John Benjamins.

Schneider, Klaus P. & María Elena Placencia. in press. (Im)politeness and regional variation. In Jonathan Culpeper, Michael Haugh & Dániel Kádár (eds.), *Palgrave Handbook of Linguistic (Im)Politeness*. London: Palgrave Macmillan.
Schneider, Klaus P. & Pawel Sickinger. 2014. Comparing pragmatic profiles of native speakers and foreign language learners of English. Paper presented at the *English Profile Seminar no. 15*, Cambridge University Press, Cambridge, UK, 6–7 February 2014.
Sickinger, Pawel & Klaus P. Schneider. 2014. Pragmatic competence and the CEFR: Pragmatic profiling as a link between theory and language use. *Linguistica* 54, 113–127.
Spencer-Oatey, Helen. 2008. Face, (im)politeness and rapport. In Helen Spencer-Oatey (ed.), *Culturally speaking: Culture, communication and politeness theory*, 11–47. London: Continuum.
Talla Sando Ouafeu, Yves. 2009. Thanking responders in Cameroon English. *World Englishes* 28(4). 544–551.
Thomas, Jenny. 1983. Cross-cultural pragmatic failure. *Applied Linguistics* 4(2). 91–112.
Timpe, Veronika. 2014. *Assessing intercultural language learning: The dependence of receptive sociopragmatic competence and discourse competence on learning opportunities and input*. Frankfurt: Lang.
Verschueren, Jef. 1999. *Understanding pragmatics*. London: Edward Arnold.
Weinreich, Uriel, William Labov & Marvin I. Herzog. 1968. Empirical foundations for a theory of language change. In Winfred P. Lehmann & Yakov Malkiel (eds.), *Directions for historical linguistics: A symposium*, 95–195. Austin: University of Texas Press.
Wierzbicka, Anna. 1985. Different cultures, different languages, different speech acts: Polish vs. English. *Journal of Pragmatics* 9(2/3). 145–178.
Wolfson, Nessa. 1988. The bulge: A theory of speech behavior and social distance. In Jonathan Fine (ed.), *Second language discourse: A textbook of current research*, 21–38. Norwood, NJ: Ablex.

Anne Barron
18 Offers in English

1 Introduction

Offers in English have been analysed from various perspectives and using a range of data sources. Studies using corpora as a database include Aijmer (1996), Barron (2011, 2017a), Leech (2014) and Schneider (2003). However, with few exceptions, these studies, some of which focus on a range of speech acts above and beyond offers, do not provide systematic information on the distribution of offer types, strategies or modification in the corpora analysed. In addition, there are no studies on offers using corpus data or other which systematically look at offer types and/ or at realisations of offer strategies and modification by offer type.

The present article, an analysis of offers in private face-to-face conversations in British English, is designed to meet these research gaps. It takes naturally-occurring data from the private face-to-face conversations of the British component of the International Corpus of English (ICE-GB) as its database and systematically investigates how offers are realised in these private conversations, what types of offers (e.g. hospitable offers, offers of assistance) occur and whether correlations exist between offer type and offer strategy, where strategies are understood as various options available to realise an offer (e.g. question desire strategy realised via conventionalised patterns such as *Do you want NP?*). Furthermore, the relationship between offer type and any pos-politeness and neg-politeness modification strategies employed is investigated. Specifically, the paper addresses the following research questions:

a) What offer types are found in private face-to-face conversation in ICE-GB?
b) Are there any correlations between offer type and offer strategy in private face-to-face conversation in ICE-GB?
c) Are there any correlations between offer type and offer modification (pos-politeness strategies, neg-politeness strategies) in private face-to-face conversation in ICE-GB?

The research adds to the limited scholarship on offers in English. In addition, by addressing the use of the speech act of offers in corpus data, the study also adds to speech act research in corpus pragmatics, an area of research which is still very much in its infancy.

The paper opens with a brief description of the speech act of offers (section 2.1) and an overview of research on offers (section 2.2). Attention then turns to issues of data and method (section 3), including a discussion of offer retrieval procedures (section 3.1) and the data source (section 3.2). The empirical analysis of offers in ICE-GB follows (section 4), and the paper concludes with a discussion and suggestions for further research.

2 Characterising offers

We begin with a characterisation of offers in section 2.1, and turn then to a brief overview of research on offers to date in section 2.2.

2.1 The blurred nature of offers

Offers represent commitments by a speaker (S) to carry out a future course of action (A). They have, thus, been categorised as commissives (Searle 1976: 11; Edmondson and House 1981: 49). At the same time, they involve attempts by S to get H to declare him/herself able and willing to engage in the proposed action A (Searle's directives) and so, given this dual nature, have been proposed to belong to the group of commissive directives, a hybrid category proposed by Hancher (1979) to deal with such speech acts which combine directive with commissive illocutionary force equally. Other researchers, however, have rejected the idea that the members of the commissive-directives category share commissive or directive illocutionary force to the same degree. Rather, a continuum of speech acts between the two poles of prototypically commissive and prototypically directive has been proposed by Pérez Hernández (2001: 78), with offers seen as closer to the commissive end of the continuum. Apart from being commissive and directive in nature, offers also involve a conditional component since the execution of an offer is always conditional on the reaction of H in which he/she indicates in some way whether he/she wishes S to carry out the deed in question A or not (Wunderlich 1977: 43).

These three components of offers, the conditional, the commissive and the directive nature of offers, are reflected in the types of overriding strategies through which offers are conventionally realised, namely, preference, execution and directive strategies (Schneider 2003: 183–185 on hospitable offers). Preference strategies, such as *Would you like some scotch?*, point to the fact that the action of offering is conditional on the will or preference of the hearer. Execution strategies, such as *Can I get you a drink?*, on the other hand, underline the role of S in carrying out A and so reflect the commissive nature of offers. Finally, offers, given their part directive nature, may also be realised using what are typically directive forms (e.g. via an imperative, such as *Have a drink*) (Schneider 2003: 183; cf. also Leech 2014: 68, 92). Within these overriding strategy types we find a wide range of subordinate offer strategies. Table 1 lists those subordinate strategies identified in the present study of ICE-GB. It also includes details of those conventionalised patterns realising each strategy in ICE-GB (cf. Barron 2005 and Barron 2017a for further details of these strategies).

Table 1. Offer strategies and conventionalised patterns in ICE-GB

Strategy	Conventionalised pattern
1. PREFERENCE	
a. Grammatically elliptical	NP?
	NP for everyone?
b. Question future act of hearer	Will you have NP?
	Are you going to have NP?
	What are you having?
	Are you having NP?
c. Question desire	Do you want NP?
	Do you want VP?
	You don't want NP.
d. Question need	Need NP?
e. Question wish	Would you like NP?
	If anyone would like NP?
	Would anybody like VP?
	What would you like?
2. EXECUTION	
a. Question future act of speaker	Shall I VP?
b. State speaker ability	I can VP
	I could VP
c. State speaker desire	I want to VP
d. State speaker obligation	I better VP
e. State speaker willingness	I don't mind if S
3. DIRECTIVE	
a. Imperative	VP
	You VP (e.g. *you try NP*)
b. State permission	You can VP
c. Suggestory formulae[1]	Why don't you VP?
	If ..., let's just VP
4. OTHER	
a. Hint	There is NP (e.g. *There's grapefruit juice as well* ...)

---

[1] In Barron (2005: 152), suggestory formulae were coded as preference strategies given that the realisations recorded were of the form *how about NP?* and thus consult H on his/her preferences. However, all of the suggestory formulae in the present corpus are of a directive nature, formally taking rather forms closely related to directives, such as suggestions or requests (*Why don't you VP?*, *Let's VP*) (cf. also Leech 2014: 138).

In Brown and Levinson's (1978, 1987) terms, the act of offering enhances H's positive face, i.e. their need to be accepted and liked by others, given that S is offering to do something for H and given that – in the case of a correct guess – s/he shows familiarity with H's needs (cf. also Leech 2014: 110). In addition, the act of offering enhances S's positive face as H is likely to look more favourably on S (cf. also Leech 2014: 110). However, at the same time, S, in offering, threatens his/her own negative face by reducing his/her own freedom of action in committing himself/herself to the action A. Also, if S offers a future act which is not welcomed by H, this may threaten H's positive face and indeed the act of second-guessing H's needs may threaten H's negative face. Finally, should the proposed act not be accepted by H, S's positive face may be threatened (although the threat is minimised given that offers are conditional speech acts; cf. Wierzbicka 1987: 96).

Building on Brown and Levinson (1978, 1987), Leech (2014: 11–13) identifies pos-politeness (positive-politeness) strategies which are employed to enhance H's face and neg-politeness (negative-politeness) strategies which mitigate a potential face-threat.[2] Offers themselves, like invitations or compliments, are an instance of pos-politeness, as they enhance the H's face (cf. above). Since pos-politeness is scalar, the positive value of such acts can be strengthened and made more difficult to refuse. Thus, an offer of cake, might be enhanced with pos-politeness by expressing it using an emphatic imperative such as *do have some cake*. Also, the use of grounders, i.e. reasons why an offer should be accepted, may be used to strengthen illocutionary force, as seen in the addition of *You've had plenty of veggies* in the offer *Uhm <,> you can break into the pears if you want to or have a piece of choccy. You've had plenty of veggies* (ICE-GB, s1a-023). Using pos-politeness, "we *magnify* or *strengthen* the expression of (positive) value" (Leech 2014: 12, original emphasis). Neg-politeness, on the other hand, "*diminish*[es] or *soften*[s] the expression of (negative) value in the transaction" (Leech 2014: 12, original emphasis). It functions to minimise potential offense and is used, for instance, when S is not completely certain if his/her offer is of value to H (cf. Leech 2014: 183). In the latter example, the explicit conditional *if you want* highlights, for instance, that it is H who decides on whether the act is carried out or not, paying heed to his/her negative face. This example also shows clearly that pos-politeness and neg-politeness may co-occur.

---

2 Leech's (2014) pos-politeness and neg-politeness strategies differ from the positive and negative strategies put forward by Brown and Levinson (1987) in a number of ways. Leech's concept does not, for instance, include strategies employed merely to reduce social distance and not to enhance H's face. The use of elliptical forms, such as *orange juice?* (ICE-GB, s1a-046), is an example (cf. also footnote 9).

Finally, from a sequential perspective, offers form the first pair part of offer-acceptance/refusal adjacency pairs, with refusals the dispreferred second pair part. From a discourse analytical perspective, we differentiate between initiative offers and reoffers. Initiative offers are defined as the first move in an initial or subsequent offer exchange (Schneider 2000: 295) where subsequent offer exchanges involve offers following an initial offer. Initiative offers in such latter exchanges frequently include the word *another* in hospitable offers (Schneider 2003: 189). Reoffers, on the other hand, are "further attempts on the part of the speaker to reiterate a particular initiative offer within one offer sequence" (Barron 2003: 127). They follow an initial refusal and when realised ritually frequently take the form of *are you sure?* The present analysis focuses exclusively on initiative offers (cf. section 3).

2.2 Offers in English

Relative to speech acts, such as requests, offers reveal a dearth of research. Nonetheless, offers in English have been analysed from various perspectives. Research on English native speaker (NS) offer realisations includes scholarship by Aijmer (1996), Curl (2006), Davidson (1984, 1990), Edmondson and House (1981: 136–137), Leech (2014: 180–186), Schneider (2003: 181–193) and also by Wierzbicka (1985), the latter on Australian English offers. In addition, research has been conducted on offers across the varieties of English within the context of variational pragmatics. In line with the principle of contrastivity in variational pragmatics (cf. Barron and Schneider 2009; Schneider 2010: 252), such analyses involve contrasts across two or more varieties of English, one of these frequently being British English given its status as the standard variety/one of the standard varieties taught around the world (cf. Seargeant 2012). Variational pragmatic analyses on offers include those by Barron (2005, 2011, 2017a). Finally, research on offers within the context of cross-cultural/ intercultural research has frequently compared offers in English with offers in other languages. Such studies include for English/Arabic Alaoui (2011) and Grainger et al. (2015), for English/Chinese Yongbing (1998), for English/German Barron (2003), for English/Greek Sifianou (1992) and for English/Japanese Fukushima and Iwata (1987).

Research on offers has employed a range of data types, among these role-play data (Edmondson and House 1981), fictional material (Schneider 2003), naturally-occurring data (Curl 2006; Davidson 1984, 1990; Sifianou 1992), intuitive/observational data (Alaoui 2011; Sifianou 1992; Wierzbicka 1987; Yongbing 1998) and production questionnaire data (Barron 2003, 2005; Fukushima and Iwata 1987). Studies based on corpus data include those by Barron (2011, 2017a), using data taken from the British and Irish components of the International Corpus of English (ICE). In addition, Leech's (2014) description of offers is based on data taken from the British National Corpus (BNC) and the Longman Corpus of Spoken American English (LCAE). Aijmer's (1996) description is based on data from the London-Lund Corpus of Spoken English (LLC), and Schneider's (2003) description of diminutive use in offers from the LLC and two further smaller corpora of everyday interactions (cf. Schneider 2003: 73). With its focus on investigating the distribution of offer types, strategies and modification in ICE-GB, the present analysis of offers in ICE-GB adds to the studies in corpus pragmatics and in particular to the corpus studies of offers in British English. We turn now to the methodological details.

3 Analysing offers in ICE-GB

The present study of offers in ICE-GB focuses on realisations of initiative offers, that is, of offers which form the first move in an initial or subsequent offer exchange (cf. section 2.1).[3] This definition thus excludes reoffers, pre-offers (involving, e.g., checks via requests for information that the preparatory conditions for realisation of an offer prevail), and also offers issued by offerees themselves in the context of negotiating an initiative offer.[4]

3.1 Offer retrieval in corpus-data

Given the lack of speech act annotation in ICE-GB, a difficulty of many present-day corpora (cf. Rühlemann and Aijmer 2014), the present analysis used an electronic form-based search of formulaic patterns or functional lexical segments. The search strings employed were based on previous research on offers by Barron (2005), and also by Searle (1975), Schiffrin (1994), Aijmer (1996) and Leech (2014: 180–186). They included the performative verb *offer*, conventionalised realisation patterns of offer strategies drawn from the literature (cf. Table 1 above for examples), frequent modification used in offers (*if you want, if you wish*),

---

[3] It should be noted that the definition of initiative offers includes offers addressed to individuals who have already received a previous general offer.
[4] An example of such an offer issued by an offeree in the context of offer negotiation is seen in s1a-045 in ICE-GB. In this transcript, an offer to use a particular book (*Would you like me to use your this book or...*) is refused with another offer (*Let's use my book <,,> because then you don't you can still use yours ...*). Such offers are not included in the analysis as these are categorised as refusals in the first instance.

common linguistic features (*for you, for everyone, anyone, anybody*), reoffer formulae (e.g. *are you sure?*, *I insist*), and routine responses to offers, such as *thanks* or *please*. Topic-oriented searches (e.g. *coffee, tea*) were also conducted and editorial comments were searched for comments such as *offered tea*. In addition, imperative forms were searched for via a POS-tagger. All forms were combined with several wildcards, symbols used to represent any one (or more) character or word, in order to minimise the possibility of not retrieving offers due to the presence of features, such as self-repair, false starts, filled hesitations or other speech related phenomenon (cf. Jucker 2009: 1623). Nonetheless, it is clear that recall errors are still possible as the forms and phrases guiding the research do not necessarily account for the full range of linguistic forms for making offers. In addition, elliptical offers taking the form of noun phrases (e.g. *wine?*), indirect non-conventionalised offers or non-verbal offers could not be searched for directly, but rather had to rely on topic-oriented searches or searches for routine responses to potentially elicit such forms (cf. Barron 2017a for an extensive discussion of the limitations of form-based functional analysis; cf. also Garcia McAllister 2015: 29).

In production questionnaire analysis, the elicited speech act is easily controlled via the situational description which provides implicit or explicit clues as to the speech act required and also via dialogue initiations and/or a hearer responses, the latter of which signal uptake (cf. Barron 2017b; Grainger and Harris 2007: 2–3). In corpus research on speech act realisations, on the other hand, situational information is frequently missing. This difficulty as well as the general difficulty of a lack of form-function equivalence in speech act realisations and also the overlap between offers and further speech acts, such as undertakings, invitations, promises and requests, makes offer identification difficult.[5] Given such obstacles, it was necessary to pay a high level of attention to the identification of offers from the concordance lines returned to ensure that the realisations at hand represented realisations of offers. To realise this aim, three broad criteria were developed and used to disambiguate an utterance's illocution and to identify offers, namely the propositional content, the context of use and hearer uptake (cf. Barron 2017a for further details). Of these, uptake was taken as an obligatory criterion (cf. Sidnell 2009). As such, the analysis captures the pragmatic effect of a particular utterance on the dialogue rather than focusing exclusively on a speaker's intention. Any unclear cases were excluded from the analysis.

---

5 Offers border on suggestions but differ from these in that offers benefit the hearer, but not clearly the speaker. They also border on invitations as both are conditional with a potential cost to S and a benefit to H. However, invitations generally deal with future participation in or attendance at a particular occasion, such as a party, hosted by the S (e.g. García 1999, 2008).

3.2 ICE-GB as a data source

The data for the present study were drawn from the British component of the International Corpus of English. The data were gathered in the early 1990s and compiled at the Survey of English Usage (SEU), University College London. The speakers of the British component of the ICE were born in England, Scotland or Wales except for a minority of cases where the informants were born elsewhere but moved to Britain early in life (cf. UCL Survey of English Usage). In addition, a limited number of speakers were exposed to continued influence from other cultures via a parent with a different mother tongue (e.g. a speaker with a Spanish father and a mother who was a gipsy). These minority cases were excluded from the present analysis. All speakers are educated speakers of English over the age of 18, where educated is defined as having at least a high school education.

The present analysis focuses on a sub-section of the overall ICE-GB corpus, namely the genre of private spoken face-to-face conversations. In total, 90 such texts exist. However, a close inspection of the data revealed that the face-to-face conversations of the British component involved a mixture of conversations of an official (e.g. interviews, service interactions) and non-official nature. In the present context, only non-official conversations were analysed. The British sub-corpus, thus, amounted to 57 texts (116,179 words) of a potential total 90 texts.

4 Offers in ICE-GB

4.1 Offer types in ICE-GB

The present analysis revealed four offer types to be present in ICE-GB, the first three of which have previously been identified in offer research. The four types include:

4.1.1 Hospitable offers

Hospitable offers have been described by Schneider (2003: 182) as being situation-specific. They are generally realised in "social gatherings such as dinners, receptions, parties" in which the role of host/hostess and guest is predefined and hosts are responsible for looking after their guests. Such offers are issued by hosts and include in the present context offers of food, drink and cigarettes and also offers to use the bathroom. They are also found in the context of the home. An example of an hospitable offer is seen in the offer of gravy in (1).

(1) ICE-GB:S1A-012
   D: Uhm who hasn't got some gravy
   D: Have some gravy Rob <,>
   A: Cheers <,,>

4.1.2 Offers of assistance

In contrast to hospitable offers, offers of assistance are situation-independent, occurring in a wide range of situations among friends, family, acquaintances, colleagues and strangers. They are defined as offers in which speakers offer to do something for H which they believe is of benefit to H. This future act may be, as Schneider (2003: 181) states, something which "in the speakers' view, may cause the hearer difficulty or inconvenience" (cf. examples (2) and (3) below, the former an offer to tape someone unable to do it themselves; the latter an offer to cancel a previous appointment due to potential time constraints). Offers of assistance may, however, also be acts of assistance which are costly to S which S believes to be potentially beneficial to H without necessarily causing him/ her difficulty. Example (4), an offer to go sight seeing with A, is a case in point.[6]

(2) ICE-GB:S1A-042 #127[7]
   C: Have you got his album
   B: Yeah
   C: I'd really love to tape it from you if you if you didn't mind
   B: Yeah
   B: If you give me a tape I've got a tape to tape and I can run it off
   C: Oh great that'd be
   C: Well
   C: I mean
   C: cos a actually thinking about it I've not got a uhm record player or anything
   C: So yeah
   C: <unclear-word>

---

[6] Despite having much in common with invitations, (3) is not classified as an invitation because it does not deal with potential attendance at a particular occasion hosted by S. (e.g. García 1999, 2008) (cf. also footnote 5).
[7] In (2), the offer to tape something is issued in response to a request for help in C carrying out the act of taping (*I'd really love to tape it from you if you if you didn't mind*) (cf. also Sidnell 2009: 218 on the presence of descriptions of *speaker-trouble* preceding offers).

B: You can make tunes from it
C: Oh good <,,>

(3) ICE-GB:S1A-048
C: So Sunday Monday keep free cos that Sunday's dinner with you <,> at your mum's
C: <unclear-word> <unclear-word>
A: Yeah
A: Listen
A: <u>If you want to put that off honestly I don't mind</u>
C: No I don't no cos you know
A: Yeah what about Rosie
A: I mean you cos you haven't got much time over here
B: No listen I I ....

(4) ICE-GB:S1A-045:
B: <u>I was wondering <,,></u>
B: <u>would you like to do some sight singing</u>
A: Mm
A: Yes
A: I'd love to

4.1.3 Gift offers

Hua, Wei, and Yuan (2000) examine gift offers in the Chinese context. They identify two functions of this offer type, a) to express friendship and b) to coerce a person into indebtedness in the context of bribery (2000: 84). Gift offers in the present corpus occur in informal situations, such as in (5), where B offers A a gift of a Labour poster (*one* stands for the poster mentioned), and also include gift offers of clothes or of jewellery. No offers were recorded in the context of gift-bringing on social occasions, such as birthdays or weddings (cf. Hua, Wei, and Yuan 1998, 2000).

(5) ICE-GB:S1A-069:
B: <u>You can have one</u> <unclear-words>
A: Thank you

Added to the above three offer types previously identified in the literature were *offers of verbal goods* identified in the present analysis.

4.1.4 Offers of verbal goods

Offers of verbal goods include offers to tell a joke as in (6). Such offers receive a response but the response may potentially be viewed as insincere and ironic (*Oh God no come on*), and the joke simply told regardless (*Why does it take ten women with P M T to change a light bulb*).

(6)　　ICE-GB:S1A-041:
   B:　　I said did you hear my joke
   B:　　<u>Do you want to hear my joke</u>
   A:　　Oh God no
   A:　　Come on <,>
   B:　　Why does it take ten women with P M T to change a light bulb

Figure 1. Offer types in ICE-GB (n=59)

Frequency-wise, most offers in the corpus were hospitable offers (55.9%) as seen in Figure 1. These were followed by offers of assistance (33.9%). Section 4.2 investigates correlations between offer types, strategies and modification. It is this analysis to which we now turn.

4.2 Offer types, offer strategies and offer modification in ICE-GB

An in-depth analysis of offer type and offer strategy reveals some interesting correlations. These are shown in Table 2 where we see a clear preference for hospitality offers to be realised using a preference strategy (p=0.000, Fisher's exact test), with 78.8% of all hospitable offers realised using this strategy type. Directive strategies are another option (18.2%) but execution strategies are not used at all in realising this offer type. In contrast, offers of assistance are realised predominantly via an execution strategy, 85% (17) of this offer type making use of these strategies (p=0.000, Fisher's exact test). On the level of the subordinate strategies, a *state speaker ability* strategy is preferred in offers of assistance (45%) (p=0.000, Fisher's exact test) as well as a *question future act of speaker* strategy (25%) (p=0.005, Fisher's exact test).

Table 2. Offer strategy type and offer strategies across hospitable offers and offers of assistance in ICE-GB

	Hospitable offers (n=33)	Offers of assistance (n=20)
Grammatically elliptical	15.2% (5)	—
Question future act of hearer	18.2% (6)	—
Question desire	21.2% (7)	5% (1)
Question need	3.0% (1)	—
Question wish	21.2% (7)	10% (2)
TOTAL PREFERENCE	78.8% (26)	15% (3)
Question future act of speaker	—	25% (5)
State speaker ability	—	45% (9)
State speaker desire	—	5% (1)
State speaker obligation	—	5% (1)
State speaker willingness	—	5% (1)
TOTAL EXECUTION	—	85% (17)
Imperative	9.1% (3)	—
State permission	3.0% (1)	—
Suggestory formulae	6.1% (2)	—
TOTAL DIRECTIVE	18.2% (6)	—
Hint	3.0% (1)	—
TOTAL OTHER	3.0% (1)	—

Turning now to offer modification, the use of modification devices to mitigate or intensify its force. From the point of view of politeness, offers enhance H's positive face (cf. section 2.1). Thus, pos-politeness modification strategies may be used to increase or intensify the force of such offers. On the other hand, given possible threats to S's and H's particular face wants (cf. also section 2.1), neg-politeness strategies may be employed to mitigate force. In addition, combinations of pos-politeness and neg-politeness may occur within one initiative offer (as seen in Table 3 by the fact that the pos-politeness or neg-politeness figures do not equal the sum of pos-politeness and neg-politeness alone).

Table 3. Pos-politeness and neg-politeness strategies employed across hospitable offers and offers of assistance in ICE-GB

	Hospitable offers (n=33)	Offers of assistance (n=20)
Pos-politeness	24.2% (8)	45% (9)
Neg-politeness	33.3% (11)	65% (13)
Pos-politeness or neg-politeness	48.5% (16)	85% (17)

Table 3 shows the use of pos-politeness and neg-politeness modification strategies with hospitable offers and offers of assistance in the corpus at hand.[8] Despite the differences on the level of the strategy type highlighted above, both pos-politeness and neg-politeness alone or in combination with each other are used with both of these main offer types. Offers of assistance do, however, show a higher use of negative politeness (65% [13] vs. 33.3% [11] for hospitable offers [Fisher's exact test, p=0.045]). In addition, the overall investment in politeness is greater in these offers of assistance, with the vast majority of offers (85% compared to 48.5% for hospitable offers) using either pos-politeness or neg-politeness in offer realisations (Fisher's exact test, p=0.009).

Table 4 summarises the individual types of pos-politeness and neg-politeness employed in these offers with examples. Neg-politeness types include conditional clauses (also termed explicit conditionals) (Aijmer 1996: 191; Barron 2005: 161; Brown and Levinson 1987: 72), conditionals (cf. Leech 2014: 183 on the hypothetical past tense serving to distance the offer from reality and thus represent a tentative formulation), impersonal constructions, lexical downtoners, subjectivisers (Leech 2014: 183), consultative devices, hesitation/restarters and clarifications of the optionality of offers. Pos-politeness types, designed to underline or increase the positive force of offers, include grounders (Aijmer 1996: 191; Barron 2005: 164–165; Brown and Levinson 1987: 128), repetition of the offer, lexical upgrading, negation (Leech 2014: 182), understaters/ diminutives (Eshreteh 2016: 142; Leech 2014: 185–186), downplaying the offer (both of the latter which downplay the cost of A to S) and the use of tags.

Table 4 also shows the level of use of each pos-politeness and neg-politeness element across offer type. Figures in this table are given as a percentage of the total number of each offer type. However, since combinations of modifiers also occurred, the overall total exceeds 100%. The use of pos-politeness strategies across offer type is broadly similar across offer type without any statistically significant differences with the exception of a slightly significantly higher use

---

8 We focus here on modifiers while at the same time recognising that the choice of a particular strategy may also orient towards pos-politeness (e.g. use of an imperative) or neg-politeness (e.g. *question ability* strategy).

of repetition in offers of assistance (Fisher's exact test, p=0.049). Within the neg-politeness strategies, conditional clauses, which explicitly underline the conditional nature of offers, are employed to a higher extent in offers of assistance relative to hospitable offers (hospitable: 9.1% vs. assistance: 35%, Fisher' exact test, p=0.030). The higher use of such conditionals also relates to strategy preferences – in this case the high use of an execution strategy in offers of assistance – given that preference strategies already include explicit reference to the conditional nature of offers, as in *Do you want NP?* and thus do not frequently include such modification (cf. Barron 2005: 161). Indeed, the only preference strategy with a conditional clause in the database was the offer *If anyone would like NP?*

Table 4. Pos-politeness and neg-politeness types employed across hospitable and offers of assistance in ICE-GB [9]

	Example	Hospitable offers (n=33)	Offers of assistance (n=20)
NEG-POLITENESS			
Conditional clauses	*I can I can dig the stuff out on it if if if there's any interest* (ICE-GB, s1a-012)	9.1% (3)	35% (7)
Conditional	*I tell you what I could look out for and that's ...* (ICE-GB, s1a-007)	21.2% (7)	25% (5)
Impersonal constructions	*if anyone would like some ice cream* (ICE-GB, s1a-073)	6.1% (2)	–
Lexical downtoner	*well I can only have a look* (ICE-GB, s1a-046)	–	5% (1)
Subjectiviser	*so why don't you have my one cos I think I might nip off shortly* (ICE-GB, s1a-042)	3.0% (1)	–
Consultative device	*Do you think you would like to eat?* (ICE-GB, s1a-046)	3.0% (1)	–
Hesitation/Re-starts	*I could uhm get you that other book* (ICE-GB, s1a-053)	9.1% (3)	10% (2)
Clarify optionality of offer	*I mean you don't have to* (ICE-GB, s1a-046)	3.0% (1)	–

---

9 As mentioned above in section 2.1 (cf. also footnote 2), Leech (2014: 99) does not include claims of common ground or solidarity in his concept of positive politeness arguing that they are employed to underline camaraderie and friendship rather than to enhance face. While it is recognised that these concepts are intricately related, the present overview does not take alerters (external elements to the offer, such as first names, which function to draw the interlocutor's attention to the offer (Blum-Kulka et al. 1989)), the use of ellipsis or the use of linguistic items designed to underline common context into account. Indeed, the use of alerters may simply function as a deictical element in large groups. For instance, there are a number of occasions of offers in my data where an offer did not receive uptake (and was thus not included in the present corpus) but was rephrased in the same way with the inclusion of an alerter and then followed by uptake (and so included in the present corpus).

Table 4. (continued)

	Example	Hospitable offers (n=33)	Offers of assistance (n=20)
POS-POLITENESS			
Grounder	*there's certain things that you can get cheaper out there* so I mean obviously if there's anything that you want me to try and get you I can get it cheaper... (ICE-GB, s1a-048)	6.1% (2)	20% (4)
Repetition	well what books shall I bring along shall I bring along some books (ICE-GB, s1a-043)	—	15% (3)
Lexical – upgrading	... if you want to put that off *honestly* I don't mind (ICE-GB, s1a-048)	6.1% (2)	25% (5)
Negation	You *don't* want any tea (ICE-GB, s1a-047)	9.1% (3)	—
Understater/ diminutive[10]	so if you feel like uh uhm trying *a bit of* walnut pastry kind of cake and putting things on it judiciously I mean let's just (ICE-GB, s1a-056)	3.0% (1)	—
Downplay that offered	*Wouldn't be very large* but it'd be big enough to ... (ICE-GB, s1a-007)	—	5% (1)
Tag	have some nuts *why don't you* (ICE-GB, s1a-057)	3.0% (1)	5% (1)

5 Conclusion

The analysis reveals ICE-GB to include a range of offer strategies and offer types. The most frequent offer types were hospitable offers followed by offers of assistance. These offer types were found to correlate with different strategy types, and modification types. Most typically, hospitable offers in ICE-GB were realised using a conventionalised preference strategy accompanied on occasion by some modification. These findings support those by Barron (2005) in which preference strategies were also revealed to be prototypical across EngE and IrE in the hospitable offer situation included in the production questionnaire analysis. The prototypical use of hearer-oriented preference strategies with hospitable offers – rather than the more indirect speaker-oriented execution strategies – is suggested to relate to the specific context of hospitable offers in which hosts have the obligation to look after their guests and in which guests are entitled – and in

---

[10] This category may include diminutives, such as *little* or indeed quantifiers, such as *drop* (drop of tea) which function as inherent diminutives (cf. Schneider 2003: 190).

some instances – obliged to accept such attention. In other words, in such situations S has a high right to offer. A hearer-oriented strategy is, thus, acceptable.

Offers of assistance in the corpus, in contrast, were realised predominantly using an execution strategy. Similarly, in Barron (2005), execution strategies, particularly the state ability strategy, were prototypical in many non-hospitable situations. Such strategies underline the role of the speaker rather than the hearer and are thus less direct relative to preference strategies. Their use reflects a higher level of negative face-threat in such situations where role relations are less standard. Neg-politeness modification and indeed overall modification is higher in offers of assistance than in the case of hospitable offers, with the vast majority of offers of assistance exhibiting some modification in the form of pos-politeness and/ or neg-politeness. Within the neg-politeness strategies, conditional clauses were used to a comparatively large extent.

Further research prospects are many. Given low occurrences of the remaining offer types identified, namely gift offers and offers of verbal goods, strategy/ modification correlations could not be carried out. This is an area ripe for future research. Further research desiderata include an analysis of the present data by gender given particularly a female bias (64.4% female; 35.6% male) in the offers identified in the present corpus. Finally, given the present form-focused analysis and the related difficulties of recall mentioned in section 3.1, a line-by-line reading of the transcripts of the corpus focused on identifying offers in context, would also be welcomed. In the British context, audio-recordings are available, which support such an analysis (cf. Garcia McAllister 2015: 32). We look forward to future analyses.

Transcription conventions

<,>	short pause
<,,>	long pause
<unclear> ... </unclear>	unclear speech

References

Aijmer, Karin. 1996. *Conversational routines in English: Convention and creativity*. London: Longman.

Alaoui, Sakina M. 2011. Politeness Principle: A comparative study of English and Moroccan Arabic requests, offers and thanks. *European Journal of Social Sciences* 20(1). 7–15.

Barron, Anne. 2003. *Acquisition in interlanguage pragmatics*. Amsterdam & Philadelphia: John Benjamins

Barron, Anne. 2005. Offering in Ireland and England. In Anne Barron & Klaus P. Schneider (eds.), *The pragmatics of Irish English*, 141–176. Berlin & New York: Mouton de Gruyter.

Barron, Anne. 2011. Variation revisited: A corpus analysis of offers in Irish English and British English. In Joachim Frenk & Lena Steveker (eds.), *Anglistentag 2010 Saarbrücken: proceedings*, 407–419. Trier: Wissenschaftlicher Verlag Trier.

Barron, Anne. 2017a. The speech act of "offers" in Irish English. *World Englishes* 36(2).

Barron, Anne. 2017b. Variational pragmatics. In Anne Barron, Gerard Steen & Gu Yueguo (eds.), *Routledge handbook of pragmatics*, 91–104. London & New York: Routledge.

Barron, Anne & Klaus P. Schneider. (eds.). 2009. Variational Pragmatics. [Special issue]. *Intercultural Pragmatics* 4(6).

Blum-Kulka, Shoshana, Juliane House & Gabriele Kasper. 1989. The CCSARP coding manual. In Shoshana Blum-Kulka, Juliane House & Gabriele Kasper (eds.), *Crosscultural pragmatics: Requests and apologies*, 273–294. Norwood, NJ: Ablex.

Brown, Penelope & Stephen C. Levinson. 1978. Universals in language usage: Politeness phenomena. In Esther N. Goody (ed.), *Questions and politeness: Strategies in social interaction*, 56–289. Cambridge: Cambridge University Press.

Brown, Penelope & Stephen C. Levinson. 1987. *Politeness: Some universals in language use*. Cambridge: Cambridge University Press.

Curl, Traci S. 2006. Offers of assistance: Constraints on syntactic design. *Journal of Pragmatics* 38. 1257–1280.

Davidson, Judy Arlene. 1984. Subsequent versions of invitations, offers, requests, and proposals dealing with potential or actual rejections. In John Maxwell Atkinson & John Heritage (eds.), *Structures of social action: Studies in conversational analysis*, 102–128. Cambridge: Cambridge University Press.

Davidson, Judy Arlene. 1990. Modifications of invitations, offers and rejections. In George Psathas (ed.), *Interaction competence* (Studies in Ethnomethodology and Conversation Analysis 1), 149–179. Washington, DC: International Institute for Ethnomethodology and Conversation Analysis, etc.

Edmondson, Willis & Juliane House. 1981. *Let's talk, and talk about it: A pedagogic interactional grammar of English*. München: Urban und Schwarzenberg.

Eshreteh, Mahmood K. M. 2016. A pragmatic analysis of diminutives in Palestinian society. *International Journal of Language Studies* 10(4). 131–148.

Fukushima, Saeko & Yuko Iwata. 1987. Politeness strategies in requesting and offering. *Japanese Association of College English Teachers Bulletin (JACET Bulletin)* 18. 31–48.

Garcia McAllister, Paula. 2015. Speech acts: A synchronic perspective. In Karin Aijmer & Christoph Rühlemann (eds.), *Corpus pragmatics. A handbook*, 29–51. Cambridge: Cambridge University Press.

García, Carmen. 1999. The three stages of Venezuelan invitations and responses. *Multilingua* 18(4). 391–433.

García, Carmen. 2008. In Klaus P. Schneider & Anne Barron (eds.), *Variational pragmatics: A focus on regional varieties in pluricentric languages*, 269–305. Amsterdam & Philadelphia: John Benjamins.

Grainger, Karen & Sandra Harris. 2007. Apologies: Introduction. [Special issue]. *Journal of Politeness Research* 3(1). 1–9.

Grainger, Karen, Zainab Kerkam, Fathia Mansor & Sara Hills. 2015. Offering and hospitality in Arabic and English. *Journal of Politeness Research* 11(1). 41–70.

Hancher, Michael. 1979. The classification of cooperative illocutionary acts. *Language in Society* 8. 1–14.

Hua, Zhu, Li Wei & Qian Yuan. 1998. Gift offer and acceptance in Chinese culture: Contexts and functions. *Journal of Asian Pacific Communication* 8(2). 87–101.

Hua, Zhu, Li Wei & Qian Yuan. 2000. The sequential organisation of gift offering and acceptance in Chinese. *Journal of Pragmatics* 32(1). 81–103.
International corpus of English. http://ice-corpora.net/ice/ (accessed 19 August 2016).
Jucker, Andreas H. 2009. Speech act research between armchair, field and laboratory: The case of compliments. *Journal of Pragmatics* 41. 1611–1635.
Leech, Geoffrey. 2014. *The pragmatics of politeness*. Oxford: Oxford University Press.
Pérez Hernández, Lorena. 2001. The directive-commissive continuum. *Miscelánea: A Journal of English and American Studies* 23. 77–98.
Rühlemann, Christoph & Karin Aijmer. 2014. Corpus pragmatics: Laying the foundations. In Karin Aijmer & Christoph Rühlemann (eds.), *Corpus pragmatics. A handbook*, 1–26. Cambridge: Cambridge University Press.
Schiffrin, Deborah. 1994. *Approaches to discourse*. Malden, MA: Blackwell.
Schneider, Klaus P. 2000. Diminutives in discourse: Sequential aspects of diminutive use in spoken interaction. In Malcolm Coulthard, Janet Cotterill & Francis Rock (eds.), *Dialogue analysis VII: Working with dialogue* (Selected papers from the 7th International Association of Dialogue Analysis Conference Birmingham 1999), 293–300. Tübingen: Niemeyer.
Schneider, Klaus P. 2003. *Diminutives in English*. Tübingen: Niemeyer.
Schneider, Klaus P. 2010. Variational pragmatics. In Mirjam Fried, Jan-Ola Östman & Jef Verschueren (eds.), *Variation and change: Pragmatic perspectives* (Handbook of Pragmatics Highlights 6), 239–267. Amsterdam & Philadelphia: John Benjamins.
Seargeant, Philip. 2012. *Exploring World Englishes. Language in a global context*. Oxon & New York: Routledge.
Searle, John R. 1975. Indirect speech acts. In Peter Cole & Jerry. L. Morgan (eds.), *Speech acts* (Syntax and Semantics 3), 59–82. New York: Academic Press.
Searle, John R. 1976. A classification of illocutionary acts. *Language in Society* 5. 1–23.
Sidnell, Jack. 2009. Sequences. In Sigurd D'hondt, Jan-Ola Östman & Jef Verschueren (eds.), *The pragmatics of interaction*, 215–239. Amsterdam & Philadelphia: John Benjamins.
Sifianou, Maria. 1992. Cross-cultural communication: Compliments and offers. *Parousia* 8. 49–69.
UCL Survey of English Usage. http://www.ucl.ac.uk/english-usage/projects/ice-gb/design.htm (accessed 10 August 2016).
Wierzbicka, Anna. 1985. Different cultures, different languages, different speech acts: Polish vs. English. *Journal of Pragmatics* 9(2–3). 145–178.
Wierzbicka, Anna. 1987. *English speech act verbs. A semantic dictionary*. Marrickville, Australia: Academic Press.
Wunderlich, Dieter. 1977. Assertions, conditional speech acts, and practical inferences. *Journal of Pragmatics* 1. 13–46.
Yongbing, Liu. 1998. A study of conversational formulas – from a cross cultural perspective. *The Internet Journal of Language, Culture and Society* 3. http://www.aaref.com.au/en/publications/journal/archived-articles/issue-03-1998/ (accessed 10 August 2016).

J. César Félix-Brasdefer
19 The intercultural speaker abroad

1 Introduction

Research on the development of intercultural competence emerged within the field of foreign language education; its focus was to provide the learner with knowledge of both language and culture. Intercultural competence is one component of the global concept of intercultural communicative competence that examines general issues related to culture, and the learner's ability to engage in an awareness of sociocultural norms (Byram 1997; Byram, Nichols, and Stevens 2001). Research on the development of intercultural competence enables teachers to provide students with sound pedagogical activities to raise learners' awareness of their own culture as well as a second, third or more cultures (Byram, Nichols, and Stevens 2001; Kramsch 2011; Wilkinson 2012). Specifically, the development of intercultural competence is crucial for the intercultural speaker who wishes to engage in critical discussions of culture and language. The intercultural speaker needs not only a knowledge of the grammatical system and vocabulary of the target language, but also pragmatic competence (pragmalinguistic and sociopragmatic knowledge) and knowledge of the culture and interactional styles of his/her own culture and other cultures. And, given the increased interest on the part of students studying abroad from different backgrounds,[1] researchers and teachers should work together to improve our understanding of the development of intercultural competence and provide the intercultural speaker with effective ways to become more culturally aware.

The aim of this chapter is to take a close look at the development of intercultural competence with particular attention to the intercultural speaker in study abroad settings. I present an analysis of two methods that can be used to raise learners' cultural awareness, namely, the diary or field-notes method and retrospective verbal reports. I conclude with pedagogical recommendations for the teaching of intercultural competence for students abroad.

---

[1] For an overview of students going abroad, see the Institute of International Education: http://www.iie.org/

2 Communicative competence

2.1 Intercultural communicative competence

Intercultural communicative competence emerged from the concept of communicative competence introduced by Hymes (1972), followed by revised models that expanded on our understanding of communicative competence with additional subcomponents which describe different abilities of the learner in various learning contexts (e.g. naturalistic, foreign language, immersion, and study abroad) (Bachman 1990; Bachman and Palmer 1996; Canale 1983; Canale and Swain 1980; Celce-Murcia 2008). In these models, some of the components of communicative competence include knowledge of grammar, discourse, culture, interaction, strategies, and pragmatics. In her most recent model of communicative competence, Celce-Murcia (2008) describes sociocultural competence as the ability "to express messages appropriately within the overall social and cultural context of communication" (p. 46). It includes knowledge of language variation (sociolinguistic knowledge), as well as knowledge of social variables such as social contextual factors, stylistic appropriateness, and cultural factors. Pragmatic knowledge falls within Celce-Murcia's (2008) component of interactional competence, which encompasses both actional competence (i.e. how to perform and recognize speech acts) and conversational competence (i.e. sequence organization, the ability to establish and change topics, how to interrupt, how to get, hold, and relinquish the floor, as well as how to collaborate and backchannel). Although intercultural competence does not feature as a subcomponent in her proposed model of communicative competence, it shares characteristics with both sociocultural and interactional competence. Overall, communicative competence refers to a composite of competences that second language learners need to improve language proficiency, including sociocultural knowledge. Of these, discourse competence represents a core component of communitive competence, as it is through discourse that second language learners interact and mediate across a second, third or more cultures.

Research dealing with intercultural competence builds on a more comprehensive approach to developing not only linguistic competence, but also cultural awareness, interaction, knowledge of the speaker's own culture and the other's culture, and his/her attitude when interacting with speakers of second, third and more languages. The concept of intercultural competence was proposed in the 1990s by Byram (1997) and subsequent revised proposals that describe the intercultural speaker as the language learner who "has an ability to interact with 'others', to accept other perspectives and perceptions of the world, to mediate between different perspectives to be conscious of their evaluations of difference" (Byram, Nichols, and Stevens 2001: 5). Developing intercultural competence, therefore, includes knowledge of cultural and global issues when interacting with speakers from other cultures.

Based on a proposed model of intercultural communicative competence, intercultural competence includes five components: knowledge, attitudes, skills of interpreting/relating, skills of discovery/interaction, and critical cultural awareness (Byram 1997, 2009; Byram, Nichols, and Stevens 2001). *Knowledge* refers to knowledge of social groups and cultures, and knowledge "about how other people see oneself as well as some knowledge about other people" (Byram, Nichols, and Stevens 2001: 6). Intercultural *attitudes* concern the speaker's curiosity, openness, and readiness to agree and disagree with other cultures, values, and beliefs. The third and fourth components concern *skills*: skills of interpreting/relating refer to how to interpret or comment on an event from another culture and contrasting them with events of the speaker's own culture; and, skills of discovery and interaction, namely, "the ability to acquire new knowledge of a culture and cultural practices and the ability to operate knowledge, attitudes and skills under the constraints of real-time communication and interaction" (p. 6). Finally, *critical cultural awareness* is placed at the center of the model because it concerns the intercultural speaker's ability to critically assess perspectives, practices, and products of his own and other cultures. Given the myriad competencies necessary to develop intercultural competence, the intercultural speaker is seen as a citizen of the world with an understanding of global issues along with his/her ability to engage in critical discussion and evaluation about his/her own culture and the other's culture.

Kramsch (2011) views the intercultural speaker as a mediator between his/her own and other cultures though discourse, and highlights the importance of developing intercultural competence in foreign language education. She describes three dimensions of symbolic competence: symbolic representation (i.e. referential function of language; conceptual meanings), symbolic action (i.e. interpersonal function; producing and interpreting speech acts), and symbolic power which concerns how learners assign meaning to social power; specifically, how learners become aware of power inequalities between natives speakers (NSs) and non-native speakers (NNSs) learning a second or third language. In Kramsch's view, intercultural competence refers to the learner's ability "to reflect critically or analytically on the symbolic systems we use to make meaning" (p. 365). According to Kramsch, the ultimate goal of studying intercultural competence is to provide teachers with pedagogical resources to help them improve the learner's intercultural competence in second and foreign contexts.

The aforementioned components of intercultural competence describe a speaker who, as a result of intercultural encounters with NSs of the target culture, is willing to relate, interact, discover, learn about global issues and events (e.g. education, politics, law, literature, ethical issues), evaluate his/her own and others' attitudes, make mistakes, express messages appropriately within the social and cultural values of both cultures, agree and disagree with NSs of the target culture on everyday topics, as well as to develop critical cultural awareness of issues related to his/her own and other cultures. The development of intercultural competence occurs gradually with constant interaction and critical awareness of cultural issues in both the speaker's and others' cultures.

In the next section I focus on the development of intercultural competence among intercultural speakers in study abroad settings.

2.2 The intercultural speaker abroad

The issue of the context of learning has received significant attention in second language acquisition (SLA). Some of the topics that have been analyzed include the learning context (e.g. naturalistic, foreign language, immersion, and study abroad), quality and quantity of input, length of stay in the target culture, intensity of interaction, acculturation and socialization, the opportunities that learners have to practice in a second language (L2) inside and outside of the classroom, proficiency level, previous contact with the target culture, and the type of instruction (e.g. explicit vs. implicit) (Bardovi-Harlig and Bastos 2011; Barron 2003; Collentine 2009; DuFon and Churchill 2006; Freed 1995; Kinginger 2015; Taguchi 2013). Further, learners of second or more languages who decide to study abroad develop different dimensions of intercultural competence while interacting with NSs of the target. As mentioned by Wilkinson (2012), the intercultural speaker is not only linguistically competent (e.g. having a command of vocabulary and grammar), but someone who is "also both sensitive towards other people and cultures and aware of his/her own cultural positioning. […] the intercultural speaker is not bound to specific cultures or languages, but is competent in mediating across multiple borders" (p. 296).

Pragmatic competence is a necessary component for developing intercultural competence in study abroad (SA) contexts. Pragmatic knowledge, according to Leech (1983) and Thomas (1983), is comprised of two components: (1) pragmalinguistic knowledge – knowledge about and performance of the conventions of language use or the linguistic resources available in a given language that convey "particular illocutions" in contextually appropriate situations (Leech 1983: 11), and (2) sociopragmatic knowledge – knowledge of and performance consistent with the social norms in specific situations in a given society, as well as familiarity with variables of social power and social distance. The intercultural speaker abroad not only needs to develop his/her ability to make form-meaning connections, but he/she also needs to consider the significance of context and the pragmatic function expressed through illocutions in pragmatically-appropriate contexts (Schmidt 1993).

Some researchers use cognitive and socialization frameworks to examine different dimensions of intercultural competence. For example, Ren (2013) studied the cognitive processes of learners of English during one academic year by means of retrospective verbal reports. His results revealed that over time, learners reported paying more attention to sociopragmatics when responding to requests, invitations, and offers in situations of equal and unequal relationships. Using natural data from a variety of service encounters in Toledo, Spain, Shively (2011) investigated the pragmatic development of requests for service among US learners over a semester (14 weeks). Unlike the previous studies, the learners in Shively's study received pedagogical intervention, specifically, explicit instruction in pragmatics with regard to requests in the context of service encounters. Results showed some changes in the opening sequences and a change from indirect (e.g. *puedo comprar...* 'can I buy') to direct requests (e.g. elliptical requests such as *cien gramos de salchichón* '100 grams of salami'), reflecting the pragmatic norms of this region of Spain. Shively's study focused on the development of intercultural competence by looking at the learners' ability to engage in face-to-face interactions during the negotiation of service. Over the course of one semester some of the learners developed awareness of cultural values of sales transaction, as well as an understanding of how to issue appropriate requests for service according to the sociocultural expectations of the culture in Spain. Further, although length of stay may be a necessary condition for improving the learner's intercultural competence, what also matters is critical awareness, reflection on cultural values, and the learner's ability to engage in conversation with NSs of the target culture about global issues related to his own culture as that of others.

In the following section, I present two methods that are effective for examining the development of intercultural competence among students studying abroad: (1) diaries or field-notes that gather impoliteness events (perceptions of impolite behavior); and (2) retrospective verbal reports to examine critical awareness and reflection of sociocultural values. I use Kecskés's (2013) socio-cognitive approach to analyze intercultural interaction between learners and NSs of the target culture. In a nutshell, the socio-cognitive approach looks at instances of intercultural interactions between NNSs and NSs or NNSs-NNSs. This model is a discourse approach that takes into account both the speaker and hearer during the negotiation of joint action in natural intercultural interactions. It considers the notion of frames or activities that are based on prior experiences.

3 Developing cultural awareness abroad

3.1 Impoliteness events

Impoliteness events yield data regarding perceptions of polite or impolite behavior. In their study, Culpeper et al. (2010) examined variation in the perception of impoliteness in five countries. Participants from China, England, Finland, Germany, and Turkey were asked to provide written narratives about an impolite situation that they had experienced. Impoliteness events have been used to examine different dimensions of impolite behavior (Culpeper 2011). Participants activate a cognitive context during an activity type. When collecting data on impoliteness events, participants are asked to remember an instance of impolite behavior that happened to them. Due to the saliency of an impolite or rude encounter, participants remember contextual information about the situation, such as where the impoliteness event took place, the participants, what was said, how it was said, and how that offense or rude behavior was perceived by the interlocutor.

The results of this section are based on a corpus of 100 impoliteness events experienced by second language learners studying in a region of the Spanish-speaking world (i.e. Spain, Mexico, Argentina, Peru, Chile, Ecuador, Venezuela, and Guatemala). The goal of this corpus is to capture impolite situations in L2 intercultural encounters between NSs and US students (NNSs) studying Spanish abroad. Based on Culpeper et al. (2010), learners completed an online questionnaire with the following information:

> Thinking about the time you spent in a Spanish-speaking country, describe a conversation in which someone said something to you that made you feel bad or uncomfortable (for example, a time that you felt hurt, offended, embarrassed, humiliated, or ostracized). Please write the conversation as a dialogue (like a play) and try to include the following information:
> – what was actually said and how it was said (for example, was there something different about the pronunciation, intonation?)
> – where the conversation took place (for example, in a class, on a bus, at a party) your relationship to the other person in the dialogue (for example, a friend, a stranger, a host family member)
> – how you reacted
> – whether other people heard the exchange, and if so,
> – how they reacted

In the second part of the questionnaire, learners were asked to describe their emotions by answering the following question:

> – Think about the event you have described and explain how it made you feel at the time and why it made you feel this way.
> – How would you describe the behavior of the person who made you feel bad (how would you label this kind of behavior)?

In the majority of the impoliteness events most learners were aware of sociocultural norms that were considered appropriate in regions in Spain and Latin America. Example (1) shows an impoliteness event reported by a male learner who lived with a host family in Spain.

(1) Impoliteness event. US male learner of Spanish interacting with his host family and friends abroad (Length of residence in Spain: 3 months)

> 01 I was visiting my host mother in Leon, Spain, whom I had known for 4 years,
> 02 shortly after I got engaged and she made it clear to me that she did not think it was
> 03 a good idea for me to get married so young. While I was discussing my proposal and
> 04 wedding plans with another friend while we were out bar-hopping as a group, my
> 05 host mother said, "Yo no me casaría; eres muy joven todavía" ('I would not get
> 06 married; you're still too young'). My host father and our friends heard what she said,
> 07 and one of the friends tried to say something positive to downplay the comment.
> 08 I reacted by ignoring the comment.
> 09 It bothered me because I was very happy to be engaged and in love, but at the same
> 10 time I had enough experience with Spanish culture to know that it is considered
> 11 okay to give opinions like that among a group of good friends, even about personal
> 12 issues, and the fact that she was willing to express such a strong opinion showed
> 13 that we have a close relationship.
> 14 My host mother did not expect me to argue with her about her opinion on my
> 15 engagement; she was merely expressing her own feelings, and so I believe it was
> 16 perfectly appropriate for me to not respond directly to what she said. She went on
> 17 to tell our friends how much I had spent on the engagement ring and compliment
> 18 me indirectly by saying something like "I don't know anyone here his age that has
> 19 [$] of dollars to buy a ring," which further told me that she really was not trying to
> 20 be offensive, just give her own analysis of the situation while at the same time
> 21 being supportive.

This example describes an intercultural encounter between the learner and NSs in Spain (host family and friends). The learner reported that he felt annoyed by the host mother's opinion that he was too young to get married (lines 05–07). In fact, when asked how this situation made him feel, the learner reported that it made him feel bad: "I was very happy about my engagement, and I wished that she would share completely in my happiness." After three months in Spain the student developed sufficient intercultural competence to realize that "expressing strong opinions" is a sociocultural trait in the Spanish culture; it enhances the degree of closeness in relationships among close friends (lines 09–13). The learner was also aware that he was not expected to argue with his host mother, and that behavior was seen as appropriate within the cultural values of the Spanish society, and not as offensive (lines 14–16). However, when asked how he described the behavior of the person who made him feel bad, his response reflects a cultural awareness of the Spanish culture: "The behavior was completely culturally acceptable. The statement that she [host mother] made is best described as very blunt or frank."

Other types of offense noted in the impoliteness events concerned the learners' perception of their weight, which is a more frequent topic of conversation in some Spanish-speaking countries than in the US. Example (2) shows an impoliteness event from a female learner who spent six months in Chile while living with a host family.

(2) Impoliteness event. US female learner of Spanish interacting with her host family abroad (Length of residence in Chile: 6 months)

>01 When I was living in Chile, after I had been there for a few months I gained weight
>02 (from all the *pan tostado*!! [toasted bread]). They (host family) were sitting in the
>03 living room when I came downstairs one day and I told my family I had to buy new
>04 pants for my school uniform.
>05 My host mom said, -¡Mary, *estás muy gorda*! [you are very fat'] (laugh laugh)
>06 –Oh thanks, (laugh) 'I know, you don't have to tell me that' (playful swat)
>07 You are eating a lot of bread.
>08 Even though we laughed during the situation, I remember being embarrassed that
>09 I had gained enough weight that people had noticed. Plus, since my whole host
>10 family was sitting around for the whole conversation and laughing with my host
>11 mom, and I remember feeling more embarrassed.

In this example, the learner's perception of rude behavior concerned an offense related to her personal traits by her host mother calling her 'fat'. In some regions of Latin America, calling someone 'fat' may not be perceived as an offense (line 05); instead, it emphasizes the links of solidarity between the interlocutors. In this case, however, the learner perceived the interaction as offensive (lines 08–11). Nonetheless, when asked how she described the behavior of the person who made her feel bad, the learner's response showed a cultural awareness of sensitive topics among family members and among close friends: "Joking around. Teasing. In Latin America they tease about different things. I have most definitely learned this over the years."

As noted from the impoliteness events in (1) and (2) and the learners' perceptions of impolite behavior, in their time abroad both learners developed cultural awareness that expressing opinions and talking about sensitive topics, such as one's weight, are markers of affiliation or involvement among family members or close friends in Spain and Chile, respectively (Félix-Brasdefer 2008a; Márquez Reiter and Placencia 2005). Although these interactions were perceived as impolite, both learners were aware of these sociocultural expectations in the target culture. The learners' comments about these events showed that they had a high level of intercultural competence as a result of their stay in Spain and Chile; in particular, through the intensity of interaction with host family members and friends belonging to the target culture.

3.2 Retrospective verbal reports

The development of learners' intercultural competence can also be analyzed by means of retrospective verbal reports (RVRs). Retrospective reporting consists of obtaining verbal reports from learners immediately after the completion of a task (e.g. role plays) when much information is still available in short-term memory and can be directly reported or used as "retrieval cues" (Cohen 2012). By administering RVRs just after a task is finished, memory traces can be partially accessed either from short-term memory, or retrieved from long-term memory (retrieval cues) and verbalized. Cohen (2004) noted that this technique can be an effective and a useful source of information if the verbal reports are collected with care. Verbal reports have been employed in ILP research because "one may learn what the respondents actually perceived about each situation (e.g. what they perceived about the relative role status of the interlocutors) and how their perceptions influenced their responses" (Cohen 2004: 321).

I will show how RVRs can be used to raise cultural awareness by reflecting on the learner's own culture and his/her perceptions of the target culture. Specifically, I will examine how learners' perceptions influence their understanding of the "insistence" that follows after refusing an invitation. Previous research has shown that among NSs of Spanish in Latin America and Spain insistence is considered polite and represents a sociocultural expectation; not insisting is viewed as rude or insincere (Félix-Brasdefer 2006, 2008a; García 1992). On the contrary, among NSs of American English a series of insistences after an invitation has been declined is often seen as impolite or face-threatening (Félix-Brasdefer 2003, 2008a). Specifically, I will examine the extent to which advanced American learners of Spanish (fourth-year undergraduate university students) perceive an insistence as polite or impolite after living in a Spanish-speaking country in Latin America.

3.2.1 Cultural awareness of the insistence after refusing an invitation

I will present an example from my corpus on role plays and verbal reports to account for perceptions of sociocultural information (Félix-Brasdefer 2004, 2007, 2008b). The role-play method is frequently used in cross-cultural and interlanguage pragmatics to examine the learner's pragmalinguistic and sociopragmatic knowledge; more importantly, verbal reports can be used after a role-play task to examine perceptions of sociocultural information and pragmatic knowledge (Félix-Brasdefer 2010; Kasper 2000).

The following learner participated in a role-play interaction with a NS of Spanish; this interaction was followed by a retrospective verbal report. The learner is a NS of US English learning Spanish who studied four years at a US university (Spanish major). He spent four months studying Spanish in Venezuela and lived with a host family. In the role play, the learner was asked to take the role of an employee and respond appropriately to his boss (a NS of Spanish; professional). The description of the role play is presented in (3):

(3)   Refusing an invitation to a boss (+ Power, + Distance)

    Imagine that you are in (Spanish-speaking country of your preference). You have been working at 3M as a sales representative for the last five years. You have a good working relationship with your boss although you do not socialize together outside the office. Your boss has always been supportive of your ideas and has been instrumental in your receiving a recent promotion. After working for him for three years, he has recently been promoted and will become the Manager of the Latin American Sales Division which will require his relocation to Mexico City next month. He is having a party next Saturday evening at a restaurant and is inviting you and other members of his sales group to celebrate his promotion and as a farewell, but you are unable to attend.

Immediately after the role-play task, the researcher asked the following questions regarding the learner's perceptions of sociocultural information of the act of refusing an invitation:

- Have you noticed any cultural differences with respect to the notion of insistence between the United States and the country you visited in Latin America?
- After declining the invitation from the boss, did you expect an insistence from him? If he did insist, how did it make you feel? Do you consider an insistence rude or acceptable in your culture?

In the following examples, I present a role-play interaction (taken from Félix-Brasdefer 2008b) between the learner and his boss (4), and the learner's perception (verbal report) regarding his sociocultural knowledge of the insistence to a refusal to an invitation (5) in both the US and in Venezuela:

(4) Role play: Declining an invitation from a boss. The learner (employee) spent four months in Venezuela; the NS of Mexican Spanish plays the role of the boss. (male-male interaction)

Boss: 01 *Hola, Adam, me imagino que sabes que me voy a mudar*
02 *a la ciudad de México con el nuevo trabajo.*
03 *Estoy organizando una reunión para nuestro departamento,*
04 *y vamos a celebrar el sábado que viene a las nueve de la noche.*
05 *y me encantaría que me acompañaras a esta fiesta.*
'Hi Adam, I imagine you already know that I'm moving
to Mexico City for my new job,
I'm organizing a gathering for our department,
and we are going to celebrate this coming Saturday at nine
p.m., and I'd love it if you could be there with me.' ⎫ Invitation-response

Learner: 06 *este sábado?*
'this Saturday?'
Boss: 07 *sí, este sábado a las nueve de la noche*
'yes, this Saturday at nine p.m.'
Learner: 08 *este sábado estoy ocupado, ya tengo planes*
'this Saturday I'm busy, I already have plans' ⎭

Boss: 09 *Qué lástima, me gustaría mucho que vengas*
'what a shame, I'd like very much for you to come'
Learner: → 10 *sí, bueno, felicidades con tu ah promoción, pero...*
11 *y que la fiesta va bien, pero no puedo asistir*
'yes, well, congratulations with your ah promotion, but...
and I hope the party goes well, but I can't attend' ⎫ Insistence-response ⎭

Boss: 12 *sí, es una lástima, me gustaría que pudieras venir*
'yes, it's a shame, I'd like it if you were able to come'
Learner: → 13 *aaay, lo siento*
'aay, I'm sorry'
Boss: 14 *bueno, okay, ni hablar, ya tienes otro compromiso,*
15 *ni modo, tal vez en otra ocasión, de acuerdo?*
'well, okay, don't mention it, you already have another
commitment, too bad, maybe another time, okay?'
Learner: → 16 (NO RESPONSE) ⎫ Insistence-response ⎭

The intercultural encounter in (4) consists of three main sequences: invitation-response (lines 01–08), followed by two insistence-response sequences initiated by the boss (lines 09–11 and 12–16). After the boss' invitation (lines 01–05), the learner issues a pre-refusal and an indirect refusal in two different turns (lines 6, 8). Next, the learner's first refusal to the insistence is mitigated: he expresses gratitude for the invitation (line 10), wishes the boss good luck with the party, and gives a direct refusal to end the refusal response ('no puedo asistir' "I can't attend') (lines 10–11). The refusal to the second insistence is realized by means of an expression of regret ('*aaay, lo siento*' 'I'm sorry') (line 13). And, after the boss' final insistence (line 14–15), the learner simply did not respond (line 16), ending the interaction with a look of uncertainty.

The example in (5) shows the learner's perception of the insistence to the invitation. Immediately after the role-play interaction, the learner in (4) was asked if he had noticed cultural differences between the US and Venezuela with regard to the notion of insistence, and whether he perceived the insistence on the part of the boss as appropriate or inappropriate behavior:

(5) Perception of the insistence after refusing an invitation (+P, +D)

> Yes, I expected the boss to insist, taken from what I've uh what I've encountered in Venezuela, they're very, very, very persistent; so uh, I was sort of prepared here. No, the insistence didn't bother me; I mean, I'm uh used to that, ya know. At first, when I was in Venezuela, I'm like, why don't these people just lay off me?, I said 'no', but that's just a cultural thing, I guess … When the boss insisted twice in the role play, it was difficult, and not having the mastery of the language that I'd like to have, I thought, 'you want me to repeat what I just said?' After the role play, I probably would've elaborated; as it gets further on, it gets more difficult."

The verbal report in (5) reflects an awareness on the part of the learner that an insistence is a sociocultural expectation in the Venezuelan context, accompanied by an awareness of his low level of linguistic ability. It appears that after four months abroad, this learner developed intercultural competence of what is considered appropriate behavior, and how it differs from the US culture. As noted by the learner, he expected the insistence in Spanish and it didn't bother him. Further, the learner's reflection shows that an awareness of cross-cultural norms when declining an invitation is often not concomitant with successful performance during an invitation-refusal interaction with a NSs of the target culture.

Other learners reported that they expected an insistence from a boss, but did not know how to negotiate an invitation-refusal response. It seems that although the learners were aware of the fact that an insistence after declining an invitation is the expected behavior in regions of Spain and Latin America (Félix-Brasdefer 2008a), they did not have the pragmatic knowledge and discourse skills necessary to perform a refusal according to the sociocultural expectations of the target culture. As a result of this inability to negotiate a refusal to an invitation, it appears that learners may benefit from explicit instruction in pragmatics to raise awareness of their pragmatic competence at the discourse level (Félix-Brasdefer & Mugford 2017).

Overall, retrospective verbal reports are instrumental in gathering supplemental information about the learners' metalinguistic knowledge and perception of sociocultural information. Specifically, by using verbal reports one can gain insights into the strategies that learners use during the planning and execution of speech acts. Verbal reports provide information with regard to: cognition (linguistic information attended to during the negotiation of a refusal), selection of the language of thought during the planning and execution of refusal, and the perception of insistence after declining an invitation in a second language (Félix-Brasdefer 2008b).

4 Pedagogical implications for teaching intercultural competence

Existing models of pragmatic instruction focus on the teaching of sociopragmatic and pragmalinguistic ability by means of pedagogical activities to raise learners' awareness of speech acts (cf. Bardovi-Harlig and Mahan-Taylor 2003; Félix-Brasdefer 2006; Félix-Brasdefer and Cohen 2012; Tatsuki and Houck 2010). However, little research has looked at the development of sociopragmatic awareness in intercultural interactions. For example, Huth and Teleghani-Nikazm (2006) proposed a pedagogical model for the teaching of sociopragmatic norms using authentic interactional exchanges in the classroom, such as telephone opening sequences. Haugh and Chang (2015) proposed a revised version of Huth and Taleghani-Nikazm's (2006) pedagogical model aimed at developing sociopragmatic awareness using an interactional approach to im/politeness through the analysis of a teasing/banter sequence. In both studies, sociopragmatic awareness consists of in-class reflection on authentic conversational practices, exposure to input at the sequential level, cross-cultural comparisons of L1 and L2 sequences, and communicative practice, followed by reflection. Additionally, Félix-Brasdefer and Mugford (2017) proposed a model for the teaching of impoliteness in the classroom consisting of the following components: raising awareness, pragmatic input (identification and reflection on im/polite behavior), teaching grammar as a communicative resource, and practicing polite and impolite behavior in the classroom. Overall, instructors should be aware of effective ways to deliver input in the classroom to enhance learners' pragmatic competence, including ways to maximize the teaching of intercultural competence in the classroom.

Wilkinson (2012) observed that the aim of intercultural competence "should be to make students aware of and sensitive to instances of cultural difference that they will inevitably encounter through foreign travel and through virtual interactions with other cultures, i.e., to create intercultural speakers with global competence" (p. 303). More specifically, for the teaching of intercultural competence an awareness-raising approach provides learners with sociocultural information about what is considered appropriate or inappropriate behavior. Awareness-raising consists of making learners conscious of the cultural values and the sociocultural expectations of the target language culture. Awareness-raising activities are often delivered through metapragmatic discussions and cross-cultural comparisons of current topics in the media, movies, technological advances, or literary novels. The delivery and reception of the input is also an important condition for developing metrapragmatic awareness (Rose and Kasper 2001). Byram, Nichols, and Stevens (2001) and Gómez Rodríguez (2015), for example, used literary texts to raise critical awareness of issues of identity, family, social class struggles, racism and discrimination, and current topics such as law and order in both the learner's own culture and in other cultures. And Kramsch (2011) takes a discourse-analytic perspective for the teaching of the intercultural dimension in the classroom: teachers should instigate reflection on the nature of language, genre, or cultural assumptions in a literary novel; reflect on what is said and not said by the students; engage the students' emotions, not just their cognition; and, discuss the social criticism implied in the book (pp. 363–64).

The following awareness-raising activities can help instructors develop intercultural competence in their students before they go abroad or during their study abroad experience. Instructors are encouraged to adopt a pragmatic-discourse approach (Félix-Brasdefer 2015) in order to engage students in discussions on cultural topics, taking into account the discourse structure of the text and the interpretations of the learner's own culture and target culture. The aim is to develop learners' global intercultural competence with respect to sociocultural topics that they may encounter abroad. Instructors should consider the following recommendations to raise the intercultural competence of students who intend to go abroad:

- Engage students in a critical discussion of the notion of culture through an analysis of knowledge and characteristics of a group: identity, tradition, religion, family, cuisine, social habits, music and arts. To achieve this goal, instructors can show films or present literary novels that prompt students' curiosity and inspire reflection on cultural topics;
- Develop students' sensitivity to everyday topics in two or more cultures through discussions of politics, education, ethics, and religion. The aim is to develop awareness of similarities and differences of how these concepts are realized in the learner's own culture and in other cultures. For instance,

comparing news in two or more newspapers would enhance the student's understanding of global competence;
- As part of the study abroad experience, instructors can teach students to be ethnographers. Ethnography "is a research methodology of professional observers and interpreters of foreign cultures" (Wilkinson 2012: 303). Students are taught to observe social activities and how people of the target culture interact, such as in schools, hospitals, and religious institutions. For example, students should be encouraged to write a reflection or a short research project about a cultural topic of their interest, such as a reflection on the educational or political system of the target culture in contrast to those of student's own culture;
- Students can be made aware of the differences between the interactional styles of customers and buyers engaged in service encounter interactions in the target culture, such as sales transactions in markets, grocery stores, coffee shops, pharmacies, or information centers. It is beneficial to expose learners to service encounter interactions with natural input and to ask them to reflect on the discourse structure of these interactions including: openings and closings, sales transactions, appropriate use of forms of address, and different ways to make a request for service (see Félix-Brasdefer [2015] for examples of service encounters in English and Spanish) with the goal of making the student cognizant of the roles of the customer and seller in the target culture and how these roles differ from the student's own culture;
- Students living with a host family are encouraged to maximize their intercultural competence through conversations and discussions of everyday topics with their host families. Students can gain insights about pragmatics from reflecting on similarities and differences between cultural values, family, directness and indirectness, and observation of manifestations of what is considered polite or impolite behavior;
- Expose learners to regional pragmatic variation (Félix-Brasdefer & Koike 2012). Instructors can compare instances of linguistic politeness or impoliteness of the learner's community abroad. For example, students can be exposed to current controversial topics (e.g. politics, education, identity, Spanish in the United States) and how they are interpreted by members of regions of Spain, Mexico, or Central or South America. For instance, students can be provided with newspaper articles from the United States, England, France, China, and Australia. Instructors can direct students' attention to features of the discourse structure, and discuss how the news is interpreted by members of each culture. The objective of this type of activity is to raise learner's awareness of linguistic (regional) variation and sociocultural norms in the learner's culture and in a second (or more) cultures.

5 Conclusion

This chapter has taken a close look at the concept of intercultural competence and its various components as a means of enhancing the learner's intercultural knowledge in a second language. The purpose of specifically targeting intercultural competence is to raise learner's global critical awareness of cultural issues related to their own culture as well as the target culture, such as identity, education, politics and law, and literary topics. To showcase the development of intercultural competence in study abroad settings, the current study presented two methods that are used to raise intercultural awareness, namely, a focus on impoliteness events (through diary or field notes) and retrospective verbal reports with data from learners abroad. These methods elicit data that offer insights into the learner's perceptions of cultural differences and raise critical cultural awareness of global issues. This chapter ended with pedagogical recommendations for enhancing the learner's intercultural competence before, during, and after the study abroad experience.

References

Bachman, Lyle, F. 1990. *Fundamental considerations in language testing*. Oxford, UK: Oxford University Press.

Bachman, Lyle F. & Adrian S. Palmer. 1996. *Language testing in practice: Designing and developing useful language tests*. Oxford, UK: Oxford University Press.

Bardovi-Harlig, Kathleen & Rebecca Mahan-Taylor. 2003. *Teaching pragmatics*. Retrieved July 13, 2015 at <http://americanenglish.state.gov/resources/teaching-pragmatics>

Bardovi-Harlig, Kathleen & Maria-Thereza Bastos. 2011. Proficiency, length of stay, and intensity of interaction and the acquisition of conventional expressions in L2 pragmatics. *Intercultural Pragmatics* 8(3). 347–384.

Barron, Anne. 2003. *Acquisition in interlanguage pragmatics. Learning how to do things with words in a study abroad context*. Amsterdam & Philadelphia: John Benjamins

Byram, Michael. 1997. *Teaching and assessing intercultural communicative competence*. Clevedon, UK: Multilingual Matters.

Byram, Michael. 2009. Intercultural competence in foreign languages: The intercultural speaker and the pedagogy of foreign language education. In Darla K. Deardorff (ed). *The SAGE handbook of intercultural competence*, 321–332. London: Sage.

Byram, Michael, Adam Nichols & David Stevens. 2001. *Developing intercultural competence in practice*. Clevedon, UK: Multilingual Matters.

Canale, Michael. 1983. From communicative competence to communicative language pedagogy. In Jack Richards & Richard Schmidt (eds.), *Language and communication*, 2–27. London: Longman.

Canale, Michael & Merrill Swain. 1980. Theoretical bases of communicative approaches to second language teaching and testing. *Applied Linguistics* 1. 1–47.

Celce-Murcia, Marianne. 2008. Rethinking the role of communicative competence in language teaching. In Eva Alcón Soler & Maria P. Safont Jordá (eds.), *Intercultural language use and language learning*, 41–57. Dordrecht, The Netherlands: Springer.
Cohen, Andrew D. 2004, Assessing speech acts in a second language. In Diana Boxer & Andrew D. Cohen (eds.) *Studying speaking to inform second language learning*, 302–327. Clevedon, UK: Multilingual Matters.
Cohen, Andrew D. 2012. Research methods for describing variation in intercultural pragmatics for cultures in contact and conflict. In J. César Félix-Brasdefer & Dale A. Koike (eds.), *Pragmatic variation in first and second language contexts: Methodological issues*,17–48. Amsterdam & Philadelphia: John Benjamins.
Collentine, Joseph. 2009. Study abroad research: Findings, implications and future directions. In Catherine Doughty & Michael Long (eds.), *Handbook of language teaching*, 218–233. Malden, MA: Blackwell.
Culpeper, Jonathan. 2011. *Impoliteness: Using language to cause offense*. Cambridge, UK: Cambridge University Press.
Culpeper, Jonathan, Leyla Marti, Meilian Mei, Minna Nevala & Gila Schauer. 2010. Cross-cultural variation in the perception of impoliteness: A study of impoliteness events reported by students in England, China, Finland, Germany, and Turkey. *Intercultural Pragmatics* 7(4). 597–624.
DuFon, Margaret A. & Eton Churchill (eds.). 2006. *Language learners in study abroad contexts*. Clevedon, England: Multilingual Matters.
Félix-Brasdefer, J. César. 2004. Interlanguage refusals: Linguistic politeness and length of residence in the target community. *Language Learning* 54(4). 587–653.
Félix-Brasdefer, J. César. 2006. Teaching the negotiation of multi-turn speech acts. Using conversation-analytic tools to teach pragmatics in the classroom. In Kathleen Bardovi-Harlig, J. César Félix-Brasdefer, & Alwiya Omar (eds.), *Pragmatics and language learning* 11, 165–197. Honolulu, HI: University of Hawai'i at Manoa.
Félix-Brasdefer, J. César. 2007. Pragmatic development in the Spanish as a FL classroom: A cross-sectional study of learner requests. *Intercultural Pragmatics* 4(2). 253–286.
Félix-Brasdefer, J. César. 2008a. *Politeness in Mexico and the United States: A contrastive study of the realization and perception of refusals*. Amsterdam & Philadelphia: John Benjamins.
Félix-Brasdefer, J. César. 2008b. Perceptions of refusals to invitations: Exploring the minds of foreign language learners. *Language Awareness* 17(3). 195–211.
Félix-Brasdefer, J. César. 2015. *The language of service encounters: A pragmatic-discursive approach*. Cambridge, UK: Cambridge University Press.
Félix-Brasdefer, J. César. & Andrew D. Cohen. 2012. Teaching pragmatics in the foreign language classroom: Grammar as a Communicative Resource. *Hispania* 95(4). 650–669.
Félix-Brasdefer, J. César & Dale A. Koike (eds.). 2012. *Pragmatic variation in first and second language contexts*. Amsterdam & Philadelphia: John Benjamins.
Félix-Brasdefer & Gerard Mugford. 2017. (Im)politeness: Learning and Teaching. In Jonathan Culpeper, Michael Haugh & Daniel Z. Kádár (eds.), *The Palgrave Handbook of Linguistic (Im)politeness*, 489–516. Basingstoke: Palgrave Macmillan.
Freed, Barbara. 1995. *Second language acquisition in a study abroad context*. Amsterdam & Philadelphia: John Benjamins.
García, Carmen. 1992. Refusing an invitation: A case study of Peruvian style. *Hispanic Linguistics* 5(1–2). 207–243.
Gómez Rodríguez. Luis F. 2015. Critical intercultural learning through topics of deep culture in an EFL classroom. *Íkala* 20(1). 43–59.

Haugh, Michael & Wei-Ling Melody Chang. 2015. Understanding im/politeness across cultures: An interactional approach to raising sociopragmatic awareness. *IRAL* 53(4). 389–414.

Huth, Thorsten & Carmen Taleghani-Nikazm. 2006. How can insights from conversation analysis be directly applied to teaching L2 pragmatics? *Language Teaching Research* 10 (1). 53–79.

Hymes, Dell. 1972. On communicative competence. In J. B. Pride & Janet Holmes (eds.)*Sociolinguistics*, 269–293. Harmonsworth, UK: Penguin Books.

Kasper, Gabriele. 2000. Data collection in pragmatics research. In Helen Spencer-Oatey (ed.), *Culturally Speaking: Managing rapport through talk across cultures*, 316–369. London: Continuum.

Kecskés, István. 2013. *Intercultural pragmatics*. Oxford: Oxford University Press.

Kinginger, Celeste. 2015. *Language learning and study abroad: A critical review of research*. Basingstoke, UK: Palgrave.

Kramsch, Claire. 2011. The symbolic dimension of the intercultural. *Language Teaching* 44(3). 354–367.

Leech, G. (1983). *Principles of pragmatics*. London: Longman.

Márquez Reiter, Rosina & María Elena Placencia. 2005. *Spanish pragmatics*. New York: Palgrave Macmillan.

Ren, Wei. (2013). A longitudinal investigation into L2 learners' cognitive processes during study abroad. *Applied Linguistics* 1. 1–21.

Rose, Ken & Gabriele Kasper. 2001. *Pragmatics in language teaching*. Cambridge, UK: Cambridge University Press.

Schmidt, Richard. 1993. Consciousness, learning, and interlanguage pragmatics. In Gabriele Kasper & Shoshana Blum-Kulka (eds.), *Interlanguage pragmatics*, 21–42. New York: Oxford University Press.

Shively, Rachel L. 2011. L2 pragmatic development in study abroad: A longitudinal study of Spanish service encounters. *Journal of Pragmatics* 43(6). 1818–1835.

Taguchi, Naoko. 2013. Production of routines in L2 English: Effect of proficiency and study-abroad experience. *System,* 41(1). 109–121.

Tatsuki, Donna & Noel Houck (eds). 2010. *Pragmatics: Teaching speech acts*. Alexandria, VA: TESOL.

Thomas, Jenny. 1983. Cross-cultural pragmatic failure. *Applied Linguistics* 4(2). 91–112.

Wilkinson, Jane. 2012. The intercultural speaker and the acquisition of intercultural global competence. In Jane Jackson (ed.), *Routledge handbook of language and intercultural communication*, 296–309. Florence, KY: Routledge.

Jörg Meibauer
20 Pragmatics and children's literature

1 Introduction

The pragmatic subfield of "pragmatics and children's literature" is still not established. While it is accepted that children's literature serves literary communication and can be looked at from the perspective of literary pragmatics (Sell 2002), the systematic link between the acquisition of pragmatics (as a part of language acquisition, see Matthews 2014, Zufferey 2015) and the specific input of children's literature seems to have been overlooked.

By pragmatics, I understand "the study of the use of language use in all its aspects" (Huang 2012: 9). This conception can be called "macro-pragmatics." Following Huang, macro-pragmatics comprises "cognitively and socially and/or culturally oriented" pragmatics. He tends to view these approaches as typical of "continental pragmatics," as opposed to "Anglo-American pragmatics," with its characteristic focus on pragmatics components, such as speech acts, implicature, deixis and reference, presupposition, information structure, and so on. However, the division between pragmatic landscapes is slightly misleading (although motivated by the recent history of pragmatics), since macro-pragmatics *must be based* on the study of pragmatic components. And pragmatics, I would like to add, has to be studied in relation to grammar, too. In the following, I will show that such a broad view of pragmatics is adequate when it comes to exploring the relation of pragmatics and children's literature.

Children's literature is literature that is usually produced by adults and targeted at children. It comprises "a broad and diverse range of texts with different addressees, forms, genres, degrees of linguistic and aesthetic elaborateness, and functions," as O'Sullivan (2010: 1) puts it. The addressees can be infants, preschoolers, middle-graders, or young adults, so the time-span covered roughly stretches from 12 months of age to 18 years.[1] Following O'Sullivan, we can state that forms of children's literature include "picture books, pop-up books, anthologies, novels, merchandising tie-ins, novelizations, and multimedia texts" and that their genres comprise "adventure stories, drama, science fiction, poetry and information books" (O'Sullivan 2010: 1). Most importantly, all these forms and genres *are accommodated* to the children's developing cognitive, social, cultural, and pragmatic abilities.

---

[1] This does not exclude the fact that some children's books are addressed to and read by adults as well.

Huang (2012: 18) mentions also the macro-pragmatic subfield of "literary pragmatics," which is characterized as the "study of use of linguistic forms in a literary text and the relationship between author, text, and reader in a sociocultural context from a pragmatic perspective, focusing on the question of what and how a literary text communicates." In this sense, the relation between children's literature and pragmatics may be seen as a study in literary pragmatics (Sell 1991; Mey 2000, 2001; de Geest 2003; Warner 2014).

Yet it seems that from the point of view of literary studies dealing with *adult literature*, children's literature is often seen as some kind of inferior literature, not worth in-depth study, or only in relation to educational purposes. This attitude is mistaken because it ignores the fact that literature acquisition goes hand in hand with language acquisition, and that children's literature paves the way for the appreciation of adult literature. With respect to language acquisition, or, closer to home, to pragmatic acquisition, it is important to stress that children's literature is a specific kind of input for the development of pragmatic abilities. Therefore, theories of pragmatic acquisition should take into account children's literature as a specific input. It is this point that I want to argue for throughout this chapter.

The outline of this chapter is as follows: In section 2, I will deal with external pragmatics, drawing largely on the pragmatics of picturebooks. External pragmatics refers to situations and contexts in which children's literature is received. Some relevant aspects will be pointed out using Margaret Wild and Anne Spudvilas's picturebook *Woolvs in the Sitee* (2006). In section 3, the focus is on internal pragmatics. By this, I understand the contents of children's literature insofar as these are relevant for pragmatics in general and pragmatic acquisition in particular. Here, I take the novel *The Curious Incident of the Dog in the Night-Time* (2003) by Mark Haddon as my prime example. Section 4 focuses on intercultural pragmatics and children's literature, drawing on findings from a recent project involving the graphic novel *The Arrival* (2006) by Shaun Tan.

2 External Pragmatics: The reading situation

In Western societies, many adults share picturebooks with their children from early on. As is the case with other social practices, this practice of joint attention to picturebooks involves some degree of variation and is dependent on a number of social and cultural factors. Nevertheless, projects aiming at enhancing family literacy show that the number of families engaged in this social practice can be increased (Bailey, Harrison and Brooks 2002). The books used in these reading situations are *early-concept books*, that is, books containing pictures of objects that are interesting for the child, for example, an apple or a ball. Such books typically contain no text at all. Yet they serve an important purpose, namely to support the child's lexical acquisition (Kümmerling-Meibauer & Meibauer 2011a, 2015c). As has been repeatedly observed, in the situation of joint attention to picturebooks, a pointing and naming game unfolds (Snow & Goldfield 1983; Moerk 1985). For example, the child points to a depicted object and the adult labels it, or the adult points to a depicted object and asks the child to label it. If the child knows the correct answer, the adult gives positive feedback, if not, he or she helps to find the correct answer or gives the correct answer himself/herself. From a pragmatic point of view, it is safe to say that the child is introduced into a specific question/answer format of discourse. Drawing on earlier work by Murphy (1978), Rohlfing, Grimminger, and Nachtigäller (2014: 101) point out that joint attention to picturebooks, including gesturing, is important for language acquisition because it raises "the expectation of interaction routines and the repeatability of the situation." Moreover, it was shown by Yont, Snow, and Vernon-Feagans (2003) that mothers finetune their interaction styles according to situational needs, e.g., joint attention to picturebooks vs. toy play.

We know that shared book reading enhances children's vocabulary (Blewitt 2014). Lexical acquisition, however, is not independent of pragmatic processes. For instance, Clark (1993) shows that pragmatic principles, such as the principle of conventionality and the principle of contrast, play an important role in lexical acquisition. The reading situation seems to support the application of such principles.

As children grow up, they are confronted with different kinds of children's literature, all of them being related to a number of pragmatic phenomena. Hence, we can assume that reading children's literature is associated with the acquisition of pragmatic abilities, such as to use indexicals correctly, to master a number of speech acts, to draw pragmatic inferences, to engage in adequate turn-taking, to tell a story, to be polite, and so on (Matthews 2014; Zufferey 2015).

Picturebooks, which play an important role in the preschool years with respect to family literacy (Cairney 2003) and are the object of shared book reading, are essentially text/picture combinations.[2] Pictures constitute a context for the text, and the text constitutes a context for the pictures. To interpret pictures is in itself a complex acquisition task, leading to visual literacy (Painter, Martin & Unsworth 2013; Bateman 2014; Bateman & Wildfeuer 2014). To interpret the text that is read correctly can also be demanding. For example, some texts are written from the perspective of a first-person narrator. Young children, still struggling with the acquisition of deixis, may have difficulties when the adult

---

2 Note that there are also complex textless picturebooks, e.g., Shaun Tan, *The Arrival* (2006).

mediator uses the first person when reading a text. They have to infer that the personal pronoun *I* does not refer to the adult mediator but to a literary character (Gressnich & Meibauer 2010). Pragmatic inferences may play a role in deriving the right perspective. Moreover, the introduction of discourse referents presupposes that a child is able to distinguish between reality and fiction, that is, she or he knows that there are ontologically different kinds of contexts (Gressnich 2011).

As an example, consider the beginning of the picturebook *Woolvs in the Sitee* (2006) by Margaret Wild and Anne Spudvilas. Admittedly, this is a so-called "challenging" picturebook (Evans 2015) that addresses a preschool audience (see also Kümmerling-Meibauer & Meibauer 2015b).[3]

> "There are **woolvs** in the sitee. Oh, yes!
> In the streets, in the parks, in the **allees**.
> In shops, in **rustee** playgrownds.
> In **howses** rite next dor.
>
> And soon they will **kum**.
> They **will kum** for me and for yoo
> And for yor **bruthers** and sisters,
> Yor muthers and **fathers**, yor arnts and unkils,
> Yor grandfathers and grandmuthers.
>
> **No won** is spared."
> (n. pag.)

When read aloud to children, the aesthetic effects of the deliberate false spelling are not relevant. When the child has already spelling knowledge, however, she may detect the mistakes and ascribe them to the narrator. In any case, the child has to solve a number of referential problems, for instance, whether the definite description *the woolvs in the sitee* are – within the fictional world – "real" or a mere product of the narrator's imagination. The narrator who is referring to himself (it is a boy, as we learn later) with *me* is hiding from the wolves whom he fears. Perspective-taking and emotional themes such as empathy with the narrator require *Theory of Mind*-related abilities. In psycholinguistics and developmental psychology, *Theory of Mind* refers to someone's belief about something in the world (first-order belief) and someone's belief about someone else's belief (second-order belief) (Miller 2012). Most researchers agree that *Theory of Mind* is acquired during the fourth year although there seem to be precursors. In addition, the acquisition of emotional vocabulary (Kauschke & Klann-Delius 1997;

---

[3] Bold face as in the original text.

Baron-Cohen et al. 2010) is important here, and can be related to the child reader's emotional development. To be sure, interpreting emotions as coded in children's literature remains a demanding task even for older children (Fries 2007, 2009; Nikolajeva 2014).

Within the reading situation, the kind of children's book matters with respect to the conversation about the content of the book. When looking at early-concept books, a game of pointing and naming unfolds. Wimmelbooks, in contrast, invite the telling of stories either by the adult mediator or by the addressees (Rémi 2011). Stark (2016) shows, on the basis of transcripts, that adults often do not read word-by-word but modify the text according to the child's needs: paraphrases, additional content, explanations of words or the story are usual. Moreover, parents try to relate the text to the experiences of the child. For instance, they may relate a book dealing with a birthday party to a past birthday party of their child. This individual shared knowledge may not be easily at hands when a reading robot acts as a mediator, or when the child reads a picturebook app. In sum, finetuning to the child's needs seems quite normal in the situation of joint looking at picturebooks.

While the first picturebooks operate on the conceptual level and introduce children to more or less abstract concepts, such as number, geometrical form, color, or conceptual classes such as animals or cars (Kümmerling-Meibauer & Meibauer 2015c), during the third year, simple narrative picturebooks are presented to the children. This means that picturebooks are designed in such a way that it makes sense to present them to children at this stage of development. This does not exclude, however, that descriptive picturebooks, that is, books that inform children about something (Kiefer & Wilson 2011; Meibauer 2015; Kümmerling-Meibauer & Meibauer 2015a), are also very interesting to children. Surprisingly, there is some evidence that descriptive picturebooks trigger more interest in the child to talk about things than narrative picturebooks (Torr & Clugston 1999). Thus, we find some variance in the interests of children; while some children find it easier to talk about how the real world is, others are more interested in fictional worlds, and still others show interest in both modalities. How such interests arise and unfold seems to be largely unknown. It is obvious that narrative picturebooks contribute to the child's emerging ability to tell stories. Certain narrative patterns can be borrowed from children's literature, for instance narrative constructions like *once upon a time*. Elaborating rudimental stories in close cooperation with an adult is a first step into the development of these conversational skills.

From a pragmatic point of view, it also matters where the reading event takes place. Thus, we distinguish reading picturebooks at home/within family life (Cairney 2003), at kindergarten (Gosen, Berenst & de Glopper 2015), or at school (Moschovaki & Meadows 2015). All these interactional settings, with their varied social and cultural backgrounds, contribute to the understanding and reflection of children's books in a different way.

When children enter school, learning to read and write makes them independent from adult co-readers. The situation of joint attention to picturebooks tends to be more and more disregarded, since children begin to read themselves. In addition, children get in contact with merely illustrated books, as opposed to a continuous picture/text relationship. The development towards literacy (not only linguistic literacy but also literary and visual literacy) does not happen suddenly, when children enter school, but begins early in their development (Lancaster 2003; Nikolajeva 2003; Snow 2006). Input from children's literature, the situation of shared attention during joint book reading, supports the path into literacy. The acquisition of pragmatic abilities always accompanies and fosters this development.

3 Internal pragmatics: Fictional input

By "internal pragmatics," I mean pragmatic phenomena as part of the input provided by children's literature. Such pragmatic content is also conveyed by books for children in the pre-school age, yet is always presented by an adult mediator in the reading situation. In contrast, with beginning literacy (that is, the ability to read and write) the child is an autonomous recipient of pragmatic input contained in children's literature, although there is a new situation of receiving literature in the classroom.[4] To be sure, children's literature is only a small proportion of the total input in a child's life. However, it is a structured input that supports pragmatic acquisition in a special way. This will be shown with respect to a number of pragmatic phenomena. It is clear that these topics, within the limits of this chapter, can only be shortly touched upon.

First, consider the acquisition of the German simple past (*Präteritum*). This tense is nearly extinct in many varieties of German. It contrasts with the present perfect (*Perfekt*), as shown in the following textbook examples:

(1) *Lola ist gerannt.* (Perfekt)
 Lola is run
 'Lola has run.'

(2) *Lola rannte.* (Präteritum)
 Lola ran
 'Lola ran.'

---

4 That children's literature is used in the classroom is still an exception.

Both tenses share the temporal meaning that the event time is located before the speech time. In picturebooks, German children come across the past tense. By way of applying the maxim of Manner/M-principle (Grice 1989; Levinson 2000) or a similar pragmatic principle (e.g., the principle of contrast, see Clark 1993), it is assumed here that children learn that the past tense is connected to a certain text type, i.e. narration. As Stark (2014, 2016) shows, the distinction between oral and written texts also plays a role. Most importantly, her research shows that adult mediators chose the simple past within the fictional context while they chose the present perfect when talking about the fictional content in the situation of shared attention to the book. This indicates that parents finetune their utterances to oral versus written contexts. Between three and five years of age, children grasp the narrative use associated with the simple past, they are increasingly able to use this tense in their own oral narratives, for example, when re-narrating a story.

Second, consider quotation. In many languages, we find complex systems of direct, indirect, and mixed quotation (Brendel, Meibauer & Steinbach 2011; Bucalić 2007). How these systems can be acquired, is largely unknown. It is assumed here that children's literature is an important input with respect to patterns of quotation that are rare in spoken language. Following Köder (2013), direct quotation is acquired before indirect quotation, and it is used more often than indirect quotation. For German children until four years of age, the most typical verb of saying (verbum dicendi) introducing indirect quotation is Germ. *sagen* ('to say'). Kümmerling-Meibauer and Meibauer (2015d) looked at the different types of quotation in 24 books of the German *Conni* series (Liane Schneider, illustrated by Eva Wenzel-Bürger, published between 1993 and 2009) addressed to children from three to seven years of age. What they found is that there are indeed more direct quotations than indirect quotations in the texts. However, contrary to the expectations of Köder (2013), indirect quotation with the finite verb in second position, as opposed to indirect quotation with the finite verb at the end of the embedded sentence, do not figure prominently in the data.[5]

(3) *Conni sagte: "Ich bin müde."* (direct quotation)
Conni said: "I am tired."
'Conni said: "I am tired."'

(4) *Conni sagte, dass sie müde ist.* (indirect quotation, verb-final)
Conni said that she tired is.
'Conni said that she is tired.'

---

[5] Note that in colloquial German indirect quotation, the indicative is used instead of subjunctive. The acquisition of the subjunctive in reported speech is yet another topic.

(5) *Conni sagte, sie ist* müde. (indirect quotation, verb-second)
Conni said, she is tired.
'Conni said that she is tired.'

In contrast, the texts offer many different verbs of saying and thinking, and, besides quotations of utterances, also many cases of quotations of thoughts. In sum, these findings allow the hypothesis that such texts foster the acquisition of different patterns of quotations, thus enabling the children to learn the syntax, semantics, and pragmatics of quotation. The latter is particularly relevant for constructing literary dialogues and attributing certain properties to literary characters.

Thirdly, consider humor. Humorous children's literature is widespread, yet attempts at explaining the interaction between children's humor acquisition and the specific input given by humorous children's literature are rare. Early acquisition of humor has to do with the detection of incongruity (Martin 2006; Hoicka 2014). The growing vocabulary and the emerging *Theory of Mind* allow children to acquire humor based on word play (for example, ambiguity) as well as humor based on shifting perspectives. Certain types of humor, for example, jokes, are acquired through narration, as Hauser (2005) shows in an empirical study of children telling jokes. Jokes, on the other hand, are also told by literary characters and may serve as a strongly contextualized input for the reading child. Children's literature displays numerous genres and types of humor which can only be enumerated here. For instance, Cross (2011: 11) mentions slapstick and visual comedy humor, oversize characters (caricatures, grotesques, and exaggerations in general), nonsense and situational humor, wordplay, wit and satire, as well as scatological ("bathroom") humor. There are many humorous genres in children's literature, for instance (some) ABC books (Torr and Griffith 2003), funny rhymes in the tradition of Wilhelm Busch or Dr Seuss, as well as comics or novels like *Le petit Nicholas* (Little Nicholas, 1959) by René Goscinny and Jean-Jacques Sempé. In addition, there are many literary characters with humorous traits, for instance anthropomorphized animals such as the boyish chimpanzee Willy in Anthony Browne's picturebooks (see also Kümmerling-Meibauer & Meibauer 2014a). In sum, the interrelation between the pragmatics of humor, both from the side of its acquisition and from the side of children's literature input, needs much more research.

With respect to "junior literature", Cross (2011: 19–20) distinguishes several strategies of "subversive-transgressive" humor. Under this notion, she subsumes the "deliberately transgressive character," "the threat of the strange in nonsensical texts," the "comic grotesque," and "comic irony." Note that some of these types may have precursors in picturebooks; for instance, the second type is connected to Pop Art picturebooks (Kümmerling-Meibauer & Meibauer 2011c). Cross (2011: 16) also stresses that there are "new compounds" of humor in junior books, "formed by the seemingly paradoxical mix of high, complex, cognitive forms of humor, along with lower forms of humor within the same text, and, even more importantly, often within the same humorous stimuli." It goes without saying that these new compounds are a challenge for pragmatic theories of humor.

Now consider the following chapter 13 (preceded by chapter 11 and followed by chapter 17 – mirroring the protagonist's preference of prime numbers) from Mark Haddons's novel *The Curious Incident of the Dog in the Night-Time* (2003: 10).

13
This will not be a funny book. I cannot tell jokes because I do not understand them. Here is a joke, as an example. It is one of father's.

His face was drawn but the curtains were real.

I know why this is meant to be funny. I asked. It is because *drawn* has three meanings, and they are **1)** drawn with a pencil, **2)** exhausted, and **3)** pulled across a window, and meaning **1** refers to both the face and the curtains, meaning **2** refers only to the face, and meaning **3** refers only to the curtains.

If I try to say the joke to myself, making the word mean the three different things at the same time, it is like hearing three different pieces of music at the same time which is uncomfortable and confusing and not nice like white noise. It is like three people trying to talk to you at the same time about different things.

And that is why there are no jokes in this book.

Obviously, the initial statement *This will not be a funny book* is in contrast to the information in the book blurb according to which Mark Haddon's depiction of the hero's world "is deeply moving, very funny and utterly convincing." The book is written from the perspective of a first-person narrator, Christopher Boone, who is fifteen years old and is living in Swindon. While never explicitly mentioned in the text, the reader is informed in the blurb that Christopher has Asperger's, a form of autism.

Basically, the content of the novel is a murder story. Christopher is the detective who wants to find the murderer of a dog. On a deeper level of interpretation the novel illuminates the world of an Asperger's patient, thus stimulating empathy in the adolescent readership. One narrative strategy to reach this goal is humor. For instance, the explanation of the difficulties in understanding jokes (which is associated to autism, see Cummings 2014), is humorous in itself. For the intended readership, it may be pragmatically quite demanding to uncover this specific sort of humor.

For Christopher, it can be difficult to compute complex visual input. In one scene (pp. 208–209), he gets a complex visual input from signs at the airport. Then, "after a few seconds," the assemblage of signs turns into a wild mixture of distorted signs, e.g., *Airport Check-In* turns to *Airpheck-I*. As Caracciolo (2014) shows, this represents the protagonist's state of mind. As Christopher reports, the signs "were too many and my brain wasn't working properly and this frightened me so I closed my eyes again and I counted slowly to 50 but without doing the cubes" (p. 210). Not only has the reader to infer pragmatically (maybe invoking the maxim of Manner) that the second, distorted version represents the protagonist's consciousness, he or she can also become aware that this comes along with humorous elements like "without doing the cubes."

Fourthly, consider the acquisition of metaphor, irony, and idioms. There is some literature on the question of how these meaning phenomena are acquired (Winner 1983; Cacciari and Chiara Levorato 1989; Pouscoulos 2014; Zufferey 2015: 97–116). And again, it is reasonable to say that children's literature provides specific forms of input. Let us focus on the somewhat neglected area of idioms. Through a careful analysis of two novels by Otfried Preußler, namely *Die kleine Hexe* (The Little Witch, 1959), addressed to 6 year-olds, and *Krabat* (1971), addressed to 12 year-olds, Finkbeiner (2011) was able to show that the author applies a pragmatic procedure of making idioms (that may be hard to grasp) understandable for the readership, i.e. to enhance comprehensibility. Finkbeiner (2011: 70) develops and tests three hypotheses. According to the first, "the phraseme types used in picturebooks are semantically and pragmatically rather 'easy' compared to those in adolescent's books." This hypothesis is borne out by the data, as embedded procedures such as accumulation, paraphrase, and modification are more frequent in *Die kleine Hexe*. The second hypothesis says that "the number of phrasemes which are accompanied by procedures of enhancing comprehensibility is higher in children's books than in adolescent's books." Again, this hypothesis is corroborated. What is not proved is the third hypothesis, according to which "the type of enhancement procedures used in children's books is different from the type of enhancement procedures used in adolescent books." By contrast, it seems that the procedures used are quite similar. In particular, the amount of paraphrases is similar in both novels under investigation. In sum, then, children's books provide an input from which idioms can be learned and authors seem to finetune their texts according to the children's needs.

Finally, consider the acquisition of lying as it is related to children's literature (Kümmerling-Meibauer & Meibauer 2011b, 2013; Silva-Díaz 2015). On closer inspection, one finds numerous children's books dealing with lying and deception. There are famous lying characters like Pippi Longstocking or Pinocchio, and there are sophisticated young adult's novels like *I ballong över stilla havet*

(In a Balloon Over the Pacific Ocean, 1994) by Mats Wahl or *Liar* (2009) by Justine Larbalestier. Due to a lack of space, I cannot elaborate on the long-standing tradition to research children's lying acquisition and behavior (see Talwar & Lee 2008; Lee 2013; Talwar forthcoming). Here it must suffice to stress that the acquisition of lying is a process that lasts until adolescence (and thus is similar to the acquisition of irony and metaphor); that it begins early and is connected to the child's emerging *Theory of Mind*; that it is connected to social, cultural, moral, and emotional development; and, on top of it, that it is a normal, healthy development. Children who do not acquire the skill of lying are pragmatically impaired.

Yet, there is a social and cultural impetus to teach children not to lie. Consequently, many narratives on lying have a didactic and moralizing overtone. Recently, researchers asked whether children get the moral message contained in some literary works. Lee et al. (2014) looked at the question whether narratives on lying can promote honesty in children aged three to seven years. They compared the stories of *Pinocchio, The Boy who Cried Wolf,* and *George Washington and the Cherry Tree*, and related them to children's peeking behavior. While the first two stories failed to promote children's lying behavior, the latter significantly increased children's honesty. The authors relate this finding to the content of the stories, since only *George Washington and the Cherry Tree* emphasizes the positive consequences of honesty. When the story was changed with a new focus on the consequences of dishonesty, there was no improvement in honesty.

In Mark Haddon's *The Curious Incident of the Dog in the Night-Time*, lying and deception are crucial for the narrative plot. Christopher Boone is not able to lie: "I do not tell lies. Mother used to say that this was because I was a good person. But this is not because I am a good person. It is because I can't tell lies" (p. 24). Christopher likes dogs because they "are faithful and they do not tell lies because they cannot talk" (p. 4). But he does not like "proper novels, because they are lies about things which didn't happen and they make me feel shaky and scared" (p. 25). Christopher is upset when he learns that his father is lying to him about the death of his mother.

Most probably, a fifteen-year-old reader will take over Christopher's perspective on his parents who care for him, yet are involved in quarrels and arguments. Being a victim of their strategies, Christopher learns to emancipate himself, to focus on his interest in mathematics, and being friend with his mentor Siobhan. Would it be better if Christopher had the normal abilities of lying and deception? The overall answer the novel suggests is that to have "normal" abilities is not really important as long as there is an individual path of development.

We do not know how such demanding stories can influence the pragmatic competence of adolescents. This is a task for experimental pragmatics.

4 Intercultural pragmatics and children's literature

As I have tried to show in the preceding sketch, there is an interface between pragmatics and children's literature that is worthy of further exploration. To take children's literature seriously as a specific input, both in the reading situation and as texts containing pragmatic information, is a worthwhile enterprise, because it fosters our understanding of pragmatic acquisition and thus pragmatics in general. It is obvious, though, that a thorough description of the relation between pragmatics and children's literature is a huge task when it comes to empirical research. We still have no complete theory about the acquisition of pragmatics, and the amount of children's literature that serves as potential input to this process is enormous. From a macropragmatic point of view, social and cultural factors play also a role when studying pragmatics and children's literature, and children's emotional and moral developments also tie in with the pragmatic development as well as the ability to understand fiction.

In addition, the study of pragmatics and children's literature might contribute to the appreciation of children's literature, which is not an inferior or merely didactic kind of literature, but the basis on which to develop more advanced techniques of text interpretation. Most linguists would agree that the study of language acquisition gives us important insights into the question of what language is. By analogy, the study of the acquisition of literary knowledge has much to offer with respect to the question what literature is. This line of reasoning has not been appreciated by literary scholars primarily dealing with works of art addressed to adults.

On a final note, I would like to point to the interface of intercultural pragmatics (cf. Kecskés 2014) and children's literature. According to Kecskés (2014: 14), "intercultural pragmatics is concerned with the way the language system is put to use in social encounters between human beings who have different first languages, communicate in a common language, and, usually, represent different cultures." One typical social encounter is the multiethnic classroom, and it is here where discussion of wordless picturebooks is valuable, because every child – independently of their knowledge in the common language – has equal access to the story told. To reconstruct a story told only by the arrangement of pictures is of course a challenge.

Arizpe, Colomer, and Martínez-Roldán (2014) explored the understanding of the masterpiece *The Arrival* (2006) by Shaun Tan, which is often referred to as a graphic novel, by children from several nations, i.e. the UK, the USA, Spain, and Australia. This book contains black-and-white drawings representing the overwhelming and sometimes frightening impressions and experiences of an immigrant family. The objective of this project was "to explore the responses of immigrant pupils from different backgrounds to wordless picturebooks in order to understand how they construct meaning from visual images in complex narratives about immigration, journeys and the visual image itself (…)" (Arizpe et al. 2014: 64). While the children had to reconstruct the content of the book for themselves, they engaged not only in interpreting the pictures but also in making meaning through retellings and inferences (Arizpe et al. 2014: 123–140). How they do this has not been investigated from a genuine pragmatic point of view; however, it seems to me, there is ample room to research their strategies with respect to their pragmatic skills. Note that this study has been undertaken with a particular intention in mind, namely "the intention of creating strategies that can develop their literacy skills, as well as help them reflect on their own or other's experience of migration" (Arizpe et al. 2014: 64). Hence intercultural pragmatics can study multilanguage interactions in families, in the kindergarten, and in the classroom with respect to the use of children's literature.

References

Arizpe, Evelyn, Teresa Colomer & Carmen Martínez-Roldán 2014. *Visual journeys through wordless narratives. An international inquiry with immigrant children and* The Arrival. London: Bloomsbury.
Bailey, Mary, Colin Harrison & Greg Brooks. 2001. The Boots Books for Babies Project: Impact on Library Registrations and Book Loans. *Journal of Early Childhood Literacy* 2.1. 45–63.
Baron-Cohen, Simon, Ofer Golan, Sally Wheelwright, Yael Granader & Jacqueline Hill. 2010. Emotion Word Comprehension from 4 to 16 Years old: A developmental study. *Frontiers in Evolutionary Neuroscience* 2 (109). 1–8.
Bateman, John A. 2014. *Text and image. A critical introduction to the verbal/visual divide*. London: Routledge.
Bateman, John A. & Janina Wildfeuer. 2014. A multimodal discourse theory of visual narrative. *Journal of Pragmatics* 74. 180–208.
Blewitt, Pamela. 2014. Growing vocabulary in the context of shared book reading. In Bettina Kümmerling-Meibauer, Jörg Meibauer, Kerstin Nachtigäller & Katharina Rohlfing (eds.), *Learning from Picturebooks. Perspectives from child development and literacy studies*, 117–136. London: Routledge.
Brendel, Elke, Jörg Meibauer & Markus Steinbach. 2011. Exploring the Meaning of Quotation. In Elke Brendel, Jörg Meibauer & Markus Steinbach (eds.), *Understanding quotation*, 1–33. Boston & Berlin: De Gruyter Mouton.
Bucalić, Tomislav. 2007. Ein typologischer Beitrag zu Formen der Redewiedergabe. In Elke Brendel, Jörg Meibauer & Markus Steinbach (eds.), *Zitat und Bedeutung*, 45–66. Hamburg: Buske.
Cacciari, Cristina & Maria Chiara Levorato. 1989. How children understand idioms in discourse. *Journal of Child Language* 16. 387–405.

Cairney, Trevor H. 2003. Literacy within Family Life. In Nigel Hall, Joanne Larson & Jackie Marsh (eds.), *Handbook of early childhood literacy*, 85–98. London: Sage.
Caracciolo, Marco. 2014. Punctuating Minds: Non-verbal cues for consciousness representation in literary narrative. *Journal of Literary Semantics* 43 (1). 43–69.
Clark, Eve V. 1993. *The lexicon in acquisition*. Cambridge: Cambridge University Press.
Cross, Julie. 2010. *Humor in contemporary junior literature*. London: Routledge.
Cummings, Louise. 2014. *Pragmatic disorders*. Dordrecht: Springer.
de Geest, Dirk. 2003. Literary Pragmatics. In Jef Verschueren, Jan-Ola Östman, Jan Blommaert & Chris Bulcaen (eds.), *Handbook of pragmatics: Manual*, 351–357. Amsterdam & Philadelphia: John Benjamins.
Evans, Janet (ed.). 2006. *Challenging and controversial picturebooks: Creative and critical responses to visual texts*. London: Routledge.
Finkbeiner, Rita. 2011. Phraseologieerwerb und Kinderliteratur. Verfahren der Verständlichmachung von Phraseologismen im Kinder- und Jugendbuch am Beispiel von Otfried Preußlers *Die kleine Hexe* und *Krabat*. *LiLi. Zeitschrift für Literaturwissenschaft und Linguistik* 162. 47–73.
Fries, Norbert. 2007. Die Kodierung von Emotionen in Texten. Teil 1: Grundlagen. *Journal of Literary Theory* 1 (2). 293–337.
Fries, Norbert. 2009. Die Kodierung von Emotionen in Texten. Teil 2: Die Spezifizierung emotionaler Bedeutung in Texten. *Journal of Literary Theory* 3 (1). 19–72.
Gosen, Myrte N., Jan Berenst & Kees de Glopper. 2015. Shared reading at kindergarten: Understanding book content through participation. *Pragmatics and Society* 6 (3). 367–397.
Gressnich, Eva. 2011. Einführung von Diskursreferenten im Bilderbuch. *LiLi. Zeitschrift für Literaturwissenschaft und Linguistik* 162. 74–92.
Gressnich, Eva & Jörg Meibauer. 2010. First-Person Narratives in Picturebooks. An Inquiry into the Acquisition of Picturebook Competence. In Teresa Colomer, Bettina Kümmerling-Meibauer & María Cecilia Silva-Díaz (eds.), *New directions in picturebook research*, 191–203. London: Routledge.
Grice, Paul. 1989. *Studies in the Way of Words*. Cambridge: Harvard University Press.
Hall, Nigel, Joanne Larson & Jackie Marsh (eds.). 2003. *Handbook of early childhood literacy*. London: Sage.
Hauser, Stefan. 2005. *Wie Kinder Witze erzählen. Eine linguistische Studie zum Erwerb narrativer Fähigkeiten*. Bern: Lang.
Hoicka, Elena. 2014. The pragmatic development of humor. In Danielle Matthews (ed.), *Pragmatic development in first language acquisition*, 219–238. Amsterdam & Philadelphia: John Benjamins.
Huang, Yan. 2012. Introduction: what is pragmatics? In Yan Huang (ed.), *The Oxford dictionary of pragmatics*. 1–19. Oxford: Oxford University Press.
Kauschke, Christina & Gisela Klann-Delius. 1997. The acquisition of verbal expressions for internal states in German. A descriptive, explorative, longitudinal study. In Susanne Niemeier & René Dirven (eds.), *The language of emotions*, 173–194. Amsterdam & Philadelphia: John Benjamins.
Kecskés, István. 2014. *Intercultural pragmatics*. Oxford: Oxford University Press.
Kiefer, Barbara & Melissa I. Wilson. 2011. Nonfiction Literature for Children. Old Assumptions and New Directions. In Shelby A. Wolf, Karen Coats, Patricia Enciso & Christine A. Jenkins (eds.), *Handbook of research on children's and young adult literature*, 290–299. London & New York: Routledge.

Köder, Franziska. 2013. How children acquire reported speech in German and Dutch: a corpus study. *Perspektiven. Diskussionsforum Linguistik in Bayern/Bavarian Working Papers in Linguistics* 2: 15–28. http://epub.ub.uni-muenchen.de/view/subjects/1407. html
Kümmerling-Meibauer, Bettina & Jörg Meibauer. 2011a. Early-concept books: Acquiring nominal and verbal concepts. In Bettina Kümmerling-Meibauer (ed.), *Emergent Literacy. Children's books from 0 to 3*, 91–114. Amsterdam & Philadelphia: John Benjamins.
Kümmerling-Meibauer, Bettina & Jörg Meibauer. 2011b. Lügenerwerb und Geschichten vom Lügen. *LiLi. Zeitschrift für Literaturwissenschaft und Linguistik* 162. 118–138.
Kümmerling-Meibauer, Bettina & Jörg Meibauer, Jörg. 2011c. On the Strangeness of Pop Art Picturebooks: Pictures, Texts, Paratexts. *New Review of Children's Literature and Librarianship* 17. 103–121.
Kümmerling-Meibauer, Bettina & Jörg Meibauer. 2013. Towards a Cognitive Theory of Picturebooks. *International Research in Children's Literature* 6 (2). 143–160.
Kümmerling-Meibauer, Bettina & Jörg Meibauer. 2014a. Understanding the Matchstick Man. Aesthetic and Narrative Properties of a Hybrid Picturebook Character. In Bettina Kümmerling-Meibauer (ed.), *Picturebooks: Representation and narration*, 139–161. London: Routledge.
Kümmerling-Meibauer, Bettina & Jörg Meibauer. 2015a. Maps in Picturebooks. Cognitive status and narrative functions. *Nordic Journal of Children's Literature Aesthetics/ Barnelitterært forskningstidsskrift* (BLFT) 5. http://dx.doi.org/10.3402/blft.v6.26970
Kümmerling-Meibauer, Bettina & Jörg Meibauer. 2015b. Beware of the fox! Emotion and deception in *Fox* by Margaret Wild and Ron Brooks. In Janet Evans (ed.), *Challenging and controversial picturebooks: Creative and critical responses to visual texts*, 144–159. London: Routledge.
Kümmerling-Meibauer, Bettina & Jörg Meibauer. 2015c. Picturebooks and early literacy. How do picturebooks support early conceptual development? In Bettina Kümmerling-Meibauer, Jörg Meibauer, Kerstin Nachtigäller & Katharina Rohlfing (eds.), *Learning from Picturebooks. Perspectives from child development and literacy studies*, 13–32. London: Routledge.
Kümmerling-Meibauer, Bettina & Jörg Meibauer. 2015d. Vorlese-Input und Redewiedergabe. In *Sprachliches Lernen durch Vorlesen*, Claudia Müller, Eva Gressnich & Linda Stark (eds.), 15–33. Tübingen: Francke.
Kümmerling-Meibauer, Bettina, Jörg Meibauer, Kerstin Nachtigäller & Katharina Rohlfing. (eds.). 2015. *Learning from picturebooks. Perspectives from child development and literacy studies*. London: Routledge.
Lancaster, Lesley. 2003. Moving into Literacy: How it All Begins. In Nigel Hall, Joanne Larson & Jackie Marsh (eds.), *Handbook of early childhood literacy*, 145–153. London: Sage.
Lee, Kang. 2013. Little liars. Development of verbal deception in children. *Child development perspective* 7. 91–96.
Lee, Kang, Victoria Talwar, Anjani McCarthy, Ilana Ross, Angela Evans & Cindy Arruda. 2014. Can classic moral stories promote honesty in children? *Psychological Science*, 1–7.
Levinson, Stephen C. 2000. *Presumptive meanings. The theory of generalized conversational implicature*. Cambridge, MA: MIT Press.
Martin, Rod A. 2006. *The psychology of humour: An integrative approach*. New York: Academic Press.
Matthews, Danielle (ed.). 2014. *Pragmatic development in first language acquisition*. Amsterdam & Philadelphia: John Benjamins.

Meibauer, Jörg. 2011. Spracherwerb und Kinderliteratur. *LiLi. Zeitschrift für Literaturwissenschaft und Linguistik* 162. 11–28.
Meibauer, Jörg. 2015. What the child can learn from simple descriptive picturebooks. An inquiry into *Lastwagen/Trucks* by Paul Stickland. In Bettina Kümmerling-Meibauer, Jörg Meibauer, Kerstin Nachtigäller & Katharina Rohlfing (eds.), *Learning from Picturebooks. Perspectives from child development and literacy studies*, 51–70. London: Routledge.
Mey, Jacob L. 2000. *When voices clash. A study in literary pragmatics*. Berlin & New York Mouton de Gruyter.
Mey, Jacob L. 2001. Literary pragmatics. In Deborah Schiffrin, Deborah Tannen & Heidi E. Hamilton (eds.), *The handbook of discourse analysis*, 787–797. Oxford: Blackwell, 787–797.
Miller, Scott A. 2012. *Theory of mind: Beyond the preschool years*. New York & Hove: Psychology Press.
Moerk, Ernst L. 1985. Picture-Book Reading by Mothers and Young Children and its Impact upon Language Development. *Journal of Pragmatics* 9. 547–566.
Moschovaki, Eleni & Sara Meadows. 2015. Affective interaction during classroom picture-book reading. In Bettina Kümmerling-Meibauer, Jörg Meibauer, Kerstin Nachtigäller & Katharina Rohlfing (eds.), *Learning from picturebooks. Perspectives from child development and literacy studies*, 156–178. London: Routledge.
Murphy, Catherine M. 1978. Pointing in the context of a shared activity. *Child Development* 49. 371–380.
Nikolajeva, Maria. 2003. Verbal and visual literacy: The role of picturebooks in the reading experience of young children. In Nigel Hall, Joanne Larson & Jackie Marsh (eds.), *Handbook of early childhood literacy*, 235–248. London: Sage.
Nikolajeva, Maria. 2014. *Reading for learning. Cognitive approaches to children's literature*. Amsterdam & Philadelphia: John Benjamins.
O'Sullivan, Emer. 2010. Introduction. In Emer O'Sullivan, *Historical dictionary of children's literature*, 1–13. Lanham, Toronto & Plymouth: The Scarecrow Press.
Painter, Clare, J.R. Martin & Len Unsworth. 2013. *Reading visual narratives. Image analysis of children's picture books*. Sheffield: Equinox.
Pouscoulous, Nausicaa. 2014. "The elevator's buttocks": Metaphorical abilities in children. In Danielle Matthews (ed.), *Pragmatic development in first language acquisition*, 239–260. Amsterdam & Philadelphia: John Benjamins.
Rémi, Cornelia. 2011. Reading as Playing: The Cognitive Challenge of the Wimmelbook. In Bettina Kümmerling-Meibauer (ed.), *Emergent literacy. Children's books from 0 to 3*, 115–140. Amsterdam & Philadelphia: John Benjamins.
Rohlfing, Katharina, Angela Grimminger & Katharina Nachtigäller. 2015. Gesturing in joint book reading. In Bettina Kümmerling-Meibauer, Jörg Meibauer, Kerstin Nachtigäller & Katharina Rohlfing (eds.), *Learning from picturebooks. Perspectives from child development and literacy studies*, 99–116. London: Routledge.
Sell, Roger D. (ed.). 1991. *Literary pragmatics*. London: Routledge.
Sell, Roger D. (ed.). 2002. *Children's literature as communication. The ChiLPA Project*. Amsterdam & Philadelphia: John Benjamins.
Silva-Díaz, María Cecilia. 2015. Picturebooks, lies and mindreading. *Nordic Journal of ChildLit Aesthetics* 6. http://dx.doi.org/10.3402/blft.v6.26972
Snow, Catherine E. and Beverly A. Goldfield. 1983. Turn the page please: situation specific language acquisition. *Journal of Child Language* 10. 531–569.

Snow, Catherine. 2006. What Counts as Literacy in Early Childhood? In Kathleen McCartney & Deborah Philips (eds.), *Blackwell handbook of early childhood development*, 274–294. Oxford: Blackwell.

Stark, Linda. 2015. Tense acquisition with picturebooks. In Bettina Kümmerling-Meibauer, Jörg Meibauer, Kerstin Nachtigäller & Katharina Rohlfing (eds.), *Learning from picturebooks. Perspectives from child development and literacy studies*, 209–227. London: Routledge.

Stark, Linda. 2016. *Vorlesen und Präteritum*. Baltmannsweiler: Schneider Verlag Hohengehren.

Talwar, Victoria. Forthcoming. Development of lying and cognitive abilities. In Jörg Meibauer (ed.), *Oxford handbook of lying*. Oxford: Oxford University Press.

Talwar, Victoria & Kang Lee. 2008. Social and Cognitive Correlates of Children's Lying Behavior. *Child Development* 79. 866–881.

Torr, Jane & Lynn Clugston. 1999. A Comparison between Informational and Narrative Picture Books as a Context for Reasoning between Caregivers and 4-year-old Children. *Early Child Development and Care* 159 (1). 25–41.

Torr, Jane & Kathlyn Griffith. 2003. An Analysis of Children's Alphabet Books: Exploring the Role Played by Nonsense in the Construction of Meaning between Text and Implied Reader. In John McKenzie, Doreen Darnell & Anna Smith (eds.), *Cinderella transformed: Multiple voices and diverse dialogues in children's literature*, 8–15. Christchurch: Centre for Children's Literature.

Warner, Chantelle. 2014. Literary pragmatics and stylistics. In Michael Burke (ed.), *Routledge handbook of stylistics*, 362–377. London & New York: Routledge.

Winner, Ellen. 1988. *The point of words: Children's understanding of metaphor and irony*. Cambridge, MA: MIT Press.

Yont, Kristine M., Catherine E. Snow & Lynne Vernon-Feagans. 2003. The role of context in mother-child interactions: An analysis of communicative intents expressed during toy play and book reading with 12-months-olds. *Journal of Pragmatics* 35. 435–211.

Zufferey, Sandrine. 2015. *Acquiring pragmatics. Social and cognitive perspectives*. London: Routledge.

Jacob L. Mey
21 Unloading the weapon: Act and tact

> "Because what happened was, he turned them [the words, JM] into weapons"
> (Cynthia Voigt, *Sons from afar*, p. 249)

1 Introduction: Of farmers and ducklings

In his 1980 book *Language, the loaded weapon*, the late Harvard professor of Romance linguistics, Dwight L. Bolinger (1902–1992), created a metaphor that was to become successful beyond the author's expectations. The book contains a reasoned and (in context of his work and times) rather spectacular critique of many contemporary linguists who only had an eye on 'the language', without taking into account any of the factors we today have come to group under the heading of 'pragmatics': to wit, the active interest of the participants in the linguistic dialogue; the societal conditions under which the participants operate; the ulterior consequences of their linguistic interactions in what is often called 'sequentiality'; Mey 2013, 2015); the pre-requirements that have to be set up before any successful interaction can happen; the wider societal background of linguistic interaction; and not least, the hidden ordinance that any language user drags with him or her to the linguistic battlefield, where all the weapons indeed are 'loaded'.

Let me expatiate a little bit on the metaphor itself. I will not criticize its perhaps overly militaristic allure; after all, violent and war-related metaphors were (and are still) current in American linguistic exemplification; the most famous instance is perhaps found in Edward Sapir's classic treatise *Language: An Introduction to the Study of Speech*: "the farmer killed the duckling" (Sapir 1921: 91) – a sentence copied *de rigueur* in any textbook of structural linguistics from the 1930 until the present day (Leonard Bloomfield's 1933 *Language* is but one instance). The example was already at the time singled out for critique by colleagues, critics, and animal lovers for its bloody implications; similarly, many years later, a new generation of linguists pilloried this skewed interest in blood and gore by taking the metaphor to its ultimate consequences, producing an example such as "Lyndon B. Johnson is an imperialist butcher", thereby bringing the political and the militarist aspects of the example together under the aegis of a self-proclaimed politically correct stance (the example is originally due to James McCawley 1968: 157).

With the advent of 'flower power' at about the same time, and its various ideological offshoots, a concept such as the 'new' (understood as 'soft, gentle, non-violent') male,[1] became emblematic for a 'new' (but not exclusively male) social consciousness: one that moved out of the 'rat race' of prestige, money, and career, and turned toward a greater appreciation of, and participation in, what earlier were dubbed 'female' chores and responsibilities: around the house, in the kitchen, with the (young and very young) children, in discussion groups and so on. The much-reviled 'group pedagogy' was one of the ways to organize and discuss these activities in a school setting, much to the dismay, then and now, of more traditionally oriented educators, including many grade school teachers, and the then Danish Minister of Education and Culture, the often reviled Bertel Haarder, who roundly rejected what they despised as *rundkredspædagogik*, 'pedagogy in the round' (teachers and students all sitting on the floor of the classroom in one big circle).[2]

2 The hidden dimension – full disclosure

Let's for a moment examine the 'loading' metaphor in more detail and see how it applies to language. If you load a weapon, you must put something in it to shoot. This applies both to the old blunderbuss, where the loading happened up front, to the modern Kalashnikov, where one just inserts a clip and is ready to continue one's shooting spree; the general idea being that something (a bullet) is placed in a hidden location (the magazine), ready to be ejected at a high velocity, with damaging effects on the objects or persons it is supposed to hit.

Full disclosure: I admit to having been fascinated, as a young boy, by the various kinds of weapons that were on display, either as souvenirs of battles or as working implements of destruction, in the homes of my parents' friends and relatives. I was always told not to touch those objects, and thereby implicitly admonished that such an interest was not appropriate. This was in my parents' vaguely socialist period, when they were pacifists and sometimes vegetarians; I do not think their attitudes changed that much though when they became Catholics of the, respectively, ardent (my mother), and lukewarm kind (my dad). I also recall how my highest desires regarding birthday presents were consistently rejected: a miniature cannon that would fire real (rubber) bullets, or an air gun. The latter I finally obtained, on the condition that I only fire at lifeless objects

---

[1] Compare the Danish expression den *bløde mand*, 'the soft man'.
[2] Most recently (December 2016), Minister Haarder became again 'past', when his party, the neo-liberal *Venstre*, sacrificed him in an effort to include members from other right-wing parties in their minority government.

such as empty cans or bottles, whereas my hunting instincts told me that the true fun of shooting was to try to hit something that moves.

With that in mind, I will now look at 'words as weapons'.

3 Loaded words

If words are considered weapons, this means that they are intended to maim and kill (either in self-defense or in aggression). It also includes a reference to the hidden character of the projectile that was mentioned above: one never knows whether or not a weapon is loaded until one has inspected, or (maybe accidentally, with fatal results) fired it. Now what do we observe when we look at our words from this perspective?

The expression 'loaded' itself has, of course, also metaphorical implications. Compare the case when a car dealer tries to sell you an old jalopy that he says is 'loaded' (meaning that the accessories and gadgets outweigh the perhaps less desirable mechanical state the car is in). Alternatively, consider a father coming back 'loaded' from his weekly visit to the pub; an older form of the verb, the partly obsolete past participle 'laden', is now only used in the positive sense of 'dad coming home laden' with Christmas presents for the family.

The next questions to ask in our case are then: what is loaded onto (or into) the words, and who does the loading?

4 'Plus' and 'minus' words

Words can be loaded either positively or negatively: they may convey a negative evaluation, like when I call a used car an 'old jalopy', or they can reflect a more optimistic view of the same vehicle, now dubbed 'a pre-owned (but loaded) automobile'. In cases such as these, the origin of the 'loading' is clear: we choose our expressions in accordance with what we think is to our best advantage in the current situation (here: a salesman trying to sell an older automobile). We prefer positively laden expressions (the 'plus' words) to the negative, 'minus', or even the 'neutral' wording, dependent on the situation of use.

But how about when our choice of words unwittingly reproduces a (positive or negative) viewpoint, an attitude, a prejudice? Or if the expression chosen actually encapsulates, or even repeats, a bit of social history, without us ever thinking of it? Take such 'plus' words as 'reform' or change'. On top of their original content, having to do with alteration in a certain state of affairs or world condition), they convey the impression of a positive possibility, a chance: something that not only is a theoretical option, but a valuable, maybe even the only alternative.

In his 2011 Presidential campaign, Barack Obama, in his use of the notions of 'change' and 'hope' (like in "A change we can believe in" – an expression dutifully embraced by his adherents and supporters both at home in the US and overseas), stressed the need for 'change', but never really specified in detail what the change was all about. As for Denmark, local 'reforms' are often expressed via the incessantly repeated mantra of a 'tax reform' whose only effect is to increase the tax burden on the individual citizen, or promoted by expressions like the infamous 2007 misnomer *kommunalreform*, lit. 'local government reform', which drastically reduced the number of cities and townships in Denmark from 271 to a mere 98, with all its negative (but few positive) effects on the general population in the form of fewer and less efficient services and reduced citizen input and influence. On these and other supposedly beneficial changes (read: bureaucratic retoolings instigated by governments to serve their own purposes), nobody is in doubt that they are not for the good: they mostly involve a serious deterioration in quality of life for the individuals whose living and working conditions have been dramatically changed (longer commutes, radical transplantation of families, disruption of social networks and local environments, and so on); for the communities as a whole, the changes involve greater distance to the centers of power, hampered access to the decision makers on the local level, less control with services such as education, transportation, care for the sick and elderly, to name a few.

As early as the 1980s, the late Swedish author Lars Gustafsson used to satirize imminent changes in postal service provided in his country. These (all negative) changes were camouflaged by the use of 'plus' words like 'progress' (Swed. *framsteg*) and 'streamlining' (Swed. *rationalisering*), whereas in reality they represented a deterioration (*försämring*) and should be called that (as when the local post office is closed down and customers are referred to a window in a nearby supermarket, manned by one of the store's mostly junior sales assistants – a tendency that became common also in Denmark a decade or so later). Similar to the 'tax cuts' that never resulted in a reduced tax burden for anybody except the rich, and the 'education reforms' that mostly led to a general lowering of the level of teaching and reduced life prospects for teachers and students, the use of 'plus' words illustrates the hidden effect of 'loading' one's linguistic weapons with apparently innocuous, but highly dangerous ordnance.

5 Know thy adversary

Just as it is useful (or even necessary) to know one's opponent when one is engaged in real battle, so, too, is it obligatory in verbal dispute to take stock of the other's verbal weaponry and ascertain its brand and origin. Knowing where the words have come from (the origin of the verbal weaponry and ammunition) may be helpful here; but much more important is a thorough understanding of how those words embody the real (but hidden) intentions of one's interlocutors. Words always reflect real stances, even if the latter are hidden or obscured; one's verbal stance is symptomatic for one's position in the world, even if it may take some effort and experience to decode the hidden, underlying reality. The reason why we try to avoid sexist or racist language is precisely that we want to avoid the use of such terminology as 'weaponry' in the verbal struggle; conversely, the use of sexually or racially tainted words (think 'broad' or 'kike') indexes our minds as being in need of a purge (like the old-fashioned schoolmarm's order to 'go wash one's mouth with soap' when one had uttered a 'no-word'). Hence, an effort to avoid using such expressions also makes it clear to our interlocutors where we stand on important matters such as gender-based discrimination, racial (in)equality, societal privilege and so on.

Since in our capitalist society, accumulation is still 'Moses and the Prophets', as Karl Marx once expressed it,[3] everything we say and do is (consciously or subconsciously) affected by this principle. Accumulation, manifested as our desire to maximize everything, steers not only our thinking in terms of profit ('what's in it for me?'); in our daily lives of supermarket-driven thinking and practice, 'more' is always considered better than 'less'. (Just consider how the neutral, unmarked order of presentation of items in a list is always top-down, with the biggest items placed on top, or mentioned first in a presentation; only in very special circumstances do we invert this order, e.g. to enhance tension, as in the presentation of the Oscar awards).

This also entails that in all our activities (specifically, in our use of language), there is a trend towards maximizing our verbal capital; and just like in the 'real' world of capital, we do this at the expense of the other agents, our interlocutors. As a consequence, while many a conversation may appear as verbal cooperation in the sense of Grice, in reality it may represent a struggle for power; rather than cooperating, we are fighting battles with words. Once we realize this potential (not always intended) duplicity, we not only try to be more circumspect in our own use of language, but will also try to 'unload' the other persons' weapons. This involves taking out, or ignoring, the potential 'sting' of the others' words

---

3 "Accumulate, accumulate! This is Moses and the Prophets!" (Marx 1974: ch. 24 sec. 3)

and conversely, endeavoring to make our own language at least neutral, but preferably positively oriented towards our partners in conversation: a language that is directed towards creating or maintaining the positive 'face' that politeness theorists have identified as one of the major paths to a mutually satisfying conversational interaction.

In all of this, there seems to be one aspect that is often overlooked, and this will be the subject of the next section.

6 Ways with words: Tact, tone, and gestures

There is more to language than just words. Research in comparative sociolinguistics has shown that so-called 'extra-linguistic' features like prosody and body movement often are very different from culture to culture; moreover, they are hard to internalize by adults whose basic language acquisition has been completed. What in one culture counts as respect (e.g. keeping silent in a congregation of one's seniors) may in another culture be interpreted as a sign of hauteur, disinterest, or even disagreement (the old adage *qui tacet consentit*, for instance, is strictly valid only in the languaculture in which it was conceived: 'cultured' speech among the Classical Roman senatorial class and its dependents).

From our very early childhood on, we all have been instructed in how to manage the expressed and unexpressed (sometimes even contradictory or irrational) niceties of conversational interaction. Since politeness and tact were the virtues most often lacking in our early, spontaneous management of language, we had to be expressly taught to say 'thank you' to an aunt whose worthless birthday gift we'd rather be without; or, if we had to leave the table to perform what we felt was a natural function, but for the adults was surrounded by all sorts of inhibitions, we had to ask for permission, using our 'nice voice'; and to avoid embarrassing potential touchy overhearers, we preferably had to use another language, in this way circumventing the adults' speaking taboos. And thus it came about that the very first French sentence I learned to say at the age of 6 was *"puis je m'absenter?"* [can I leave?] – a standard formula whose proper morphemic analysis had to wait until much later, when I finally got familiar with the language itself.

That tabooized words and 'dangerous' speech acts have to be 'massaged' or 'hidden' in order to be effective, is something that we all are familiar with; yet, this fact has not received the attention it deserves in the official literature on speech acting. More interesting perhaps, in relation to gestures, is the observation that speech acts must be appropriately formulated; conversely, gestures must be commensurate with the speech act they express or accompany. A classical demonstration is due to my late friend Karl-Erich Heidolph, of the (then East) German *Zentralinstitut für Sprachwissenschaft* in (East) Berlin, who during a lunch break illustrated the need of having the proper 'tone' to one's speech acts by bringing down his fist on the luncheon table while exclaiming '*Vielleicht!*' ['Perhaps!]

Also, as is well known, a good wish or congratulation proffered in a tombstone voice rather misses the point; a 'friendly' offer made with a deprecatory intonation is likely not to be gladly accepted; and smiles can be used to validate or reinforce, or conversely nullify and void whatever speech act they are accompanying (here I'm not talking about the universal 'cheesy' smile that is often seen on photographs made 'on demand', and was even stipulated as desirable on certain official documents such as passports: "The State Department welcomes a relaxed, smiling face", as it used to read in the *Instructions for Applying for a US Passport*).

While a lot has been done studying the realm of gestures and facial expressions as accompaniments to speech acting, very little has been written about these expressive features in their own rights. Yet (to remain in the metaphorical micro-universe of this paper), as weapons, these non-verbal features are as effective and lethal as are the bullets we gather in our secret verbal armories, to be released when the occasion presents itself – in fact, they are even more effective, precisely because they remain hidden.

Recall the case of the famous British cricketer who was given three months' quarantine because of a shrug produced in response to the referee's determining him 'LBW' during a match at Lords'? In a personal remembrance, I recall how I almost got myself arrested one day in 1943, when I had heard Winston Churchill's famous announcement on the BBC Home Service (illegally monitored by me at home in the coal cellar, for fear of the German reprisal): "I can now formally announce to the House the end of the campaign in North Africa". I was walking the family dog past the German sentries standing guard next to our house (where they had occupied the adjacent private High School), when I was suddenly stopped by a German guard and asked to explain why I was smiling to myself. The soldier rightly surmised that I had been listening to an 'enemy broadcast' (actually a capital offense during the occupation), but not being a linguist, he was unable to prove the connection – even though my (pragmatic) act of 'triumphant assertion' was valid enough in itself, perhaps thanks to my 'Duchenne smile'.[4]

---

[4] A 'cheesy' smile (as when one says 'cheese' in response to the photographer's admonition) is often described as "a smile that doesn't reach the eyes" (Mayle 1997: 35). By contrast, the smile that does reach the eyes is technically termed a 'Duchenne smile' (named for the French psychologist Guillaume Duchenne; 1806–1875). For the concept of 'pragmatic act', see Mey 2001, chapter 8.

7 Conclusion

> The hidden knowledge of act and tact, or
> 'How to succeed in language without really trying'

What we should learn from the above is that a word seldom comes alone: it is always wrapped in history, in our past, present, and future situations of use. In the word's use, the speaker's entire situation is compromised: speech, body movements, personal feelings, social ties. No matter how much we try to 'sanitize' our words, making them into abstract representations à la Leibniz' *characteristica universalis*, or into symbolic renderings as in Frege's (1879) *Begriffsschrift*, our history, with all it implies, will show through (and the more so, the more efforts we spend in covering it up). Conversely, accepting and mastering one's 'historical' expression, emotional, social, facial, and bodily, is one of the major factors in successful communication, to the extent that popular wisdom (as propagated in airline magazine advertisements) tells us that '95 % of your message is body talk, and only 5 % is accounted for by the words'.

Recent research on gestures has emphasized the importance of such 'body talk'; what I still miss is a consistent and exhaustive investigation into the ways in which particular speech acts and other communicative features (such as intonation or body movements) interact in loading (or unloading, as the case may be) our verbal ordnance. A theoretical framework for such an approach has been suggested in the form of the concept of the 'pragmeme': a superordinate notion meant to encompass precisely, in addition to the speech phenomena themselves, the pragmatic acts that we all are accustomed to use even without being aware of it, along with their historic implications (in the sense defined above).

In this connection, it is useful to remind oneself that the original concept of 'tact', mentioned earlier as a supernomer for everything that facilitates communication between people 'without really trying', goes back to the Latin verb for 'feel, touch': *tangere* (in particular, its related substantive, *tactus*). 'Feeling' our interlocutors includes not only the need to 'feel them out', as the popular saying goes, but more importantly, to 'have a feeling' for the situation in its entire historic complexity: what is conducive to the speech acting in question, what is not, and in particular, how can we 'touch base' with our respondents while we avoid to 'hurt their feelings'.

And finally: note that I'm not advocating a 'feel-good' pragmatics that is devoid of real, history-based social and linguistic content. I only want to indicate here some of the ways in which we can put our 'hidden knowledge' of situations and people to work in the service of communication – a project that has been close to István Kecskés' heart for the entire time I have had the privilege of working with him on his various, eminently successful projects (the journal

Intercultural Pragmatics comes to mind, as do the other initiatives he undertook or inspired in order to extend the theoretical findings and practical results of our common pragmatic endeavors across several continents – most conspicuously in his founding of the American Pragmatics Association, AMPRA, a decade or so ago).

Hearkening back to the motto at the beginning of this piece, then, rather than turning words into weapons, István Kecskés, by unloading those weapons, repurposing our linguistic swords into useful tilling tools (Isaiah 2:4), is making us all into better ploughmen and –women of the verbal fields. May the septuagenarian István's intellectual prowess, contagious enthusiasm, and dogged persistence continue to serve our community well in the years and decades to come!

References

Bloomfield, Leonard. 1933. *Language*. Chicago: University of Chicago Press.
Bolinger, Dwight L. 1980. *Language, the loaded weapon: the use and abuse of language today*. London & New York: Longman.
Frege, Gottlob. 1879. *Begriffsschrift: eine der Mathematik nachgebildete Formelsprache des reinen Denkens*. Halle a.d.S.: Louis Nebert.
Marx, Karl. 1974 [1867]. *Capital*. Vol. 1: *A Critical Analysis of Capitalist Production*. London: Lawrence & Wishart.
Mayle, Peter. 1997. *Chasing Cézanne*. New York: Vintage Books.
McCawley, James D. 1968. The role of semantics in grammar. In Emmon Bach & Robert T. Harms (eds.), *Universals in linguistic theory*, 125–169. New York: Holt, Rinehart & Winston.
Mey, Jacob L. 2001. *Pragmatics: An introduction* (2nd edn). Oxford: Blackwell.
Mey, Jacob L. 2013. The well-timed speech act: Bourrée for Bache. *A Rule of Thumb: For Carl Bache. RASK: International Journal of Language and Linguistics* 38. 265–278.
Mey, Jacob L. 2015. Sequentiality and follow-ups. In Anita Fetzer, Elda Weizman & Lawrence N. Berlin (eds.), *The dynamics of political discourse: Forms and functions of follow-ups*, 17–32. Amsterdam & Philadelphia: John Benjamins.
Sapir, Edward. 1921. *Language: An introduction to the study of speech*. New York: Norton.
Voigt, Cynthia. 1987. *Sons from afar*. New York: Simon & Schuster.

Kepa Korta
22 The meanings and contents of aesthetic statements

1 Introduction

Suppose that, after watching a movie, Peter and Carole have the following conversation:

(1) Peter: It's beautiful.

(2) Carole: No, it's not.

They have different opinions; that seems quite clear. But do they disagree? Do they actually contradict each other? If they do, *prima facie*, one statement is true, the other is false; and, therefore, either Peter is right and Carole is wrong, or vice versa.

There is, however, another way to interpret (1) and (2). Admittedly, Peter and Carole seem to disagree, but they do not *really*. They are just expressing different personal tastes and, as the famous maxim says, *De gustibus non disputandum est* ('in matters of taste, there can be no disputes'). Peter liked the movie, Carole did not. There is no contradiction here. If they are talking sincerely, as expressions of their personal tastes, both statements are true, if they are statements at all.

And there is a still different take on Peter and Carole's exchange. Admitting that in uttering (1) and (2) Peter and Carole disagree and contradict each other (i.e., that Peter asserts that p, and Carole that not p), it may be maintained that both statements can be true (or false), because their truth (falsity) is relative to a perspective or a context assessment.

This last approach, usually presented under the label of "relativism", has been forcefully defended by Kölbel (2003), MacFarlane (2007), and Lassersohn (2005), among others, for dealing with cases of what they call "faultless disagreement".

The debate concerns various kinds of issues with impacts at different levels that are often entangled. First, there are the metaphysical issues as to whether there are any objective aesthetic facts out there, any real property called "beautiful", for instance, present or absent in the objects in the world. Aesthetic realists would reply affirmatively, but different types of subjectivism or inter-subjectivism seem to prevail among the participants in the debate about faultless disagreements. Perhaps David Hume's ambivalence on the topic has had its influence here.[1] Perhaps Kölbel's argument that realist approaches are incompatible with the existence of faultless disagreements has had a greater impact recently. I take a different route. I broadly adopt a realist approach on aesthetic properties, fundamentally inspired by Peter Kivy's work on aesthetics and the philosophy of art, and, especially, by his recent monograph *De Gustibus* (2015). I do not present an argument for aesthetic realism, but I hope that, at the end, this realist approach, though somewhat sketchy and programmatic, provides a reasonable account of what we are talking and disputing about when we talk and dispute about art.

The debate on faultless disagreements involves epistemological and normative issues about the concepts of truth, assertion and rejection, which, no doubt, have notable sophistication and interest in themselves, but which need not be dealt with from our perspective. We should note, anyhow, that much of the debate has been about so-called "predicates of personal taste" like "delicious" or "tasty", and that aesthetic predicates like "beautiful" have been included in the list without further argument, when not directly excluded (by Lasersohn 2005, for instance) to avoid entering into "fundamental issues" in aesthetics. My strategy is different. I adopt a clear position regarding some of those fundamental issues in aesthetics, trying to clarify what is at stake when people (philosophers of art, art-critics, and art lovers in general) make different claims about the beauty of an artwork.

The aim of this essay, then, is not to enter directly into the discussion of the best semantic and/or epistemological account of faultless disagreements about taste, but to discuss the meaning, content and use of utterances of the form "X is beautiful" when X denotes a particular work of art.

To do that, I draw, on the one hand, from aesthetics and the philosophy of art, broadly adopting Peter Kivy's aesthetic realism about aesthetic properties as well as his distinction between the analysis, the interpretation, and the evaluation of artworks as presented in his recent work *De Gustibus* (2015). And, on

---

[1] In "Of the Standard of Taste", Hume initially presents a radical subjective view on taste:

> Beauty is no quality in things themselves: It exists merely in the mind which contemplates them; and each mind perceives a different beauty. One person may even perceive deformity, where another is sensible of beauty; and every individual ought to acquiesce in his own sentiment, without pretending to regulate those of others. (Hume 1987 [1757]: 230)

However, he immediately watered this extreme subjectivism down and pointed to inter-subjectivist standards when he claimed that "the joint verdict" of "the true judge[s] in the finer arts" – who are characterized by "strong sense, united to delicate sentiment, improved by practice, perfected by comparison, and cleared of all prejudice – is the true standard of taste and beauty" (Hume [1987 [1757]: 241]).

the other hand, I also consider McNally and Stojanovic's (forthcoming) groundbreaking work on aesthetic adjectives and, in particular, on the term "beautiful" (see also Liao, McNally, and Meshin [2016] and Sundell [2016]).

I focus on utterances of declarative sentences of the form "X is beautiful" (when X is used to refer to an artwork), which, for convenience, I call "aesthetic assertions". Among aesthetic assertions, we should distinguish between aesthetic *judgments* and aesthetic or artistic *appraisals* (or *verdicts*). The former belongs to the *analysis* of the artwork and by "beautiful" we denote a certain aesthetic property of it. The latter belongs to the *evaluation* of the artwork and "beautiful" behaves as a purely evaluative term, roughly equivalent to "aesthetically or artistically good"; a property that all artworks share qua artworks, if they are aesthetically or artistically successful. In this essay, I clarify the difference between these two senses of "beautiful" and the corresponding difference between judgments and appraisals, and I show how these distinctions help us to understand the content of our disputes about artworks, and the extent to which our disagreements constitute cases of genuine or merely apparent disagreements or, perhaps, disagreements without fault. I also show that the meaning and content of aesthetic assertions involving the predicate "beautiful" and other aesthetic predicates, as employed by philosophers of art, art critics and art lovers in general, is even more complex than what current studies of the semantics and pragmatics of aesthetic adjectives may initially suggest.

To motivate the discussion, I start, in the next section, by showing a real example of a public disagreement on a recent movie between a film critic for *The Guardian* and a writer and regular contributor for *The Observer* – Peter Bradshaw and Carole Cadwalladr, respectively. They did not utter anything as explicit as (1) and (2), but it is fair to attribute that sort of exchange to them. Then, in section 3, I summarize the results of McNally and Stojanovic's (forthcoming) analysis of "beautiful" that, as we shall see, fall short of explaining the two main senses or uses of the predicate in aesthetic or artistic discourse: its sense or use in aesthetic analysis (where the assertions constitute judgments), on the one hand, and its sense or use in aesthetic or artistic evaluation (where they constitute aesthetic or artistic appraisals), on the other. These uses or senses are introduced in section 4. As the careful reader may have surely noticed, I use a systematic disjunction when talking about aesthetic *or* artistic appraisals. Section 5, which deals with the *interpretation* of artworks, explains why. I also keep using a cautious disjunction between "sense" and "use" of "beautiful". The reason for that tedious "or" is my current agnosticism as to what is the best way to linguistically deal with the distinction. Although I consider various options in the seventh and last section, more investigation is needed, I think, to reach more solid conclusions.

As I have said, the characters in our initial example, Peter and Carole, are based on real people: Peter Bradshaw, a film critic, and Carole Cadwalladr, a writer. They both wrote in *The Guardian* about the same movie, Alejandro González Iñárritu's *The Revenant*, shortly after its opening in Europe. They seemed to disagree. Judge for yourself.

2 Reviewing *The Revenant*

González Iñárritu's film is based on the true story of Hugh Glass, a fur trapper of the 19th century American West (portrayed by Leonardo DiCaprio) who is attacked by a bear and undergoes an incredible story of survival and revenge.

Of course, Bradshaw (2015) and Cadwalladr (2016) did not write anything as simple as (1) or (2).[2] The titles of their pieces, however, make clear their difference of opinion:

> Bradshaw: "The Revenant review – gut-churningly brutal, beautiful storytelling".
> Cadwalladr: "The Revenant is meaningless pain porn".

It is clear that Bradshaw thinks it is a beautiful movie. After summarizing the plot, he describes his experience watching the movie:

> I clenched into a whimperingly foetal ball so tight that afterwards I practically had to be rolled out of the cinema auditorium. (...) I also felt every droplet of bear spittle, every serration of tooth, and I understood what it feels like when parts of your ribcage are exposed to fresh air and light rain.

Not everybody would take those experiences as exactly positive, but Bradshaw clearly does so. He not only talks about his experiences but especially about the features of the movie itself, using a variety of adjectives. It is quite clear, for instance, that he has a very positive view on Iñarritu's direction and Lubezki's cinematography:

> The images that the movie conjures are ones of staggering, crystalline beauty: gasp-inducing landscapes and beautifully wrought closeups, such as the leaves in bulbous freezing mounds, and a tiny crescent moon, all unsentimentally rendered. But there is

---

[2] Interestingly, Stojanovic claims that "[i]n aesthetics, art critics hardly ever use adjectives like 'beautiful' to express a positive evaluation of a work of art" (Stojanovic, forthcoming: 5). I'm not that sure. In his review, Bradshaw uses the adjective twice, the adverb "beautifully" once, and even the noun "beauty". In her op-ed, Cadwalladr uses none of these.

also something hallucinatory and unwholesome about these images, as if hunger and pain has brought Glass to the secularised state of a medieval saint tormented with visions. (...) what is so distinctive about this Iñárritu picture is its unitary control and its fluency: no matter how extended, the film's tense story is under the director's complete control and he unspools great meandering, bravura travelling shots to tell it.

So, it seems fair to attribute to Bradshaw an utterance like (1). He believes that *The Revenant* is a beautiful movie.

On the other hand, Cadwalladr, who has read Bradshaw's review, makes it clear she thinks it's not. The first paragraph announces the severity of Cadwalladr's opinion:

Ritualised brutality. Vengeful blood lust. Vicious savagery justified by medieval notions of retribution. We all know how dark the world can be these days. A world where men are garrotted and impaled. Where they're speared and disembowelled and have their necks slashed and their genitals sliced off. Where they're killed for no other reason than revenge. This isn't Raqqa, though, it's *The Revenant*.

The summary of her experience as a viewer is no less blunt:

I saw it at a press screening (...) to spend what felt like several weeks in a dark room waiting – oh dear God, do you wait – for Leo [DiCaprio] to just get on and hack the other man to death so I could finally go home.

She really saw little value in the movie:

Director Alejandro González Iñárritu's idea was for it to look as *real* as possible. Which would have been magnificent if there was something in the way of a story or any meditation on the nature of retribution or anyone – *anyone* – that you could give one toss about, but there's not. So the landscape is chilling and the violence is pointless and the whole thing is meaningless. A vacuous revenge tale that is simply pain as spectacle.

It is clear enough that Bradshaw and Cadwalladr disagree and they do it blatantly. But what do they disagree about? It is quite obvious that the former liked the movie, the latter did not; she disliked it. But their differences amount to more than that. They refer to various aspects of the movie to make their point. It seems fair to say that they intend to describe the film's virtues (or vices), merits (or demerits). And that, if pressed, they would be willing to give further arguments for the truth of (1) and falsity of (2), and vice versa.

I think it is just too simplistic to take this as a case of faultless disagreement, and say that, even if they contradict each other, they can both be perfectly right. We need to clarify, first, what exactly they are talking about to be able to determine whether they contradict each other and/or whether they can simultaneously be making true assertions about the beauty (or lack thereof) of *The Revenant*. Looking at the meaning of the adjective "beautiful" seems a good start in the inquiry.

3 McNally and Stojanovic on "beautiful"

McNally and Stojanovic (forthcoming) characterize the adjective "beautiful" as gradable, multidimensional, and non-measurable (because it is evaluative). Let us see what they mean.

3.1 Gradability

Gradable adjectives allow us to compare two objects according to the degree to which they show the property denoted by the adjectives. So, it is perfectly right to claim of any two objects X and Y that "X is more beautiful than Y". On the other hand, for the correct application of the adjective, "it is typically not enough that the property in question be held just to any degree; rather it must be held to a degree that passes a *threshold* or meets a *standard*. For example, if something is long, it has a certain, usually substantial length" (p. 2).[3] Moreover, "beautiful" passes the two linguistic tests used for gradable adjectives: it is compatible with "very" (e.g., "X is very beautiful") and allows a *for*-phrase ("X is beautiful for a three-star hotel").

McNally and Stojanovic (forthcoming) hypothesize that most aesthetic adjectives are gradable, though they leave it open whether all of them are. Of course, this depends on what we take aesthetic adjectives to be, but, since we are mainly concerned with "beautiful", whose status as an aesthetic predicate is not questioned, we need not deal with it.

3.2 Multidimensionality

Unidimensional adjectives are those for which there is only one criterion by which to order the individuals according to the property in question. They include adjectives like "long", "tall", "slow", and "old" that order objects accord-

---

[3] It is not clear to me whether the same works with "beautiful". It's odd to say that we do not call an object "beautiful" unless it is "substantially beautiful". The distinction between the two senses or uses of the adjective that I introduce in section 4 may be relevant here, but I will leave this issue aside.

ing to length, height, speed, and age, respectively. Multidimensional adjectives, on the other hand, are those for which there is more than one criterion used to order the objects bearing the property. "Deciding whether an adjective describing a multidimensional property holds of some individual involves not only determining a threshold of applicability but also determining the relative weight of each of the dimensions that contribute to the property in question" (p. 4). The tests for multidimensionality include compatibility with phrases like "in some/every way/respect" or "except for A", which "beautiful" seems to pass: "X is beautiful in every respect", "X is beautiful except for the color".

McNally and Stojanovic's (forthcoming) hypothesis is strong concerning this aspect. They venture that all aesthetic adjectives are multidimensional. Again, this depends on the delimitation of aesthetic adjectives, but, regarding "beautiful", we need to make further considerations about its multidimensionality.

3.3 Measurability

According to McNally and Stojanovic (forthcoming), most unidimensional adjectives are measurable. We can order the objects to which we attribute the property in question. Some multidimensional adjectives are also measurable. Among the latter, they include "intelligent" and "simple" along with "big", "large" and "small". In the case of intelligence, they allude to IQ tests but, admitting that they are questionable, they observe that "intelligence can be measured non-numerically, for example, by checking which sorts of problems an individual is capable of solving or how quickly they can be solved" (p. 5).

One might think that if "intelligent" is taken as measurable (in this last non-numerical sense), "beautiful" could also be regarded as measurable in an analogous way.[4] But McNally and Stojanovic do not, their main reason being that while "[m]easurability, as [they] understand it, allows in principle for the objective use of an adjective", non-measurable adjectives introduce subjectiv-

---

[4] When discussing aesthetic terms Sibley (1959) contrasts aesthetic terms which, according to him, are *non-condition-governed*, with "intelligent", which is *condition-governed*. Briefly put, in the relevant sense here, I take it that Sibley's "condition-governed" terms are those which denote complex qualities analyzable as an "open-ended" set of component properties, which, taken separately, are neither necessary nor sufficient, but which jointly are sufficient for the complex quality to occur. According to Sibley, "intelligent" denotes such a quality; "beautiful" does not. This is extensively discussed by Kivy (1979) who, *pace* Sibley, takes aesthetic terms like "unified", "delicate" and "beautiful" to be analogous to "intelligent": either "intelligent" is non-condition-governed or they are all condition-governed. Analogously, I contend that either "intelligent" is non-measurable or "beautiful" is also measurable.

ity, because they either involve properties entailing an experiencer or "imply a positive or negative evaluation on the part of the speaker" (p. 5). They think that "beautiful" does not entail an experiencer, but that, being evaluative, introduces subjectivity, and, therefore, is non-measurable.[5]

Their hypothesis is that all aesthetic adjectives are non-measurable, and that "the entailment of an experiencer is neither sufficient nor necessary for an adjective to be properly aesthetic" (p. 9). They leave open the question of whether all aesthetic predicates are evaluative.

McNally and Stojanovic's (forthcoming) thorough analysis of "beautiful" seems quite compatible with a realist account like Kivy's. Gradability and multidimensionality might need some further clarification, but I do not attempt to discuss that here. From Kivy's realist point of view, there are at least two objections to the non-measurability of "beautiful", even before we distinguish between its two senses or uses. First, if "measurable" means to be "condition-governed" à la Sibley, and "intelligent" is measurable, then "beautiful" is measurable too.[6] If measurability is what allows the objective use of an adjective, then "beautiful" is measurable, because "beautiful" can be and is objectively used. I leave the discussion here –though I will discuss evaluativity later in sections four and seven – to turn to the main theme of the essay: the two senses or uses of "beautiful".

4 Two senses or uses of "beautiful"

From our point of view, the first and most important distinction has to do with two uses or senses of the predicate "beautiful" that are well rooted in the history of aesthetics and the philosophy of art. They are present in artistic contexts at least from the 18th century. There is, on the one hand, the general artistic or aesthetic sense or use in which "any great work of art ... calls forth the appellation 'beautiful', regardless of its specific features ... (Thus the eighteenth century called the fine arts "beaux arts", indicating that their essential feature, at least when they are well-executed, is beauty)" (Kivy 2015: 37).

In this sense or use of the predicate, to use Kivy's own examples, both the *Iliad* and the *Aeneid* are beautiful; Beethoven's *Grosse Fuge* and Grünwald's

---

[5] McNally and Stojanovic (forthcoming), on the other hand, admit that numbers can be assigned to the beauty of a woman or an exercise in a figure skating contest, but they take these cases not "to involve some sort of external criterion" but "to express an ordinal ranked preference" (p. 6).
[6] See footnote 5.

Christ on the Cross are both beautiful as well. Hume would be using the word in this general evaluative sense in his essays on taste. And perhaps this is the main sense or use of the adjective by non-specialized art lovers when talking about telling *good* and *bad* artworks apart. "Beautiful" in this use can be paraphrased as "artistically or aesthetically good, or successful". Let's call this use or sense of the adjective "beautiful$_{EVAL}$"; an assertion of the form "X is beautiful$_{EVAL}$", then, constitutes an aesthetic or artistic appraisal, and belongs to the evaluation of the artwork.

There is a second, more specific, use or sense of "beautiful" with more descriptive content, which helps us in contrasting "a pretty face with a beautiful one, a sublime composition with a beautiful one" (Kivy 2015: 37). In this use or sense of the adjective, the *Iliad* is not beautiful but sublime; the *Aeneid* is not sublime but beautiful; Beethoven's *Gross Fuge* and Grünwald's *Christ on the Cross* are both ugly.

This second use or sense (let's call it "beautiful$_{DESCR}$") is strictly aesthetic and situates "beautiful" among the aesthetic predicates along with "unified", "balanced", "integrated", "lifeless", "serene", "somber", "dynamic", "powerful", "vivid", "delicate", "moving", "trite", "sentimental", "tragic" and the like.[7] The properties they denote are aesthetic properties absent or present in the artwork. I call them "second-level" aesthetic properties, since they are distinguished from purely "technical" – musical, literary, pictorial, cinematographic, … which, naturally, I call "first-level" – like the number of characters in a plot, the use of pale colors in a painting, the inversed theme in a fugue, that there is a stretto at some point, that the plot of a story takes place in the span of one day or that there is a reconciliation scene at the end.[8] According to Kivy (2015), second-level aesthetic properties such as serenity, balance, and being tightly-knit emerge from, or supervene on, first-order aesthetic properties such as a stretto or inversion in a fugue, and a reconciliation scene in a plot. Thus, the presence of second-order properties is dependent upon the presence of first-order properties. But Kivy points to another important difference between the two: first-order properties are non-evaluative; second-order properties are evaluative; and among the latter, he distinguishes those that are both descriptive and evaluative (or thick) features such as being balanced or graceful, and purely evaluative (thin) ones such as being good.

---

[7] The list is taken from Sibley's initial examples. As he observes, there are many more, of many types that can be grouped in "various kinds of sub-species" (Sibley 1959: 127).
[8] Again, this list is Sibley's (1959). He takes these to be non-aesthetic "concepts". I follow Kivy (2015), and take them as aesthetic too. (See also Kivy 1973, 1975, 1979.)

Regarding the predicate "beautiful" in its specific use or sense, by "beautiful$_{DESCR}$" we denote the thick (second-order) property *beautiful*, which, of course, has a positive value[9] and also describes some perceptible or experiential feature of the artwork, which is describable in purely descriptive first-order terms, the stretto in the fugue at that point or the melodic inversion at that other point, and so on. All the aesthetic features pertain to the analysis of the artwork.

> I take it that all aesthetic features of artworks, both the non-value and the value features, are, to put it one way, art-relevant structural and phenomenological features of them. And these features are, of course, the subject of "analysis". (Kivy 2015: 124)

"Beautiful$_{DESCR}$", then, is a thick aesthetic term with both descriptive and evaluative (positive) contents, denoting a thick aesthetic property of artworks, which depends on the presence or absence of first-order aesthetic features in the artworks. An assertion of the form "X is beautiful$_{DESCR}$" constitutes an aesthetic judgment,[10] which belongs to the analysis of the artwork, that is, to "an explication of how the artwork 'works', what makes it tick." (Kivy 2015: 124)

To recapitulate, an assertion of the form "X is beautiful", when X is used to refer to an artwork, is either an aesthetic judgment ("beautiful$_{DESCR}$") or an aesthetic or artistic appraisal ("beautiful$_{EVAL}$"). If the former, "beautiful$_{DESCR}$" denotes a second-level thick aesthetic property of the artwork which emerges from certain first-level or technical features of it. If the latter, "beautiful$_{EVAL}$" provides a fully evaluative general property of the artwork that is based on the aesthetic or art-relevant properties of the artwork.

A note of caution might be in order here. I am not claiming that *beautiful$_{DESCR}$* and *beautiful$_{EVAL}$* are totally independent properties, as I am not claiming that the analysis and evaluation of an artwork are independent tasks, or that an aesthetic judgment of a particular artwork is irrelevant to its aesthetic (or artistic) appraisal. If we find an artwork to be *beautiful$_{DESCR}$*, that depends on first-level technical properties which make it beautiful and not just pretty, and not sublime. Since being *beautiful$_{DESCR}$* is *prima facie* a positive property, in general, it counts for a positive evaluation as a good artwork, but it is neither sufficient not necessary for it. Given the presence or absence of other aesthetic (and other non-aesthetic but art-relevant) properties, a *beautiful$_{DESCR}$* artwork, might not be *beautiful$_{EVAL}$* – as in the case of *Gone with the Wind*, discussed below –

---

9 Following Kivy (2015: 122–123), I take the valence of thick aesthetic predicates like "beautiful" to be positive *prima facie*. In general, being *beautiful$_{DESCR}$* is an artistic merit of and artwork, but that valence is defeasible. In particular instances, it can have a neutral or even a negative valence.

10 See also Kivy (1975).

or an *ugly*$_{DESCR}$ artwork might be *beautiful*$_{EVAL}$ – as in the cases of Beethoven's *Gross Fuge* and Grünwald's *Christ on the Cross* mentioned above. To put it short, the presence of absence *beautiful*$_{DESCR}$ is relevant to the presence or absence of *beautiful*$_{EVAL}$, but it is just one property among many properties that are jointly relevant.

As I have said, McNally and Stojanovic (forthcoming) do not distinguish between "beautiful$_{EVAL}$" and "beautiful$_{DESCR}$", and I do not discuss how their analysis could be recast in terms of this distinction. A couple of remarks seem relevant, though. When they talk about the evaluativity of "beautiful" and compare it to "good" and "bad" as "[p]erhaps the most basic examples of evaluative adjectives" (p. 9), they seem to point to "beautiful$_{EVAL}$", i.e., the thin, purely evaluative sense or use, proper to the artwork's evaluation. But, when they immediately include "beautiful" along with "pretty", "gorgeous", "handsome" and "ugly", they are pointing to our "beautiful$_{DESCR}$", that is, the adjective's thick (evaluative and descriptive) use or sense. Actually, they acknowledge that there are not any strictly evaluative readings of "beautiful" when, for instance, it is embedded under "find" or look (p. 12, fn 11). So, implicitly at least, they are also pointing to two different uses or senses of the adjective.

I want now to say a bit more about "beautiful$_{EVAL}$" or the sense or use of the predicate "beautiful" in aesthetic and artistic appraisals. It is about time to clarify, in particular, why I keep systematically using a disjunction when talking about aesthetic *or* artistic appraisals.

In many art forms, the aesthetic appraisal of the artwork, based on its aesthetic properties, is all there is to its artistic appraisal. So, in this case, the disjunction would amount to the mutual interchangeability of "aesthetic" and "artistic". If we hold an autonomist conception of art, an *art for the art's sake* kind of view, this generalizes to all arts disciplines and works. All that matters when evaluating a work of art is to consider its aesthetic properties.

But, if we go with an anti-autonomist view like Kivy's, there is more to the evaluation of an artwork *qua* artwork than the analysis of its aesthetic properties, because some artworks have meanings, and an *interpretation* of the meaning of the artwork is also part of its evaluation *qua* artwork. Given the interpretation of an artwork, the aesthetic appraisal of the work (let's say, "beautiful") can be different from its artistic appraisal ("not beautiful"). To understand this, we need to clarify the notion of the meaning of an artwork.

5 The meaning of an artwork

The artistic appraisal of an artwork involves all the *art-relevant* properties of the artwork:

> The art-relevant properties of a work I take to be those properties of the work that are the ones we appreciate in it qua artwork. They are the properties that are relevant to its merit or demerit as an artwork; the properties we mention as contributing to its merit or demerit as an artwork. (Kivy 2015: 59)

And the propositional or representational content of an art-work, if it has one, is, according to Kivy, art-relevant: it is relevant for its overall evaluation as an artwork, as constituting a beautiful, that is, an artistically good or successful work of art.

It is commonplace to admit that artworks can have a meaning, that is, that they can assert, convey or suggest propositions purported to be true. Absolute music (i.e. music alone, without program and without text) asserts or conveys nothing. Literary artworks such as novels, poems and plays often make assertions and suggestions, and music with text, visual representational arts and movies can also do so. They often have propositional and representational content. These contents, though not aesthetic, are art-relevant properties of the work.[11]

Kivy gives an example that illustrates his view on the contribution of the non-aesthetic art-relevant properties to the evaluation of the artwork, which helps us with the discussion of our motivating example about *The Revenant*: the movie *Gone with the Wind*. On the one hand, at the level of analysis it is quite obvious that it has positive aesthetic qualities:

> With its stunning cinematic technique, its narrative sweep, spectacular special effects, and performances by some of the most talented movie actors and actresses of its day, it is on every cinema buffs list of cinema greats, at least of the Hollywood variety. (Kivy 2015: 60–61)

From the point of view of its aesthetic appraisal, then, Kivy agrees – with everybody else, I think – that *Gone with the Wind* is a beautiful ("beautiful$_{EVAL}$") movie.

---

[11] If one takes meaning-properties to be aesthetic properties of the artwork, like, for instance, Gaut (2007) does when he equates aesthetic properties with art-relevant properties, then there would be no difference between aesthetic and artistic appraisals. But, of course, meaning-properties would always be relevant for the aesthetic appraisals of artworks with meaning. Both Kivy's and Gaut's views deny the *autonomy* of art posed by *art for the art's sake* views that see meaning properties irrelevant for the artistic appraisal. I follow Kivy's anti-autonomist view here.

But there are other art-relevant properties, non-aesthetic properties having to do with the movie's meaning that affect the final artistic verdict:

> It advances an idealized picture of the ante-bellum, slave-supported Southern culture; and the depiction of the African-American slave as a dithering incompetent ... the depiction of the South's "noble" struggle against Northern oppression, during the Civil War, ... leaves out the fact that the South's "noble struggle" was a struggle to preserve one of the most morally depraved institutions in human history, namely the chattel-slavery of a race. (Kivy 2015: 61)

Kivy's artistic appraisal is clear. He thinks that *Gone with Wind* is not good as an artwork, it is not *beautiful*$_{EVAL}$, after all; it is not artistically good. Here is why:

> I find *Gone with Wind* an utterly repellent work of cinematic art, *on moral grounds*. All its aesthetic merits, which are in abundance, are not enough, for my taste, to weigh the balance of artistic merit in its favor, against its moral defects. (Kivy 2015: 61)[12]

In other words, from an exclusively aesthetic point of view, the movie is *beautiful*$_{EVAL}$, but, from an artistic point of view, it is not. Thus, for artworks with meaning, we should distinguish two further uses or senses of "*beautiful*$_{EVAL}$": one that only evaluates the aesthetic merits of the artwork ("*beautiful*$_{EVAL\text{-}AES}$", for short); another that also includes in the evaluation the art-relevant non-aesthetic meaning properties belonging to the artwork's interpretation ("*beautiful*$_{EVAL\text{-}ART}$").

Of course, there is room for disagreement in the determination of the precise meaning of a particular artwork and its weight vis a vis its aesthetic merits. For instance, Handel's *Messiah* has been interpreted as anti-semitic; and so has Wagner's *Meistersinger*.[13] But, whatever their meaning, the point is that they have one, and that it is relevant for the artistic appraisal as an artwork. To take another well-known case, Picasso's *Guernica* has abundant aesthetic merits (though we can hardly say that it is *beautiful*$_{DESCR}$), but, no doubt, the fact that it represents the bombing of Gernika, one of the first raids on a defenseless civilian population, adds to its artistic appraisal as one of the most beautiful (*beautiful*$_{EVAL\text{-}ART}$) paintings of the 20th century.

With all these distinctions at hand, let us turn to assess Peter Bradshaw's and Carole Cadwalladr's conflicting views about *The Revenant*.

---

12 Kivy's qualification "for my taste" should not be taken as a sign that he takes appraisals to be subjective. From his realistic point of view, aesthetic and artistic appraisals are true (or false) according to matters of fact, i.e., the presence (or absence) of a positive aesthetic or artistic value in the artwork.
13 Kivy rejects those interpretations in Kivy (2012) and (2007), respectively.

6 Back to *The Revenant*

Bradshaw thinks that *The Revenant* is beautiful ("gut-churningly brutal, beautiful storytelling" he says in the title), and Cadwalladr thinks it's not ("[it] is meaningless pain porn"). An immediate conclusion is that the consideration of the movie's meaning plays a very different role in each case.

Bradshaw has no substantial claim to make about the interpretation of the movie. He is almost exclusively focused on its aesthetic properties, both first-level and second-level: the images are "ones of staggering, crystalline beauty: gasp-inducing landscapes and beautifully wrought closeups, such as the leaves in bulbous freezing mounds, and a tiny crescent moon, all unsentimentally rendered". Or again: "what is so distinctive about this Iñárritu picture is its unitary control and its fluency: no matter how extended, the film's tense story is under the director's complete control and he unspools great meandering, bravura travelling shots to tell it."

We can safely say that, if we asked him, all the aesthetic merits emphasized by Bradshaw would lead him to assent that "*The Revenant* is *beautiful*$_{EVAL-AES}$".

It is quite clear, on the other hand, that Cadwalladr's main focus is on the interpretation of *The Revenant*, its meaning. She is mainly discussing what the movie represents, which she summarizes as "Ritualised brutality. Vengeful blood lust. Vicious savagery justified by medieval notions of retribution."

She does not deny the movie's aesthetic merits. She describes the cinematography not as beautiful, but as gorgeous: "Emmanuel Lubezki's cinematography – all shot in just a few hours of natural light each day – really is gorgeous." It is true that she shows some skepticism about the seemingly positive valence carried by Bradshaw's description, when she says that "It's ..., according to the *Guardian's* Peter Bradshaw, 'as thrilling and painful as a sheet of ice held to the skin'. This is praise, by the way." But we have no reason to think she would deny that "*The Revenant* is *beautiful*$_{EVAL-AES}$". We have strong reasons, however, to suspect that things are very different when it comes to the movie's artistic evaluation.

Cadwalladr, when it comes to the artistic appraisal of *The Revenant*, believes that the demerits of its interpretation outbalance its aesthetic merits. In her own words, the director's "idea ... for it to look as *real* as possible would have been magnificent if there was something in the way of a story or any meditation on the nature of retribution or anyone – *anyone* – that you could give one toss about, but there's not".

Cadwalladr thinks that the violence of the movie, its pointlessness, is immoral and that it weighs more than the cinematography, the landscapes or the acting. Like Peter Kivy with *Gone with the Wind*, Cadwalladr thinks that, given its moral defects, *The Revenant* is not *beautiful*$_{EVAL-ART}$: "So the landscape is chilling and the violence is pointless and the whole thing is meaningless. A vacuous revenge tale that is simply pain as spectacle."

To sum up, Bradshaw and Calwaladr do not seem to disagree about its first-level aesthetic properties. They pretty much agree as well about the second-level properties (the cinematography is "beautiful$_{DESCR}$" for Bradshaw, "gorgeous" for Cadwalladr). We can also take them to agree pretty much on the film's aesthetic appraisal. Even if Calwalladr would not take "thrilling and painful as a sheet of ice held to the skin" to provide a positive value, we may venture that they both agree that *The Revenant* is *beautiful*$_{EVAL-AES}$. Their disagreement must be about the artistic appraisal; that is, Bradshaw, perhaps, believes that *The Revenant* is *beautiful*$_{EVAL-ART}$; Cadwalladr clearly believes it is not.

Cadwalladr's position is clear; her reasons too. We have to speculate about Bradshaw's position and his reasons. If he indeed believes that *The Revenant* is *beautiful*$_{EVAL-ART}$, he may have three reasons for disagreeing with Cadwalladr: a) he thinks that *The Revenant* does not have the meaning that Cadwalladr attributes to it, so he sees no reason for the artistic merit to be affected by it; or b) he agrees that it has that meaning, but he does not take it to outweigh its indubitable aesthetic merits; or, finally, c) whatever his beliefs about the meaning of the film, he is an autonomist, and believes that non-aesthetic properties are irrelevant for artistic evaluation, and therefore being *beautiful*$_{EVAL-AES}$ and being *beautiful*$_{EVAL-ART}$ are equivalent.

Whatever Bradshaw actually believes, it is clear now what he and Cadwalladr agree and disagree about, if they agree or disagree, when they each (virtually) claim about *The Revenant* that it is beautiful (1), and it is not (2). Cadwalladr claims that

(3) *The Revenant* is beautiful$_{DESCR}$

(4) *The Revenant* is beautiful$_{EVAL-AES}$

(5) *The Revenant* is not beautiful$_{EVAL-ART}$

and Bradshaw agrees on (3) and (4). If there is any disagreement between them, it is about (5), and, as we just said, there can be at least three different reasons having to do with the interpretation of the film and the place of that interpretation in the overall artistic appraisal of it. If they disagree, however, the disagreement is real and somebody is at fault. Either Bradshaw is right about the interpretation of *The Revenant* and Cadwalladr wrong, or viceversa. No doubt, it may difficult to decide one way or the other (and I am not going to pursue the issue here) but at least we have a better understanding about what the disagreement is about.

In general, then, when two people assert about an artwork that it is or it is not beautiful, there is much to clarify before concluding that they just faultlessly disagree. The aesthetic assertion can be an aesthetic judgment describing a second-level aesthetic property of the artwork, or an appraisal. If the former, the judgment is about the presence or absence of *beautiful*$_{DESCR}$, and pointing to the first-level technical properties is the way to clarify its content. Making this dimension explicit, that is, its multi-dimensional properties (the cinematography, the landscapes, the plot...), will help in clarifying the truth-conditions of the judgments and determining whether their apparent disagreement is genuine or not. Being a matter of degree, the dispute might be about whether the right property is *beautiful*$_{DESCR}$ rather than pretty or sublime; a case that can be difficult to resolve. Or it can be a bold genuine opposition, with dimensions fixed, to the effect that one judges it to be *beautiful*$_{DESCR}$ while the other considers it *ugly*$_{DESCR}$. An aesthetic realist claims that in this case one would be right, the other wrong.

If the latter, if the assertion is an appraisal, it can be an aesthetic appraisal or an artistic one. If the artwork has no meaning, there will no difference between the last two. If the artwork has a meaning, the artwork's interpretation plays a role in its artistic evaluation. And this opens various sources of possible disagreement and contradiction.

Exchanges like (1) and (2) may simply be taken as expressions of personal taste. But often they are not. When talking about artworks, they are just the beginning of complex arguments about their aesthetic properties and their non-aesthetic but art-relevant properties. I hope to have shown that this is at least a reasonable enough account of what is going on in our aesthetic and artistic disputes about the beauty of an artwork.

7 Semantics or pragmatics?

Throughout this essay, the systematic use of both "sense" and "use" when talking about "beautiful$_{EVAL-AES/ART}$" and "beautiful$_{DESCR}$" has been deliberate. I wanted to avoid a premature decision about whether this difference should be assimilated to the semantics or the pragmatics of the adjective. Or, perhaps, the distinction is better handled as a difference in the practices of analyzing (i.e. producing aesthetic judgments) versus evaluating (producing aesthetic or artistic appraisals about) works of art, than by assigning special semantic or pragmatic features to "beautiful". More research is of course needed to argue in one direction or the other, but I will dare to venture some general hypotheses that could accord with the general realistic account of aesthetic and artistic properties and values sketched here.

First of all, a negative semantic hypothesis: the meaning of "beautiful" does not include the expression of personal taste or preference on the part of the speaker. It is an element that the speaker often conveys without asserting. More precisely, in uttering (1) Peter does not state that he likes *The Revenant*, but he implicates it, in the sense of Grice (1967a, b). That he likes the movie is not a component of the conventional meaning of the sentence uttered, but something that arises from the fact that Peter utters (1). We can venture that it constitutes what Grice called a "generalized conversational implicature" – generalized because it is identified without reference to a particular context. In normal circumstances, we infer that the statement "X is beautiful" typically conveys that "the speaker likes X". The inference is cancellable explicitly, since there is no contradiction, or even oddness, in claiming "X is beautiful, but I don't like it".[14]

Now, the positive hypothesis: what does "beautiful" (semantically) mean? We have said that it can denote either a thick second-level aesthetic property or a thin purely evaluative one. That might make us think that the predicate is systematically ambiguous with two general meanings ("beautiful$_{DESCR}$" and "beautiful$_{EVAL\text{-}AES/ART}$"), which need to be contextually determined (recognizing the speaker's intention when using the term). That's probably the most obvious direction to take. The two senses have various aspects in common. I agree with McNally and Stojanovic (forthcoming) that gradability, multidimensionality and evaluativity may well be semantic features of "beautiful", that is to say, that they are encoded as its lexical conventional meaning, though I have some qualms with non-measurability, as I have said above. I will not pursue the matter here. But I want to make a couple of remarks about the evaluativity of "beautiful" and other aesthetic terms.

It might well be the case that genuine aesthetic adjectives like "beautiful", in contrast with predicates that have aesthetic and non-aesthetic uses like "dynamic", "somber" or "moving", have it built into their lexical meaning that their role is to assign a certain aesthetic value to the object of which we predicate it. But we should note that an aesthetic/artistic positive evaluation is all there is to the meaning of "beautiful$_{EVAL\text{-}AES/ART}$", while in the case of "beautiful$_{DESCR}$" there is both description and (positive) evaluation involved. This situates "beautiful$_{DESCR}$" closer to "dynamic", "somber", and "moving", because all describe and evaluate different properties of the artwork. "Somber" usually denotes a negative property of an artwork, "dynamic" typically a positive one, and "moving" and "beautiful$_{DESCR}$" always positive ones. But none of them is either necessary or sufficient for the artwork to be evaluated as "beautiful$_{EVAL\text{-}AES/ART}$".

---

14 Grice's test of non-detachability also applies. In relevance theory (Sperber and Wilson 1995 [1986]; Carston 2002), it would possibly be regarded as a higher-order explicature.

Once again, the evaluative aspect of "beautiful" that describes a second-level aesthetic property of the artwork, and that is part of our aesthetic judgments, is one thing; the evaluative aspect of the "beautiful" we employ in our aesthetic or artistic appraisals is a different thing. Admitting in the analysis that an artwork has (or has not) the property *beautiful*$_{DESCR}$ does not imply admitting in its evaluation that it is (or it is not) beautiful$_{EVAL\text{-}AES/ART}$; and admitting from a purely aesthetic evaluative point of view that an artwork is (not) beautiful$_{EVAL\text{-}AES}$ does not imply admitting that it is (not) beautiful$_{EVAL\text{-}ART}$.

Now, does evaluativity involve subjectivity? Not necessarily. If aesthetic realism is a viable option, as I think it is, aesthetic and artistic appraisals, that is, our claims about the aesthetic or artistic value of an artwork, state matters of fact. So, there is no direct and inevitable route from evaluativity to subjectivity.

Finally, concerning the semantics and pragmatics of aesthetic assertions, there are other options to explore. One may contend that all these differences between our aesthetic judgments and appraisals come, not from the encoded semantic meaning of an ambiguous adjective, but from the fact that when asserting the beauty of an artwork we can be making different speech acts – aesthetically describing and aesthetically or artistically evaluating. Or one could maintain that it is the conversational context or background that determines whether we are talking about one aesthetic property of the object or we are talking about the object's aesthetic or artistic value, or about both. Current semantic and pragmatic theories offer a variety of possible answers to these issues, but moving further along any of these courses exceeds my current limits of time and competence, and I have no choice but to leave it for a future occasion.

Acknowledgements: I am obliged to Rachel Giora and Michael Haugh for inviting me to participate in this volume, and thus to express my admiration for Professor Kecskés's immense contribution to pragmatics. My general view on the topic discussed here is highly influenced by Peter Kivy's (2015) defense of aesthetic realism. The entire paper reflects my possibly idiosyncratic take on his approach. I apologize in advance for my poor rendering of his rich and elaborate account, while at the same time I acknowledge his help and support. I am also grateful to Eros Corazza, María de Ponte, Joana Garmendia, Larraitz Zubeldia and two anonymous referees for their comments and criticisms. This work has been partially supported by a grant of the Spanish Ministry of Economy and Competitivity (FFI2015-63719-P (MINECO/FEDER)), and the Basque Government (IT1032-16). I dedicate this work to the memory of Peter Kivy (1934–2017).

References

Bradshaw, Peter. 2015. The Revenant review – gut-churningly brutal, beautiful storytelling. *The Guardian*, 4 December, 2015. https://www.theguardian.com/film/2015/dec/04/the-revenant-review-gut-churningly-brutal-beautiful-storytelling (accessed 21 July 2016)

Cadwalladr, Carole. 2016. The Revenant is meningless pain porn. *The Guardian*, 17 January, 2016. https://www.theguardian.com/commentisfree/2016/jan/17/revenant-leonardo-dicaprio-violent-meaningless-glorification-pain (accessed 21 July 2016)

Carston, Robyn. 2002. *Thoughts and utterances. The pragmatics of explicit communication.* Oxford: Blackwell.

Gaut, Berys. 2007. *Art, emotion, and ethics.* Oxford: Oxford University Press.

Grice, H. Paul. 1989a [1967a]. Logic and conversation. In Peter Cole and Jerry L. Morgan (eds.). 1975. *Syntax and semantics 3: Speech acts*, 41–58. New York: Academic Press. Reprinted in Paul Grice, 1989, *Studies in the way of words*, 22–40. Harvard: Harvard University Press.

Grice, H. Paul. 1989b [1967b]. Further notes on logic and conversation. In Peter Cole (ed.), *Syntax and semantics 9: Pragmatics*, 147–170. New York: Academic Press, 1978. Reprinted in Paul Grice, 1989, *Studies in the way of words*, 41–57. Harvard: Harvard University Press.

Hume, David. 1987 [1757]. Of the Standard of Taste. In Eugene F. Miller (ed.), *Essays moral, political and literary*, 226–249. Indianapolis: Liberty Fund.

Kivy, Peter. 1973. *Speaking of art*. The Hague: Martinus Nijhoff.

Kivy, Peter. 1975. What makes "aesthetic" terms aesthetic? *Philosophy and Phenomenological Research* 36(2). 197–211.

Kivy, Peter. 1979. Aesthetic concepts: some fresh considerations. *The Journal of Aesthetics and Art Criticism* 37(4). 423–432.

Kivy, Peter. 2007. Anti-semitism in *Meistersinger*? In Peter Kivy, *Music, language, and cognition*, 44–50. Oxford: Oxford University Press.

Kivy, Peter. 2012. *Messiah*'s message. In Peter Kivy *Sounding off*, 113–130. Oxford: Oxford University Press.

Kivy, Peter. 2015. *De Gustibus. Arguing about taste and why we do it.* Oxford: Oxford University Press.

Kölbel, Max. 2003. Faultless disagreement. *Proceedings of the Aristotelian society* 104. 55–73.

Lasersohn, Peter. 2005. Context dependence, disagreement, and predicates of personal taste. *Linguistics and Philosophy* 28. 643–686.

Liao, Shen-Yi, Louise McNally & Aaron Meskin. 2016. Aesthetic adjectives lack uniform behavior. *Inquiry* 59. 618–631.

MacFarlane, John. 2007. Relativism and disagreement. *Philosophical Studies* 132. 17–31.

McNally, Louise & Isidora Stojanovic (forthcoming). Aesthetic adjectives. In James Young (ed.), *The semantics of aesthetic judgment*. Oxford: Oxford University Press.

Sibley, Frank. 1959. Aesthetic Concepts. *Philosophical Review* 68: 421–450. Reprinted in Peter Lamarque & Stein Haugom Olson (eds.), *Aesthetics and the philosophy of art. The analytic tradition*, 127–141. Oxford: Blackwell, 2004.

Sperber, Dan & Deirdre Wilson. 1986. *Relevance: Communication and cognition*, Oxford: Blackwell.

Stojanovic, Isidora (forthcoming). Evaluative adjectives and evaluative uses of ordinary adjectives. In Daisuke Bekki & EricMcCready (eds.), *Proceedings of Language Engineering and Natural Language Semantics*. Tokyo.

Sundell, Tim. 2016. The tasty, the bold, and the beautiful. *Inquiry* 59. 793–818.

Index

acategorical 7, 255, 256, 258–262, 264–266
adaptive management 7, 255–259, 265
additive multimodality 301
aesthetic property 400, 401, 407–416
age 5, 41, 42, 121–123, 126–132, 168, 320, 322, 323, 326, 342, 359, 371, 376, 377, 394, 405, 418
algorithms 82–84, 86, 87, 92
ambiguity 6, 57, 66, 70, 72, 74, 109, 178, 180, 181, 185, 193, 198, 200–202, 208, 212, 230, 378
aspectual matching 93, 233
assertion 6, 154, 156, 158, 162, 165, 171, 293, 298, 395, 400, 401, 404, 407, 408, 410, 414, 416

bare objective noun 233, 234, 240–243, 245

cardinals 163, 164
cartoon 5, 18, 122, 123, 126, 127, 129, 132
child language v, 8, 127, 131, 132, 180, 371, 372, 377, 382
children's literature 8, 371–383
Chinese perfective LE 6, 233–253
common ground vi, 3, 4, 7, 13–19, 21–27, 31, 33, 38, 40–43, 45–53, 57, 139, 179, 187, 270, 279, 280, 288, 289, 348
comparability 42, 325, 327, 330
compositionality 6, 91, 175, 176, 185, 186, 193, 195, 197, 198, 201–203, 212, 269
conceptual meaning 85, 88, 258, 355
contextual sifting 257
contrastive discourse relation 7, 269–289
conventional act(s) 165, 297, 337
conventional implicature 164, 165, 170, 196, 198, 199, 205, 229
conventions (of language use) 315, 329, 356
conversational implicature 13, 98, 100, 162, 164, 217, 223, 415
corpus pragmatics 335, 340
cultural awareness 329, 353–368

data collection 128, 140, 324, 325
default semantics 186, 187

de se thought 177, 179, 184, 188
disagreement 65, 394, 399–401, 403, 411, 413, 414
discourse
  ~ connective 269, 272, 274–278, 281–287, 289
  ~ relation 7, 269, 270, 272, 275, 276, 278, 289
  ~ semantics 186, 269–271
discursive glue 270, 273–275, 288
dovetailedness 271–273
dynamic model of meaning 14, 20, 27, 58, 257
dynamical systems 4, 23–27, 418

editing-based task 7, 269, 278, 279, 289
egocentrism vi, 22, 33, 56, 58, 59, 62, 66, 67, 69, 73, 74, 175
equilibrium semantics 186
evaluation 5, 22, 58, 63, 121, 122, 129, 140, 168, 354, 355, 391, 400–402, 406–416
experimental pragmatics 4, 17, 135, 139, 228, 381
explicated inferences 5, 97, 98, 100–102, 104, 107–109, 112–119
explicature 5, 6, 84, 86, 89, 97–100, 103–105, 107–110, 114–116, 118, 171, 215, 224–228, 415

fictional input 376, 377
foreign language v, 257, 291, 315, 316, 319, 329, 353–356
functional categories 80–89, 91, 92, 179

genre 270, 272–274, 278, 279, 289, 298, 318
gesture 8, 51, 88, 294–297, 299, 301, 305–309, 394–396
grammar 80, 88, 92, 93, 179, 185, 197, 258, 266, 269, 271, 274, 301, 306, 317, 318, 354, 356, 365, 371

heat maps 141–143
honorifics 179
humour
  conversational ~ 5, 55, 65, 69, 73
  failed ~ 55, 65, 66, 74

idioms vi, 6, 193, 201–205, 210–212, 380
　fixed-form ~ 202, 203, 205, 212
　free-form ~ 6, 193, 204, 210–212
IEM (immunity to error through misidentification) 182–184, 188
implicature vi, 5, 6, 13, 63, 83, 84, 97, 98, 100, 101, 103–105, 107, 109, 111, 117–119, 154, 155, 157–160, 162–165, 170, 171, 195, 196, 198–200, 204–206, 212, 215–225, 227–229, 371, 415
impoliteness 5, 8, 67, 135–143, 145, 357–360, 365, 367, 368
　~ event 8, 141, 357–360, 368
indexical expressions 176, 178
indexical/nonindexical distinction 176, 187, 188
inference 5, 40, 51, 57, 71, 72, 83, 84, 97–109, 112–119, 158, 162, 175, 187, 229, 230, 240, 270, 274, 275, 373, 374, 383, 415
interactional
　~ collaboration 21, 22, 25, 56
　~ effort 31–33, 38
　~ obligation 32, 38
　~ resolution 117
intercultural
　~ competence 315, 353–357, 359, 361, 364–368
　~ speaker 8, 353–356, 366
interfaces 5, 81–83, 91, 93, 151, 257, 382
International Corpus of English 8, 335–338, 340, 342–349
intersectional multimodality 306, 308, 309
irregular negatives 193, 194, 197, 198, 202, 204, 208, 210, 211

lexical categories 80–83, 85, 87, 88, 91
literary character 374, 378
literature 8, 32, 55, 60, 66, 112, 136, 138, 139, 141, 144, 171, 175, 177, 182, 184, 206, 217, 233, 234, 255, 319, 321–323, 325, 327, 340, 344, 356, 371–373, 375–378, 380, 382, 383, 394
loanword 5, 121–123, 132
lying 6, 151–171, 199, 200, 380, 381

maximalists 5, 98–101, 110, 113, 115, 116
metalanguage 135–137, 145, 233, 238

metalinguistic negation 195, 196
metaphor 8, 58, 59, 70, 71, 74, 154, 166, 168, 175, 296, 299, 305, 380, 381, 389–391, 395
metapragmatics 136–138, 145
minimalists 5, 83, 98–101, 109, 115, 116
miscommunication 4, 5, 55, 58–62, 65, 66, 73, 74
misleading 6, 70, 110, 151, 152, 154, 155, 157, 160–164, 170, 171, 199, 220, 371
misunderstanding 4, 5, 21, 23, 31, 55, 56, 58–62, 65–67, 69–74, 228, 257
modification 8, 269, 335, 340, 345–350, 380
multimodality 7, 293–298, 300, 301, 304–310
multimodal text 7, 295, 310

non-natural meaning 155, 216
non-verbal communication 51, 293, 297

offers 8, 23, 31, 101, 186, 220, 259, 335, 336, 338–350, 357, 419, 420
　~ hospitable 8, 335, 336, 339, 342, 343, 345–350
　~ of assistance 8, 335, 343, 345–350
offer strategies 335, 337, 340, 345, 346, 349
offer types 8, 335, 340, 342, 344, 345, 347, 349, 350
opaque interpretation 193, 206–208, 210

perfective aspect 6, 233–236, 240, 243, 244, 246, 250, 253
perjury 152, 155, 156, 160–163, 166, 170, 171
politeness 5, 32, 36, 135–145, 147, 181, 300, 319, 326, 346–348, 365, 367, 394
　negative ~ 138, 142, 300, 338, 347, 350
　positive ~ 142, 145, 300, 338, 346–348, 394
power 6, 8, 23, 38, 39, 50, 80, 139–145, 158, 185, 211, 235, 243, 293, 308, 319, 355, 356, 362, 392, 393
pragmalinguistic
　~ competence 7, 257, 321, 323
　~ knowledge 3, 13, 317, 321–323, 353, 356, 362, 365
pragmalinguistics v, 3, 13, 121, 293, 296, 317
pragmastylistic features 295, 298
pragmastylistics 7, 293, 296, 298, 300, 310

pragmatic
- ~ competence 7, 8, 257, 315–323, 325, 327–330, 353, 356, 364, 365, 381
- ~ conventions 31, 93, 171, 297, 315, 319, 327, 329, 330, 356, 373; see also conventions (of language use)
- ~ fossilisation 257
- ~ markers 7, 255, 256, 258–260, 262, 264–266, 274

pragmaticography 7, 318, 320
privileged interactional interpretation 5, 99, 100, 102, 103, 112, 117, 119
procedural meaning 5, 79, 80, 84–89, 91–93, 215, 258
propositional attitude reports 6, 193, 206–208, 211, 212
prosody 24, 139, 141, 144, 256, 265, 394
prototype theory 297

rating scales 135, 136, 139–142, 144
realization marker 250
regional variation 322, 324, 330
relevance 32, 35–37, 58, 79, 81, 84, 86, 88, 89, 97–100, 109, 118, 171, 216, 248, 256, 258, 289, 297, 300, 304, 415
Relevance theory 32, 35, 79, 88, 99, 171, 216, 256, 258, 297, 415
requests 15, 25, 26, 35, 44, 48, 139, 140, 337, 339–341, 343, 357, 367, 420
rhetorical covenant 34, 37, 39, 40, 43, 46, 52

scalar implicature 6, 111, 159, 215, 218–222, 228
self-organization 4, 14, 24–27

self-reference 6, 175–177, 180, 182, 184, 187, 188
semantics-pragmatics boundary 176, 185
situational variation 319, 321, 323
societal pragmatics 7, 8, 175, 313, 389
sociopragmatic competence 317, 321–323
sociopragmatic knowledge 353, 356, 362, 365
sociopragmatics 317, 357
speaker-hearer difference 4, 31–42, 52, 170
speaker-hearer motivation 36, 74
speaker meaning 6, 73, 156, 187, 215–217, 219, 221–223, 226–229
study abroad 353, 354, 356, 366–368

tact 8, 389, 394, 396
taste 183, 184, 399, 400, 407, 411, 414, 415
teaching pragmatics 316, 327, 329
thematic analysis 7, 255, 258
theme zone 269, 277, 278, 281, 282, 287, 289
time-scale 4, 25
topical themes 259, 260, 265
transparent interpretation 193, 206–212
truth-evaluable proposition 98

understanding troubles 31–34, 38–42, 49, 51, 52

verbal reports 8, 353, 357, 361, 362, 364, 365, 368

what is said 5, 6, 20, 97–101, 105, 106, 115–117, 119, 151, 157, 159, 162–164, 171, 215, 217, 221–223, 225, 226, 366

www.ingramcontent.com/pod-product-compliance
Lightning Source LLC
Chambersburg PA
CBHW061341300426
44116CB00011B/1943